D0881807

WORLD PHYSICAL MAP

ARCTIC OCEAN

Scandinavia

Baltic Sea

Volga R.

Ob R.

Yenisei R.

Lena R.

S i b e r i a

Bering Sea

EUROPE

Alps

Danube R.

E u r a s i a n   S t e p p e

A S I A

Baikal

Black Sea

Caspian Sea

L. Balkhash

Manchuria

Sea of Japan

Anatolia

Zagros Mts.

Central Asia

Tarim Basin

Gobi Desert

Sicily

Mediterranean Sea

Southwest Asia

Persian Gulf

Tigris R.

Euphrates R.

Himalaya Mountains

East Asia

Yellow Sea

Yangzi R.

reb

Syrian Desert

Strait of Hormuz

Indus R.

Ganges R.

ahara

Nile R.

Red Sea

Arabian Desert

South Asia

Deccan

Southeast Asia

South China Sea

Philippines

PACIFIC OCEAN

hel

Bab al-Mandab

Arabian Sea

Bay of Bengal

Sri Lanka

AFRICA

Ethiopian Highlands

Central Africa

Congo R.

L. Victoria

East Africa

Zambezi R.

Madagascar

Straits of Malacca

Sumatra

Borneo

Java

New Guinea

INDIAN OCEAN

Coral Sea

Great Sandy Desert

A U S T R A L I A

Southern Africa

Cape of Good Hope

Tasmania

New Zealand

0   1,000   2,000 mi
0   1,000   2,000 km

A N T A R C T I C A

THIS REGISTRATION CODE GIVES YOU ACCESS TO

📘 Ebook | 🔲 InQuizitive | 🏛 History Skills Tutorials | ▦ Map & Primary Source Exercises | ◎ Student Site

FOR *The Webs of Humankind*, Volume Two, Seagull Edition

ACTIVATE YOUR REGISTRATION CODE!

1) Scratch the foil to view your code

2) Go to digital.wwnorton.com/websseagullv2
3) Follow the instructions to register your code

A code can be registered to only one user. Used codes are nontransferable and nonrefundable.

For more help, see the back of this card.

What if my code is scratched off?

You can purchase access at
digital.wwnorton.com/webssseagullv2

What if I need more help?

For additional support, visit **support.wwnorton.com**

ISBN 978-0-393-41753-1

9 780393 417531

9 0 0 0 0

THE WEBS *of* HUMANKIND

A WORLD HISTORY

SEAGULL EDITION

Volume Two

JOHN McNEILL

THE WEBS *of* HUMANKIND

A WORLD HISTORY

SEAGULL EDITION

Volume Two

W. W. NORTON & COMPANY

Independent Publishers Since 1923

W. W. Norton & Company has been independent since its founding in 1923, when William Warder Norton and Mary D. Herter Norton first published lectures delivered at the People's Institute, the adult education division of New York City's Cooper Union. The firm soon expanded its program beyond the Institute, publishing books by celebrated academics from America and abroad. By midcentury, the two major pillars of Norton's publishing—trade books and college texts—were firmly established. In the 1950s, the Norton family transferred control of the company to its employees, and today—with a staff of five hundred and hundreds of trade, college, and professional titles published each year—W. W. Norton & Company stands as the largest and oldest publishing house owned wholly by its employees.

Senior Editor: Steve Forman
Editor: Justin Cahill
Senior Associate Managing Editor: Melissa Atkin
Manuscript Editor: Alice Vigliani
Senior Associate Editor: Gerra Goff
Assistant Editors: Lily Gellman and Angie Merila
Cartographic Editor: Charlotte Miller
Copyeditor: Marne Evans
Managing Editor, College: Marian Johnson
Managing Editor, College Digital Media: Kim Yi
Director of Production, College: Jane Searle
Media Editor: Carson Russell
Media Project Editor: Rachel Mayer
Media Associate Editor: Alexander Lee
Media Assistant Editor: Alexandra Malakhoff
Photo Editor: Stephanie Romeo
Photo Researcher: Lynn Gadson
Associate Art Director: Jillian Burr
Permissions Manager: Bethany Salminen
Permissions Specialist: Josh Garvin
Layout Artist: Brad Walrod/Kenoza Type, Inc.
Cartographer and Illustrator: Mapping Specialists—Fitchburg, WI
Manufacturing: Transcontintental Interglobe Inc.—Beauceville, QC

ISBN for this Edition: 978-0-393-41756-2

The Library of Congress has cataloged another edition as follows:

Names: McNeill, John Robert, author.
Title: The webs of humankind : a world history / J. R. McNeill.
Description: First edition. | New York : W. W. Norton & Company, [2021] |
     Includes index.
Identifiers: LCCN 2019045123 | ISBN 9780393979114 (hardcover)
Subjects: LCSH: World history—Textbooks. | Human ecology—History—Textbooks. |
     Globalization—History—Textbooks.
Classification: LCC D20.M4843 2021 | DDC 909—dc23
LC record available at https://lccn.loc.gov/2019045123

W. W. Norton & Company, Inc., 500 Fifth Avenue, New York, NY 10110

wwnorton.com

W. W. Norton & Company Ltd., 15 Carlisle Street, London W1D 3BS

1 2 3 4 5 6 7 8 9 0

This book is dedicated to families: especially the one into which I was born, the one that Julie and I created, and the one that is the community of historians at Georgetown University—students and teachers, past and present.

ABOUT THE AUTHOR

 **J. R. McNEILL** studied at Swarthmore College and Duke University, where he completed a Ph.D. in 1981. Since 1985 he has taught at Georgetown University, in the History Department and School of Foreign Service, where he held the Cinco Hermanos Chair in Environmental and International Affairs before becoming University Professor in 2006. He has taught roughly 3,000 Georgetown students in courses on world history, international relations history, and environmental history.

McNeill's books include: *The Atlantic Empires of France and Spain* (1985); *The Mountains of the Mediterranean World: An Environmental History* (1992); *Something New under the Sun: An Environmental History of the Twentieth-Century World* (2000), co-winner of the World History Association book prize and the Forest History Society book prize; *The Human Web: A Bird's-Eye View of World History* (2003), co-authored with his father, William McNeill; and *Mosquito Empires: Ecology and War in the Greater Caribbean, 1620–1914* (2010), which won the Beveridge Prize from the American Historical Association. His latest book, *The Great Acceleration: An Environmental History of the Anthropocene, 1945–2015*, appeared in 2016. He has edited or co-edited 15 other books, including two volumes of *The Cambridge World History* (2015).

In 2010, McNeill was awarded the Toynbee Prize for "academic and public contributions to humanity." In 2014, the World History Association awarded him its annual prize for achievement in that field; in 2019, the American Society for Environmental History presented him with its Distinguished Scholar Award. The Royal Netherlands Academy of Arts and Sciences awarded him the Heineken Prize for history in 2018. In 2011–2013, he served as President of the American Society for Environmental History, and in 2019 as President of the American Historical Association. He is a member of the American Academy of Arts and Sciences.

CONTENTS IN BRIEF

CONTENTS

MAPS

FEATURES

The Webs of Humankind Seagull Edition offers two text features that reinforce and enrich the book's presentation of world history. They are meant to support student work with primary sources and strengthen their engagement with world history questions.

The first is a primary source feature called **Considering the Evidence**, which appears in every chapter. Authored by Daren Ray (Auburn University), Considering the Evidence presents text documents and images of art and artifacts for analysis by students. Each box includes a contextual headnote and study questions. The primary sources all shed light on the events and developments of each chapter.

The second feature, **The Human Web**, is a map feature that combines text and maps to illustrate webs of interaction at key periods. Each volume of the textbook offers three Human Web features. Each one is built around a central map of an important web, including an introductory headnote by J. R. McNeill and study questions based on the feature and the chapter reading.

FEATURE CONTENTS

PEDAGOGY

The Webs of Humankind Seagull Edition presents a set of pedagogical features intended to guide introductory students through the chapters and support their understanding of world history.

All chapters open with a list of **Focus Questions** that correspond to the major section headings in the chapter. These questions, which appear also in the relevant running heads at the tops of pages, are meant to alert students to the key developments in each section. All chapters also open with a **Chronology** of major events and an **immersive narrative vignette** to draw students into the reading. The chapters end with a summary **Conclusion** and a **Chapter Review** page that includes **Review Questions** and a list of the **Key Terms** (with page references) that appear in bold in the chapter. A **Further Reading** list compiled and annotated by J. R. McNeill appears at the end of the book, along with a **Glossary** including definitions of all key terms and a pronunciation guide.

The author also collaborated on the art program, which includes more than 350 images, and more than 150 original maps, all with captions by the author.

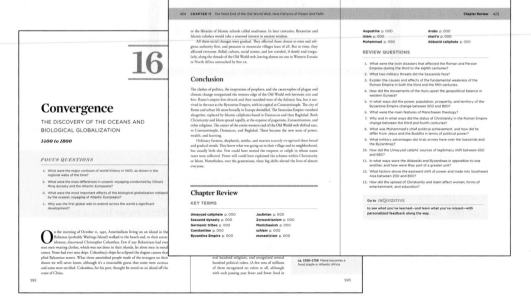

DIGITAL RESOURCES FOR TEACHING AND LEARNING

W. W. Norton has a long history of delivering robust and carefully designed digital resource packages to support teaching and learning. The resources described here have been built from the ground up—with guidance and input from active world history instructors—specifically for use with *The Webs of Humankind* by J. R. McNeill.

RESOURCES FOR STUDENTS

The following resources are available using the access card at the front of this text.

InQuizitive

InQuizitive is Norton's award-winning adaptive learning tool that personalizes the learning experience for students and enhances their understanding of the key themes and objectives from each chapter. This new InQuizitive course, written for *The Webs of Humankind*, features hundreds of interactive questions tagged to each chapter's Focus Questions—including questions based on maps, historical images, and primary source documents—all of which are delivered in an engaging game-like environment with detailed, answer-specific feedback. InQuizitive can be integrated directly into your existing learning management system for easy student access.

▶ **Increased student scores by 16%**

In efficacy studies, when history students completed InQuizitive activities prior to taking a summative quiz, their quiz grades increased by an average of 16 percentage points. Go to www.wwnorton.com/inquizitive for more information.

History Skills Tutorials

The History Skills Tutorials are interactive, online modules that support student development of key skills for the world history course—such as analysis and interpretation of primary source documents, images, and maps. With interactive practice assessments, helpful guiding feedback, and videos with John McNeill modeling source analysis, these tutorials teach students the critical analysis skills that they will put to use in their academic and professional careers. These tutorials can be integrated directly into your existing learning management system for easy student access.

Primary Source and Map Exercises

Building from the critical analysis skills developed in the History Skills Tutorials (above), a series of assignable Primary Source Exercises and Map Exercises provide students the opportunity to practice these skills in every week of the course. Each exercise includes 5 to 10 interactive questions based on documents, images, and maps found in the chapter reading. These exercises can be integrated directly into your existing learning management system for easy student access.

Student Site

The online Student Site offers additional study and review materials for students to use outside of class. Resources include:

- An Online Reader features over 100 additional primary source documents and images, with introductory headnotes, sample short-answer questions, discussion prompts, and activity ideas for easy assignability.
- Author videos featuring John McNeill help students understand the webs of interaction that shape world history.
- Flashcards invite students to review the key terms from the textbook.
- Chapter outlines give students a detailed snapshot of the key topics of each chapter.

Ebook

Norton Ebooks give students and instructors an enhanced reading experience at a fraction of the price of a print textbook. Students are able to have an active reading experience and can take notes, bookmark, search, highlight, and even read offline. Instructors can add notes for students to see as they read the text. Norton Ebooks can be viewed on—and synced among—all computers and mobile devices. Features in the ebook include:

- Enlargeable maps and art
- Embedded videos
- Pop-up key term definitions

RESOURCES FOR INSTRUCTORS

All instructor resources are available for download after free registration at

wwnorton.com/catalog/instructor-resources

Resources for Your LMS

Easily add high-quality Norton digital resources to your online, hybrid, or lecture courses. Get started building your course with our easy-to-use integrated resources; all activities can be accessed right within your existing learning management system. The downloadable file includes integration links to the following resources, organized by chapter:

- Ebook
- InQuizitive
- History Skills Tutorials
- Primary Source Exercises & Map Exercises
- Student Site Resources

Test Bank

The Test Bank features more than 1,500 questions—including multiple choice, true/false, and short-answer questions—aligned with the chapter's

Focus Questions. This bank of quiz and exam content provides multiple avenues for comprehension and skill assessment.

Norton Testmaker brings Norton's high-quality testing materials online. Create assessments from anywhere with an Internet connection, without downloading files or installing specialized software. Search and filter test bank questions by chapter, type, difficulty, learning objectives, and other criteria. You can also customize questions to fit your course. Then, easily export your tests to Microsoft Word or Common Cartridge files for import into your LMS.

Instructor's Manual

The Instructor's Manual contains:

- Detailed chapter summaries
- Chapter outlines
- Discussion/forum prompts
- Lecture ideas
- Sample responses to Questions for Analysis in the text, and more

Lecture and Art PowerPoint Slides

The lecture PowerPoint slides combine chapter review, images, maps, and lecture notes, and are easily customizable. Art PowerPoint slides and JPEGs are available separately for every image and map in the text. Alt-text is provided for each item.

PREFACE

How did our world get to be the way it is? Why are some parts of the world so much richer than others? Is gender inequality universal, or have societies ever existed without it? Why are empires, so common throughout most of world history, so rare today? Why in both the Americas and Eurasia—which developed in isolation from each other—did many early cities feature monumental architecture, grid patterns, and open public spaces? When and why did slavery begin, and why, after thousands of years, was it abolished almost everywhere in the nineteenth century? What role has climate change played in history, and has that role changed in recent decades?

The study of world history can provide answers to big questions like these. Almost any variety of history can help explain how and why societies have changed over time. However, world history (or global history—I make no distinction between the two terms) is a special kind of history. It is not the sum of all history: it is in fact more than the sum of its parts.

WHAT IS DISTINCTIVE ABOUT WORLD HISTORY?

World history is comparative: it helps distinguish what is commonplace from what is distinctive about societies. In the early chapters of this book, we will notice that places where people raised crops that store well were much more likely to develop kingdoms, empires, and other states than places where people relied on crops that spoil too quickly to be stored and distributed. An important pattern like this would be harder to see if we were looking at the histories of China, India, Africa, and South America separately, without comparison. So too with several religious movements of the sixteenth and seventeenth centuries. The Protestant Reformation in Europe, the birth of the Sikh religion in India, and the Shi'a Islamic revival in seventeenth-century Iran all emphasized personal relationships with divinity, and valued intuition over institutions in matters of faith. Comparing these (as Chapter 18 does) suggests a common pattern despite the different contexts.

World history is also selective. Because the past is virtually infinite, all historians must choose what to include in their accounts and what to leave out. World historians must be more selective to avoid having their subject become a giant jumble of facts. World history tends to foreground parallels, contrasts, and connections among societies rather than the details of national history. So, for example, Chapter 9 considers the impact of iron working on both northern Europe and sub-Saharan Africa after 1000 BCE. In Africa, iron making and iron tools tended to bring societies closer through trade, but in northern Europe it had the opposite effect, weakening linkages. A world historical lens on international politics similarly shows that on every continent in the sixteenth and seventeenth centuries a handful of big empires grew much larger, eliminating hundreds of smaller states. In Chapter 19, we see that this was not an accident but a result of faster flows of new technologies and techniques of warfare through a globalizing world.

In the process of being selective, world history can also highlight the global trends that are distinctive across long stretches of time. For thousands of years, powerful states saw fit to build and maintain empires as long as their power lasted. But after 1960 or so, the idea of empire lost its appeal, and ever since the powerful have preferred to avoid formal empires. That is a historically unique development, although not necessarily a permanent change. On even longer time scales, we can see, as Chapter 29 explains, that the modern rise in greenhouse gas concentrations in the atmosphere has been faster—by far—than any other such rise in the historical or geological record. These two examples of distinctive, and even peculiar, aspects of our own period are best understood in the long sweep of world history.

THE APPROACH OF THIS TEXTBOOK

This book differs from most world history textbooks in a few ways. It has one author, not several, which has been hard on that author but might be good for the reader because it raises the odds of achieving a consistent viewpoint and framework. I hope I have achieved that because it might compensate for the chief disadvantage of a single-authored world history: no author can know everything. I do not have the same command of human evolution, ancient Chinese history, medieval Russian history, or modern U.S. history that specialists in these fields have. However, I have taught world history for decades and learned a fair bit along the way, not least from my students. I've also written global-scale histories before, mainly environmental histories. This book reflects my own background as a historian, giving frequent attention to matters of geography and environment.

This book features a particular framework for understanding world history. Having an effective framework is essential because it helps organize information and put it into a context—avoiding that giant jumble of facts. The framework here is based on the concept of webs of social interaction.

It's an approach that, I hope, will provide readers with a strong sense of the connectedness, but also the contrasts, of world history—and in an easily accessible way.

THE WEBS OF HUMANKIND: AN OVERVIEW

People always and everywhere have been connected to others. These connections have taken many forms, ranging from kinship and friendship to economic exchange and military confrontation. In all such relationships, people exchanged information and used it to guide their future behavior. They often also exchanged technologies, religious beliefs, artistic visions, trade goods, food crops, violent threats, lethal infections, and much else. These exchanges shaped what people could do and could imagine. When exchanges and connections became regular, I call them webs of interaction.

For most of human history—from the dawn of our species' existence some 300,000 years ago until roughly 13,000 years ago—our ancestors lived in a very loose, far-flung human web. Their communities were normally small migratory bands that only occasionally mixed with others. That way of life only rarely presented them with the stimulus of new ideas and objects to consider. By later standards, the pace of change in arenas such as technology or social organization was glacially slow. This doesn't mean nothing happened, though: this was the time when humans invented religion and language, and migrated from their place of origin in Africa to settle every habitable continent. These were momentous changes, even if they happened extremely slowly.

Beginning around 13,000 years ago (or roughly 11,000 BCE), a handful of changes occurred that encouraged the weaving of much tighter webs of interaction. While the loose and far-flung human web continued in the background, new, tighter webs developed where people began to settle into permanent, sedentary communities. Sedentary life in those times worked best beside a seashore with abundant edible marine life (as on the coasts of Japan, for example) or amid wild grasses that yielded reliable and nutritious seeds (as in what is now southeastern Turkey). Some of these now-sedentary people domesticated wild animals and plants, converting them genetically into livestock and crops, respectively. Farming, the first evidence of which comes from Southwest Asia, encouraged larger communities, denser populations, and more vibrant, if still local, interactive webs—"local" here means several villages and a few thousand people. Changes in technology and social organization now came more rapidly than before.

Around 5,500 years ago (3500 BCE), much bigger and tighter webs formed when people first clustered together into cities, and then built networks of cities linked by regular trade and communication. This too happened first in Southwest Asia, specifically in what is now southern Iraq. But it didn't take long—a thousand years at most—before cities and regional webs linking multiple cities emerged elsewhere—in northeast Africa, South Asia, and East Asia, and by 200 CE in the Americas, especially in Meso-america and the Andes region of South America. Each of these regional webs, between roughly 2500 BCE and 200 CE, would grow to contain a few million people, dozens of cities, and thousands of villages. Within these emerging webs, changes in ideas, technologies, and social structures came faster than before, and faster than among people not connected to webs. Cities—nodes in these larger webs where people with different outlooks, religions, skills, and technologies rubbed shoulders every day—became hothouses of innovation and adaptation.

Mainly through the expansion of long-distance trade, those urban-based webs gradually linked up to one another. The biggest one formed between the Nile and the Ganges, and the next biggest in East Asia. By roughly 200 CE, sprawling webs of interaction spanned continents. By far the biggest, called the Old World web in this book, was anchored at either end by China and Egypt, stretching over most of Eurasia and North Africa. (Scholars often refer to Eurasia and Africa as the Old World, a usage I adopt because human occupation of those continents predates that anywhere else.) In 200 CE, it encompassed tens of millions of people living in cities and villages especially along rivers such as the Huang He (Yellow River), the Yangzi, the Ganges, the Indus, the Tigris and Euphrates, and the Nile. All of these rivers served as sources of irrigation water and arteries of transport, per-mitting more productive farming, larger food supplies, more people, more trade—and more frequent and sustained interaction of all sorts. The Old World web eventually—by 1400 CE—grew to include almost everyone living within a space the edges of which were Japan and Java in the east, and Iceland and West Africa in the west. At the time, that area included at least three-quarters of humankind, or more than 200 million people.

Smaller but still sizeable regional webs grew up elsewhere. In Africa, the northeastern region along the Nile and the Red Sea coast was enmeshed in the Old World web early on—by 1500 BCE if not before. Elsewhere in Africa, much smaller webs developed, especially along the Niger River in West Africa. That one merged with the Old World web by about 800 CE, mainly through the trans-Saharan trade routes that linked North Africa and West Africa as never before.

In the Americas, local webs developed based around irrigation agricul-ture, the first of them starting as early as 3000 BCE in the Andes. Bigger regional webs formed in the Andes by about 100 CE and another in Meso-america by about 200 CE. Both the Mesoamerican and Andean webs grew, but intermittently with many reversals. The outer threads of these two webs by 1450 CE extended far across the Americas and linked both continents very loosely through trade and migrations.

In Oceania, as people sailed from what is now Indonesia out to remote Pacific islands, a process that began around 2000 BCE, they formed thin webs linking island communities, bringing thousands of people into contact with one another over vast distances.

In character, these smaller webs bore many similarities to the Old World web: they were held together by trade, travel, and communication, and clusters of people—whether in cities or tightly packed villages—served as key nodes for the transmission of ideas, goods, and everything else. But in size, the Old World web, from its beginning around 200 CE, always outstripped all others.

A GLOBAL WEB

Beginning in the fifteenth century, breakthroughs in transport and communication fused all these webs into a single global one. Breakthroughs in ship design and in information storage, especially printing technology, contributed to a bigger breakthrough: sailors accumulated enough information to crack the code of the planet's winds and currents, enabling them to navigate the deep oceans much more securely than ever before. That launched an era of intercontinental navigation that wove the world's coastlands together into a global web. Beginning with Chapter 16, which overlaps both volumes of the text, this Global web is the main story of the book.

This new Global web triggered thorough-going and accelerating changes in the sixteenth through the eighteenth centuries, the first of which I call biological globalization. Infectious diseases such as measles and smallpox spread to populations with no acquired immunity, especially in the Americas and on Pacific islands, cutting populations by 50 to 95 percent. Sailors and ships also carried crops to new environments. Potatoes, for example, native to the Andes, gradually became part of the diet in northern Europe, and eventually in China and north India as well. Maize, originally from Mexico, became Africa's most important crop.

The Global web brought changes that extended far beyond biological transfers. New information and ideas from the four corners of the Earth led people to reconsider long-cherished beliefs, altering religious landscapes in Europe and Asia, as Chapter 18 details. The variety of political formats in which people lived diminished as small polities gave way to growing empires. The productive techniques and technologies that underpinned industrialization spread widely within decades after their introduction during the eighteenth and nineteenth centuries, reflecting the accelerating flow of information characteristic of the Global web. So too with new ideas about freedom, justice, and sovereignty that underlay political revolutions around the world, from the United States and France in the late eighteenth century to Mexico, Russia, and China in the early twentieth.

Throughout the last 150 years, with telegraphs, telephones, and networked computers, the Global web has grown tighter, its communications faster, its linkages stronger. Cities, which were home to about 10 percent of humankind in 1800, by 2010 accounted for more than half of the world's population. Today, almost everyone lives within a single, unified, global-scale web of interaction, competition, and cooperation. Different people experience this differently, but almost no one (aside from a few thousand people deep in rain forests) lives outside it.

WEB MAKING: A GLOBALIZING PROCESS

The long process of web making over thousands of years is in effect a globalizing one. The first webs launched a long-term trend—with reversals—toward greater connectedness. In this sense, world history has a direction to it. Several motors drove the web-making process. Among them were the economic advantages of specialization and exchange, which inspired trade. The desire of monarchs, whether Macedonian kings such as Alexander the Great or Chinese emperors such as Han Wudi, to expand their power and influence also extended the reach of webs. So did the ambition of missionaries to spread their religions. Merchants, monarchs, and missionaries weren't trying to extend webs—they didn't think in these terms at all. But their ambitions and actions had that effect. So did the routine movements of travelers, pilgrims, refugees, soldiers, sailors, pastoral nomads, and everyone else who moved around, interacted with strangers, and—unintentionally—helped to build sustained webs of interaction.

The long-term trend of webs growing, tightening, and consolidating was far from consistent. At times, when empires fell apart, plagues swept through, or trade routes shifted, contacts and connections might languish and webs unravel. This happened after the fifth century CE in western Europe when the Roman Empire fell. Webs might also fray as a result of deliberate choices, as in East Asia in the late eighth century CE when the rulers of China's Tang dynasty decided to reduce foreign contacts of all sorts. The complete disappearance of webs occurred often on local scales, probably more often in the Americas than elsewhere. But bigger webs, although they often frayed or shrank, rarely disappeared altogether and normally rebounded within a century or two, as happened in East Asia after new dynasties replaced the Tang.

The expansion of webs was often a brutal process. It frequently involved warfare and epidemics. Both occurred at once in many cases—as, for example, after Christopher Columbus's voyages of the 1490s when the Americas

Major Webs of World History

NAME AND EXPLANATION	LOCATION	APPROXIMATE DATES
Human web This refers to the faint and intermittent ties that have linked all, or almost all, humans throughout our species' entire career. But its connections were weak compared to the tighter local and regional webs, and to the Global web of the last five centuries.	Everywhere people have lived, except in the few cases where groups became genuinely isolated	From human origins ca. 300,000 years ago until today
Southwest Asian web This formed in the Tigris-Euphrates valley beginning about 5000 BCE. It extended into surrounding uplands by 3500 BCE, lasting until 2500 BCE when it was subsumed into the Nile-Indus web.	Mesopotamia and neighboring areas	5000 BCE to 2500 BCE
Nile-Indus web This was an expansion of the Southwest Asian web to both the east and the west.	From Egypt, and at times its southern neighbor Nubia, across Southwest Asia to the Indus valley	2500 BCE to 1500 BCE
Nile-Ganges web A further expansion across north India.	From Egypt across Southwest Asia and north India	1500 BCE to 200 CE
East Asian web Originated in China but extended to neighboring societies.	North and central China, with strands reaching into Korea, Japan, Central Asia, and northernmost Vietnam	1000 BCE to 200 CE
Old World web This is the fusion of the East Asian web and the Nile-Ganges web, with extensions into Europe and Africa.	From Senegal and Scotland in the west to Japan and Java in the east, including the Indian Ocean world	200 CE to 1500 CE
Andean web This formed in South America from the Moche and Tiwanaku cultures.	From the Altiplano in Bolivia to the coasts of Peru, straddling the high Andes	100 CE to 1500 CE
Mesoamerican web This developed with the interactions among the Maya, the Zapotecs, and Teotihuacán.	Central and southern Mexico and the Maya lands of Yucatán and northern Guatemala	200 CE to 1500 CE
Global web This is the fusion of the Old World web, the American webs, and all other local and regional webs.	Global, but tiny uncontacted communities deep in rain forests such as Amazonia remain outside it.	1500 CE to the present. It began to take shape with oceanic voyagers in the fifteenth and sixteenth centuries and is still tightening in the twenty-first.

were firmly linked to the Old World web. Newly introduced diseases in combination with warfare killed tens of millions of people in the Americas. Peoples who had lived outside of webs, such as the indigenous populations of the Americas, Australia, Polynesia, or Siberia, often suffered heavily for a century or more once they became entangled in webs.

As a rule, the expansion of webs, especially the Global web in recent centuries, has worked to reduce cultural diversity. The number of languages spoken has fallen by about half since 1500, while English, Spanish, Hindi, Arabic, Chinese, and a few others have acquired more speakers. The number of legal traditions too has declined: more and more people live under fewer and fewer legal systems, many of them now based on English common law or Islam's code of shari'a. Farmers' fields feature fewer strains of wheat, maize, and rice than they did 100 years ago, partly because farmers now have more information about which crop varieties yield best in their environments.

The table at left summarizes the main webs featured in this book. Many smaller ones that involved thousands, but not millions, of people are left out of the table. The dates are given in round numbers and are approximate because webs formed and merged gradually, with no sharp beginnings or end points.

ORGANIZATION OF THE BOOK

With the globalizing process of web making at work throughout, this book takes a largely regional organization in Volume 1 and a largely global one in Volume 2. The schemes of regionalization it adopts change as the world changed, reflecting the formation, and occasional decay, of webs. So, for example, "Africa" in some periods is treated as a continental unit, but at other times regions of Africa appear as parts of larger maritime webs. In Chapter 13, the coasts of eastern Africa are presented as a key element of a region called the Indian Ocean world. In Chapter 21, parts of Africa appear as components of a different region, the Atlantic world, united by trade, travel, and exchanges among the coastlands of the Americas, Europe, and Africa. The book often avoids the vocabulary of regions as we typically see them today. A conventional regionalization of the world takes the continents as regions, with a few additions such as "Middle East" and lately "Asia-Pacific." In emphasizing webs of interaction, this book minimizes the projection onto the past of today's conventional regions. So there is no "Middle East" until the twentieth century here, and no "Latin America" until the nineteenth century. It is worth noting too that in this world history some of the most important regions are defined by water, not land. There is no perfect way to regionalize the globe for all time periods. The different regionalization schemes used in this book reflect the changing reality of web connections among people in the past.

PARTS AND PERIODS

This book is divided into six parts, each of which corresponds to a period of time.

Part 1 (Chapters 1–3) takes on the longest sweep of time, from human origins to about 1500 BCE. For most of this period, all people lived in Africa. When some migrated to other continents, beginning about 70,000 years ago, we follow them wherever they went, which included every habitable continent by 12,000 BCE. Part 1 is global in the sense that it considers the experience of the entire human population. The very thin and faint web uniting our entire species endured despite the inter-continental wanderings of peoples.

Part 2 (Chapters 4–10) deals mainly with the period between 3500 BCE and 200 CE and shifts to a regional scheme of organization. It addresses the emergence of regional webs in parts of Eurasia, Africa, and the Americas, as outlined in the table above. In so doing, it examines the rise of cities, states, organized religions, and stratified, hierarchical societies. In places such as China, India, or Egypt—among others—these millennia also saw the formation of durable cultural traditions anchored in religion. By 200 CE, several regional webs in Eurasia and North Africa had fused into the single, sprawling Old World web. Chapter 9 pairs two places not often drawn together for comparison: northern Europe and sub-Saharan Africa. They were similar in that they stood on the frontiers of the big webs in the millennia before 200 CE. Among the resulting commonalities were smaller polities, a slower pace of technological change, and better health than that of people living in the larger webs. Slowly, though, they too became entangled in the Nile-Ganges web and, eventually, the full Old World web. The Americas and Oceania, the focus of Chapter 10, remained autonomous, unaffected by the formation of the Old World web until well beyond 200 CE. So this chapter continues up to 1000 CE, by which time a big web linking both North and South America had taken shape.

Part 3 (Chapters 11–15) maintains a regional organization and takes up the centuries between 200 CE and 1400 CE—and in one chapter to 1500. Most of it is devoted to developments within the Old World web, in East and South Asia, Africa, and Europe. It deals with several aspects of the maturation of regional webs—such as improvements in transport and navigation, and the accelerated spread of cultural traditions such as Buddhism, Christianity, and Islam. The final chapter of Part 3 returns to the Americas and Oceania, each of them still standing apart with no significant links to the Old World web until 1492 in the Americas and about 1770 in Oceania. Both built, or extended, webs of their own, which developed in accordance with prevailing conditions: the vast distances of the Pacific, for example, rewarded the navigational skills that islanders developed, while the paucity of domesticable animals in the Americas encouraged agriculture that did not require plowing. Yet strong, thought-provoking parallels existed between the societies in the Old World web and those of the Americas—as, for example, in the relationships between religious and political power, or the prevalence of gender inequality.

With **Part 4** (Chapters 16–20), the book becomes global in scope again because the links connecting every large population strengthened so much between 1400 and 1800 with the weaving of the Global web. Chapter 16, a pivotal chapter that ends Volume 1 and begins Volume 2, focuses on the convergence of the world's webs into a single Global web and the wave of biological exchanges that followed. This biological globalization set some of the basic conditions for world history in the next centuries, mainly through major shifts in agriculture and population. The connections of the Global web meant that the oceans no longer separated peoples as much as before. The histories of Angola and Brazil, as we see in Chapter 17, were firmly linked by a slave trade that established African culture in much of Brazil. As we see in Chapter 19, the effective use of guns in sixteenth-century Japan illustrates the effects of the Global web in distributing techniques and technology around the world. In Chapter 20, we see that the histories of China and Mexico developed a tie through transpacific trades in silver, silk, and porcelain routed through the Philippines. Part 4 considers the comparatively sudden changes resulting from this surge of globalization in the realms of ecology, ideas and culture, economies, and political competition.

With one exception, the chapters of **Part 5** (21–25) are also global in scope and organized by theme. They span the centuries between 1620 and 1920. The exception is Chapter 21, which is devoted to political revolutions in the Atlantic world—Africa, Europe, and the Americas. Collectively, these Atlantic revolutions were momentous enough, and their legacies global enough, to merit treatment as a unit unto themselves. The balance of Part 5 considers fundamental changes such as industrialization, the near-elimination of slavery and other forms of forced labor, and the rise of such political trends as nationalism and imperialism. It also treats some major political revolutions—in part, efforts to resist imperialism and industrialization—in India, China, Mexico, and Russia. Its main theme is the many political and social realignments and revolutions encouraged by the formation, and tightening, of the Global web. It seeks to find some balance between global currents and local factors in explaining these turbulent times.

Part 6 (Chapters 26–29) takes on a mere century and a half, from 1870 to the present—an era of accelerating globalization and episodes of fierce resistance against it. Maintaining the pattern of chapters that are global in scope and focused on themes, it takes up international politics more than earlier parts do, including two world wars, the Cold War, and decolonization. It also explores the global economy, particularly the rapid rise of East Asia; global ecological shifts including recent climate change; and social and cultural transformations such as migration, urbanization, or the rise of globalized popular music and sport. The pace and scope of global integration in this last century and a half is extraordinary, and many peoples and communities found the rapidity of changes wrenching or the direction of change unwelcome. Part 6 explains why the pace was so fast and the process so disruptive.

CONSIDERING THE EVIDENCE OF WORLD HISTORY

One last point to bear in mind before the story begins. Understanding history is like assembling a challenging jigsaw puzzle. Some of the pieces clearly fit together in obvious ways. Most of them don't, and it is not easy to know what to make of them. Many of the pieces are missing, hidden under the rugs of time. All this means that history is an exercise in creating plausible interpretations from incomplete evidence.

One needs to use imagination disciplined by evidence to arrive at a reliable reconstruction of the past. It is evidence—written texts, works of art, archeology, oral traditions, historical linguistics, and now also genetic analysis—that helps us figure out what is plausible and what isn't, what arguments to accept and what to reject. Among the skills history teaches are the abilities to assess evidence thoughtfully and to recognize when the evidence is insufficient or contradictory, making strong conclusions difficult.

When multiple pieces of evidence seem to be saying the same thing, and especially when different types of evidence harmonize, we can be more confident of our conclusions. So, for example, when linguistic evidence, genetic evidence, and pottery fragments all suggest that people from West Africa filtered into central and southern Africa beginning roughly 1500 BCE, we can be confident that something historians call the Bantu migration took place—even though there is not a single written document that says anything about it. If pottery were the only evidence, we could not be sure about the migration—people can trade pots over long distances, one person to the next, without migrating. If we had only the genetic or the linguistic evidence, we would have only the fuzziest idea about when the migration occurred.

For the deeper past, we have fewer written records, and none more than 5,000 years old. In some places—the Americas, Oceania, and most of sub-Saharan Africa, for example—written records are non-existent or at best extremely rare until 500 years ago. In these situations, other forms of evidence such as archeological remains or genetic analysis become much more important in underpinning interpretations of the past.

Keep in mind too that written documents almost always reflect the viewpoints of adults rather than children, men rather than women, rich rather than poor, powerful rather than weak, and literate rather than illiterate. In archeology, as well, we are likelier to find the remains of royal palaces built of stone than peasant huts made of thatched reeds. Historians (and other scholars) have shown some ingenuity in overcoming these inherent biases, "reading against the grain" as historians often put it. But these asymmetries of information remain, and it is important to remain aware of them.

Sifting, evaluating, and interpreting incomplete and sometimes contradictory evidence, and evidence of different types, are crucial intellectual skills. The study of history, and especially world history, hones those skills. As Ziauddin Barani, a scholar of the fourteenth century writing in Persian but working in India, said: "I have not observed such advantages from any branch of learning as I have from history." The branches of learning have changed since his day, as a grounding in history would lead you to expect, but he could still be right.

ACKNOWLEDGMENTS

During the years devoted to researching, writing, and revising this book, I have accumulated deep debts to many people. First to acknowledge are those to my former students who have read parts of the text and suggested improvements: Kwabenah Akuamoah-Boateng, Dan Brendtro, Adrienne Kates, Michelle Melton, Ani Muradyan, and Michael Samway. Then various classes of History 007 and History 008 in recent years, undergraduates who collectively made thousands of (anonymous) comments on a first draft of the book. Because the book is written for students, their feedback proved enormously valuable. I also wish to thank—enormously—Robynne Mellor and Javier Puente, who worked as teaching assistants in my world history classes and provided their own advice on drafts of the book. And Benan Grams, a PhD student who helped me with medieval Arabic passages.

I am fortunate to have family members willing to share their unvarnished opinions of my prose. These include Katriona McNeill and Patrick McNeill, Mairead MacRae, Leila Meymand, and especially my sister and brother-in-law Ruth McNeill and Bart Jones. They read every word of every chapter and were not stingy with their advice. My sister taught me to read before I went to school and ever since, it seems, has felt a responsibility to improve my facility with the English language. When she read my PhD dissertation, she wrote that it could be improved if I added 20 commas per page, and it would hardly matter where I put them. I must have taken her suggestion too strongly, because when she read this book she said I should remove most of its commas. My wife, Julie Billingsley, also read passages and suggested, tactfully, that I should try to make the book more amusing.

Another family member earned my deepest thanks although he never read a word of this book. In his final years my father, William McNeill, never failed to ask me when I would finish it, which spurred me along. Debating with him how best to present the big picture in our short, co-authored book, *The Human Web: A Bird's-Eye View of World History* (2003), influenced the thinking behind this book more strongly than anything else—other than my years teaching world history.

Several professional colleagues also earned my deep gratitude. Three experienced world history teachers helped shape my understanding of how to introduce the subject to students: Alan Karras of the University of California and Merry Wiesner-Hanks of the University of Wisconsin–Milwaukee, with both of whom I served for several years creating and vetting questions for the Advanced Placement world history examination; and the late Jerry Bentley of the University of Hawaii. Rick Potts of the American Museum of Natural History, an expert in human evolution, helped me avoid missteps in the first chapter. At the Foundation for Civic Space and Public Policy in Warsaw, Poland, professors Spasimir Domaradzki, Maciej Janowski, Dariusz Kołodziejczyk, and Jan Szemiński critiqued parts of the manuscript, correcting some of my misconceptions especially about central and eastern European history. My colleagues in the History Department and Walsh School of Foreign Service at Georgetown University have contributed to my education in countless ways over the past 30-plus years. Their insights, perspectives, knowledge, and encouragement have enabled me to come to grips with world history in ways unimaginable to me without their help.

I wish to acknowledge as well the superb work of a team of colleagues at W. W. Norton, beginning with Steve Forman, who has patiently supervised the entire project from start to finish, read multiple drafts, and made thousands of valuable suggestions—of which I probably should have taken more than I did. Lily Gellman was invaluable in her orchestration of myriad details in the publishing process. Alice Vigliani, the excellent manuscript editor, improved and tightened my prose and eliminated some of those extraneous commas to which I am now apparently prone. Charlotte Miller, our outstanding cartographer, created an ambitious map program with insight and vigor, and politely tolerated my endless suggestions for revisions. Gerra Goff and Stephanie Romeo were creative and resourceful in building the extensive illustrations program. Melissa Atkin brought order to the puzzle pieces of the book as project editor. Jillian Burr, our brilliant designer, created beautiful book and jacket designs. Sarah Bartley gave us timely advice from the perspectives of marketing and sales. Carson Russell, our media editor, planned and implemented the important digital resources that support the book; and Jane Searle, our production manager, kept this big train running on schedule.

REVIEWERS OF THE FIRST EDITION

Other professional colleagues, most of whom I have never met, have also worked wonders for this book. World history teachers and scholars from many colleges in the United States and abroad have read draft chapters and made useful suggestions:

Anthony Barbieri-Low, University of California, Santa Barbara
Hayden Bellenoit, United States Naval Academy
David Biggs, University of California, Riverside
Beau Bowers, Central Piedmont Community College—Levine
Kevin Brady, Tidewater Community College—Chesapeake Campus
Gary Burgess, United States Naval Academy
Annette Chamberlin, Virginia Western Community College
Stephen Chappell, James Madison University
Katy Clay, Shippensburg University
Sean C.D. Colbert-Lewis, Sr., North Carolina Central University
Phyllis Conn, St. John's University
Judith Davis, Three Rivers College
Peter De Rosa, Bridgewater State University
Eric Dursteler, Brigham Young University
Gregory Ference, Salisbury University
Allen Fromherz, Georgia State University
Denis Gainty, Georgia State University
Jessica Gerard, Ozarks Technical Community College
Rachael Goldman, Rutgers University
Noah Goode, Central Piedmont Community College—Levine
Andrew Goss, University of New Orleans
Candice Goucher, Washington State University
Hans Hägerdal, Linnaeus University
Sarah Hamilton, Auburn University
Ann Hardgrove, University of Texas at San Antonio
Matthew Herbst, University of California, San Diego
Carsten Hjort Lange, Aalborg University
Stephanie Holyfield, Wesley College
Paul Stephen Hudson, Georgia State Perimeter College
John Hyland, Newport University
Joanna Jury, Georgia State University
Sofia Laurein, San Diego City College
Jess LeVine, Brookdale Community College
Scott Lloyd, University of Arkansas
Anthony Makowski, Delaware County Community College—
    Marple Campus
Harold Marcuse, University of California, Santa Barbara
Matthew McCoy, University of Arkansas—Fort Smith Campus
Ian Miller, St John's University—Queens Campus
Elizabeth Milliken, Mount Hood Community College
Philip Misevich, St. John's University
Lance Nolde, California State University, Channel Islands

Hosok O, Dixie State University

Annette Palmer, Morgan State University

Alejandro Quintana, St John's University—Queens Campus

Daren Ray, Auburn University

Charles V. Reed, Elizabeth City State University

Thomas J. Rushford, Northern Virginia Community College—
    Annandale Campus

Ruma N. Salhi, Northern Virginia Community College—
    Annandale Campus

Christine Senecal, Shippensburg State University

Michael Seth, James Madison University

Emily Story, Salisbury University

Barbara Syrrakos, City College of New York

Peter Utgaard, Cuyamaca College

Evan Ward, Brigham Young University

Molly Warsh, University of Pittsburgh

James Webb, Colby College

Andre Wink, University of Wisconsin

Jennifer Winters, Northern Virginia Community College—
    Annandale Campus

In a book that aims to explore the history of the world from the origins of humans until today, there are sure to be more than a few lapses. Those are all my fault and no one else's.

J. R. McNeill, *Georgetown University*

THE WEBS *of* HUMANKIND

A WORLD HISTORY

SEAGULL EDITION

Volume Two

WEAVING THE GLOBAL WEB

1400 to 1800

Chapters 16 through 20 cover world history between 1400 and 1800. During that period, human history became genuinely global for the first time. Events in South America, such as a discovery of silver, affected China, and changes in Chinese tax policies affected silver miners in South America. The regional webs featured in Part 3 fused into a single global web.

The great economist Adam Smith in his famous work, *The Wealth of Nations* (1776), wrote that:

> The discovery of America, and that of a passage to the East Indies by the Cape of Good Hope, are the two greatest and most important events recorded in the history of mankind....By uniting, in some measure, the most distant parts of the world, by enabling them to relieve one another's wants, to increase one another's enjoyments, and to encourage one another's industry, their general tendency would seem to be beneficial.

Now, two and half centuries after Adam Smith, it's a bit easier to see the full significance of "uniting, in some measure, the most distant parts of the world." In Part 4 we focus on just how this "uniting" happened, and its consequences—economic, political, intellectual, social, and biological. From here on in the book, as history became more globalized, our portrayal of it also becomes more global in scope.

The First Pulse of Globalization

Before starting in, one further point is worth establishing. Although Smith refers to the discovery of America, in fact America—the Western Hemisphere—already had tens of millions of people in it, and neither the Vikings nor Columbus actually discovered it. What Columbus did discover was a practical route between Europe and America. What he and dozens of other mariners collectively discovered was how to sail the world's oceans by exploiting the prevailing winds and currents. Before the fifteenth century, almost all sailors except Polynesians and Vikings hugged the shorelines. Polynesians in the tropical Pacific, and Vikings in the North Atlantic, had learned how to navigate and survive at sea for many weeks without sighting land. But even they did not establish enduring routes over the seas they sailed.

Between 1400 and 1800, mariners traversed all the world's seas and linked all the world's inhabited coastlines and hinterlands. They discovered oceanic routes, unlocked the secrets of the globe's wind patterns, and, armed with this knowledge, spun the first genuinely global web of humankind. That was the first pulse of true globalization, and its events belong—just as Smith said—among the most important in history.

New Crossroads

One aspect of the new global connections deserves underlining at the start. For thousands of years before the 1490s, the best place on Earth in which to learn about other places was Southwest Asia. Its connections, by land and sea, brought its peoples into at least intermittent touch with others in Africa, Europe, South Asia, and to a lesser extent Southeast and East Asia as well. Southwest Asian societies enjoyed access to the Mediterranean, Black, and Red Seas, the Indian Ocean world, and the overland routes of the Eurasian steppe. Southwest Asia was the land bridge connecting world regions, the closest thing to a center of the Old World web. This geographical position put Southwest Asian societies in a situation that was sometimes dangerous but often advantageous. Their position exposed them at times to more epidemics and perhaps more invasions than most peoples elsewhere. But it also enabled them to learn more from more places, and this they could turn to their advantage.

Southwest Asia gradually lost this dangerous but privileged position after the 1490s. Seaborne communications and trade enabled Atlantic Europeans gradually to take over this role. Increasingly they, rather than Southwest Asians, learned more about technologies in use around the world. Atlantic Europeans could now adopt useful technologies from a larger menu of options than others had done. And now they, rather than Arabs, Armenians, and Persians, knew more about relative prices in different markets, enabling them to make money in trade more reliably, buying low and selling high in different parts of the world.

Global History

In Part 3, the chapters each addressed a separate region, but they shared common themes. Here, in Part 4, with the world drawing together into a single web, the chapters address separate themes with a global scope. Chapter 16 explores the navigation advances that wove the world together and the biological exchanges among regions that resulted. Chapter 17 considers the impacts of the newly formed global web on societies previously enmeshed in smaller webs. All of these societies faced severe challenges that some survived but others did not. Chapters 18 through 20 deal with the cultural, political, and economic implications, respectively, of weaving a global web.

So how did all this weaving start? The answer lies with sailors.

Convergence

THE DISCOVERY OF THE OCEANS AND BIOLOGICAL GLOBALIZATION

1400 to 1800

FOCUS QUESTIONS

1. What were the major contours of world history in 1400, as shown in the regional webs of the time?

2. What were the main differences in oceanic voyaging conducted by China's Ming dynasty and the Atlantic Europeans?

3. What were the most important effects of the biological globalization initiated by the oceanic voyaging of Atlantic Europeans?

4. Why was the first global web to extend across the world a significant development?

On the morning of October 11, 1492, Amerindians living on an island in the Bahamas (probably Watlings Island) walked to the beach and, to their astonishment, discovered Christopher Columbus. Few if any Bahamians had ever seen men wearing clothes, which was not done in their islands, let alone men in metal armor. None had ever seen ships. Columbus's ships far eclipsed the dugout canoes that plied Bahamian waters. What those astonished people made of the strangers on their shores we will never know, although it's a reasonable guess that some were curious and some were terrified. Columbus, for his part, thought he stood on an island off the coast of China.

Nearly six years later, in 1498, residents of the Indian port city of Calicut, strolling along the harbor-front, were almost as astonished to discover Portuguese ships approaching. They had seen Europeans before, although not many. But they had never seen European ships anywhere in the Indian Ocean, nor any ships carrying big cannon as these did. The ships' commander, Vasco da Gama, soon found occasion to use the big cannon.

These two encounters in the 1490s symbolize the opening of a new era in world history. Before the 1490s, the Americas and Afro-Eurasia remained essentially separate hemispheres. Before the 1490s, the Old World web relied heavily on overland connections together with the maritime links centered on the Indian Ocean. After the 1490s, the world's coastlands quickly (well, over two centuries) became integrated as never before, thanks to seaborne trade. Indeed, the world's populated coasts, with scant exceptions, came to form the first genuinely global web of human interaction, channeling the flow of ideas, technologies, goods, crops, diseases, and much else.

But before we get to the story of several sailors and the seven seas, let's pause and look at the lands on which people lived as of the fifteenth century, and specifically, the webs of interaction within which they lived. Before examining the formation of a global web, it helps to remember its constituent parts.

The World's Webs in the Fifteenth Century

As of 1400, the 350 to 450 million people on Earth spoke several thousand languages, followed several hundred religions, and recognized several hundred political rulers. (A few tens of millions of them recognized no rulers at all, although with each passing year fewer and fewer lived in

CHRONOLOGY

1291 Italian sailors attempt to circumnavigate Africa

ca. 1300–1400 European and Moroccan sailors reach the Canary Islands

1368–1644 Ming dynasty in China

1402–1424 Reign of Yongle Emperor

1402–1496 Spanish conquest of the Guanches in the Canary Islands

1405–1433 Zheng He organizes and leads seven maritime voyages

1415 Portuguese army captures Moroccan port of Ceuta

ca. 1430–1440 Henry the Navigator organizes systematic voyaging along the coasts of Atlantic Africa

ca. 1480 Knowledge of how to make great ships is lost in China; Portuguese sailors establish a fort in West Africa

1492 Christopher Columbus lands in the Bahamas

1492–1650 Populations in the Americas fall by 70 to 95 percent

1494 Spain and Portugal sign the Treaty of Tordesillas

1497 Vasco da Gama embarks on expedition to India; John Cabot makes round trip from England to Newfoundland

1500 Pedro de Cabral claims Brazil for Portugal

1519–1522 Ferdinand Magellan's surviving crew members circumnavigate the globe

ca. 1550–1750 Maize becomes a food staple in Atlantic Africa

By 1570 The Pacific Ocean wind system is deciphered

ca. 1650 Population of the Americas begins to recover

ca. 1670 Military expansion of Asante kingdom begins

so-called stateless societies.) Despite nearly 5,000 years of states, cities, and empires, and some 2,000 years of expanding, proselytizing religions, the human race remained politically and culturally fragmented. It was in no deep sense a community. Even within the Old World web, spectacular diversity prevailed—from the refined world of Confucian scholars in urban China, with its leisured philosophy and gorgeous calligraphy, to the austere and dangerous world of illiterate fisherfolk on the coasts of Scotland.

The Old World Web

That diversity resulted partly from the sheer size of the Old World web. Its frontiers, in 1400, stretched from Greenland to Japan and from Indonesia to West Africa. Three-fourths of humanity lived within it. Thousands of caravan tracks, navigable rivers, and sea routes held the web together. It included hubs or nodes, such as Malacca, Calicut, Hormuz, Cairo, Constantinople, or Venice, where people heard many languages and where the silks of China crossed paths with the ivory of East Africa or the amber of Scandinavia. But it also included spaces where people kept to themselves, deep in the forests of Siberia or high in the Himalaya mountains, minimally connected to empires, trade routes, or major religions. These people, comparatively few in number, lived within the Old World web's frontiers, but they were not part of its fabric—at least, not yet in 1400.

Interactions within the Old World Web The Old World web had two main trunk routes. The overland caravan routes, collectively known as the Silk Road, linked eastern and western Eurasia. The caravan routes flourished in times of peace, when strong empires kept brigands in check and prevented dozens of local rulers from demanding payment from traders in exchange for safe passage. The best example is the Pax Mongolica (ca. 1260–1350), when the short-lived Mongol Empire stamped out brigandage almost everywhere along routes between Korea and Iraq, making travel safer for merchants.

The second main trunk route, also in reality a series of connected routes, was by sea. It extended from the East Asian ports through the waters of Southeast Asia and into the Indian Ocean, as far west as the coasts of Africa. Via a short overland passage in Egypt, these routes connected to the Mediterranean. Mastery of the monsoon winds had opened this trunk route in ancient times.

The traffic within the Old World web, along these trunk routes and countless lesser ones, served as a homogenizing force. Cultural interaction and political conquests reduced the number of different languages spoken. Meanwhile, more and more people chose (sometimes under duress) to follow fewer and fewer religions, and so Buddhism, Hinduism, Christianity, and Islam (some people would include Confucianism as a religion too) each acquired tens of millions of believers, while many other religions disappeared. Of course, at the same time, the big religions fractured, developing internal splits such as the Sunni–Shi'a divide in Islam or the Orthodox–Catholic schism in Christianity. And the big languages fractured too, although slowly. They developed dialects, so the Arabic spoken in Morocco gradually came to seem strange to Arabs in Iraq because it sounded so different from their own. So the process of homogenization in the Old World web had its limits and counter-currents.

A Thickening Web During the fifteenth century, the eastern and western edges of the Old World web were rapidly consolidating and thickening as a result of maritime trade. In earlier centuries, mastery of the arts of camel management had boosted the connectivity of the central regions of the Old World web, making desert crossings in Central Asia, Arabia, and Africa much more practical. Mastery of the monsoon winds had given sea traders in the Indian Ocean world a precocious start in developing long-distance networks. But now, from at least 1200 onward, improving ship design and navigational skill in both western Europe and eastern Asia were fast accumulating, reducing the risks of sea travel and making trade and economic specialization yet more rewarding. Sailing the western Pacific waters from Japan to Java, or the eastern Atlantic from Scandinavia to Spain, was dangerous indeed. Both seas featured frequent, furious storms, not to mention (especially in the western Pacific) bold, enterprising pirates. But bigger and better ships helped sailors overcome their understandable fears of these hazards.

Overland and Seaborne Trade These two fifteenth-century images show contrasting sides of the long-distance trade circuits of the Old World web. The image at left shows overland transport of Chinese ceramics to Southwest Asia; the image at right shows the seaborne spice trade from Southeast or South Asia as imagined by a French painter. Only high-value items could justify the costs and risks of transport, whether by land or sea, over thousands of miles.

The rewards to risking one's life and cargo at sea were genuine and growing. Both western Europe and eastern Asia produced a wide diversity of resources and goods. Markets had sprung up offering tempting prices at which to sell scarce goods from afar, whether Spanish wine in the Netherlands or Moluccan spices in China. At times, even bulk goods such as rice, salt, and timber could justify voyages in these two sea rooms.

Both these emerging maritime worlds drew additional traffic from networks of navigable rivers. In Europe, the big rivers flow fairly evenly throughout the year and permit ship or barge traffic well inland. In East and Southeast Asia, the big rivers are more seasonal because of the pattern of summer monsoon rain. But with painstaking construction of canals, dikes, and dams, these rivers too served as reliable avenues of commerce, linking interior regions with the sea.

So, in 1400, the eastern and western edges of the Old World web were humming with riverine and seaborne trade. Knowledge of geography, winds, and currents, of ship design, cartography, and navigation, of goods, markets, and prices was growing at ever faster rates. Both regions were developing a more maritime and commercial culture. Populations were recovering from the disease and climate disasters of the fourteenth century, and cities were expanding rapidly.

Local Webs

In 1400, some 60 to 120 million people in Oceania, the Americas, and the southern third of Africa lived outside the Old World web altogether. They too, of course, took part in trade networks, military conquests, and the same sorts of activities as people in the Old World web. But their scales of operations were smaller. In Oceania, people in Polynesia and Micronesia had built their own small webs of interaction. Archipelagoes like that of Hawaii, or Tonga and Fiji, hosted constant interactions among hundreds of thousands of people. In the Caroline Islands of Micronesia by 1400 or 1450, a well-integrated exchange network had grown up, using big stone discs as money—some of them heavier than a car. But this little web probably involved at most tens of thousands of people. In demographic terms, these Oceanic networks were tiny compared to the Old World web.

Webs in the Americas

In the Americas, as we saw in Chapter 15, much larger webs had developed around the dense populations in the Andes and in Mesoamerica. In 1400, perhaps 40 to 70 million people lived in the Americas, and about half were in either the Andes or Mesoamerica. Most Amerindians, and all those in the Andes or Mesoamerica, took part in interactive webs. In the absence of pack animals (outside of llamas and alpacas in the high Andes), goods could travel only by watercraft or human porters in the American webs. Canoes and rafts linked peoples on riverbanks and shorelines. Elsewhere, people had to carry everything themselves.

So the character of the American webs was slightly different from that of the Old World web, with less bulk commerce in transit. Crops such as maize diffused widely within this web, and so did some cultural practices such as ball games and mound building. But the volume and intensity of the exchanges of goods over long distances were modest compared to what occurred in the Old World web with its caravans and shipping. Buzzing markets did exist, but mainly on the local level—as in the Basin of Mexico, the region around today's Mexico City. As in the Old World web, those societies enmeshed in the American web featured more specialization and exchange, greater wealth, greater inequality, greater military power, than those societies outside the web.

Like its counterparts, the American webs left some people out entirely. In the far south of South America and in the northern reaches of North America, scattered populations lived essentially subsistence lives. In pockets of Central American or Amazonian rain forest too, there were some people living substantially in isolation.

Webs in Africa

Most of the northern half of Africa, by 1400, lay within the Old World web. Egypt had long been one of its linchpins. Trade and cultural exchange, most notably the spread of Islam, tied the East African coast as far south as Kilwa and Sofala, the Mediterranean lands, and the West African Sahel firmly to the rest of the Old World web. Where rivers made travel easy, as along the Nile and Niger, tendrils of the Old World web reached further still.

But the southern third of Africa, like sizeable parts of the Americas, or Siberia, stood apart from any big web. People there were not importing shiploads of luxury goods from Egypt or India; they were not sending young men to study Islam in Cairo or Baghdad. They were not experimenting with Indian Ocean world technology such as sugar mills or lateen-rigged sails. Instead, they were producing food and clothing for themselves or for local use, they were following their own religions, and they were using the same technologies—perhaps with minor alterations—that their ancestors had employed for many generations. They lived outside the Old World web, but within much smaller webs of their own making.

As in the Americas, these little webs in southern Africa were better for circulating ideas than goods. Without pack animals, wheeled vehicles, or ships, people here had to move everything on their backs, on their heads, or in canoes.

So in 1400 the world included one giant interactive web in Eurasia and the northern half of Africa, a large one in the Americas, and small, local ones elsewhere. The Old World web was home to most of the world's people, and to its most formidable states and societies. It alone had sailing ships capable of carrying hundreds of tons of cargo. It alone had many kinds of pack animals suited to almost any terrain. It alone had wheeled vehicles. By 1400, it had fewer obstacles to interaction, especially to trade, than did the other, smaller webs around the world.

The Old World web was not necessarily a pleasant place to live—certainly not if life expectancy or social equality are the measures—but it is where people had built the most powerful militaries, the most efficient communications networks, and the most sophisticated technologies. Therefore, it comes as no surprise that the people who brought the world's webs together, who forged the first truly global web, came from the edges of the Old World web.

The Discovery of the Open Sea

Before 1400, as earlier chapters explained, several peoples had developed maritime cultures. The most extraordinary of these was the Polynesian, which carried colonists throughout the archipelagoes of the tropical Pacific and as far south as New Zealand. However, by 1400 its farthest outposts had become cut off and sea traffic took place mainly within archipelagoes. The Vikings, too, had a seafaring history several centuries long, although by 1400 they had stopped exploring the North Atlantic and their Greenland colony was on the verge of extinction. Many other peoples sailed routinely on more protected seas, such as the Mediterranean, the Arabian Gulf, the Bay of Bengal, the South China Sea, or the Sea of Japan. The islands of Indonesia, and adjacent coasts of Southeast Asia, hosted sizeable regular traffic by 1000 CE. The traffic in all these seas was much thicker and more regular than in the Polynesian Pacific or the Viking North Atlantic. The vessels were often larger, and some could carry hundreds of tons of cargo. The routes were well established and studded with commercial seaports. Those who plied these routes usually hugged the shores, although certain passages, such as from East Africa to India and back, took sailors far from land for a week or two.

Sailors had accumulated a considerable, if fragmented, knowledge of winds and currents. Polynesians knew how to ride the currents and the trade winds of the Pacific. People all around the Indian Ocean knew how to use the monsoon to sail north in the summer and south in the winter. Everywhere, sailors had mastered the local tides, currents, and winds for the short voyages that made up the great majority of seafaring. But no one knew the overall pattern of the planet's winds. No one knew how it might be possible, in the Atlantic and Pacific as well as the Indian Ocean, to find winds that would reliably take ships far out to sea, thousands of miles from land, and then safely home again. In the fifteenth and sixteenth centuries, people learned where to find these winds, unlocking the secrets of oceanic navigation.

The ocean winds form gigantic merry-go-rounds. In the North Atlantic, for example, the prevailing winds spin in a clockwise fashion. Its westerlies (winds are named for the direction *from* which they blow, unlike ocean currents; so a westerly wind and an easterly current are going the same way) whip across from North America to Europe. Further south, the trade winds blow along the northwestern coasts of Africa and then whistle across to the Caribbean. In the South Atlantic, the merry-go-round

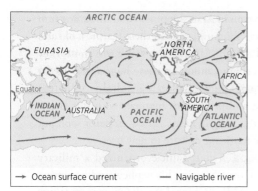 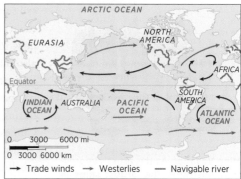

Prevailing Winds and Ocean Currents Mariners of the fifteenth and sixteenth centuries figured out the global system of winds and ocean currents, enabling them to plot the routes of sailing ships that tied the Global web together.

spins counterclockwise, so the westerlies lie far to the south and the trade winds cross from Angola to Brazil. The North and South Pacific have their own spinning wheels, as does the southern Indian Ocean. (The winds of the northern part of the Indian Ocean are governed by the monsoon.) The whole system slides north by a few hundred miles from April to August and slips back south from September to March. Thus there is a general pattern to the world's winds. But nobody knew that in 1400.

The Ming Voyages, 1405–1433

In 1400, the biggest ships and perhaps the best navigators were Chinese. Under the Song, the Yuan, and then the Ming (1368–1644) dynasties, the Chinese had rapidly developed ship and navigation technology, and Chinese merchants had taken a large role in the booming trade between East and Southeast Asia. The Ming maintained a state shipyard that employed between 20,000 and 30,000 workers. Their ships were by far the biggest in the world, capable of carrying a thousand people. Chinese tinkerers had invented the compass, and Chinese sailors used it more than sailors elsewhere. Their maritime culture was developing rapidly, thanks to constant voyaging to the islands of Southeast Asia, to Japan, and to every coast in between. By 1400, that maritime culture and Ming finances had reached a point at which they could support large, expensive, showy voyages to overawe just about everyone from Vietnam to East Africa.

Two crucial components of that maturing maritime culture were ship design and navigational tools. Chinese mariners had long used sternpost rudders and double-hulled construction. Rudders improved the steering of ships, and double hulls saved them from sinking if rammed or smashed on rocks. Chinese sailors also used the space between hulls to carry fresh water. During the Song dynasty, their seaborne trade links to the Indian Ocean acquainted them with new rigging and sails—particularly the lateen

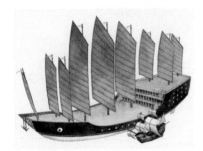

Ming Voyages As this artist's impression illustrates, the largest ships in Zheng He's fleet were 10 times the size of Columbus's flagship. The size of Ming ships was symbolic, enabling the emperor to advertise his power widely.

sail common in Arab shipping, good for sailing into the wind. Shipbuilders used these features, old and new, to design seagoing ships of 2,500 tons. They also put small cannon on these huge ships. As for navigation, Chinese sailors were already using the compass and printed sea manuals with star charts during the Song dynasty. A new emperor soon put Chinese maritime culture to new uses.

In 1402, a crafty uncle organized a military rebellion, overthrowing his nephew and becoming emperor of Ming China. Like all Chinese emperors, he took a reign name upon ascending the throne: the Yongle Emperor. To help consolidate his position, he promoted loyal eunuchs into positions of power. Eunuchs had minimal family connections of their own and therefore depended entirely on the emperor, making them highly reliable administrators. One of these eunuchs, **Zheng He**, became Yongle's indispensable adviser and political fixer. Ruling with an iron fist, Yongle moved the capital from the south to Beijing, launched campaigns against the Mongols (in which Zheng He distinguished himself), invaded and annexed part of Vietnam, and chased down and executed everyone loyal to his nephew.

Yongle also made his devoted aide Zheng He an admiral. Even though he had probably never smelled the sea, Zheng He organized a massive maritime expedition the likes of which China—and the world—had never seen. His official errand was to find and capture Yongle's nephew, who according to rumor had escaped his uncle's extermination campaign. But the scale of the undertaking indicates that Yongle had additional motives. In 1405, Zheng He set sail from Suzhou with roughly 300 ships, newly built in the shipyards of Nanjing along the Yangzi. They carried 28,000 men, both sailors and soldiers, a crew larger than the population of any city they would visit. His biggest ships, if we can believe the Chinese sources, were gigantic, about 400 feet (125 m) by 160 feet (50 m) and displacing 20,000 tons—far larger than any yet built anywhere and 10 times the size of Columbus's flagship. They were the largest wooden ships ever built.

Zheng He sailed well-traveled seas from China into the Indian Ocean. He used persuasion, intimidation, and military power to oust unfriendly rulers in Sumatra, Sri Lanka, and elsewhere, and install replacements more willing to acknowledge Yongle's overlordship and pay him tribute. In Sri Lanka he deposited a giant stone slab with inscriptions in Chinese, Persian, and Tamíl (a South Asian language in use in Sri Lanka after 1000 CE) commemorating his visit as an emissary of "the supreme overlord of kings"—lest anyone fail to appreciate Yongle's stature. Zheng He annihilated pirates—or maybe just merchant princes who failed to show proper enthusiasm for the emperor and so earned the title "pirate" in Chinese accounts. Perhaps Zheng He was also looking for allies against steppe nomads, almost always the Ming's main enemies.

Whatever his purposes, Zheng He was not attempting to find new routes. On his first six expeditions (1405–1424) he commanded similar-sized fleets, and on more than one occasion he sailed as far as the Swahili coast of Kenya. But in every case he visited ports and coasts well known to the maritime merchants of the Indian Ocean world, places where the occasional Chinese trader, and certainly Chinese goods, were familiar.

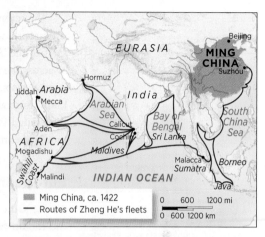

It was a traditional priority of Chinese statecraft to defend the empire's landward frontiers. Yongle mounted and personally led many expeditions into the Mongolian steppe and sent several embassies to Central Asia trying to improve the political situation on his frontiers. Overawing distant foreigners by sea ranked well behind

Voyages of Zheng He, 1405–1433 The Chinese admiral Zheng He led seven massive fleets into the Indian Ocean, following routes long familiar to merchants in these waters. Zheng He and his captains knew how to ride the monsoon winds, navigate with star charts, and find safe harbors. His routes extended to the far edges of the Indian Ocean world, the Swahili coast, the Arabian Peninsula, Java, and his home, China.

this priority, so the logic of doing it again and again came into question. Zheng He himself was an outsider in Chinese politics, a Muslim, a eunuch, and not even Chinese (he came from an ethnic minority population and had Persian ancestry as well). His career hinged entirely on the emperor's favor. When Yongle died in 1424, factions came to power that did not favor overseas voyaging.

Those factions eventually prevailed. Voyaging was costly and did not contribute to the security or virtue of the empire, nor much to its prosperity. Repairs to the Grand Canal, finished in 1411, made seafaring less important to the Ming state and Chinese society, since shipping could flow more safely on the canal than on the sea. Yongle's successor judged the oceanic voyaging wasteful and ended it in 1424. Under a later emperor, Zheng He and the eunuch faction prevailed one last time and launched a seventh voyage (1431–1433), again reaching Africa. But Zheng He died en route home, and his remaining supporters lost influence. The Ming eventually broke up the great fleet and sold it for fuelwood. By 1480, the skills needed to build such great ships had vanished.

The geographical and other knowledge accumulated on Zheng He's voyages found its way into Chinese charts, maps, and books. But it did not vastly expand, or fundamentally alter, Chinese understanding of the world. It temporarily lubricated the wheels of commerce that connected China to the Indian Ocean trading ports, but only for a few decades. The **Ming voyages** left scant enduring legacy.

Ming Giraffe Giraffes are native to Africa, but here one appears as an illustration in a Ming manuscript, indicating the reach of Chinese maritime voyaging during the Ming period. Like other luxury goods, exotic animals could be brought back from voyages as status objects and prizes.

The scale of the Ming maritime effort before 1433 suggests that the Chinese had the ships and skills to sail around Africa to Europe, or south to Australia, or across the Pacific to the Americas. But they had no good reason to try to reach Europe. They didn't yet know Australia or the Americas existed. So, instead, they sailed familiar waters in grand style with enormous government support. Then, in 1433, they stopped.

European Voyaging, 1400–1700

At the same time that the Ming were gliding into the Indian Ocean, western Europeans were probing the Atlantic. Some of them dreamed of sailing to the Indian Ocean too. They lacked the massive state support that Zheng He had enjoyed, and the states that helped them could mobilize only a tiny fraction of the resources the Ming could. These mariners were lucky if they could cobble together a tiny flotilla.

But European mariners usually had a good idea where they were heading. Navigational skill had accumulated slowly but surely over the centuries in Atlantic Europe. In Iberia especially, the practical experience of sailors combined with Arab mathematics and astronomy to create a more reliable—if by no means fully reliable—art of navigation. European sailors used the compass by the thirteenth century to find direction on cloudy days. By the fourteenth, they had translated Arabic texts on the use of astrolabes to help determine latitude. Soon they were authoring their own manuals on astrolabes—the English writer Geoffrey Chaucer penned one—and building the devices themselves. But even perfect navigational skill would have meant little without seaworthy ships.

Like the Chinese, Atlantic Europeans for a century or more had been rapidly refining their ship designs. More frequent connections in the fourteenth and fifteenth centuries between sailors in the North Atlantic and the Mediterranean yielded a hybrid in hull design and rigging. Shipbuilders combined the economical hull structure typical of Mediterranean ships—in which planks were nailed to ribs rather than to one another—with the sternpost rudder invented in the Baltic. This led to stronger, cheaper, and more maneuverable vessels. In addition, mariners supplemented square sails typical of northern waters with lateen sails characteristic of Arab seas to create the so-called fully rigged ship, which could sail swiftly before the wind and tack close to the wind.

Portolan Charts This innovation in cartography helped explorers to navigate the routes between ports. A 1571 Portolan chart of West Africa shows numerous ports along the coastline, with crests indicating the powers—especially Portugal, the red and white shield—that controlled them.

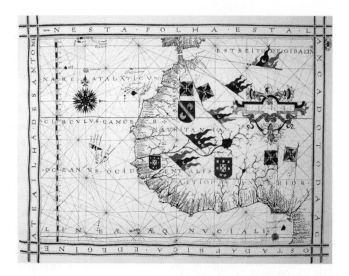

With these advances, European sailors could dispense with oars and oarsmen and rely entirely on the wind. Ships became cheaper to operate because much less was needed in the way of food, water, and wages to mount a voyage. So by the early fifteenth century, European shipwrights knew how to make sturdy, swift, and cheap ships, capable of carrying lightweight cannon and sailing anywhere in the world even in heavy weather. Their ships were far smaller than those of Zheng He, but no less seaworthy. And by 1500, they built ships large enough to carry heavy cannon capable of battering down walls or sinking any ship afloat.

Atlantic European mariners also had incentives to gamble on sailing the open seas. They, rather than the Chinese, began to unlock the secrets of the world's winds. And once they started, unlike the Ming they did not stop.

European Mariners' Motives Atlantic Europeans launched onto the high seas primarily in quest of wealth, fame, and the greater glory of their God. They started by sailing south into unfamiliar waters, looking for a practical route to African gold or Asian spices and silks, the most valuable trade goods they knew of. Merchants from Italian city-states such as Venice and Genoa had tapped into these trades, acquiring gold in Morocco or Tunisia and spices in Egypt or Syria, after the goods had changed hands many times. Merchants who could get these goods closer to the source could buy them for less and make a fortune by cutting out several middlemen.

The search for glory and fame also propelled European navigators. Fifteenth-century Europeans, especially Iberians, were steeped in a culture of adventure and chivalry as proper male pursuits. Owing in part to the centuries-long **Reconquista**—in which Christians retook Iberia from Muslim rulers—Iberian books, songs, poems, and folk tales celebrated the deeds of heroes who took daunting risks and either triumphed or, if they died young, at least won lasting fame. Young males eager to vault several rungs up the social ladder learned that they could do so through acts of reckless heroism.

The Atlantic Europeans' third reason for taking the risks of oceanic seafaring was simultaneously religious and political. It appealed especially to Christian rulers, for whom victories against Muslim states meant more glory, political legitimacy, and support from the Pope. European voyagers who could find Christian allies in Africa or Asia against Muslim foes might tip the balance of power in favor of Christian kingdoms. Helping to find sea routes that deprived Muslim states of their trade revenues served the same purposes. If successful, quests for Christian allies might set the stage for renewed conquest of the Holy Land, in the tradition of the Crusaders of a few centuries before. For Iberians, voyaging south along the African Atlantic coast seemed an extension of the Reconquista and the loot and glory it provided. Although the last Muslim rulers in Spain were ousted in 1492, there were more targets nearby in North Africa. Indeed, the Portuguese had already begun to attack Muslim strongholds in Morocco as early as 1415.

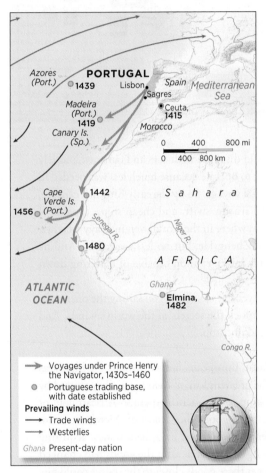

Early Exploration of the Atlantic, 1400–1480 In the fifteenth century, Iberian mariners figured out how to use the winds to venture far out into the Atlantic and get home safely. This accomplishment took navigation well beyond the familiar practice of hugging coastlines, and eventually led to successful crossings of the Atlantic and the discovery of routes linking the Atlantic and Indian Oceans.

Learning the Atlantic After about 1200, European and Moroccan mariners sailed hundreds of miles west into the uncharted Atlantic. By the fourteenth century, if not before, some stumbled across the Canary Islands, Madeira, and the Azores. The Canaries' population, called the **Guanches**, descended from North African Berber settlers who had arrived about 1000 BCE. Madeira and the Azores were uninhabited.

By the early fifteenth century, Europeans were attempting settlement of these islands, which in the Canaries required Spain to undertake military conquest of the Guanches. They fought fiercely, but their long isolation meant the Guanches had never acquired metallurgy: they used only stone, bone, and wooden weapons. Moreover, with no experience of infectious diseases by now familiar to Spaniards, they suffered repeated epidemics. The conquest of the Guanches, begun in 1402, ended in 1496. Many isolated peoples around the world would soon share their fate.

Shuttling to and from these little archipelagoes helped European sailors grow accustomed to the open Atlantic. The Canaries were crucial because they served as the entrance ramp to the northeast trade winds, which would prove to be the highway to the Americas.

At the same time as they were learning about, and starting to settle, these archipelagoes, European sailors were also edging down the coast of Africa. A pair of Italian brothers, the Vivaldis, tried to circumnavigate Africa in 1291—but they were never heard from again. Others, mainly Portuguese, followed more cautiously. The northwest coast of Africa offered little fresh water, and the northeast trade winds, which made outbound journeys simple, made it hard to get back home to Portugal. Improved ship design helped with that problem, as did the gradual discovery that sailors could follow the trade winds as far south as the Canaries and then swing north to the latitude of the Azores and catch the prevailing westerlies to get home. This was the first step in deciphering the code of the oceanic wind pattern.

African Coasts Portuguese efforts along the African coast quickened when in 1415 an army captured the Moroccan port of Ceuta. One of the leaders of that expedition, a prince known generously as Henry the Navigator, began to organize and support systematic voyaging along the coasts of Atlantic Africa in the 1430s. Henry was a seeker after honor and fame, which he once said were life's highest goals after salvation. He had strong religious convictions, influenced by chivalric notions of crusades against infidels. He also took astrology to heart and interpreted it to mean he was destined for great deeds. Henry the Navigator only put to sea two or three times in his life, but he siphoned off some of the modest resources of a threadbare dynasty in a poor country to pay for sea voyages along the northwest African coast, hoping to get at the source of West African gold.

The Portuguese voyages along the northwest coasts of Africa formed part of a larger, haphazard program that was full of failures. Several Portuguese sailors tried heading west from the Azores, out into the Atlantic, but either were pushed back by the westerly winds or lost at sea. Others tried to cross the Sahara on foot, but none returned. Henry encouraged various assaults on strongholds in Morocco, most of which failed.

All these efforts were dwarfed by the simultaneous voyaging of Zheng He, who commanded far greater resources than any Portuguese sea captain ever did. The tiny size of its investment, perhaps, explains why the Portuguese Crown did not give up and put a stop to the whole enterprise, as the Ming did with Zheng He's journeys. In

Elmina Castle The basement of the Portuguese fort of Elmina, located in present-day Ghana, was originally built as a pen to hold the enslaved people who were traded on the West African coast.

any case, the Portuguese kept at it, even after Henry's death in 1460, despite meager returns on their investment for half a century.

By the 1480s, their efforts began to pay off. Sailors reached the West African coast of what is now Ghana and established a fort—called Elmina—through which they traded for gold. Soon they found they could buy slaves on the coast and export them from Elmina to Iberia, or the sugar plantations of the Canaries or Madeira in a lucrative supplement to the gold trade. After nearly a century of meager returns, the Portuguese monarchy now had a profitable toehold in African trade. Soon every kingdom in Atlantic Europe would be sponsoring sea captains trying to get in on African commerce. One captain would also try, as several luckless Portuguese had before, to sail to China by heading west across the Atlantic.

Columbus Crosses the Atlantic   In 1477, a ship broke up in a storm off the southern coast of Portugal. Almost everyone aboard drowned, but a 23-year-old sailor swam ashore. That sailor was **Christopher Columbus**.

Columbus was the son of a weaver from Genoa in northern Italy. He was a bit of a dreamer, easily lost in popular literature with its tales of adventure. He turned to the sea as a teenager, escaping the narrow horizons of an artisan's life in Genoa. As a sailor, he first roamed the Mediterranean and then made forays into the Atlantic. He became a trader too, and sometimes made lush profits in walrus tusk, whale blubber, and other items of Atlantic trade. After he washed up in Portugal in 1477, he went to Lisbon, where he had a brother working as a mapmaker. Through his brother, Columbus began to meet people with all sorts of tall tales about what lay over the western horizon.

Columbus was working in the sugar trade, shuttling between the eastern Mediterranean and the eastern Atlantic, when in the 1480s he began to peddle schemes for a voyage further west. Sometimes he said he would find new islands, as profitable as the Canaries or Madeira. Sometimes he said he would sail to China, which he claimed

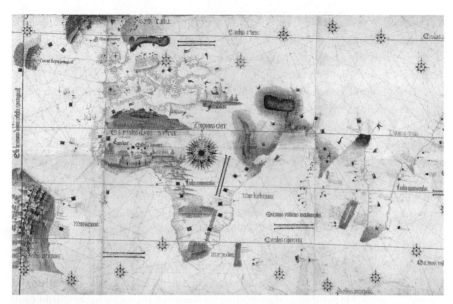

The Cantino Planisphere This Portuguese map was drawn by hand in 1502. Its rendering of the African coastline is especially detailed, an indication of how quickly and how well Portuguese mapmakers and navigators accumulated geographical information.

was a "few days" away. He had learned of the equatorial trade winds blowing to the west from Africa's northwest shores, and of the westerlies (blowing to the east) at higher latitudes. These prevailing winds, he figured, would allow a round-trip voyage to China. They would also allow him, the weaver's son, to join the titled aristocracy, which seems to have been his primary ambition. Columbus was at heart a social climber, willing to take great risks in his quest for status, wealth, and glory. But to get anywhere, he needed backers.

Like any would-be entrepreneur, Columbus pitched his schemes to anyone who would listen. He failed to convince the Portuguese monarchy to invest in his plans, so he went next door to Spain, where he proved more persuasive. Funded by Italian bankers residing in Spain, he secured permission from Ferdinand and Isabella, the king and queen of Castile (the largest region of Spain), to sail under their flag. The story that Queen Isabella pawned her jewels to finance the voyage is, sadly, mere whimsy. Some of her courtiers did invest in the voyage, using funds confiscated from Jews recently expelled from Castile.

Columbus promised the investors that he would forge a route to and from China by sailing west with the trade winds and then back home with the westerlies. He figured that Japan, which he had read about in Marco Polo's book of travels, lay about 2,500 miles (4,000 km) west of Spain. His estimate was off by about 10,000 miles. Had he calculated correctly, he surely would have stayed home.

Instead, he gathered sailors in the small Spanish port of Palos, acquired three little ships, and set out on the well-worn route to the Canary Islands. From there he ventured west into the open sea, seeing no land for 35 days before bumping into an island, perhaps Watlings Island in the Bahamas.

What he found looked nothing like Japan or China. Far from sporting silken robes, the locals stood stark naked and seemed unashamed of it. They had dugout canoes but no ships, and huts instead of palaces. Still hopeful, Columbus quickly moved on and in two weeks was in Cuba. He later stopped at the island of Hispaniola, where he met the more familiar trappings of complex society—dense populations, intensive agriculture, trade networks, and rumors of great kings. On Hispaniola, someone presented him with a few lumps of gold, something he could bring back for his investors. Upon his return home, he insisted to his backers that he had found a direct route to islands off the coast of Asia—and he probably believed it.

The Spanish Crown rewarded him with the title Admiral of the Ocean Sea and granted him broad powers to operate as he saw fit on subsequent voyages. He returned three more times to the Caribbean, even reaching the mainland shores of South and Central America. He engaged in slave trading (of Amerindians native to the Caribbean), bloody reprisals, and several sorts of atrocity in his eagerness for gold. His conduct met with rebukes among his followers and back in Spain. He hanged several Spaniards who defied his authority. A Spanish woman who reminded everyone that the Admiral of the Ocean Sea was the son of a weaver had her tongue cut out.

Columbus's Landfall In this 1493 engraving from *La lettera dell'isole*, Columbus's first account of his voyage, King Ferdinand observes from afar as Columbus and his crew land on an island in the Caribbean. The island's native inhabitants appear to flee.

Columbus's final years were filled with recriminations, lawsuits, bankruptcy, imprisonment, and bitter disappointment that he had found few riches and had not made it to China. He died in 1506, still convinced he had reached the doorstep of the Great Khan. No one else in history has had so many streets, squares, schools, and hotels named after him for making such a big mistake.

Columbus was wrong and he was brutal, but he was nonetheless a central historical figure. His voyages inaugurated a new age of connection among worlds long separate.

Soon after Columbus returned from the second of his four transatlantic voyages, another Italian, Giovani Caboto, was proposing voyages to China across the Atlantic. John Cabot, as he is known, approached merchants in Bristol, England, who were growing rich on the whale and walrus trade of the North Atlantic. Cabot also enlisted support from the English court, and in 1497 he made it across the Atlantic to Newfoundland and back in a tiny ship, about 3 percent the size of Zheng He's flagship. His crew numbered about 18. Among the treasures Cabot reported, mostly fanciful, were the very real and stupendously rich cod fisheries off of Newfoundland. Like Columbus, he recruited more investors, fitted out more and bigger ships, and set sail across the Atlantic a second time. Unlike Columbus, he never came back. Nevertheless, from soon after Cabot's time, Europeans would sail regularly to the fishing grounds off of Newfoundland, creating an enduring link—something the Viking voyaging to Newfoundland, some 500 years before, had not done.

Da Gama Sails to India In 1497, the same year that Cabot sailed, the Portuguese court fitted out an expedition of four ships and 170 men under the command of a low-ranking provincial noble named **Vasco da Gama**. Just a few years before, a Portuguese captain, Bartholomew Dias, had sailed from Lisbon to the shores of South Africa and returned safely. Dias discovered the belt of westerly winds in the Southern Hemisphere that enabled ships to sidestep adverse currents and ride into the Indian Ocean from the South Atlantic. Counting on this information, da Gama sailed way out into the South Atlantic to catch the westerlies and made it safely to the tip of South Africa and into the Indian Ocean. He worked his way up Africa's southeast coast and soon found evidence, in the form of Indian cloth and glassware, that he was where he hoped to be—in the Indian Ocean.

The ultimate prize, a practical route to and from the rich trade of Asia, lay almost within da Gama's grasp. He and his men resorted to piracy and the kidnapping of local pilots to help them find their way. On the shore of what is now Kenya they found a pilot who showed them the easiest route to **Calicut**, a trading city on the coast of India, where the Portuguese hoped to find—as one of da Gama's captains put it—Christians and spices.

The Portuguese expedition under da Gama had two main goals. The Portuguese Crown hoped to win glory, papal favor, and some practical political advantage by finding Christian allies somewhere in the Indian Ocean world, friends who would help in struggles against Muslim states of North Africa and Southwest Asia. The Crown also hoped to boost its finances by trading in spices, peppers, cloves, nutmeg, and more, items that were plentiful in India but scarce and expensive in Europe. Some Italian traders had done well in the spice trade, linking Venetian markets, through Egypt or Syria, with sources of supply in India and even further afield in Southeast Asia. The Portuguese hoped to help themselves to a share of this trade by sailing around Africa and going directly to the source of spices. Da Gama encountered no politically useful Christians in Calicut, but he found plenty of spice traders.

Da Gama and his crew did not linger long in India. The trade goods they had brought with them didn't interest the merchants of Calicut. The local prince wanted da

Gama to pay customs fees like any trader, whereas da Gama regarded himself as a royal emissary and above such things. After three disappointing months the Portuguese left, kidnapping a few Indians and sailing back toward Africa. Portuguese–Indian relations were off to a rocky start.

Da Gama left in a huff, pointing his prows into the teeth of the summer monsoon. The route that had taken three weeks with the winds at his back now took him four months on the return. Half the crew died before they reached Africa, and only 55 remained alive when da Gama returned to Lisbon more than two years after departing. He had sailed more than 25,000 miles (40,000 km), equal to the circumference of the Earth. He had confirmed the understanding of the winds of the South Atlantic and had pioneered a practical, if slow, route between western Europe and South Asia. And he had brought back enough spices to inspire investors, especially the Portuguese Crown, to send him back again.

In subsequent voyages, da Gama helped set up a lasting Portuguese presence in India and East Africa. It consisted of small trading enclaves, always fortified, sometimes under the protection of local rulers and sometimes at odds with them. The rivalries among rulers on the Indian and African coasts ensured that da Gama, and later Portuguese as well, could always find allies. Da Gama committed remarkable acts of cruelty, especially against Muslims making the pilgrimage to Mecca. He understood his mission to include piracy against Muslim shipping and did not mind making enemies. (He was not beloved by his own men either—at least, not after he ordered them to rinse their mouths with their own urine to combat scurvy, a gum disease resulting from vitamin shortage, one that often beset sailors on long voyages.)

The Portuguese commercial presence did not matter much to Indians and Africans, who continued their business much as before. But to Portugal, a poor kingdom of fewer than a million people, the occasional trading voyage to India meant infusions of riches, especially for the Crown. The trade to the Indian Ocean also affected Portuguese culture and self-image. Portuguese monumental architecture developed a distinctive style, called Manueline after Manuel I (r. 1495–1521), the king at the time of the first voyages to the Indian Ocean. It celebrates those voyages and nautical life, using artistic motifs from sailing ships and from Indian temples and mosques. The Portuguese national saga, known as *The Lusiads*, is an epic poem, first printed in 1572. It is modeled on ancient epics, especially the *Iliad*, but based loosely on the experience of da Gama and other sea captains.

One of the voyages to India missed its target. In 1500, on his swing out into the Atlantic in search of the Southern Hemisphere's westerlies, Pedro de Cabral and his fleet of 13 ships accidentally bumped into Brazil. Cabral claimed it for Portugal, despite the fact that people already lived there. After a brief look around, he continued on across the South Atlantic, around Africa, to India. Like da Gama, he ran into trouble in India with Arab merchants unhappy with competition and engaged in a vengeful massacre in Calicut before heading home in 1501.

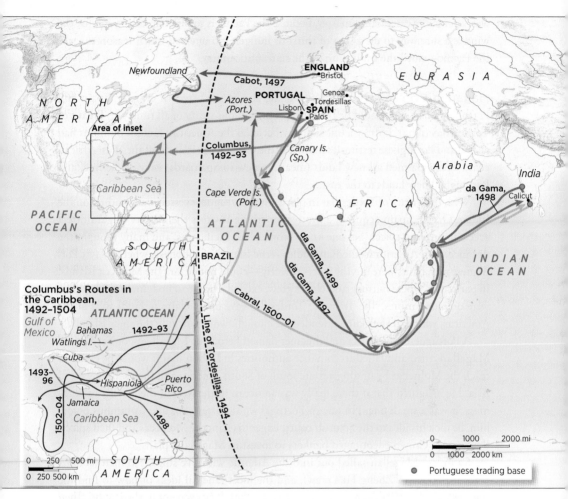

Navigation in the Atlantic and Indian Oceans, 1492–1500 This map shows the new routes pioneered by Columbus, Cabot, da Gama, and Cabral, which began the process of tying together the coasts of Europe, the Americas, Africa, and South Asia. The Line of Tordesillas, established in 1494, divided all "new" lands between Portugal and Spain.

Sailors such as Columbus, da Gama, and Cabral made the years 1492–1501 as pivotal as any decade in world history. Mariners from Atlantic Europe learned how to ride the winds back and forth between Europe and America, between Africa and America, and between Europe and South Asia. They found viable routes across the open ocean linking coastlines of continents formerly out of touch with one another.

The discovery of the oceans did not stop in the 1490s. Mariners had now solved the mysteries of the wind system of the Atlantic, as they had long ago the monsoon winds of the Indian Ocean. But the broad Pacific was another matter. Its winds and currents were even more essential to master, because the Pacific is so big that sailing against the wind is a sure way to die at sea of thirst or hunger. No one had much reason to cross the Pacific—until the beginning of the sixteenth century.

Magellan Crosses the Pacific   At the end of the fifteenth century, Spain and Portugal signed what could be the most presumptuous treaty of all time, the **Treaty of Tordesillas** (1494). It drew a line halfway between the American lands Columbus had visited and Portuguese territories known as the Cape Verde Islands off the West African coast. Spain claimed all new lands (meaning new to Spaniards) west of the line, and Portugal all new lands to the east.

With the Treaty of Tordesillas in place, once Portuguese vessels were trading on the Indian Ocean, Spain acquired a motive for trying to cross the Pacific: to gain direct access to precious spices. No one knew how big the Pacific was, and many thought the distance from America to the East Indies—the islands of Indonesia where by 1515 Portuguese merchants were buying spices directly—could not be far. The Molucca Islands, in particular, where nutmeg and cloves grew, excited European imaginations as if they were diamond mines. The Treaty of Tordesillas gave Spain claim to lands west of the Americas, which, if the claim extended far enough, would include the spice islands.

A Portuguese adventurer and dreamer named Fernão de Magalhães, or **Ferdinand Magellan**, tried and failed to convince authorities in Lisbon that it would be easier to reach the **Moluccas** by finding a route south of South America and then sailing west to Asia. He imagined that if there really was an ocean to the west of the American landmass, it was a small one. No one in Portugal would listen. So, like Columbus before him, he took his idea to the Spanish court. Eager to claim the Moluccas and their spices, the Spanish Crown encouraged bankers to invest in Magellan's plans.

So in 1519 Magellan sailed out into the Atlantic with five ships, 250 men (about 1 percent the size of Zheng He's crew), and the most fanciful ideas of how to find the spice islands. Magellan's crew mutinied twice before they even got to the Pacific. Then things went south in a hurry. Magellan thought he could cross from South America to the spice islands easily, but he had been on the ocean for 14 weeks, out of food and fresh water, before his men sighted Guam—they had sailed across an ocean with hundreds of inhabited islands and by bad luck had missed them all. One of the crew explained their suffering:

> We only ate old biscuit reduced to powder, full of grubs and stinking from the dirt, which the rats had made on it when eating the good biscuit and we drank water that was yellow and stinking. We also ate the ox hides which were under the main-yard, so that the yard should not break the rigging: they were very hard on account of the sun, rain, and wind, and we left them for four or five days in the sea, and then we put them a little on the embers, and so ate them; also the sawdust of wood, and rats which cost half-a-crown each, moreover enough of them were not to be got.

CONSIDERING THE EVIDENCE

Portuguese Reasoning about Skin Color

As Portuguese ships explored the oceans, they also recorded observations about geography and people that contradicted traditions handed down from classical scholars. The Portuguese sea captain Duarte Pacheco Pereira (1460–1533) discussed some of these contradictions in his manuscript *Esmeraldo de Situ Orbis*. Pereira had voyaged nearly everywhere the Portuguese reached. He defended Portuguese forts in India, governed Elmina off the coast of West Africa, and captured a French pirate in the Atlantic. He was also the first person to mention Brazil in a navigation book. In the following excerpt, he draws on personal observations to reconsider the classical Greek assumption that skin color was determined by latitude.

[D]uring the many years we have sailed and operated in this part of the Ethiopias of Guinea [i.e., West Africa], experience has taught us how to take the height of the sun and its declination in order to tell the degrees of latitude by which each place is separated from the Equator and one of the poles. And we have found that this promontory lies directly over the Equator, and have discovered that in this place the days and nights throughout the year are equal....

Many of the ancients said that if two lands lie to the east and west of one another, both would have the same degree of sun and would be in all things alike. As to their equal share of the sun this is true, but such is the great variety employed by the majesty of nature in her work of creation and procreation that we find, from experience, that the inhabitants of this promontory of Lopo Gonçalves and of the rest of Guinea are very black, whereas the people who live beyond the Ocean Sea to the west (who have an equal amount of sun with the blacks of Guinea) are brown, and some almost white. These are the people who live in the land of Brazil....If any want to claim that these are protected from the heat of the sun because there are many trees in that region, I would say that there are also many trees as great and as thick in this land of Guinea on the eastern side of the ocean. And if any should say that they are black because they go around naked and that the others are white because they go clothed, I would say that both of them ...go around just as they were born. So we can say that the sun does not affect one more than the others. Now it only remains to find out if they are both descended from Adam.

Questions for Analysis

1. What evidence does Pereira rely on to challenge the conclusions of "the ancients"?

2. After dismissing possible explanations for the differences in skin color between people in Africa and those in Brazil, what direction does he suggest for future research?

3. Does this excerpt suggest that the Portuguese of Pereira's time considered people whose skin color differed from theirs to be inferior in any way?

Source: "Duarte Pacheco Pereira Tries to Come to Terms with 'Difference,'" in Malyn Newitt, ed., *The Portuguese in West Africa, 1415–1670: A Documentary History* (Cambridge, 2010).

On Guam, Magellan guessed he was just off the shore of China. He was 2,500 miles (4,000 km) from it. He next blundered into the Philippines, where he got mixed up in a local war and died in battle.

Magellan's surviving crew kept going west, sailing through the islands of Indonesia, where they picked up a cargo of spices, and into the Indian Ocean, around Africa, and home to Spain. The trip had taken three years, and only about 10 percent of the crew survived. They were the first humans to circumnavigate the globe—although they had intended only to find a route to the Moluccas and spices.

It took many decades before anything practical came of Magellan's quixotic quest. Magellan had showed how big the Pacific really was, and that it—like the Atlantic—had trade winds blowing east to west. Some 40 years later, another captain showed how one could cross the Pacific west to east, from Asia to America, by riding the westerlies, found at the same latitudes as those of the Atlantic. By 1570, Atlantic Europeans had deciphered the wind system of the Pacific too.

Weaving a Maritime Web

Every coastline in the world was now more accessible than ever before to those who knew the secrets of the winds. While Magellan sailed the wide Pacific, other mariners in less dramatic fashion brought more of the world into a tighter web of connections. Portuguese captains began to visit China and Japan, following routes that Asian sailors had used for centuries. From the East African coast, Portuguese adventurers pushed inland, developing a previously small-scale trade in slaves and ivory in Mozambique and making contact with fellow Christians in Ethiopia. These Portuguese travels followed the beaten paths of Asian and African traders.

While European sailors were gathering up knowledge of routes and coasts in Africa and Asia, as far as Australia and Japan, others were adding further information from the Americas. Columbus had begun the process, but dozens of others, mainly Spaniards, followed. They sailed the coastlines, probed the river mouths, and, despite language barriers, absorbed what they could from Amerindian informants. By 1520, they had accumulated a good knowledge of the Caribbean and South America coasts. It took much longer for mariners to figure out the coasts of North America, but by 1620 sailors, mainly English and Dutch, had charted the eastern shoreline all the way north to the fogbound and iceberg-strewn coasts of Hudson Bay. To their dismay, they established that here too there was no good route to the riches of Asia. That dream died hard. As late as the 1630s, Jean Nicolet, a French fur trader, walked and canoed through Wisconsin wearing flowing Chinese robes in hopes of meeting someone who knew the way to China.

Gradually, mariners filled in the remaining blank spots on the map of the oceans. Dutch and English ship captains sailed around New Zealand and Australia in the seventeenth century, charting the coasts. But finding the Maori unwelcoming and the Aborigines poor, they left these lands alone for another 150 years. In the eighteenth

Namban Screen This six-fold Japanese screen from around 1600 likely illustrates the arrival of a Portuguese merchant ship in Japan. Portuguese sea captains began to visit Japan in 1543, bringing Christianity, guns, and Chinese silks and porcelain. They bought thousands of Japanese slaves to sell in Macao, Goa, or other Portuguese enclaves until the trade ended soon after 1600.

century, European sailors refined their knowledge of Pacific shores and blundered into most of the inhabited Pacific islands, including the remotest outposts of Polynesia in Easter Island and Hawaii. They charted the American coastlines from Alaska to Chile. By 1780, every significant coast of every ocean had been mapped, and every important island located. For all intents and purposes, the discovery of the winds and the oceans was complete.

European mariners failed in their quest to find a direct route from Europe to Asian spices and failed to find powerful Christian allies against Islamic polities. But they succeeded at something they did not consciously attempt, which was to unite the world's coasts and harbors into a single network and to build geographical knowledge so that any competent navigator, with the right equipment and ship, could go anywhere on the sea with a reasonably good idea of where he was and what lay ahead. The confidence with which merchants had long sailed the South China Sea, the Arabian Gulf, or the Mediterranean, European merchants (and for a long while only European ones) now extended to the deep oceans. The first pulse of true globalization, achieved partly by accident, was accomplished mainly by Europeans—specifically, those from Atlantic Europe.

Biological Globalization, 1492–1800

One of the most important consequences of the discovery of the oceans and their winds, and the establishment of regular traffic linking the world's shores, was a surge in **biological globalization**. This process reshuffled the continents' flora and fauna,

Waldseemüller World Map Created by German mapmaker Martin Waldseemüller in 1507, this map was the first to encompass the full Western Hemisphere. It was also the first—on the lower portion of South America—to mention the name "America."

bringing both searing new epidemics and useful new food crops to many peoples. It changed the world's demographic balance and altered political and economic fortunes. By and large, it eased life for millions in Eurasia and Africa, and ended it prematurely for millions in the Americas and Oceania. It provides an excellent example of the fact that in world history major consequences often flow from events in ways that no one intended or foresaw.

As earlier chapters have noted, over the centuries people moved plants, animals, and microbes around the world. Sometimes they did it on purpose, like the first settlers of North America who brought dogs with them, or the Polynesians who ferried crops and animals to uninhabited Pacific islands. Sometimes they did it by accident, like the anonymous people who brought the plague bacillus from northeast Africa to the Byzantine Empire in the time of Justinian. Biological exchange has long been an important part of history, with powerful effects on food supplies and disease burdens.

The pace of biological exchange sped up whenever web connections boosted trade and migration. It slowed down when webs withered. So, for example, when the Roman and Han Empires were at their height, and trans-Eurasian trade and travel reached a temporary peak along the Silk Roads, so did biological exchange. China acquired camels, donkeys, and grapes. Mediterranean peoples added cherries, apricots, and walnuts to their gardens and diets. When commerce quickened in the Arabian Sea after 800 CE, the exchange of crops among India, East Africa, and the Mediterranean picked up speed.

Biologically, as in other respects, the Americas had remained a realm apart from these Old World web exchanges. Aside from the import of the dog (from Siberia about

15,000 years ago) and the export of sweet potato (to Polynesia about 1,000 years ago), the American hemisphere before 1492 exchanged nothing consequential with the wider world. American plants and animals included many unknown elsewhere—tobacco, armadillos, and grizzly bears, for instance. Australia and New Zealand, even more isolated, each hosted flora and fauna—eucalyptus trees, kangaroos, and moas, for example—found nowhere else on Earth.

After the voyages of Columbus, mariners linked almost every nook and cranny of the humanly habitable Earth into a biologically interactive web. The world's oceans no longer served to isolate ecosystems from one another. It became a world without biological borders, as plants, animals, and disease-causing pathogens scattered wherever ecological conditions permitted their spread. They went wherever people took them, and sometimes even further on their own.

Columbus inaugurated regular exchanges across the Atlantic in 1492. On his second voyage, he deliberately brought a ship full of species new to the Americas and brought home to Spain some biological souvenirs. Over the next few centuries, his followers did the same in an ongoing process known to historians as the Columbian Exchange. The most conspicuous result was that Amerindians acquired hundreds of new plants and animals from Eurasia and Africa, as well as a dozen devastating diseases formerly unfamiliar to them. At first, between 1492 and 1700, the spread of diseases was the most important part of biological globalization, mainly because of their horrific impact on the peoples of the Americas.

Deadly Diseases

Upon arrival in the Americas, transatlantic travelers coughed and sneezed billions of deadly microbes into the air that Amerindians breathed. Among them were the pathogens (viruses, mainly) that cause smallpox, measles, mumps, whooping cough, and influenza. All of these had become fairly widespread in the Old World web. From West Africa to East Asia, they were usually endemic, childhood diseases, sometimes now called crowd diseases (discussed in Chapter 5), that killed huge numbers of small children. But in the Old World web, most adults were survivors, and either resistant or fully immune to most or all of these viral infections. In addition to the crowd diseases, the Columbian Exchange brought some lethal vector-borne African diseases to the Americas. The two deadliest were yellow fever and falciparum malaria (the worst form of **malaria**), both spread by mosquitos.

In the Americas in 1492, none of the 40 to 70 million people had any prior experience with, and therefore no acquired immunity to, any of these diseases. Their immune systems did not instantly "recognize" and neutralize the exotic pathogens. This vulnerability was compounded by the weakening of their nutrition and health by Atlantic European colonization—which, as we'll see, included loss of farmlands, enslavement, and forced migration.

The cascade of unfamiliar pathogens brought suffering and death on the largest scale. Here is how one Amerindian, in Mexico, recalled it:

> The illness was so dreadful that no one could walk or move. The sick were so utterly helpless that they could only lie on their beds like corpses, unable to move their limbs or even their heads. A great many died from this plague, and many others died of hunger. They would not get up to search for food, and everyone else was too sick to care for them, so they starved to death in their beds.

In many Amerindian communities, the social fabric dissolved under this onslaught. People lost all hope. Few wanted to bring children into a world such as theirs had become, dominated by sickness and pain, and few were healthy enough to do so.

The scale of epidemics and death was gigantic. Between 1492 and 1650, populations in the Americas fell by 70 to 95 percent in one of the two largest-scale demographic disasters in world history. (The other was the Black Death of the fourteenth century in the Old World web.) The sharp decline in population in the Americas had many consequences that we will meet repeatedly in the chapters ahead.

The Amerindians had little in the way of lethal infectious disease that transferred to Africa and Eurasia. The first migrants to arrive in North America had passed through northeastern Siberia and Alaska during an ice age. The brutal cold probably killed off some pathogens. And since they left Siberia when no animals but dogs had been domesticated, the human infections shared with herd animals (e.g., smallpox, measles, influenza) had not yet appeared. Thus the first Amerindians arrived relatively free from infection.

Once in the Americas, Amerindians did not domesticate any herd animals other than alpacas and llamas, which seem, by chance, not to have hosted pathogens that evolved into agents of human disease. If Eurasia and Africa acquired any new diseases from the Americas at all (syphilis is the leading candidate, but the evidence is far from conclusive), they had trivial consequences. So, as regards disease, the Columbian Exchange was a notably one-sided affair.

The one-sidedness of the health consequences of the Columbian Exchange led Europeans who witnessed this devastation to see divine purpose at work. Francisco de Aguilar, who was present when Spaniards and their allies conquered the Aztec capital of Tenochtitlán, wrote: "When the Christians were exhausted from war, God saw fit to send the Indians smallpox, and there was a great pestilence in the city." More than a century later in New England, John Winthrop, the first governor of the

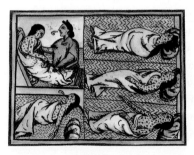

Epidemics in the Americas This illustration of Aztecs suffering and dying from the smallpox brought by Spanish colonists appears in the Florentine Codex, a Spanish missionary's sixteenth-century treatise about the Spanish conquest of Mexico in 1519–21.

Massachusetts Bay Colony, saw the disaster as divine endorsement of the seizure of land: "For the natives, they are neere all dead of small Poxe, so as the Lord hathe cleared our title to what we possess."

Useful Animals

The Columbian Exchange was almost as one-sided with respect to domesticated animals. People transported turkeys and guinea pigs from the Americas to other continents, but nowhere did they become important. Alpacas and llamas never prospered outside their native Andes, although scattered populations do exist elsewhere. The Amerindians had little in the way of domesticated animals, and those they had did not travel well.

In contrast, Eurasian and African animal species flourished when transported to the Americas. Cattle, goats, sheep, pigs, and horses were the most important animal immigrants. They all found empty niche space in the Americas, especially cattle and horses on the vast grasslands of both North and South America. The new animals provided surviving Amerindians with new sources of hides, wool, and animal protein. Horses and oxen made plowing feasible in the Americas for the first time, allowed transportation through wheeled vehicles, and, together with donkeys and mules, provided a greater variety of pack animals. Animal-powered transport extended the potential of commerce and economic specialization, which over centuries raised overall production levels considerably.

In addition to economic growth, the new animals brought unwelcome frictions to the Americas. They munched and trampled crops, provoking quarrels between herders and farmers of the sort familiar in Africa and Eurasia but almost unknown in the Americas before 1492. In this respect, the Columbian Exchange helped make the Americas a bit more like the rest of the world, where such quarrels had long been routine.

In North America, the introduction of horses upset the political order. The Amerindians of the prairies, from Texas to Manitoba, acquired horses from newly Spanish Mexico in the seventeenth century, and some of them quickly mastered riding and horse breeding. On horseback, they became far more adept as bison hunters, solving any subsistence problems as long as the bison lasted. Moreover, those with horses easily inflicted military defeats on those without. Amerindian peoples such as the Sioux and Comanche eventually built considerable empires on the basis of mounted warfare, as Mongol and Malian horsemen had recently done in Asia and Africa. In this respect too, the Americas became less distinctive, more like the rest of the world, thanks to the Columbian Exchange and biological globalization.

Key Crops

The Columbian Exchange was more even-handed when it came to crops. The Eurasian staples of wheat, rye, barley, and rice flourished in the Americas. Some of the new crops could survive in cold and dry landscapes where the indigenous crops fared poorly: North Dakota and Saskatchewan do better growing wheat than maize. Others, such as rice, transplanted from both Asia and Africa, required heavy labor in order to produce bumper crops. Rice became a plantation crop in the Americas, worked mainly by imported African slave labor. Aside from grains, the Americas also acquired citrus fruits, grapes, and figs from Eurasia, and millets, sorghums, yams, bananas, okra, and watermelon from Africa. So the new crops extended the possibilities of American agriculture somewhat and allowed a more varied diet. But in many places they brought only a small improvement in nutrition, because people in the Americas already had maize or potatoes (or both) and plenty of fruits and vegetables.

New drug crops changed the Americas at least as profoundly as the new food crops. Sugar, originally from New Guinea but a commercial crop in South Asia, China, and the Mediterranean, came to Brazil and the Caribbean in the sixteenth and seventeenth centuries. Both a mild drug and a food, it became, as we shall see, the mainstay of a plantation economy based on African slave labor. Coffee, from Ethiopia and Arabia, also became a plantation crop in the eighteenth century. We will see the full importance of these crops in a later chapter when we encounter the plantation system in the Americas.

The Americas' contributions to global cuisine included the staples maize, potatoes, sweet potatoes, and cassava, together with tomatoes, cacao, peanuts, pumpkins, squashes, pineapples, and a handful of other food crops. Some of these crops had revolutionary consequences in sizeable regions of Africa and Eurasia. Potatoes, for example, which nicely suited soil and climate conditions from Ireland to Russia, led to a spurt of population growth in northern Europe after 1730.

Maize This staple had a broader impact than potatoes. It did well in conditions as varied as those of southern Europe, southern and central China, and much of Africa. **Maize** allowed new lands to be brought under cultivation, because it prospered where grains and tubers would not. It soon undergirded population growth and famine resistance in China and southern Europe. But nowhere was it more influential than in Africa, where today it remains the single most important food crop. In the two centuries after 1550, maize became a staple in Atlantic Africa, from Angola to Senegambia. Different maize varieties suited the several different rainfall regimes in Africa and improved African peoples' chances of surviving drought.

While maize helped feed generations of Africans, it had bleaker consequences too. Maize stores much better than millets, sorghums, or tubers, the traditional crops in most of Africa. It thus allowed chiefs and kings to maximize their power by centralizing the storage and distribution of food. In the West African forest zone, south of the Sahel, maize encouraged the formation of larger states than ever before. The Asante kingdom, for example, embarked on a program of military expansion after the 1670s, spearheaded by maize-eating armies that could carry their food with them on distant campaigns. Maize also served well as a portable food for merchant caravans, which contributed to commercialization in Atlantic Africa, including an expansion of existing slave trades.

Slave traders could operate over longer distances if they, and their human property, had an easily portable food supply that stored well. Maize in Africa increased the practicality of the slave trade. As we shall see, it helped make slaving an intercontinental business, linking Europe, Africa, and the Americas.

Cassava   Also known as manioc, **cassava** was the Americas' other great contribution to African agriculture. A native of Brazil, cassava is admirably suited to drought and poor soils, and resistant to many insect crop pests. It too did well in many parts of Africa, and like maize provided a portable, storable food that underlay state formation and expansion in West Africa and Angola. Cassava, like potatoes, need not be harvested at a particular season but may be left in the ground for weeks or more. So it is an ideal crop for people who might need to run away for their own safety and abandon their fields—for example, people routinely subject to slave raiding. In this respect, it had the opposite effect of maize: it helped peasantries to flee and survive slave raids, while maize helped slavers to conduct raids and wars.

The impact of American food crops on Africa was so great that it makes sense to think of African history, especially Atlantic African history, as divided into pre-Columbian and post-Columbian phases—as is normally done for the Americas. Maize, cassava, and a cornucopia of other crops from the Americas, including peanuts, pineapple, chili peppers, sweet potato, avocado, cacao, and a dozen others, gradually re-fashioned African cuisine and agriculture. This was the second time in African history that imported crops made a big difference—recall the impact of bananas, acquired from Southeast Asia, many centuries before.

African farmers took to the new American crops eagerly, seeing them as either useful additions or even replacements for their old ones. The greater variety of food crops provided a form of insurance against crop failure due to insect pests or bad weather. Maize had the further attraction that birds usually find it too much trouble to poke through the husks to get at the grain. Birds don't bother with cassava either. Ripe millet and sorghum, in contrast, provide tempting targets for birds, and people must defend these crops day and night if they wish to enjoy a harvest. The American crops undergirded a slow expansion of farming, state making, and perhaps even population growth in Africa after 1650—despite the demographic effects of the transatlantic slave trade.

Cassava in Africa This illustration of the cassava plant appears in a French book about Caribbean plants from 1688. Originating in the Americas, cassava became an even more successful crop in West Africa and Angola, where it was well suited to the climate, soils, and the needs of farming communities.

The Columbian Exchange

1492–1800

horses

potatoes

EUROPE

NORTH AMERICA

Rocky Mts.

Colorado R.

Mississippi R.

Appalachian Mts.

grains

Danube R.

maize

influenza, measles, mumps, smallpox, whooping cough
cattle, goats, horses, pigs, sheep
barley, oats, rye, wheat, citrus, cotton, figs, grapes
sugar

maize

cotton

cassava, maize, potatoes, avocadoes, cacao, chili peppers,
peanuts, pineapples, pumpkins, squashes, sweet potatoes, tomatoes
syphilis? tobacco

Mexico

sugar

coffee
sugar

horses

malaria, yellow fever
rice, millets, sorghums, bananas, cotton, okra, watermelon, yams
coffee

Senegambia

Niger R.

Nile R.

Arabia

cassava
maize

coffee
sugar

AFRICA Ethiopia

Andes Mts.

Amazon R.

SOUTH AMERICA

Brazil

sugar

ATLANTIC OCEAN

Congo R.

cassava
maize

Angola

Zambezi R.

sugar

PACIFIC OCEAN

Andes Mts.

Parana R.

coffee
sugar

horses

KEY

Organisms originating
in the Old World

Organisms originating
in the Americas

Organism transferred

measles Pathogen

horses Livestock

maize Food and fiber crop

sugar Drug crop

Population decline due to
introduction of pathogens

■ 90% or more

□ Less than 90%

Areas of greatest impact
of livestock and crops

■ Horses

□ Food and fiber crops

■ Drug crops

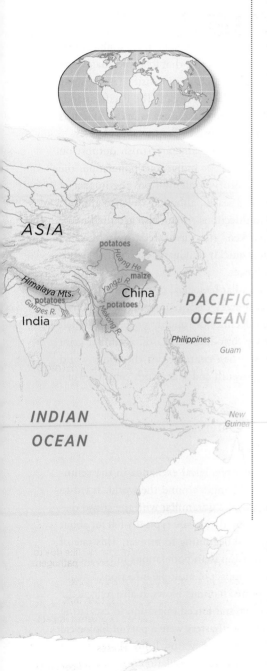

ASIA

potatoes

Huang He

Himalaya Mts.
potatoes
Ganges R.

India

Yangzi R.

maize

China

Mekong R.

potatoes

PACIFIC
OCEAN

Philippines

Guam

INDIAN
OCEAN

New
Guinea

BETWEEN 1492 AND 1800, mariners tied together the shores of the Atlantic into an especially vibrant part of the emerging Global web. Their voyages created an Atlantic world, similar in many respects to the Indian Ocean world, another lively part of a larger web, built long before. But in one respect—the Columbian Exchange—the Atlantic world had no true parallels in world history.

The Columbian Exchange of plants, animals, and lethal pathogens was the biggest pulse of biological exchange in world history. Anytime that webs extended across vast distances, people—intentionally and accidentally—carried some species to new homes. When the Silk Roads opened, for example, China acquired grapes, sorghum, donkeys, and camels from Southwest Asia. But no other such episode approaches the Columbian Exchange which suddenly united biological communities that had been separate for 50 million years.

The impacts of the Columbian Exchange included drastic changes in population, agriculture, and the economies of the Americas, Africa, and Europe. For some people, such as Amerindians, the Columbian Exchange brought disaster in the form of new diseases. For others, such as southern Europeans or southern Africans, it brought a new, high-energy food crop: maize. The introduction of maize and cassava to African agriculture and diet was so important that for Atlantic Africa at least, it makes sense to think in terms of pre-Columbian and post-Columbian phases, just as scholars routinely do for the Americas.

Questions for Analysis

Based on this feature and your chapter reading, consider the following questions:

1. Why did some peoples suffer and some peoples benefit from the Columbian Exchange?

2. What regions within the Atlantic world felt the strongest impacts of the Columbian Exchange?

Biological Globalization in the Pacific

The **Columbian Exchange** was the largest-scale, fastest, and most important set of intercontinental biological transfers in world history. But it was only part of the surge in biological globalization that followed upon the navigational exploits of Columbus's generation. A modest transpacific exchange resulted from traffic that followed Magellan's voyages, at first affecting chiefly the Philippines. That exchange intensified in the wake of later sea captains' travels throughout the world's largest ocean. The Pacific islands themselves, rather than the ocean's rim, felt the greatest effects, and as in the Americas the most striking result was sharp depopulation in the wake of repeated epidemics.

Guam, for example, in the seventeenth century became a Spanish outpost on the route between the Philippines and the Americas. Its indigenous population, the Chamorro, fell by about 90 percent within a century—mainly from the impact of smallpox, measles, tuberculosis, and other new diseases, although violence and loss of lands raised the Chamorros' vulnerability to infections. Guam also acquired many new plants and animals, such as cattle, hogs, chickens, rice, citrus trees, and a Mexican shrub tree called Tangantangan. The latter grew quickly on Guam, especially in lands no longer farmed because of the population disaster.

Later on, other Pacific islands experienced similar biological disruptions when put into sustained contact with the wider world. In every case, the demographic consequences overshadowed all others. Population declines of roughly 90 percent befell many archipelagoes, primarily a result of newly introduced diseases. A similar grim history befell aboriginal Australians after 1788 when contact with the wider world became routine. But this was a story of the eighteenth and nineteenth centuries, one that belongs to a later chapter.

The Impact of Biological Exchange

Taken together, the whirlwind of intercontinental biological exchange in the centuries between 1492 and 1800 brought astounding changes around the world. It led to long-lasting demographic catastrophes among peoples unfamiliar with the crowd diseases. In the Americas and Oceania, indigenous population size typically fell for about six or seven generations before bottoming out and beginning to recover. This rate of recovery was slow compared to the experience of Eurasian populations in the face of most epidemics. That is testimony to the terrible impact of multiple infections assaulting peoples in the Americas and Oceania in repeated hammer blows. It also reflects the significance of loss of the best lands, enslavement, and forced migration in escalating mortality and suppressing fertility. The population disasters were a part of biological globalization, but they were not just biological processes: they arose from the interaction of biological and social processes. They represent a penalty of isolation from the bigger webs of world history, a theme we have encountered before.

The surge in biological exchange eventually improved the quantity and reliability of food supplies almost everywhere. This process slowly reduced the frequency of starvation and the toll of epidemics (because well-fed people survive most diseases better than malnourished ones). The world's population almost doubled between 1500 and 1800, from about 500 million to about 950 million, and a big reason was improved nutrition thanks to food-crop globalization.

One agreeable way of thinking about the whole (admittedly often grim) subject of biological globalization in the wake of Columbus is to contemplate food. Can you imagine Italian food without tomatoes? Or Polish cuisine without potatoes? What would the South African diet be without mealie maize, or West Africa's without peanuts? Argentina's without beef? New Zealand's or southern China's without sweet potatoes? What would Korean kimchi taste like without chili peppers? If we are what we eat, then the Columbian Exchange and biological globalization not only shaped empires and demography but also helped to make us what we are.

The Beginnings of a Global Web

The oceanic voyaging of the fifteenth and sixteenth centuries united continents into a single global web for the first time in human history. The web-making process—at work from the very earliest human settlements onward—had developed an extended, multilayered fabric of connections across Eurasia and North Africa. Significant webs had developed also in the Americas, and smaller, local ones elsewhere. But for thousands of years before 1492, the Americas had largely stood apart from Africa and Eurasia, notwithstanding the brief Viking and Polynesian visits. Now the history of the Americas unfolded in continuing connection with the Old World web. Similarly, after the secrets of oceanic navigation spread and mariners sailed regularly among all the world's inhabited shores, the islands of the Pacific, the coastlands of South Africa, and a few other spots around the world became linked as never before to the new, global web now in formation.

The oceanic voyaging also tightened linkages within the Old World web. In some cases, the tighter links proved temporary, as with Zheng He's voyages to India and East Africa between 1405 and 1433. But in others they endured much longer, as with Portuguese ties to African coasts, India, and the spice islands of Southeast Asia. So the three centuries after the 1490s saw a sudden spurt in web building, one that transformed human history and inaugurated a global age in which we still live.

The spinning of the first truly global web had many consequences. The most enduring and important of these was the biological globalization that reshuffled the distribution of economically significant plants and animals around the world and brought devastating infections to the Americas and Oceania. Another important consequence flowed from the fact that it was mainly Atlantic Europeans—not Chinese,

Africans, Polynesians, or anyone else—who first fully deciphered the oceanic winds and currents. As a result, they were the first to sail the seven seas and learn of new long-distance trade possibilities. They also found new opportunities to conquer peoples less militarily formidable than themselves. The role of Europeans, especially seafaring Atlantic Europeans, in influencing world history rose to new levels. Over the prior millennia, only rarely could such a small minority of humankind exercise such out-sized influence upon world history as Atlantic Europeans would wield in the three or four centuries to come.

The penalties of isolation for societies with few or no connections to the Old World web were now felt as never before. These societies typically hosted a narrower range of infectious diseases than did peoples in the web that enveloped Eurasia and North Africa, leaving them vulnerable to shattering epidemics when European ships arrived with new pathogens. They typically possessed a less formidable array of weaponry than existed in China, India, or Europe, using less metal, no firearms, and no horses. These societies had not needed or developed institutions and technologies that equipped them to deal with the challenges posed by seafaring, horse-riding, disease-bearing, well-armed strangers.

The spinning of the first truly global web proved transformational in other respects too. It continued the longstanding process by which cultural diversity narrowed. The major religions, especially Christianity and Islam, spread to new ground. They became slightly more diverse themselves as a result, because in every case they adopted some local features; but they reduced the overall diversity of religion with their conversions in Asia, Africa, the Americas, and Oceania. The spread of Arabic, Spanish, and English also, on balance, reduced the variety of languages spoken around the world, even if the English spoken in Australia or Barbados was not the same as that spoken in London. Many languages would gradually go extinct in the centuries after oceanic voyaging linked up the world. The next few chapters will detail the formation of the global web and how it affected political, economic, and cultural life throughout the world.

Conclusion

The world in 1400 included one big web and several smaller ones. The Old World web was the big one, containing the majority of humankind and stretching across Eurasia and North Africa from Senegal to Japan. A smaller one existed in the Americas, and local ones existed in several places around the world. In the course of the fifteenth century, however, this longstanding pattern underwent a major reorganization.

Beginning early in the fifteenth century, Chinese and Atlantic European mariners undertook oceanic voyages that brought the world together as never before. The most decisive changes came with the European, mainly Iberian, voyaging. From 1460 onward, this voyaging brought an increasing number of African maritime ports (e.g., Elmina) into direct contact with communities of the Old World web. From 1492 onward, it brought the Americas and the Old World web together on a sustained basis. From the early sixteenth century onward, it brought an increasing number of Pacific islands into enduring touch with the Old World web. Thus those mariners, in seeking fortune and glory for themselves and their monarchs, created the first truly global web.

Biological globalization in some respects was the deepest of all the global web's consequences, affecting as it did the life and death of hundreds of millions of people during the sixteenth and seventeenth centuries. Exchanges of food crops resulted in changes to agriculture and diets and, in more cases than not, improvements in nutrition. People in Africa and Eurasia acquired maize and potatoes from the Americas, while those in the Americas acquired wheat, rye, barley, and new varieties of rice. Exchanges of domesticated animals brought horses, cattle, pigs, sheep, and goats (to name only the most significant) to the Americas. These plant and animal exchanges were important in the sixteenth century and remain so today.

The other major component of biological globalization was the exchange of disease pathogens. It was extremely one-sided—and extremely costly to peoples of the Americas and Oceania. Its toll varied from case to case, but generally was on the order of one-half to nine-tenths of populations affected. The population catastrophe, made more costly by violence, loss of lands, and other stresses, generally lasted for the first 150 years after sustained contact with peoples of the Old World web.

The oceanic voyaging of the fifteenth through the seventeenth centuries did not start biological globalization, which can be traced back many thousands of years. But it launched the biggest and most consequential spurt of it in world history.

Chapter Review

KEY TERMS

REVIEW QUESTIONS

1. What were the main trading routes in Eurasia and North Africa in the fifteenth century?

2. What were the other three, smaller trade networks that existed apart from the main Eurasian and North African trading routes?

3. In what two ways were the Ming voyages exceptional?

4. Identify the three main reasons European explorers sailed west into the Atlantic Ocean during this period.

5. Why was knowledge of the Atlantic Ocean's wind patterns essential for sailors?

6. What was Columbus looking for when he journeyed across the Atlantic?

7. How did the Treaty of Tordesillas spur Spanish exploration of the Pacific Ocean?

8. Why was the transfer of malaria and yellow fever to the Americas so deadly?

9. How did prairie Amerindians, such as the Sioux and the Comanche, use horses to build empires?

10. Which crops that were indigenous to the Old World web became significant plantation crops in the Americas?

11. How did maize support the growth of larger states in West Africa?

12. In what two ways did the global exchange of crops improve food supply around the world?

13. Explain the major consequences of biological globalization in the sixteenth and seventeenth centuries.

Go to INQUIZITIVE

to see what you've learned—and learn what you've missed—with personalized feedback along the way.

Disruption

AFRICA, THE AMERICAS, SIBERIA, AND OCEANIA

1492 to 1850

FOCUS QUESTIONS

1. What were the major effects in Africa of joining the Global web?

2. What were the major effects in the Americas of joining the Global web?

3. What major changes came to Siberia once it was integrated into the Old World web?

4. How did entry into the Global web affect Oceania and Australia?

Trucanini, who died in 1876, was one of the last of the Tasmanians. She was witness to a grim and frequent process in world history.

Tasmania is an island 150 miles (240 km) off the southern coast of Australia. People first arrived there about 40,000 years ago, when lower sea levels allowed them to walk from Australia. When rising sea levels divided Tasmania from the Australian mainland around 6000 BCE, the Tasmanians were cut off. For nearly 8,000 years, until a few centuries ago, they had no known contacts with the rest of humankind. They gradually lost the skills to catch fish, make bone tools, and even to make fire. Their technological decay is striking evidence of the costs of isolation in small groups.

In 1642, a Dutch sea captain, Abel Tasman, sighted the island that bears his name but did not disembark. British whalers began to use it as a base in 1798, ending the long isolation of Tasmania, and in 1803 British authorities decided to locate a penal

629

CHRONOLOGY

1441 Portuguese begin selling Africans as slaves

1462 Portuguese mariners establish Elmina in West Africa

1519 Hernán Cortés attacks Tenochtitlán

1519–ca. 1860 The transatlantic slave trade

1524 Waves of epidemics begin in the Andes

1532 Francisco Pizarro overthrows Inka emperor

1580s Yermak spearheads fur trade in Siberia

ca. 1600–1694 Palmares maroon community in Brazil

1652 Dutch East India Company founds outpost at Cape of Good Hope

1680 Pueblo kill or expel all Spanish from what is now New Mexico

1689 Russian and Chinese Empires sign treaty dividing Siberian and East Asian spaces

1713 Smallpox epidemic kills up to 90 percent of Khoi

ca. 1780–1810 King Hamehamea unites Hawaii

1788–1868 Britain sends convict settlers to Australia

1807–1845 Musket Wars in New Zealand

1840 Treaty of Waitangi

1845–1872 Intermittent land wars between Maori and pakeha

1876 Trucanini dies

1898 United States annexes Hawaii

colony there. At that time, there were about 5,000 to 15,000 Tasmanians in existence. By 1830, only some 300 remained. The British prisoners and their keepers had brought new diseases, casual attitudes to murderous violence, and weaponry far superior to what the Tasmanians could muster. Most of Trucanini's family was abducted, enslaved, or killed. She became an outlaw in her 20s, was shot in the head and imprisoned, but lived into her 60s. Meanwhile, British officials gathered the last of the Tasmanians together with the stated intent of protecting them, but influenza and other infections continued to wreak deadly havoc. With the death of Trucanini, a 40,000-year-old language and culture died as well, after a mere three-quarters of a century of contact with the outside world.

This chapter presents the ways in which peoples previously outside the Old World web found themselves rapidly enmeshed in the Global web in its formative centuries. The processes behind these new connections were simultaneously political and military, economic and technological, religious and cultural, biological and demographic. In most cases, they involved episodes of great brutality. The focus here is on sub-Saharan Africa, the Americas, Siberia, and Oceania and Australia. Later chapters will take up the story of how this globalizing, web-expanding process played out within the former Old World web itself—that is, within Eurasia and North Africa.

Entry into the expanding global web for peoples long isolated was always hard, and sometimes fully as disastrous as for Tasmanians. Most peoples suffered demographic losses due to **disease disasters**, violence, and declines in fertility. Most also experienced wrenching cultural and political changes, and yet somehow made the adjustments necessary to survive in their new worlds as participants in the Global web. They had a lot to learn

The Last Tasmanians In the mid-nineteenth century, British authorities took this studio photograph of four of the last surviving Tasmanians, dressed in British fashions. Trucanini is seated on the far right.

about operating in new and larger economic and political contexts, and the people who knew most about global contexts often preferred to kill or enslave them rather than instruct them.

The opening of the oceans to navigation, and the sudden spread of information, diseases, migrants, and much else, reshuffled fortunes dramatically. Just about everyone sought to take advantage of the new situation, including the peoples of Africa, the Americas, Oceania, and Siberia, although they were rarely well placed to do so. The people best positioned to seize the opportunities of the globalizing world were those who had the fullest information about routes, goods, prices, technologies, languages, and religions. These were the people who traveled the seas for themselves—mainly but not exclusively Atlantic Europeans.

European sailors, soldiers, settlers, merchants, and missionaries often knew, or knew how to find out, roughly how much a pound of pepper would fetch in Lisbon markets or whether customers in Calicut preferred pearls over ponies. This enabled them to trade more profitably than others could. They also knew, or could make educated guesses, whether or not their weapons would give them an edge against peoples around the world, and thus whether attacking them might be foolish or not. There was of course much they did not know, and they made many miscalculations. But on average they had a more global perspective than anyone else, and they took advantage of that where they could.

Atlantic Europeans were only the latest example of people in position to exploit the information advantages of web connections. Ancient Carthaginians usually knew more about distant markets and new technologies than anyone in Spain, and they too took advantage of that when they could. The same was true of the Chola merchants and kings in south India in their relations with landlocked neighbors, or of Arabs with respect to East Africans living inland from the Swahili coast. The difference here is one of scale: the Atlantic Europeans enjoyed information advantages over many peoples around the world and could harvest information from every continent.

And information advantages were only part of their edge. Atlantic European mariners were in effect the Mongols of the sea. Like horse nomads, they didn't always have military advantages over potential rivals, but thanks to their mobility they could choose when and where they might wish to fight, when and where they preferred to flee. With their big shipboard cannon, they could attack enemies from a safe distance, as horse nomads could with their bows. Like the mobile Mongols, they could, when it suited them, engage in acts of unspeakable cruelty, knowing they could get away safely, never to return and face the consequences. This is not to suggest that either Mongols or sea-going Europeans were by nature crueler than anyone else; only that they could indulge in cruelty and escape retribution more easily than others who lacked superior mobility. And, like the Mongols, Atlantic Europeans' conquests, massacres, co-optations, and absorptions of other peoples helped prepare the way for unprecedented consolidation of webs of economic, cultural, and biological interaction.

It is important to recognize that this process of globalization, even if on balance it led to European domination of large parts of the world, reshuffled fortunes in complicated ways. In Africa and the Americas especially, some rulers, clans, and peoples found ways to turn the linkages presented by European seafaring to their advantage. Some, for example, monopolized European trade goods and got rich. Others managed to control access to firearms and became more powerful. Still others translated support from Christian missionaries into prestige and power. And some, such as the kings of Kongo in West Central Africa, did all of the above, if only for a while. Trucanini and the Tasmanians, mainly because of the penalties of isolation in small groups, did none of the above.

Africa and the Global Web

Sub-Saharan Africa in 1400 already had considerable links to the Old World web, across the Sahara and via the sailing routes of the Indian Ocean. Only the southernmost reaches, and a few pockets here and there, may be said to have been truly isolated from the wider world. However, after 1450, as trans-Saharan travel became more common and Portuguese mariners began to visit its coasts, nearly every part of Africa tightened its connections to what was rapidly becoming a global web. The process, as usual, was a rough one, featuring war, empire building, epidemics, and enslavement, as well as heightened trade and cultural exchange. The main components of the process were, first, the gradual and ongoing spread of Islam through the northern half of Africa, which in places was coupled with wider use of the Arabic language. Second, in a few locations, small colonies of European settlers took root, creating altogether new societies. Third,

Africans, especially those living near the coasts, became increasingly active in maritime trade circuits, not only of the Indian Ocean (which had been going on for centuries) but also of the Atlantic. The largest part of this commerce was the transatlantic slave trade.

Islam in Africa

Islam, as we have seen, spread from its Arabian homeland into North Africa, largely by conquest, during the seventh century. It subsequently seeped into sub-Saharan Africa along two main paths: by sea to the Swahili coast and across the desert into the western and central Sahel (the southern edge of the Sahara). In both cases, Islam's spread usually occurred not by conquest but through efforts of merchants, rulers, and missionaries—categories that overlapped in many cases.

Merchants from North Africa and Arabia brought their varieties of Islam with them when visiting Sahelian towns or Swahili ports. Since they generally stayed for months and interacted daily with locals, they had plenty of opportunity to demonstrate the attractions of Islam to urban Africans. Merchants in Africa, as in South, Southeast, and Central Asia, often found it both agreeable and convenient to adopt Islam. Many were naturally curious about an unfamiliar religion and welcomed instruction. For many, Islam's tenets held genuine appeal. The Qur'an portrays commerce and merchants (Muhammad was one, after all) in a favorable light. It spells out suitable practices with respect to contracts, money lending, and other business procedures. In addition, treating visiting Muslims and Islam with respect was good for business. Converting to Islam was even better, as it smoothed relations by binding all parties together with the same concepts of law spelled out in shari'a.

Rulers, too, often found advantage in becoming Muslim and proclaiming themselves sultan or emir. They too, no doubt, embraced Islam out of genuine conviction. But doing so could also improve their political position, providing prestige through connections to distant centers of power and learning. Having literate people around was always helpful to monarchs, so Muslim scholars often found employment at African courts. Islam also suited rulers, as all durable religions do, by offering justification (or spiritual compensation) for hierarchy and inequality. Kings and chiefs needed less raw power or personal charisma if their subjects believed it was normal, natural, and divine will that they should be subjects.

The experiences of East and West Africa illustrate the economic and political factors at work in the spread of Islam. In East Africa, the influence of Islam was already widespread before 1400. After 1500, the Portuguese incursions on the Swahili coast that began with Vasco da Gama inadvertently helped to promote Islam, which provided a rallying point for resistance to Portuguese attacks. By the seventeenth century, growing trade links with Oman tightened Swahili cultural connections to the Arabian Peninsula. Swahili and Omani forces drove the Portuguese out of East African coastal cities between 1650 and 1730, opening the door to a wave of immigrants from southern Arabia. Omani merchants, generally trading cloth for ivory and slaves, took up residence on the coast, especially its offshore islands such as Zanzibar. Clerics and holy men, often Sufi mystics, came too. The Omanis gradually extended their operations into the East African interior. Everywhere they went, they interested locals in their religion.

In West Africa, Muslim traders crossing the Sahara had found a welcome reception since at least the eighth century, as we have seen in the history of Ghana and Mali.

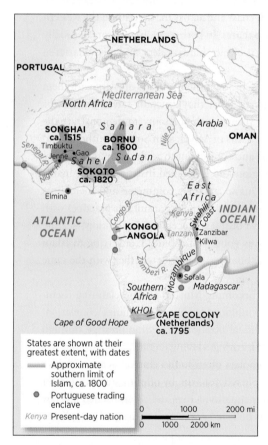

The Songhai Empire, a successor to Mali that took shape in the 1460s and 1470s, became an active promoter of Islam. Its founder, Sunni Ali, based his new state at Gao and soon conquered the other Niger River trading cities including Timbuktu and Jenne. By most accounts, he practiced multiple religions, was an indifferent Muslim, and clashed with the Islamic scholars of Timbuktu. But under his rule, and especially that of a later king, Askia Muhammad (r. 1493–1528), Songhai used all available means to spread Islam. A firm Muslim, Askia Muhammad supported Islamic scholars, built mosques, and encouraged conversion. He launched wars against infidels wherever they might be found. His success helped to spread Islam widely in the West African Sahel and to revive Timbuktu as a major center of Islamic learning. A Moroccan army, invading across the Sahara, ended the Songhai Empire in 1591, but smaller successor states continued to promote Islam in West Africa.

Africa: The Spread of Islam and the European Presence, 1450–1800 Connections between Africa and other parts of the world strengthened in the centuries after 1450. Many Africans along the Swahili Coast and across the Sahel embraced Islam, typically modifying its practices to suit their own traditions. Meanwhile, European mariners, especially Portuguese and Dutch, set up fortified trading posts (and in the Dutch case, an entire colony) in places along coastal Africa.

To the east, in the central Sudan, other, smaller, Muslim states, most notably Bornu in the sixteenth through the eighteenth centuries, promoted Islam much as Songhai had done. South of the Sahel, in West Africa's forest zone, Muslim traders (called

Dyula or Juula in West Africa) served as informal ambassadors of Islam. Muslim communities developed along the trade routes. Where trade and states did not figure prominently, Islam had less impact in West Africa before 1800.

Merchants and rulers both, when accepting Islam, did not necessarily renounce their former ways. From their point of view, Islam was one of several spiritual options. Many continued to celebrate feasts; venerate stars, sun, moon, and ancestors; or call upon spirits long familiar to them. Like Sunni Ali, rulers especially might find it politically prudent to become bicultural, both Islamic and non-Islamic, for different audiences and occasions.

Wherever Islam spread in Africa, it acquired local characteristics: just as parts of Africa were Islamized, Islam was in those places Africanized. African Muslims built mosques out of mud brick in the western Sahel or of coral on the Swahili coast. Muslim African women rarely dressed as modestly as women did in Islam's heartlands. In what is now northern Nigeria, African Muslims designated some non-Muslim Africans as "people of the book," a category that previously in Islam was used only for Jews, Christians, and Zoroastrians, and in India for Hindus and Buddhists.

Such adjustments to Islam offended purists. Ibn Battuta, the great world traveler, was one of many outsiders irritated by the unorthodox, Africanized versions of Islam practiced on the Swahili coast and in the West African Sahel. Centuries later in what is now northern Nigeria, a poet, scholar, and reformer, Uthuman dan Fodio, launched a rebellion against rulers he judged insufficiently Islamic and went on to found the Sokoto caliphate in 1804. He condemned the local sultans as unbelievers who "raise the flag of a worldly kingdom above the banner of Islam." His daughter, Nana Asma'u (1793–1864), a considerable scholar and poet, carried on the work of purifying the practice of Islam in West Africa, organizing Qur'anic schools for girls and women. Tensions persisted between champions of Islamic orthodoxy and supporters of a more adaptable and Africanized Islam.

In the process of Africanizing Islam, many prominent African Muslims claimed descent from the Prophet or from his inner circle. Prestigious ancestors were important credentials in most African societies, as in most Islamic communities. Even if these claims were not genealogically correct, over time some came to be believed and therefore served their purpose. For example, the ruling house of Mali, the sprawling empire in West Africa, claimed descent from Bilal, one of the Prophet's faithful companions and originally an Ethiopian slave. In these ways and many more, Islam acquired new forms and features drawn from African traditions and practices.

European and Christian Influences on Coastal Africa

While Islamic and Arab influence trickled into both East and West Africa, after 1440 Portuguese and then Dutch influence crashed into coastal Africa. In 1462, Portuguese mariners established a fortified post called Elmina on West Africa's coast. Their impact

CONSIDERING THE EVIDENCE

The Perils of Trade in Kongo

After Afonso I defeated his half-brother to gain control of Kongo, he emulated the Catholic king of Portugal. Though Kongolese, Afonso appointed officials with Portuguese titles, corresponded with the Pope, and requested priests to conduct Christian Mass with wine and grain imported from Portugal. He also bolstered his prestige by distributing merchandise imported from Portugal that he paid for with ivory, copper, and enslaved men and women who had followed his political rivals. Although Afonso initially benefited from the slave trade, the following letters between him and King João III of Portugal show that he had reservations about the trade. In the end, Afonso agreed with King João III that the slave trade should be continued, but he appointed officials to witness every sale in an effort to ensure that merchants would not capture and sell his own subjects.

Letter of the King of Kongo to [King of Portugal] Dom João III, 1526

[O]ur kingdom is being lost in so many ways...; this is caused by the boldness your... officials give to the... merchants who come to this kingdom to set up shops with merchandise... that we forbid, which they spread... in so great abundance that many vassals that we held in our obedience elevate themselves [i.e., are no longer obedient] by obtaining those things in greater quantities than we possess. With those things we had kept them content, and subjected under our vassalage and jurisdiction, so now there is great damage to the service of God as well as for the security and orderliness of our kingdoms and state.

And we cannot reckon how great this damage is, since these same merchants each day take our native people, sons of the land and sons of our nobles and vassals, and our relatives, because the thieves... steal them with the desire to have the things and merchandise of this kingdom that they covet.... [O]ur lands are entirely depopulated.... [W]e do not need... merchandise, other than wine and bread for the holy sacrament. For this

was greater still farther south, in the region of Kongo and Angola, and on the Indian Ocean coasts of Mozambique. Dutch involvement in Africa focused on the area around the Cape of Good Hope.

Kongo and Angola Just south of the mammoth Congo (or Zaire) River's mouth, Portuguese seagoing expeditions encountered a welcoming king, whom they called the *manicongo*. He ruled over half a million people in a kingdom that had been founded late in the fourteenth century. In the 1490s, Portuguese missionaries convinced a *manicongo* to convert to Catholicism. His son learned to speak, read, and write Portuguese, adopted European dress, and took the name Afonso. The Portuguese we are asking of Your Highness . . . not to send either merchants or merchandise, because our will is that in these kingdoms there is no trade in slaves nor outlet for them.

Letter of Dom João III to the King of Kongo, 1529

You say in your letters that you do not want there to be any slave trade in your kingdom because it is depopulating your land. . . . I am told of the great size of Kongo and how it is so populated that it appears that not a single slave has left it. They also tell me that you send to buy them [slaves] outside [the country] and that you marry them and make them Christian. . . .

If . . . as you request, . . . there shall not be any trade in slaves in your kingdom, I will still want to provide wheat and wine for use at Mass, and for this only one caravel [ship] a year will be

necessary. . . . However, . . . it would be more praiseworthy to draw each year from the Kongo 10,000 slaves and 10,000 *manilhas* [copper bracelets] and as many tusks of ivory. . . . If you do not want anyone to bring merchandise to Kongo, this would be against the custom of every country. . . . [A]nd if a *fidalgo* [noble] of yours rebels against you and receives merchandise from Portugal, where will be your power and greatness. . . .

Questions for Analysis

1. How did trade in merchandise, as well as enslaved people, threaten Afonso I's rule?

2. What arguments did the king of Portugal use to convince the king of Kongo to continue trading?

3. Do these letters indicate that these kings dealt with each other as equals?

Sources: "Letter of the King of Kongo to [King of Portugal] Dom João III, 6 July 1526," trans. Jared Staller, in *Converging on Cannibals: Terrors of Slaving in Atlantic Africa, 1509-1670* (Athens, OH: 2019); "The Slave Trade Is Good for the Kongo, Extract from a letter of Dom João III to the King of Kongo, 1529," trans. Malyn Newitt, in *The Portuguese in West Africa, 1415-1670* (Cambridge: 2010).

helped Afonso to seize the throne in conflicts with his brothers. Subsequently, **King Afonso** (r. 1506–1543) prospered with their continuing help, using Portuguese advisors, military officers, and muskets against neighboring peoples whose weaponry did not include firearms.

Part of the Portuguese interest in Kongo was religious, and in King Afonso they had an eager partner. While Askia Muhammad was using his power in Songhai to spread Islam in West Africa, King Afonso made Catholicism the state religion in Kongo, using it to bolster his legitimacy as ruler. By the 1520s the Pope named King Afonso's son Henrique, who had studied theology in Portugal, bishop of Kongo. Thereafter missionaries from Portugal poured into the kingdom, although most of them quickly

Christianity in West Central Africa
A bronze crucifix from sixteenth-
or seventeenth-century Kongo
demonstrates how Christianity
had become an integral part of
Kongolese artistic and cultural
tradition.

died from malaria, yellow fever, or other unfamiliar diseases. Catholicism gradually blended with local traditions and became the dominant religion.

Eventually the kings of Kongo and Portugal fell out, and Portuguese interest in West Central Africa shifted south to Angola. Here too Portugal allied with a local king, called the *ngola*, which became the name for the country. Portuguese helped him in his political struggles and in exchange won the right to preach Catholicism and conduct trade. Soon several local leaders accepted baptism, although they often kept their old ways as well, to the dismay of Catholic missionaries. Rumors of vast silver mines proved unfounded, and efforts to establish Portuguese immigrants as farmers failed miserably, mainly the result of the disease environment.

So in Angola, as in Kongo, the Portuguese turned to the economic activity that yielded the most reliable profit: slaving. They encouraged wars and slave raids among peoples in Kongo and Angola. Local kings (and one highly successful queen, known as Nzinga or Njinga), seeking Portuguese support and military expertise, eagerly enslaved their enemies. They sold war captives to Afro-Portuguese slave traders, the sons of Portuguese men and African women. As we shall see, Angola became one of the biggest sources of slaves sent to the Americas. Kongo too became a major exporter. By 1660, half the population of Kongo were slaves captured from neighboring peoples.

The Portuguese also brought new strains of smallpox to Kongo and Angola. Sub-Saharan Africans had long experience with the virus, and many peoples regularly used inoculation (the practice of deliberately infecting bodies with weak strains of a pathogen in hopes of triggering immunity without a serious case of disease). But apparently mariners brought a new variety, for major epidemics struck the region in the years 1625–1628 and 1655–1660. Some evidence suggests that tuberculosis and a form of pneumonia also hit Angola in the seventeenth century. For Kongo and Angola, inclusion into the Global web meant new diseases, one additional religion, and much more trade, enslavement, and warfare.

Mozambique   The Portuguese also took a strong interest in Mozambique. Unlike Angola or Kongo, Mozambique—located in southeastern Africa—had a history of involvement in maritime trade circuits. When da Gama passed by in 1498, its seaborne trade was in the hands of Swahili, Arab, and Indian merchants based at Sofala and Kilwa. Sea power enabled Portuguese merchants to convert Sofala into their own trade enclave, exporting gold and ivory and importing Indian cloth. The Portuguese occasionally sent military missions inland, hoping to seize the goldfields, but these efforts always met with disaster in the form of African armed resistance and deadly disease.

The Portuguese Crown issued land grants to Portuguese settlers who made themselves into local lords and merchants. Their connections to India and Europe—market knowledge and military hardware proved most useful—gave them an edge in dealing with African populations. Unlike Kongo and Angola, Mozambique's commerce consisted mainly of gold and ivory until after 1700, when demand for slaves in the Americas led to a growing slave trade in Mozambique. Meanwhile, Christian conversion made little headway there, and indeed many Portuguese and Afro-Portuguese abandoned Catholicism for either Islam or local African religious culture.

The Cape of Good Hope From the 1620s onward, the Portuguese had a seafaring rival, the Dutch, seeking toeholds in southern Africa. They conquered, and briefly held, some Portuguese coastal outposts in the 1630s and 1640s. But in 1652 the Dutch East India Company—a quasi-governmental trading company known by its Dutch initials as the VOC—founded a base near the southern tip of Africa, at the Cape of Good Hope. It originated as a way station for ships headed from Dutch ports to the East Indies (mainly Java), supplying water, fresh fruit, vegetables, wine, and meat to desperate crews—the death rate on these long voyages ran at 15 to 20 percent. The Cape grew into a full-fledged colony of settlement. Here, unlike in most of tropical Africa, there was no malaria or yellow fever, and foreigners could flourish. While Portuguese traders and missionaries frequently died soon after arrival in Kongo or Mozambique— mainly from mosquito-borne diseases—Dutch settlers at the Cape survived about as well as their relatives at home.

The Africans who lived at the Cape, hunters and cattle keepers called the **Khoi**, numbered perhaps 50,000 to 100,000 in 1652. At first, the Khoi and the Dutch found they could coexist: the Dutch would buy any extra cattle the Khoi could raise and would pay the Khoi to work on their farms. But soon the Dutch were claiming more land and seeking more labor. The Khoi recognized the threat and attacked the Dutch in 1659 and 1673—unsuccessfully.

The Dutch began to import slaves, mainly from Madagascar, Indonesia, and India in the seventeenth century, and from Mozambique in the eighteenth. This arrangement set the Cape on the path toward a sharply stratified society in which concepts of race mattered fundamentally. By 1700, the colony officially contained some 4,000 people—not including the Khoi, whom officials didn't bother to count. During the next century, population surged because of slave imports, immigration from Europe (often French or German), and social norms of early marriage and big families. With

European women scarce, marriage often crossed racial lines, making the Cape not just racially stratified but also racially complex. By the mid-eighteenth century, the whites came to call themselves Afrikaners.

For the Khoi, despite new goods and opportunities, the Dutch colony proved a disaster. They lost control of the best lands to the newcomers. They lost their autonomy if they integrated themselves into Dutch society as laborers. In 1713, a large proportion of them lost their lives in a smallpox epidemic. Within weeks the virus killed a quarter of the Dutch colonists, many of whom had enjoyed rural childhoods without exposure to smallpox and thus remained vulnerable as adults. All the Khoi were equally vulnerable, and as many as 90 percent died in the epidemic of 1713–1714, a mortality rate possible only because of widespread malnutrition. Further epidemics in 1755, 1767, and the 1780s burned through the remaining Khoi population. Little of their way of life survived, and Dutch settlers moved into the interior of South Africa with less resistance than ever before. They also imported more slaves to do the work the Khoi no longer could: as in the Caribbean, the disastrous decline of indigenous population inspired an expanded slave trade. By 1800, the Cape region contained about 20,000 settlers, maybe 25,000 slaves, and very few Khoi. In the taverns of Cape Town, which one VOC official described as the "mother of all scandalous practices," one might hear Malay, Tamil, Arabic, Portuguese, German, Dutch, and a dozen other languages. But one was unlikely to hear Khoi. The Cape settlement was an island of cosmopolitan, globalized society, now thoroughly enmeshed in the Global web.

The Transatlantic Slave Trade

The most visible, and for world history the most important, way in which large parts of Africa joined the Global web was through the slave trade. As in most lands, slavery had been a fact of life in Africa long before 1400. In Africa, people became slaves if captured by slave raiders or in war, if they couldn't pay their debts, or if their family or lineage gave them away as compensation for harm done to another family or lineage. In some societies, enslavement was also punishment for certain crimes. Most children of slaves were legally free (a big difference from many other slave systems), but these children could perform useful labor for slave owners, their families, and their communities. Slave owners in Africa preferred women and children for working in the fields, tending animals, making cloth, and doing domestic chores. Above all, they valued young women for reproduction. Only in a few places were male slaves more valued than females, such as the salt mines of the Sahara.

African slave exports to the Mediterranean world, Southwest Asia, and India had a long history. Ancient Egypt had imported African slaves. During the eighth and ninth centuries, many thousands of African slaves had been sold to landowners in Abbasid Iraq. Between 1400 and 1900, perhaps 5 to 6 million Africans were enslaved for sale to these markets.

Dimensions of the Trade The size and significance of African slave exports changed when European mariners connected Africa's coasts to the Americas. Portuguese sailors seized Africans beginning in 1441 and sold some of them on islands such as Madeira—500 miles (800 km) west of Morocco—where sugar plantations were developing. Meanwhile, Moroccan entrepreneurs organized sugar-and-slave plantations supplied with labor by trans-Saharan slave caravans. The success of sugar plantations worked by enslaved Africans in Morocco and Madeira inspired larger-scale imitation, first on the island of São Tomé off the coast of Kongo.

Then, in 1518, a king of Spain authorized the first direct slave trading voyages from Africa to the Americas. The first recorded voyage arrived in Puerto Rico in 1519, and others to Caribbean islands followed. The population catastrophe in the Caribbean that we saw in the previous chapters was already well under way. The Spanish interest in transatlantic slaving arose from concern that mines and agricultural estates in the Caribbean might languish for lack of labor. In this way, the misfortune of the Americas became the misfortune of Africa.

The first transatlantic slaving voyages to Brazil's sugar plantations began in 1534. Thereafter, the size of the transatlantic trade began to grow rapidly. Before long, the African coast from Senegal to Angola was exporting slaves across the Atlantic, and by the late seventeenth century the coasts of Mozambique and Madagascar were as well.

The **transatlantic slave trade**, the largest forced migration in world history, lasted until about 1860. In all, some 12 to 14 million slaves departed Africa's shores, of whom about 85 to 88 percent—10 to 11 million—survived what is called the **Middle Passage** across the Atlantic. The survival rate improved over the centuries, but the voyage

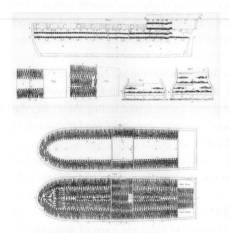 

The Middle Passage The conditions aboard slave ships on the Middle Passage are evident in these two illustrations: a diagram prepared by British antislavery activists in 1808, and a watercolor made in 1846 by a British naval officer who assisted in the capture of an illegal slave ship. Both show enslaved men and women packed together in inhumane conditions.

remained hazardous to the end, especially lengthy crossings. The average trip required about two months at sea, after which food and fresh water often ran short. A three- or four-month trip usually killed a large proportion of both slaves and crew. Slaves were kept below decks, usually naked, packed like "books on a shelf" as one observer put it. Men were often kept in chains for most of the voyage, women usually not. Sanitation was negligible. Dysentery was the foremost killer on the Middle Passage, but violence and other diseases took their toll as well.

Slaves attempted uprisings on perhaps as many as one in ten slave ships. Ottobah Cugoano, born in what is now Ghana, survived the Middle Passage in 1770 en route to the Caribbean and remembered a planned uprising: "And when we found ourselves at last taken away, death was more preferable than life, and a plan was concerted amongst us, that we might burn and blow up the ship, and to perish all together in the flames; but we were betrayed by one of our own countrywomen, who slept with some of the head men of the ship, for it was common for the dirty filthy sailors to take the African women and lie upon their bodies; but the men were chained and pent up in holes." Successful uprisings were rare.

Of the 10 to 11 million Africans who survived the Middle Passage, about 44 percent landed in Brazil, another 40 percent in the Caribbean, and 4 percent in what would become the United States. The remainder were scattered among Mexico, Colombia, and other parts of mainland Spanish America. Among slaves sold across the Atlantic, about two-thirds were male and one-third female. Children constituted one-fifth to one-quarter.

The transatlantic traffic peaked in the 1780s at nearly 87,000 slaves per year. It gradually became illegal, outlawed by various countries beginning in 1807, but a secondary peak occurred in the 1820s at 86,000 annually. During the seventeenth century, the transatlantic trade outstripped the size of the combined trans-Saharan, Red Sea, and Indian Ocean slave trades, and cumulatively between 1400 and 1900 was twice as large.

The Slaving Business   The transatlantic slave trade was big business. In 1750, about one-third of the British merchant fleet took part, and for Portugal it was even bigger. In West African states such as Oyo or Dahomey, capturing and selling slaves was the main source of mercantile wealth. European slavers, with their newfound global reach, had much to offer African dealers. Cloth from India became the chief West African import, supplemented by iron, copper, guns, tobacco, liquor, and cowrie shells collected in the Indian Ocean. Ottobah Cugoano, enslaved at age 13, recalled that he was sold for "a gun, a piece of cloth, and some lead." A slaver visiting the coast of what is now Nigeria in about 1680 noted that one could buy a male slave for about the same price as 40 baskets of plantains. Cowrie shells came to serve as money in parts of West Africa, and by 1720 about one-third of slaves bought on West Africa's coasts were purchased for cowries. To acquire the cloth and cowries from the Indian Ocean world, European

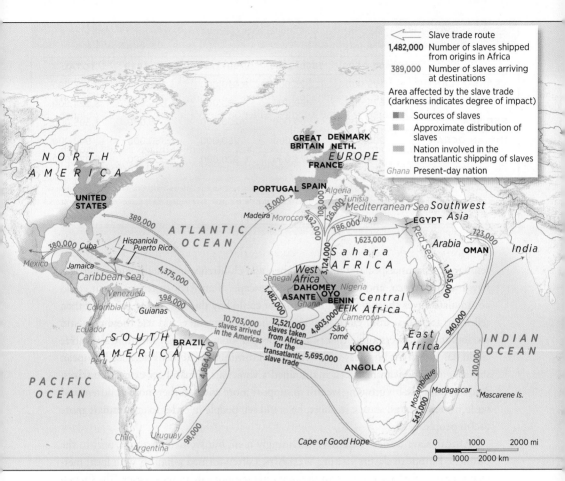

African Slave Trades, 1400–1900 Over these 500 years, roughly 16 million sub-Saharan Africans were enslaved and exported. Brazil, the Caribbean, and Egypt purchased the most Africans. West Central and West Africa supplied the most. The width of the arrows in this map is proportional to the number of people sold on each route.

merchants generally sold silver mined in the Americas. Thus the slave trade evolved into a large-scale business linked to trade circuits spanning three oceans and all continents except Australia and Antarctica.

The cloth, cowries, and other items on offer provided reason enough for African rulers and entrepreneurs to capture and enslave as many people as possible. In Africa, as we saw in Chapter 9, ambitious men normally sought prosperity in the form of people—wives, children, servants, slaves—as was typical of places where land was abundant and people scarce. Accumulating large numbers of dependent followers meant status, power, wealth, and security. To achieve such a following, paradoxically, it made

Estimated Volume of the Slave Trades from Africa, 1400–1900

	1400–1599	1600–1699	1700–1799	1800–1899	TOTAL
TRANS-ATLANTIC	199,000	1,523,000	5,610,000	3,371,000	10,703,000
TRANS-SAHARAN	675,000	450,000	900,000	1,099,000	3,124,000
RED SEA	400,000	200,000	200,000	505,000	1,305,000
INDIAN OCEAN	200,000	100,000	260,000	380,000	940,000
TOTAL	1,474,000	2,273,000	6,970,000	5,355,000	16,072,000

Sources: Nathan Nunn, "The Long-Term Effects of Africa's Slave Trades" (2007), Data Appendix, http://scholar.harvard.edu/files/nunn/files/empirical_slavery_appendix.pdf; and the Slave Trade Database maintained by David Eltis: https://www.slavevoyages.org/voyage/database

Note: The reliability of the transatlantic estimates is much greater than that for the other slave trades. These figures represent disembarkations: those who arrived alive.

sense to sell slaves, especially males. Women and children were usually more useful as slaves within Africa, and less likely to try to escape. If an African entrepreneur could accumulate slaves cheaply through capture or could buy them at a good price and then sell them for guns, iron, cloth, cowries, or horses, then he could use these goods to attract more followers and either purchase or raid more effectively for more slaves. He could reinvest in his business with little risk of diminishing returns because European slavers, and American markets, maintained a voracious demand for ever more slaves. And he could use his growing wealth to support more wives, father more children, and build his retinue and status: in short, he could sell people in order to accumulate more useful people.

African slave traders were overwhelmingly men, but women also took part in the business. European slavers visiting West Africa often formed alliances with local merchant families by "marrying" into them, if only temporarily in most cases. The French called women in these marriages *signares*; the English called them wives of the coast. As European slavers died or moved away, wives of the coast found replacements, new European men, who needed the business connections these women and their families provided. Most wives of the coast were content to remain informal wives or married according to local practices. But some insisted that representatives of a Christian church recognize their marriages.

Two men who knew the slave trade inside out were Little Ephraim Robin John and his nephew Ancona Robin Robin John. They were elite men of the Efik people, living at the mouth of the Cross River (in today's Nigeria). They made a fine living seizing and buying Africans, usually Igbo-speakers, and selling them to English ship captains. They spoke, wrote, and read English, and when dealing with English slavers they dressed as English gentlemen and followed English manners and customs. In 1767, to their horror, an English captain seized them, crossed the Atlantic, and sold them to a French doctor in the Caribbean. They soon escaped, but instead of freedom they found themselves sold again, this time in Virginia. After further misadventures brought them to England, a judge ruled them free men. They took ship back home to Cross River, where, well acquainted with the horrors of American slavery, they returned to their old business and sold thousands more Africans into the Atlantic slave trade. There was no surer way to sustain elite status on the West African coast than to deal in slaves.

Consequences in Africa The impact of the slave trade on the population of Africa is a controversial subject among historians. In the 1780s, at the height of the trade, 87,000 slaves crossed the Atlantic annually—roughly 1/1,000 (or 0.1 percent) of Africa's estimated population of 75 to 125 million. However, for each slave who stepped off a ship in the Americas, two Africans had been enslaved, and one had died en route to the African coast or on the Middle Passage. So on account of the transatlantic slave trade, Africans in the worst years stood a 1/500 chance of being enslaved. On a continental basis, the transatlantic slave trade probably did not have much impact on the size of Africa's population; but at certain times and places, such as Angola between 1750 and 1850, the demographic effects were substantial.

The transatlantic slave trade also spurred the growth of slavery within Africa. During the centuries of the slave trade, far more enslaved Africans lived out their lives within Africa than were transported across the Atlantic. The typical fate of an enslaved African was to be traded (or given to someone) somewhere else within Africa. But the scale of slavery within Africa grew as a result of the export trade, which provided strong incentives for slavers to build their businesses in order to reap economies of scale. The more slaves became available in Africa, the more uses were found for them.

The transatlantic slave trade had other major impacts on Africa. Politically, it encouraged the development of larger and more militaristic states. Stateless societies with weak defenses, such as the Igbo of what is now southeastern Nigeria, suffered as a result. Igbo farmers had to take weapons with them into their fields and lock children in fortified places at night. Predatory states prospered, such as Asante (Ashante) and Dahomey in West Africa, which specialized in seizing people from less militarily adept neighbors. One state that refused to export male slaves, the Kingdom of Benin after 1516, built up a slave army to defend itself.

Economically, the slave trade encouraged predatory people—African warlord-entrepreneurs who invested in guns, horses, and violence. This diverted effort and investment from other endeavors that might have proven more socially useful than slaving. It also promoted commercialization, adding traffic to long-distance trade routes. As we have seen, the slave trade also affected African agriculture, making both maize and manioc more appealing crops.

Culturally, the slave trade hastened the spread of Islam in Africa. By law, Muslims may not enslave fellow Muslims, so in those areas where slave raiders were mainly Muslims, such as the western and central Sahel, people fearing enslavement had strong incentives to become Muslim themselves. Socially, the slave trade was divisive. Some people became extremely rich and powerful by conducting it; ordinary people who didn't became more fearful and mistrustful. To this day in many parts of Africa, people remember whose ancestors were slave traders and whose were slaves.

The effects of the slave trade were geographically uneven, as the map on page 643 shows. Peoples within reach of armed horsemen, as in the Sahelian regions, were at great risk. The region most affected was Atlantic Africa, from Angola to Senegal—and within that, Angola itself and West Africa from what is now Ghana across to Cameroon. People living deep in central African rain forests remained almost fully out of reach.

The growth in maritime trade and the spread of Islam helped tighten Africa's connections to the Global web after 1450. Both developments brought some regions that had formerly been remarkably isolated, such as the zone around the Cape of Good Hope, into sustained contact with the wider world. The new maritime links undercut the Sahelian empires that had for centuries enjoyed a stranglehold on the trans-Saharan gold, salt, horse, and slave trades. After Songhai's demise at the end of the sixteenth century, no great Sahelian empire arose again. Instead, many smaller kingdoms emerged, competing for influence, subjects, and control over trade.

For Atlantic Africa, the slave trade stood at the center of tightening webs of interaction. Together with the importance of American food crops explained in Chapter 16, the slave trade's impacts make it sensible to think of pre-Columbian and post-Columbian periods in African history (which Africanists do not typically do) as well as in the history of the Americas (as is commonly done).

The Americas Join the Global Web

Millions of African slaves experienced the brutal rigors of the Middle Passage because in the wake of Columbus the newly transformed economies of the Americas needed labor. The European discovery of sea routes, and the subsequent surge in globalization, disrupted the Americas much more than Africa. The first stage, following upon Columbus's voyages, involved wave after wave of lethal epidemics in tandem with military conquests led by small bands of Spaniards, Portuguese, French, Dutch, and British.

Disease and Depopulation: Regional Variations

As we saw in Chapter 16, the crowd diseases brought to the Americas by European mariners proved extremely lethal to native populations, who had no prior exposure for protection. Here we will take a closer look at the post-Columbian catastrophe, considering some of the regional variations in the Americas and the role of factors outside of biology.

The Caribbean The severity of the calamity varied considerably across the Americas. People in the warm coastlands of the Caribbean had the worst of it. The more densely populated islands, such as Hispaniola, where pathogens could most easily find new bodies to infect, suffered losses of more than 99 percent within three generations. Before Columbus arrived in 1492, the **Taíno** (as the Amerindians of this part of the Caribbean are called) on Hispaniola numbered several hundred thousand, perhaps a million or more. By 1514, an attempt to count them recorded only 26,000. By 1550, when malaria inadvertently brought from Africa had joined the crowd diseases, perhaps 5,000 Taíno remained.

Spanish violence and enslavement of the Taíno added to the deadly effect of unfamiliar diseases. Some Spaniards would stop at nothing in their efforts to find gold or seize farmland. Others, meanwhile, tried to convert Taíno to Christianity, which caused divisions within Taíno communities. Their social structures fell apart. Death of spouses, separations, and demoralization led birth rates to plummet. Young Taíno women became wives or concubines of Spaniards. The net effect of the Spanish efforts to make money on Hispaniola and save Taíno souls was to compound the disease disaster and hasten the demographic decline. On Hispaniola and several other islands, Taíno society, language, culture, and identity virtually disappeared—much as would happen later to the Tasmanians with whom this chapter began.

Immigrants from Europe and slaves from Africa came to dominate Hispaniola demographically, and its culture—religion, language, food, dress—evolved, like so many others, as a blended, or creole, culture. Pottery shows how rapid this process was on Hispaniola: in 1515, most pots bore the marks of Taíno potters. By 1530, none did, and the island's pottery was made by Africans. The demographic story on other big Caribbean islands such as Cuba, Jamaica, and Puerto Rico was broadly similar.

Mesoamerica and the Andes The major centers of Amerindian population— Mesoamerica and the Andes—suffered smaller losses in proportional terms than the Caribbean, but in absolute terms they lost more population than anywhere else in the Americas. Repeated battering from epidemics and disruption of family routines, village life, and the political order cost each region roughly 70 to 90 percent of its population. In Mesoamerica, where perhaps 15 to 20 million people lived in 1492, the disaster began in 1519 when a Spanish adventurer, Hernán Cortés, and a band of a few hundred Spaniards rallied some of the subject peoples of the Aztec Empire in an assault on Tenochtitlán. A raging smallpox epidemic scythed down millions of Amerindians but left Spaniards—normally survivors of childhood bouts with the virus—unscathed. Epidemics recurred time and again, birth rates fell, and by 1620 Mesoamerica held fewer than a million people.

In the Andes, waves of epidemics began in 1524, preceding the arrival of Spaniards. A civil war over succession to the throne divided the Inka Empire when in 1532 a distant kinsman of Cortés named Francisco Pizarro led a band of 168 men into the Andes. The combined effect of epidemic and civil war enabled Pizarro to engineer a coup d'état, overthrowing the Inka Empire. For a hundred years after Pizarro, native

Cortés and the Aztecs
A pictographic Aztec chronicle recorded the events of the conquest of Tenochtitlán. In the illustration, Cortés—shown on horseback carrying a large cross—and his troops arrive in the Aztec capital and slaughter the local inhabitants.

population continued to plummet, from perhaps 12 to 15 million in 1532 to under 1 million by 1630.

The demographic disaster in the Americas was least severe in those regions where people were few and pathogens could not easily find new bodies to infect. The Arctic is one such example, where the toll of disease was smaller (closer to 50 percent) and came later, in the eighteenth and nineteenth centuries. The Mapuche of southern Chile, whose armies kept Spanish conquistadores at bay, as they had done with the Inka before, also seemed to have survived better than most.

Ecological, Social, and Economic Factors   The demographic catastrophe varied in its intensity from place to place partly for ecological reasons. Malaria, a warm-weather disease carried by mosquitos and introduced from Africa, became entrenched in some parts of the Americas but not others. Higher elevations and higher latitudes, which are colder than lower ones, hosted fewer mosquitos and less malaria.

The variability of the population catastrophe also had to do with social factors. In some cases, the ravages of introduced diseases began before European conquerors or settlers turned up, as in the Andes. In New England, in the years 1616–1619, epidemics took a terrible toll before the first English settlement at Plymouth Rock (1620). More often, however, social chaos created by European settlement compounded the effects of epidemics, as in Hispaniola during the early sixteenth century.

Warfare, loss of lands, and enslavement magnified the population losses. Wars of conquest, as in Mexico and Peru, were widespread. Although small in scale, these wars often involved Amerindians on both sides. In addition, Amerindian peoples when hit by epidemics often sought to recover their losses by seizing people, normally women and children, from their neighbors. The Iroquois, for example, who began to suffer heavily from epidemics in 1645, launched attacks on the Huron starting in 1648 partly to replenish their own numbers.

Almost everywhere in the Americas, sooner or later, Amerindians lost their best farmland to encroaching Europeans. That created additional problems of food supply and brought the demoralization that people typically experience when forced from their homes. Hunger and demoralization both can weaken disease resistance.

In many parts of the Americas, forced labor and enslavement added to the toll. Recent estimates suggest that between 1500 and 1800, some 2 to 4 million Amerindians were enslaved. Although slavery had existed in the Americas for millennia, its scale increased just when the population of the Americas was collapsing. This was no accident: population collapse created intense demand for labor, filled by both the transatlantic slave trade from Africa and the enslavement of Amerindians.

In particular, the newly developing mining and plantation economies (of which more below) relied on forced labor, both African and Amerindian. Spanish rule in South America continued the Inka practice of the *mita*, the forced labor draft imposed on Andean peoples, using it to provide workers for silver mines—where high mortality prevailed. Silver mines in Mexico, pearl fisheries off the coast of Venezuela, and early plantations in what would become the southeast of the United States also drew upon enslaved Amerindians. Charleston, South Carolina, in the seventeenth century even exported Amerindian slaves to plantations on the Caribbean island of Barbados.

The enslavement of Amerindians was repeatedly prohibited by European authorities. The Spanish did so throughout their empire early in the sixteenth century, but with important exceptions—for peoples judged cannibals, such as the Caribs (of the eastern Caribbean), or for those like the Mapuche of Chile, whose resistance to Spanish rule was especially fierce. Spanish law also permitted slavery for everyone already enslaved. This created incentives for Amerindians to capture their neighbors and sell them to Spanish mining or plantation enterprises.

Where Spanish authorities tried hardest to save Amerindians' souls, death rates were especially high. Catholic missions throughout Spanish America clustered Amerindians together in

Forced Labor in the Americas Across the Americas, European settlers enslaved indigenous people as well as importing enslaved people from Africa. In this 1522 Spanish illustration, enslaved indigenous people are being forced to lay the foundations for the Spanish capital of Mexico City.

agricultural villages to hasten their conversion to Christianity. Clustering, however, sped the transmission of most infectious diseases. The California missions begun in 1769, for example, suffered population losses that exceeded 90 percent over 50 years. Here too, few babies were born to take the place of the dead and dying.

Effect on Climate   All in all, the fate of Amerindians after 1492 was among the most dismal chapters in world history. The experience of depopulation and displacement was shared with Tasmanians, the Khoi of southern Africa, and several other peoples around the world. But the scale of the population disaster was larger in the Americas than anywhere else—large enough, perhaps, to affect the Earth's climate.

The loss of population in the Americas from 1492 to 1700 may have deepened the chill of the Little Ice Age. Where some 40 to 70 million people had once lived, in 1700 fewer than 5 million remained. Former farmland became forest over broad patches of the Americas. As the forests grew, they absorbed carbon dioxide from the atmosphere, lowering its concentration and weakening (ever so slightly) the greenhouse effect. This (along with big volcanic eruptions and reduced energy output from the sun) probably helps to explain why the coldest spells in the Little Ice Age occurred between 1590 and 1710.

New Empires

The arrival of Europeans and the disastrous depopulation in the Americas had political consequences that varied from place to place. Where large empires had existed, as in the Andes and Mesoamerica, new, Spanish-led ones instantly replaced them. Where smaller-scale political structures had existed, as in most of the Americas, guerilla resistance was more common and European control took far longer to establish.

The largest-scale conquests took place in Mexico and Peru. In both cases, small bands of conquistadores allied with big armies of Amerindians, such as the Tlaxcalans who joined Cortés. Locals often out-numbered Spaniards in the armies of conquest by 100:1. So, in effect, Mesoamaerican conquerors used Cortés and his men to overthrow a hated Aztec Empire. Indeed, Tlaxcalans in the mid-sixteenth century considered that they, not Spaniards, had conquered the Aztecs. Similarly, in Peru, Spanish conquistadores made common cause with dissident subjects of the Inkas. When "Spanish" conquerors later marched into Chile, their armies consisted mainly of former Inka soldiers; and when Spaniards led armies into Guatemala or fought the Chichimecs in northern Mexico, it was mainly Aztecs and Tlaxcalans who followed.

In Mesoamerica, when Cortés and his allies overthrew the Aztec state (1519–1521), he and his followers proclaimed the Viceroyalty of New Spain. Pizarro created a Viceroyalty of Peru. In some ways, these Spanish colonial states were just the latest successors in native imperial traditions that stretched back centuries. The Spanish in Peru, for example, not only continued the Inka forced labor system, but they also maintained the

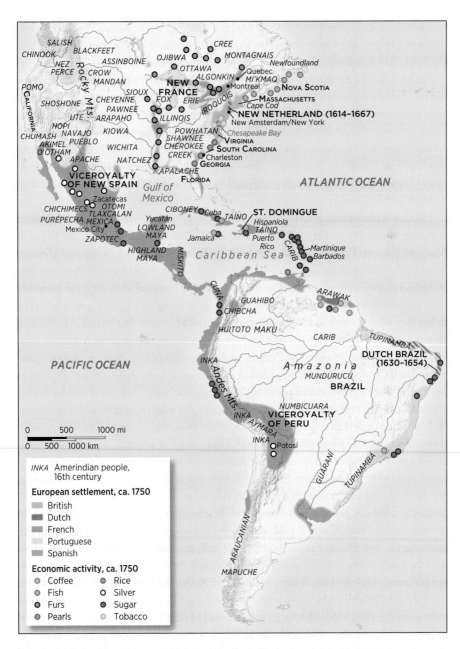

European Presence in the Americas, ca. 1750 By 1750, most of the land in the Americas was claimed by one or another European state. However, the degree to which they actually controlled American territory varied greatly. Where Amerindians remained numerically dominant, as in the heart of North America, they often exercised economic and territorial power and European claims carried little weight. The new export economy of furs had a longer reach and was a collaboration of Amerindians and Europeans.

reciprocal exchange networks among lineages that had underpinned Andean society under the Inkas, and before them the Moche. They fought on the same frontiers that the Inkas had a century before, using mainly Inka soldiers.

In Mexico, the Spanish re-built an empire on the foundations they seized from the Aztecs. Tribute payments from surrounding districts, formerly sent to Aztec Tenochtitlán, now went to Spanish Mexico City. The Spanish governed together with indigenous elites, splitting the resulting revenues and other perks of power. They did not exact tribute from the Tlaxcalans, their co-conquerors. In Mexico, as in Peru, the Spanish were too few to conquer and govern alone. Spaniards supplied superior armament and global knowledge; indigenous elites supplied local knowledge and manpower. Together, Spanish and local elites could rule the rapidly declining mass of the population.

Where Amerindian polities were small or absent, Europeans encountered more enduring resistance to their rule. The Mapuche of southern Chile and the Maya of Mexico's Yucatán Peninsula, for example, who did not have much in the way of states, fought long and hard against Spanish control. Unlike the populations of Peru and central Mexico, they had no tradition of deference to any imperial authority. For centuries they succeeded in keeping themselves independent in most respects; and when they failed they often mounted rebellions, especially the Mapuche. In general, Amerindian revolts happened more often in northern New Spain and in the southern Andes. In what is now New Mexico in 1680, the Pueblo, an Amerindian people, rose up against Spanish authority and either killed or expelled all Spaniards from their area for the next 12 years. The biggest Amerindian uprising, however, took place in the heart of the Andes, around Cuzco in 1781–1783, led by a descendant of the Inka royal family, Túpac Amaru II. It failed, at a cost of more than 100,000 lives. Nonetheless, the Spanish Empire in America was a patchy one with firm control only in a few centers.

The other European empires in the Americas were smaller than the Spanish. Portugal claimed Brazil but controlled only stretches of coastline and their hinterlands as late as 1600. When the Dutch decided to take a bit of Brazil for themselves in 1618, Portugal could not prevent it. Almost all of Brazil remained Amerindian country into the eighteenth century, when gold and diamond strikes brought a wave of European immigrants. The Dutch Empire was smaller still, confined to a few small Caribbean islands, a tiny settlement of New Netherlands (now New York), and for 30 years a corner of Brazil. And the Dutch surrendered New Netherlands to English rule in 1667.

Like the Spanish and Dutch, both the French and British claimed some Caribbean territories. They founded colonies on several small islands and some of the big ones, such as Jamaica, that Spain could not hold. In North America, they took gradual control of the eastern seaboard from the dwindling Amerindian populations. The French settled at Quebec after 1608 but struggled to populate their colony, called New France, with farmers. By 1750, New France had about 50,000 people. British settlement began in 1607 in Virginia and 1620 in Massachusetts, and soon spread everywhere from Georgia to Nova Scotia. These colonies grew quickly, expanding to the Appalachian Mountains by 1750, at which time they held a population of perhaps 2 million. In economic and strategic terms, Caribbean islands such as Jamaica and even tiny Martinique were worth a lot more than the North American colonies—because of the money made selling sugar from slave plantations.

Settlement and Transoceanic Economies

The sudden loss of native population in the Americas played havoc with economic life and increased the scale of slavery. Labor grew ever scarcer, and ambitious businessmen despaired over how to mine ores or raise crops without sufficient labor. The main motive behind both the African and Amerindian slave trades was to provide cheap labor for the economies of the Americas. European laborers crossed the Atlantic too, a few as slaves, many as indentured servants—meaning they had to work for no wages for a set period, often seven years. But up to 1820, roughly four enslaved Africans had come to the Americas for each European migrant whether indentured or free. It wouldn't be until 1880 that the cumulative number of European arrivals in the Americas equaled the number of enslaved Africans who survived the Middle Passage.

With African and European migrants joining the Amerindian populations, building a new economy in the Americas became possible. The new connections to transatlantic markets, and in some cases new crops or technologies, presented novel opportunities. All the European powers hoped to find precious metals, as the Spanish did in great quantities. Where that failed, the new empires sought other ways to realize the economic potential of the Americas.

Fisheries and Furs One opportunity lay in the world's richest cod fisheries, from Cape Cod to Newfoundland. From the 1520s onward, British, French, and Basque (and eventually American and Canadian) fishermen, free men working for wages, caught thousands of tons of cod annually. Most of it was salted or dried and shipped to Europe for sale. On the mainland of North America, at least its northern half, beaver fur offered another way to make money. Amerindians had long hunted and trapped fur-bearing animals. An export trade began around 1630, funneled through Montreal and New Amsterdam (New York after 1667) to Europe. Amerindians still did most of the trapping, but they now sold most of their fur harvest to French, Dutch, or British merchants. Agents for European fur merchants eventually ranged far into the interior of North America—especially those based in New France, often marrying into Amerindian communities in arrangements broadly parallel to those with wives of the coast in the African slave trade. By 1800, the North American fur trade extended as far west as the Rocky Mountains.

The Plantation Zone Another transatlantic economy, even more lucrative than the fishery or fur trade, took root in the warmer regions from the Chesapeake south to

Brazil. This became the **plantation zone** of the Americas, the destination of the great majority of enslaved Africans shipped across the Atlantic. In the Chesapeake, where English settlement began in 1607, the money-making crop was tobacco. In South Carolina and Georgia, a rice plantation economy flourished after 1690, also based on slave labor and to some extent slave know-how in rice cultivation: some slaves came from rice-growing regions of West Africa and brought their techniques of irrigation and planting with them.

The heart of the plantation zone lay in the Caribbean and northeastern Brazil. Sugar became the most rewarding plantation crop. Unlike fishing, fur trapping, or even tobacco farming, sugar cultivation only made sense on a large scale. Sugarcane juice has to be crystallized within days after the cane is cut, which required elaborate machinery to press juice out of the cane and boiling houses to convert the cane juice to sugar crystals. Because it called for hefty capital investment, sugar production became a business dominated by big planters with connections to European merchant houses. Dozens of Caribbean islands, including British Barbados and Jamaica, Spanish Cuba, and French Saint-Domingue (part of Hispaniola), produced sugar, as did Portuguese Brazil. From 1650 to 1800, sugar islands were the second-most valuable possessions in the Americas. Sugar plantation workers suffered the highest mortality rates of slaves anywhere in the plantation zone. Millions of Africans died on these plantations. Planters bought millions more to take their places.

Silver Precious metals formed the most valuable transatlantic economy. Cortés and Pizarro sought gold and silver, and found both in envy-provoking quantities. They and their successors used all the tools they had—imagination, guile, technology, brutality—to coax more gold and silver out of Mexico and Peru. Spanish authorities organized large-scale silver mining in Zacatecas, Mexico, and at **Potosí** in the Andes. Potosí alone yielded 40,000 tons of silver between the 1540s and 1780s. Potosí temporarily became one of the world's largest cities, despite an elevation of more than 13,000 feet (4,000 m).

By 1600, some 20,000 Amerindians—both wage workers and mita forced laborers—mined, processed, and minted silver into coins. Wage workers were well paid by local standards but their lives were brutal and short on account of harsh conditions, frequent accidents, and poisoning from mercury used in the refining process. Laborers in the Potosí mines performed heavy work in darkness relieved only by candlelight. They breathed air laced with dust that over time brought on silicosis and other lung diseases. Many of them spent their shifts carrying 55lb (25-kilo) sacks of ore up rickety ladders, climbing more than 650 feet (200 m)—no wonder they wouldn't work without a wad of coca leaves in their cheek to dull their pain, hunger, thirst, and minds.

Additional unfree Amerindian workers were dragooned from as much as 350 miles (600 km) away to replace the sick, maimed, and killed. Andean peasant communities held the equivalent of funerals for men drafted for the mita, knowing what lay ahead.

By 1608 the mita could no longer deliver enough workers, and mine-owners bought

African slaves for work at Potosí. They generally toiled above ground in transport or refining. Life expectancies were so short for miners, and slaves so expensive, that employers preferred to see mita recruits do the lethal work below ground. One Spanish friar wrote in 1628, "Every peso coin minted in Potosí has cost the lives of ten Indians who died in the depths of the mines." This exaggerated the toll but underlines the human cost of the silver business.

Mule caravans and coastal shipping carried most Mexican and Andean silver to port cities for transport through the Caribbean to Spain. Some went directly from Mexico to Manila in the Philippines. Much of the silver that Spain extracted from the Americas eventually found its way to China or India, as we shall see in a later chapter.

Agriculture But people couldn't eat furs or silver: agriculture fed almost everyone from French Quebec to Spanish Chile. Amerindian peoples everywhere grew their own food when they could avoid being dragged off to plantations, mines, or missions. They took up the raising of livestock with newly introduced species such as sheep, goats, and cattle. In seventeenth-century New Mexico, for example, the Navajo economy combined sheep herding with farming and raiding. Amerindians sometimes added Old World crops to their gardens too. Settlers from Pennsylvania to New England to Quebec also raised their own food, often planting American maize alongside European varieties of wheat. Farther south, in the plantation zone, the richer European settlers obliged slaves to do all farm work. Poor families in the plantation zone, whatever their racial identity, worked the land themselves. In Spanish America, settlers created big agricultural estates (*haciendas*), and the Crown granted them the right (an ***encomienda***) to conscript Amerindians as unpaid laborers.

By and large, everyone ate local food. But by 1750, locally raised food might well consist of crops and animals that had been introduced from other continents in the Columbian Exchange and integrated into the farms and fields of the Americas.

Hybrid Societies

With lucrative transatlantic (and in cases transpacific) export economies linking the Americas to Africa, Asia, and Europe, the Americas developed creole societies and cultures that blended elements from these distant places. The changing languages of the Americas were a good measure of broader social and cultural change.

Creole Languages and Cultures Many Amerindian tongues spoken in 1492 gradually died out as the number of speakers dwindled. By 1800, perhaps one-third of the roughly 25 million people living in the Americas spoke an Amerindian language. Maybe one-tenth—generally, people born in Africa—spoke an African language. The great majority spoke a European language, although sometimes not as a native tongue. In the plantation zone especially, new, creole languages developed that typically

Missionaries This eighteenth-century manuscript illustration celebrates Spanish Dominican friars for their missionary efforts among Amerindian people. At top a friar gathers his congregants in a church away from attacking demons.

combined features from European and African tongues. (Most people in the Caribbean today speak one or more creole languages.) Haitian Creole combined mainly French vocabulary with grammar based on West African languages such as Fon. Papiamento, spoken in Aruba, Bonaire, and Curaçao, is a blend of Portuguese, Spanish, Dutch, and indigenous Amerindian languages.

Similar blending took place in religious beliefs and practices. Most people in the Americas practiced one or another form of Christianity, but in ways that might have raised eyebrows in Christianity's homelands. European colonization in the Americas included substantial efforts at conversion and religious education, especially in lands controlled by Catholic kingdoms such as Portugal, Spain, or France. They tended to entrust religion to one or several orders of the Catholic Church, such as the Jesuits, Franciscans, or Dominicans. Missionaries of these orders often accepted great hardship and suffered high on-the-job mortality rates: in New Mexico over the course of the seventeenth century, about 40 percent of Franciscans were killed by the people they were trying to convert, the Pueblo. Members of these orders built missions in French Canada, Portuguese Brazil, and throughout Spanish America, especially in frontier regions: Texas had 30 missions and California 21. Priests and friars, more than officials of the state, brokered the relations between Amerindian and European societies in the Catholic domains. In lands controlled by the mainly Protestant British and Dutch, Christianization of the indigenous population carried a far lower priority.

Amerindians who were attracted to Christianity generally preferred to meld the old with the new, to adopt Christian forms and belief selectively and mix them with their own practices—as Africans did with Islam or Chinese with Buddhism.

In the plantation zone, African religions entered the mix and often dominated it. Vodun, a polytheistic religion with a prominent role for female deities, was imported by enslaved Fon- and Ewe-speakers from West Africa. It took root in the Caribbean, Brazil, and Louisiana, acquiring new features, often from Catholicism, in each locale. Slaves (and former slaves) created new religions, such as Santería in the Spanish Caribbean or Candomblé in Brazil, based on West African spiritual practices but with components adapted from Christianity or Amerindian traditions. Yoruba religion played an especially large role in shaping religious practice in the plantation zone. Its tradition of orishas—spirits that guide people to live properly and help win favor from Olorun, the Yoruba creator god—blended fluidly with Catholicism's emphasis on saints. Slaves and former slaves adjusted their spiritual lives to fit the challenges of plantation society.

Shifting Social Hierarchies The social structures of colonial societies in the Americas were complex and shifting hierarchies. Status depended on a long roster of variables. Gender and age mattered here much as everywhere else. Legal status (i.e., slave or free) and wealth mattered a lot in the Americas, as almost everywhere else. Skin color and presumed ancestry mattered more here than almost anywhere else because the Americas was one of the few places (the Dutch settlement at the Cape of Good Hope was another) where people from multiple continents and with notably different superficial characteristics (e.g., skin color) coexisted.

But every place calculated social status differently because so many variables were involved. For example, in the eighteenth century in the French plantation colony of Saint-Domingue (Haiti today), the social pyramid featured slaves—roughly 90 percent of the population—at the bottom. Above them stood free blacks of African birth; free blacks of Caribbean birth; *gens de couleur libre,* or free people of mixed African and European ancestry; poor whites; and at the top, prosperous whites. However, in some contexts wealthy *gens de couleur libre* might outrank poor whites. A lengthy vocabulary existed to distinguish among people depending on ancestry.

In Brazil, Mexico, or Peru, even more complex hierarchies existed, because—unlike in Saint-Domingue—Amerindians survived in large numbers. Many people had African, Amerindian, and European ancestors in every imaginable proportion, all captured in a correspondingly detailed vocabulary. In all three of these societies, slaves were on the bottom and wealthy Europeans on top of the social pyramid, but what lay in between was more complicated, and more fluid, than in Saint-Domingue.

New France and New England had different social hierarchies from the rest of the Americas. In 1750, New England had about 350,000 people, of whom roughly 330,000 were free, Christian, and of European descent. About 13,000 were of African descent, slave or free, and fewer were Amerindian. Social distinctions beyond those of age and

New Social Hierarchies An eighteenth-century portrait by Brunias, *Free Women of Color with their Children and Servants in a Landscape* (ca. 1764–1796), depicts a group of wealthy mixed-race women—*gens de couleur libre*—surrounded by their children and a large retinue of enslaved people of African descent. Both the enslaved people's unfree status and their darker skin color marked them as being of lower status in the complex social hierarchy of the Caribbean.

gender rested mainly on wealth, the prestige of one's ancestry, and one's religious sect. But in New France and farther west, around the Great Lakes, there were only 70,000 French people in 1750 and about 1,200 of African descent. Amerindians outnumbered everyone else until about 1830. Many Amerindian groups retained their old social structures with hierarchies based on age, gender, and achievement. But increasingly they took part in market transactions with frontier settlers—providing furs and hides, for example—and as a result became part of larger societies in which they occupied subordinate roles.

Independent Groups Some peoples in the Americas managed to keep their distance from the new European empires. The Mapuche and Maya, and the so-called Plains Indians of North America, successfully resisted encroaching empires until the nineteenth century, as did the peoples of the Northwest coast. But even these groups experienced some rearrangements of their social hierarchies. With war and trade more common, specialists in these pursuits could more easily gain status. Many Amerindian tribes in Amazonia evaded contact with outsiders altogether for centuries (some of them even until this day) and probably underwent no sharp changes in their social structures.

Communities of runaway slaves, called maroons in the English-speaking colonies, secured their freedom for decades, often in mountains or jungles. Brazil had many such communities, usually short-lived. The largest, Palmares, was home to 30,000 former slaves and lasted from about 1600 until 1694, when Portuguese forces overwhelmed it in an artillery assault. Other such communities were much smaller, mostly composed of young men eking out a living hunting, fishing, and sometimes raiding plantations from which they had escaped.

Maroons were not the only ones who temporarily escaped the reach of the new empires. Until about 1730, many coastlands of the Americas hosted pirates who operated on the margins of the new empires, preying on merchant ships and occasionally on settlements. Most were Europeans themselves, usually runaway sailors fleeing the harsh discipline of naval or merchant vessels, but perhaps one in three were African or of partly African descent. In general, piracy flourishes when a lucrative maritime trade springs up without powerful naval states nearby. The spurt of seaborne trade in the wake of Columbus and da Gama provided such an opportunity, and pirates multiplied in the Caribbean, the Mediterranean, the Indian Ocean, and in East Asian waters. Pirates in the Caribbean enjoyed considerable success from the 1570s until the 1720s, by which time European navies became too large and efficient for piracy to flourish.

The entanglement of the Americas in the growing Global web was an extremely disruptive process. It entailed the dismantling of the pre-Columbian American webs of interaction—mainly through the massive loss of native populations, but also through compulsory labor, forced migration, and other hardships visited upon Amerindians. Meanwhile, merchants, migrants, missionaries, and others forged new linkages both within the Americas and between the Americas and the wider world of Atlantic Europe,

Atlantic Africa, and East Asia. A true global web was spun in the centuries after Columbus, for the first time in the history of the world. The newly refashioned Americas provided much of the thread in the form of silver, sugar, furs, fish, and other commodities traded far and wide.

Siberia Absorbed

Expansion of the Old World web proceeded by land as well as sea. One of the largest territorial expansions took place in Siberia. Nearly the size of South America, Siberia (now Russian territory) lies between the Arctic Ocean to the north and the steppe of Central Asia and Mongolia to the south. It is stunningly cold during its long winter. In 1500, most of it was tall forest or shrubby, coniferous, and often swampy forest called taiga. Getting around within Siberia was a challenge, and getting anything useful out of it was no easier. A strong motive would be required to tempt outsiders to tackle Siberia.

The people of Siberia, some of whose ancestors had been the first migrants to the Americas 15,000 to 20,000 years before, numbered only a few hundred thousand in 1500. They were divided into about a hundred linguistic groups, and most followed a variety of shamanistic religions. Some, in southern Siberia, were Buddhist or at least influenced by Buddhist beliefs acquired from Mongols, whose empire had included parts of southernmost Siberia. Siberians drew their living from the forest: fishing, hunting, trapping, and reindeer herding. In southern Siberia they also raised what crops they could in the brief growing season and traded occasionally with the steppe peoples to their south.

Fur: A Lucrative Export

The main thing outsiders wanted from Siberia was fur. Several million foxes, ermine, squirrels, and sables, all with thick pelts, wandered the woods and swamps. For centuries, a tiny proportion of those pelts were traded to China, the steppe peoples, or the Baltic lands and Russia. In the sixteenth century, as more people in those lands became more prosperous, demand for Siberian furs grew. Eventually this demand provoked a growing export trade, providing the motive for outsiders to try to control Siberia.

The outsiders who took this step were Russians and Cossacks. Russians were Slavic-speakers who in 1480 had won independence from the Mongol Golden Horde and formed a state called Muscovy, centered on Moscow. Muscovy grew as Mongol

Siberian Fur The large fur piece decorating the crown of the tsar Ivan V from the seventeenth century is indicative of the growing status of Siberian fur as a luxury commodity and a symbol of Russian power.

power waned, and its leaders aimed to "gather all the Russias" into a larger empire at the expense of neighbors. The aptly named Ivan the Terrible (r. 1553–1584 as Ivan IV) championed this enterprise, never missing an opportunity to flay or boil an enemy alive. By the late sixteenth century, Muscovy's princes called themselves tsars (derived from the word *Caesar*), or emperors of Russia, and ruled 8 to 12 million people. Most of those were unfree peasants, called serfs, bound to landed estates and in effect owned by landlords.

Cossacks were mainly serfs (or their descendants) who managed to run away from their owners in what is now Russia and Ukraine. They settled in the river valleys of the steppes north and east of the Black Sea, forming their own self-governing communities beginning in the fifteenth and sixteenth centuries. They were roughly analogous to the escaped former slaves known as maroons in the plantation zone of the Americas. Cossacks lived by farming, raiding, and piracy on rivers and the Black Sea, or by hiring

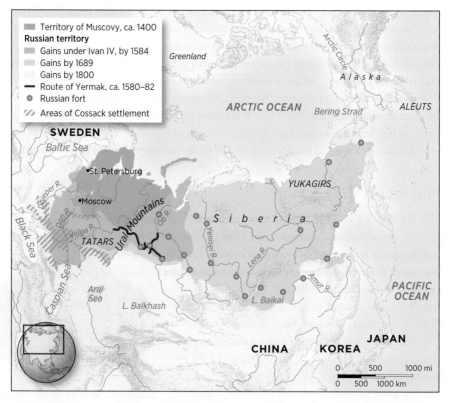

Muscovy, Russia, and Siberia, 1400–1800   The expansion of Muscovy and Russia included the incorporation of Siberia, beginning with the incursions of the Cossacks and Russians led by Yermak starting around 1580. Motivated by a quest for furs, by 1640 Russians had built scattered forts across Siberia to the Pacific shores. By 1730, Russians had crossed the Bering Strait and extended their fur trade to Alaska.

themselves out as mercenaries. In the sixteenth century, Cossacks were often enemies of the Russian state, but sometimes protectors of Russian frontiers against Tatar raiders from the steppe. At all times they were military specialists. Their population was probably no more than 100,000 in 1600.

The spearhead of the process by which Siberia joined the Global web, and the Russian Empire, was a Cossack named **Yermak**. He was successful as a river pirate, but about 1580 he became the equivalent of a conquistador. It was not silver that drew him into Siberia, but fur. An entrepreneurial family with close ties to the tsars, the Stroganovs, hired Yermak to expand their fur trade from Siberia. To do so he had to battle through a Tatar khanate in southwestern Siberia, a legacy of Mongol rule. With a band of about 800—just a few more than the number of Spaniards Cortés led in his assault on Mexico—Yermak defeated the Tatars, thanks to guns and riverboats provided by the Stroganovs. Within a couple of years, Yermak and his roughnecks had reached the Ob River. They sent back enough furs to please the Stroganovs and Tsar Ivan, who—sensing a business opportunity—removed the price he had put on Yermak's head and became his biggest supporter.

Yermak died in 1585 in a scrap with Tatars, but his success inspired a stream of Cossacks and Russians to flow into Siberia. By 1640, they had built wooden forts at key portages and river junctions across Siberia all the way to the Pacific shores. The conquest of Siberia paid handsome rewards for Russia. Soon one-tenth to one-third of the tsar's revenues came from the sale of furs. Yermak became a hero in Russia, memorialized over time with postage stamps and public statues.

Like Spain's conquistadores, Yermak and his successors enjoyed the advantages of living inside the world's biggest web. They had the latest military technologies, thanks to the Stroganovs and the tsars. They knew how to build boats that could operate on Siberia's rivers, and how to put small cannon on their boats. They knew the market price of trade goods—tobacco, alcohol, flour—as well as that of furs. At least some of them could read and write, enabling them to communicate and coordinate the actions of scattered parties over vast distances. And by virtue of childhood exposure, they carried immunities to the standard crowd diseases, which indigenous Siberians generally did not.

The Russification of Siberia

The Russian conquest carried hard consequences for the native populations of Siberia. In 1600, they numbered over 300,000 people, with 120 languages among them. Like Amerindians, many Siberians died from exposure to unfamiliar diseases. One group, the Yukaghirs in eastern Siberia, lost two-thirds of their population to disease, probably smallpox in the main. By 1700, the Yakut and Tunguz peoples had lost 80 percent of their population of a century before. As in the Americas, brutal treatment compounded the effects of diseases. Cossacks, following Yermak's lead, demanded tribute in the form of furs from all adult males (an arrangement with no parallel in the North American fur trade). As the Siberian population fell, Cossacks and Russians required more tribute from each man. Many Siberians resisted Cossack and Russian demands, and countless ambushes, skirmishes, and battles resulted. The patriarch of Moscow, the top religious official of the Russian Orthodox Church, complained in 1662 that Russian men were neglecting their Christian duties, mistreating native Siberian women, even buying and selling them. In the end, a few thousand Cossacks and Russians subdued a few hundred thousand Siberians, over 5 million square miles of forest and taiga. Together, they trapped and skinned millions of sables, ermines, and foxes—and helped make the Russian tsars richer and more powerful than ever before.

Over time, Siberia entered the Global web and became increasingly Russian. Military and political control came first. Creole versions of Russian gradually developed and occasionally took the place of indigenous languages. Russian Orthodoxy joined the several forms of shamanism formerly practiced, creating blended religious practices as in the Americas. Siberia in the seventeenth and eighteenth centuries was creating new hybrid cultures, with ever stronger Russian components. By 1795, population surpassed 1 million, mostly Russian in language and culture. Many Siberian women took Russian (or Cossack) husbands, and their children often preferred the identity of their fathers, which conferred more advantages in life. And in later centuries, mainly after 1860, millions of Russians migrated to Siberia, swamping what remained of the indigenous peoples, their languages, and religion, so that Siberian culture became highly Russified.

Russians and Cossacks pushed farther eastward. Clashes with China led to a 1689 treaty that divided vast uncharted Siberian and East Asian spaces between the Russian and Chinese Empires. By 1730, Russians were seeking furs in Alaska. Within decades, they mobilized Alaskan natives—Aleuts, mainly—to hunt fur seals along the Pacific coast from the Aleutian Islands south to San Francisco Bay. These shores of North America, like Siberia, also joined the world's web in part through Russian enterprise.

Oceania and Australia Enmeshed

Probably the most isolated peoples in the world in the years between 1500 and 1750 were those living on the continent of Australia and the islands of Remote Oceania. In Australia, as we have seen, people had arrived at least 50,000 years ago and learned to manage a challenging environment. The archeological evidence suggests that by 1750 they numbered 500,000 to 1 million. The islands of Remote Oceania acquired human population as early as 6,000 years ago in some cases and as recently as 750 years ago in others. The most populated archipelagoes, as of 1750, were Hawaii and New Caledonia, each with perhaps 400,000 people, Fiji with 150,000, and Tahiti and New Zealand, each with maybe 100,000. Taken together, the population of Australia plus all the Pacific Islands in 1750 came to less than 4 million people.

Another Disease Disaster

Except for some island chains of Near Oceania (meaning New Guinea, the Bismarck Archipelago, and the Solomon Islands) where malaria lurked, Pacific islands, like Australia, harbored few infectious diseases. By global standards, people lived unusually healthy lives. That did not mean they lived especially long: droughts, storms, tsunamis, and other natural hazards took a considerable toll. The islanders' minimal experience with infectious disease had long been a blessing, but in the late eighteenth century it became a curse.

In the 1760s, European mariners, especially British and French, began to sail the Pacific more frequently. They increasingly found commodities that, with their knowledge of distant markets, they could sell: sealskins, whale oil, sea cucumber (a delicacy in China), and sandalwood (a luxury in China). Sustained contact between Pacific Island populations and Europeans began between 1767 and 1778 in most cases, and in Australia in 1788.

In every case, the contact brought demographic catastrophe. Unfamiliar diseases had the same effect as in the Americas, Siberia, and among the Khoi of South Africa. The precise scale of these disasters is uncertain, but it appears that the Marquesas Islands were among the hardest hit, losing about 96 percent of their population between roughly 1770 and 1920. Small archipelagoes, where everyone was in regular contact with everyone else, allowed killer diseases to spread quickly. Epidemics hit again and again, sometimes killing a quarter or a third of an island's people each time. As late as 1875, a measles outbreak in Fiji carried off one-third of all remaining Fijians.

Larger archipelagoes, with more dispersed populations, fared somewhat better but still suffered disastrous losses. New Zealand lost about half its Maori population between 1769 and 1870. Australia probably lost more than half of its Aboriginal people between 1788 and 1900. No one had much in the way of useful medicine to combat the epidemics.

Part of the demographic catastrophe, in the Pacific as in the Americas, resulted from falling birth rates. This too had something to do with disease. The arrival of European (and after 1780, American) sailors spurred a sex trade that spread venereal diseases far and wide from Hawaii to New Zealand. These infections made many women infertile. Sometimes women voluntarily took sailors as lovers while a ship anchored offshore, receiving gifts they valued and, as they saw it, enhancing their *mana*, or spiritual prestige, through sex with powerful strangers. Sometimes they did so under duress, compelled by fathers, brothers, or husbands to trade sex for iron nails, liquor, guns, or other items. In New Zealand by the 1820s, Maori clans fought wars to capture and enslave women. Their captors then sold these women's favors to visiting sailors for guns to fight rival clans more effectively.

Just about everywhere in the Pacific, as in Siberia and the Americas, indigenous populations fell for about 150 years after the onset of first contact with the wider world. Then they stabilized and slowly began to grow. Despite this recovery, in many cases, most notably Australia, New Zealand, and Hawaii, immigrant peoples came to outnumber indigenous populations.

Christianity and Trade Goods

Contact with the wider world brought much more than disease and disaster to Oceania and Australia. Christianity was a popular import. Catholic and Protestant missionaries flocked to many Pacific islands, and although easily horrified by local attitudes to clothing (too little) and sex (too much), in time they proved highly successful in making converts. Missionaries had invisible allies in the murderous microbes they and others brought with them: everyone could see that newcomers suffered far less from disease, and many islanders concluded that the Christian God offered better protection than their own deities could. Missionaries had highly visible, if inadvertent, allies in the sailors and whalers who vividly illustrated some of Christianity's seven deadly sins. Within a century of contact, almost all Pacific Islanders and Australian Aborigines had accepted Christianity, although they adapted their new religion to their own traditions and circumstances, as converts normally do.

Trade goods and introduced plants and animals proved as popular as Christianity. European mariners brought such useful novelties as iron fishhooks and farming tools, guns, cattle, horses, goats, and sheep. Pacific peoples traded for these goods and increasingly worked specifically to get them. The new goods increased the economic potential of island (and Australian) landscapes.

Australia

In Australia during the eighteenth century, the Aboriginal population of half a million to 1 million divided into roughly 250 groups, each with its own language. According to one of the first foreigners ever to meet them, Captain James Cook in 1770, "They may appear to some to be the most wretched people on earth, but in reality they are far happier than we Europeans. They live in a tranquility which is not disturbed by the inequality in condition: the earth and the sea of their own accord furnish them with all things necessary for life." Cook may have failed to recognize social inequalities among Aboriginal Australians, which surely existed, even if muted by the standards Cook knew from his native Scotland. Protocols governed inter-group behavior, usually keeping conflict under control.

However, no protocols could protect Aboriginal Australians from what
came their way in 1788: a fleet of 11
ships bearing more than 1,000 settlers
backed by the British government.
Most of the settlers were convicts.
Transportation of convicts continued
until 1868, totaling 160,000 in all, of
whom about 15 percent were women.
Once in Australia, a few were freed,
and one rose to become a magistrate.
Free migrants—mostly English, but
one-quarter of them Irish—came
in larger numbers by the 1820s, and
population spilled out of the original settlements near Sydney onto the
tablelands of the interior. Squatters, as
Australians who helped themselves to
land were called, pushed Aboriginals
off the best lands, often violently.

Over the next century, skirmishes
and wars between settlers and Aborigines claimed about 27,000 lives, 90
percent of them Aboriginal. The
Aboriginal Australians fought with

Australia and New Zealand, ca. 1770–1900 Aboriginal Australians had to adjust to British settlement
from 1788 onward, as did Maori in New Zealand
from about 1800. They often found trade goods
attractive, and Christianity too. But like Amerindians, native Siberians, and the Khoi in South Africa,
they suffered greatly from imported diseases and
attacks by better-armed newcomers. Within a century, both lands were demographically dominated
by the newcomers and were securely part of the
British Empire.

spears and shields; the newcomers had muskets and, soon, artillery. Scattered guerilla
wars flared up now and again, but the tide flowed in favor of the settlers. As in Siberia,
South Africa's Cape, and the Americas, the toll of disease and advantages in military
technology made the difference.

By 1850, the rising population of Euro-Australians outnumbered the falling one of
Aboriginal Australians among the continent's half million residents. Aborigines increasingly lived in the dryer or more tropical parts of the country that the immigrants did
not want. Having lost the best lands, many Aborigines made their peace with the settlers and worked as cooks or stockmen (cowboys) on cattle or sheep stations (ranches).
Aboriginal women often married (often informally) immigrant men, especially in the
early years of settlement when European women were scarce. Australia now had sprawling wheat fields, millions of sheep and cattle, and a prosperous wool export trade. All
this seemed right to most Euro-Australians: as one settler asked in 1845, "which has
the better right—the savage, born in a country, which he runs over but can scarcely
be said to occupy...or the civilized man, who comes to introduce into this...unpro-
ductive country, the industry which supports life...?" By 1850, the southern continent

had undergone a radical transformation, similar in its broad outlines to the fate of the Americas and Siberia, if different in the particulars.

New Zealand

In New Zealand, the entry into the Global web also came suddenly and wrenchingly. As we've seen, Maori—Polynesians who settled New Zealand about 1250—lived as farmers, fishers, foragers, and hunters, in groups that since 1500 or so had become more competitive and often warlike. They had had no significant interactions with peoples from outside New Zealand and its neighboring small islands for many centuries. In 1642, the Dutch sea captain Abel Tasman sighted New Zealand, stayed for a few hours, and was driven away by Maori. In 1769, two European ships visited. Settlers began to dig in about 1800, at first living among, and more or less as, Maori. But by 1840 organized colonization was under way, and the *pakeha* (as people of European origin are termed in New Zealand) population ballooned to half a million by 1885. Maori population continued to fall due to introduced diseases and violence until about 1890.

As in the Americas, Siberia, and Australia, the local population in New Zealand alternately welcomed and resisted the settler presence. Some Maori went to work on

sailing ships to see the wider world. Many more traded eagerly for exotic goods such as iron nails (useful as chisels for the Maori tradition of wood carving), blankets, and guns. Maori also adopted pig raising and potato farming, markedly improving their nutrition by making new animals and plants their own.

Maori took up firearms with both enthusiasm and desperation. Martial prowess had long been important to male Maori. Now their internal wars became deadlier. As in Africa during the time of the Atlantic slave trade, it often became necessary to acquire guns to defend oneself against others already equipped with them. In the early nineteenth century, Maori with guns terrorized Maori without guns, until the point came when all surviving Maori peoples had guns. In the process, 20,000 to 40,000 were killed in the so-called Musket Wars (1807–1845), and many thousand women and children captured and enslaved. Women captives, as noted above, could be put to use in the sex trade to acquire more guns. Maori also turned their weapons on visiting whalers and sealers. On one occasion in 1821, they captured six Americans and forced some to eat

Maori Culture A nineteenth-century illustration of a Maori warrior carrying a musket is suggestive of the destructive impact that European firearms had on Maori society.

others (according to Joseph Price of Wilmington, Delaware, who survived this ordeal, his shipmates "tasted very much like roasted pork").

It comes as no surprise that Maori did not often welcome newcomers. For half a century after contact in 1769, Maori exposure to the wider world came mainly via two sorts of men: Australian convicts eager to shed their pasts and gamble on a rough life skinning seals on New Zealand's shores, and sex-starved British, Australian, and American whalers.

But over time, as the newcomers came to include more and more missionaries and even families, Maori found more to welcome. They embraced Christianity with remarkable gusto from the 1830s. Missionaries' Christian messages made sense to many Maori, who witnessed the conspicuous sinfulness of visiting whalers and sealers.

In 1840, in the **Treaty of Waitangi**, most Maori chiefs agreed to put down their weapons and become British subjects in return for guarantees of their land. Large-scale British settlement soon followed; and treaty or no treaty, Maori and *pakeha* engaged in intermittent land wars (1845–1872), which ultimately ended Maori independence and confirmed New Zealand's future as a British settler colony. Epidemics, warfare, and dispossession: the entry of New Zealand into the Global web bore a family resemblance to the experience of Australia, Siberia, and the Americas.

Hawaii

Before contact, Hawaii's roughly 400,000 people lived—mainly on a diet of taro, yams, sweet potatoes, and fish—in a handful of small and competitive kingdoms long isolated from the rest of the world. When Captain Cook and British sailors turned up in 1778, Hawaiian kings sought to exploit the opportunity presented by the strangers' tools and weapons. One king, Kamehameha, scored a brilliant success when he murdered all but one of a ship's crew and invited the sole survivor to instruct his warriors in the arts of using firearms and sailing European vessels. His soldiers learned well, and between the 1780s and 1810 he defeated all his rivals and unified Hawaii as a single monarchy. Unlike the chiefs of New Zealand's rival clans, **King Kamehameha** managed to keep tight control over imported weaponry and thus could vault himself into supreme power over his fellow Hawaiians. He ruled as an autocrat, made a fortune on sandalwood exports, banned human sacrifice, and imposed peace.

Despite the peace, his subjects diminished in number. Whalers, traders, and sailors brought the same infections to Hawaii that ravaged the rest of the Pacific. Venereal disease, previously unknown, spread widely and lowered birth rates. The native Hawaiian population plunged to about 75,000 in 1850 and 40,000 in 1890. As this demographic catastrophe unfolded, many Hawaiians came to wonder whether their old ways were best and whether their familiar gods could still protect them.

After King Kamehameha died in 1819, missionaries arrived in force and met with much success. The most politically ambitious of the deceased king's 22 wives,

Hawaiian Monarchy An official portrait recorded Queen Liliʻuokalani sitting on her throne in 1892, shortly before Americans deposed her monarchy.

Kaʻahumanu, adopted a Protestant faith. She served as regent for her son, King Kamehameha II, and did her best to suppress both Hawaiian religion and Catholicism until her death in 1832.

Settlers came late to Hawaii—mainly after 1850—but by 1870 they outnumbered Polynesian (native) Hawaiians. They brought cattle, sugarcane, and a new export economy that bound Hawaii mainly to U.S. markets. Sugarcane in particular required labor, which came in the form of nearly 50,000 Chinese and tens of thousands more Japanese, Koreans, Filipinos, and Portuguese. Hawaii too became a hybrid society and culture. Newspapers in Chinese appeared in 1881. The quintessential Hawaiian musical instrument, the ukulele, was first made about 1880 by Portuguese immigrants. In the 1890s, American businessmen resident in Hawaii deposed the reigning monarch, Queen Liliʻuokalani, and ended the Hawaiian monarchy. The United States annexed the islands in 1898.

Between the 1760s and 1850, the Global web ensnared the Pacific world from Australia to Hawaii. Formerly isolated peoples now found themselves in regular contact with the wider world, thanks to European mariners often seeking goods for Chinese, European, or U.S. markets. The roughly 4 million people affected entered a new epidemiological world full of dangerous new diseases. They entered a new cultural world dominated by European outlooks, languages, and Christianity, to which many Pacific peoples were strongly attracted. They also entered a political realm in which their small numbers, limited state organization, and stone- and wood-based military technologies put them at an acute disadvantage. Even those most determined to fight domination, such as New Zealand's Maori, were vanquished.

Conclusion

When people from Eurasia crossed the seas to the Americas, southern Africa, Australia, and Oceania and pierced the forests into the interior of Siberia, they created the first truly global web. In demographic and political terms, this process proved a disaster for indigenous peoples. In cultural terms, it was a disaster for people who preferred the old, familiar ways. Introduced crowd diseases wrought havoc for five or six generations. People lost hope and initiative. Social networks, institutions, collective memory, and expertise were all eroded or entirely lost. Some peoples—like the Tasmanians with whom this chapter began—were effectively wiped out, and stray survivors attached themselves to new families, tribes, and groups.

In most cases in the Americas and Siberia, the creation of the Global web entailed the destruction of political orders. Empires such as those of the Aztecs and Inkas crumbled. New polities took their place, usually dominated by Europeans, as in the Americas, Siberia, and South Africa's Cape, but sometimes run by opportunistic locals, such as Hawaii's King Kamehameha.

In Africa north of the Cape settlement, the new links to oceanic trade and the Global web had political consequences too, but less radical ones. States rose and fell, and on balance more militaristic states prospered in the new situation, which brought with it the risks and opportunities of the expanded slave trade. But basic political formats held up better than elsewhere. So did population. In most of Africa, as in most of Eurasia, crowd diseases were familiar childhood diseases that rarely caused massive epidemics.

Vast cultural changes resulted from the formation of a globalizing web. These normally led to hybrid, **creole cultures**, with varying mixtures of traditions from Europe and from local populations. In the plantation zone of the Americas, the mix also included a large share of African culture—religion, languages, foodways—carried across the Atlantic by slaves. And in Hawaii it included strong infusions of East Asian cultures, carried across the Pacific mainly by immigrant laborers.

The economies that underpinned all the societies in question also underwent radical restructuring. Oceanic trade reached almost every coast and navigable river, inspiring stepped-up (or altogether new) production or extraction of furs in Siberia and North America, slaves and ivory in Africa, wool in Australia, sealskins in New Zealand, whale oil throughout Polynesian waters, fish from the northwest Atlantic, sugar from the plantation zone of the Americas and Hawaii, and silver from the Andes and Mexico—just to name a few. The growing scale, scope, and pace of commerce created opportunities for survivors, at the same time that unprecedented demographic disasters were unfolding.

Such demographic, political, cultural, and economic tumult around the globe added fuel to the dynamics of change in the heartlands of Eurasia, to which we turn next.

‖‖

Chapter Review

KEY TERMS

disease disasters p. 630

King Afonso p. 637

Khoi p. 639

transatlantic slave trade p. 641

Middle Passage p. 641

Taíno p. 647

mita p. 649

plantation zone p. 654

Potosí p. 654

encomienda p. 655

Yermak p. 661

Treaty of Waitangi p. 667

King Kamehameha p. 667

creole cultures p. 669

REVIEW QUESTIONS

1. Why were Atlantic Europeans in the best position to take advantage of the opportunities that the globalizing world offered?

2. Identify the three main components of the process of globalization in Africa.

3. What motivated merchants and rulers in East and West Africa to convert to Islam?

4. How did the Portuguese economic and religious presence in Angola and Kongo differ from that in Mozambique?

5. Explain the major political, economic, cultural, and social impacts of the slave trade in Africa.

6. What interrelated factors contributed to demographic catastrophes in the Americas?

7. Compare and contrast the Spanish conquest in the Americas in large empires versus smaller polities.

8. How did silver grease the wheels of global commerce?

9. What happened to the native Siberian population after becoming part of the Russian Empire and the world's largest web, and why?

10. What caused birth rates in the Pacific to plummet following sustained contact with Europeans?

11. How did European military technology affect Maori and Hawaiian society and politics?

12. What were the overarching cultural and economic changes that globalization caused?

Go to INQUIZITIVE

to see what you've learned—and learn what you've missed—with personalized feedback along the way.

18

Cultural Upheavals

RELIGIOUS AND INTELLECTUAL MOVEMENTS

1500 to 1750

FOCUS QUESTIONS

1. Why was this a period of intellectual upheaval?

2. How were the Renaissance, the Reformation, and the Scientific Revolution disruptions of European culture and society?

3. How did the Safavids enable Shi'a Islam to triumph in Iran?

4. What factors led to the rise of Sikhism in India?

5. How did China's Confucian traditions undergo change in the sixteenth century?

6. How did ruling elites attempt to roll back new religious and intellectual movements?

7. Why was the intellectual upheaval of the period uneven across Eurasia?

About 1545, a Japanese samurai named Anjirō killed someone in a brawl. His remorse led to the introduction of Christianity into Japan. Although sorry for his deed, Anjirō chose to flee and live as an outlaw. In 1547 he met a Portuguese sea captain in the port of Kagoshima on Japan's southern island of Kyushu—Portuguese sailors had recently started looking for trade opportunities in Japan. The sea captain suggested that Anjirō might feel better about his crime if he consulted a priest, specifically a Spanish Jesuit named Francis Xavier. The **Jesuits** were a newly founded

CHRONOLOGY

1430–1450 Johannes Gutenberg develops moveable type and printing press

ca. 1450 Safavis embrace Shi'a Islam

1469–1539 Lifetime of Nanak

1472–1529 Lifetime of Wang Yangming

1501 Ismail establishes a Safavid state in Iran

1514 Nicolas Copernicus writes down his heliocentric system

1517 Martin Luther writes Ninety-Five Theses

1540 Founding of the order of Jesuits

1542 Re-establishment of the Inquisition

1555 Treaty of Amasya; Peace of Augsburg

ca. 1580 Reaction against Wang Yingming's followers

1587–1629 Reign of Shah Abbas I

1597 Christianity is banned in Japan

1603 First academy of science is founded in Rome

1606 Sikhs abandon pacifism and begin military tradition

1608 Invention of the telescope

1618–1648 Thirty Years War

ca. 1620 Peak of European witch hunts

1687 Newton publishes his *Mathematical Principles of Natural Philosophy*

1702 First daily newspaper

1724 Christianity is banned in China

(1540) order of priests within the Catholic Church dedicated to evangelizing non-Catholics and to rigorous education.

Francis Xavier worked as a missionary throughout the Portuguese Empire in Asia. Anjirō met him in 1547 at Malacca, the cosmopolitan city on the Malayan Peninsula where shipping passed between the Indian Ocean and the South China Sea. While Xavier explained to him the merits of Catholicism, Anjirō—in broken Portuguese—convinced Xavier that the people of Japan might be willing to try a new religion. Together they went to Goa, the Portuguese enclave in India, where Anjirō studied Catholic theology and the Portuguese language at a Jesuit college. In 1548 he was baptized a Christian. Then they returned to Malacca, boarded a Chinese pirate ship (the only one they could find heading to Japan), and arrived at Kagoshima in 1549, intending to convert Japan to Catholicism.

Japan was fragmented politically and religiously at the time. Buddhism was the primary spiritual path, and several different Buddhist sects competed for followers. They also competed with ritual-rich Shinto, Japan's oldest religion. Xavier and Anjirō drew crowds in Kagoshima. Anjirō translated the Christian concept of God as *Dainichi*, one of the Japanese terms for the Buddha. That and the fact that they had come from India, the home of the Buddha, added to the interest Japanese took in their preaching. The Japanese at first understood Catholicism as another version of Buddhism coming straight from the Buddha's homeland.

Xavier and Anjirō met with a warm reception from the local authorities until, two years into their mission work, Xavier concluded that Anjirō's translation did not convey the true nature of God. He started using the Latin word *Deus* instead and began to denounce Dainichi as a creature of the devil. His reception in Kagoshima cooled quickly.

Xavier left Kagoshima for the capital city of Kyoto, where he hoped to convert the emperor. But he never received an imperial audience, and in 1552 was recalled by the Jesuits to Goa. He died en route. Anjirō, meanwhile, lost most of his following in Kagoshima and returned to a life of crime, taking up piracy. He died at sea.

Nonetheless, his followers won many converts, and by 1579 some 130,000 Japanese came to call themselves Christians. The oceanic voyaging of the Portuguese, together with Anjirō's remorse and Xavier's ambition, brought new ideas to Japan, shaking up its spiritual and political order.

Forging the Global web was a disruptive and destructive process, but also a creative one. As we saw in Chapter 17, joining the web wrought havoc on peoples in Africa, the Americas, Siberia, and Oceania, but in time generated new, hybrid societies and cultures. Within the Old World web, the process was disruptive and creative too, not least in the realm of ideas. During the centuries from 1500 to 1750, the convergence of the webs helped to drive major challenges to established patterns of thought, leading to new religions, schisms in old religions, new paths within old philosophies—and to the beginnings of modern science. These are the subjects of this chapter.

Information Flows and Intellectual Ferments

With the advent of oceanic voyaging, and the simultaneous quickening of commerce, information moved farther and faster than ever before. Although shipping had carried ideas and information around for millennia, the linking of formerly separate worlds after the 1490s enabled Confucian and Daoist thought to filter (faintly) into Europe, Christianity to take root in China, and Islam to reach Brazil and coastal South Carolina. Sometimes these exchanges were the work of elites operating at the highest rungs of society, such as the Jesuits who brought European cartography and cannon-making skills to the Ming imperial court in China. In other cases, they involved humbler folk, such as the enslaved West Africans who carried Islam to the Americas.

This swirl of new information from around the globe challenged existing systems of thought. In one important realm, astronomy, new and disruptive information also came from well beyond the far corners of the Earth. When glasses-makers in northern Europe invented telescopes, starting around 1608, it soon became possible to see the craters of the moon and the rings of Saturn. Heavenly bodies, it turned out, were rather different from what people had long imagined. By 1625 microscopes were also in use in northwestern Europe. Soon people could see all sorts of unexpected things, such as corpuscles in blood, crystals in frost, and cells in plant tissues (named cells because they reminded their discoverer of monastic quarters). Telescopes and microscopes, like the Americas and the coasts of Africa, furnished Europeans with unfamiliar observations in every realm from astronomy to zoology. Wherever it came from, new information often proved difficult to fit into prevailing religions and philosophies. That inspired great intellectual effort to resolve the new data with the old systems, sometimes convincing, sometimes not.

In this situation, the authority of existing intellectual traditions, religions included, weakened. New versions of truth had an opening. The odds of a new religion, a new wrinkle in moral philosophy, or a new paradigm in science attracting a following improved sharply. This intellectual and cultural ferment took place in several places around the world, but in Europe more than anywhere else. As we've seen, Atlantic Europeans were the ones who completed the linking up of the world's shorelines through oceanic navigation and so came into possession of wider knowledge of the world sooner than others. And they were the ones who first developed the telescope and the microscope, bringing knowledge of worlds unknown to anyone else.

Two other developments, one global and one mainly European, helped create widespread intellectual ferment during these centuries. The first was faster urbanization. As we have seen at many points already, cities served as hothouses for ideas because people could interact so easily with so many others. Between 1500 and 1750, commerce (among other things) drove the growth of cities, especially port cities, almost everywhere. Here people could rub shoulders with strangers from other continents and exchange their understandings of medicine, metallurgy, morality, and everything else. Most of the time, no doubt, language barriers and preference for familiar ideas prevented meaningful exchange. But every now and then they did not. The second development was entirely new, and its impact for centuries focused within Europe: the **printing press**.

Information Technology: The Printing Press

Around the years 1430–1450, a few people including Johannes Gutenberg, a goldsmith and gem cutter in the German town of Mainz, started work on casting metal type for use in printing. At that time printing involved the use of wood blocks, painstakingly carved by skilled woodworkers. Gutenberg gradually developed movable and reusable type, better ink, and a better press. His invention, one of the most consequential in world history and one of the first for whom we know the name of the primary inventor, made possible the ever-cheaper transmission of information.

Gutenberg was not the first to come up with moveable metal type. Chinese in the Song dynasty had used bronze plates to print paper money. Similar technology filtered into Korea in the thirteenth century. But metal type was not a useful advance over woodblock printing when writing in Chinese, because one needs to make thousands of characters to create a text. When Korea introduced an alphabet with only 24 letters in the 1430s, it made more sense to use moveable metal type. That led to a small flurry of publishing there. But literacy was rare in Korea, and some of the elite resisted the

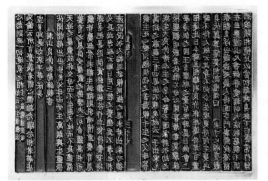

Moveable Type Sets of metal type like that above—from Korea in the fourteenth century—had been developed to print text in Chinese as early as the late thirteenth century. But moveable type was more transformative in Europe, where it enhanced the efficiency of producing and distributing texts like the Bible. At right is a page from a fifteenth-century Bible, printed and subsequently hand-illuminated.

new alphabet, preferring the traditional Chinese characters. So even with moveable type, Korea experienced no revolution in reading, publishing, or the circulation of information: the prior invention of moveable metal type in East Asia had none of the consequences that Gutenberg's did. Given the trans-Eurasian traffic in the wake of the Mongols, it's conceivable that Gutenberg was inspired to experiment with casting type after hearing of the Korean innovation—but there is no evidence for that. This case is a reminder that it is not always the first invention of something that matters.

In Europe, conditions different from Korea's led to an explosion in printing once Gutenberg had shown the way. By 1500, 236 towns in Europe had printing presses, and on those presses hundreds or thousands of copies of over 30,000 different books had been printed. This came to about 20 million books in all, in at least a dozen languages. Venice alone had 417 printers. The first presses using the Cyrillic (for Russian and some other Slavic languages) alphabet debuted in 1483, and in 1501 the first ones using Greek. Regular newspapers appeared by 1605, specializing in business news. The first women's magazine started publication in 1693 (in England), and the first daily newspaper in 1702. By 1753, British readers bought 20,000 newspapers daily, each one probably read by several people. By 1800, European presses had released some 2 million different book titles.

Europeans carried this new device overseas. (The typical press, made of wood, was 6 to 8 feet high and weighed several hundred pounds.) Spanish Mexico acquired a press by 1539, Portuguese Goa (where Anjirō studied) had one by the 1550s, and the Spanish

Philippines by 1593. Jesuits brought one to Japan in 1590. The first in English North America was set up by Elizabeth Glover, a widow with five children, in 1638 upon her arrival in Massachusetts.

At first, even printed books were expensive. Gutenberg's printed Bible, published in 1455, cost about a year's wages for an ordinary laborer. But gradual improvements in the alloys of lead used, in the oil-based ink, and cheaper paper kept pushing the price of printed material downward. Cheaper books raised the demand for education: literacy rates began to climb.

In Gutenberg's time, only 5 to 15 percent of adult Europeans could read. Two-thirds or more of those were male. By 1500, however, the literacy rate had begun to climb, and by 1650 it reached about 25 to 50 percent. In the Netherlands and Britain, and in New England too, it was slightly above 50 percent; in Sweden and Italy, just below 25 percent. The gender gap remained wide until the twentieth century. The market for books and pamphlets ranged from the Bible (easily the best seller) and texts of Christian instruction such as catechisms, to manuals of farming and mining and light entertainments of every sort.

Scribes and manuscripts did not disappear. They coexisted with print technology for a few centuries. Yet printing was truly revolutionary, lowering the costs of information while improving its accuracy by reducing copying errors.

For centuries, the printing revolution encompassed only Europe and European outposts. The great states of Asia preferred to rely on scribes and hand copying of texts. For written languages that used thousands of ideographic characters rather than alphabets, such as Chinese, moveable type did not seem an advantage. Muslim authorities until the eighteenth century generally thought that the sacred language of the Qur'an should only be copied by hand, that printing it would amount to desecration. In many settings, scribes and literate elites regarded printing as a challenge to their position. Rulers feared that printers would be harder to keep under watch and control than scribes—and they could not have been more correct. Printing made ideas harder to control.

Europe: Extreme Turbulence

As we've seen in previous chapters, it was primarily Atlantic Europeans who made the voyages that forged the Global web. So it was primarily in European societies that the global harvest of new information arrived first, sped forward by the printing press. These circumstances colored three great disruptions in the intellectual sphere in early-modern Europe, major developments that we now call the Renaissance, the Protestant Reformation, and the Scientific Revolution. The first deeply affected European thought but did not travel well beyond Europe's shores. The second involved far more people than the others, brought fierce conflict, and motivated spasms of violence. The third involved only a tiny few but brought far larger, and more global, consequences in the long run.

The Renaissance

In an earlier chapter we saw how exposure to Arab and Byzantine Greek learning helped to stimulate new thinking in twelfth- and thirteenth-century Europe, especially challenges to longstanding Christian dogmas within the newly invented institution of the university. Knowledge of Arabic and Greek gave access to bodies of thought from the ancient world that were otherwise out of reach. Political and military pressure on the waning Byzantine Empire motivated many learned Greeks to seek safe spaces in Italian universities in the early fifteenth century, bringing perspectives, and manuscripts, previously unknown there. The growing fascination with ancient Greek and Roman wisdom brought what historians since the nineteenth century have called the Renaissance, meaning a re-birth of ancient learning. Of course, ancient learning was never dead. It was alive and well in Greek and Arab lands. But in western Europe much had vanished, and it is from that perspective that the term *Renaissance* makes sense.

The heart of the Renaissance was a re-engagement with the literatures, histories, philosophies, and art of the ancient Greeks and Romans. Their emphasis on human affairs and human achievement—as opposed to more spiritual matters—found a ready audience among the literate classes and their wealthy patrons. Plato and Cicero came back into style. Translations of the histories of Herodotus and Thucydides appeared, as did the work of ancient Greek playwrights. Sculptors imitated the ancients' marble statuary, with its emphasis on accurate human form.

The **Renaissance** began in Italy, especially in the city-state of Florence. The political fragmentation of northern Italy probably helped the movement along because local dukes and princes supported artists, architects, and scholars in their competition for political prestige. By the mid-fifteenth century, Italian architects and scholars were in demand elsewhere in Europe too. In Hungary, Poland, and even Russia,

Renaissance Art The Italian artist Carlo Crivelli made this painting of the Annunciation for a church altarpiece in 1486. The painting includes artistic motifs such as the use of perspective as well as small scenes of everyday life, both hallmarks of Renaissance art.

rulers hired Italians to build magnificent buildings, such as the Cathedral of the Dormition in Moscow's Kremlin. Aided in part by the printing press, Renaissance texts—literature, history, philosophy—circulated swiftly in sixteenth- and seventeenth-century Europe. Renaissance art, using geometry to achieve perspective and depicting everyday life as well as traditional subjects such as Bible scenes and stories of saints, spread almost as quickly.

Renaissance ideals, especially humanism—the view that human affairs were worthy of careful study and suitable themes for art and literature—also took root in the Netherlands, the German lands, France, England, and beyond. Erasmus of Rotterdam, educated and employed at universities in Paris, Cambridge, Turin, Oxford, and Leuven (now in Belgium), used his extraordinary talents in ancient languages and well-honed powers of reason to produce more coherent translations of the New Testament and to call the Catholic Church to account on some of its inconsistencies. Even the study of politics took on a humanistic tone as writers such as Niccolò Machiavelli, a diplomat in Florence in the early sixteenth century, sought to depict political life as it really was rather than in relation to ideal worlds. The Renaissance affected European elites strongly, especially those who read Latin, and to some extent those in lands elsewhere controlled by Europeans. It did not resonate deeply anywhere else—unlike the upheavals in Christianity, which had more widespread repercussions.

Religion: Protestant and Catholic Reformations

By 1500, the Catholic Church in Europe had met and mastered many challenges. Since the so-called Great Schism in 1054, when the Church of Rome and the Orthodox Church parted ways, Catholicism had spawned many innovations. The church authorities regarded most of these innovations as heresies. It almost invariably succeeded in stamping them out or confining them to remote mountain districts, often using armed force provided by secular rulers. However, in 1517 Martin Luther (1483–1546) launched a new heresy that proved too popular to uproot. It evolved into a new branch of Christianity, called Protestantism.

Luther and Protestantism   Luther was born to middle-class parents. His father leased and operated mines in a part of Germany known as Saxony. His parents' ambitions for young Martin extended to sending him to the University of Erfurt. He completed his degree by age 21 and entered law school at his father's insistence. He hated it, dropped out, and seeking deeper truths, decided to become an Augustinian friar. His father was outraged, considering that path a waste of a good university education. Martin, however, recalled the University of Erfurt as "a beer hall and whorehouse" and preferred to devote himself to confession, prayer, and pilgrimage.

But Luther was not done with education. His Augustinian mentors encouraged him to study theology, and after acquiring a few university degrees, Luther joined the theology faculty at the newly founded University of Wittenberg just before his thirtieth birthday. He remained employed there all his life.

In his schooling, writings, preaching, and teaching, Luther developed two main ideas. One was the primacy of scripture over the traditions of the church. So, for example, Luther noted that celibacy for priests has no basis in the Bible (it became required practice in the late fourth century CE). Nor, he argued, did the ritual of confession, or the concept of purgatory—in Catholic theology, an anteroom to heaven in which all but the sinless souls must linger for as long as it takes to burn away their sins. He came to regard these (and much else) as obstacles to the proper practice of Christianity. Rather than follow traditions unsanctioned in the Bible, believers should, Luther said, read scripture themselves and decide for themselves just what it meant. To make that easier, he translated the Bible into German, finishing in 1534. In effect, said Luther, Christians should be their own priests.

Martin Luther Luther's friend Lucas Cranach painted this portrait of him in his friar's habit in 1533, when the Protestant movement was becoming increasingly widespread across Europe.

The second idea is known as justification by faith alone. This meant that salvation of one's soul could result only from a full embrace of the Christian faith and the gift of divine mercy. For Luther, true Christianity was an inward commitment. He took issue with the church's position that one could ensure salvation through "good works," such as donating money to the church, although he thought that people who had that inward commitment would likely want to perform good works. Luther held fast to these two ideas, arguing for his beliefs with both skill and ferocity.

Earlier reformers had foreshadowed some of Luther's ideas. Jan Hus, a university rector in Prague (in today's Czech Republic), challenged the privileges of the clergy and the church's quests for money. Hus also preached a more intimate, personal commitment as the core of Christianity. In 1415, he was burned at the stake at the command of a bishop. Hus and his followers had drawn much of their outlook from John Wycliffe, who preached, taught, and wrote mainly at Oxford University. He oversaw the first translation of the Bible into English, completed in 1382. Wycliffe railed at the wealth and power of the clergy and Papacy, recommending a more personal Christianity and the primacy of scripture over church and tradition. The Pope denounced him, and the head of Oxford University had him imprisoned for his views. Wycliffe died of natural causes in England in 1384, but in 1431 a pope ordered that his corpse be dug up and burned, as befitted a heretic.

Luther found it particularly offensive that the church, in need of money to pay for the building of St. Peter's Basilica in Rome, had sent churchmen around Europe offering promises of expedited salvation in exchange for donations. This practice, not so different from the deals forged between holy men and the Gupta kings in India (noted in Chapter 13), was called the sale of indulgences. The practice was invented in the 1090s to persuade people to join the Crusades. It was never official policy, but it had become routine procedure by Luther's time. In effect, the gates of heaven were treated like a tollbooth. Sinners who paid could escape a painful term in purgatory. The most successful salesmen of indulgences promised that even the most unspeakable sins could be wiped away for a suitable fee.

Luther wrote up his objections, in Latin, in a document now called his Ninety-five Theses. This was not quite the undertaking it might seem: most of his theses were only a sentence long. He did not seek to challenge the church directly, but the implications of some of his theses aroused the ire of Rome. Number 86, for example, which he described as a shrewd question of lay people, read: "Why does the Pope, whose wealth today is greater than the wealth of the richest Crassus, build the basilica of St. Peter with the money of poor believers rather than with his own money?"

Legend has it that Luther nailed his theses to the door of the cathedral at Wittenberg in 1517. The door often served as a bulletin board. Whether the story is true or not (it probably is not), he did allow friends to translate his text into German and print it in early 1518 as a pamphlet. By 1519, it had circulated all over Europe.

Here it is important to note the political landscape surrounding Luther and his ideas. Germany was not a unified state but a mosaic of dozens of small states, most of them offering a cautious allegiance to the Holy Roman Empire. The Holy Roman Empire was nominally the successor to Charlemagne's kingdom of the ninth century, but in fact it was a loose and weak collection of duchies and principalities whose rulers enjoyed great autonomy. It also comprised about 100 self-governing "free cities," not subject to any duke or prince. The Holy Roman Empire's territory had been shrinking for centuries (and would continue to do so until it was wiped off the map in 1806). It was, however, usually the political force most inclined to serve the interests of the Pope. The political fragmentation of Germany made it hard for authorities to do anything, such as executing Luther, unless every prince, duke, and free city agreed.

By Luther's day, the Papacy had plenty of experience in handling upstarts and heretics. It gave Luther a few chances to recant his positions, which he refused, most dramatically in 1521 at the Diet of Worms (not a college meal plan, but an assembly of officials of the Holy Roman Empire held in the town of Worms). Luther stood his ground, and soon the Pope excommunicated him from the church, calling Luther a "wild boar in the vineyards of the Lord." The Pope's political allies called for Luther's murder. Luther responded to efforts to muzzle him by taking more radical positions, including denying the legitimacy of the Papacy altogether and calling the Pope the antichrist and "servant of the devil." He denounced several important church rituals as unchristian. This was a quarrel that could not be patched up.

Despite having enemies in high places, Luther lived on, in effect an outlaw protected by German princes who liked his ideas, and by his university. He produced his German-language edition of the Bible, wrote many hymns and pamphlets, read a translation of the Qur'an and supported its publication (on the grounds that its errors should be held to scrutiny), and in his last years wrote violent screeds against Jews, few of whom he had ever seen. Always bull-headed, by the end of his life he zealously courted controversy and confrontation.

The printing press and spreading literacy, discussed above, made it more difficult for the church to extinguish an appealing heresy. Luther's many pamphlets found receptive readers all over Europe, and he became a celebrity professor. Even an organization as vast and staffed with talent as the church could not keep Luther's ideas in check.

Variations on Luther's themes soon appeared in Swiss cities. In Zurich, a Catholic priest, Ulrich Zwingli, preached a message similar to Luther's and won over the town leaders. In Geneva, John Calvin took up Luther's cause and gave it his own spin based on the gloomy idea that everyone's fate—heaven or hell—was predestined and no amount of good behavior (or donations to the church) could improve one's odds of salvation. Bad behavior such as blasphemy, witchcraft, adultery, or heresy, in contrast, brought a parade of executions by drowning, beheading, and burning in Calvin's Geneva after 1536. Calvin's uncompromising formula, much influenced by St. Augustine, claimed to be the sole authentic form of Christianity. It spread further than Lutheranism in the sixteenth century, taking root in parts of Switzerland, France, Britain, Germany, and the Low Countries. Emigrants from these lands carried it to South Africa and North America in the seventeenth century.

Various groups of Protestants (the term was in use by 1530) formed in pockets across Europe. Those who embraced it tended to be more urban and literate than average. Cities with printing presses were particularly likely to turn Protestant. But village peasants too, especially in Germany, often found **Protestantism** appealing. They felt its emphasis on "God's law" justified their revolt in 1524–1525 against taxes and levies imposed by princes and the church. Luther disavowed the revolt, and it was crushed.

In general, Protestants shared the view that salvation rested on personal commitment to God and that the Catholic Church had grown stale, stolid, and corrupt, standing as a barrier between individuals and God. Several rulers embraced this new creed, finding it appealing in its own right and often advantageous in political terms—it provided grounds for confiscating church and monastic property, a tempting target. Many German princes had chosen Protestantism by 1530. By 1560, the rulers of Denmark, Sweden, England, and Scotland had become Protestant and encouraged or obliged their subjects to follow suit. In France maybe 10 to 20 percent of the population was Protestant, and in German lands closer to 80 percent. Most of the German speakers in Poland—a sizeable minority there—were as well. Protestantism in the mid-sixteenth century seemed an unstoppable force in Europe north of Italy, Spain, and Portugal.

The Catholic Reformation Yet between 1550 and 1620 the Catholic Church did manage to check the spread of Protestantism. Indeed, the church and its allies regained

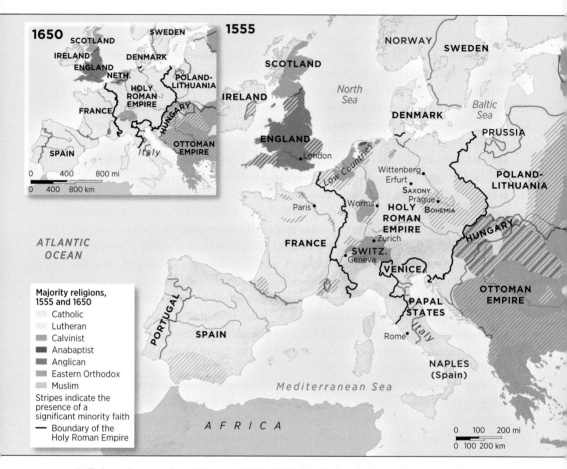

Religious Geography of Europe, 1555–1650 Beginning in the early sixteenth century, the Protestant Reformation added new Christian sects that by 1555 (main map) had acquired millions of followers in western and central Europe. But, as the inset shows, by 1650 the Catholic Reformation, supported by powerful rulers such as the Habsburgs and the kings of France, had won back certain populations. Some lands remained thereafter a patchwork of religions, with multiple Christian minority sects.

some lost ground, winning back people in the southern part of the Netherlands (now Belgium) and a good share of Germans. The Catholic Church nearly stamped out Protestantism in Poland and France, and it crushed the followers of Jan Hus in Bohemia (now part of the Czech Republic). Part of its success came through war. The Pope had armies in those days, and so did the house of Habsburg, a firmly Catholic family that held the Spanish and Austrian thrones, as well as a few other duchies and provinces.

The Protestants could not unify their resistance. Splinter sects popped up constantly, much to the annoyance of Luther and Calvin, none more hated than those Anabaptists who regarded polygamy, pacifism, and communal property (as opposed to private property) as acceptable. Protestant sects and princes quarreled fiercely among themselves over fine points of doctrine and over political advantage, which made it harder to fight effectively against Catholic powers. Struggles abated somewhat after an agreement of 1555, the Peace of Augsburg, in which Catholic and Lutheran rulers in central Europe agreed on the principle that rulers should be free to require either Catholicism or Lutheranism of their populations.

The church also undertook major reforms in response to the Protestant Reformation. Beginning in the 1540s, in a movement called the **Catholic Reformation** (or the Counter-Reformation), the church cleaned up its act considerably. No more libertine popes, living in luxury, fathering children and making a mockery of Christian morals. Bishops and abbots cut back on high living. The church grew more centralized and standardized, settling on a single required script for mass, for example. Popes became more powerful over bishops and priests, abbots and monks. The Papacy re-established its Inquisition (1542), an office tasked with rooting out heresy, and created the so-called Index of banned books (1559). The Index stopped work in 1966.

The church also went global. While Luther and Calvin were diverting souls in Europe from Catholicism, missionaries found fertile fields for the salvation of different souls overseas. In the first half of the sixteenth century, Catholic priests ventured to the Americas, Africa, India, China, Japan, and almost everywhere in between. Religious orders such as Augustinians, Dominicans, and Franciscans came to specialize in converting unbelievers around the world, usually focusing their efforts on the poor. The Jesuits also took to evangelical work, generally working from the top down, trying to convert rulers and courts. They led the rollback of Protestantism in Poland, helped lead it in Germany, brought Catholicism to Japan, and were especially active in China.

By 1620, the Catholic Church had revitalized itself and stopped the Protestant surge. Divisions in Europe—intellectual, cultural, political—became more entrenched. Vicious religious wars only deepened cleavages and resentments, culminating in the Thirty Years War (1618–1648) in western and central Europe, which reduced population there by as much as one-third. As the French mathematician and philosopher Blaise Pascal noted in the 1650s, people "never do so much harm so happily as when they do it through religious conviction." The convulsions in religious life in sixteenth-century Europe created divisions and sectarian identities that live on to this day—less lethally— in Europe itself, wherever European migrants have settled and wherever Christian missionaries made converts.

All durable religions develop schisms and rival sects that get tangled up in struggles for wealth and power. Islam's two largest factions broke apart soon after Muhammad's death, and both Sunni and Shi'a communities subsequently fragmented into many sub-groups. Buddhism's two leading forms, Theravada and Mahayana, also fragmented into smaller sects. Christianity splintered into several churches early in its history. While every schism and sect is different, the human capacity for religious innovation, and reform, makes the process commonplace.

Witch Hunts The competition between Catholicism and Protestantism proved Pascal's point in another respect. It fueled a craze for witch trials. Accusations of witchcraft—typically understood as working with the devil to obtain supernatural powers to use against neighbors or family—had been rare in Europe until 1550, by which time they reached a few hundred annually. The next century, however, brought a flurry of accusations, trials, and executions, reaching a peak about 1620 with more than 5,000 trials and 2,000 executions annually. In total, between 1500 and 1700, about 40,000 to 60,000 people were hanged, drowned, or burned as witches, often after confessions extracted with torture. Of these, 75 to 80 percent were women, usually over 40 years of age; although in parts of northernmost Europe—Iceland, Finland, Estonia, and Russia—the majority of those accused and killed were men.

Historians still struggle to explain why the **witch hunts** arose and why they stopped. Nearly nine-tenths of the executions took place in Germany (about 42 percent), Switzerland (35 percent), or France (10 percent), mainly in areas where Protestants and Catholics were vigorously competing for allegiance. One way a ruler could demonstrate the logic of accepting his (or, in rare cases, her) preferred religion was to encourage trials and convictions of witches, so as to appear committed to defending the people against the devil's mischief. King James VI of Scotland personally oversaw some cases and published a book in 1597 about witchcraft, which explained the justice of persecuting witches in a Christian community. (Shakespeare borrowed liberally from this book in writing *Macbeth*.) Countries with little Catholic-Protestant rivalry saw far fewer cases. Staunchly Catholic Portugal, Spain, and Italy together accounted for only 6 percent of witchcraft executions.

The fact that the majority of victims were women, in Protestant and Catholic lands alike, requires a different explanation, one anchored in demography. A rise in the proportion of unmarried women likely played a big role. Unmarried women, especially those not under the authority of an adult male, seemed a threat to the sanctioned social order. But the ongoing religious struggles contributed to the visibility of unmarried women: Protestant rulers often seized convents' property and pushed nuns out into society at large.

The Scientific Revolution

While both the Renaissance and the Reformation were gathering pace, shaking up the European intellectual landscape, the **Scientific Revolution** began. The term itself is controversial among experts, some of whom see the gradual pace of change in scientific thinking as reason to avoid the term *revolution*. But if significance rather than pace is the key criterion, then the term is warranted.

Two deep principles underlay the Scientific Revolution. The first was accepting that religious scripture and ancient texts did not contain everything worth knowing after all. The logic of accepting this principle strengthened as unfamiliar and baffling information arrived from overseas. Neither scripture nor the ancients had said anything about the existence of manatees and llamas, or hurricanes and typhoons. The second deep principle was the embrace of mathematics and a quantitative culture. In most fields of scientific endeavor, the book of nature was written in the language of mathematics, as the Italian astronomer Galileo put it.

The Scientific Revolution began roughly around 1500, although it is possible to find evidence of new directions in science before that. It too began mainly in northern Italy, like the Renaissance, but quickly leapfrogged to towns, especially university towns, all over Europe. Again, urbanization, universities, printing, and the challenge of new information from overseas helped to create and sustain the Scientific Revolution. So did political fragmentation, in the sense that it was hard for anyone to crush ideas they didn't like when people could easily move to another city or duchy. In addition, the widespread use of Latin helped advance the Scientific Revolution because scholars all over Europe, whatever their native tongue, wrote and read the language.

Historians sometimes say the Scientific Revolution ended around 1700, because many of the fundamental principles of modern science had by then been articulated. But in one sense the Scientific Revolution has never stopped, because its core procedures and deep principles have remained behind scientific inquiry ever since.

One final factor behind the Scientific Revolution deserves emphasis. European scientists in 1500 had no great body of wisdom to protect against new ideas and information. In this they were like the Arab intellectuals after the early Islamic conquests of the seventh and eighth centuries who suddenly came into possession of philosophy and science from India, Persia, and the Greek and Jewish worlds. This situation had led to daring new syntheses, as Arab thinkers tried to reconcile discordant ideas and data and fit them to their own religion. Their emirs and sultans had not felt required to quash this new thinking, because it offered no threat to them or their supporters. Something similar happened in Europe after 1500. Novel ideas, some of them very ancient but new to Europeans, jostled together. New observations from distant continents, and even some from distant planets, challenged old wisdom. But European intellectuals and rulers rarely felt they needed to protect existing ideas (at least, scientific ones) from competitors. And thanks to political fragmentation, intellectual protectionism, when tried, did not fully succeed.

Systematic observation and experimentation lay at the heart of the Scientific Revolution. Scientifically minded men (and a few women) increasingly sought to find the true essence of things by careful study and designed experiments, rather than relying on the theories of Aristotle and his interpreters. They sought, like many before them, to understand the workings of the heavens, the nature of matter, the secret of human health—but with different methods.

The Scientific Revolution was not anti-religion. Every one of its prominent figures considered himself a Christian. Many of them were priests. Most of them sought to reveal God's glory by revealing the perfection of creation in the precise, regular, harmonious workings of the universe. They aimed to read the book of nature alongside the book of scripture, as early Christian writers had put it. The seventeenth-century English scientist Robert Boyle regarded the study of God's creation as a form of religious worship and enjoyed conducting experiments on Sundays. Boyle's father was the second-richest man in England, so Robert could afford to study chemistry and physics every day of the week.

Since the early nineteenth century we have divided science into fields called disciplines, but no one did that in the sixteenth and seventeenth centuries. Many thinkers ranged across fields, considering all of science to be one. But to see its long-term impact, it is helpful to look at a few particular fields before returning to the whole.

Astronomy and Heliocentrism Let's begin with astronomy. In 1500, most people supposed that the sun moved around the Earth because that's what their eyes told them every day. Ancient Greek philosophers, notably Ptolemy, had explained how and why that was so (although one or two ancient Greeks had suggested the Earth might move around the sun instead). Careful observation of the movements of planets and stars raised questions about Ptolemy's system. One of those puzzled by discordant observations was a Polish-German student in northern Italy, known by his Latinized name as Nicholas Copernicus (1473–1543). He knew Latin and Greek, as well as Polish, German, and Italian, giving him access to a wide intellectual heritage. In 1514, he wrote up an alternative explanation based on a **heliocentric system** in which planets spin around the sun. He tinkered with it for decades, while working in Poland as a cathedral administrator. Just before his death he overcame his fears of persecution and his perfectionist tendencies and published his work in 1543. In it he cited both ancient and recent Islamic astronomers and was clearly influenced by both.

Copernicus's heliocentric system did not catch on quickly. It violated common sense as well as the wisdom of the ancients. Nor did it arouse the ire of the church, as Copernicus had feared. It was useful for astrologers because it simplified calculations about future positions of the planets. Astrology was a prestigious branch of science in those days. When Elizabeth I of England chose a day for her coronation, she consulted a mathematician and an astrologer. So did the Pope when choosing an auspicious day for laying the cornerstone of the Basilica of St. Peter's in Rome in 1506. It took some 200 years, and many further observations and refinements of Copernicus's system, before all serious students of the heavens had abandoned Ptolemaic astronomy.

The three scientists whose work did the most to confirm Copernicus's heliocentric view were Johannes Kepler (1571–1630), Galileo Galilei (1564–1642), and Isaac Newton (1643–1727). Kepler, whose major works were published between 1609 and 1627, used careful mathematics to show that planets revolved around the sun in elliptical, not circular, orbits. That helped resolve some discrepancies between observations and Copernicus's theories, although it took decades to become accepted. Kepler lived in German cities and, although he considered himself a proper Christian, had to overcome occasional persecution at the hands of Lutheran churchmen, Catholic authorities, and political leaders alike. His mother, Katharina Guldemann, was tried for witchcraft.

Kepler's contemporary, Galileo, lived in northern Italy and provided detailed observations of the planets using homemade telescopes. In 1615 Catholic officials warned him to stop writing in favor of the heliocentric view, and in 1632 they put him on trial. He officially recanted when faced with the prospect of torture. His works were banned by the church, but this did not stop their spread. The church abandoned its objections to heliocentrism in 1835.

Two generations later, Isaac Newton, a professor of mathematics at Cambridge University, clinched the case for heliocentrism. In the 1660s and 1670s he formulated his laws of motion and gravity, accounting in detailed mathematical proofs for the movement of planets, comets, the tides, and much else. He too considered himself a devout Christian and maintained that his work, published by 1687, laid out the elegance and beauty of God's creation as revealed by mathematics. The official Anglican Church did not bother trying to dispute or suppress his work. The scientific battle launched by Copernicus in 1543 was over, and heliocentrists had won.

Astronomical Revolution In his 1543 book *On the Revolution of the Spheres*, Copernicus published his theory of a solar system in which (as this diagram indicates) the planets revolved around the sun.

Chemistry and Experimentation As astrology was to astronomy, so was alchemy to chemistry. The greatest motivation behind experiments and new thinking in chemistry during the Scientific Revolution was the hope that cheap metals could be transformed into valuable ones—for example, lead into gold. Boyle dabbled in alchemy and claimed to have seen base metals changed into gold. Alchemy, unlike astrology, did not carry much prestige and was often scorned at universities, although Newton, at Cambridge, was fascinated by it. It had no classical pedigree from ancient Greeks or Romans, it was messy, and its practitioners had reputations as con men.

But, working on their own, sometimes in their own kitchens, sixteenth- and seventeenth-century chemists developed a tradition of experimentation and precise recording of results. We now consider most of the ideas they advanced to be wrong, but their methods proved enduringly useful. One prominent chemist, physician, and astrologer was the Swiss-born Philippus Aureolus Theophrastus Bombastus von Hohenheim, who, understandably, preferred to go by the name Paracelsus (1493–1541). He entered and quickly exited six universities before earning a degree at Ferrara, in northern Italy, in 1516. Along the way he developed the view that all disease results from too much of either sulfur, mercury, or salt, three chemicals that he considered central to all matter. Disdaining tradition in favor of experimentation, he claimed that "my shoe buckles are more learned than Galen and Avicenna [Ibn Sina]." Although often wrong in his conclusions, his insistence on experimentation to show the medical uses of chemicals and minerals helped establish genuinely scientific methods. More than any other branch of science, it was in chemistry that the methodology of experimentation evolved.

Medicine Unlike chemistry, medicine was among the prestigious subjects and professions. It too underwent major revision, in both methods and concepts. The most important new methods paralleled changes everywhere in science: greater reliance on observation and experiment, and less deference to ancient authors. The most significant new concept was the principle of the circulation of the blood, detailed by the Englishman William Harvey.

Harvey (1578–1657), the son of a small-town mayor, entered Cambridge University at age 15. After studying medicine for six years, he moved on to northern Italy (like Copernicus and Paracelsus before him), where he learned the fine points of dissection of human cadavers and live animals. In 1628, now a prosperous physician in London, Harvey published his book on the circulation of the blood, showing that the heart pumped blood through arteries into capillaries, and that veins returned the same blood to the heart. Like Copernicus, Harvey showed what others had earlier guessed—notably, Ibn al-Nafis in thirteenth-century Cairo. He built on assertions made by medical men in Italy and Egypt, using systematic observation, in this case based on dissections. In his work, as in Copernicus's, we can see the circulation of knowledge between the Islamic and Christian worlds, made possible by the longstanding connections of the Old World web.

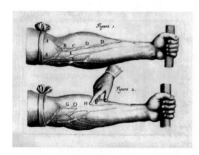

Anatomical Innovation William Harvey's 1628 book *The Motion of the Heart and Blood in Living Beings* was accompanied by detailed diagrams illustrating how the heart pumped blood throughout the body.

Institutions and Connections Every field of science, from astronomy to zoology, experienced some upheaval during the Scientific Revolution. Those most influenced by the global harvest of information and ideas were probably botany and zoology, due to the large number of strange species attested to in distant lands. Ideas and principles from China, India, and the Islamic world, as well as observations made elsewhere, brought challenges to received wisdom in Europe.

The links between science and technology were weaker in those days than ours, but nonetheless the new scientific outlook filtered into fields such as mining, cartography, navigation, and clock making. In particular, more precise mathematics and a culture of quantification helped these fields develop. Technical advances in these fields helped, in turn, to promote commerce and connections within Europe and between Europe and other lands, contributing to the tightening of the Global web.

The Scientific Revolution was a permanent revolution: it continues to this day. Part of the reason for that is the institutionalization of scientific inquiry that began in the late seventeenth century. Academies of science sprouted first in Italy. An 18-year-old from a wealthy family in Rome founded the first one in 1603, but it folded in 1630 upon his death. More durable academies, enjoying royal support, were created in London (1662) and Paris (1666). Others followed in the eighteenth century in Uppsala (Sweden), Berlin, St. Petersburg, and Philadelphia. Networks of scientists solidified, based on correspondence and travel from one city or university town to another, and eased by the shared use of Latin. Carl Linnaeus, the eighteenth-century Swedish botanist who developed a system for naming, ranking, and classifying organisms, maintained a correspondence with nearly a thousand people. Such networks, combined with print technology, prepared the way for publication of scientific journals, the first of which appeared in England in 1665 and is still going strong. These academies, networks, and journals helped to entrench the Scientific Revolution in European thought and society by 1700. In later centuries similar institutions would underpin science around the world, helping to make modern science a global undertaking.

The World of Islam: A Shi'a Reformation

The intellectual world of Islam, like that of India and China, underwent less turbulence than Europe in the centuries between 1500 and 1700. Its cities were less affected by newly forged links to distant lands than Seville or Amsterdam were. Its religious and scientific establishments by now had a great deal of established belief, practice, and knowledge to protect from novelty. But nonetheless, human creativity, the rise of commerce, and the advance of urbanization helped bring about some intellectual realignments in Islamdom. The most important of these was the success of the Shi'a branch of Islam in Iran.

Shi'ism

Shi'ism is almost as old as Islam itself. Its followers regard descendants of Muhammad through his daughter Fatima and his son-in-law Ali to be especially endowed with religious and political authority. Only members of Muhammad's lineage could provide proper earthly guidance.

In the early years of Islam, Sunni caliphs crushed Shi'a factions in battle, and they survived only as a tiny minority. For 800 years Shi'ism suffered frequent persecution from Sunni rulers, who regarded it as heresy, and its followers often kept their convictions secret. Many Shi'a felt disdain for power, authority, and sometimes wealth, seeing virtue in humility and commitment to justice. The most important dynasties to embrace Shi'ism were the Fatimids in Egypt (909–1171) and the Buyids in southern Iran and Iraq (934–1048), but they did not impose it upon their populations. Iran in 1450 had very few Shi'a Muslims.

Shi'a Islam triumphed in Iran for political reasons. In the chaotic conditions of the late fourteenth century, following the decline of Il-Khanid Mongol overlords in northern Iran, charismatic religious leaders competed for influence. They won followers through demonstrations of religious power and military success. Most of them were Sufis.

Sufism (see Chapter 14) is an umbrella term for philosophical, theological, and literary traditions within Islam that emphasize a mystical, intense, and personal engagement with God. Sufi leaders, who usually called themselves sheiks, did not need much formal education in Islamic theology or law. They attracted followers by convincing people that they had a special connection to God. They flourished in regions where states, law, and the *ulema* (the learned interpreters of Islam) were weak. They built solidarity with their followers through rituals involving dance and music—attractions that had no place in more formal versions of Islam. They sometimes added distinctive practices in order to stand out from the competition. As from time to time with various sects in Christianity, Jainism, and Buddhism, these practices could include extreme self-denial and the acceptance of self-inflicted pain. The Riffaiyya, a Sufi sect whose followers lived mainly in Egypt and Syria, felt they could improve their relationship with God by biting the heads off living snakes, thrusting iron spikes into their own bodies, and climbing into hot ovens. Theirs was probably the most eccentric set of practices among hundreds of Sufi brotherhoods. Sufi sheikhs usually required unquestioning obedience among their followers, so Sufi organizations were very hierarchical.

As Iran (and neighboring parts of Anatolia and

Sufi Warriors A history book from seventeenth-century Iran shows Safavi soldiers (with their distinctive red headgear) fighting Sunni troops, as part of the conflict that saw Ismail and his descendants assume control over Iran.

the Caucasus) became more chaotic in the fourteenth and fifteenth centuries, Sufi movements increasingly coalesced into orders or brotherhoods, often for self-protection. To the extent they could provide protection, they attracted more followers. The most successful, by 1450, were the Safavis, a Sunni and Sufi brotherhood. They organized herders, former soldiers, and anyone else willing to pledge loyalty into a formidable warrior band, distinguished by their red headgear, which earned them the name *kizilbash* ("red head").

Safavids and Shi'ism in Iran

At some point after 1450, the leader of the Safavis decided to embrace Shi'a Islam, perhaps to mark his leadership off from all the competition. He began to claim descent from Ali. His grandson Ismail—at age 14—led *kizilbash* warriors to several victories and in 1501 established a dynastic state with the northwestern Iranian city of Tabriz as its capital. By 1510 Ismail had taken over all of Iran and much of Iraq as well. He declared himself the Hidden Imam—in Shi'a theology, the messiah who will return at the right moment to bring justice to humankind. Ismail sought to cloak himself in the mantle of prestigious religious and political figures to enhance his legitimacy as ruler:

> My name is Shah Ismail.
> I am on God's side, the leader of warriors.
> My mother is Fatima, my father Ali.
> I too am one of the twelve Imams....
> Know that I am the true coin of Haidar [i.e., Ali]
> Ever-living Khezer, and Jesus son of Mary.
> I am the Alexander of the people of this era.

Before he died in 1524, Ismail set about converting the entire population to Shi'a Islam, something prior Shi'a rulers had not attempted. He had to import scholars from afar because Iran had so few Shi'a. His son, Tahmasp, who ruled for 52 years (r. 1524–1576), took this program further. He closed brothels, taverns, and gambling dens and forbade shaving beards. He banned music from his court. The **Safavids** (Safavis as a Sufi brotherhood, Safavids as a ruling dynasty) executed or exiled Muslims who overtly resisted their religious program and instituted harsh penalties for rule-breakers—a bit like Calvin's Geneva, but on a larger scale.

As with many an embattled theocracy, relations with hostile neighbors made the Safavids sterner at home. They faced a powerful foe in the Ottoman Empire to the west, a champion of Sunni orthodoxy with whom they fought for most of the first half of the sixteenth century. They also fought another Sunni polity to their northeast, the Uzbeks. Despite a difficult military situation, the Safavids obtained a peace treaty with

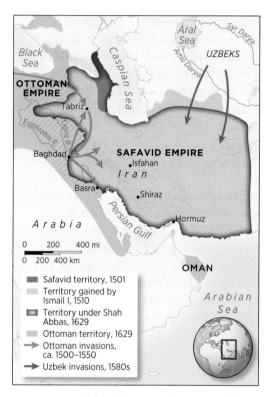

Safavid Iran, 1500-1630 The Safavid dynasty, originally from the southwestern shores of the Caspian Sea, imposed its Shi'a form of Islam as thoroughly as it could within its domain. This sharpened conflicts with Sunni rulers on its borders—notably the Ottomans and Uzbeks, with whom the Safavids warred frequently. The Treaty of Amasya (1555) reduced tensions with the Ottomans.

the Ottomans that recognized them as Shi'a Muslims rather than heretics or unbelievers. The Treaty of Amasya, signed in 1555, also secured the right of shahs in Iran to enforce the religion of their choice within their domain—coincidentally, the same year as the Peace of Augsburg that cemented similar rights for central European rulers. Both agreements soothed half a century of deadly religious rivalry by granting opponents legitimacy and allowing monarchs to impose their religions upon their subjects. The Safavids eventually endorsed forced conversion of Jews, Zoroastrians, and most Christians in their quest for uniform religious purity—and political security. The Safavids even turned on Sufis and massacred thousands.

Shi'ism under the Safavids

Under Safavid rule, Iran experienced a philosophical and religious reorientation. State power was at the center of it. The most effective of Safavid rulers, Shah Abbas I (r. 1587–1629), enjoyed great economic and military success, and supported artists and thinkers, at least of the sort he preferred—not Sufi sheikhs, whom he preferred to execute. He built a new capital at Isfahan, in west-central Iran, with lavish mosques and palaces. He supported painters, especially the miniaturists who became all the rage in Iran and northern India (Shah Tahmasp had been trained to paint in this tradition). Shah Abbas I also encouraged Shi'a theologians, who worked out a new religious orthodoxy that provided some much-needed glue for Safavid society and equally needed legitimacy for the state.

The most prominent of these theologians was Ṣadr ad-Dīn Muḥammad Shīrāzī (or **Mulla Sadra**, 1571–1640). He was born to a courtly family and moved to the capital of Isfahan for study as a young man. He developed unorthodox ideas that resulted in many years of exile to a village, where he began his writing career, trying to reconcile Sufi emotion and intuition with a more reasoned and intellectual Islam. A provincial governor who liked Mulla Sadra's message installed him as the head of a school in Shiraz, in southwestern Iran, where he built an arts and sciences curriculum. An English traveler who passed through in 1629 wrote: "Shyraz has a colledge wherein is read Philosophy, Astrology, Physick, Chemistry and the Mathematicks; so as 'tis the more famoused through Persia."

Mulla Sadra wrote prolifically on deep metaphysical and theological issues, squaring mystical Sufi impulses with the thought of earlier Muslim philosophers such as Ibn Sina (Avicenna). He leaned toward a personal, reflective engagement with the world and with God, and taught that one must live by the principles one's philosophy reveals. He died in Basra while en route to Mecca to perform his seventh hajj. He may fairly be considered the most influential Shi'a philosopher and, despite his early troubles with the authorities, the most important intellectual of Safavid Iran.

The Wider Islamic World The reformulation of Shi'a belief and its adoption as the state religion in Iran was the most important intellectual current within the Islamic world in these centuries, but it was far from the only one. Iranian refugees from Safavid persecution brought many new wrinkles in philosophy, art, and literature to northern India, including the tradition of miniatures in painting. Scholars in Timbuktu, which had some 150 Qur'anic schools in the sixteenth century, brought ideas and practices from Egypt to West Africa, often when returning from a hajj to Mecca. The annual practice of pilgrimage drew pious Muslims from West Africa to Southeast Asia together in Mecca, where they mingled for weeks or months, prayed together, and debated the fine points of religion. Muslim traders traveled far and wide, bringing their particular beliefs in their saddlebags. The quickening of commerce and the growth of cities, especially port and caravan cities, led to faster circulation of ideas and more friction among faiths and sects. Political turmoil in the Islamic world, as we will see in the next chapter, encouraged rulers to embrace legitimating ideologies, including religion above all, as the Safavids did when embracing Shi'a Islam.

West African Scholarship Scholars in Timbuktu in the sixteenth and seventeenth centuries created tens of thousands of manuscripts that recorded knowledge from across the Islamic world. This page is from a sixteenth-century Qur'an.

Sikhism in India: The Birth of a New Religion

New information and ideas from afar affected intellectual life in South Asia too, but not as disruptively as in lands to the west. The greatest departure came in the form of a new religion, now called **Sikhism**. It is a blend of Hindu and Islamic traditions with several innovative twists all its own.

Islam had first come to India in the eighth century. By the end of the tenth century it emerged a powerful political force, the religion of conquerors and rulers from Central Asia. Thereafter its followers jostled with India's more numerous followers of Hinduism, sometimes congenially, sometimes violently. Some thinkers emphasized the compatible features of the two religions to try to achieve a synthesis. This became a little easier with the rise of Sufism within Islam. Sufi sheikhs acquired saint-like status and their tombs attracted worshippers, similar to the shrines of the many Hindu gods. In the fifteenth century, a few thinkers arose in northwestern India claiming that Hinduism and Islam were two approaches to the same sacred truth.

Nanak's Teachings

The most influential of these was Nanak (1469–1539). He was born into a Hindu family of a merchant caste near Lahore, in Punjab, in today's Pakistan. He had a Muslim teacher, however, and showed keen interest as a youth in theology, philosophy, and poetry. He learned Sanskrit, the ancient language of the Hindu Vedas, as well as Arabic and Persian, giving him access to vast learning—not so different from his contemporary, Copernicus. His father tried to install him in positions as an accountant, his own line of work, but Nanak found keeping track of money tedious compared to the timeless questions of religion, righteousness, and truth. So, like Luther, he disappointed his father and sought elusive truths rather than a safe career. At age 27 he experienced a vision in which God told him that he, Nanak, was to be the prophet of the true religion. Nanak summarized his new message in the phrase "there is no Muslim, there is no Hindu." He left a wife and children to begin a long journey that purportedly took him all over India, to Tibet and Arabia. Everywhere he discussed the big questions about truth, existence, reality, and divinity, refining his message as he went.

Nanak's followers became known as Sikhs ("disciples" in the Punjabi language). They accepted his message that Hindusim and Islam are really one, and several other tenets that gave Sikhism a special character. Sikhs, like Muslims, accepted that there is but one God, the creator of all things. In contrast to most Indian religions, Sikhism held that God's supreme creation is humankind, and other living creatures are lesser beings. So Sikhs have no problem with eating meat, which followers of other Indian

CONSIDERING THE EVIDENCE

A Hymn by Kabir in the *Adi Granth*

India had no shortage of holy men when Guru Nanak founded the community that would become the Sikh religion. *Pirs, bhagats, mullahs, sants, qazis, swamis, brahmins, pandits,* and *gurus;* these devotees all defended their doctrine and practices with arguments from the Hindu Vedas and the Muslim Qur'an, just as Protestants and Catholics turned to the Bible for support in their debates. Yet, both Hinduism and Islam also inspired mystics who tired of orthodox religion and the sectarian squabbling it inspired. They rejected rational arguments and the external rituals of fasting, prayer, and pilgrimage as being inferior to an intense, internal devotion to God. Kabir, for instance, was a weaver born in the early fifteenth century to Muslim parents who became the disciples of a Hindu holy man. He lived hundreds of miles away and decades before Guru Nanak; but the Sikh gurus who compiled the *Adi Granth* as their faith's scripture decided to include over 500 of Kabir's songs alongside their own teachings. As shown in the following hymn, Kabir taught that both Hinduism and Islam point to the same God, but everyone needs a personal guru to awaken them to the presence of God in their own hearts.

If Allah lives in a mosque,
to whom belongs the rest of the land?
Hindus say His name dwells in an idol:
I see the truth in neither.

Allah, Ram, I live by Your name.
Be merciful, O Sain. (Rest)

The south is Hari's abode;
   Allah's camp
is in the west. Look inside your own
   heart—
inside your heart of hearts—
there is His abode, His camp.

Brahmins fast twice a month
   twenty-four times;
qazis fast in the month of Ramadan:
Neglecting the remaining eleven
   months,
they search for treasure in one month.

Why go and bathe in Orissa?
Why bow heads in a mosque?
You're a thug at heart.

Why pray and go on a *hajj* to the
   Ka'aba.

All these men and women—
they are Your forms.
Kabir is the infant of Ram-Allah;
everyone is my guru, my *pir*.

Kabir says, "Listen, O men and women,
seek only one shelter:
Repeat His name, O mortals.
Only then will you swim across."

Questions for Analysis

1. Does Kabir want Hindus and Muslims to stop praying or fasting, or is he more concerned about their intentions during worship?
2. How do Kabir's critiques of both Hindus and Muslims help him find the common ground of both faiths?
3. Which lines in Kabir's hymn would have appealed to the Sikh gurus who compiled the *Adi Granth*?

Source: Nirmal Dass, *Songs of Kabir from the Adi Granth* (Albany, 1991), pp. 251–252.

religions often avoid. Sikhism did accept reincarnation, more or less along the lines of Hinduism's principle of karma.

Nanak explicitly rejected the elaborate ceremonies of both Hinduism and Islam, just as Protestants scrapped much Catholic ritual. He preferred a more ascetic, personal, plain approach to God, without priests and their arcane knowledge. He regarded religious commitment as something one accepted as an adult, which Sikhs mark with a simple ceremony, rather than something one is born into—again, like some branches of Protestantism. Nanak rejected caste as well and preached an egalitarian creed in which the same moral codes applied to all regardless of birth, family, and status. He extended this to gender, claiming men and women were equal before God. Nanak also preached a strict pacifism, in line with some strains of Hindusim and a few sects of Protestantism. The parallels with Protestantism are not mere coincidence. Nanak and Luther both reacted against religions that seemed to them too ornate, remote, attentive to worldly concerns, and devoted to the self-interest of priests and officials.

The Development of Sikhism

Nanak Guru (meaning "leader" to Sikhs) died in 1539, but his religion lived on. He left behind an enormous number of hymns, which with a few additions are collectively called the *Adi Granth* (meaning "the first book"), the scripture for Sikhs. It is written mainly in Punjabi, not Sanskrit, and so was accessible to most any literate person in Nanak's part of India, rather as the translations of the Bible by Wycliffe and Luther made Christian scripture accessible to people who had not studied Latin, Greek, or Hebrew.

Subsequent gurus modified Nanak's teachings, most notably in response to persecution of Sikhs by Muslim princes in the early seventeenth century. After one guru was tortured to death in 1606, his son, Guru Har Gobind, the sixth guru, abandoned pacifism and started a Sikh military tradition that survives to this day. Any Sikh male of any background could become a member of a warrior class, called *singhs* ("lions"). They became famous for their valor in battle, which ensured the survival of Sikhism against many threats. Soon Sikh warriors were working as mercenaries here and there throughout South Asia.

Sikhism survived and flourished in north India. It held special attraction for women and low-caste Hindus, for whom it promised some degree of liberation. It also appealed to cosmopolitan urban and merchant groups, who had some exposure to the diversity of religion in the Indian subcontinent and Indian Ocean world. It made a sufficiently good impression on the most powerful Muslim ruler of India, the Mughal emperor Akbar (r. 1556–1605), that he donated land for what would become the most important Sikh shrine, the Golden Temple in Amritsar, in the 1570s.

Ideas and information from the Americas or Oceania contributed nothing to the

Golden Temple Built in the 1570s, the Golden Temple at Amritsar became the most important site of worship for Sikhs. An anonymous Indian artist painted this watercolor of the temple around 1840.

ferment from which Sikhism evolved. Instead, it represents an innovation favored by the tightening of the existing Old World web, rather than its expansion. Increased trade and urbanization created a social milieu in which Sikhism prospered. The constant frictions between Islam and Hindusim provided the spark that inspired Nanak to his quest for reconciliation.

China and Japan: Confucian Reformation and Imported Christianity

In East Asia, as in India, Iran, and Europe, intellectual life had a long and refined formal tradition. Here too the new linkages of the sixteenth century jolted established ideas.

Wang Yangming

In China since the late Song dynasty (960–1279), a coherent ideology held sway among the intellectual elite, one historians now call **neo-Confucianism**. It built on the ancient sages, Confucius and Mencius, but added an even stronger emphasis on self-cultivation and study in the quest for moral rectitude. It formed the core of the civil service examination, so every ambitious young man sought to master this philosophy in hopes of winning a prestigious place in the bureaucracy. Neo-Confucianism survived the downfall of the Song, the Mongol invasion of China, and the Yuan dynasty set up by the Mongols (1279–1368), and it was flourishing under the Ming dynasty (1368–1644).

But in the early sixteenth century, just when Luther and Nanak were shaking up Europe and India, a Chinese philosopher, **Wang Yangming**, mounted a challenge to the reigning ideology. He did not seek to repudiate Confucianism, but to improve upon it, so he too is called a neo-Confucian thinker.

Wang Yangming (1472–1529) was born to a family of the bureaucratic and intellectual class. His father had come in first in the civil service examinations in 1481, and Wang himself did well too, earning degrees at age 19 and 26 when many other men studied into their thirties trying to pass the examinations. He served in the imperial government in middling roles until he offended the palace eunuchs in 1506 (an offense his father had committed in his day as well). For his transgressions, Wang was publicly flogged and banished far from the capital.

Exile and isolation proved productive for Wang, as it would for Mulla Sadra in Iran. During his three-year banishment, Wang developed his distinctive brand of neo-Confucian thought. His fortunes revived and he won government appointments in southern China, where he distinguished himself by crushing rebellions. He still maintained an active scholarly career while holding official posts and holding forth to many admiring students.

Wang Yangming rejected one of the main tenets of the neo-Confucianism of his youth, which treated knowledge as available only through dedicated study. Although himself a champion at book learning, Wang began to argue that true knowledge could not be separated from action and experience. Indeed, he maintained, one did not need book learning to understand truth and morality. Ordinary people, Wang claimed, could as readily obtain wisdom and act ethically as the most learned of scholars. He believed "the nature of all humans is good" and that anyone, however humble, has innate knowledge and could attain moral perfection. All that stood between people and moral perfection was selfish desire, so freeing oneself from that was key. One can see undertones of Buddhist philosophy, familiar to many Chinese intellectuals, in his logic.

This viewpoint was revolutionary in the context of the Confucian tradition and made Wang in effect a traitor to his class. His confidence in ordinary folk led him to maintain that "all the people filling the street are sages"—a heretical thought in China. His philosophy bore some resemblance to Lutheranism or Sikhism, which held that people could achieve spiritual perfection on their own without guidance from priests.

Wang's philosophy attracted many adherents during the sixteenth century, and in retrospect he stands among the most influential thinkers in the Confucian tradition. Young strivers of modest means found his message liberating. Wang Yangming study groups proliferated for decades after his death. His philosophy won admirers in Japan too.

Wang Yangming's revision to neo-Confucianism was only one strand in the tapestry of Chinese thought and belief, but it was the most influential and enduring. Other developments included a Buddhist revival among elites that spread in the late sixteenth century with support from an empress, and the arrival of Christianity, brought by missionaries beginning in 1583.

Christianity in China and Japan

In China, Christianity came mainly with the Jesuits, of whom about 900 made the perilous trip from Europe. In the early seventeenth century they met with some success, converting three high officials and thereby acquiring some protection. The Jesuits generally concentrated on the top rungs, the high literati, of Chinese society and used technical knowledge to get a hearing. At the Ming court, Jesuit skills in map making and cannon casting were of particular interest.

In general, however, Christianity was a hard sell to the Confucian literati. They had spent decades mastering a philosophical-religious system that carried immense prestige in China and had no need to exchange it for another. As a practical matter, Christian morality was often a sticking point, as many Chinese literati had concubines in their households. At a maximum, Christianity won over about 1 percent of the Chinese population, and the proportion fell after the late seventeenth century when the Jesuits tried to embrace a new dynasty of conquerors from Manchuria, the Qing. The Jesuits achieved some success with the Qing imperial household, especially that of the great emperor Kangxi (r. 1661–1722), but they never found broad adherence among the Chinese elite.

Christianity also took root in Japan, as we saw at the start of this chapter. Europeans first arrived, shipwrecked on southern islands, in 1543, and missionaries, mainly Spanish and Portuguese, arrived in 1549 beginning with Francis Xavier and Anjirō. As in China, missionaries in Japan focused first on the upper classes, especially the great landowners called *daimyo* who in the sixteenth century dominated the country. Francis Xavier considered the Japanese to be "of very good manners, good in general and not malicious." Most Japanese, however, regarded missionaries, and other Europeans, as "southern barbarians" and wanted little to do with them except perhaps trade. Missionaries found it convenient to double as importers of exotic goods. Japan was among the world's most urbanized societies, which made the business of conversion a little easier because missionaries could reach bigger audiences in cities. Japan's political divisions also helped the missionaries by preventing any single authority from banning the southern barbarians.

Mission efforts—staffed mainly by Japanese who had already embraced Christianity—converted some 2 to 3 percent of Japan's population, or 200,00 to 300,000 people, by 1590. Christians lived in every province. Hundreds of churches opened. Even some of Christianity's less appealing practices caught on, such as self-flagellation with whips as a way to compensate for sin. But after 1590, rulers of an increasingly unified Japan, including men who had formerly shown some interest in Christianity, tried to prevent conversion. Eager to minimize foreign influence, the government officially banned Christianity in 1597 and again, more effectively, in 1614. Churches were torn down, missionaries expelled, Christian communities conquered by force of arms, and roughly 4,000 converts executed. By 1640, Christianity in Japan was on the edge of extinction, surviving only as an underground religion.

Repression and Persecution

Reactions against novel religious and intellectual movements, like the suppression of Christianity in Japan, were routine among elites and rulers wedded to existing ideologies. The most secure rulers, however, showed great interest in diverse religions—rather like the Mongol court in the thirteenth century. Among these were Shah Abbas I in Safavid Iran, and two whom we'll see more of in the next chapter—Akbar the Great in Mughal India and Mehmet the Conqueror in the Ottoman Empire. But their successors, often feeling less secure in their power, generally organized clampdowns and persecutions. In Europe, Catholic authorities revitalized the Inquisition in the sixteenth century and supported religious wars against Protestants, and Protestant kings did their best to reciprocate. In Iran, the Safavids eventually attacked just about all religious groups and movements other than their preferred version of Shi'a Islam. Sunni Muslims, Sufis, Christians, Jews, and Zoroastrians all felt the consequences. In India in the early seventeenth century, the Sikhs went from being pacifists to militarists in response to assaults from Muslim princes.

In China, by 1580 a concerted reaction against Wang Yangming's followers took shape, and many were imprisoned or executed. Catholicism in China also provoked official reaction. The Jesuits backed a losing candidate in an imperial succession struggle, and the winner, the Yongzheng Emperor, banned Christianity in China in 1724.

Anti-Christian Reaction In this seventeenth-century Japanese illustration of the turn against Christianity in unified Japan that started in 1597, dozens of Christians—including several European missionaries—are beheaded and burned at the stake.

The Scientific Revolution, compared to the several religious movements discussed in this chapter, provoked less official reaction. Galileo and Kepler both met with hostility from church authorities, but Galileo had initially found support from the Pope and the Jesuits when attacked by the Inquisition. Only after he went to some lengths to offend the Pope was he forced to renounce his views and confined to house arrest. But most of the new science did not trouble the church, and indeed much of it was conducted by churchmen or devout Christians like Boyle and Newton. About half the mathematics professors in seventeenth-century Europe were Jesuits.

In any case, the political divisions within Europe made clampdowns on new ideas ineffective in comparison with comparable efforts in China after 1580 or Japan after 1590. Religious disunity flourished in Europe, as in India, as did rival schools of scientific thought, and no prince, however determined, could change that. In Europe, unlike in India, easy access to information, a result of the spread of the printing press and the shared use of Latin among scholars, also made it hard for authorities to clamp down.

Intellectual Upheaval:
Parallels and Contrasts

The entire process of intellectual upheaval in Eurasia was uneven in three main respects. First, as we have seen, it was geographically uneven, affecting Europe more than the rest of Eurasia, and within Europe some parts more than others. Part of the unevenness within Eurasia had to do with Europe's political fragmentation and Atlantic Europe's greater involvement in global circuits than anywhere else. Much of the unevenness within Europe had to do with local circumstances such as the fact that Calvin took refuge in Geneva rather than somewhere else.

Second, everywhere the intellectual upheaval affected cities and especially trading cities, more—or at least sooner—than the countryside. Remote mountain villages in Asia were less likely to be buffeted by the currents of Sikhism or neo-Confucianism than were the cities, where new ideas arrived more frequently and were likelier to win followers.

Third, intellectual upheaval was socially uneven. Although the religious transformations of the Reformation(s) and the conversion of Iran to Shi'ism rippled through all levels of society, and the spread of Sikhism touched the lower classes first and foremost, much of this turbulence shook only the elite. Chinese peasants, with the rarest of exceptions, did not know that Wang Yangming and his followers considered them equally as capable of moral perfection as the most learned Confucian scholar. Polish peasants remained entirely unaware that Copernicus was charting a new map of the heavens. English peasants did not know that Newton was formulating an elegantly precise mathematical account of the force of gravity. They and their counterparts, 90 percent of the population of Eurasia, had hungry children, sick babies, tired muscles, fickle weather, ravenous tax collectors, and a hundred other things on their minds every day. Although they worried about what might follow upon death, whether or not to do what priests told them to do, and even contemplated the mysteries of divinity, they generally could not spare much time for moral philosophy or mathematical equations.

There is a fourth respect in which the intellectual and religious turbulence of these centuries was uneven, but consistently so across Eurasia. None of the great religious reformers, philosophers, or scientists mentioned in this chapter were women.

Women Intellectuals The German entomologist and botanist Maria Sibylla Merian, shown here in a 1679 portrait alongside one of her detailed color paintings of butterflies and caterpillars, was one of the women whose work contributed to the Scientific Revolution and other early modern intellectual movements.

Some European women did make contributions to scientific work, such as Margaret Cavendish (1623–1673), an English duchess who wrote poetry, plays, and several works on moral philosophy. She undertook scientific experiments and was once—controversially—permitted to attend a meeting of the Royal Society. Maria Sibylla Merian (1647–1717) was a German entomologist and botanist who published the first detailed work on caterpillars and their metamorphosis into butterflies. She also undertook a self-funded scientific expedition to South America and produced a landmark study of the insects of Surinam.

But the truth is none of them were anywhere near as influential as Copernicus, Galileo, Harvey, or Newton. No women in Iran, India, or China had anything like the impact on religion or philosophy of Mulla Sadra, Nanak, or Wang Yangming. We can be sure that some women were just as interested in truth, the heavens, health, alchemy, morality, divinity, as any man—as the record of more recent centuries shows. But fewer women than men could act upon an interest in these and other intellectual matters. Women were less likely to be able to read than were men, and in most places far less likely. They were much more likely to face discouragement from family and society if they showed inclination toward deep thinking. A French aristocrat, Martine Berterau, who published a book on mining engineering, was charged with witchcraft, as was her husband.

Women were often forbidden to be members of universities, madrasas, and academies. When in 1678 the University of Padua awarded a PhD to Elena Cornaro, a Venetian noblewoman, the university promptly revised its statutes to prevent women from taking degrees. The Swedish aristocrat Eva Ekeblad in 1748 was elected to the Swedish Royal Academy of Sciences for her successful distillation of alcohol from potatoes. But in 1751 she was demoted to honorary membership, on the principle that full academicians should be men. The rare exception was Laura Bassi, the second woman anywhere to earn a doctorate, which she did in 1732 at age 20 from the University of Bologna in Italy. That same year she was appointed there as a chaired professor of physics. She taught science for the next 45 years and conducted experiments in electricity—meanwhile bearing 12 children. But by and large, women could not and did not hold positions like Bassi's; and whatever their inclinations and talents, they did not influence intellectual agendas and paths in major ways. So the religious schisms and revivals, the philosophical twists and turns, the Scientific Revolution—as well as all the efforts to suppress these novelties—were overwhelmingly the work of men.

Conclusion

The Eurasian landmass in the sixteenth and seventeenth centuries experienced unusual intellectual and religious turbulence. Ideas, ideologies, and religions are of course changing all the time. But sometimes they change faster and more radically, and this was such a time. This turbulence always had important local causes bound up in the politics and social changes of particular places, such as the demographic trends that underlay the witch craze or the fragmentation of Japan that gave Christian missionaries an opening. But it also had larger, looser causes connected to both the expansion and the consolidation of what was becoming the Global web.

Those general causes included the difficulty of making sense of new data within old systems of thought. Observations from distant continents after 1492, and distant planets after 1608 (the date of the invention of the telescope), called old wisdom into question and set curious minds to work. This particular source of intellectual turbulence was strongest in Europe, because Europe was much more involved in overseas linkages to hitherto isolated lands than was anywhere else in Eurasia. And the telescope and microscope were European inventions.

At the same time that new information was flooding into the minds of Europeans, the flow of ideas and information more generally sped up. In Europe, the printing press played a big role in that. But everywhere in the sixteenth and seventeenth centuries, even in those parts of Eurasia least affected by seaborne commerce to the Americas, the pace of trade, travel, and urbanization crept upward. More people came into more frequent contact with strangers bearing exotic notions. While new ideas were usually shunned, from time to time they appealed to people, who explored them and sometimes adopted them. Or, more often, adapted them into their prior schemes of religion and thought, and in so doing altered those schemes.

Despite their local causes and distinctive characters, these new intellectual and religious movements—many of them—shared some common features. In most of them one can find an emphasis on personal responsibility and personal approaches to truth or God, with minimal mediation from priests, as in Lutheranism, Sikhism, and to some extent the Shi'a movement in Iran. One can find an appeal to the value of experience, as in Wang Yangming's thought and the Scientific Revolution. These common threads reflect not so much interaction among these movements, but similar reactions to dissatisfaction with the entrenched, institutionalized, stolid religions and ideologies, all of them seemingly slow to adapt to changing times.

Most of these intellectual and religious innovations survived into the twenty-first century. Today, in retrospect, we can say that the most important among them was the Scientific Revolution, as it laid the foundations for the technological transformations that distinguish modern times. At the time, however, the religious upheavals seemed most important. They meant more to more people. And they helped to animate the political struggles of the early modern centuries, to which we turn in the next chapter.

‖‖

Chapter Review

KEY TERMS

Jesuits p. 671

printing press p. 674

Renaissance p. 677

Protestantism p. 681

Catholic Reformation p. 683

witch hunts p. 684

Scientific Revolution p. 684

heliocentric system p. 686

Shi'a Islam p. 690

Safavids p. 691

Mulla Sadra p. 692

Sikhism p. 694

Adi Granth p. 696

neo-Confucianism p. 697

Wang Yangming p. 697

REVIEW QUESTIONS

1. How did new geographic and scientific discoveries lead to the weakening of existing intellectual traditions?

2. Why was the printing revolution mainly confined to Europe and European colonies for many centuries?

3. What was the source and the main emphasis of the Renaissance?

4. What political and technological conditions helped Luther and his ideas evade Catholic persecution?

5. What principles formed the basis of the Scientific Revolution, and what procedures were at its heart?

6. What measures did the Safavids introduce to transform Iran into a Shi'a theocracy?

7. Whom did Sikhism attract, and why?

8. Why was conversion to Christianity unpopular in China and Japan?

9. Why was it more difficult for authorities to clamp down on new ideas in Europe than it was in China, Japan, and India?

10. What were the three main ways in which intellectual upheaval in Eurasia was uneven?

11. What common features did new intellectual and religious movements share, and what widespread trends did these commonalities reflect?

Go to INQUIZITIVE

to see what you've learned—and learn what you've missed—with personalized feedback along the way.

19

University of War

EMPIRES AND POWER

1450 to 1800

FOCUS QUESTIONS

1. What general conditions contributed to the growth of empires in the early modern period?

2. What were the most important components of the military revolution during this period?

3. What role did firearms play in the consolidation of power in Japan?

4. Why was the Qing dynasty so effective over its first century and a half?

5. How were the Mughals able to create a multireligious empire in India?

6. What policies helped in the expansion of Ottoman rule during this period?

7. What initiatives of Ivan III and Peter the Great strengthened the power of the Russian state?

8. How did the Habsburgs become rulers of the first global empire?

9. What was the "university of war," and how did it strengthen European states?

10. How did smaller states adapt to the changes wrought by the military revolution?

11. How did nomads and pirates fare during this period of growing state power?

Zheng Zhilong and his son were the most successful pirates in world history. Zheng the elder was born to a Chinese gentry family. In 1622, at age 18, unhappy with his schooling, he ran off to Macao (a Portuguese trading post in southern China), where he had an uncle. He learned Portuguese, was baptized a Christian, and soon took up trade and piracy. Sent by his uncle to Japan, he married a Japanese woman, Tagawa Matsu. Their son, Zheng Chenggong (1624–1662), although born and raised in Japan, was sent to study in a Chinese Confucian academy in hopes that he would qualify for the Ming dynasty's bureaucratic elite. But Zheng Chenggong (also known as Koxinga or Coxinga) eventually joined the family business.

Active along the southeastern coasts of China, from Nanjing to Macao, the Zheng family ran an international trade and piracy operation. In 1628, they captured nearly half of the recorded Chinese ships returning from the Philippines laden with silver. A Chinese governor explained why:

> The Zheng pirate gang is very clever and tricky, and good at sea fighting. Their pirate troops...consist mainly of Chinese bandits, with some Japanese and Europeans. Their war ships and weapons are manufactured by the distant barbarians [i.e., the Dutch]. Their ships are tall and solid, and their cannon can hit targets miles away.

From the late 1620s to the 1680s, no one could trade safely on the southeast China coast without permission from the Zheng family. In the 1650s, they employed some 400,000 sailors and soldiers, mostly Chinese and Japanese, but also some Europeans and a 300-man East African bodyguard. Their fleets included 5,000 ships.

The Zhengs and their sea captains raided and traded far and wide in East Asian waters. When the Chinese Empire tried to deny him supplies

CHRONOLOGY

1453 Ottomans besiege Constantinople

ca. 1490 Very large cannon introduced

1508–1519 Emperor Maximilian I's reign

1516–1517 Ottomans defeat Mamluks and conquer Egypt and the Hejaz

1520–1566 Suleiman's reign

1526 Mughals conquer sultanate of Delhi

1543 Chinese ship brings Portuguese guns to Japan

1547–1584 Ivan the Terrible's reign

1550s Habsburgs acquire windfall of silver from Americas

1556–1605 Akbar's reign

ca. 1590 Introduction of disciplined and drilled standing armies

1591 Saadians conquer Songhai in West Africa

1592–1598 Toyotomi Hideyoshi's Korea campaign

ca. 1600 Japan is unified; start of Tokugawa shogunate

ca. 1620–1680 Zheng family flourishes

1638 Manchus conquer Korea

1644 End of Ming dynasty and start of Qing dynasty

1658–1707 Aurangzeb's reign

1662–1722 Kangxi emperor's reign

1682–1725 Peter the Great's reign

1694 National banks invented

1719–1722 Bartholomew Roberts captures 400 ships in the Atlantic and Caribbean

1735–1796 Qianlong emperor's reign

ca. 1750 Qing crush Zunghars

and bases on the mainland, Zheng Chenggong conquered the island of Taiwan, then held by the Dutch East India Company. His captains controlled 80 percent of the trade to Japan, carried cargoes from Cambodia and Thailand, and raided as far afield as the Philippines. He organized his own bank and minted coins.

The Zhengs were in effect building their own maritime state when Zheng Chenggong died, probably of malaria, at age 39 in 1662. They used all the resources at hand in their quest for power and wealth: Dutch and Chinese shipbuilding skills; Dutch and Portuguese cannon; Chinese and Japanese manpower; their own wide knowledge of East Asian coasts, islands, and waters; and their deep fund of daring. They ultimately lost, crushed by China's improving military in the early 1680s.

The Zhengs were among many such losers in the centuries between 1450 and 1800, often called the early modern period. Pirates, nomads, and the rulers of hundreds of small states, few of them as powerful as the Zheng clan at its height, lost out to larger, imperial states. These empires flourished as they grew more successful at winning over subject people's loyalties, more skilled at tax collection, and above all, more effective in using new technologies and techniques of violence.

This chapter deals with political, military, and economic history in an age of imperial consolidation. It explains how a handful of great powers arose, how they sometimes competed with one another, and how they shared (often unwillingly) technologies and techniques useful to states. In particular, it focuses on Tokugawa Japan, Qing China, Mughal India, the Ottoman Empire, Russia, and the Habsburg Empire. It includes more about military matters than any previous chapter, because in these centuries military innovations came thick and fast, spread throughout the Global web, and carried greater consequences for the global distribution of wealth and power than ever before.

These imperial powers used their improved skills and technologies to destroy hundreds of smaller states, crush pirates like the Zhengs, suppress bandits, and overwhelm tribal peoples—anyone who stood in their way. They took over lands formerly filled with peoples living in principalities, city-states, tribal confederations, or in no state whatsoever. In political terms, the big got bigger. The small polities and the peoples without states became fewer, surviving mainly in nooks and crannies of world politics such as high mountains, barren deserts, or unhealthy swamps—outside the nodes and threads of the Global web. The variety of political formats in which people lived became smaller—another example of how the globalizing web-building process reduced diversity.

Early Modern Empire in Global Perspective

The main reason that the big political fish gobbled up the small fish in the early modern period is that the economics of power evolved in ways that favored big fish. In almost every part of the world, the costs of projecting power rose, especially the technologies and techniques of warfare. Big states could bear those costs with less difficulty than small ones.

The history of empire gives us a valuable perspective on these developments. Today, there are very few states conventionally called empires, so it is easy to regard them as abnormal. But between Sargon of Akkad and today—and especially since the formation of the Roman and Han empires roughly 2,000 years ago—most of the world's people most of the time lived in empires. Most empires came and went quickly, even powerful ones such as those of Alexander the Great or Genghis Khan. Only a few endured, such as the Chinese, dynasty after dynasty—and even it experienced interludes of chaos and disunity.

World history shows two main periods when big empires grew bigger. The first occurred between about 600 BCE and 100 CE, when Achaemenid Persia, Mauryan India, Rome, and Han China emerged and expanded. For the first time, single states controlled big territories, including all the most populous parts of the world. The second period was the one under consideration in this chapter, roughly the period 1450–1800.

Seen within a single national or imperial tradition, these surges in empire may appear to be accidental or the work of extraordinarily great leaders. Seen in world-historical perspective, they appear as parallel processes with some connections uniting them. In the first era of imperial growth and consolidation (600 BCE–100 CE), the challenge of steppe warriors helped inspire people to band together into larger and larger agrarian states in places such as Persia and China.

In the second era (1450–1800 CE), as we shall soon see, the parallels and connections were even stronger, showing the Global web in action. Empires learned military and fiscal techniques from one another, adopted technologies used effectively by others, and in the process came to resemble one another more as time went on. Improved printing technology sped the flow of information generally, including manuals on naval ship-building, army maneuvers, and other military topics. The mobility of experts, especially military architects and shipwrights, promoted the spread of information as well. Although rulers in possession of the best military technologies and expertise generally tried to keep it for themselves, by 1600 it had become harder than ever to keep useful secrets of power from one's neighbors.

Population figures help illustrate the growth of big states (see table on page 710). In 1500, about 36 percent of the global population lived in the six most populous states; by

Proportion of Global Population in the Most Populous States, 1500–1800

DATE	GLOBAL POPULATION	PROPORTION LIVING IN THE SIX MOST POPULOUS STATES
1500	438 million	36% (China, Muscovy/Russia, Aztec Empire, Inka Empire, France, Ottoman Empire)
1600	556 million	55% (China, Russia, Japan, Mughal India, Ottoman Empire, Habsburg Empire)
1700	603 million	60% (China, Russia, Japan, Mughal India, Ottoman Empire, Habsburg Empire)
1800	950 million	57% (China, Russia, Japan, Mughal India, Ottoman Empire, France)

Sources: Colin McEvedy and Richard Jones, *Atlas of World Population History* (1978), 55–60, 78–82, 137, 166–75, 179–89; Angus Maddison, *The World Economy* (2001), 241–43; Max Roser's website Our World in Data: https://ourworldindata.org/world-population-growth.

1700, by which time the roster of most populous states had changed, that proportion was 60 percent. Two main developments underlay this trend: the Inka and Aztec empires had disappeared from the list of most populous states, to be replaced by the Habsburg Empire and Japan; and the big states in Eurasia had gotten bigger.

Warfare and Its Price: The Military Revolution

Every state and society conducted war in its own way, shaped by its own culture, traditions, and constraints. Societies without horses—as in the pre-Columbian Americas, for example—fought on foot. Mongols and other steppe peoples fought on horseback. South Asians often used war elephants. Some states had navies, but most did not. The reasons for war also differed, and often went no deeper than a monarch's quest for glory. But states also fought in the name of religion—or at least their ruler's religion. Most wars were also fought for control over land or people, and the wealth and prestige that control might bring. Vikings and the kings of Kongo often fought to acquire slaves for sale. And, as we've seen, the Aztecs fought to acquire captives for sacrifice.

All these approaches to warfare had proven effective in their specific settings. Now, however, with the formation of the Global web, several new and useful technologies and techniques of fighting spread widely, replacing some of the local variations. War elephants and big armored horses, for example, gradually became obsolete.

In the years between 1450 and 1800, war grew more expensive and complex just about everywhere. Historians call this development the **military revolution**. It happened at different times, and at different paces, in different places. Many trends underpinned the military revolution. Here we will touch on six.

Bigger Battalions, Higher Taxes

In the seventeenth century French soldiers had a saying: "God is on the side of the bigger battalions." The first reason warfare became so costly was the expansion of the scale of military operations, with larger armies and, in some cases, navies. In the sixteenth and seventeenth centuries, big empires spent 60 to 90 percent of their state budgets on their armed forces. (Today, the U.S. government spends about 15 to 20 percent of its budget on its military.) By 1700, several states around the world had learned how to organize, equip, and field armies of more than 100,000 men, and a few, mostly Atlantic European states of modest size, boasted battle fleets of dozens of large ships each studded with 40, 50, even 100 heavy cannon.

A second trend was the availability of greater funding for war. It was both a cause and a consequence of the trend toward bigger and costlier militaries. More money supported more expensive forms of warfare for kings, but costlier forms of warfare also required monarchs to find more funding. Usually, this entailed making taxation more efficient. It often also involved financial practices that made it easier for states to borrow money, either through the invention of national banks (beginning in 1694), the courting of private bankers, or the practice of tax farming—an arrangement in which an entrepreneur advanced money to a ruler in exchange for permission to extract taxes in the future.

The vast expansion of commerce around the world beginning in the sixteenth century enlarged the tax base for monarchs. It also made it feasible for kings and emperors to demand taxes in the form of money, rather than in rice, maize, or labor. The monetization of taxes enabled rulers to pay more professional soldiers and buy more equipment.

Despite these innovations and opportunities, most successful monarchs teetered on the edge of bankruptcy in wartime. They had to negotiate, often in a hurry, with anyone who had vast wealth, in hopes of getting cash quickly in order to pay troops. This financial desperation proved a consistent check on monarchs' power, and it gave people with ready cash, such as big merchants and bankers, great leverage with which to pursue their own interests. In short, the rise of trade and finance—again, the Global web in action—made the military revolution affordable for a fortunate few monarchs, with the effect of often putting rulers at the mercy of bankers.

Navies and Artillery

A third trend of the military revolution that made war more complex and expensive was the emergence of oceanic navies. Local navies operating close to home had existed for more than 2,000 years, but oceanic navies were novel. As we saw in Chapter 16, Ming

Oceanic Navies States that built ocean-going fleets in the early seventeenth century included Japan (left) and the Ottoman Empire (right), whose galleys were better suited to the quieter waters of the Mediterranean.

China built one beginning in 1405 but abandoned it after 1433. Over the next four centuries, China's navy stayed close to home, patrolling rivers, canals, and inshore waters, battling pirates such as the Zhengs but not sailing the open sea. Atlantic European states, however, began to build ocean-going navies and kept expanding and improving them.

Their main innovation was to build ships big and sturdy enough to serve as gun platforms for heavy cannon. Building such ships was expensive and took great expertise. The workhorse of the British Royal Navy in 1780, the 74-gun ship, cost ten times as much to build as the largest factory in Britain. But such ships allowed monarchs to project power—through bombardments—anywhere on Earth within reach of the sea. This capacity more than anything else accounts for the rise to global power of five small Atlantic European states: Portugal, Spain, France, the Netherlands, and Britain.

Other Eurasian and North African states built navies too, but usually with galleys and small craft, not ocean-going cannon platforms. An exception was Japan between about 1600 and 1635: it built a few hundred armed merchant vessels that each carried about six or eight cannon, used mainly in trading with Southeast Asia. But these ships were small and unsuited to naval warfare, and in any case in 1635 Japan stopped making them.

Most rulers preferred not to compete at sea and to focus their efforts on land. An English doctor wrote of Aurangzeb, the last of the powerful emperors of Mughal India, in the 1670s, "if the King's Fleet be but ordinary, considering so great a Monarch..., it is because he minds it not; he [is] contenting himself in the enjoyment of the *continent* [India], and styles the Christians Lions of the Sea; saying that God has allotted that Unstable Element for their Rule." Heavy cannon mounted on sturdy ships enabled "Christians"—more precisely, Atlantic Europeans—to become the lions of the sea.

A fourth trend was the development of **field artillery and fortification**. Beginning in the early fifteenth century, armies lugged cannon into battle. By the 1490s, they used cannon so large that teams of horses or oxen, or a couple of elephants, might be needed to haul them around. To counter the power of such weapons, military architects built new kinds of fortresses with thick walls—those at the fortress of Kumbharlgarh in northwest India, built in the fifteenth century, were 15 feet (4.5 m) thick. The new fortresses had to be big, bristling with artillery, and designed according to geometric principles. It often took 20 years to construct one. In Italy, both Michelangelo and Leonardo da Vinci used their architectural skills designing fortresses before succeeding as artists. The new fortresses also needed garrisons, supplies, and plenty of cannon of their own, all of which made them extremely costly. But the cost of not building them, if one's neighbors had capable field artillery, was surrender.

Standing Armies

A fifth trend came later, in the 1590s: the formation of disciplined and drilled standing armies. Most monarchs before 1590 recruited men for fighting only when they needed them. They paid military entrepreneurs to raise armies of mercenaries. When there was no war brewing, monarchs didn't want to pay for an army. From the 1590s onward, this system began to give way to one of standing, professional armies that rulers had to pay in times of both war and peace.

The main reason for this change was the effectiveness of drilled and disciplined infantry armed with reasonably accurate muskets—long, smoothbore guns developed in the sixteenth century. Dutch and Ottoman war captains pioneered drill, apparently independently of one another. They found, as had Japanese and others, that musket fire was devastatingly effective in volleys. They arranged musketeers in parallel lines (ranks) and taught them to fire, reload, and fire on command. While one rank fired, another was busy reloading. To do this quickly, without injuring one's fellows, and while one's closest comrades were being wounded and killed, required iron discipline. To achieve it, Dutch captains obliged their troops to drill endlessly on parade grounds until their choreographed motions were second nature. Close-order drill took years to master, so men had to be housed, fed, and clothed in

Ottoman Drill A painting shows Ottoman troops from the era of the sixteenth-century sultan Suleiman in battle. It took years of drilling to achieve coordination among the ranks of artillery, infantry, and cavalry attacking in formation.

peacetime at government expense. If unpaid, these men could turn their violent skills against civilians or kings. So wherever armies adopted drill, and therefore became standing armies, monarchs had to pay soldiers in peacetime and wartime alike to avoid chaos.

A sixth trend underlying the military revolution was the development of a more sophisticated logistical apparatus. With bigger armies and navies, someone had to come up with more horses, oxen, mules, camels, elephants, and their food; and more iron, steel, bronze, tin, wood, leather, and saltpeter (used in gunpowder) to be made into weapons and other war materiel. More men had to be transported to the right places at the right times, and in the right proportions of infantry to cavalry to artillerymen, not to mention cooks, gunsmiths, engineers, and muleteers, camel drivers, or elephant handlers. All these animals, supplies, and people had to get across rivers, over mountains, or through deserts on schedule. Creating, maintaining, and deploying a big military machine required a military bureaucracy, made up of literate and numerate people with desk skills usually despised by men at arms.

To summarize, the innovations that made up the military revolution consisted of a hardware package of ships, cannon, muskets, gunpowder, and fortification, and a software package of improved financial systems, military engineering, infantry drill, and logistical bureaucracy. Rulers adopted those innovations that they could afford and that addressed the threats they faced.

Let's look at a few examples of states that to one degree or another adopted the innovations of the military revolution to become more powerful. This approach focuses on the winners in military competition. Some of the many losers are mentioned along the way, but there were many more that aren't.

The Tokugawa Consolidation of Power in Japan

An archipelago of perhaps 12 to 18 million people in 1500, Japan was politically fragmented. Any semblance of unity had vanished by the late fifteenth century, and thereafter numerous warlords fought one another for territory, resources, influence, and glory. None could count on the allegiance of, or extract taxes from, more than a couple of million people. But within 140 years Japan became a unified country. The process was bloody.

Locked in ruthless competition, Japan's warlords were open to innovations that might give them an edge. After 1500 their armies grew in size, and they turned increasingly to unskilled foot soldiers—ordinary peasants with no training or socialization in military culture. Warlords learned to integrate massed infantry into battle tactics. Sieges and elaborate fortification became the rule. Samurai (an elite warrior class that took shape in the twelfth century) infantry and horsemen, formerly the cutting edge of Japanese warfare, now played smaller roles.

The Introduction of Firearms

In 1543, a Chinese pirate ship introduced Portuguese guns to Japan's vortex of violence. Guns required little training or skill to use, and so were well suited to the ordinary infantryman. Soon there were hundreds of thousands of firearms in Japan, and every warlord had to have plenty of them and figure out how to integrate them into his tactics.

In order to obtain guns, many warlords sold slaves. Chinese, Japanese, and Korean pirates had been enslaving coastal villagers off and on for centuries and selling them far from home. Now, Japanese warlords turned to slave exports, especially of young women, to Portuguese merchants, who in turn sold them in China or in Portuguese trading posts such as Macao or Goa. The Portuguese slave trade from Japan probably involved a few hundred people annually until the trade was outlawed soon after 1600. Many more slaves remained in Japan. As in West Africa and New Zealand, in Japan more guns meant more enslavement.

Nobunaga and Hideyoshi

The most successful warlord at exploiting the political potential of guns was **Oda Nobunaga**, whose battlefield successes unified the southern half of Japan by 1580. He arranged his gunmen in tight formations to maximize their firepower, and perhaps—accounts are unclear on this—invented the tactic of volley fire. Nobunaga and his successors unified Japan by mobilizing hundreds of thousands of peasants and giving them guns manufactured by Japanese smiths. For a few decades, Japan made more guns than any other country in the world. A great change was taking place in Japan, a country where formerly only exquisitely trained warriors—samurai—could win battles. This change in the social foundation of war loosely resembled the transition in the ancient world from aristocratic warriors armed with bronze armor and weapons to mass armies using iron.

Oda Nobunaga's career exemplifies a pattern that would become increasingly common after 1500. As the Global web connected distant regions, ambitious rulers time and again borrowed useful techniques and technologies from afar. They mastered them, modified them as needed, integrated them into local culture, and used them to smash or enslave rivals and neighbors, and build empires. The pattern was not new: the adoption of horses or iron in earlier times sometimes had had similar effects. From the sixteenth century onward, the adoption of guns produced this result in many cases around the world, including, as we saw, with King Kamehameha in Hawaii.

Upon Nobunaga's death in 1582, a former foot soldier and servant, **Toyotomi Hideyoshi**, out-maneuvered all rivals to succeed Nobunaga. In 1592, he decided to

The Unification of Tokugawa Japan, 1580–1603
The Japanese archipelago was politically fragmented for most of its history. But in the late sixteenth century, local leaders or warlords found ways to use guns effectively, destroy rivals, and create—by 1603—a politically unified Japan in the heavily populated islands of Honshu and Kyushu. The northernmost island, Hokkaido, became part of Japan only later.

invade Korea and then China with 160,000 soldiers, a quarter of them gunmen. Japanese armies succeeded in Korea, where guns remained rare. Hideyoshi, who had tried to restrict the export of Japanese slaves in 1587, now eagerly enslaved and sold thousands of Koreans to Japanese and Portuguese buyers. In the end, China sent an army to Korea, and it became clear that Japan's sea power was not up to the task of supplying an overseas army against a large force. In 1598, Hideyoshi's Korea campaign ended in retreat.

At the same time that his soldiers ravaged Korea, Hideyoshi was defeating rival warlords in Japan. By his death in 1598, he had just about unified the country. That task was completed by his successor, a samurai, Tokugawa Ieyasu, who crushed rival forces loyal to Hideyoshi's young son. Only the sparsely populated northern island, Hokkaido, remained outside his realm.

Establishing the Tokugawa Shogunate

By 1600, Tokugawa Ieyasu stood supreme over a unified Japan. In 1603 he acquired the title of shogun (roughly: top general), which meant he was the de facto ruler of Japan. His descendants continued in that role until 1868 in a dynasty called the **Tokugawa shogunate**. With the country unified after 1600, and peace imposed (except on Hokkaido), Japan ceased to be a center of military innovation. Hideyoshi, despite his common origins, had begun the process of restoring samurai to their former status by banning peasants from owning weapons in 1588. Under the Tokugawa, that became entrenched policy, and only samurai could own and use weapons. The shoguns with their new military policy after 1600 reversed a social, democratizing—but bloody—revolution that helped bring them to power.

The process of consolidation continued into southernmost Hokkaido. There an indigenous population called the Ainu, who had only rudimentary technology by

Japanese standards, resisted centralized control off and on until about 1700. War and newly introduced diseases reduced their numbers to about 25,000 by 1800, and eventually ethnic Japanese from the southern islands colonized Hokkaido, swamping the Ainu demographically.

The Tokugawa shoguns consolidated their power before 1600 by using new technologies and techniques of war. After 1600 they kept the peace, and kept themselves in power, by time-honored tactics including threats of force and keeping regional elites either content or cowed. Successful monarchs elsewhere did similar things.

The Qing Consolidation in China

China's Ming dynasty (1368–1644) ruled over a quarter of the world's population, perhaps 175 million people, by 1600. As we have seen in earlier chapters, it launched great oceanic voyages under the command of Zheng He and presided over a buzzing hive of intellectual activity, including the neo-Confucian revival associated with Wang Yangming. The Ming also found ways to profit from international trade opportunities (see Chapter 20) brought by European sailing ships. Sales of silk and porcelain for silver from Japan and Mexico fueled an economic expansion that extended from 1520 to 1580. In general, despite droughts, rebellions, and frontier struggles with pastoral peoples to the north, the Ming governed well enough to remain in power for 200 years.

Tokugawa Shogunate A painting on silk from the seventeenth century illustrates the importance of the samurai to supporting and legitimating the Tokugawa shoguns' rule. It shows the shogun at court, surrounded by samurai from the 16 most noble families.

The Fall of the Ming

But by the end of the sixteenth century, their troubles mounted. The Ming's campaign against Hideyoshi in Korea in the 1590s depleted the treasury. Adverse climate change—long spells of drought and cold of the Little Ice Age—brought more famines and lowered state revenues. When an emperor granted palace eunuchs the right to collect taxes, he precipitated a crisis between the eunuchs and the gentry. His successor allowed the eunuchs free rein in the early seventeenth century, provoking determined hostility from the gentry. At the same time, the overseas supplies of silver dried up when mining output in Spanish America and Japan fell, starving Chinese commerce of its medium of exchange and making it harder for anyone to pay their taxes—which by law had to be paid in silver. By the 1630s, China was fracturing and civil war loomed.

Then things went from bad to worse for the Ming: an enterprising steppe leader from Manchuria, Nurhaci, and his son, Hong Taiji, united many of the tribes of the eastern steppe, forged a new ethnic identity (called Manchu), built an efficient army in ways that recalled Genghis Khan, conquered Korea (1638), and threatened China. When one faction in China's civil war invited the Manchus to help, they helped themselves, occupying Beijing and refusing to leave. The last Ming emperor hanged himself from a garden tree in 1644, an ignominious end for one of China's great dynasties.

The Qing Conquest

The Manchu elite renamed themselves the Qing, ruling China as the **Qing dynasty** until 1911. But first they had to consolidate their power, eliminating pockets of Ming loyalists in battle. Then they had to win over elite Chinese, the literati, without whom routine administration and tax collection was next to impossible. The literati, who admired elegant handwriting more than good horsemanship, normally found the Qing foreign barbarians with undistinguished ancestry and strange customs. Male Qing shaved the front part of the top of their heads and wore a long braid, a style they made a legal requirement for all Han Chinese men. It took most literati families several generations to overcome their resentment of Qing rule.

The Qing faced two main military challenges during their first century in power. One was the naval power of the pirate king and Ming loyalist Zheng Chenggong and his clan, with which this chapter began. The Qing finished them off by 1683. The other was the perennial problem of Chinese dynasties: confederations of steppe nomads to the north. In the late seventeenth and early eighteenth centuries, a subset of the Mongols, the Zunghars, forged large confederacies, threatening the security of northern China. At the same time, Tibetans to the southwest showed signs of hostility to the Qing and supported their fellow Buddhists in Mongolia.

The Qing's answer to the challenge from the steppe came in the form of army campaigns to the north and west, which, combined with smallpox epidemics, decisively broke Mongol power in the 1750s. Soon thereafter they added more territory, including the desert and oasis lands in the far northwest now known as Xinjiang, and the high plateau of Tibet. The Qing campaigns doubled the territorial size of their empire and secured their frontiers. They also made their empire more multicultural, multilingual, and multiethnic than the Ming or most previous Chinese empires. By 1800 it counted some 350 million people, roughly a third of the global population.

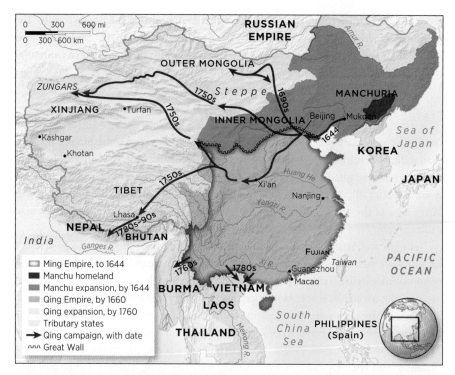

The Qing Empire, ca. 1600–1800 From their homeland in eastern Manchuria, the Manchu expanded militarily in the steppe and woodlands of northeastern Asia. They intervened in a power struggle in China's declining Ming Empire, and between 1644 and 1683 they took over most of the Ming territory. As rulers of China they took the name Qing, and for another century proved effective in war and diplomacy, expanding their empire westward.

The Qing also fought expansionist campaigns in the south, against Burma and Vietnam, but with no success. Mountain terrain and rain forest hamstrung the Qing cavalry. Malaria killed many thousand Qing soldiers. Combined with stern resistance, these factors—after multiple failed campaigns—persuaded the Qing that southern expansion was not worth the cost.

The Qing were led by two long-lived, vigorous, conscientious, clever, and ruthless emperors, conventionally reckoned among the greatest in Chinese history. The Kangxi emperor, who reigned for some sixty years (r. 1662–1722), was the first Qing emperor born and raised on Chinese soil rather than in Manchuria. His grandson, the Qianlong emperor, reigned from 1735 to 1796, abdicating at age 85 in order not to outdo his grandfather. Of the 265 years of Qing dynastic rule, about 125 took place under these two men. They were both cultivated, multilingual, highly literate political wizards—and mercilessly brutal when it suited them. The Kangxi emperor, for example, welcomed foreign Jesuits to his court, but he also obliged the people of Fujian province to evacuate the entire coastal district in his effort to undermine the Zheng family. The Qianlong emperor spoke six languages, took a deep interest in Tibetan Buddhism, and hired Italian and French Jesuits to build palaces—but also ordered the extermination of Zunghar Mongols as a people in 1755.

Statecraft and Military Innovation

The Qing consolidation of power and expansion of empire owed something to the Eurasian military revolution, but much less than the Tokugawa did. The Ming had already used guns and adapted them into their military system—gunpowder was a Chinese invention, after all. As early as 1400, about 10 percent of Ming soldiers used firearms. By the time of the war against Japan in Korea (1590s), the Ming had a formidable field artillery force.

Yet guns and artillery mattered much less in China than in Japan. Siege artillery did not work well in China, because cities typically had earthen walls thick enough to stop cannonballs. Neither guns nor artillery were much use against China's main enemies, the Mongols, whose ponies enabled them to scamper out of range quickly. So although firearms were invented in China, and used by both the Ming and the Qing, the Chinese did not always keep pace with other states in firearm quality. In 1644, when the Qing took power, the best muskets, according to the Chinese, were Ottoman, and the best cannon were Portuguese. The Qing military sometimes imitated the best technologies, and in some cases made small improvements upon them. Like the Ming before them, they studied cannon making with Jesuit teachers skilled in European casting techniques. But they did not rely on firearms to the extent that other early modern empires did.

The Qing's military secret sauce, more than new technology, was new technique. Even before they came to power, Nurhaci and Hong Taiji had organized their steppe

Qing Military Strategy A large eighteenth-century scroll painting illustrates a scene from the imperial hunt, a ritualized court event. Here athletes train in a circle at the center of the camp, as the emperor and numerous spectators look on. Such activities allowed the Qing army to practice the logistical competence and military readiness for which it was renowned.

warriors into units, called banners, that cut across kin lines and strengthened central-ized command—just as Genghis Khan had done with Mongol tribes 400 years before. In their campaigns in China, the Qing effectively integrated cavalry, their own strong suit, with infantry, artillery, and siege skills. They learned, from the Ming, to conduct naval warfare along the rivers and coasts. And when they chose to attack the Zunghar Mongols in the eighteenth century, they combined canny diplomacy that divided their enemy together with brilliant logistics that enabled them to campaign out on the steppe grasslands without running out of food and water.

The Qing emphasized military virtues in their efforts to influence Chinese culture. They boosted military spending and highlighted military achievements in art and archi-tecture to a degree unusual in China, where cultured people tended to regard military men as uncouth. The Qianlong emperor in his first year on the throne (1736) stressed the importance of military preparedness even in peacetime.

Keeping the military paid was a high priority for the Qing. They knew their own rise to power rested in part on disaffected Ming army units rising in rebellion. So they boosted the military's budget, even while lowering taxes overall. They improved the efficiency of tax collection. They also encouraged "voluntary" contributions of silver from big merchants, who knew better than to refuse. And they encouraged the military to go into business for itself to bolster its finances.

All these initiatives, more than new technologies, helped the Qing consolidate their power and expand their empire. They did not disdain foreign military technology. But their most effective statecraft and military innovations came locally, from within China and the Qing homeland of the eastern steppe, and not from contact with the wider world. This was unique among the great powers in the early modern centuries.

The Mughal Empire in India

The Mughal Empire took shape in the early sixteenth century in northern India. Its Muslim founders came from Central Asia and identified with the Turkic and Mongol (hence "Mughal") warriors of the steppe. After taking a beating from an Uzbek emir in Central Asian warfare, they invaded northern India and, after four failed attempts, conquered the much-decayed Delhi sultanate in 1526. A forceful emperor, Abu'l-Fath Jalal ud-din Muhammad Akbar (usually just called **Akbar**, which in Arabic means "the great one"), stabilized the Mughal state and launched it on a path to expansion. He took power as a teenager in 1556 and reigned to his death in 1605, almost as long as Kangxi or Qianlong. Soon the Mughal Empire controlled, although loosely, most of South Asia—like the Mauryans (fourth to second centuries BCE) and the Gupta (fourth to sixth centuries CE) before them.

No state in a thousand years had been able to unify as much of South Asia as the Mughals. Akbar ruled over perhaps 60 million people. A century of geographical expansion later, his great-grandson, Aurangzeb, ruled about 120 million, about 20 percent of the world's total. At its height the Mughal Empire was the second most populous state in the world, trailing only China, and controlled all but southernmost India.

Mughal Might

Mughal success rested in part on military innovations. Like the Qing, they found effective combinations of old and new. Warfare in India for five centuries before the Mughals had hinged on foot soldiers, mounted archers, war elephants, and sieges. Indians also used bamboo rockets fired from iron tubes. Guns first arrived, via Central Asia and Iran, about 1450, but were not yet effective enough to catch on widely. Then, in the 1520s, the Mughals introduced larger quantities of guns and cannon in their North India campaigns, and figured out how to combine these new weapons with cavalry archers. Akbar recruited skilled gunsmiths from the Ottoman Empire and Europe to improve the quality of his weaponry, and soon Mughal smiths and guncasters were making excellent muskets and cannon. Now firearms spread widely in India, including among enemies of the Mughals. To maintain a military edge, the Mughals also had to ensure access to horse-producing regions in Central Asia—and deny it to enemies. Lacking enough good grassland, India itself could not raise enough horses. The Mughals imported up to 16,000 annually via Afghanistan. By 1560, in the early years of Akbar's reign, the Mughals had perfected the combination of horses and guns—cavalry, infantry, and artillery—and added to that a mastery of both siegecraft and fortification.

Mughal Conquests The Mughal emperor Akbar owed his military success in part to the combination of old and new technologies: on the one hand, war elephants and horses, seen here (left) crossing the Ganges in a 1600 manuscript; on the other, advanced siege artillery, shown here (right) being used to attack a hill fort in central India in 1568.

The Mughals also learned to use the navigable rivers, especially the Ganges and Indus, to move their military machinery around. In the watery landscapes of Bengal, which in the monsoon season could become a maze of swampy creeks and ponds, they conducted warfare from boats. On rivers and inshore seas, they used gunboats in support of their army. They never built a navy capable of projecting power on the high seas—recall Aurangzeb's willingness to concede the oceans to the "lions of the sea." At all times, the Mughal navy was subordinate to their army in importance and in prestige within Mughal society.

The careful integration of infantry with firearms together with cavalry, field artillery, siegecraft, and armed river boats made the Mughals more formidable at war than any South Asian rival. In Akbar's time, and throughout the seventeenth century, the Mughals generally crushed those who resisted them. They met stern resistance from some Indian rulers, however, such as those of the sultanate of Ahmadnagar in west-central India. In the late 1590s, its armies were led by a female regent, Chand Bibi, who beat back Mughal attacks on her capital for four years. Despite the Mughal conquest of Ahmadnagar city, resistance continued under the leadership of an Ethiopian slave, Malik Ambar. Born in Africa, sold by his impoverished parents to Arabs, shipped to Iraq, Arabia, and finally India, Malik Ambar became a slave soldier and through skill and guile rose to be the leading minister of Ahmadnagar by 1607. He masterminded guerilla resistance to Mughal expansion for two decades before his successors succumbed to the superior power of the Mughals. Just about everyone else in South Asia also bowed before Mughal power sooner or later.

Malik Ambar An anonymous artist made this portrait of the Ethiopian slave-turned-military-leader near the end of his life, in about 1620.

Mughal Consolidation

The Mughals needed all the raw power they could amass because, as Muslim invaders in an overwhelmingly Hindu land, they faced a legitimacy problem. Akbar addressed this not only with military force, but with a tolerant religious policy as well. Although illiterate himself, Akbar supported scholars and libraries and seems to have been genuinely curious about and tolerant of multiple religions, like some of the Mongol khans and the Kangxi emperor in China. He enjoyed discussions with Sufis, Jesuits, Jains,

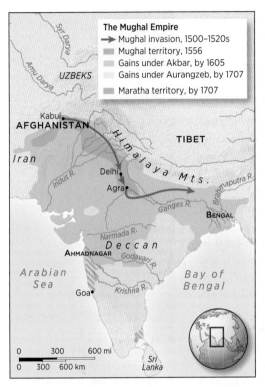

The Mughal Empire
→ Mughal invasion, 1500–1520s
▨ Mughal territory, 1556
▨ Gains under Akbar, by 1605
▨ Gains under Aurangzeb, by 1707
▨ Maratha territory, by 1707

The Mughal Empire, ca. 1500–1707 The Mughal dynasty, originally from Central Asia, became one of the great powers of the early modern world. Once they dominated the fertile Ganges basin, they had the resources to bring most of South Asia under their control. By 1600, their territorial success rivaled that of the Gupta Empire a thousand years earlier. But by 1700, other polities, such as the Maratha states, were adapting to the Mughals' technologies and techniques, and their empire was in retreat.

and Buddhists. When the Mughals had first arrived in South Asia in the 1520s, they allowed only Muslims to serve in their military. Akbar recruited Hindus too, and relaxed other forms of religious discrimination. He suspended the normal Islamic policy of taxing non-Muslims at higher rates, allowed Hindu landowners to hold high office, welcomed Hindus at his court, celebrated Hindu holidays such as Diwali, and married a Hindu woman, Mariam-uz-Zamani (one of his 14 wives). The Mughal religious policy, with a few adjustments in favor of Islamic orthodoxy, remained in effect until the time of Aurangzeb (r. 1658–1707).

Like every early modern state, the Mughals needed huge sums to pay for their military. Like every successful early modern state, the Mughals made tax collection more efficient. They also raised money by negotiation with, and occasional intimidation of, local elites, typically landowners who took a share of what the toiling peasantry produced. Under Akbar they also encouraged foreign trade and benefited from custom duties. As they conquered new territories, they used the plunder to lower tax rates and win their subjects' loyalty. They could dole out conquered lands to reliable followers, who gave a share of their income to the Mughals.

As long as new conquests kept coming, this system worked admirably—as a similar one had worked for the Roman Republic and Empire long before. The early Mughals rarely lacked for money, and this underwrote their military and political success. Shah Jahan, who ruled from 1627 to 1658, was able to field an army of a million men and pay for a glorious mausoleum, the Taj Mahal, built to honor his favorite wife, Mumtaz Mahal, who died while giving birth to her fourteenth child in 1631. When Emperor Aurangzeb (the sixth of Mumtaz Mahal's children) went on campaign in Afghanistan in the 1670s, he brought 300 camels carrying gold and silver to cover his expenses.

Mughal Decline

In Aurangzeb's later years, the Mughal Empire weakened. Having imprisoned his father and defeated his brothers on the battlefield, he took the throne at age 29. Aurangzeb sought legitimacy by burnishing his credentials as a Muslim ruler. By all accounts he was pious and knew the Qur'an by heart. His religious devotion—and misguided political calculation—led him to adopt a policy that emphasized Sunni orthodoxy and instituted Islamic law (shari'a) throughout his empire. He forbade construction of new Hindu temples, permitted destruction of some existing ones, and imposed higher taxes on non-Muslims. This departure from Mughal tradition alienated Hindus, Sikhs, Jains, Shi'a Muslims—as well as everyone who enjoyed music, dancing, drinking, and gambling.

As a result, the Mughal state faced more frequent rebellions and tax revolts. Eventually it could not control its southern frontiers. In a region called the Deccan, Hindu warriors known as Marathas gradually rolled back Mughal control. Starting in the 1660s, a successful guerilla captain, Shivaji Bhonsle, built up a Maratha state, including a navy. His state building was a rough equivalent to that of the Zheng family on the southeast coasts of China. But whereas the Qing ultimately vanquished the upstart Zhengs, the Mughals could not overcome the Marathas, despite the efforts of Aurangzeb, who personally campaigned against them for 25 years. By 1770, the Marathas controlled half of India. Aurangzeb's absence from the empire's heartlands in north India led elites there to experiment with keeping bigger chunks of revenue for themselves, and central control, never very strong, weakened.

After Aurangzeb's death in 1707, with the empire under less able successors, the Mughal retreat gathered pace. Princes and warlords broke free and carved out their own states. In 1739, Nader Shah, a former slave from northeastern Iran who had just overthrown the Safavid dynasty and made himself shah of Iran, sacked Delhi. He massacred tens of thousands, looted the city, and carried off the Mughals' peacock throne. India became more politically fragmented, and the Mughals held only small parts of the country until their final collapse in 1857.

Like the Qing in China, the Mughals were originally foreign invaders who built a formidable multiethnic and multireligious empire within 40 years. Also like the Qing, they focused their efforts on their landward frontiers, leaving the sea to others, and took advantage of innovations in the military sphere to expand their territory. But unlike the Qing—more like the warlord Oda Nobunaga in Japan—their innovations included major elements adopted from abroad, notably firearms. They integrated artillery and muskets into their existing military traditions, while monopolizing the import of horses, helping them to dominate South Asia for two centuries and to survive for three.

The Ottoman Empire

While the Mughals lasted some 300 years, the Ottomans, another Turkic and Muslim dynasty that traced its origins to Central Asia, lasted over 600. Their success rested on factors important to the Mughals as well: canny integration of new weaponry into existing military culture, liberal religious policy, and healthy finances.

The Ottomans began as a community of Turkish-speaking mobile pastoralists, followers of a tribal chieftain named Osman. They began to enjoy military success in northwest Anatolia against Byzantine Greeks in the fourteenth century. They may have benefited politically from the bubonic plague pandemic of 1346–1351 which probably killed urban and agrarian populations faster than it did pastoralists. In any case, the Ottomans gradually expanded their domain in Anatolia and the Balkans at the expense of the Byzantine Empire and several smaller polities. By 1453, under a 21-year-old sultan known as Mehmet the Conqueror, they successfully besieged Constantinople, the best-fortified city in all Europe. That brought the Byzantine Empire to its knees, and within eight years its last remnants disappeared.

The Ottomans made Constantinople, also called **Istanbul**, their capital and exploited its geographic location astride the straits connecting the Black and Mediterranean Seas. They now controlled one of the world's most lucrative trade routes. Their conquests continued after 1453, notably in the Balkans and along the Black Sea coasts.

Ottoman Expansion

Then between 1514 and 1526 Ottoman good fortune multiplied. Battlefield victories stabilized their eastern frontier with the Safavids of Iran, the Shi'a dynasty with whom the Sunni Ottomans competed for power and prestige. With that frontier secured, in 1517 they conquered Egypt and the Hejaz, the strip of Arabia where Mecca and Medina lie. This was a double windfall for the Ottomans. Egypt yielded reliable surpluses of grain and revenue. The Ottomans used Egypt, as Achaemenids, Romans, Byzantines, and others had before them, as a means to feed their armies and cities, and to help finance wars and administration. By some calculations, conquering Egypt doubled the revenues of the Ottoman state. On top of that, when drought afflicted the eastern Mediterranean region and crops failed, those of Egypt did not—because the Nile flowed from the mountains of Ethiopia, where rain is more reliable and determined by different weather systems. So Egypt not only provided grain and revenue, it also provided insurance against the droughts common in the other lands of the Ottoman Empire.

Taking over the holy places, Mecca and Medina, might have doubled the prestige of the Ottomans. Soon Ottoman sultans (as their leaders were called) took the title of caliph, proclaiming themselves the successors of the Prophet Muhammad and the spiritual leaders of all Muslims. Not all Muslims agreed. But nonetheless, most Sunni Muslims—always a majority within Islamdom—regarded the Ottoman caliphs as the guardians of the Islamic community. This prestige won considerable cooperation and deference.

Moreover, a long spell of good rains in the Ottoman heartland of Anatolia, around the years 1520–1590, boosted livestock herds, grain harvests, population, and imperial revenues. Whereas both the Qing and the Mughals had to import horses, the Ottoman lands produced all the horses, grain, timber, and important mineral ores that the empire's population and military might need.

These circumstances contributed to the notable success of the empire's longest-reigning sultan, Suleiman (r. 1520–1566), who consolidated Ottoman control over vast territories and added several more—most importantly, Iran and Hungary. Both yielded grain surpluses in most years, and Hungary also provided great herds of horses and cattle. Controlling Hungary meant the Ottomans could use the Danube River as a transport artery to tighten their hold on southeastern Europe. Controlling the Tigris

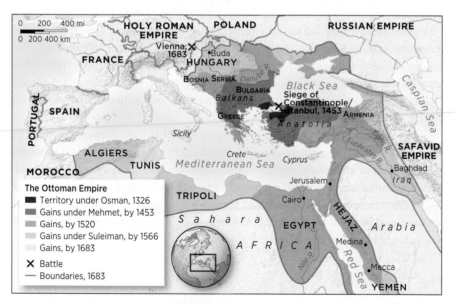

The Expansion of the Ottoman Empire, ca. 1320s–1683 From their beginnings in northwest Anatolia early in the fourteenth century, the followers of Osman—the Ottomans—expanded their domain for three centuries into southeastern Europe, Southwest Asia, and North Africa. Under sultans such as Mehmet and Suleiman, the Ottomans wielded the techniques and technologies of power effectively, becoming one of the great powers of Eurasia.

and Euphrates rivers enabled them to move troops and supplies easily along their eastern frontier with Iran.

The Ottoman Empire reached its territorial peak in the late sixteenth and seventeenth centuries. Stretching from Iraq to Algeria and from Yemen to Hungary, it contained nearly 30 million people, about 7 percent of humankind.

Ottoman Consolidation

Like that of the Mughals, Ottoman political success rested on military, financial, and religious power. Like the Qing and the Mughals, the Ottomans integrated firearms into their military culture. They used guns as early as the 1390s and artillery by the 1420s. They quickly mastered the fine points of siege warfare and fortification, demonstrated in the capture and rebuilding of Istanbul in 1453. They recruited an elite infantry force, called the janissaries, from Christian communities of the western Balkans. The **janissaries** were taken from their homes as boys, trained in the arts of war and administration, and deployed, nominally as slaves of the sultans, in the army or bureaucracy. Although slaves, many of them rose to powerful positions. As gun-wielding infantry (by 1560 more than half of the janissaries carried firearms), they played a key role in many battlefield triumphs, such as the defeat of the Safavid army, which did not yet use guns, in 1514. Most states equipped their least skilled soldiers with guns, because they did not take much practice to learn to use. The Ottomans did the reverse, arming their elite and best-trained soldiers with muskets. By the 1560s, the janissaries had developed the technique of volley fire with muskets, like Hideyoshi's troops. To equip their forces, the Ottomans built up military industries and produced high-quality artillery and small arms. They blended all their military innovations with cavalry, their traditional strength.

The Ottoman military machine grew bigger as well as more efficient. During the reign of Suleiman, the artillery corps tripled in size. Until the 1690s, the Ottomans could usually put more men, horses, and weapons in the field than any of their enemies. They also built a big navy of galleys propelled by oarsmen, suited to the conditions of the Mediterranean and Black Seas, but also active in the Indian Ocean, at times as far afield as Mombasa and Malacca. As everywhere, fielding such an expanded and well-equipped military was extremely expensive.

The Tax System

Like every other empire, the Ottomans sought to tighten up their tax system. Mehmet the Conqueror (r. 1451–1481) attempted to centralize taxation and bureaucracy, and to take a bigger chunk of the revenues of provincial elites. He even tried to impose fixed prices on items bought and sold in the markets, which proved hard to enforce. The local elites, often quite different from one province to another, proved resilient. With the scale and cost of warfare expanding so quickly during the sixteenth century, Mehmet and his successors had to strike bargains with them.

The fiscal windfall of expansion, especially the conquest of Egypt, helped. But the state also turned increasingly to tax farming—selling to private entrepreneurs the right to collect taxes from Ottoman subjects. And the Ottomans in the sixteenth century encouraged the monetization and commercialization of the economy, which enabled them to collect more revenue in cash rather than in produce—always preferable for governments. After territorial expansion and plunder stopped, the sultans had to become more efficient to keep solvent.

The Millet System Ottoman religious policy helped reduce the costs of ruling. From the beginning, the sultans happily recruited Christians into their military and bureaucracy. They valued loyalty wherever they found it. They welcomed tens of thousands of Jewish refugees from Spain, expelled in 1492 by Ferdinand and Isabella. Mehmet the Conqueror was genuinely curious, like Akbar, about religions other than Islam and at times tried to present himself as a worthy successor to Byzantine (Christian) emperors. Although they taxed non-Muslims at higher rates, the Ottomans by and large left Christian and Jewish communities to adjudicate their own affairs until the nineteenth century. Sometimes called the **millet system**, this tolerant religious policy, like Akbar's, made the empire a bit easier to govern.

With these measures, the Ottomans managed to stay afloat, to field and finance a military equal to foreign challenges and internal rebellions through the end of the seventeenth century. After a defeat by the combined forces of the Habsburg Empire and Poland-Lithuania in 1683, their position relative to their neighbors and rivals weakened, and after the 1770s the tide was running against them. They could not keep up with their neighbors, especially Russia and the Habsburgs, and their neighbors more often formed coalitions against them. The empire shrank after every lost war. But the Ottomans, like the Qing, lasted into the early twentieth century. So did the Russian Empire.

Imperial Consolidation in Russia

Russia is another case of **imperial consolidation** and territorial expansion at the expense of weaker neighbors. In earlier chapters we saw how the original Russian state emerged on trade routes linking the Baltic and Black Seas, how the Muscovite princes served as clients of Mongol khans for a while, and how, in the sixteenth century, the Russian state sponsored expansion into Siberia. The conquest of Siberia and its fur trade bolstered Russian state revenues almost as much as the conquest of Egypt helped Ottoman finances. By 1600, Russia was a large and—in ethnic and religious terms—highly diverse state, an empire in all but name. It was, however, sparsely settled, with a population of only 10 million.

CONSIDERING THE EVIDENCE

An Ottoman Register in Ukraine

In addition to training janissaries to run its war machine, the Ottoman Empire hired thousands of scribes and tax farmers to keep money flowing. Census takers (*muharrir*) determined tax levels by interviewing farmers, traders, herders, bakers, ferrymen, and even alcohol distillers to estimate what they produced in a normal year. Then they wrote everything in duplicate registers: one for the imperial archive in Istanbul and one for local officials to reference. The excerpt below is from a register for the Ukrainian province of Kamaniçe near the Black Sea, which the Ottoman Empire took from the Polish-Lithuanian Commonwealth in 1672. The imperial government wanted to protect its productive settlements on the nearby Black Sea.

The introduction to the register begins with two lists. The first list describes collections from tax farmers reserved for the Ottoman sultan: poll taxes from Christian and Jewish immigrants, fees from a boat toll, and prepaid taxes on fishponds. The second list, shown below, summarizes the collections from tax farmers that the *beylerbeyi*—the governor—would retain. Although additional taxes pushed annual revenue to over 5 million silver coins (*akçe*), this amount was not nearly enough to pay the 6,000 soldiers garrisoned in the border province. So, each year, the empire subsidized military salaries with nearly 13 million *akçe* from the central treasury in Istanbul until it abandoned Kamaniçe in 1699.

The domains of the *beylerbeyi* [governor] of the province of Kamaniçe

[Tax collections] from market dues on horses, mules, oxen, sheep, goats, and

others in Kamaniçe ... Žvanec', and ... Mohyliv: yearly 54,000 [silver coins]

[and] from weighing and measuring fees in Kamaniçe, except for the rent of the

---

While the princes of Moscow, who after 1547 took the title **tsar**, were underwriting Siberian expansion, they also took large parts of Ukraine and the Muslim lands of the lower Volga. These were more fertile than their home region around Moscow. This territorial expansion helped boost the population to about 14 million in 1700. During the next century, natural increase helped propel it to 40 million. By 1800, the tsars ruled about 5 percent of the global population.

The early tsars faced difficult conditions—the harsh climate of the Little Ice Age, frequent famines and rebellions, and formidable neighbors such as Poland-Lithuania to the west and Muslim khanates to the east and south. Their response was to grab all the power they could. That meant forcing regional elites, mainly landed aristocrats called *boyars*, to knuckle under to the tsars. The tsars drew upon their revenues from the fur trade, the plunder from newly conquered lands, politically astute marriages, buildings [where the weighing and measuring was done]: yearly 42,000

[and] income from coffee-roasting in Kamaniçe: yearly 19,000

[and] from market tolls, coffee-houses, candle works, slaughterhouses, sheep [herders], eating houses, cookshops with dye-houses and others in Kamaniçe and from the fair-brokers' fees in Žvanec': yearly 52,200

[and] from the head-broker's fee in the "black" market ... [and the] head-broker's fee in the horse and cattle [market] in Kamaniçe ...: yearly [scribe did not record amount]

[and] from the fees of the [drivers] of oxen, sheep, goats and with the pasturage and passage fee [collected] from the [drivers] in Žvanec': yearly 25,300

[and] from the [unclaimed] property devolved upon the imperial treasury, left by ordinary subjects and state servants except for *janissaries*, ... and from the property of missing and absent persons, stray and run-away [slaves, arrested and sold in auction] in [Kamaniçe] with the fee from the [wineries] and distillery kettles and with the cask fee in Žvanec' and ... Mohyliv: yearly 50,000

Questions for Analysis

1. What products and activities did the Ottoman Empire tax?
2. Besides adding a new revenue stream, what could have motivated the Ottoman Empire to tax coffee and alcohol production?
3. Why would the Ottoman Empire conquer territory that provided less revenue than it cost to maintain?

Source: Dariusz Kołodziejczyk, trans., "Appendix 1: Translation of the Beginning of the *Defter*," The Ottoman Survey Register of Podolia (ca. 1681), *Defter-i Mufassal-i Eyalet-i Kamaniçe* (Cambridge, MA: Harvard Ukrainian Research Institute, 2004).

and the legitimacy conferred by the Russian Orthodox Church to build a remarkably centralized state over their sprawling domain.

Ivan IV

Much of that was the work of Ivan IV, called Ivan the Terrible (although Ivan the Tough might be a better translation of *groznyi*). He reigned for nearly four decades (r. 1547–1584) and more than anyone else brought the nobility to heel and gave imperial Russia its political character. He oversaw conquests (and defeats), required military service of his population, wrapped himself in the mantle of the Russian Orthodox Church, married eight or nine times, killed his son and heir in a tantrum, spent lavishly on war and monumental architecture—following in many ways the age-old emperor's playbook.

But Ivan the Terrible was also an innovator. He helped set up the first printing press in Russia. He sought overseas contacts, especially with England. Most important in the context of this chapter, he built up a huge army and an armaments industry to match. His engineers and craftsmen manufactured countless guns and cannon, and his officers (selected for talent rather than ancestry) refined the blending of infantry, cavalry, and artillery into a cohesive force. Russian engineers even invented mobile fortifications, made of wood, which could be dragged or floated here or there as needed, like a set of giant Lincoln logs. In conquering the lower Volga, Ivan made that great river into a Russian transport artery, like the Danube in the Ottoman Empire. It gave Russia easy access to the Caspian Sea and trade with Iran. After he died—while playing chess—Russia almost fell apart.

Peter the Great

A later tsar, Peter the Great (r. 1682–1725), was equally innovative. After surviving murderous power struggles within the imperial family, now the Romanovs, Peter inherited an unstable country as a 17-year-old. He had studied military matters, mathematics, and navigation keenly as a teenager, grew to be 6'8" (2.03 m) tall, and scorned the soft, courtly life. After becoming tsar, he took the extraordinary step of visiting western Europe, and at one point he worked as an apprentice carpenter in a Dutch shipyard to learn the ins and outs of shipbuilding. As an English politician of the seventeenth century so brilliantly put it, "A prince who will not undergo the difficulty of understanding must undergo the danger of trusting." Peter studied hard, undergoing the difficulty of understanding, fearing there were few he could trust.

Like Ivan the Terrible, Peter felt the need to make Russia strong lest its enemies destroy it. Like Ivan, his reforms put Russia through great stress, but left the country more formidable than before. He too put the *boyars* on a short leash, modernized the military, and nourished military industries. (He also killed one of his sons, like Ivan.) Like the Qianlong emperor in China, he encouraged a military culture especially among the elite of society. He built Russia's first real navy and introduced drill into the army. He reined in the power of the Orthodox Church, which had grown politically powerful under weaker tsars, winning for himself the right to appoint bishops. In building a new capital on the Baltic, called St. Petersburg, he gave Russia an outlet to the Baltic Sea as Ivan's conquests had given Russia an outlet on the Caspian Sea. Access to the Baltic brought better trade connections with all of northern Europe and enabled the use of the navy in wars with Russia's Baltic neighbors such as Sweden. Reveling in his conquests, Peter formally declared Russia to be an empire, which indeed it was.

Despite initially controlling little in the way of natural resources beyond timber and furs, the Russian state flourished politically under the tsars. The dedicated and energetic ones found ways to mobilize the population and resources of the country, increase tax

St. Petersburg The Summer Palace in St. Petersburg, built in the early eighteenth century on the banks of the Neva River where it flows into the Baltic Sea, suggests the grandeur that Peter the Great imagined for his new imperial capital.

revenues, control regional elites, and integrate military innovation—especially guns, cannon, army drill, and ships—into the cultural fabric of Russia, all in the service of their own power.

The Habsburg Empire: The First Global Power

The **Habsburgs**, a clan of modest nobles from southwest Germany and Switzerland, managed to join the winner's circle of Eurasian empires through their mastery of the new technologies and techniques of power. In the thirteenth century, good fortune in war added Austria to their domains. Silver from mines in the Austrian Alps helped finance their ambitions. In the fourteenth century, through war and strategic marriages, they garnered new territories here and there in central Europe, creating a patchwork empire with Vienna as its capital. Between 1477 and 1526 they enjoyed a run of excellent political marriages, which brought them Burgundy (a sizeable piece of France), territories in the Low Countries (today's Belgium and the Netherlands), northern Hungary, and Bohemia (the Czech lands). These were comparatively productive provinces. Through another marriage they inherited the kingdom of Spain, a comparatively poor land with about 6 million people.

With Spain came its overseas empire in the Americas and the Philippines. This was worth little at first, but in the 1550s silver began to cascade out of Mexico and the Andes. The windfall was analogous to what the Ottomans enjoyed after taking Egypt with its vast surpluses of grain. By the mid-sixteenth century, the Habsburgs were the strongest dynasty in Europe and a power on the global stage. With territories in Europe, the Americas, and Asia (the Philippines), the Habsburgs count as the first true global power in history, the first empire on which the sun never set.

Habsburg Patrons The Habsburg archduke Leopold Wilhelm (in hat) appears in this 1647 painting in his own art gallery, surrounded by artists and their works. Habsburg patronage of the arts helped burnish their dynasty's prestige.

Soft Power

The Habsburgs became justly famous for finding marriage partners for their eligible princes and princesses that brought new territories to the empire. An irritated king of Hungary wrote of them, "What kingdoms Mars gives to others, Venus gives to thee." The grandmaster of strategic matchmaking was Emperor Maximilian I (r. 1508–1519), who used marriages—his own, his children's, and his grandchildren's—to add Spain, Bohemia, and northern Hungary, and a few other useful slivers of Europe to the Habsburg collection. He would have been especially pleased with his daughter-in-law Anna, who bore 15 children, potential political assets all, before she died at age 44.

In addition to marriages, the Habsburgs used image-making to good effect. As rulers of a hodge-podge of territories, they had to work hard to win their subjects' loyalty. They became champions of the Roman Catholic faith, sometimes militantly so. They paid painters, sculptors, architects, and composers to create art that boosted the reputation of the dynasty. Patronage of the arts was expected of rulers in Europe, as in India or China, and the Habsburgs cannily played that role. In another effort to amass prestige, several of them contrived to be elected as Holy Roman Emperor, linking themselves to the legacy of Charlemagne, who ruled much of Europe and was the first to hold this office. They used every form of soft power to try to burnish their image, inspire loyalty or awe, and thereby reduce their reliance upon brute force to rule.

Hard Power

But they could not neglect hard power. They were full participants in the military revolution of Eurasia. The Spanish branch of the Habsburgs built an oceanic navy in the sixteenth century and took part in all the innovations of marine warfare. They also oversaw the creation of infantry units called *tercios* that combined musketeers and pikemen to become Europe's most feared soldiers. Pikemen wielded long spears and were effective in protecting musketeers from cavalry charges. In the Austrian domains, Maximilian took a special interest in developing a formidable body of infantry, the *Landsknechte*, German mercenaries who fought in most central European Habsburg campaigns. Until about 1650, the Habsburg army still consisted largely of units recruited by private entrepreneurs and rented out to monarchs. The Habsburgs, like the Ottomans and the Mughals, fielded larger and larger armies. Habsburg military architects and commanders mastered the expensive business of building fortresses and the use of field artillery. Their many wars with the Ottomans, France, and other powers ensured that they kept up to date on military technology and technique.

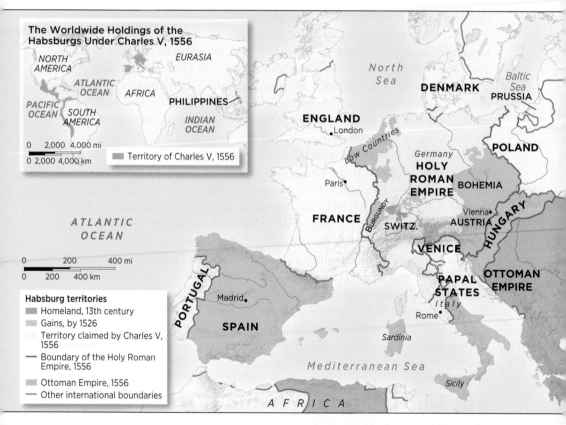

The Growth of Habsburg Territories, Thirteenth through Sixteenth Centuries The Habsburgs built an unusual empire consisting of scattered territories throughout central Europe, soon supplemented in the sixteenth century by others in western Europe, the Americas, and the Philippines. The Habsburgs, like the other great powers of the early modern world, adopted most of the innovations of the Eurasian military revolution to acquire their new lands and defend a stable frontier against their great rival, the Ottomans.

The Habsburgs needed all the military power and money they could get to wage war. There were rebellions to stamp out. There were religious wars to fight, against Protestants and against Muslims, to protect the interests of Catholicism. And there were dynastic wars to fight in the interest of the Habsburg family. Through the sixteenth century, these wars more often than not went well for the Habsburgs. After 1620 or so they went less well and the dynasty reeled from crisis to crisis, almost collapsing a few times. But fortunately for the Habsburgs, their most formidable neighbor, the Ottomans, also faced many crises after 1620.

A Patchwork Empire

The patchwork character of most of their empire made the Habsburgs more dependent than most rulers upon the consent of their elites. They could not easily launch aggressive wars, unlike the Ottoman sultans or Qing emperors. They could rally all the many kings, princes, dukes, and counts—nominally their subjects—for defensive wars and could often build coalitions among neighbors to resist the Ottomans or France when it became powerful. After the 1520s, the Spanish and the Austrian parts of the dynasty ruled their domains separately, more allies than a single state. The Habsburgs never achieved the cohesion within their empire that smaller European states, or the Qing, the Ottomans, or Russia's Romanovs, managed.

Nonetheless, between the 1530s and 1556, Charles V, both king of Spain and Holy Roman Emperor, almost became emperor of all Europe. Several of the world's other big concentrations of population were undergoing violent unification in the sixteenth century: Japan, India, and, under the Ottomans, the eastern Mediterranean. China remained unified, and when it fragmented in the early seventeenth century the Qing soon put it back together again. The Habsburgs made a bid to be the unifiers of Europe. They tried to crush Protestant princes in Germany, drive the Ottomans back in southeastern Europe, and defeat a rival dynasty, the Valois, in France. Charles V financed, directed, and in cases personally fought in these campaigns. In the end, his enemies made common cause against him, and he could not pull it off. He abdicated his thrones in 1556 and died three years later. The Habsburgs remained a major power in Europe until 1918, but never again could they realistically consider creating a pan-European empire.

The University of War and the Rise of Europe

Nor could anyone else create a pan-European empire. Europe remained a cockpit of pitiless political competition. It was, as one Dutch observer put it, a **"university of war."** In this respect it resembled China of the Warring States period (771–256 BCE) before its first unification, or, on a much smaller scale, the independent, rivalrous Greek city-states of the fifth century BCE. These were terrible circumstances in which to live. War, rapine, and epidemics (many of them associated with armies at war) flourished in Europe.

Military Competition and State Power

One result of this constant military competition was a gradual growth in the power of surviving European states. Many small ones disappeared, absorbed by the Habsburgs, the Ottomans, the French, the English, the Swedes, the Prussians, or the Russians. But, despite Charles V's best efforts, none of these successful states could destroy all others, establish an empire across the entire region, enforce peace at home, and confine warfare to its frontiers, as did the Qing in East Asia, the Mughals in South Asia, and the Ottomans in the lands around the eastern Mediterranean. Europe, in the sixteenth through the eighteenth centuries, was out of step with the other major population centers of Eurasia because competition among near equals prevailed.

This university of war provided strong incentives for every ruler to maximize the efficiency of revenue collection and military operations. Those who were not successful in these tasks were typically crushed by their neighbors. So European states were forced to get better and better at taxing their subjects and fighting their neighbors. This brutal pressure lasted for centuries—unlike the situation for the Qing and the Mughals, whose success at unification and expansion meant they no longer had to compete with equals. By 1750, this unusual circumstance enabled a handful of European states—Spain, France, the Netherlands, Prussia, Habsburg Austria, and Britain—to attain world-class efficiency in taxing and fighting.

Political Fragmentation and Global Reach

As we've seen, world history includes several examples of regions divided politically and engulfed in ceaseless warfare. But early modern Europe was unique in the combination of political fragmentation with global reach, global knowledge, and low information costs because of printing. Their maritime prowess and their role in weaving the first Global web gave Europeans access to information from all over the world. They quickly learned of best practices in use elsewhere. If Italian architects showed there was a better way to build a fortress, other Europeans learned about it quickly. If Ottoman commanders showed there was a better way to combine light cavalry, field artillery, and disciplined infantry, Europeans learned about it quickly. The terrible experience of incessant war and chaos in Europe during the sixteenth through the eighteenth centuries provided states strong incentives to learn and adapt. These early modern advances helped set the stage for European global power in the nineteenth and twentieth centuries.

The Rise of Big States: Leadership or Circumstance?

The early modern centuries raise a question that has long divided historians: how much importance to give to individuals in shaping history. It may seem that the big empires prospered because they had a run of great emperors—Kangxi and Qianlong, Ivan the Terrible and Peter the Great, Akbar and Aurangzeb, Mehmet and Suleiman, Maximilian I and Charles V—all men of intellect, vision, ambition, and political savvy. Seen from the perspective of a single state or empire, that conclusion appears hard to dispute.

But if one steps back and takes a world history perspective, another possibility appears: it could be that the greatness of these emperors was owing mainly to the situations of their rule. They all came to power when circumstances, especially those connected to the exercise of military power, favored big states. They could expand at the expense of little states more easily than at most times in history. While conquests lasted, these emperors had the prestige, revenue, land, and armed power to keep their subjects in line and negotiate with regional elites through strength—and generosity if they wished. So the extraordinary longevity and political success of an Akbar, Suleiman, or Kangxi can in part be explained by the circumstances of their historical moment.

Responses of the Smaller Powers

While the Qing, the Mughals, the Ottomans, the Russians, and the Habsburgs became the biggest of the big fish, they did not devour all the little fish. Smaller states could survive by playing the great powers off against one another, although this was a hazardous game that required skill and luck. To succeed, the small fish had to embrace at least parts of the military revolution—streamlining tax collection and improving their bureaucracies and militaries. Let's look briefly at some that did—and some that didn't.

Iran and Southeast Asia

Some were successful. The Safavids in Iran, sandwiched uncomfortably between the Ottomans and the Mughals, faced enormous pressure to keep up with their neighbors' military innovations. They had to transition from a strictly cavalry-based military (defeated by the gun-using Ottomans in 1514) to one that used the full arsenal of the military revolution: gun-wielding infantry, field artillery, fortresses, as well as cavalry. And they had to raise all the money they could to finance campaigns, which they accomplished in part by promoting and taxing long-distance trade in silks, silver, and porcelain through their territory. The Safavids survived in power until 1736.

Smaller powers elsewhere survived, and often grew larger and more powerful, by modernizing their militaries and boosting their revenues. In Southeast Asia, Vietnam, after suffering invasion by the forces of Ming China early in the fifteenth century, adopted firearms and used them effectively against its neighbors. Other small kingdoms such as Burma and Thailand took shape and prospered at the expense of their immediate neighbors. In Burma, firearms and centralization of taxation helped to build the Toungoo dynasty (1510–1752) into the largest empire in the history of Southeast Asia for a few decades (ca. 1540–1580). In the late seventeenth century, a kingdom in Thailand briefly attained similar success after imitating Burmese military methods and securing access to weaponry from European merchants trading in the Indian Ocean.

Kongo and Morocco

In Africa, a few states such as Kongo or Morocco took advantage of new opportunities presented by firearms to build their power. Kongo, as we've seen, was a major participant in the transatlantic slave trade. Through contacts with Europeans, mainly Portuguese, the kings of Kongo maintained a privileged position (not quite a monopoly) on imported guns. That gave them the power to attack and enslave neighboring peoples and to make their kingdom the most powerful in southern Africa in the seventeenth century.

In Morocco in the sixteenth century, ambitious dynasts called the **Saadians** used revenues from trans-Saharan trade and sugar plantations to build their power. They studied Ottoman military tactics and acquired firearms and, from England, cannon. They demolished a Portuguese assault in 1578, and in 1591 sent an expedition across the Sahara to the Middle Niger to crush the last of the great West African Sahel states, called Songhai. The Songhai Empire had ruled for about a century, had centralized its bureaucracy and military, but did not adopt firearms. Gunpowder weapons were decisive in the encounter between the Saadian army and Songhai.

The Moroccans, aware of their military advantages, were probably aiming to control the West African goldfields, and perhaps to create a caliphate to rival the Ottomans. They achieved neither. Moroccan troops died quickly of diseases along the Niger; and although they held the cities for many years, they could not end resistance and never came close to the goldfields. One Saadian ruler, al-Mansur, in 1601 proposed to England's Queen Elizabeth I that they should join forces and divide Spain's American empire between them. Unable to corner West Africa's gold, he set his sights on Spanish America's silver. His plan came to nothing. Mastery of firearms enabled the Saadians to unify Morocco, destroy enemies across the Sahara, and dream of greater conquests—but firearms alone could not guarantee that those dreams would come true.

Moroccan Battles A seventeenth-century engraving shows Moroccan troops (right) facing off against Portuguese opponents (left) during the unsuccessful 1578 Portuguese invasion.

North America and Hawaii

In North America, several Amerindian peoples exploited the potential of firearms to strengthen themselves and assault their neighbors. The most successful examples came in the nineteenth century, when Plains Indians confederacies, the Comanche and the Lakota Sioux, for example, built up power through access to guns and horses. As we saw in Chapter 17, in Hawaii King Kamehameha forged his kingdom with the help of a monopoly on imported firearms.

From Hawaii to Morocco to Burma, the same broad pattern prevailed. Local states were created or expanded through prudent adoption of new technologies and techniques of warfare. An edge, even if temporary, in military formidability enabled ambitious rulers to extend their domains. Obtaining such an edge was much easier in times of flux, when technologies and techniques were changing faster than usual. The resulting states and empires were often fleeting, as neighbors formed coalitions or adopted new and effective military techniques and technologies themselves.

The broad pattern was a smaller-scale version of the pattern among the great Eurasian powers from the Qing to the Habsburgs: the big got bigger because they were better able to realize the potential of expensive new technologies and techniques. Kamehameha I was not a big chief in global terms, but he was in his own neighborhood of the Hawaiian Islands. And he used the opportunity that presented, once firearms were introduced, to get bigger, make himself a king, and dominate the archipelago, as Oda Nobunaga and Hideyoshi did in the Japanese islands and the Mughals in their (larger) neighborhood, or the Ottomans in theirs.

The Costs of Maintaining Tradition: Poland and Egypt's Mamluk Sultanate

The costs of not following the trend are illustrated by the case of the Polish-Lithuanian Commonwealth (Poland for short). Poland took shape in the fifteenth century, officially merged with the Grand Duchy of Lithuania in 1569, and enjoyed its greatest power in the mid-seventeenth century. Its kings were elected by members of the nobility, who tenaciously guarded their liberties from central control. The Polish military relied on cavalry composed chiefly of nobles, which proved effective against Muscovy, Sweden, and the Ottomans, if less so against Tatar raiders. The Polish nobility kept alive traditions of chivalry long after other states had built up large infantries composed of peasants and had invested in fortresses, artillery, and navies. The Polish elite long resisted these trends: it did not wish to help pay for fortresses and ships, nor did it want to see common foot soldiers or the architects of fortresses siphon off any prestige or glory. One Polish nobleman dismissed siege warfare as "mole's work." The nobles particularly did not wish to see the king equipped with a standing army, rightly fearing that kings with armies would trample upon the nobility's liberties.

Unfortunately for the liberty-loving Polish elite, by 1690 their military did not match, in size or technique, that of Russia or the Habsburgs, and gallant cavalry charges could not make up for that. Their decentralized, consensual political system prevented the military and fiscal reforms that might have preserved their state. Between 1772 and 1795, Poland's neighbors—Russia, Prussia, and Habsburg Austria—partitioned it three times.

The Polish nobility was not alone in clinging to cherished traditions. Slave soldiers of the Mamluk sultanate, based in Egypt, did so too with similar consequences. In the thirteenth century, Mamluk forces had defeated the Mongols (1260) and become the most powerful military in the Islamic world. The sultans' soldiers mastered archery, swordsmanship, and horsemanship. But their commitment to, and success with, these skills and weapons led them to scorn firearms. When one sultan organized a corps of infantry with muskets in 1498, the slave soldiers attacked it. In 1516–1517, Ottoman armies using all manner of firearms crushed the Mamluks and took Egypt.

The Mamluk and Polish-Lithuanian cases show the dangers of disdaining military modernization in a time of rapid change. In both, elites—whether nobles or slave soldiers—prized their identity as skilled horsemen and the status that conferred, and could not contemplate adjusting to the times.

Nomads and Pirates in a World of Expanding States

The broad pattern of centralization and expansion of state power through fiscal and military reform was hard on smaller states, but harder still on nomads and pirates. On the world's grasslands and seas, nomad confederations and pirate gangs were for many centuries important political and military forces. But between 1650 and 1890, their power was decisively broken by the armies and navies of agrarian states. Nomads and pirates still existed afterward, but never again exercised much influence in history.

Nomad Power

Nomads—or more properly, mobile pastoralists—had operated on the grassy steppes of Asia and North Africa for millennia, and as we have seen time and again, they interacted both peacefully and violently with settled, agrarian populations and states. They often enjoyed considerable political and military power, thanks to their mobility and their capacities for surprise attack and tactical retreat. They could, when unified, defeat great empires. During the tenth through the thirteenth centuries, steppe pastoralists took over China, North India, and Iran, and North African pastoralists did roughly the same in Morocco and Egypt.

Nomads (Left) A large-scale painting executed collaboratively by Chinese and European painters shows Qing forces decisively defeating the nomadic Zunghars in their camp. (Right) In the United States, in 1876 Lakota Sioux, Cheyenne, and Arapaho forces defeated U.S. troops at the Battle of Little Bighorn, as this 1900 image by Lakota artist Amos Bad Heart Buffalo records—but they ultimately lost the war.

But by the seventeenth and eighteenth centuries, settled agrarian states were re-inventing themselves and the nomads could not follow suit. Mobile peoples could not develop more efficient tax collection, manufacture cannon, build elaborate fortifications, or add navies to their arsenals. They became increasingly dependent upon agrarian empires and less menacing to them. Their fighters more often served kings and emperors as auxiliary cavalry in exchange for cash, cloth, food, or weaponry. The Russians and Ottomans, for example, made good use of steppe peoples such as the Tatars. The Ming and the Qing hired Mongols to do some of their fighting for them. But the steppe warriors sometimes proved disobedient and dangerous allies, leading decision makers in Beijing or Istanbul to conclude that it would be wiser to crush pastoralists than to continue to risk keeping them in service and supplied with weaponry.

So, roughly between 1700 and 1850, hundreds of campaigns, small and large, took place from Manchuria to Morocco in which emperors and kings sent their armies against pastoralists and nomads. They built strings of forts in the steppes and deserts. Their armies at times managed to surround or trap a group of nomads and disarm them, slaughter them, or sell them into slavery. Guns played a role in this—although nomads often had guns too—but logistics, money, and manpower played larger ones. The Saadians, Ottomans, Russians, Safavids, Mughals, and Qing all mounted intermittent wars against nomads and pastoralists. The last large-scale confederacy of nomads was that of the Zunghars in Mongolia, about 750,000 people, which was crushed militarily and then slaughtered by the Qing in the 1750s.

On a smaller scale, and in a compressed time frame, a similar saga played out in the Americas. With the introduction of horses and guns, after 1800 peoples such as the Comanche and Lakota Sioux created mobile and militarized ways of life that bore some resemblance to that of steppe peoples in Asia. The Comanche and Lakota Sioux were not pastoralists on any scale; they did not keep livestock except horses. They lived more by hunting than stock raising. But they became a political force in North America and terrorized settled, farming peoples—mainly other Amerindians—with frequent brutal raids.

In South America, horse cultures arose in northern Patagonia during the seventeenth and eighteenth centuries among peoples such as the Tehuelche. They took to hunting guanacos (close relatives of llamas) and rheas (big flightless birds), raising cattle and sheep, and raiding neighboring settlements. They used lances, guns, and a weapon called the bolo, two stones tied together with a hide rope, in hunting and warfare. The basis of their newfound power, as for the Comanche and Lakota Sioux, was the mobility conferred by horses.

The age of nomad (or semi-nomad) power in the Americas came late compared to Asia and North Africa, beginning only in the eighteenth or nineteenth century. It ended in the second half of the nineteenth century, when the armies of settled agrarian societies—Argentina, Chile, Mexico, the United States, Canada—crushed the last remnants of nomad power in world history. This after-echo of the Qing obliteration of Zunghar power brought to a close a 3,000-year epoch in world history in which nomads and mobile pastoralists were a force to be reckoned with.

The relentless competition among agrarian states, their swift exchange (often unwilling) of information about the technologies and techniques of warfare, and their growth in size and capacity—all directly or indirectly resulting from the tightening of the Global web—spelled the end for nomads. They could not keep up with their agrarian neighbors, and their courage, horsemanship, and marksmanship no longer mattered.

Pirates

Pirates played a far smaller role in world history. They probably existed even earlier than mobile pastoralists, from soon after the beginning of waterborne trade. Conditions generally suited pirates best when and where long-distance seaborne trade flourished, navies were weak, and at least a few good bays or inlets with minimal population could serve as bases. Access to markets was also important for piracy: when pirates grabbed a cargo of porcelain or sugar, they couldn't use much of it themselves and needed to sell it for money or swap it for what they wanted.

The early centuries of the Global web were a golden age for pirates. The linking up of the world's coastlines by European mariners led to a vast expansion in long-distance maritime trade. Port cities everywhere did a thriving business, and stolen cargoes could find ready buyers. Navies remained too small to patrol the world's oceans, leaving extensive safe space for pirates. Navies were so weak that in wartime they often inadvertently created pirates by recruiting sailors to assault enemy shipping—they were called privateers. In peacetime privateers were out of work, and many chose to stay afloat as pirates. The distinctions between pirate and privateer were sometimes fuzzy.

The Caribbean and Indian Ocean   Although pirates might roam anywhere, they preferred certain locations. The Caribbean met their requirements nicely, and from the 1550s to the 1720s it was a hotbed of piracy and privateering. Spanish ships bearing silver exports from Mexico passed through the Caribbean, attracting pirates and privateers such as the Dutch privateer Piet Heyn, who captured a silver fleet off of Cuba's coast in 1628. Bartholomew Roberts, a Welsh-born pirate, captured 400 merchant ships in the Atlantic and Caribbean between 1719 and 1722. In the early eighteenth century, about one-third of pirates were Africans or of African descent, and at least two—Mary Read and Anne Bonny—were women.

The Indian Ocean, from the Red Sea to the Straits of Malacca, also presented pirates with splendid opportunities. These were exploited both by interlopers from the Atlantic, such as the Scottish-born Captain Kidd who built a base in Madagascar, and by locals, such as the Arakan (or Magh) pirates based on the shores of Burma who feasted on Bengali shipping and coastal settlements. Even better hunting grounds for pirates lay in the South and East China seas. The largest-scale pirate operation was that of the Zheng family on the southeastern coasts of China from Nanjing to Macao, the story of which began this chapter.

The Barbary Pirates   Other large operations were based in the North African cities of Algiers, Tunis, and Tripoli from the sixteenth century onward. The Mediterranean suited pirates because of its abundant shipping and lively slave markets where captives could be sold. With Ottoman encouragement, local officials, called *beys*, organized pirate/privateer forces to prey on shipping and coastal settlements mainly in Spain and Italy. The Barbary pirates, as they are known, sought cargoes and Christian captives to sell in North African markets. By one estimate, over the years from 1500 to 1800 they seized and enslaved about 1 million captives. On occasion they ventured farther afield, raiding Iceland in 1627, Ireland in 1631, and even the coast of Argentina in 1720. The Barbary pirates were at the height of their power in the early and mid-seventeenth century. Moroccan rulers offered similar support for pirates/privateers operating in eastern Atlantic waters from their base in Salé.

Christian kingdoms such as Spain and France encouraged European piracy and privateering against North African shipping and ports, and by 1630 used their navies against the Barbary pirates with some effect. But they did not yet have the power to close them down. Piracy flared up in the 1780s and 1790s, and now the targets included American merchant ships in the Mediterranean. For several years, the U.S. government paid protection money to get the pirates to desist—as much as 20 percent of the U.S. federal budget in 1800. The United States launched attacks in 1805 and 1815, and a British-Dutch force bombarded North African ports in 1816. By 1830 the naval power of their foes had become too great and the Barbary pirates were just about out of business.

The same fate befell pirates elsewhere. The Mughals routed pirates from their coastal lairs, mainly in Bengal and Burma, in the seventeenth century. British naval power largely eliminated pirates in the Caribbean by 1730. Everywhere around the world, from Taiwan to Jamaica, pirates were hunted down and piracy declined. It did not entirely disappear—indeed, a few pirates are active today in the Arabian Sea and Southeast Asian waters—but they never again attained anything like the power and wealth of the Zhengs or the *beys* of North Africa. Like the mobile pastoralists, the pirates of the world ran afoul of the ever-growing power of big empires.

Conclusion

The turmoil of the early modern centuries may seem a confusing blur of wars won and lost, dynasties rising and falling, states and empires appearing and vanishing, but there is a general pattern behind it. If one steps back from the details, it is possible to see a brutal political shakeout in which a few polities prospered and many disappeared. This pattern showed up more strongly in Eurasia than elsewhere, but it can also be found on smaller scales in places such as Hawaii and Morocco. As the technologies and techniques of war and power grew more complex and costly, the big got bigger, usually at the expense of the small. A handful of empires dominated Eurasia, and increasingly—a development without precedent in world history—the whole world.

The history of war and empire in these centuries reveals two other significant developments. First is the eccentricity of Europe. Despite the Habsburgs' best efforts, no state could build a pan-European empire. The other great centers of population in Eurasia—China, North India, and the Ottoman lands—all became the seats of gigantic empires far stronger than most of their frontier neighbors. Europe's eccentricity led to relentless competition—the university of war—and, in the long run, to stronger, more efficient, more formidable states. It also led to exceedingly difficult times for ordinary people caught up in the maelstrom. This peculiarity, combined with the access Atlantic Europeans had to information and commercial opportunity all over the world, helps to explain the rise of European power, specifically the Atlantic European powers, in the global political arena.

The second notable development was the destruction of nomad power and the marginalization of piracy. In the eighteenth and early nineteenth centuries, the big states developed sufficient capacity—logistics more than firepower—to abandon their at times cozy relations with nomads and pirates and to turn forcefully against them. This simplified international politics, by reducing the role of non-state actors and leaving the stage, increasingly, to a smaller number of bigger players.

Part of the reason for the general pattern of consolidation of power around the world came from a quickening of world trade in the early modern centuries. Ships and caravans carried valuable goods and money—often, silver from the Americas or Japan. Any ruler could take a cut, and those located at choke points on long-distance routes could take big ones. In the next chapter we will see how this came to pass by turning to the new global economy made possible by the formation of a truly global web.

Chapter Review

KEY TERMS

military revolution p. 710

field artillery and fortification p. 712

Oda Nobunaga p. 715

Toyotomi Hideyoshi p. 715

Tokugawa shogunate p. 716

Qing dynasty p. 718

Akbar p. 721

Istanbul p. 726

janissaries p. 728

millet system p. 729

imperial consolidation p. 729

tsar p. 730

Habsburgs p. 733

university of war p. 736

Saadians p. 739

pirates p. 743

REVIEW QUESTIONS

1. What is the main reason that large imperial states were able to destroy hundreds of smaller states during the early modern period?

2. What six trends making up the military revolution caused warfare to become more complex and expensive?

3. How did Oda Nobunaga and his successors use guns to unify Japan?

4. Identify the Qing's most successful military innovations, and explain what was unique about these initiatives.

5. What military, religious, and economic techniques did the Mughals employ to consolidate power?

6. Describe how Istanbul, Egypt, the Hejaz, Mesopotamia, and Hungary contributed to Ottoman power.

7. What social, political, and military reforms did Ivan the Terrible and Peter the Great introduce in Russia?

8. What were the main forms of soft power the Habsburgs employed to expand their power in Europe?

9. How did constant political competition in Europe affect successful European states?

10. Explain the main technologies and techniques that small states adopted in order to survive.

11. What was the contribution of the elite class to the downfall of Poland and the Mamluk sultanate?

12. Why did the relationship between nomads and agrarian states change during the early modern period?

13. What was the chief reason for the loss of power among pirates?

14. What two significant developments does the history of war and empire in the early modern period reveal?

Go to INQUIZITIVE

to see what you've learned—and learn what you've missed—with personalized feedback along the way.

||||||||||||||||||||||||||||||||||||||||||||||||

20

||||||||||||||||||||||||||||||||||||||||||||||||

The First Global Economy

1500 to 1800

FOCUS QUESTIONS

....

1. What broad factors drove the increases in world population and economic growth between 1500 and 1800?

2. What evidence is there that economic growth in this period mainly benefited elites?

3. How did the spice, cotton, and silver trades help integrate the global economy?

4. What was the significance of the new business formats that emerged during this period?

5. Which world regions experienced commercial revolutions, and why?

Jakob Fugger (1459–1525) and Virji Vora (ca. 1590–1670) knew how to make money. When Fugger died, his net worth was equivalent to about 2 percent of Europe's total annual economic output. Vora's trading partners reckoned he was the richest man in the world. Both men had acquired the knowledge and contacts to take full advantage of two recent changes that came with the formation of a truly global web: rulers' growing need to borrow money for wars (discussed in Chapter 19) and the expanding scale of long-distance trade.

Fugger was the tenth of eleven children in a merchant family in Augsburg in southern Germany. At age 14 he was sent to represent his family's business in Venice, and he ended up living there for 14 years. Most of his older brothers died young, and he took over the family business, shifting its focus from textiles to mining. He invested in copper and silver mines all over central Europe and traded copper to markets as far away as Russia and India. He also invested in a successful voyage from Portugal to India that returned with cargoes of spices. But his core business was mining, and he eventually controlled most of Europe's copper output.

Banking became another core business for Fugger. He made loans to dukes, emperors, and popes. He financed the rise of the House of Habsburg. He paid for the Pope's Swiss guards. Fugger earned interest on his loans and also the cooperation of the powerful, which he used to win control over more mines throughout Habsburg Europe. Mining, banking, and political influence underlay Fugger's success.

A similar formula worked for Virji Vora a century and a half later. Trade, banking, and political influence underpinned his prosperity. He was probably a Jain and lived in Surat, in northwest India. He first appears in the written record in 1619 and for the next half-century figured prominently in Indian commerce of almost every variety. Commodity trading was a core business for Vora. Documents record him either buying or selling cloth, silver, gold, mercury, lead, pearls, diamonds, rubies, ivory, tea, opium, indigo, coral, and many kinds of spices. His agents had offices in eight Indian cities and as far afield as the shores of the Persian Gulf, the Red Sea, and Malacca in Southeast Asia. He was a master of cornering a market—buying up the entire supply of a certain good and then re-selling it on his own terms. He dominated trade with English, Dutch, and French merchants, who often complained of his business tactics.

Like Fugger, Vora was also a banker. He lent money to aristocrats of the Mughal court and to Mughal governors. He lent to European traders, even while he competed with them. Like Fugger,

CHRONOLOGY

1490s Portuguese mariners settle São Tomé

1511 Portugese defeat the Muslim sultanate of Malacca

1520s–1540s Silver strikes in Japan

1530s Portuguese introduce sugar plantations in northeastern Brazil

1545–1558 Silver strikes in Mexico

1550s Sultan of Aceh begins to compete with Portuguese spice merchants

1555 English Muscovy Company founded

1560s Ming China rescinds foreign trade band

1570s Ming China requires everyone to pay taxes in silver

1590s Brazil leads world's sugar production

1602–1799 Dutch East India Company (VOC)

1609 Bank of Amsterdam founded

1621 Japanese silver production peaks

By 1640s Sugar and slavery are booming in Caribbean

1684–1715 Shipping from south China to Manila triples

1720 British Parliament forbids the wearing and use of imported calico cloth

ca. 1750 China has enough silver in circulation to satisfy demand

1750–1800 Laborers' wages in Beijing, Delhi, and Florence bottom out

1760 Tacky's War in Jamaica threatens plantation regime

he translated his banking role into favors from politically powerful people, both Mughal officials and those of the English East India Company.

Both Fugger and Vora became immensely rich at a time when—as we shall see—most people around them were poor and getting poorer. These men exploited their knowledge of distant markets and prices and their connections with rising political powers, taking advantage of opportunities presented by changes in the world economy.

This chapter takes up economic history in the sixteenth to the eighteenth centuries. It begins with some data about global population, economic growth, and welfare. It emphasizes the big changes—for example, the rise of long-distance trades in spices, cotton, and silver. It also emphasizes the innovative features of the world's economy, including business and financial organizations such as large-scale slave plantations, joint-stock companies, and banks. In focusing on long-distance trade and innovation, the chapter tilts toward the European experience, because Europeans, mainly Atlantic Europeans, specialized in intercontinental trade and in innovative business organizations. This was no accident: long-distance trade encouraged novel business formats, and novel business formats eased long-distance trade.

For all this economic history to make sense, we need to remember three points in particular. First, that for several millennia before 1500, Southwest Asia was the region most connected to the world's largest web—the Old World web. That region stood at the center of connections among the northern half of Africa, South and Southeast Asia, Europe, and the Mediterranean. It lay close to the steppe corridor of Eurasia. The least well connected regions in the Old World web were probably Siberia, the interior of sub-Saharan Africa, and the European subcontinent. But after the 1490s, as we've seen, all that changed and Atlantic Europe became the best-connected place on Earth.

The second point to remember is that Atlantic European mariners and merchants had forged most of the intercontinental connections after 1490. This gave them an information edge that translated into more available technologies for adoption, and more opportunities for profit based on knowledge of prices in different markets. This information edge, combined with the military advantage of shipboard cannon, goes far toward explaining the rising prominence of Atlantic European societies and states in global economic history after 1500. Atlantic Europeans were not richer than everyone else in 1500. But they, more than anyone else, changed the course of economic history in the three centuries after 1500. And, very gradually, their societies began to grow richer faster than others around the world. To put this another way, Atlantic Europeans took the lead in forming the Global web and knitting it together with trade. They derived greater wealth and power from it than anyone else between 1500 and 1800.

The third point to remember is that despite the long-distance trade and economic innovations, most people between 1500 and 1800 lived much as their ancestors had for centuries. Whether in China, Russia, West Africa, Scotland, or Peru, most people lived in villages, farmed for a living, ate most of what they produced, and rarely ventured far from home. Their economic existence—indeed, their entire existence—was precarious. It depended on the weather and the harvest, as well as the health of their animals (if they had any) and of the able-bodied members of their families. If they were free people, as most were, they turned over a bit of what their hard work produced to landlords or tax collectors, or both. The unfree—whether slaves, serfs, indentured laborers, or in some other bonded status—turned over most of what their work produced to lords and masters. Some of these people, both free and unfree, did additional work on the side, especially in the slack seasons of the farming year, perhaps making cloth or cutting timber. Few of them used money regularly, knew about the business empires of men like Fugger or Vora, or were aware of the commercial webs spanning the globe.

Of course, most people's lives were not exactly the same as their ancestors'. They might raise different crops or animals, perhaps ones newly introduced via the Columbian Exchange. Some technological improvements took place on farms during these three centuries—perhaps most important, in the means of draining swampland. A slightly larger proportion of farming families sold some of their harvest or even all of it. A few million people worked to produce spices, cotton, silk, sugar, tea, tobacco, or some other agricultural commodity that someone else traded to distant markets, a way of life rare among their ancestors. And a small but growing proportion did no farmwork and specialized in other tasks, such as spinning cotton or mining silver. But for most people alive before 1800, the routines of life changed little and slowly and remained centered on farming. Nonetheless, this chapter will focus on the new developments in economic life that changed the course of world history.

World Population and the Global Economy

Despite some terrible demographic catastrophes, in the three centuries between 1500 and 1800 global population more than doubled. Although slow by the standards of our time, this growth was faster than in any previous era of world history. Improvements in agriculture and food supply helped spark the **population surge**. The Columbian Exchange enabled farmers to raise crops well suited to their local environments that had not been available before, such as maize in Africa or wheat in the Americas. Minor improvements in agricultural technology or practice in some parts of the world also helped. But there were no transformative technical breakthroughs in food production anywhere.

A second reason for the surge was what one historian has called the "microbial unification of the world." As travelers spread pathogens around the globe, the resulting diseases at first had terrible consequences, most notably in the Americas. But over time, populations developed resistance to a wider array of infections than before. More infections became childhood diseases, endemic in communities and only rarely sparking epidemics. No one understood it at the time, but this process of biological adjustment was speeding up by 1700 or 1750.

Global Population Growth, 1500–1800

DATE	GLOBAL POPULATION	AVERAGE ANNUAL GROWTH RATE (ROUNDED)	
1500	438 million		
1600	556 million	0.25%	(1500–1600)
1700	603 million	0.1%	(1600–1700)
1800	950 million	0.6%	(1700–1800)

Source: Angus Maddison, *The World Economy: Historical Statistics* (2003), 256.

As more infections became endemic, they killed children without immunities even if antibodies now protected more disease-experienced adults. As before, families had to expect about half their children would die of disease before reaching adulthood. So they did their best to produce plenty of them, and fertility rates stayed high in most societies. Globally, mortality diminished slightly between 1500 and 1800. Before 1800, medical improvements remained trivial everywhere in their demographic impact.

The table above gives a rough idea of the trajectory of world population growth over these three centuries. Bear in mind the figures are educated guesswork.

The sixteenth century, as we have seen, was catastrophic for many Amerindian peoples. But elsewhere, as best we can judge, populations grew despite repeated epidemics and famines. In Europe and China, where the estimates are more reliable than elsewhere, that was clearly true. Population levels recovered from the losses of the fourteenth-century plague pandemic and kept growing briskly.

But the seventeenth century saw slower growth due mainly to enormous disasters. In the Americas, the effects of imported and unfamiliar diseases such as smallpox, measles, influenza, and malaria were still making themselves felt. More broadly, the seventeenth century brought the chilliest and driest years of the Little Ice Age. The years between 1618 and 1697 were ones of recurrent crisis in food supplies, the result mainly of a cluster of volcanic eruptions and their "dust veils." Sharp cold snaps and repeated droughts led to crop failures and starvation, resulting in more epidemics (worsened by malnutrition) and more warfare than normal. Political violence spiked in China, where the invading Manchus battled the collapsing Ming dynasty; in Ottoman lands, unsettled by internal rebellions; and in Europe, with its bloody religious wars and rebellions. In Gujarat and the Deccan, in India, an official Mughal chronicle described severe famines:

> ... [A] perfect drought prevailed.... [H]igh and low were clamouring for their bread and dying from sheer exhaustion.... the streets and marketplaces were so thronged by the immense number of corpses that [one] could scarcely make [one's] way through them.

More broadly, infanticide and suicide apparently peaked in several societies around the world during the seventeenth century. On a global basis, the 1640s were probably the worst decade for humankind since the plague pandemic of the 1340s.

A Population Landmark

The eighteenth century, in contrast, brought faster population growth than our species had ever before experienced. China more than doubled its population, a result partly of the spread of American food crops such as sweet potatoes and maize, but also of a reduction in deadly epidemics and political violence. In the Americas, the ravages of introduced diseases abated and millions of immigrants—mostly enslaved Africans—arrived. Europe's population increased by roughly 50 percent, with Ireland's growing the fastest. It more than doubled to about 5 million, fueled by the introduction of the potato from the Americas, a crop that suited Irish conditions well and allowed a family to survive—in poverty—on a small patch of land. The populations of India, Southwest Asia, and Africa grew more slowly—in Africa's case, probably by very little compared to China, the Americas, and Europe. Nobody knew it at the time, but in the eighteenth century the world began its modern rise of population that is still ongoing. From about 1750, if not a decade or two before, growth rates tilted upward at steeper and steeper rates through the late twentieth century, as we will see.

The Size of the World Economy

The size of the world economy, the total value of goods and services produced, is called the **gross world product**, or GWP. We have only educated guesses of GWP, but by 1500 those estimates become more reliable.

So let's look at the numbers. The table below uses index numbers, with GWP in 1500 set at 100. (GWP in later years is presented relative to GWP in 1500—so a value of 150 in the year 1700 means the economy was half again as large as in 1500.) In today's money, the size of the world economy in 1500 was about U.S. $250 billion, equivalent to that of Louisiana or Finland or Bangladesh in 2018.

The world economy more than doubled in size between 1500 and 1800. It grew by about one-third in the sixteenth century, probably a record at that time. The seventeenth century, marked by crop failures, epidemics, and mass violence, posted a far weaker rate, but the eighteenth century showed resurgent growth.

The growth rates in global population resemble those of GWP, as they should: most economic growth was merely the result of more people living and working. But some of it derived

Gross World Product, 1500–1800

DATE	SIZE	AVERAGE ANNUAL GROWTH RATE (ROUNDED)	
1500	100		
1600	133	0.3%	(1500–1600)
1700	150	0.1%	(1600–1700)
1800	250	0.7%	(1700–1800)

Source: Elaborated from Angus Maddison, *The World Economy: Historical Statistics* (2003), 259.

from small technical advances in farming, and from more important ones in textile manufacturing, mining, and other arenas. A larger spur to economic growth came from the efficiencies of specialization and exchange, whereby more people than before were doing what they did best and trading the fruits of their labor for goods that others produced. After 1500, long-distance trade flourished as never before, quickened by the gradual extension of the Global web into almost every nook and cranny of the globe.

The Distribution of Economic Benefits

But the gains from expansion of trade and technical improvements mainly benefited a fortunate few. There are several ways to estimate how well off people were in the past. Two of the better methods use data on people's heights and incomes. They suggest that although societies in the aggregate grew slightly richer between 1500 and 1800, most people did not.

Incredible Shrinking Humans

Changes in the average heights of populations are a good indication of changes in the childhood nutrition and disease burden in a society. Well-fed and healthy children reach their genetic height potential. Malnourished ones ravaged by chronic disease don't. The raw data on stature generally come from archeology (skeletons) or, more often, records of military recruits. Let's consider some data from around the world on average heights.

The largest sample available comes from northern Europe: Scandinavia, the Netherlands, and Britain. These data in the table below show that on average northern Europeans shrank from medieval times until the late eighteenth century by nearly 3 inches (7.5 cm), with the fastest declines in the seventeenth through the eighteenth centuries. By 1800, northern Europeans were smaller than at any time before or since. This loss of stature is extreme in the annals of human height history. Populations in southern Germany (Bavaria), the Habsburg Empire, and northern Italy also shrank a bit between 1730 and 1780. We don't have earlier data for them.

In Russia, matters were apparently similar. The average height of military

Average Male Heights in Samples from Northern Europe

PERIOD	AVERAGE HEIGHT
9th to 11th century	173.4 centimeters (just under 5'7")
12th to 14th century	171.5 cm
17th to 18th century	167.5 cm
18th century	166.2 cm (or 5'4½")

Source: Richard Steckel, "Health and Nutrition in the Pre-Industrial Era: Insights from a Millennium of Average Heights in Northern Europe," in *Living Standards in the Past: New Perspectives on Well-Being in Asia and Europe*, eds. R. C. Allen, T. Bengtsson, and M. Dribe (2005), 242.

Note: 1 inch = 2.54 cm

recruits, most of whom would not have come up to Peter the Great's armpit, fell during the eighteenth century by 2 inches (5 cm). These were glorious times for Russia's rulers and its elites, who managed to corral the benefits of a growing economy and territorial expansion, but times of grinding hunger and economic hardship for regular people. Russia, like many other places, grew richer in the aggregate and on average, yet at the same time more miserable for most people.

In Mexico, data on army recruits suggest the male population was shorter in 1840 than in 1740 by an average of 1.6 inches (4 cm). Argentine male heights shrank by about half as much in the same years. In both countries, the population and economy grew while stature declined.

In Korea, the only East Asian society for which we have data prior to 1800, army recruits on average grew taller through the sixteenth century and the beginning of the seventeenth, despite the devastating Japanese invasion of Korea in the 1590s. But during the late seventeenth and early eighteenth centuries, recruits lost 1.6 inches (4 cm) in height on average.

All these cases of declining average heights reflect poorer nutrition and heavier burdens of stunting diseases. The main reason for these trends was probably lower protein supply for children. Urbanization may also have played a role: city folk everywhere averaged an inch or two shorter than their country cousins, again a reflection of nutrition and disease.

Army recruit records only pertain to men. If we had more data for women, they would probably show just as much, or even more, loss of stature during the period from 1500 to 1800. In most cultures, when families were short of food, they usually gave more to boys than to girls—as remains true today where food is scarce.

In British North America, the history of stature tells a different and happier story about nutrition and welfare. The population of European descent grew taller on average between 1710 and 1810, by about 0.8 inches (2 cm). British army recruits born and raised in North American colonies towered over their cousins born in Britain, by about 3 to 5 inches (8 to 12 cm) on average, an indication of the superior nutrition and health in the lands that would become the United States and Canada. Enslaved people's average heights fell slightly before 1800 in the United States, but from 1800 to 1840 average male slave heights climbed 1.5 inches (4 cm) to 5′8½″, suggesting they benefited from improving nutrition in those decades.

Meanwhile, the nutrition experience of Amerindians in North America was mixed. Skeletons show that the Iroquois, Cherokee, Delaware, and Ottawa all grew taller, by about 2 to 3 inches (4 to 7 cm), between 1650 and 1800. President Thomas Jefferson in 1804, upon meeting a delegation of Osage from the Kansas plains, wrote that they were "certainly the most gigantic men we have ever seen." While it is hard to imagine this reflected better nutrition, given the rough fate of Amerindians in these years, it is either that or else short people (and their genes) were ruthlessly weeded out by violence, hunger, and disease, which over a mere 150 years is unlikely.

Probably improved protein supply played a role. To judge by their skeletons, the equestrian buffalo hunters of the plains were the tallest and healthiest Amerindian populations anywhere in the Americas. Indeed, by the mid-nineteenth century, Plains Indians were the tallest people in the world for whom data exist, probably a reflection of a meat-rich diet. In contrast, Amerindians who clustered around Spanish missions in California shrank, especially males. That probably registers a change of boys' diet toward cereals and away from meat. Just as human populations in the deeper past shrank when they transitioned from hunting and foraging to farming, so, perhaps, the buffalo hunters of the plains grew in stature from an increasingly protein-rich diet.

While we don't have data yet for Africa, China, and India before the nineteenth century, it appears that the global trend—to which North America was an exception—was that people grew smaller even as economies grew larger. The benefits of expanding economies (outside of North America) seem to have flowed overwhelmingly to elites while the standard of living for most people fell between 1500 and 1800.

Falling Incomes for Wage Laborers

The evidence on incomes for ordinary city folk supports this discouraging conclusion. In Beijing, Delhi, London, Amsterdam, and Florence, laborers' real incomes climbed during the fourteenth and fifteenth centuries. The plague pandemic of the 1340s had had one silver lining for survivors: the resulting scarcity of people drove wages up. Unskilled laborers earned three to four times what they required for subsistence in 1450, which meant each one could support a small family. But in the late fifteenth century, laborers' incomes began a long slide, which in Beijing, Delhi, and Florence bottomed out around the years 1750–1800. At that point, a laborer barely earned enough to feed one mouth, which meant in families everyone had to work. In Amsterdam and London, laborers'

The Laboring Poor Both peasants and laborers—ordinary people—were hit hardest by major environmental, demographic, and economic shifts. A seventeenth-century French painting depicts the realities of subsistence life for a peasant family: ragged clothing and a few basic dishes empty of food.

incomes slipped rather less; they climbed a bit in the seventeenth century, before falling again in the eighteenth. Everywhere, the constraints of an economy based on human and animal muscle meant that the great majority of people lived close to subsistence levels. Britain's North American colonies, again, were an exception to the dismal trend. In the mid-eighteenth century, unskilled free laborers in Boston and Philadelphia earned four or five times what they needed for subsistence, more than anywhere else in the world for which data exist.

Why did ordinary people grow poorer while economies grew faster than ever before? At any time of large-scale economic reorganization, some people are better situated to benefit from change than others. Most of the economic growth from 1500 to 1800 created rewards for those involved in trade, finance, and government. Ordinary peasants and laborers, outside of a few favored locations such as eastern North America, saw their economic position weaken as their numbers grew.

Trade

The burst of oceanic voyaging after the 1490s linked markets as never before. This created opportunities for buying cheap in one market and selling dear in another. To do this optimally, one needs more market knowledge than competitors have—exactly what the people who made the voyages acquired. These voyagers were mainly Atlantic Europeans, not the maritime traders of the East China Sea or the Indian Ocean, nor the caravan merchants of Iran or Central Asia, who by and large did not go global.

Certain trades, such as cotton, rewarded market knowledge more than others. You needed to know a lot in order not to lose your shirt in the cotton business. On the production side, some varieties of cotton plants produced better fiber than others. Spinners and weavers had several techniques for making yarns and cloths of different quality and cost. Different dyestuffs and printing methods produced an array of colors and patterns. And at every stage, spinners, weavers, and other workers had varying skill levels. So "cotton" amounted to dozens of different products.

On the demand side, communities of consumers had particular preferences, and these might change over time. During the early modern centuries, most Chinese markets valued plain white cotton. West African markets preferred vivid hues, while Latin American consumers paid more for floral motifs. But beneath these generalizations, specific villages and individuals had different preferences. Knowledge of these complexities helped people make money in the long-distance cotton trade. This favored literate people and those who actually did the voyaging and trading: they accumulated broader knowledge faster.

Atlantic Europeans had another important edge in long-distance trade, noted in the previous chapter. Their sturdy ships, built to withstand Atlantic gales, accommodated heavy cannon. European merchants active in oceanic trade almost always

Cotton Production Technological advances and market know-how enabled Europeans to begin to compete in the global cotton trade. In this painting, mid-seventeenth-century French peasants spin cotton on a spinning wheel and weave it into cloth on a large frame loom within their own cottage—the typical form of cotton production at the time.

carried serious armament. They could fight back against pirates and hope to prevail. They could engage in piracy themselves when it suited them, attacking, say, Bengali or Malay ships and seizing their cargoes. They could threaten to bombard port cities until local princes and merchants offered their goods at lower prices. Well-armed ship captains could sell "protection" to the less well armed, allowing them to live in peace for a price. These twin advantages, in information and seaborne firepower, went a long way toward enriching Atlantic Europe's merchant classes.

Before 1500, the Indian Ocean world, from China to Egypt, was the central arena of long-distance seaborne trade. The sea lanes of the Atlantic, the Baltic Sea, North Sea, and the coasts as far south as Senegal were busy too, but not on the same scale. Regular transatlantic traffic began in the wake of Columbus, and the slave trade extended it to African coasts as far south as Angola and Mozambique. Almost all Atlantic trade took place in ships owned and operated by Atlantic Europeans. By the 1550s, this burgeoning Atlantic trade was increasingly linked to the Indian Ocean commerce. European merchants gradually got involved in the trade circuits of Indian Ocean and East Asian waters, although never outstripping Asian trading communities.

Three commodities accounted for a sizeable chunk of world trade during the early modern centuries: spices, cotton, and silver. While many other things (as well as millions of people) were traded, these three played central roles in tightening the commercial webs of the world, integrating far-flung regions in particular.

Spices and the Spice Trade

Cooks have flavored food with spices for several thousand years. When people thought that good health rested on a proper balance of hot and cold influences, spices such as pepper, ginger, and cinnamon acquired reputations as health foods. (In fact, many spices are rich in micronutrients and antioxidants.) The lands that produced the most spices were the islands of Southeast Asia. Spices featured prominently in local diets, but more than 2,000 years ago they also became staples in long-distance trade to both India and China. Ancient Rome imported spices too, as did, later on, the Muslim caliphates based in Damascus and Baghdad, and Byzantine markets in Constantinople. Eventually, spices, especially peppers, were grown in south India as well as Southeast Asia. In addition to peppers, the most marketable spices included nutmeg, cinnamon, and cloves, valued for their flavor and purported medicinal value. The port cities of the Indian Ocean world, from Malacca to Basra, all had spice bazaars.

In 1400, China and India remained the chief markets for spices. Europe's supply, maybe 2,000 tons annually, came mainly via Egypt to Venice. Vasco da Gama sought a route to the Indian Ocean around Africa in the 1490s, with the backing of the Portuguese Crown, in part to cut out the middlemen in the **spice trade** and get to the source—Southeast Asia and India. An all-sea route lowered the price of spices in Europe, boosting demand. After da Gama's return in 1498, Lisbon soon became one of the world's great spice markets.

The best spices grew wild on islands such as the Moluccas and the Bandas, now parts of Indonesia. Much of the trade flowed through the port of Malacca, a great

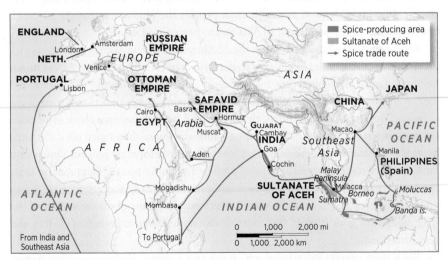

The Spice Trade, ca. 1600 The spice trade had flowed along the maritime routes of the Indian Ocean world for millennia. The main production zones were Southeast Asian islands such as the Moluccas and Bandas, and eventually southwestern India. The biggest markets by 1600 were China, India, Southwest Asia, and Europe. Before the Portuguese voyages around the southern tip of Africa, spices had arrived in Europe overland via Ottoman territories. By 1600, the Ottomans were losing that trade to seagoing European merchants. The sultans of Aceh kept their grip on the trade passing west from the spice islands through the Straits of Malacca until 1600.

trading city with perhaps 100,000 people by 1500. Superior firepower enabled the Portuguese to defeat the Muslim sultanate of Malacca in 1511 with a force of only 1,200 men. This strategic conquest was the most important step in the Portuguese quest for a commanding position in the spice trade. Tomé Pires, a Portuguese who visited Malacca in 1511, wrote that one could hear 84 languages spoken on its streets on any given day. Its connections with northwest India were so strong that Pires wrote: "Melaka cannot survive without Cambay, nor Cambay without Melaka." Portuguese merchants now carried increasing shares of the trade not only to Lisbon, but also to markets in India and China. The Portuguese language became the lingua franca of the spice trade. Superior market knowledge and naval firepower permitted tiny Portugal to play this outsized role.

The spice trade initially brought spectacular profits for merchants who survived the dangers of long sea voyages. When da Gama first arrived in India, the market price of pepper there was 4 percent of the price in Europe. In the Moluccas, spices could be had for 1/700 the Lisbon price. In the years from 1500 to 1630, an average of seven Portuguese ships set out each year for Asian spice markets. Storms, shipwrecks, and pirates claimed an average of three, but the surviving four brought magnificent profits.

The quantities of spices going to China, India, and Islamic lands remained greater than that headed to Europe. In the pepper trade perhaps a quarter or a third went to Lisbon, while the rest found its way to Asian markets, often in Portuguese ships. For cloves, more expensive and profitable than pepper, the proportion (for the sixteenth century) was roughly 90 percent to Asia and 10 percent to Europe.

After 1550, the sultan of Aceh (on the northern end of Sumatra) sought to control the spice trade. With allies in Gujarati traders and even Ottoman sultans, Aceh's sultan became a formidable competitor for Portuguese merchants after 1550. They acquired more competitors after 1590 when the Dutch, and soon English traders too, tried to get a share of the spice trade. By 1620, the Dutch and English between them sent about ten ships laden with spices back to Europe annually, more than twice what Portugal managed. The more competitive market meant less profit for everyone, but Dutch data show the spice trade returned an annual profit averaging 27 percent from 1602 to 1650. By the late seventeenth century, Amsterdam prices were only about 5 times Malacca prices for pepper, and 15 times for cloves. The fabulous profits of the early years of the spice trade were gone forever. But more people were able to enjoy spices' flavors and healthful effects.

With their market knowledge and shipboard cannon, Portuguese, Dutch, and English merchants won a large share of the world's spice trade after 1511. They cut Egyptian and Venetian middlemen out of the trade to Europe. By 1615, English merchants were trading pepper to Ottoman markets in the eastern Mediterranean, where a century before Venetians had purchased pepper to sell in Europe. Portuguese, Dutch, and English traders also carried spices from Southeast Asia to Japan, China, and India, competing with Malay, Gujarati, and other Asian merchants on their home turf. The spice trade continued to grow into the eighteenth century. But its relative importance in global trade dwindled as cotton became the staple of the long-distance trade between the Indian Ocean world and the Atlantic.

Cotton and the Cotton Trade

Cotton grows only in lands where there are at least 200 frost-free days and either 20 inches (50 cm) of rainfall annually or irrigation water. The earliest evidence we have of cotton cultivation comes from the ancient Indus valley about 5,000 years ago. Its cultivation spread outside of India to Southwest Asia and Egypt mainly during the era of Islamic expansion, the eighth through the tenth centuries. But world production remained centered on India. Chinese farmers in the southeastern province of Fujian grew cotton too. When the Ming decided to accept cotton as a means of paying taxes in the fourteenth century, the crop spread widely in southern China.

Before 1450, cotton was raised, spun, and woven into cloth, and traded chiefly in India and China. It was grown mainly on small farms, spun into thread by women and children in villages, and woven into cloth usually by men in village workshops.

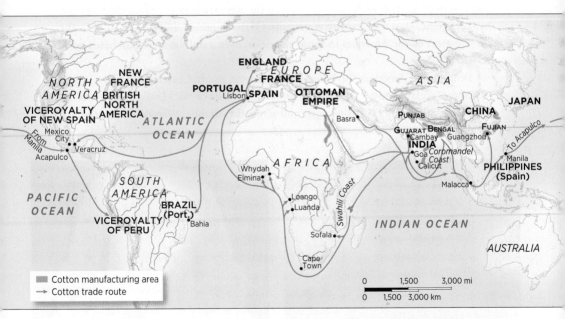

The Cotton Trade, ca. 1700 Cotton grew well in several zones around the world in 1700, but India was the biggest producer. With markets almost everywhere, cotton was one of the first truly global trade commodities. The seaborne circuits shown here include both transatlantic and transpacific routes to markets in the Americas. Southeast Asia, both East and West Africa, the Ottoman lands, and Atlantic Europe were also major importers of cotton.

During the fifteenth through the seventeenth centuries, India's cotton farming and manufacturing was concentrated in the regions of Gujarat and Punjab, in northwest India, which specialized in cheap cottons; and in Coromandel, in the southeast; and Bengal, in the northeast, both of which specialized in fine muslins and high-quality printed cloth such as calicoes and chintzes.

High-quality cotton, like silk, was well suited for long-distance trade. It was lightweight and durable, and it could be folded or rolled into nearly any shape. In the fifteenth century it was valued from Japan to Spain to East Africa. Merchants traded it by land and sea, including along caravan routes of Asia, many of which were "cotton roads" as much as "silk roads." In the mid-seventeenth century, Iran imported 25 to 30 thousand camel loads of cotton annually from India.

As with spices, it was European oceanic merchants who most conspicuously expanded the scope of the world cotton trade. They carried it to new markets in Africa, Europe, and the Americas. They also competed with Asian traders carrying cotton from one Asian port to another.

In the course of the sixteenth century, the Atlantic slave trade came to involve cotton. West Africans already had a taste for Indian cottons, available at considerable cost via trans-Saharan routes from North Africa and Egypt. Between 1500 and 1800, some 50 to 60 percent of African imports in the slave trade were Indian cloth offered by Portuguese, Dutch, or English merchants. Of the roughly 8 million Africans bought for shipment to the Americas in those centuries, over 4 million were purchased with Indian textiles.

People in the Americas also bought Indian cotton goods. Cotton cloth, like Chinese silk and porcelain, crossed the Pacific to Spanish America via Manila and Acapulco. But it also came through Spain's ports and across the Atlantic. Women in Mexico City

The Cotton Trade Painted cloth from the Madras region of India shows an Indian woman (center)—perhaps a cotton-spinner herself—conversing with European traders. Traders shipped Indian textiles to western Europe, where they became the basis for luxury commodities such as this fashionable eighteenth-century gown made of Indian muslin. The pleated, floor-length fabric at the back falls loosely as a slight train.

wore fine calicoes from India. According to one eighteenth-century account, even slave women in Veracruz (Mexico) wore skirts of embroidered muslin. Portuguese merchants sold Indian cotton cloth in Brazil.

European markets eventually bought more Asian cottons than did either Africa or the Americas. The Portuguese trade to Indian Ocean ports had initially focused on spices, but by 1620 textiles—mainly cotton—made up 60 percent of it (by value). In 1708, the English man of letters Daniel Defoe (author of *Robinson Crusoe*) complained that imported cotton had "crept into our Houses, our Closets and Bed Chambers, Curtains, Cushions, Chairs, and at last Beds themselves were nothing but Calicoes or Indian stuffs." Indian cotton was sufficiently good and cheap that it menaced Europe's wool and linen business and put thousands of weavers out of work. Responding to weavers' riots and complaints voiced by men such as Defoe, France and Britain enacted tariffs and outright bans on Indian cloth imports, starting in the 1680s. In 1720, the British Parliament passed a law forbidding the use or wearing of imported calico cloth.

These protectionist measures spurred domestic cotton manufacturing industries in England and France, using imported raw cotton. By the 1760s, European cotton mills could compete successfully against Indian producers in African and American markets. Cotton was now a global business—one that, as much as anything else, brought the Indian Ocean and Atlantic Ocean into a unified trading world, providing a strong strand in the Global web.

Silver and the Silver Trade

Silver became another of the first global trade commodities, but with a difference. It served primarily as money, whereas cotton was most often used for clothing and only occasionally as money. There were two main reasons for silver's expanded role. First, governments, always in need of revenue, found it advantageous to demand that taxes be paid in silver as opposed to grain, cotton, livestock, labor, or anything else. Silver gave them the flexibility to pay for weapons, soldiers, or whatever else they might need on short notice. The Mughals gradually put tax payments in India on a silver basis. The Ming did the same in China, where tax had previously come most often in the form of rice. In the 1570s they changed the laws to require everyone, even peasant families, to pay taxes in silver. A huge proportion of the world's population now needed silver.

The second reason for the rise of silver as a global commodity was that it solved a problem of mistrust that hampered long-distance trade. When people don't know and trust one another, they need money that everyone trusts. In practice, the cash of the early modern world, as before, came in the form of precious metals such as gold, silver, and copper. In long-distance trade, silver emerged as the best option because copper wasn't valued enough, gold was too rare, and paper money or promises of future payment were unreliable.

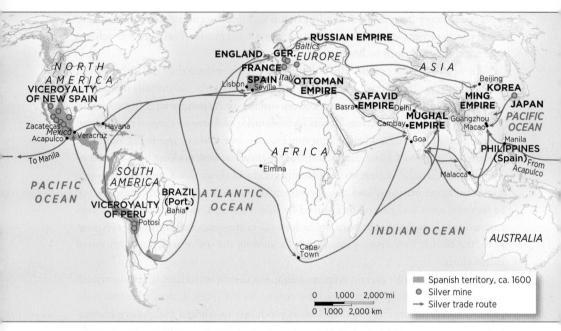

The Silver Trade, ca. 1600 Silver became a truly global commodity in the sixteenth century. The main silver-mining zones were in Japan, central Europe, and Spanish America—especially in Zacatecas, Mexico, and Potosí. Silver was crucial to the Spanish Empire's finances. However, it commanded a higher price in India and China than anywhere else, so silver flowed across land and sea to the Mughal and Ming empires. Silver was so prized in China that it could bear the high transport costs across the length of Asia by overland caravan.

The silver needed to keep governments going and long-distance trade humming came mainly from Spanish America, central Europe, and Japan. New silver strikes took place in Japan in the 1520s through the 1540s, in Mexico during the years 1545 through 1558, and the biggest of all—as we've seen—at Potosí (in today's Bolivia) high in the Andes, in 1545. In Japan, Chinese and Korean mining technology adopted in the 1550s improved the yield of silver veins. In the Americas, the latest German technology was applied in Mexico in the 1550s and at Potosí in the 1570s. Japan's mines adopted it, via Mexico, by 1580, leading to a peak in production from 1602 to 1630.

These technologies, especially the so-called *patío* **process** in Spanish America, made it easier to separate silver from its surrounding rock, so lower-grade ores became worth mining. Japan in the sixteenth century mined about 30 percent of the world's silver, and in the seventeenth century about 15 percent. Spanish American mines produced a good deal more, and Potosí alone accounted for 60 percent of world silver production between 1550 and 1650. Thus the transmission of technology along international circuits helped advance a silver mining boom on three continents. The effects enabled some monarchs to spend as never before and tightened the Global web through the enhanced use of silver in global trade.

Financing the Spanish and Japanese States The rising tide of silver production floated the Spanish and Japanese states and tempted them to overreach. Despite Spain's small population (about 7 million) and poverty of natural resources, it became a great power in Europe and controlled much of the Americas and the Philippines after the mid-sixteenth century. In Europe, the Spanish Crown—a branch of the Habsburg dynasty from 1519 to 1700—used its silver bonanza to fight endless wars and champion the Catholic effort to roll back Protestantism. Spanish monarchs also committed to continual warfare against the Ottomans (and Muslims more generally) in the Mediterranean. A Spanish friar writing in 1638 put it this way: "Potosí lives in order to serve the imposing aspirations of Spain: it serves to chastise the Turk, humble the Moor, make Flanders tremble and terrify England." By law, the Crown was entitled to one-fifth of all silver production in the Spanish Empire. At times, upward of 40 percent of Spain's government revenue came from Potosí alone.

The silver mountain's bounty peaked in the 1590s and slipped sharply after about 1640. Spanish kings managed to spend all the silver that crossed the Atlantic on royal account and then some. When pinched for funds after production started to fall, they sometimes grabbed private traders' silver as it came ashore. Felipe IV (r. 1621–1665) said, "Nothing do I regret more than having to seize silver." But he did it anyway to fight wars.

Similarly, in Japan, the military entrepreneurs who unified the country—Oda Nobunaga (1534–1582), Toyotomi Hideyoshi (ca. 1536–1598), and Tokugawa Ieyasu (1543–1616)—financed their campaigns against rival warlords with silver. They converted the mines into a state monopoly exploiting convict labor. Silver revenues also helped pay for Hideyoshi's unsuccessful invasion of Korea in the 1590s. Like Habsburg Spain (and, for that matter, like Athens of the fifth century BCE), Tokugawa Japan's hard power rested largely on military force supported by the yields of silver mines while they lasted. By 1640, Japan's silver production had shrunk to half its peak levels of 1621.

Promoting Economic Growth in China and India The silver that was mined in Spanish America and Japan traveled around the world. Most of it eventually went to China or India, where it served to promote commerce and underpin economic growth. When both the Ming and the Mughals insisted on silver for tax payments in the sixteenth century, silver became more valuable in those lands than anywhere else. People could exchange silver for more goods, or more gold, in India and China than elsewhere. Anyone who could survive the risks of trading across the seas could do well exchanging silver for Indian cotton cloth and pepper, or Chinese silk and porcelain. As a

Chinese Ceramics The export of Chinese luxury goods, like this intricate Ming-era painted and enameled porcelain box, brought the silver needed for coinage and tax payments in China.

Portuguese official in Macau, Manuel de Comara de Noronha, put it in 1630, "When the Chinese smell silver, they will bring mountains of merchandise." In the same year, He Qiaoyuan, a Ming scholar and official, remarked that silver acquired through foreign trade resulted in massive exports, thereby ensuring "employment for weavers, potters, and merchants, whose waxing affluence augured higher standards of living for all." The ceramic kilns at the southern town of Jingdezhen employed more than 10,000 workers during the late Ming. Silver flows helped to bolster both the Chinese economy and world trade.

Merchants sent Japanese silver to China, often in Dutch or Portuguese ships because Japanese were officially forbidden to trade with foreigners. American silver flowed along many pathways. Some bullion crossed the Pacific via Acapulco to Manila in the Philippines, and on to China from there. In this way, Chinese silk and ceramics entered markets in Mexico and Spanish America generally. The bulk of American silver crossed the Atlantic, usually via Cuba's main port of Havana, to Seville in Spain. But it did not rest there long. Some of Spain's incoming silver went to repay loans from Italian and German bankers, including the house of Fugger. After the 1560s, plenty of it went to finance Spain's army, which was at war with the Dutch. Once delivered to bankers or the Spanish army, American silver flowed through Ottoman lands, the Baltic, and Russia, or traveled in European ships sailing around Africa, always heading for India and China, as if pulled by a magnetic attraction.

For two centuries nothing produced in the rest of the world, except at times European cannon, interested Chinese and Indian merchants as much as silver. But by 1750 or so, China had enough silver in circulation to satisfy demand and reduce its price to about the same as the world price. Silver flows slowed and no longer quickened global commerce.

Silver, cotton, and spices: they could be produced only in some places but were in demand everywhere. They formed the lifeblood of global trade between 1500 and 1750, and they exemplify the process by which merchants connected far-flung markets in a global commercial web. Tea, sugar, silk, gold, ivory, and many other items—even dried fish—were traded across the oceans as well. So were millions of slaves. At any given time after 1550, hundreds of ships were sailing on well-traveled routes, linking ports such as Guangzhou, Manila, Cambay, Goa, Basra, Cape Town, Elmina, Seville, Amsterdam, London, Bahia, Havana, Acapulco, and many others. Year after year ships and cargoes sailed, tightening the web of global commerce.

New Business Formats: Plantations, Companies, Banks

The quickening pace of global commerce invited creative entrepreneurs to invent or refine the institutions through which they did business. Three of the most important in the early modern centuries were plantations, trading companies, and banks.

Plantations

A seventeenth-century Barbadian slave was quoted in 1676 as saying, "The devil was in the Englishman that he makes everything work; he makes the Negro work, he makes the horse work, the ass work, the wood work, the water work and the wind work." But it was not the devil that inspired Englishmen on Barbados to try to force everyone and everything to make sugar. It was the opportunity to get rich by selling sugar grown, harvested, and processed by enslaved labor on plantations.

Plantations are large-scale commercial farming operations with labor forces of dozens or hundreds of people—sometimes free wage workers, sometimes unfree laborers, and often both. They have existed here and there since ancient times. But the interconnected commercial world that developed after the 1490s improved the economic logic of plantations. When many markets were within reach, the rewards to large-scale production (known as **economies of scale**) multiplied. Nothing worked better as a plantation crop than sugar.

Sugar is a grass native to Southeast Asia. It will grow in tropical and subtropical latitudes where temperatures are warm for most of the year. It needs either abundant rain or irrigation, and fertile soils. In the harvest season, it needs a burst of labor. Its economies of scale came in the processes of milling and refining, in which juice is squeezed by rollers from sugar cane and then boiled into a goopy mass that dries into crystals. To make sugar pay, one needed to make big investments in land, labor, machinery, buildings, and other infrastructure. Sugar is rarely a small farmer's crop, and for the last thousand years it has been mainly a plantation crop.

Sugar was grown on a modest scale in China and India in ancient times. By 650 CE it had appeared in Iraq and Egypt. By 800 its cultivation had spread to several Mediterranean islands, southern (Islamic) Spain, and river valleys of Morocco. In the Muslim lands of the Mediterranean, slaves—mainly captives from Christian Europe—formed the backbone of the sugar labor force. In Morocco by 1450, entrepreneurs and emirs imported African slaves across the Sahara to work on sugar plantations. Portuguese and Spaniards did the same on Atlantic islands such as Madeira, the Canaries, and São Tomé.

The Spread of the Sugar Plantation São Tomé, in the Gulf of Guinea, pointed the way toward a large-scale slave-and-sugar complex. Portuguese mariners settled the formerly uninhabited island in the 1490s. Its volcanic, nutrient-rich soils and rainy climate proved ideal for sugar. By the 1550s, the island's economy focused so tightly on sugar that it raised too little food for its population. Merchants brought food from Portugal, a month away by sail. The plantations required a constant influx of people—slaves from Kongo on the mainland of Africa, and settlers, often unwilling migrants, mostly from the communities of Portuguese Jews, debtors, and criminals, and other populations the Portuguese Crown was happy to deport. For nearly half a century, São Tomé served as the leading example of a new business format, the large-scale slave plantation.

In the 1530s, Portuguese businessmen took the plantation format to the northeast of Brazil. There they found good soils and climate for sugar cultivation, but a

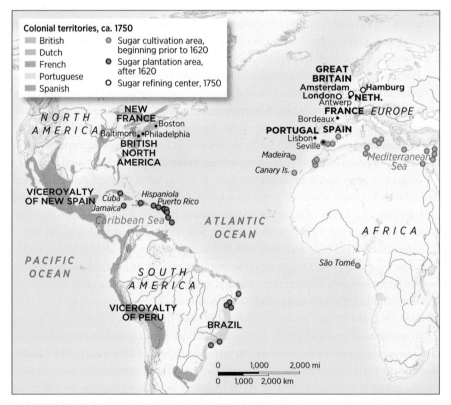

The Sugar Industry, ca. 1750 People had been cultivating sugar for millennia, but it became a major commodity, produced on plantations with slave labor, in the Mediterranean world around 1000 CE. In the sixteenth century, Portuguese and Spanish entrepreneurs brought sugar plantations into the Atlantic world, first to islands such as Madeira, the Canaries, and São Tomé, then across the ocean to the Caribbean and coastal Brazil. Sugar refining was concentrated in Hamburg, Amsterdam, and London, with smaller centers elsewhere in Europe and in British North America, especially Boston and Philadelphia.

shortage of labor. They tried enslaving the Amerindian population, but extremely high death rates from disease and maltreatment convinced them that the answer to their problem was massive imports of African slaves. By the 1590s, Brazil led the world in sugar production. By the 1640s, the tandem of sugar and slavery was booming in the Caribbean too, where planters on Spanish, French, British, and Dutch islands all raised cane in quantity. Some Caribbean planters at first tried using enslaved Scots and Irish, but too few could be found. Next came indentured European laborers, who were bound to work for a fixed number of years in exchange for free passage across the Atlantic. But too few volunteered (or could be kidnapped), and once in the Caribbean they died fast from diseases. So, as in Brazil, Caribbean planters turned to Atlantic Africa, where local merchants offered slaves in great numbers at advantageous prices. Thereafter, for 200 years, Brazil and the Caribbean led the world in sugar exports and slave imports.

The **slave-and-sugar plantations** in Brazil and the Caribbean were a novel form of enterprise, far larger and more efficient than their predecessors in São Tomé or the Mediterranean. The plantations, at least on the smaller islands of the Caribbean such as Barbados, imported most of their food from afar, as had São Tomé—so they could specialize on one product, sugar. Plantations usually held between 100 and 500 slaves, and sugar districts supported the densest rural populations anywhere in the Americas. They were all located near the seacoasts because sugar was an export crop, destined for European markets in Lisbon, Seville, Bordeaux, Antwerp, Amsterdam, or London— and after 1730 or so also North American ones such as Baltimore, Philadelphia, or Boston. They were often enormously profitable for planters.

Sugar and Plantation Slavery Sugar profits rested on a double exploitation. Sugar monoculture depleted soil nutrients, so planters periodically had to move to virgin fields, usually to forested land. In time, often about 50 to 75 years, plantations on smaller Caribbean islands became unprofitable due to nutrient loss, and the sugar industry gradually shifted to bigger islands such as Jamaica, Hispaniola, and Cuba. The big islands had more land and forests that, when burned, released in their ash a pulse of nutrients to the soil from which a bumper crop could spring for a few years.

The exploitation of people was more consequential. From 1550 to 1850, about half of the nearly 11 million Africans shipped across the Atlantic went to sugar plantations in Brazil and the Caribbean. The majority were field slaves who worked long hours in labor gangs overseen by armed men. During the harvest and milling seasons, men, women, and children worked around the clock with scant rest. A combination of strenuous work, brutality, and a lethal disease environment made sugar plantations notoriously unhealthy and contributed to the short life expectancy of slaves on these plantations: shorter than anywhere else in the Americas, averaging about 10 years after arrival for those born in Africa. (Free blacks' life expectancy was marginally longer, indentured Europeans' slightly shorter.) Among slaves on sugar plantations, deaths outstripped births until the nineteenth century. So, after more than two centuries of continuous slave imports, the population on sugar plantations in the Americas in 1790 stood at about 2 million people, 90 to 95 percent of them slaves.

Brutality stood at the core of sugar plantation society. Masters and overseers resorted to violence and the threat of violence as the chief means of enforcing discipline among the labor force. Thomas Thistlewood, an overseer on a Jamaican plantation starting in 1750, left a diary in which he detailed the various punishments and tortures he inflicted on slaves. His diary also recounts his sex life with slave women, showing him to be a sexual predator and a rapist. Thistlewood's conduct was not unusual for overseers and slavemasters. Their brutalities were calculated to make slaves choose obedience over defiance. That calculation worked most but not all of the time. Slaves defied Thistlewood on occasion, for which he made them suffer.

Slaves from time to time risked everything on attempts to run away or rebel. In 1760, some 1,500 slaves, led by Akan-speakers from what is now Ghana, tried to take over the island of Jamaica. **Tacky's War**, as it is called, lasted a few months and shook the foundations of the plantation regime on that island. As we've seen, in northeast Brazil a community of runaway slaves, Palmares, managed to defend its independence from 1605 to the 1690s. The greatest of all slave risings took place in the 1790s in the French sugar colony of St. Domingue, as we will see in Chapter 21. By and large, slaves on the smaller islands were less likely to try to run away because recapture was more likely there than on bigger islands or in Brazil, where sparsely populated forests beckoned slaves yearning to escape the plantation.

Sugar was not quite the global commodity that silver or cotton was. Because it does not keep as well as silver or cotton, and could be grown widely, it was not traded from the Atlantic basin into the Indian Ocean or Pacific on any scale. The primary significance of sugar for the global economy was that it demonstrated the viability of the large-scale slave plantation.

Other crops in the Americas, notably tobacco, cotton, rice, and indigo, would also be produced on the plantation model. The particulars varied from place to place and from crop to crop. But plantation owners all used slave labor, relied heavily on terror for labor discipline, systematically sought economies of scale, and filled distant markets with their products. By the mid-eighteenth century, some of the richest men in the world made their money this way.

Chartered Joint-Stock Companies

The commercial opportunities of the Global web offered economies of scale in long-distance trade as well as in cash-crop production. Just as the slave plantation brought new levels of efficiency, human suffering, and profit to the business of sugar production, so the joint-stock company did for oceanic trade.

Intercontinental shipping was risky business. Storms, pirates, disease outbreaks, and other hazards could ruin any voyage. To make business sense, ventures needed to be big: big enough to fight off pirates, negotiate bulk discounts on trade goods, and ensure that *some* ships would surely survive a storm. Sending several ships together made sense, and sending a fleet was better still.

To achieve economies of scale in long-distance trade, merchants found ways to cooperate and pool their resources. Traders and businessmen had done this for millennia, usually with family members or close friends because mutual trust was crucial. These kin-based concerns could be gigantic, like the Zheng family operations along the coast of China or the merchant empire of Virji Vora in India.

Origins During the sixteenth century, more anonymous forms of partnership developed to spread and share the risks of long-distance trade. Some were chartered companies, granted monopoly rights over certain trades by governments. Others were joint-stock companies in which hundreds or thousands of investors might own shares, as in modern corporations. Some were both, such as the English Muscovy Company, founded in 1555, or the Levant Company, chartered by England's Queen Elizabeth in 1581 to conduct trade with Ottoman lands. All had professional managers. This was a business model that could expand to indefinite size more readily than the kin-based business empires of the Zhengs or Virji Vora.

The English pioneered **chartered joint-stock companies**. France and the Netherlands soon followed, and during the eighteenth century Spain, Denmark, and others did too. One of these, the Hudson's Bay Company, begun in 1670 to handle the fur trade in Canada, still exists, albeit in much different form. The gold standard of chartered joint-stock trading companies was the **Dutch East India Company**, the VOC, founded in 1602, which we've already encountered in South Africa and in East Asian waters.

The Dutch East India Company (VOC) The VOC was a chartered joint-stock company, formed to share the risk of voyages to the spice islands of Indonesia. Voyages in the seventeenth

Stock Exchanges The Dutch painter Emanuel de Witte made this painting of the Beurs, or Amsterdam stock exchange, in 1653. Investors met in this busy courtyard to trade shares in increasingly popular and profitable joint-stock companies.

century from Amsterdam to Indonesia and back typically took 200 to 300 days outbound, and more than 300 on the return. About 3 to 5 percent never returned, better than the 40 percent rate for Portuguese ships in the sixteenth century.

The VOC proved a spectacular success for nearly 200 years. Between 1602 and 1796, the company sent nearly 5,000 ships around Africa to the Indian Ocean. They brought back some 2.5 million tons of trade goods and exchanged countless cargoes between Asian ports. Detailed records for a 300-ton ship, the *Ceulen*, which sailed from Java to Amsterdam in 1697, reveal something of the business: in addition to a crew of 105 seamen and 30 soldiers, it carried a cargo of Japanese copper, tin from Thailand, ceramics from China, aromatic wood, saltpeter, tea, ginger, nutmeg, cloves, cardamom (another spice), bird's nests, cotton, silk yarn—and black pepper equal to the ship's weight. The *Ceulen* was small as VOC East Indies ships went, less than one-third the size of a typical East Indiaman, as the biggest ships were called. The VOC's most lucrative trade was buying Indian cloth and selling it for spices destined for European or Chinese markets.

As part of its strategy, the VOC captured port cities, many such as Malacca in 1641 taken from the Portuguese, and built others, such as Cape Town, founded in 1652. It held dozens of fortified posts and at times had as many as 100 hundred heavily armed merchant ships cruising Indian Ocean waters. By 1669 it had 50,000 employees, 10,000 soldiers, and a navy of 40 warships. It constituted a privately funded, state-sanctioned, maritime empire devoted to commercial gain, a smaller version of the Zheng family business empire but with more global reach and governmental support.

The VOC captains enjoyed a military edge in the Indonesian archipelago. VOC forces were frequently outnumbered, but rarely outgunned. Wherever they could maneuver their big floating fortresses, they could concentrate firepower enough to destroy a city in hours. In order to found their center of operations on Java, they destroyed a local town and rebuilt it as Batavia in 1619. In an effort to monopolize the clove and nutmeg trades in the 1620s, they attempted to kill the entire population of the Banda Islands and replace them with loyal settlers. They tried to burn all pepper vines and clove or nutmeg trees not under their control to undermine their competition. They took part in a slave trade in Southeast Asia that specialized in the sale of women from the island of Bali.

In general, the VOC's business model consisted of using force or the threat of force to extract favorable terms of trade—preferably a monopoly—from local rulers and merchants. The approach was backed up with merciless punishment of anyone who traded with rivals. The centrality of violence to their business is captured in a letter from the governor general of the Dutch East Indies, Jan Pieterszoon Coen, in 1614 to the directors of the VOC. Coen, the man later responsible for the effort to exterminate the Banda Islanders, wrote: "You gentlemen ought to know from experience that trade in Asia should be conducted and maintained under the protection and with the aid of your own weapons, and those weapons must be wielded with the profits gained by the

Dutch Colonists Some merchants settled down in VOC colonies—such as the Dutch merchant Pieter Cnoll, who managed trade in Batavia, the capital of the Dutch East Indies. Cnoll is shown here with his half-Dutch, half-Japanese wife, their children, and their servants.

trade. So trade cannot be maintained without war, nor war without trade." Violence half a world away was part of the price for adding a pinch of nutmeg to millions of cakes, sauces, and glasses of cider.

This business strategy worked brilliantly for Coen and the VOC. Before it was liquidated amid a morass of corruption in 1799, the VOC averaged roughly 18 percent annual profit on the totality of its business. Other companies imitated its formula, most notably the English East India Company (EIC). But in its entire career, 1600 to 1857, the EIC managed to carry only about one-fifth the goods traded by the VOC.

Banks

As long-distance trade grew in volume and reach, businesses more often needed to finance their operations by borrowing money. They borrowed to mount large trading ventures that could realize economies of scale. They also borrowed to cover the period between their purchase of goods and the subsequent sale of those goods, which might be years in trade between Europe and Southeast Asia or China. So the demand for private finance grew dramatically after 1500.

New institutions evolved quickly in response to this demand and governments' constant need for cash to pay military expenses. Most notable among these institutions were modern banks, bond markets (in which people traded governments' debt), and stock exchanges (in which people traded shares of companies). All these institutions helped both governments and merchants get cash when they needed it and earn a return on their money when they didn't need cash.

Lending at Interest Of these, the most important were banks. To have a flourishing banking sector, societies first had to discard the idea that lending money at interest

CONSIDERING THE EVIDENCE

On the Circulation of Blood and Money

Usually, the value of a commodity drops when more of it is in circulation. However, as the gold and silver mined in the Americas became more plentiful in Europe, their value increased because more people demanded cold hard cash instead of accepting bartered goods. Some people even began shaving small slivers of metal off of coins before passing them on. Bankers and loan sharks simply lent the money they had in return for a larger amount of money later. Today that difference is known as interest, but European theologians and politicians saw interest as a euphemism for the sin of usury (i.e., lending at interest) that should be banned, or at least regulated. It seemed right to be paid for a hard day's work or a risky investment in overseas trade, but making money from money struck Christians, Jews, and Muslims alike as immoral.

For the Italian scholar Bernardo Davanzati, usury was just one of the mischiefs people could make with money. In a 1588 lecture on coins, he described money as the lifeblood of states to illustrate why money must circulate to retain its value. Although a scientific description of blood circulation eluded Europeans until William Harvey published his research on the subject in 1628, it was commonly understood that blood moved through the heart and lungs to nourish the rest of the body. Over a century after Davanzati delivered his lecture, a British philosopher named John Toland translated it into English, introducing Davanzati's ideas to a new generation of thinkers and bankers on the other side of the continent. As the center of banking moved from Italy to England, so did the demand for ideas about how to deal with money problems.

Some grave and famous Authors have call'd Money the Sinews of War and Government; but, in my Opinion, it may be more properly stil'd the Second Blood thereof. [F]or as Blood, which is the Juice and Substance of Meat in the

was immoral. Hindu, Buddhist, Islamic, and Christian scripture and tradition include objections to the practice of charging interest, or too much interest, for loans. Jewish law prohibits lending at interest to fellow Jews, although not to others. Plato, Aristotle, Cicero, the Buddha, Jesus, Muhammad, and Aquinas all denounced lending at interest, and Confucius disdained money-grubbing of all sorts. Luther got his start railing against usury, and early Protestants generally regarded lending at interest as sinful. So robust banking required cultural change.

In Europe the moral objections and legal prohibitions against lending at interest weakened in places such as northern Italy, where small family banks emerged as early as the thirteenth century, and Barcelona (northeastern Spain), where a city-owned bank natural Body, does, by circulating out of the greater into the lesser Vessels, moisten all the Flesh, which drinks it up as parch'd Ground soaks Rain Water; so it nourishes and restores as much of it as was dri'd up and evaporated by the natural Heat: In like manner, Money, ... does, by circulating out of the richer Purses into the poorer, furnish all the Nation. ... From the poorer it returns again into the richer Purses; and thus circulating without Intermission, it preserves alive the Civil Body of the Common-wealth. Hence ... every State must have a quantity of Money, as every Body a quantity of Blood to circulate therein. But as the Blood stopping in the Head or the larger Vessels puts the Body naturally into a Consumption, Dropsy, or Apoplexy, etc. so [if] all the Money be only in a few Hands, as in those of the rich for Example, the State falls unavoidably into Convulsions, and other dangerous Distempers.... We ought therefore to set a high Value upon the living Member of the Common-wealth, and to preserve it from those Mischiefs which usually befal it, when not carefully look'd after; such as Counterfeiting, Monopolizing, Simony [buying religious privileges], Usury, and the like, already decri'd, and known everywhere. But, ... I shall now confine my Discourse only to ... debasing of Coin.

Questions for Analysis

1. How is the circulation of money in a state like the circulation of blood in a body?
2. Why does Davanzati think that concentrating money in a few hands is dangerous?
3. In what ways did ideas about how to manage money, and money problems, circulate in Europe?

Source: Bernardo Davanzati, *A Discourse upon Coins*, trans. John Toland (London: 1696).

appeared by 1381. Elsewhere in Europe, those objections eroded during the sixteenth and seventeenth centuries. The intellectual climate in which old truths were subject to renewed questioning, combined with economic changes that heightened the demand for finance, probably both contributed to this cultural trend. Lending at interest gradually lost its taint among Protestants, and eventually Catholics as well, despite repeated papal pronouncements about the evils of usury.

The Bank of Amsterdam, founded in 1609, was the first modern bank. It attracted depositors, cleared debts, offered quick transactions, and maintained public trust by reliably allowing anyone to withdraw a deposit on demand. In 1609, at least 800 different coins circulated in Amsterdam, including copper, silver, and gold coins from dozens of countries as far away as Japan. Doing business amid this diversity of money—like conducting conversations in 800 languages—was enormously inefficient. The city council of Amsterdam sought to solve this problem by creating a new bank that kept accounts of merchants' deposits and converted them to a single standard, at first a tally of who owed whom how much of an abstract accounting unit, called bank money. This practice reduced transaction costs and attracted yet more business to Amsterdam. The city required merchants to use the bank for all big transactions. Soon the bank routinely lent out more money than it held, a practice typical of modern banks called **fractional reserve banking**. This innovative, expansive practice had the effect of creating money in the form of credit; although if all depositors demanded their money at the same time, the bank would be unable to pay. To avoid this problem, any bank engaged in this practice had to maintain a solid reputation, as the Bank of Amsterdam did for nearly 200 years. Fractional reserve banking helped lubricate the wheels of commerce by making credit more easily available to merchants.

Bank Notes and Credit Bank notes boosted commerce too. The Bank of Amsterdam did not issue paper money. Other banks had tried and found customers mistrustful, often rightly so. Banks sometimes would print too many notes and then refuse to honor them. But the Bank of Sweden in the 1670s, and then the Bank of England, founded in 1694, managed to win public trust in bank notes. They successfully lobbied for government monopoly rights on printing bank notes and issued them only in modest quantity. Both fractional reserve banking and the use of paper money—if trusted—expanded the amount of money in circulation and reduced the transaction costs of commerce.

Banks often found that their best customers were kings. As we've seen, the spiraling costs of warfare, navies, and standing armies put pressure on royal treasuries. Borrowing was one of the few solutions monarchs could find. If the costs of, say, five years of campaigning could be spread out over the next 50 years, then the need to raise taxes would not be so sharp, making tax revolts less likely. Early modern monarchs had every reason to wish to see healthy banking systems in their countries. The Habsburgs had relied heavily on the banking house of Fugger to attain and retain power.

In practice, northwestern European monarchs, and the Dutch Republic, had the most extensive banking systems to draw upon. Creditworthiness became a strategic asset for states: in the eighteenth century, bankers lent the British government money at half the rate they charged the French Crown. Indeed, the British government's reputation for repaying debts enabled it to spend as much on war as could the far larger Qing empire: it could borrow at low rates and the Qing could not borrow at all. Banks kept kings and governments solvent, and kings and governments, if they paid their debts, helped keep banks profitable. Governments without access to banks, or deemed poor credit risks by bankers, struggled financially.

Large-scale plantations, joint-stock companies, and banks were among the new business formats that developed in response to the opportunities and challenges presented by the Global web. Partnerships and family-run businesses survived, of course. But they could not take full advantage of potential economies of scale in production, commerce, and finance that resulted from the newly global reach of ships, the connections among far-flung markets, and the frequent need for ready cash on the part of kings and merchants.

Global Links and Commercial Revolutions

In eastern Canada about 1680, a Mi'kmaq told a French priest, "In truth, my friend, the beaver does everything to perfection. He makes for us kettles, axes, swords, knives, and gives us drink and food without the trouble of cultivating the ground." By trapping beaver and selling fur, Mi'kmaqs and other Amerindians could buy an array of useful goods produced across the Atlantic in Europe. A Khoisan raising cattle in South Africa or a Dayak in Borneo gathering sandalwood might have said much the same thing. They all found advantages in taking part in global commerce, selling something they were good at producing in order to buy other things they could not easily produce. People had taken part in such exchanges for millennia before 1500. But now more people did so more often, and over longer distances.

During the early modern centuries (1500–1800) the world's trade networks fused into one giant, but patchy, commercial web. Regular shipping linked places that had previously been isolated, such as Caribbean islands or southernmost Africa. Strong links emerged across the Atlantic where none had existed before, such as the trade routes between Mexico and Spain, or Angola and Brazil. New routes also spanned the Pacific between Acapulco and Manila. Strong links also developed where only weak ones had existed before, such as between south China and the Philippines or between Atlantic Europe and West Africa.

These links and shifts to a more commercial orientation touched some places more than others. The commercial transformation ran deepest in coastal China and Atlantic Europe, at the two ends of the Eurasian landmass.

China

Between 1550 and 1800, China underwent a second **commercial revolution**. The first one had occurred during the Song dynasty (960–1279). This second one, under the

力田巧機事利
器由心匠翻〱
轉圜摳叐〱鳴〱
翠浪三春欲盡
萬頃平如掌
漸暄牛已喘長
懷兩丞相

Chinese Commercial Revolution In this 1696 painting, a peasant and a water buffalo prepare the soil for rice planting. The poem in the upper left praises the farm tool depicted, which flattens the ground. New, intensive agricultural practices enabled late Ming and Qing China to become more commercialized.

late Ming and then the Qing, was something of an economic miracle. China doubled its population without impoverishing it. This was achieved partly by conquest of new lands, not only in Mongolia and Tibet (economically not all that helpful) but also in western Sichuan and other southwestern lands populated by non-Han minorities. China absorbed, killed off, or pushed out these peoples and put their lands to more intensive use with state-of-the-art agricultural technologies. This resulted in more rice paddies and millet fields, and less swampland, forestland, and grassland—hence a bigger economy and more tax receipts for the emperors.

But even more than frontier conquest and territorial expansion, China built its economy through increased commercialization of both agriculture and manufacturing. Regions came to specialize more in certain products, such as tea or cotton, and to import their food from elsewhere in China or even Vietnam. Most of this specialization and exchange took place within China. But some of it linked up to foreign markets, especially for silk and porcelain.

The Ming and Qing governments had ambivalent views about foreign trade. Sometimes they tried to ban it, and sometimes they encouraged it. In the 1560s the Ming rescinded an earlier ban, helping to create a surge in foreign trade. Restrictions returned, but under the Qing between the 1680s and 1760s foreign trade again generally met with official approval and grew apace. Shipping from south China to Manila tripled from 1684 to 1715, to some 20 ships per year. Silver imports increased by nearly sixfold between 1728 and 1800, and exports increased by a similar proportion. By 1800, some 10 percent of Chinese grain, 25 percent of cotton, 90 percent of silk, and 95 percent of tea was produced for markets, whether domestic or foreign. Only a few other spots in the world matched this degree of commercialization.

Atlantic Europe

One was Atlantic Europe, which also underwent a commercial revolution. Here, as in China, frontier expansion played a role. Some settlement and agricultural expansion took place in drained wetlands in Europe, especially in England, the Netherlands, and along Baltic shores. But the main thrust came overseas. The plantation zones of Brazil and the Caribbean were under the control of Atlantic Europeans. By the 1690s, smaller plantation regions were taking shape in South Carolina (rice) and around the shores of the Chesapeake (tobacco). Most of the wealth squeezed from plantations enriched Atlantic Europeans.

But, as in China, the heart of the commercial revolution in Atlantic Europe took place at home. Ever-larger shares of agricultural harvests went to nearby markets. Wool and cotton textile businesses expanded. In Atlantic Europe as a whole, the proportion of people working the land in 1500 was about 75 to 80 percent—less in the Netherlands, more in Iberia. By 1750 that proportion had fallen to about 60 percent, and in England and the Netherlands was well under half. Manufacturing and services made up the rest, both attuned almost entirely to market production. Market towns sprouted and financial centers, such as Antwerp, Amsterdam, and London, flourished. By 1600, even bulk items were traded over long distances, such as grain from Poland to Amsterdam or to north Italian cities.

This slow but steady march toward market societies in China and Atlantic Europe distinguished them from the rest of the world. Elsewhere, except in the plantation zones and India's cotton districts, markets and commercial production existed in pockets but did not pervade societies. This did not mean ordinary people in Atlantic Europe and coastal China were better off than those elsewhere. By and large they were not. But their societies were richer and included more prosperous families, generally merchant families and owners of agricultural estates. In Atlantic Europe, but less so in China, rulers became more responsive to the wishes of commercial elites, nowhere more so than the Dutch Republic, where the rulers and the commercial elite were the same people.

Other Regions in the Global Economy

India's connections also expanded after 1500, thanks above all to the cotton trade. They now reached to the Americas and West Africa, although rather thinly. The older links to Southeast Asia, East Africa, and Southwest Asia only strengthened, although some of the actual connecting was now done by European merchants, including the VOC. In general, India's position with respect to the world's webs changed less than coastal China's or Atlantic Europe's: it had long been tightly linked throughout the Indian Ocean trading world, by foreigners—Malays, Persians, and Arabs mainly—as much as by Indian merchants, and that remained true after 1500, although the foreigners involved now sometimes included Europeans. Those parts of India where cotton growing, spinning, and weaving were concentrated—Gujarat and Bengal especially—became yet more commercial in orientation. So did Kerala, in the southwest, where peasants and landowners found that raising peppers for export and buying food was a preferable strategy to subsistence food production.

Europe east of the Elbe River also underwent a shift to a more commercial economy after 1500 or 1550. Landowners in Prussia, Poland-Lithuania, and Russia developed big grain-producing estates and sold their harvests to cities around the Baltic and in Atlantic Europe. Like the plantations of the Americas, these estates relied on forced labor. Peasants—called **serfs** because they were legally tied to the land and not free to leave—increasingly were required to work several days a week on their landlord's estate. In Russia, serfs could also be bought and sold, and their status differed little from that of slaves in Brazil or the Caribbean. Landlords also monopolized the right to make alcohol from excess grain and sell it. Commercialization in eastern Europe was agrarian: it did not lead to rapid urban growth but to the proliferation of big estates, each one a world unto itself but with ties to ports and through them to overseas urban markets—again like the plantations of the Americas.

Southwest Asia before the 1490s had stood at the center of the Old World web, a crossroads of trade, travel, and information. Under Ottoman control by 1550, this region together with Egypt had long been among the most commercialized in the world—since the cloth workshops of ancient Sumer. By 1800, it was still closely linked to neighboring lands, and by sea to the Indian Ocean's ports. But the biggest flows of world trade now passed it by. The relative importance of caravan trade across the steppe lands of Asia declined, even if absolute quantities did not. Trade and information flows elsewhere in the world—across the Atlantic, for example, or between China and Southeast Asia— grew far faster than anything involving Southwest Asia. Its economic importance in

The Fur Trade An 1845 watercolor depicts a white trapper and his Amerindian family navigating the waters of interior North America. Mixed families like this worked at the source of what was a transatlantic trade in furs.

the world dwindled, and its former advantages in access to information about distant markets and foreign technologies disappeared. In a sense, Atlantic Europe dethroned Southwest Asia between 1500 and 1800.

One indication of that change is the connections in which Africa was enmeshed. Before 1500, Africa's strongest linkages, by far, were with Southwest Asia, both by land via Egypt and by sea. But in the course of the next few centuries, while these connections persisted, stronger ones developed linking Africa to Atlantic Europe and to India, mainly in the form of the slave and cotton trades.

Nonetheless, the bulk of Africa's economies, devoted to farming and pastoralism, bore little connection to the outside world except for the gradual spread of American food crops. Most families produced for themselves. Few sought to maximize production in the ways that Chinese or Indian cotton-producing peasants did in response to market incentives. The African entrepreneurs attuned to distant markets were mainly slave traders or in the elephant-hunting and ivory export business. They were just as ruthless profit-maximizers as Dutch VOC traders or Gujarati cotton merchants, but this culture of commercialism was a rarity in Africa. Where the violence and commercial opportunities of the slave trade did not intrude, African economic life was more stable, less dynamic and disruptive, and less market oriented than in either coastal China or Atlantic Europe.

The Americas, in contrast, became much more powerfully, and disruptively, connected to the wider world between 1500 and 1800. The plantation zones, the mining regions, and the northern lands devoted to the fur trade were thoroughly enmeshed in the commercial web that now spanned the globe. By 1800 even some small-farming districts, such as those of southern New England, were substantially market oriented and took part in a transatlantic economy that extended not only to Atlantic Europe but to the Caribbean and West Africa too. Many of the Amerindian peoples had also linked up to market economies, whether through the mines of the Spanish Empire, the fur trade of French North America, or a deerskin trade that thrived in the Carolinas in the eighteenth century. Only a few people in 1800, maybe 2 to 4 million in all the Americas, conducted their economic lives locally without reference to distant markets.

This patchiness of the global economic web carried consequences that we will return to in later chapters. The most momentous of them flowed from the fact that by the late eighteenth century the most connected place of all—not the happiest, not the most just, not the best in any moral sense, but the most connected—was Atlantic Europe.

Conclusion

In the three centuries after 1500, a true global economy developed for the first time in world history. Like all economic shifts, it benefited some and hurt others.

During these centuries, world population and the world economy more than doubled in size. Some people, like Jakob Fugger and Virji Vora, became unimaginably rich by taking advantage of new opportunities in trade and banking. Most people, however, grew poorer over these centuries, as evidenced by data on both shrinking average heights and falling wages.

The most dramatic economic change in these centuries was the rise of transoceanic trading in commodities such as spices, cotton, and silver. All three had existed for many centuries on smaller scales, but now all three expanded in size and scope, flowing along the new circuits of global commerce. New business formats arose in response to the globalizing economy and to the growing financial distress of rulers. Plantations, joint-stock companies, and modern banks all fit the new realities. They could mobilize resources on a scale unavailable to most family businesses and partnerships.

The new global economy rewarded those people who could gather the most information about conditions, prices, and politics around the world. Such people could buy cheap and sell dear in different markets. Or they could lend money wisely—rather than to a prince about to be defeated or a merchant about to go broke. Such people might live almost anywhere, including in Augsburg and Surat, like Fugger and Vora. But, increasingly, they were likelier to be found in Atlantic Europe. Flows of information and goods combined to make Atlantic Europe's economy, by 1800 and probably by 1750 if not 1700, more innovative, dynamic, and disruptive than that anywhere else, including the other parts of Europe. The next century and a half of world history, from roughly 1750 until 1918, may be seen in many ways. But one of those ways is as an age of Atlantic European pre-eminence.

Chapter Review

KEY TERMS

population surge p. 751

gross world product (GWP) p. 753

spice trade p. 759

cotton p. 761

silver p. 763

patío process p. 764

economies of scale p. 767

slave-and-sugar plantations p. 769

Tacky's War p. 770

chartered joint-stock companies p. 771

Dutch East India Company (VOC) p. 771

fractional reserve banking p. 776

commercial revolution p. 777

serfs p. 780

REVIEW QUESTIONS

1. What accounts for the rising prominence of Atlantic European societies in global economic history after 1500?

2. Why did global population more than double between 1500 and 1800?

3. What spurred the massive growth of the world economy between 1500 and 1800?

4. Why did most ordinary people around the world grow smaller in stature while economies grew faster than ever before?

5. In what ways did European oceanic merchants change the scope of the spice and cotton trades?

6. Explain the two main reasons for silver's expanded role.

7. How and why did sugar profits rest on the exploitation of environments and people?

8. Describe the novel tactics merchants used to reduce the risks of long-distance trade beginning in the sixteenth century.

9. Who relied heavily on banks, and why?

10. What were the similarities and differences between the commercial revolutions in China and those in Atlantic Europe?

11. Compare how the global economic connections of India, eastern Europe, Southwest Asia, Africa, and the Americas changed after 1500.

12. What was the most dramatic economic change between 1500 and 1800?

Go to INQUIZITIVE

to see what you've learned—and learn what you've missed—with personalized feedback along the way.

REVOLUTIONS

1640 to 1920

The weaving of the Global web between 1450 and 1800, the subject of Part 4, had several revolutionary consequences. Some of them, such as the formation of a global economy and the advance of commercialization, were part of the process of web building itself. Others, no less revolutionary, were not. Part 5, which includes Chapters 21 through 25 and deals with the years 1640 to 1920, takes up some major transformations that followed—and to some degree, resulted from—the spinning of the Global web. They were all interconnected and overlapping.

Transformations: Political, Economic, Social

The first of these major transformations involved politics and violence. Several political revolutions reverberated throughout the world during these centuries, rearranging hierarchies but never—revolutionary rhetoric notwithstanding—eliminating them. The most consequential of these political revolutions took place around the shores of the Atlantic Ocean, in West Central Africa, western Europe, eastern North America, and Spanish America. They all shared some general features, although they led to different outcomes. Together, they established ambitions for self-rule that have reverberated around the world ever since. They are the subject of Chapter 21.

The second transformation was, and remains, the most important: the industrial revolutions, the first of which took place in England. Several more followed, all of which changed the ways things were made, affected living conditions and health, reshuffled geopolitical relationships, and brought new impacts on the environment. At the heart of this economic transformation was a shift in energy regime—specifically, the widespread adoption of fossil fuels beginning with coal. Industrialization included important changes in transport and communications, such as railroads, that sped up connections in the Global web. This transformation is the focus of Chapter 22.

The third transformation partly flowed from the second: it was a pair of liberations helped along by industrialization. The first of these, a partial liberation from disease and early death, translated into giant improvements in human health and life expectancy between 1750 and 1950. The other liberation was the abolition of legal slavery and serfdom, which began in the late eighteenth century. For thousands of years, most societies had recognized forced labor systems such as slavery or serfdom as legal and just. Then, from about 1780 to 1920, almost every society changed its laws on this. Some came to regard slavery or serfdom as immoral or a sign of backwardness. Others, such as the southern states of the United States, abandoned slavery only by force, after losing a war over it. But one way or another, slavery and serfdom were abolished, a dramatic departure from the patterns of the deeper past. In a sense it is as if history was speeding up. Social changes—and big ones fundamental to the human condition such as health and freedom—were now coming thick and fast, as Chapter 23 shows.

Chapter 24 considers nationalism and imperialism between 1800 and 1920. Both of these major developments were also helped along by industrialization. Nationalism, which is at root a sense of shared identity among the people of a nation-state, or people hoping to create one, was rare or non-existent before 1600. After 1790, however, it emerged in several settings, and by 1900 was felt strongly by hundreds of millions of people around the world. Its emergence strengthened some countries such as Japan but weakened ethnically diverse empires such as the Ottoman Empire. Nationalism together with industrialization made some societies far more formidable than others in economic and military terms. The strong took advantage of the weak, acquiring new territories and incorporating them as subordinate colonies in a political system that is often called modern imperialism. The Global web came to include ever more direct political relationships, as the most industrialized states—including Britain, France, and other European states, the United States, and Japan—built overseas empires in Asia, Africa, and the islands of the Pacific.

Empires provoked resistance. So did nationalism when it seemed to trample on other forms of identity. Several kinds of resistance, especially rebellions and political revolutions, reverberated around the world between 1850 and 1920—the subject of Chapter 25. It first considers several uprisings against imperial power in the nineteenth century, from small-scale examples in the U.S. West and the Brazilian backcountry to giant struggles such as the Taiping Rebellion, the Indian Rebellion, and the U.S. Civil War. The chapter moves on to a threesome of large-scale political and social revolutions in the early twentieth century, in China, Mexico, and Russia.

In Part 5 we see some of the indirect effects of the formation of the Global web. Old certainties, such as the acceptability of slavery or of monarchical rule, came in for questioning. Old hierarchies and social orders sometimes now seemed unjust—or merely unfavorable to new coalitions of people who were acquiring the wealth, power, and ambition to change them. Meanwhile, industrialization and changes in health and labor regimes profoundly affected millions of people worldwide. Social and economic changes, such as the rise of commercial classes or the formation of an urban working class, were coming faster than ever. The foundations of longstanding political orders shook and often crumbled as a result, opening the door to new kinds of politics. That crumbling began in the Atlantic world.

The Best and Worst of Times

ATLANTIC REVOLUTIONS

1640 to 1830

FOCUS QUESTIONS

1. In what ways was the Atlantic world becoming more densely connected after 1600?

2. What were the key similarities between the revolutions in Kongo and Britain in the seventeenth century?

3. What tensions between Britain and its American colonies led to the American Revolution?

4. What were the major outcomes of the French Revolution?

5. In what ways was the Haitian Revolution a distinctively Atlantic revolution?

6. What tensions contributed to the wave of revolutions in Spanish America?

7. What features did all of these Atlantic revolutions share?

On July 14, 1789, a crowd of 900 artisans and workers attacked a 400-year-old prison in eastern Paris. The Bastille, as it was known, had once held important political prisoners, including aristocratic enemies of French kings such as the satirical author Voltaire. As prisons went, it was a nice place, complete with a library—it held 389 books in 1787—a garden, and curtained windows in most cells. In the eighteenth century, the French Crown used the Bastille in its attempts to control unruly publishers—as a place to store books it had banned and printing presses it had seized. The Bastille had acquired public notoriety in part through banned, and therefore prized, memoirs of prisoners such as Henri Latude, a soldier and mathematics student who had done time for, among other things, sending a box of poison to the mistress of King Louis XV. But by the summer of 1789, the Bastille's best days were behind it: the expense of keeping it up seemed too great to those in charge of French finance, who hoped to close it. Its 82-man garrison guarded only four counterfeiters, two madmen, one nobleman accused by his family of sexual depravity—and 250 barrels of gunpowder. It was the gunpowder the crowd of 900 was after.

At the cost of several dozen deaths, the crowd fought its way into the Bastille, killed its governor (prison warden), liberated its surprised prisoners, and seized the gunpowder—igniting an urban uprising in Paris. The uprising grew into a revolution, and its opening act, the storming of the Bastille, became the pre-eminent symbol of liberation in France. A sharp-eyed businessman got permission to tear down the prison and sell its fragments, which then were taken on tours of France as icons of the toppling of an unjust despotism. July 14, Bastille Day, has been France's national holiday for over 120 years. But the Bastille was only one of several symbols, and the French Revolution only one of several Atlantic revolutions. Something was afoot around the shores of the Atlantic.

CHRONOLOGY

1576 Establishment of Portuguese trading colony at Luanda

1641–1649 British Civil Wars

1641–1660 Garcia II reigns in Kongo

1649–1660 Commonwealth and Protectorate in Britain

1661–1685 British Restoration

1665–1709 Fragmentation of power in Kongo

ca. 1684–1706 Lifetime of Beatriz Kimpa Vita

1688–1689 Glorious Revolution

1707 Union of Scotland and England

ca. 1743–1803 Lifetime of Toussaint L'Ouverture

1756–1763 Seven Years' War

1763–1765 Pontiac's War

1764 Britain imposes new taxes on American colonies

1767 Bourbon Reforms begin in Spanish America

1774 Continental Congress assembles

1775–1781 American Revolution

1780–1783 Revolt in Andes led by Túpac Amaru

1787–1789 American Constitution drafted and adopted

1789–1799 French Revolution

1790 Slave uprising in St. Domingue

1791–1804 Haitian Revolution

1793 Jacobins end elections; French royal family is executed

1793–1798 British troops fight Haitian revolutionaries

1799–1815 Napoleon Bonaparte heads French government, becomes emperor

1807–1814 Napoleon Bonaparte occupies Spain

1815 Spanish king sends large armies to Colombia and Venezuela

1825 Formal recognition of Brazilian independence

1826 Spain's American empire is reduced to two islands

This chapter explores six revolutions around the Atlantic and tries to explain both what they shared and each one's particular elements.

The Atlantic World in Global Perspective

As we've seen in recent chapters, a Global web formed in the centuries after 1500 as oceanic trade, travel, and biological and intellectual exchanges knitted the world together as never before. The process affected coastal communities, especially port cities, more than anywhere else. But it touched every society and every state involved in oceanic links.

The Atlantic world was forging new connections faster than anywhere else after 1600. New circuits of Atlantic trade reshuffled fortunes and misfortunes. Men and some women of modest origins became rich by trading slaves, sugar, cottons, indigo, wine, fish, and other goods. Those lifted by the new commerce wanted liberty to make more money faster than before, liberty in some cases to practice minority religions, and liberty in the form of guarantees against arbitrary measures by old political elites. To secure these liberties they sought a greater political voice. Many of them, ironically, were slaveowners or slave traders who would never consider liberty for slaves.

The quests for new liberties developed alongside new political ideas. These ideas, often about freedom, sovereignty, and the sharing of power, spread with ships, sailors, and merchants from port to port. Coffee houses and taverns, custom houses and dockyards witnessed arguments about tyranny and liberty. Where people could read, cheap pamphlets and newspapers, as well as word of mouth, served to spread the new political principles. Even if merchants, sailors, cobblers, peasants, and slaves did not agree on just what liberty or freedom might mean, increasing numbers of them felt that they had a right to more of it.

Outside the Atlantic world, the new oceanic connections proved less politically disruptive, for several reasons. In some cases, such as in Qing China or Mughal India, oceanic trade accounted for a smaller proportion of the economy as a whole than in most Atlantic societies. Some merchants grew rich in these lands, as we saw in Chapter 20; but overall they were few and weak compared to the thousands of landlords living off of rents paid by peasants, and the ruling elites living off of taxes or war loot. As long as these landlords could control their laborers and in turn supported the state, the basic arrangements of political life endured. Newly rich merchants had a tough time banding together as an interest group against such well-entrenched incumbents—landowners, bureaucrats, military castes, and imperial courts. Instead, they gradually joined the old elites, if they did not come from those groups to begin with.

In general, merchants around the Indian Ocean and the South China Sea were already plugged in to the circuits of power, the result of centuries-long negotiations with kings, sultans, emperors, and their bureaucrats. They had mastered the arts of securing political favors through generous gifts to rulers and savvy marriages of their daughters to princelings. They could reach their goals within the system and rarely wished to overthrow it.

Although they faced many challenges, the ruling elites in Tokugawa Japan, Qing China, Mughal India, and the Ottoman, Russian (Romanov), and Habsburg empires proved adept enough at adjusting to a globalizing world to avoid revolutions before 1850. In these places, the underlying principle of monarchical rule survived intact. These ruling elites contained, co-opted, or destroyed rival coalitions of power in their own domains more successfully than did several of the old elites in the Atlantic world.

In some Atlantic societies, the new pressures and opportunities coming from the new circuits of commerce and ideas proved enough to spark revolution. In others, they didn't. To understand why, let's zoom in on specific Atlantic societies.

Kongo and Britain, 1640–1709

In the decades after 1640, the kingdom of Kongo in West Central Africa and the British kingdoms of England and Scotland experienced revolutions. After costly civil wars and eras of religious strife, by 1710 merchant elites in both settings had sharply reduced royal power and expanded their own.

Civil War and Revolution in Kongo, 1640–1709

Kongo, as we've seen, was an African kingdom formed in the fourteenth and fifteenth centuries and centered on the south bank of the Congo River. Its subjects were mainly from an ethno-linguistic group called Bakongo and spoke a language called Kikongo. After 1483, its kings forged ties with Portuguese mariners to bolster their royal power. That led to sustained trade links, Christianization of the royal lineage, expansionary warfare, and occasional reliance on Portuguese military power. It also led to one of the best-documented histories anywhere in sub-Saharan Africa before 1800. The Kongo elite left Portuguese-language documents from about 1520 onward, and European missionaries and traders who learned local languages, and took part in Kongo life, wrote down their observations and experiences beginning about 1580, giving us a richer understanding of history here than in most places in Africa.

Monarchy and the Slave Trade   Kongo kings maintained diplomatic relations with Catholic countries of Europe and with the Papacy. Their power rested on their ability to use Portuguese trade goods, including firearms, to maintain a military, win prestige, and buy and raid for slaves. The Kongo state also controlled other exports such as ivory and copper, and it maintained the firm loyalty of lineage heads who themselves controlled, at least loosely, the labor of the common people. Most of those people farmed cassava and maize, American food crops first acquired via Atlantic trade. The geographic base of royal power was the fertile, productive, and densely populated vicinity of the capital, São Salvador. It was, by African standards, an unusually centralized state, thanks to the concentrated resources and population around the capital.

The **Kongo monarchy** was not hereditary but, in theory, elective. In practice, each time a king died a power struggle took place, often bringing brief civil wars, the winner of which became king. To stay alive and in power, kings had to negotiate a challenging diplomatic and military landscape. They faced problems of internal cohesion, as in any kingdom; border troubles, mainly to the east and south; and after the 1570s, the presence of a Portuguese colony based in the northern Angolan city of Luanda.

One particular responsibility of Kongo's kings was to protect their subjects from enslavement. A large part of the kings' legitimacy and support depended on it. One king in the 1580s went so far as to ransom some of his subjects who had been enslaved and shipped to the offshore Portuguese sugar island of São Tomé. In Kongo society, subjects explicitly expected kings to protect them; if kings could not, their authority collapsed.

In this regard, the establishment in 1576 of a Portuguese trading colony just south of Kongo, at Luanda, created an enduring problem for Kongo kings. The Portuguese eagerly traded in slaves and would happily buy anyone, including subjects of Kongo. To protect their Kongo subjects, the kings needed income, weapons, and loyal followers—and to get all that, they had to continue to trade slaves on their own account. They tried hard to get them from neighboring societies or from the ranks of rebels within Kongo, and not from their own loyal subjects. They had succeeded in this while Kongo was expanding at the expense of neighbors; but by the 1590s, when expansion slowed and then ceased, kings of Kongo found it harder to get slaves to sell for weapons.

After 1590, most royal reigns in Kongo were short and many more Kongo subjects were captured in civil wars or rebellions and enslaved. Then a particularly

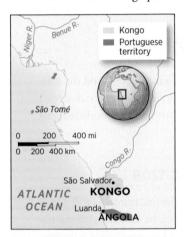

The Kingdom of Kongo, ca. 1640
One of many African kingdoms, Kongo took shape in the fourteenth and fifteenth centuries. Its rulers strengthened their grip through participation in Atlantic trade, especially by acquiring firearms from Portugal. When Portugal established a base at Luanda in 1576 and expanded its slave trade to Brazil, it gradually destabilized Kongo.

Portuguese Kongo By the late seventeenth century, the Portuguese colony based in Luanda in northern Kongo was itself a large planned city, as this image from the period suggests. Figures in the foreground highlight the centrality of the slave trade to the city's economy.

skilled and lucky king, Garcia II, took over in 1641. When he acceded to the throne, his subjects spelled out their expectations: "You shall be king, be no thief, neither covetous nor revengeful, but be a friend of the poor: You shall also give alms for the release of prisoners or slaves." He ruled over roughly half a million people, most of them speakers of the Kikongo language. Garcia, a graduate of a Jesuit school in the capital city of São Salvador (today's M'banza-Kongo in northernmost Angola), took power by force and constantly had to fight rebels to maintain his kingdom. His success represented a high point in the history of the Kongo monarchy. The stability of his reign allowed trade to prosper, boosting the fortunes of some of his lieutenants and supporters. Part of that trade was in slaves, generally captured or purchased on the frontiers of the kingdom. Like earlier kings of Kongo, Garcia II traded in slaves himself. On one occasion, he sold 700 slaves to the Dutch in exchange for an attack on Portugal's Luanda colony.

Fragmentation of Power Things fell apart for Kongo soon after the death of Garcia II in 1660. His successor renewed war with Portuguese forces—made up mainly of African soldiers serving the Portuguese colonial governor in Luanda—and was killed together with most of his high-ranking followers in 1665. Various contenders for power emerged, many of them men who had become empowered and enriched by trade during Garcia's reign. For decades none could vanquish all rivals, and Kongo fell into civil war. Neighboring states took advantage of the chaos to try to put their puppets on the throne. São Salvador was sacked several times.

The fragmentation of power had something to do with Kongo's Atlantic connections. Rival factions competed for alliances with the Portuguese and briefly with the Dutch. They tried to use European missionaries to bolster their authority. They struggled to win advantageous positions in the trade for foreign goods such as cloth, iron, and guns. That inspired them to try to monopolize exports of slaves, ivory, and copper. During the violent decades of fragmentation (1665–1709), the volume of slaves exported from Kongo

Kongo and the Atlantic This portrait of Kongolese diplomat Miguel de Castro shows him wearing Dutch garb. The portrait speaks to Kongo's embeddedness within the Atlantic world during the period.

increased sharply, and Kongo warlord-entrepreneurs increasingly financed their quests for political power by capturing and selling their fellow Bakongo—which had rarely happened before the kingdom fell apart. In 1701, one Kongo warlord wrote a letter to the Pope asking permission to sell Kongo Catholics so he could afford to defend his territory. (There is no record of any papal response.) At this point, the old prohibition in Kongo against enslaving subjects of the kingdom had vanished, and all were at risk.

Beatriz Kimpa Vita's Movement for Re-unification

A young woman inspired by a Christian saint tried to bring the chaos in Kongo to an end. **Beatriz Kimpa Vita**, born about 1684 to a prominent Kongo family, sought to re-unite the kingdom. Women had long played behind-the-scenes roles in Kongo politics, and after the breakdown of the kingdom following 1665, some took more direct parts in the ensuing power struggles. Beatriz was apparently a high-spirited youth who preferred to think for herself. Two early marriages did not work out, and in her late teenage years she became more interested in faith than husbands. She had some training in local religious traditions, but by 1700 or so felt more attracted by Catholicism. She soon felt possessed by the spirit of St. Anthony, a medieval Portuguese priest and the patron saint for the recovery of lost goods or people. She believed that Christ was unhappy with the fragmentation of Kongo and preached that it must be re-united. She approached two claimants to the throne, one after the other, but both declined her help. So she decided to do it herself.

She convinced thousands that God spoke through her and that all should work for the re-unification of Kongo. She took the unorthodox view that Jesus, Mary, and other central figures in Christianity were all Bakongo, which offended European missionaries but won supporters in Kongo. By 1705, she and her followers had taken up residence among the ruins of São Salvador, where she established herself in the wreckage of the cathedral. One rival sent an army against her, but she converted its commander and the wife of the would-be king who sent it. She had become a major force in Kongo politics by age 21, commanding strong loyalties among masses of poor people and an increasing number of prosperous ones.

Beatriz Kimpa Vita did not, however, command much of an army. Her movement threatened all other aspirants to power in Kongo, and in 1706 one of them launched his forces against her. She was captured, declared a witch and a heretic, and burned at the stake. Her followers were defeated in battle, and 30,000 of them sold into the Atlantic slave trade. By 1709, a much weaker Kongo was nominally under the control of a new king. In reality, the king had little authority and local rulers held sway. Kongo became a highly decentralized polity with power residing in provincial families and warlords, not in the court or the king in São Salvador. Civil war, partly a routine power struggle and partly an outgrowth of changes brought on by Kongo's participation in the Atlantic world, especially the slave trade, destroyed the old kingdom of the Kongo and gave rise, after decades of violent anarchy, to a new, different, and weaker state. This was a revolution that constrained royal authority sharply and shifted power to local elites.

The old political principle undergirding the legitimacy of kings, one that obliged them to see to the security and welfare of their Bakongo subjects, was gone. After 1665, no one was secure, and anyone in Kongo might be enslaved. The political contract between ruler and ruled had changed. Kongo's troubles had loose parallels elsewhere.

The British Civil Wars and Revolution, 1640–1707

Another land beset by religious strife and civil war was England. Here again a **rising class of merchants** enriched by Atlantic trade were at the center of events. And here again they and their allies upset the structures of power, weakened kingly authority, and in the process put their country through a bloodbath. A charismatic religious zealot tried to unite the country—and briefly succeeded rather better than Beatriz Kimpa Vita in Kongo.

These events are traditionally called the English Civil War (or Civil Wars), lasting from 1641 to 1649, followed by the Commonwealth and Protectorate (1649–1660), the Restoration (1660–1685), and the Glorious Revolution (1688–1689). But because Scotland and Ireland took such a large part in these struggles, it makes more sense to see them as British Civil Wars or a British Revolution. At issue was how much power monarchs should have, whether there should be monarchs at all, and how much religious liberty to allow Britons, as well as the proper relation of Scotland and Ireland to England.

England and Wales in 1600 counted about 4 million inhabitants, mostly Protestant in religion. Both were ruled by a long-lived queen, Elizabeth I, who reigned with a strong hand, although not quite the iron fist favored by her father, Henry VIII. She consolidated the position of the Protestant religion in England, giving rise to what would become the Church of England (Anglicanism), headed by herself. Elizabeth lasted 44 years on the throne, providing stability. But she died, unmarried and childless, in 1603, the last monarch of the Tudor dynasty.

Her throne passed to her cousin James, a Scottish king from the Stuart dynasty, long in power in Scotland. James had keenly awaited this moment, because Scotland was a small kingdom with under a million inhabitants, most of them dirt-poor, and most

Elizabeth I of England Painted in 1588 at the height of her reign, this portrait depicts Elizabeth I surrounded by symbols of her country's rising naval power and its supremacy over its rival, Spain.

of them Protestants of a Calvinist sort, called Presbyterians. As James I of England, he would rule a much larger and richer kingdom. Ireland came with his inheritance. Ireland was also poor, with a population of 2 million, almost all Catholics. The three kingdoms had long histories of warfare among them, and many of their subjects had long memories and strong attachments to their preferred sect of Christianity.

James balanced the interests of his three kingdoms reasonably successfully for a while, although a Catholic conspiracy tried to blow him up in 1605. In his later years, when he was drinking heavily and his health slipping, he indulged his taste for arbitrary rule and alienated some of the elite who felt entitled to a larger voice in political matters. He was a learned man, conversant in Latin and French, and liked to lecture everyone within earshot on the "absolute prerogative of kings." And in fact his legal authority, like that of the Tudor monarchs before him, was close to absolute. His biggest problem was finance: he needed the consent of **Parliament**—a legislative assembly partly elected by property owners (House of Commons) and partly composed of hereditary nobles (House of Lords)—to raise enough revenue. In 1625 James died, and his son Charles took the throne with a firm belief in the right of kings to rule as they pleased.

King versus Parliament Charles I (r. 1625–1649) came to power at age 24 and had not learned to play well with others. He quarreled with Parliament, which in 1628 officially forbade taxation without its consent. No one was willing to lend to the Crown. Desperate for money, Charles resorted to seizing property and selling it. To many of his subjects, he appeared too sympathetic to Catholics—his wife, a French princess, was one. He was less popular than his father, who had been less popular than Elizabeth. The monarchy's stock fell further when Charles tried to force the Scots Presbyterian

Church to adopt a new prayer book based on Anglican tradition. Many Scots rose in rebellion. Now in urgent need of armies and money, Charles I could no longer ignore Parliament.

His timing could hardly have been worse. The entire seventeenth century in Britain was marked by rising prices and stagnant standards of living. Fuelwood and coal prices climbed especially fast. And the 1640s was one of the coldest decades of the Little Ice Age in Britain, with bad harvests and pervasive hunger. Ordinary people had plenty to complain about.

So did the more comfortable ones elected to Parliament. A torrent of complaints, mainly about royal overreach, flooded the body when it met in 1640. Many in Parliament were Puritans, zealous Protestants who felt that bishops and royal power over the church were illegitimate. Compromise did

Death Warrant of Charles I A detail of the death warrant that was signed by representatives of Parliament in 1648. Oliver Cromwell was among the signatories.

not come easily to them. When an Irish rebellion flared up in 1641 and the king needed even more money and men, he could not get the cooperation he wanted. Soon both he and members of Parliament were recruiting their own armies, and by 1642 they were at war. The king set up his headquarters in a college of Oxford University.

Warfare now ravaged England as well as Ireland and Scotland. Allegiances were chaotic. Every county had its own civil war. But in general English Catholics sided with the king, and Puritans with Parliament. The people of London, and the urban middle classes, tended to support Parliament. Royalists, as those loyal to the Crown were called, seemed to be getting the upper hand in the early 1640s, but Scottish armies helping the forces of Parliament turned the tide. King Charles was captured, and in 1649 tried for treason and publicly beheaded, maintaining to the end the right of kings to rule unhindered and that no court could try a king for any crime.

The Commonwealth The victors set up a republic called the Commonwealth of England. It soon slid into military dictatorship, ruled by Oliver Cromwell. Cromwell, a parliamentarian and Puritan, distinguished himself in warfare against the royalists. Confident that God endorsed his every move, he was among those who signed the death warrant of King Charles. He led a brutal suppression of Ireland in 1649–1650 and managed to subdue Scotland by 1653. By force of arms he had achieved what kings could not: a unified Britain under the near-absolute power of one man. But his religious zealotry alienated all those who did not share his Puritanism. His persecution of Catholics in Ireland and Scotland bordered on genocide. After a while, many who had opposed Charles I and welcomed a republic began to think kings weren't so bad after all. The wars and their attendant epidemics and famines, between 1639 and 1653, cost England about 4 percent of its population, Scotland 6 percent, and Ireland a staggering 40 percent.

When Cromwell died of malaria in 1658, the republic gradually fell apart. After an interval of chaos, Parliament invited the son of the beheaded king to rule over England, Scotland, and Ireland. Charles II ascended the throne in 1661. His followers dug up Cromwell's body and beheaded it on the anniversary of the beheading of Charles I. Cromwell's severed head remained on display in London until 1685.

The Restoration   The principle of monarchy was restored and endures to this day in Britain. But Parliament and the propertied classes it represented—landowners, merchants, lawyers, and others—had successfully asserted their privileges. The monarchy henceforth was weaker than it had been in Elizabeth's time, and it would weaken further. Cromwell's political revolution had been overturned, but the result was a decentralization of power. As in Kongo, the British Civil Wars weakened central authority; unlike Kongo, Britain restored internal peace—and exported only a few thousand of its people to the Americas as forced laborers, mostly Irish and Scottish vagrants and rebels.

King Charles II lived until 1685, devoting at least as much attention to his mistresses as to affairs of state. He sought to reduce discrimination against Catholics and lost a war with the Dutch, provoking his own struggles with Parliament. His younger brother, James II, was a Catholic, and his succession brought a new crisis. Once on the throne, James showed signs of trying to re-establish a more centralized monarchy and of treating religious minorities, chiefly Catholics, with toleration. But Protestant elites, fearful of what James might do, invited a Dutch aristocrat, William of Orange (who was married to James II's eldest daughter, Mary), to invade the country. Eager to improve the Dutch position against France in European geopolitics, William accepted the invitation, overthrowing his father-in-law in 1688–1689.

The Glorious Revolution   William's English allies, members of the Protestant elite, intended to prevent James II from solidifying royal power at their expense. In effect, they wanted to preserve the principles established in the wars between Parliament and king in the 1640s. Their remarkable act of conspiracy and treason became known as the **Glorious Revolution**. Almost bloodless, in sharp contrast to the wars of four decades before, it consolidated the position of Protestants in England and Scotland and the strength of Parliament with respect to monarchs. Parliament made it illegal for Catholics to ascend the throne, a law not changed until 2013. Partly to ensure that no Catholic could come to power in Scotland, Parliament in 1707 undertook the union of Scotland and England, ruled ever since by a single government seated in London.

The British Revolution, spanning the period 1640–1707, ultimately established the principle that Parliament ruled over England and Scotland. Kings and queens increasingly became symbols, sovereign only in name, while their ministers and the people's representatives in Parliament governed. The British Revolution resulted in the triumph of both mercantile elites and landed gentry, but above all of Protestants, especially Anglicans, at the expense of Catholics, who were denied the right to serve in Parliament or as officers in the military. These arrangements at first inspired some rebellions, especially among Catholics in Scotland, which ended in 1746. The settlement of 1707 provided the basis for a stable polity in Great Britain for centuries to come.

North America, 1750–1790

The British Civil Wars and Revolution left most British subjects with the impression that property-owning adult males should enjoy some political rights, and that government should be based on consent of the governed. Many who left Britain for North America brought these convictions with them. The literate and best connected among them also kept in touch with friends and relatives in Britain, and a few, mostly merchants, had ties with other lands as well. As a result, they knew something of the political struggles ongoing in Europe over the proper forms of government and the extent of royal power.

North America in 1750 remained home to a substantial, if falling, Amerindian population, almost all of whom lived west of the Appalachians. These lands were claimed by Britain or France, but not yet occupied by either power except for a few wooden forts. The Amerindians, however, had long been fighting losing battles for their land—indeed, since the first English and French settlements in 1607 (Virginia) and 1608 (Quebec).

By 1750, North America's eastern seaboard was dominated demographically by European immigrant settlers and their slaves, all but a few of whom were at least partly of African descent. It was dominated politically by Great Britain and included 14 British colonies stretching from Georgia to Nova Scotia. The colonies' population was about 1.3 million—but growing fast. Migrants kept pouring in from Britain, and to a lesser extent, Germany and elsewhere. Land was cheap, and free people, usually with enough to eat, were remarkably healthy. Families with 6 to 10 children were common. Even the most downtrodden, the slave population of the plantation colonies (South Carolina and Virginia chief among them), was growing through natural increase, reaching about 230,000 in 1750. French settlements along the St. Lawrence River, called Quebec or Canada, counted about 60,000 people, also growing quickly. An even smaller population existed in Spanish outposts in Florida and along the Gulf Coast. Virginia was the biggest of all these colonies, with nearly half a million people in 1750, 40 percent of whom were slaves.

In 1750, no one supposed that any of these colonies would soon become independent. None of the mainland colonies, not even Virginia, was as important to Britain as Jamaica or even tiny Barbados, with their profitable sugar plantations.

North America, 1750–1783 The peace settlement of the Seven Years' War (1756–1763) left Britain in nominal control of all eastern North America. France ceded all its territorial claims there, and Spain traded Florida for the return of Havana in Cuba and Manila in the Philippines. Amerindian populations, most of them west of the Appalachian Mountains, had no voice in the settlement. The grievances of American colonists grew steadily during the late 1760s and led to the American Revolution, which effectively ended with the siege of Yorktown. Thirteen of the British mainland colonies became independent as the United States. Spain recovered Florida for another 35 years, and thousands of loyalists fled the United States for British colonies in Canada or the Caribbean.

The North American colonies were squabbling constantly. But within a quarter-century, 13 of them would be fighting for freedom from British rule.

Growing Tensions with Britain

Broad economic and social changes would lead some Americans to aspire to independence from Britain. Many of these changes came from Atlantic connections. Not only did colonists share in some of the political ideas in circulation in Britain, but trade links created prosperous elites with ambitions. In the southern colonies, rice and tobacco plantations, based on slave labor, supported a class of rich planters who considered themselves every bit as good as English aristocrats. In New England, New York, and Pennsylvania, successful merchants and professionals, including some whose fortunes came from slave trading, increasingly thought of themselves as equal to their counterparts in England and deserving of the same political rights.

That situation alone probably would not have led to anything much, but in 1754 a 22-year-old Virginian unintentionally started what would become the first global war. In the summer of that year, authorities in London instructed the colonies in North America to coordinate an effort to check French expansion west of the Appalachians. The colonial assembly in Virginia decided to send its militia, commanded by a youthful George Washington, into what is now western Pennsylvania. After he attacked a French post, Britain and France declared war on one another, and eventually fought on three continents and the high seas in the Seven Years' War (1756–1763, sometimes called the French and Indian War in the United States). Britain's superior sea power and better state finance enabled it to prevail, acquiring nominal title to lands west of the Appalachians from France.

But British victory led to new tensions in North America. Most of the British colonies soon felt that Britain was treating them unfairly. The colonials' irritation with Britain focused on two main issues.

Amerindian Lands First was access to the lands in the interior of North America. Now claimed by Britain, these lands were populated by Amerindians. Authorities in London tried to control that vast space from the Gulf Coast to Canada with some 500 soldiers, whose conduct alienated many Amerindian chiefs accustomed to reasonably smooth relations with French traders. Meanwhile, the Euro-American population of the eastern seaboard, whose numbers were growing fast, wanted to push Amerindians off their lands and farm them or profit from their sale. Britain wanted to reserve most of those lands for Amerindians in the interest of maintaining peace.

A large Amerindian uprising confirmed the British concern over unrest in the region. Irritated by British soldiers, and in some cases fearful of losing their land to settlers, many Amerindians—groups from the Ottawa, Delaware, Seneca, and Huron among them—joined in what is called Pontiac's War in 1763. Pontiac, an Ottawa chief, was only one of many leaders. They took eight British forts around the Great Lakes during the years 1763–1764 in a loosely coordinated set of campaigns. Their assaults on colonial settlements in Pennsylvania and Virginia brought counterattacks on Amerindian villages. A few thousand people were killed, many in grotesque ways. British tactics included deliberately trying to infect Amerindians with smallpox at Fort Pitt (now Pittsburgh) and paying a bounty for scalps of any Amerindians over age 10, a response to the scalping of white children by Amerindian war parties.

Militarily it was a standoff, but politically Pontiac and his followers won a significant victory. In the early months of the struggle, the British issued a proclamation that designated North America, from the Appalachians to the Mississippi River and from Florida to Quebec, as an "Indian reserve." Negotiations ended **Pontiac's War** in 1764–1765, confirming Amerindian rights to lands west of the Appalachians.

For many colonists, especially in Virginia, Pennsylvania, and New York, the settlement seemed a betrayal of their rights and interests by a distant king. The Crown, as they saw it, had taken the side of savages who had massacred hundreds of colonists, rather than allow British subjects to occupy western lands. The king, or at least his ministers, had larger strategic interests to consider, and those were incompatible with colonial expansion sure to inflame Amerindian resentment.

British Taxes   The second issue was taxes. The British government in 1764 began to impose new taxes on the American colonies in order to help pay debts incurred in winning the Seven Years' War. After all, their armies and navy had protected the colonists from assaults by the French and their Amerindian allies. Many colonials, however, saw the matter differently. After 1763, there was no French threat anymore. With no further need for British protection, the colonists didn't want to pay for it, especially considering that they had no representation in the British Parliament that decided upon taxes. This irritation at new taxes was gradually framed as a matter of principle: British subjects in North America should have the same rights as British subjects in Britain, and therefore should be taxed only by their consent, by representative assemblies of their own choosing. "No taxation without representation" became a popular slogan.

Colonial Americans organized boycotts of sugar, official documents, and tea—items on which Britain hoped to collect new taxes. Some proclaimed that they would be no better than slaves if they permitted themselves to be taxed with no say in the matter. In Boston especially they rioted now and again, on one occasion dumping valuable cargoes of tea into the harbor in what became known as the Boston Tea Party. In 1768, the British government chose to send two army regiments to Boston to keep the peace. Ben Franklin, the Boston-born, Philadelphia-based printer and all-purpose intellectual, warned that this was as prudent as "setting up a smith's forge in a magazine of gunpowder." And so it was.

Frictions in Boston flared up into violence in the early 1770s. On the coasts, the British Royal Navy fell into conflict with merchants and fishermen. British governors tried to keep colonists out of the Indian reserve, but with little success. Virginia's governor, Lord Dunmore, complained that he could not "restrain the Americans [who] do and will [move west] as their avidity and restlessness incite them." Farmers in North Carolina, who called themselves the Regulators, refused to recognize British courts and tried to establish their own system of justice. From Massachusetts to Georgia, colonists who before 1763 could agree on nothing now agreed that they deserved the full "rights of Englishmen" and should not be taxed without their consent.

In 1774, their representatives came together in a new assembly called the Continental Congress. They petitioned Parliament to reconsider several of its policies. But fighting broke out around Boston in the spring of 1775 between local militias and British regiments, leading to six years of warfare.

The American Revolution

The **American Revolution** (1775–1781) was a revolutionary war and a civil war. It was a revolutionary war in that the American forces—mainly poor men—were led by elites who sought fundamental political changes. In the summer of 1776, representatives of 13 colonies gathered in Philadelphia as the Second Continental Congress. The representatives cited grievances going back to 1764 and principles that separated just government,

Revolution in North America In this French engraving, New Yorkers tear down a statue of King George III following approval of the Declaration of Independence in July 1776.

with the consent of the governed, from "absolute despotism." The second sentence of their Declaration of Independence read: "We hold these truths to be self-evident, that all men are created equal, that they are endowed by their Creator with certain unalienable Rights, that among these are Life, Liberty and the pursuit of Happiness." The author of these words, Thomas Jefferson, ironically was a Virginia slaveowner.

The American Revolution was a civil war in that about 15 to 20 percent of Americans were loyalists who wanted to remain within the British Empire. Rebels and loyalists occasionally indulged in bloodbaths, especially in the Carolinas. It was an unpopular war in Britain, where most of the population wanted peace and favored making concessions to get it—as Britain had done in Pontiac's War.

Keys to American Victory The war was a close contest. The Americans won because the fighting was an ocean away from Britain, and because France, Spain, and the Netherlands all joined in against Britain. They provided the Americans with much of the money, weaponry, and engineering expertise they needed, and almost all the naval power. Their entry sapped political support for the war in Britain. There the Crown was mainly concerned about preserving its colonies in the Caribbean, its position in India, and its naval superiority in the waters close to Britain. The rebellious lands from Georgia to Massachusetts just weren't worth that much in comparison.

The Americans also won because their leaders, in particular George Washington, had the good sense to fight a patient war. He avoided major battles, which, as he knew, the better-trained, better-armed, and better-disciplined British Army was almost sure to win. When he did get trapped into giving battle, he normally lost. His volunteer army sometimes threatened to melt away. Most of his foot soldiers had signed on for a cash enlistment bonus or the promise of land after the war, and not for principles of representative government. Keeping them together as an army was a remarkable feat.

In 1781, Washington had to shoot the ringleaders of mutinous New Jersey troops, who were owed money that Congress could not pay.

Washington also had the wisdom to require inoculation against smallpox for every man in the Continental Army when an epidemic was threatening to destroy it. Diseases killed about 10 times as many men as did combat in the war, and so reducing losses to infection made a big impact.

Major combat operations ended in 1781. The French navy coordinated with both the French and the Continental armies to pin the bulk of the British forces in a swampy, malarial spot at Yorktown, Virginia, where they surrendered. When a peace treaty was negotiated confirming American independence in 1783, some of Washington's followers urged him to declare himself king and establish a monarchy. Instead, Washington resigned his commission and retired to his Virginia plantation.

Only thirteen British colonies had joined the war. The Caribbean island colonies, such as Jamaica and Barbados, and the northernmost—Nova Scotia, Prince Edward Island, and Quebec—chose to remain British. Seventy thousand loyalists fled during and after the war, mainly north to what would become Canada. They took about 2,000 slaves with them.

Outcomes of the Revolution

Those who remained in the newly independent United States had many differences among them. It took years of politicking before Americans could agree on the principles underlying their new country, formalized in a constitution drafted in 1787 and adopted in 1789. Based on the belief that just government required the consent of the governed, it established a federal structure balancing the authority of a central government against that of constituent states. It also carefully divided power among three branches of government: a judiciary, a legislature, and an executive—a president, the first of whom would be Washington, coaxed from retirement. Its first ten amendments, called the Bill of Rights, added in 1791, guaranteed certain liberties for citizens, such as the freedom of religion, of speech, to bear arms, and to a jury trial. Voting rights were left up to the states, most of which allowed only property-owning adult white males, about 6 percent of the population, to vote.

Women's Rights Political rights for women hardly crossed men's minds. In early 1776, while her husband John was away in Philadelphia hatching plans for rebellion from Britain, Abigail Adams tried to alert him to an oversight. She wrote to him:

> I long to hear you have delivered [independence]—and by the way in the new Code of Laws which I suppose it will be necessary for you to make I desire you would remember the Ladies and be more generous and favourable to them than your

ancestors. Do not put such unlimited power into the hands of Husbands. Remember all Men would be tyrants if they could.

When her husband replied and dismissed her concerns, in another letter (with the inconsistent capitalization normal in the eighteenth century) she added:

> I cannot say that I think you are very generous to the Ladies, for whilst you are proclaiming peace and goodwill to Men, Emancipating all Nations, you insist upon retaining absolute power over Wives. But you must remember that Arbitrary power is like most other things which are very hard, very liable to be broken.

Neither the Declaration of Independence nor the Constitution reflected any of Abigail Adams's views. In general, the American Revolution left the matter of women's political rights untouched, despite the participation of women in the boycotts of the 1770s and the support they gave the Continental Army as cooks, nurses, and washerwomen—indeed, a few had even managed to serve as soldiers by disguising themselves as men.

Compromising on Slavery The Revolution was no more revolutionary on the issue of slavery, although it came in for more discussion. After much debate, and difficult compromise, the framers of the Constitution decided to permit slavery where it already existed and to allow the continuation of the Atlantic slave trade until 1808. States, however, were free to make their own rules, and Vermont and Massachusetts, which had relatively few slaves, soon passed laws making slavery illegal. But the states where most of the Republic's half a million slaves lived passed no such laws, and those states' political strength ensured that the federal government could not either. Jefferson in 1782 had written that slavery was an "unremitting despotism" and that "I tremble for my country when I reflect that God is just." But he did not even free his own slaves. Ironically, slavery lasted in the United States until 1865, long after it had ended in the British Empire against which Americans had fought for freedom.

France, 1780–1815

The **French Revolution** led to the formation of another republic at the expense of another monarch. It led to deeper changes in France than had the American Revolution in the United States. The revolutionaries in France overthrew the principle of monarchy, proclaimed the sovereignty of the people, established a secular republic, killed a king, seized most of the property of the Catholic Church, abolished slavery throughout the French Empire, abolished all they could of feudalism, legalized divorce, established freedom of religion, and even instituted a new calendar. The French did all this, and then undid most of it.

Origins of the French Revolution

The origins of the French Revolution make up one of historians' favorite puzzles. Like all the revolutions considered in this chapter, the French Revolution had deep and tangled roots. Some of them were intellectual, anchored in what is called the Enlightenment. Some were socioeconomic, based in slow changes in French society. Other, shallower, roots were financial, and even climatic.

The Enlightenment   The European Enlightenment took shape in the early eighteenth century. Its center lay in France, but participants lived in most parts of Europe, from Poland to Spain and from Italy to Scotland. It was, in essence, an intellectual movement involving a few thousand well-educated people, although to some extent their ideas affected others, even people who could not read or write—the majority everywhere. In France, its chief targets for reform—or perhaps for elimination—were the twin institutions of monarchy and church. To supporters of the Enlightenment, both seemed out of date and obstacles to human progress. The ideals of the Enlightenment included reliance on reason and science, wider political liberty, and religious toleration for Christians of all sorts and often for Jews. Its exponents were thinkers such as François-Marie Arouet (1694–1778), who mocked the institutions and traditions of France under the pen name Voltaire; Denis Diderot (1713–1784), who tried to compile all knowledge in a 28-volume encyclopedia, published between 1751 and 1778; and Immanuel Kant (1724–1804), a German philosopher who claimed that morality derives from reason. Its sponsors were mainly wealthy patrons, often women who organized "salons" dedicated to discussion of political questions as well as to art and literature. The most prominent was Suzanne Necker (ca. 1737–1794), a Swiss Protestant of modest origins. An intellectual in her own right, she was particularly interested in hospital reform and the question of whether divorce should be legal. She married a successful financier and ran a Paris salon in the 1770s and 1780s that attracted the most active thinkers, writers, and artists.

Salons In this engraving from the eighteenth century, Suzanne Necker is shown seated with her daughter at one of her famous Parisian salons, listening to a writer read his work aloud. The spaces created by *salonnières* such as Necker helped Enlightenment ideas to develop and spread.

Socioeconomic Changes   The intellectual currents of the Enlightenment flowed together with socioeconomic changes in France. In the late eighteenth century, the French, like other Europeans, divided their society legally, politically, and culturally into three "estates." The clergy constituted the First Estate, about 0.5 percent of the population of 28 million as of 1789. It owned 10 percent of the farmland and pastureland in France and had the right to impose taxes (tithes) on peasants. The nobility made up the Second Estate, about 1 to 2 percent of the French public. They owned about 25 percent of the productive land and enjoyed exemption from most taxes. The Third Estate included everybody else—except the landless poor, who were outside this system altogether. Peasant farmers made up most of the Third Estate, which paid almost all the taxes and had the least political influence in France. They owned at most 40 percent of the useful land in France, usually in small plots. Urban artisans and professionals were also in the Third Estate; many urban families owned farmland too. There was little social mobility in this system: only rarely did anyone change their status as a member of one or another estate. This system of social and political hierarchy, all subject to the authority of the French king, is often called the Old Regime.

Over the course of the eighteenth century, France became more urbanized. Atlantic trade played some role in this shift, especially in western France. Cities such as Bordeaux and Nantes rose to prominence on Atlantic trade, including the slave trade. Merchant and professional classes grew in number, strength, and ambition. They resented the grip on social status and political influence held by the nobility. For many in these classes, monarchy and church seemed hostile to their ambitions.

Meanwhile, the French aristocratic elite—the nobility and the top ranks of the clergy—began to divide against itself by 1770. Like all elites, it had always had its lines of fracture. But now some came to share doubts about the Old Regime system, particularly about the efficiency of the monarchy, which wasted money, employed incompetent bunglers, and lost most wars. Voltaire recommended following the Chinese example and staffing government offices not with well-connected aristocrats but with smart young men selected by examination. Many among the elite thought the Catholic Church suffocated society and culture. Others thought that aristocratic lords (often, their own friends and relatives) did the same to agriculture and the economy by resisting innovations, whether in crop rotations or technologies.

Other Pressures Other pressures were slowly building in the lower echelons of society. France's population grew from 20 million to 28 million between 1700 and 1789. Unlike the situation in the colonies in North America, where land was plentiful, in France population growth did not enhance prosperity for ordinary folk. Land was growing scarce, and much of it was already owned by nobles and the church. Population growth did not mean expansion so much as overcrowding. The prospects for poor peasants were getting bleaker.

All of this might have come to nothing without short-term financial and climatic stresses. The French Crown, like most monarchies, had perpetual money problems

Food Riots One of the catalysts of the French Revolution was a poor harvest and astronomically high food prices. The price of bread impelled hundreds of women of all social classes to march on the royal palace of Versailles in 1789, as illustrated in this engraving.

worsened by the heavy costs of war. After 1778, French involvement in the American Revolution drained what was left in the French treasury, now deep in debt. Neither bankers, nobles, nor the Catholic Church would lend money to the king except at the most exorbitant interest rates. In France, the body with the authority to vote taxes was the Estates-General. No French king had consulted it for over 170 years. When the king, desperate for revenue, summoned the Estates-General in 1789, he ignited a political wildfire, blown this way and that by swirling winds beyond anyone's control.

To add to the pressures, in the 1780s bad weather brought meager harvests and widespread hunger. An Icelandic volcano erupted in 1783–1784, spewing dust into the atmosphere and blocking sunlight. Its effect lasted two or three years, reducing harvests and raising grain prices in northern Europe. In 1788, drought hit France—and then a cold winter. Ordinary people normally spent about half their income on food, but by 1789 that was up to 90 percent. Now people who had never heard of Voltaire or discussed ideas of sovereignty rioted over bread prices and clamored for lower taxes—the last thing King Louis XVI wanted. The food crisis brought poor people—men and women—together as nothing else could, and briefly made them a political force in France.

The Early Revolution

The French Revolution began when the Estates-General, composed of representatives of the three estates, met in 1789. Its members understood that they, like England's Parliament in 1641, had bargaining power because the king needed money desperately. Soon the Third Estate declared itself to be a National Assembly, embodying the will of the people. Some clergymen joined it. The king tried offering some concessions, but in the summer of 1789 he fired his most reform-minded ministers, a signal that he hoped to face down the Third Estate. Then the poor artisans, clerks, and petty shopkeepers of Paris stormed the Bastille, hungry people rioted in other cities, and peasants began to attack the property of their landlords and the church. The Revolution was under way, and no one knew where it would lead.

The Declaration of the Rights of Man and Citizen   In August 1789, the National Assembly decided to abolish the feudal privileges of the clergy and nobility. All citizens of France would henceforth be legally equal. No more tax exemptions for the nobility. No more dues owed by peasants to nobles or tithes to the church. The Assembly adopted an extraordinary document entitled The Declaration of the Rights of Man and Citizen, which borrowed from Enlightenment thought and from the American Declaration of Independence. The first of its 17 Articles proclaimed that "Men are born and remain free and equal in rights." The third stated that "The principle of sovereignty resides essentially in the nation," which meant adult males.

Some French women objected to being excluded. In the fall of 1789, one group wrote a pamphlet intended for the National Assembly asking why 13 million females should be the slaves of 13 million males (they underestimated the national population slightly). In 1791, Olympe de Gouges, a woman of modest origins from the southwest of France who had moved to Paris and become a playwright, a political intellectual, and a fierce opponent of the enslavement of Africans, wrote a counterblast that she called Declaration of the Rights of Woman and Citizen. Although de Gouges won little popular support among either men or women in her call for equality, women soon achieved the right to divorce husbands and to equality in matters of inheritance. But not to vote or hold office.

Men did a little better with political rights in the first years of the Revolution. At first only men over age 25 who paid taxes were allowed to vote—about 4 to 5 million Frenchmen, around 15 to 18 percent of the population. By 1792, almost all males over age 21 could vote. But in 1793 they elected representatives, most of them young men, who allowed no further elections.

Targeting Church and Monarchy   Securing political rights was only one part of the Revolution. In the late fall of 1789, the National Assembly confiscated most of the lands and buildings of the Catholic Church and sold them. It forced most clergy to retire and made the others employees of the state. It made Protestants and Jews equal citizens with Catholics. The church in France eventually recovered some of its property, but never the power it lost in 1789.

From 1789 to 1791, the National Assembly ruled France in uneasy harness with King Louis XVI. But the king, sensing his position weakening, attempted to flee the country. He was caught, eventually put on trial, and executed. This earned the revolutionaries many enemies within France and in Europe. The French royal family had kinship ties with royalty in Austria. Kings everywhere felt threatened. By early 1792, revolutionary France was at war with the monarchs of Austria and Prussia.

A Radical Turn

Now the Revolution entered a much more radical and violent phase. The wars against foreign monarchies required unity among the French. But unity could not be achieved by consensus, as many sympathized with the dead king and the dispossessed church, especially in the provinces. So the revolutionaries sought unity through compulsion. The executive machinery of government (called a Legislative Assembly in 1791–1792 and the National Convention in 1792–1795) was increasingly dominated by men called **Jacobins**, mostly middle-class, many of them lawyers, who were prepared to take drastic measures to prevent the Revolution from collapsing. They often allied with the urban poor, usually called *sans-culottes* because they wore trousers rather than the more fashionable knee-breeches. The Jacobins ended elections in 1793 and ruled with an iron hand.

Jacobin Reforms Jacobin members of the revolutionary government sought to change almost everything. Sometimes they aimed to improve the human condition, sometimes to save the Revolution from its enemies, sometimes to destroy one another in their competition for power. One of them, Louis Antoine de Saint-Just, a 26-year-old law school dropout and poet, declared that "everything that is not new in a time of innovation is pernicious." The Jacobins instituted a tax reform whereby the wealthier paid more, a popular move. They created a mass army through conscription, an unpopular one. They tried to create a new religion, sometimes called the Cult of the Supreme Being, based on concepts of civic virtue and an abstract God who preferred reason to faith. They promulgated a new calendar in which the beginning of the Republic in fall 1792 became Year I. It divided years into 12 months, each of three 10-day weeks. No longer would ordinary people get one day in seven off; the calendar was never popular. Days were divided into 10 hours, and hours into 100 minutes of 100 seconds, part of an effort to replace tradition with reason. The Jacobins instituted the metric system of weights and measures. They banned aristocratic fashions such as men's powdered wigs and women's velvet dresses. They abolished slavery in France and French colonies. They encouraged people to destroy statues of kings and bishops and melt them down to be turned into weapons for the army. And they made it clear they would tolerate no dissent. By late 1793, citizens who did not have a "certificate of public virtue" issued by the state could be arrested on sight. The unfortunate Madame de Gouges, suspected of disloyalty to the Revolution, was among those guillotined in Paris.

The Committee of Public Safety The Revolution now reached a stage that historians call the Terror. The government, dominated by a so-called Committee of Public Safety, itself soon dominated by a 34-year-old lawyer, Maximilien Robespierre, found enemies everywhere. Robespierre, who liked to be called "The Incorruptible," was a man of principle at any cost. In early 1794, he wrote that "the spring of government during a revolution is virtue combined with terror: virtue, without which terror is destructive; terror, without which virtue is impotent. Terror is only justice prompt, severe and inflexible; it is ... a natural consequence of the general principle of democracy, applied to the most pressing wants of the country." Saint-Just told the deputies of the Convention that "a nation creates itself only upon heaps of corpses."

He and Robespierre did their part to build those heaps. The Committee of Public Safety ordered the arrest of half a million people and had some 20,000 executed. Everyone now lived in fear. Some 150,000 people, mostly nobles and clergy, fled France, many of them for America. Rebellions in the countryside, prompted by conscription as much as anything else, cost tens of thousands of lives. Ambitious revolutionaries denounced one another, hoping to climb the slippery pole of political power at one another's expense. Robespierre turned on his friends and comrades at the slightest suspicion of dissent. As one observer put it, "Like Saturn [of ancient Greek mythology] the revolution devours its children." In the summer of 1794, the Terror reached a climax with public executions in Paris averaging about two dozen daily.

Unfortunately for Robespierre, Saint-Just, and the Committee of Public Safety, the military situation for France improved, weakening their main justification for relentless execution of their political enemies. In a few dramatic days, they lost much of their support in the Convention and, together with their closest supporters, lost their heads at the guillotine in late July 1794.

The Convention created a new government called the Directory (1795–1799), which excluded men under age 30 from office. It faced many challenges, from hunger riots to coup d'état conspiracies to rampant inflation. Political turmoil declined but did not disappear. The Directory re-instituted elections but was appalled when royalists won. Some of its members in 1799 mounted a coup against their own government. They installed a military man, **Napoleon Bonaparte**, who gradually made himself a dictator—in the name of liberty and equality.

Napoleon Bonaparte: Expansion and Overreach

Bonaparte (1769–1821), who had served in France's revolutionary army, rose from obscurity through talent and ambition. He made his name by crushing a royalist rebellion in Paris in 1795 and became a general at age 26. He won a string of astounding victories against foreign armies beginning in 1796.

The revolutionary republic had been at war since 1792. While fighting for its life against reactionary foreign monarchs, it was nonetheless pursuing traditional French foreign policy, conquering and occupying the same neighboring lands that French kings had previously tried to subdue. Under Bonaparte, however, the French army roamed farther afield and with startling success, especially in Italy, Austria, and Germany. Everywhere it went, Bonaparte's army tried to set up new governments. They were supposedly embodiments of universal principles proclaimed by the Revolution,

Napoleon's Russian Campaign A dramatic 1808 painting depicts the bleak aftermath of the 1807 Battle of Eylau in East Prussia, which Napoleon's forces lost. Napoleon appears at the center on horseback, while bodies lie piled in the snow and farms and villages burn in the distance.

but in practice mainly puppets of Napoleon, sometimes ruled by his relatives. They always found local people who joined them enthusiastically against their own kings and princes. Thus Bonaparte's armies and agents re-wove the fabric of European politics, spreading some of the ideals and practices of the French Revolution.

Bonaparte's military success was part genius and part system. He knew his business well and was especially effective in coordinating field artillery with infantry and cavalry. Thanks to conscription and the size of the French population, he usually had a bigger army than his enemies. Big armies were hard to feed, but Bonaparte found that his could live off the land, buying or stealing food from farms and villages. This worked well as long as the army kept moving and operated in the agriculturally richer parts of Europe that produced enough surplus food.

Bonaparte's system failed when his armies entered poorer lands without much surplus food. Unfortunately for him, for France, and for the Revolution, Bonaparte could not stop attacking other countries, even poor ones with slender surplus. He had a bottomless need for glory. And he rightly feared what would happen, to him and to France, if he discharged a million men with military skills. When he attacked Spain in 1807, his army became bogged down in endless anti-guerilla operations. When he attacked Russia in 1812 and occupied much of the country, his army of 600,000 dwindled to 25,000 within months through starvation, typhus and other diseases, and an unexpectedly stiff resistance from Russians. As the French novelist Victor Hugo put it, Bonaparte was "conquered by his conquests."

These and other disasters undermined his political support at home, and by 1814 he had to abdicate the imperial throne he had earlier awarded himself. In France, the nobility soon recovered most of its former lands, and the monarchy and church returned atop society, although less powerful than before 1789. Some changes, such as the Napoleonic law code, remained in force. In Europe, all the revolutionary governments installed

From French Revolution to French Empire, 1789–1814 The government guiding the French Revolution declared war on Austria and Prussia in April 1792, igniting more than two decades of warfare. Under Napoleon Bonaparte, the French set up sympathetic rulers in Italy, Germany, Spain, and Poland, but none survived his downfall. The inset shows the location of key sites in revolutionary Paris.

by Bonaparte's army were overthrown, and monarchs across Europe climbed back onto thrones—even in France in 1815. But in most cases they had to share power with legislatures.

The Revolution was dead, politically and militarily defeated, but it lived on in the hearts and minds of millions of people in Europe. The ideas it unleashed, however imperfectly brought into practice, retained some of their appeal. Revolutions and republics since 1789 have drawn inspiration from the French experience. And the stated political principles, like those of the American Revolution, remain compelling to billions of people today who cherish freedom, justice, and equality before the law—even if everyone understands these concepts differently.

Haiti, 1780–1804

The French Revolution proved inspirational in the French colony of St. Domingue (today's Haiti), where a revolution exploded in 1791. Like the French Revolution, the Haitian Revolution attacked a hierarchical social and political order. But, in contrast to the French revolution, race and slavery were at the center in Haiti.

A Plantation Colony: Sugar, Coffee, Slaves

Acquired in war from Spain in 1697, St. Domingue soon became France's most valuable colony. Its lowland plains proved excellent for raising sugar, and its hills equally good for less profitable crops such as coffee. By the 1780s, St. Domingue had 8,000 plantations. It produced nearly half the sugar and coffee harvested in the Atlantic world. Thirty ships a week used its ports, carrying its products to France and bringing in human cargoes from Africa.

Its population, about 550,000 in all, was nearly 90 percent slaves, two-thirds of whom were born in Africa. In the 1780s, some 30,000 slaves arrived annually, largely from Kongo. Two-thirds were male. They worked mainly on the plantations. About 5 percent of St. Domingue's people were free blacks or people of mixed African and European ancestry, called *gens de couleur*. Some of them were rich planters and slaveholders—indeed, they owned one-quarter of the colony's slaves—but most were artisans, petty merchants, or laborers. Another roughly 5 percent of the total population were whites, mainly born in France, 80 percent of whom were men. Some were rich planters, others wage laborers. All whites enjoyed legal privileges based on skin color, such as the right to bear arms or to hold political office. Almost all hoped to get rich and get back to France. Few succeeded.

St. Domingue was a tinderbox of unfulfilled ambitions. Whites wanted political representation in Paris, much as in British North America colonists a few years earlier had wanted representation in London. They wanted to be free to trade their sugar and coffee anywhere, not just to France. The *gens de couleur* wanted equality with whites. Slaves wanted freedom. Word of the revolution unfolding in France in 1789 provided a spark. The first uprising involved the *gens de couleur* in 1790, led by one of the richest men in the colony. Colonial authorities crushed it.

Toussaint and the Haitian Revolution

A far bigger one, involving at its outset about 100,000 slaves, erupted in the summer of 1791. It took the whites and *gens de couleur* by surprise. Most slave risings in the Americas failed before they started because someone betrayed the plans in advance. Somehow this one, the biggest of all, was kept secret.

The primary leader of the revolution, **Toussaint L'Ouverture**, was born a slave in the north of St. Domingue, probably in 1743. He grew up handling animals and became an expert horseman. He also learned the healing arts. His master freed him when Toussaint was about 30, and as a free man he sometimes owned slaves himself. He spoke French, Ewe (the West African language of his father), and the French-based creole (*kreyol*)

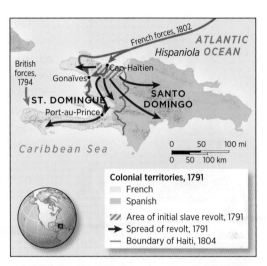

The Haitian Revolution, 1791–1804 Enslaved Africans, and others of African descent, engineered the largest slave revolt in world history beginning in 1791, turning the French sugar colony of St. Domingue into a new country, Haiti, by 1804. The uprising began on sugar plantations in the north and prospered especially in difficult, mountainous terrain where guerilla warfare was practical. French armies, arriving in force in 1802, controlled the ports but could not crush the revolution in the countryside. What little remained of them departed in 1804.

that was the lingua franca of St. Domingue. He was a practicing Catholic and learned to read and write as an adult. It turned out that as a middle-aged man he had remarkable physical stamina, courage in the face of death, and the smarts and flexible principles of a master politician. By 1792, he was one of the top commanders of the slave insurrection.

French planters in St. Domingue could not get much help from France against the uprising. Many Jacobins sympathized with the slave insurrection. And by the spring of 1792, revolutionary France was fighting for its survival in Europe. War with Britain and its powerful navy made it hard for the French army to reach Haiti. So French planters invited Britain to occupy St. Domingue and crush the slave insurgency, which Britain agreed to attempt lest the uprising spread to its own slave and sugar colonies in the Caribbean. British troops arrived in 1793.

After a couple of years of shifting allegiances, Toussaint organized an army that gradually swelled to 20,000 poorly equipped men to fight the British occupation. Like Washington a generation earlier, he could not afford to fight set-piece battles against the British army and knew it. He fought a guerilla campaign, moving as needed, attacking when he saw an opening, and prudently allowing yellow fever to scythe down his enemy.

Toussaint L'Ouverture The leader of the Haitian Revolution appears in uniform on horseback—cast in the role of a heroic general—in a French engraving from the period.

Toussaint recognized that he had an ally in yellow fever. Most of his men had acquired immunity to the lethal disease either in Africa or in St. Domingue, where just about everyone faced it in childhood. Virtually no one in the British Army had ever encountered it. Two-thirds of the British soldiers who landed in St. Domingue died of it. Those who survived left in 1798.

French Intervention The French then tried to undo the revolution in St. Domingue. A peace treaty with Britain opened the seas to French navigation in 1802, and soon Bonaparte's brother-in-law, leading an army about 65,000 strong, arrived. Bonaparte gave instructions to defeat the insurgents, then re-install the plantation system and slavery, less than a decade after France's revolutionary government had abolished it. Things went well at first for the French. But Toussaint and his ragtag army ("naked as earthworms," as he put it) had other ideas and knew time was on their side. He drew inspiration from the slave revolt of Spartacus two thousand years before (Toussaint owned books on Roman history). The army of former slaves, many of whom had prior military experience in Africa, tried to pin the French down in the unhealthy lowlands while keeping the mountains to themselves. Although Toussaint was captured in 1802 and died the following year in a French prison, his strategy worked again.

Toussaint's followers stunned France and the world by winning their revolutionary war against an army—Bonaparte's—that had humbled the kings of Europe. The French had spared no effort and still lost. Once again, the Haitians used their ally, yellow fever, which killed about 75 percent of the French army. The Haitians lost many as well, to combat, disease, and massacres (of which there were many on all sides). But they could recruit from the local population, which the French found difficult to do after it was revealed that Napoleon had re-legalized slavery in the French Caribbean.

Aftermath The **Haitian Revolution** triumphed by 1804. It ended both French colonial rule and legal slavery in Haiti. It was, perhaps more than any other, an Atlantic revolution. Some of its animating ideas came from the revolutions in America and France. Nearly a thousand *gens de couleur* had fought in the American Revolution against Britain. Between 1789 and 1804, events in Haiti and France directly affected one another. Some of the Haitian Revolution's soldiers came from the civil wars in Kongo, via the slave trade. And its victors would soon give advice and arms to revolutionaries in what is now Venezuela.

The Haitian Revolution, like the French, devoured its children. Toussaint's most prominent lieutenant, Jean-Jacques Dessalines, organized massacres of the remaining French and of his political rivals—and declared himself emperor. His own troops killed him in 1806. His successors, also leaders of the revolution, fought one another in civil wars, created regional despotisms, and, without calling it slavery, re-established forced labor on plantations where they could.

Toussaint and his followers had pulled off the largest slave rebellion in history, won wars against two of Europe's great powers, and established the second independent country in the Americas. But the Haitian Revolution still left the great majority of Haitians poor and powerless.

Spanish America, 1765–1825

Spanish America underwent a set of revolutions in the early nineteenth century. They were anti-colonial, like the American and Haitian revolutions, and resulted in several new republics. They led to abolitions of slavery and in places a degree of popular rule. But in most cases, they resulted in unstable autocracies or military rule.

A Diverse Society

At the end of the eighteenth century, Spanish America included most of South America, Central and North America as far north as Texas and California, plus several Caribbean islands. Social and economic conditions were extremely diverse over this vast terrain. Some 13 to 15 million people lived there. About 5 million lived in the Viceroyalty of New Spain (today's Mexico), with smaller centers of population elsewhere.

Ever since the conquests of the sixteenth century, people of Spanish birth (*peninsulares*) or Spanish descent (*criollos*, or creoles) dominated Spanish American society politically and economically. They held all public offices, filled the officer corps of the military, and staffed the top positions in the Catholic Church. They made up most, though not all, of the merchant class. Most parts of Spanish America included in their populations Amerindians—usually the demographic majority except in the Caribbean—slaves, free blacks, as well as large and growing communities of mixed descent. *Mestizos* were of Spanish and Amerindian ancestry; *mulattos* of African and European descent; *zambos* of African and Amerindian parentage. These groupings were fluid around the edges, and to some extent people could claim whatever status they wanted if they could make others believe it. These designations mattered, partly because of social prejudices and partly because of law: various privileges were reserved for *peninsulares* and *criollos*, and various legal handicaps for people of African descent, whether free or enslaved.

By 1760, the Spanish Empire in America was about 250 years old. This empire was essential to Spain's standing in Europe and the world, the source of about a quarter of its revenues. From Spain's viewpoint, its American empire had two great vulnerabilities. First, it was threatened by rising British military power. Second, its merchants objected to a monopoly trade system that required them to trade only with Spain. They wanted to trade with foreigners too. The rise of Atlantic commerce tempted them with opportunities they were legally forbidden to take.

The Bourbon Reforms

Spain's anxiety about British power, and its failures in the Seven Years' War (1756–1763), including a defeat at its major port of Havana, led to reforms coming from Madrid beginning in 1767. Known as the **Bourbon Reforms**, after the name of the ruling family in Spain, these were intended to strengthen the empire. Their backers had read Enlightenment thinkers and preferred reason to tradition as a guide to action. They were, in effect, technocrats, convinced they could make Spain's rule more efficient and productive, but in cases also idealists, hoping to improve human welfare. Under these reformist influences, the Crown allowed more cities to trade with Spain but cracked down on illegal trade with other empires. It reserved a larger proportion of political appointments for Spaniards at the expense of *criollos*. And it tried to curtail the power of the Catholic Church, most notably by expelling all Jesuits from the Americas in 1767. With these reforms, the Crown hoped in particular to strengthen colonial defenses,

Race in Spanish America Intermarriage between people of Amerindian, European, and African heritage in Spanish America created new categories of racial difference and hierarchy. Many images from the period show families of mixed racial heritage, such as these eighteenth-century paintings of families in everyday scenes.

pump up the economy, and increase the wealth flowing to Spain through new taxes and other means. The Bourbon Reforms, like most dynamic reform programs, pleased some and irritated many—rather like the reforms Britain enacted (new taxes and restrictions on westward migration) in the wake of the Seven Years' War.

Túpac Amaru's Revolt Almost nobody liked the higher taxes. In 1780, a giant tax revolt broke out in the Andes. It was led by an elite, Jesuit-educated *mestizo*, **Túpac Amaru II**, a descendant of the Inka Empire's ruling family. He proposed a return to the supposedly good old days of the Inka Empire. He promised justice, an end to oppression of Amerindians and *mestizos* by Spaniards, and the elimination of all distinctions based on ethnicity. He also called for fully free trade. His wife, Micaela Bastidas, was one of several Amerindian women who helped organize the rebellion. She took charge of military logistics.

This revolutionary agenda provoked firm and at times ruthlessly violent responses from Spanish authorities, which in turn made Túpac Amaru and his followers more radical still. Many of them concluded that the only route to justice involved full independence from Spain and the murder of all Spaniards. The revolt lasted until 1783 and cost the Viceroyalty of Peru about 10 percent of its population. It was suppressed with maximal cruelty, including a gruesome public execution of Túpac Amaru. Of the 73 leaders killed by Spanish authorities, 32 were women. Like many smaller revolts of Amerindians and *mestizos* before, it failed militarily but its memory lived on, among both those who welcomed it and those who defeated it.

Túpac Amaru's failed revolution frightened everyone committed to the future of the Spanish Empire in the Americas. It had almost deprived Spain of the wealth of the Andean silver mines. Ministers in Madrid, and their agents in the colonies, trembling with relief, redoubled their commitment to reform.

Amerindians generally found little to like in the Bourbon Reforms. They lost some legal protections. The Crown's efforts to unshackle the economy led to new opportunities for entrepreneurs, especially on the frontiers such as northern Mexico. To exploit those opportunities businessmen needed laborers, and they found ways to require Amerindians (among others) to work for them in mines, on ranches, and on farming estates. Debt peonage was one such technique, whereby poor people were encouraged to borrow money and obliged to pay off their debts through labor.

The reforms also increased the scope for slavery in Spanish America. In the 1770s, the Crown opened the Atlantic slave trade to all merchants. For three decades, the traffic boomed and over a million slaves were sold to the mines of Mexico, the plantations of the Caribbean, and elsewhere in Spanish America. An internal document of the Spanish government from 1802 acknowledged that "the opulence of [Spanish] America . . . could not exist without the slave trade."

The *criollo,* or creole, elites found plenty to dislike in the Bourbon Reforms too. They lost access to many political offices, which henceforth were open only to men born in Spain. Those creoles who had enjoyed privileged positions in the old monopoly

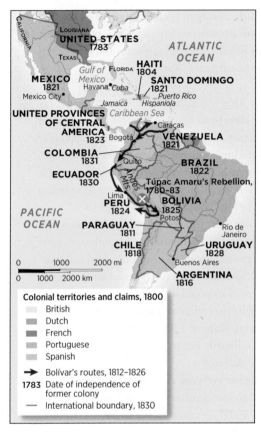

Spanish America, 1800–1830 In 1800, most of the American hemisphere was claimed by European powers, the greater part of it by Spain. Nevertheless, Amerindian peoples actually controlled sizeable parts of both continents; moreover, the United States was already an independent country, and Haiti would soon be. Spanish rule was shaken by the revolt led by Túpac Amaru in the Andes in the 1780s, and further uprisings against Spanish rule began in 1808, centered on what is now Mexico, Venezuela, Colombia, and Peru. By 1826, 17 new republics had emerged from the ruins of the Spanish Empire in the Americas.

trade system—the merchant guilds of Lima, Mexico City, and Havana, for example—lost out when the Crown permitted more free trade.

Tensions over Trade The Crown's experiment with freer trade was perhaps its most destabilizing step. Formerly only a few merchant guilds in the Americas were allowed to conduct transatlantic trade, and only with the merchant guild in Cadiz, a city in southwestern Spain. These rules, although widely flouted by smugglers, severely constrained the chances to make money in commerce. Beginning in 1765, the rules grew looser. By 1789, nine Spanish cities were allowed to trade with almost anyone in Spanish America, but no one was permitted to trade with foreigners. This program worked, but in a sense too well. Some creole merchants prospered mightily but grew ever more frustrated by their reduced political voice.

Thus, as in Haiti, few in Spanish America found political arrangements to their liking by the end of the 1780s. All sorts of suggestions arose for reworking relations with Madrid. A very few thought that independence from Spain was the best course. One such was Francisco Miranda (1750–1816), from what is now Venezuela. He had fought with Spanish forces in Florida against Britain in the American Revolution. In the 1790s, he fought for the Revolution in France and became a marshal of the French army. His military service, wide travels, and very wide reading led him to the conclusion that Spanish America ought to be free from Madrid's control. Miranda, tireless though he was in his efforts, had little direct effect on the politics of Spanish America while making his tour of revolutions around the Atlantic, and few others shared his view about independence.

Geopolitical Shifts

In the 1790s, matters grew more urgent as the wars of the French Revolution at times cut into Atlantic commerce. This was bad for creole merchants in Spanish America, whose discontent deepened. It was worse for the Spanish Crown, which needed the revenues from its American possessions. Everyone concerned was still searching for a new compromise between Spain and Spanish America, a new version of the empire.

Then in 1807–1808 Bonaparte's armies marched into Spain and Portugal and forced King Fernando VII to abdicate the Spanish throne. Bonaparte eventually installed his brother Joseph as the new king of Spain, which few Spaniards welcomed. Having lost St. Domingue in 1804, Bonaparte might have had his eye on the silver mines of Spanish America. He got, instead, six years of vicious guerilla war in Spain.

Now Spain and Spanish America were cut off from one another more than ever. This created a power vacuum in Spanish America, giving rise to countless factions. In cities such as Caracas, Bogotá, and Buenos Aires, local elites began to debate politics with the vigor of Jacobin clubs in Paris. Many wanted liberties of the sort Bonaparte often promised and rarely delivered, such as freedom from censorship, and fully free trade—in this case meaning trade outside the Spanish Empire, with Britain and the United States, for instance. From 1808 to 1814 the situation was fluid, although few yet thought in terms of independence.

In 1814, Bonaparte's army left Spain in defeat. King Fernando VII returned to power and immediately tried to restore Spain's hold over Spanish America. He hoped to turn back the clock. Many of the elites in Spanish America, now accustomed to greater liberties, especially in foreign trade, objected to the king's plans and embraced independence as a goal. Others, however, remained loyal to Spain. Civil wars soon erupted between revolutionaries and loyalists. As in North America in the 1770s, clumsy royal policy brought matters to a head quickly, converting reformists into revolutionaries.

Spain's efforts to bring its American colonies back into the fold failed spectacularly. In 1815, the king sent a large army to what is now Colombia and Venezuela, where, like the European armies in Haiti, it suffered epidemics of yellow fever and malaria. More than 90 percent of the army never came home. This was the only place where sizeable armies fought. Combat took place also in Mexico, Peru, and Chile, and around the city of Buenos Aires, but it involved small armies of a few thousand.

Bolívar and the Spanish American Republics

Revolutionary leaders, such as **Simón Bolívar** (1783–1830), a wealthy, aristocratic creole from Venezuela, forged coalitions of creole elites, free blacks, and *mestizos*. Bolívar was educated in Spain and France in his youth and admired Enlightenment ideas as well as the French and American revolutions. He supported women's political rights and made one woman, Manuela Sáenz, a general in his army. During a period of exile, he

Simón Bolívar A contemporaneous portrait of the Venezuelan creole revolutionary depicts him clad in military dress.

went to Haiti and learned about the revolution there. Bolívar and other revolutionaries often promised slaves freedom if they joined their forces.

Spain had little power to deploy in the Americas. Loyalists in Spanish America, although numerous in the upper ranks of society, could not drum up much support among the common people. Bolívar's and other ragtag revolutionary armies trudged far and wide across Spanish America, showing a determination that Spain's troops lacked. In addition, the revolutionaries enjoyed British support. The Royal Navy made it difficult for Spain to carry men and supplies across the Atlantic. Fighting waned after 1826, and soon Spain gave up entirely. Only Cuba and Puerto Rico remained of Spain's American empire.

Bolívar was hoping to achieve a united states of South America. Instead, seventeen new republics were born from the ruins of the Spanish Empire in America—a greater number than the leaders of the revolutions had hoped for. Confederations in Central America, in northern South America, and between Argentina and Uruguay fell apart a few years after independence. Bolívar expressed his disappointment with this fragmentation when he wrote that all who had served the revolution had only "plowed the sea."

In most of the newly independent republics, creole factions feuded for power. In most cases the new rulers reduced the sway of the church, leaving the military often as the only institution with any prestige. Military dictatorships were frequent. Only Chile managed some measure of stability in the coming decades. Amerindians generally found the revolutions did nothing for them. But the republics, whether dictatorships or not, abolished slavery within a few years or decades—whereas it lasted until 1874 in Puerto Rico and 1886 in Cuba. Spain, exhausted by recurrent warfare and with its American empire reduced to two islands, was finished as a world power and even as a great power within Europe.

The Atlantic Revolutions in Broader Perspective

Other Atlantic societies, such as Portugal, Spain, and Brazil, also underwent revolutionary changes. Bonaparte as we've seen invaded Spain and Portugal in 1808, creating conditions that led not only to independence across the Atlantic, but to struggles in Iberia. Absolutists supported restoration of monarchical rule, while liberals sought either republics or constitutional monarchies with representative legislatures. By the 1830s, after 20 years of instability, both Spain and Portugal emerged as constitutional monarchies. Brazil won its independence from Portugal when in 1807 the Portuguese Crown and court moved from Lisbon to Rio de Janeiro and governed the Portuguese Empire from that Brazilian city. When the king and court returned to Lisbon in 1822, they lacked the power to keep Brazil under their control. A prince, Dom Pedro I, defied his father and declared Brazil an independent monarchy, with constitutional limits upon royal power. After a few small battles, the Portuguese gave up, confirming the independence of Brazil in 1825.

Atlantic Connections

All of these revolutions, from Kongo and Britain in the late seventeenth century to Spanish America and Brazil in the early nineteenth, had their own local causes. At the same time, they all shared Atlantic roots: the reshuffling of fortunes resulting from expanding Atlantic commerce proved destabilizing almost everywhere around the ocean's shores. Rising merchant classes increasingly objected to the monopoly on state power held by monarchs and their traditional allies.

By and large, the Atlantic revolutions brought **political decentralization** of two sorts. First, they undermined highly centralized kingdoms such as Kongo and England before 1640, and France before 1789. Second, they dissolved some of the bonds of transatlantic empires by giving birth to newly independent countries in the Americas. In Kongo and England, the revolutions were in effect national, reducing royal authority and empowering commercial elites. In France, the revolution began that way, but it became international when Bonaparte invaded much of Europe and St. Domingue as well. In the Americas, the revolutions were anti-imperial, with the effect of creating newly independent countries, generally republics in place of colonies subject to European monarchs.

This pan-Atlantic movement did not sweep all before it. Many West African polities, even some deeply involved in Atlantic trade, managed to survive—partly because they were not so centralized to begin with. Several Caribbean colonies such as Jamaica and Barbados, as well as Cuba and Puerto Rico, remained colonies long after the era of Atlantic revolutions. So did the British colonies that are now in eastern Canada.

Nonetheless, the Atlantic record of revolution after revolution, establishing new principles of sovereignty, contrasts sharply with most of the rest of the world, where older polities and older principles held up better. In the big centers of population, such as China, north India, or Southwest Asia, the effects of oceanic commerce were less sudden and disruptive. Existing institutions and elites withstood better whatever revolutionary pressures bubbled up, even if specific dynasties came and went. Not so around the Atlantic.

This Atlantic taproot was not the only element that all these revolutions had in

CONSIDERING THE EVIDENCE

A Revolutionary's Letter from Jamaica

The revolutions in North America, France, and Haiti inspired revolutionaries in Spanish America, including Simón Bolívar (1783–1830). Bolívar was Spanish by descent, but his birth in South America made him part of the creole class that the Spanish Empire excluded from political offices after the Bourbon Reforms of 1767. For Bolívar, who had studied Enlightenment writings in Europe as a young man, the tyranny of imperial rule was distressing, but he also found it attractive because it commanded respect. He felt that if Americans like him could rule, instead of distant Spain, they could build a better future by unifying the provinces of South America. While living as an exile in Jamaica in 1815, he set down his reasons for revolting against Spain in a letter to a British gentleman.

We are still in a position lower than slavery, and therefore it is more difficult for us to rise to the enjoyment of freedom. ...A people is therefore enslaved when the government...usurps the rights of the citizen or subject. Applying these principles, we find that [Spanish] America was denied not only its freedom but even an active and effective tyranny. Let me explain. Under absolutism there are no recognized limits to the exercise of governmental powers. The will of the great sultan [is] carried out more or less arbitrarily by the lesser pashas, khans, and satraps of Turkey and Persia.... But ...the rulers of Ispahan are Persians; the viziers of the Grand Turk are Turks....

How different is our situation! We have been...kept...in a sort of permanent infancy with regard to public affairs. If we could at least have managed our domestic affairs...[w]e should also have enjoyed...unconscious respect from the people, which is so necessary

common. They also had direct links in the form of mobile ideas and personnel, and interlocking events. The ideas of limited royal sovereignty that animated the British Revolution filtered into British North America, France, and at least indirectly into St. Domingue and Spanish America. Similarly, the principles embodied in the American Declaration of Independence and France's Declaration of the Rights of Man and Citizen were prominent in the revolutions in Haiti and Spanish America.

People such as Francisco Miranda moved from revolution to revolution. Many of the fighters in Toussaint's armies in Haiti came from Kongo, bringing not only military skills but ideas about proper exercise of power. Similarly, thousands of Frenchmen fought in the American Revolution, and many of them just a few years later took part in the French Revolution. And a few thousand veterans of the wars of the French Revolution fought for independence in Spanish America.

In some cases, the events of the Atlantic revolutions were interlinked. The French to preserve amidst revolutions. That is why I say we have even been deprived of an active tyranny, since we have not been permitted to exercise its functions.

Americans...who live within the Spanish system occupy a position in society no better than...serfs destined for labor, or at best...that of mere consumers. Yet even this status is surrounded with galling restrictions, such as being forbidden to grow European crops, or to store products which are royal monopolies, or to establish factories of a type the Peninsula [Spain] itself does not possess. To this add the exclusive trading privileges [of merchants favored by Spain]...and the barriers between American provinces.... [D]o you wish to know what our future held?—simply the cultivation of [cash crops]; cattle raising on the broad plains; hunting wild game in the jungles; digging in the earth to mine its gold—but even these limitations could never satisfy the greed of Spain.... Is it not an outrage and a violation of human rights to expect a land so...vast, rich, and populous, to remain merely passive?

Questions for Analysis

1. For Bolívar, what restrictions in the Spanish system justified revolution?
2. What reason does Bolívar give for asserting that Americans, instead of the government in Spain, should exercise "active tyranny"?
3. How do Bolívar's references to rights, slavery, and commercial restrictions reflect the influence of earlier revolutions?

Source: Harold A. Bierck Jr., ed., *Selected Writings of Bolívar, Vol. 1: 1810–1822*, trans. Lewis Bertrand (New York: 1951).

and the Haitian revolutions, overlapping in time and both involving the French Empire, directly affected one another's course. The French Revolution, via Bonaparte's invasion of Spain in 1808, opened the political vacuum in Spanish America that ultimately brought independence there. And French involvement in the American Revolution deepened debts that pushed the French king to summon the Estates-General, setting in motion events he would regret.

Different Outcomes

For all their common roots and interconnections, the Atlantic revolutions produced differing results. Some decentralization occurred everywhere, but beyond that each situation had its own character. Kongo became more unstable, violent, and enmeshed in the slave trade. Britain achieved considerable stability after 1689. So, too, the United

Liberty in the Atlantic World This 1792 painting uses an Atlantic world setting—including a globe, a liberty cap, and trading ships—to convey its message of freedom and the abolition of slavery.

States after a rocky start, although the issue of slavery would bring on a civil war a few decades later—as we shall see. In France, the revolution collapsed into dictatorship, and in 1815 a restoration of royal power followed Bonaparte's exile. Haiti also collapsed into dictatorship and then a very unstable republic. In Spanish America, unstable republics alternating with intervals of military dictatorship became the norm.

The Atlantic revolutions also brought different results for the most disenfranchised members of society. In Kongo, the United States, and France, women took part in various ways, and some of them hoped that revolution would usher in a new age for women. In Britain, Haiti, and Spanish America, the evidence for women's involvement is thinner. None of the revolutions immediately changed the political circumstances of women, although in New Jersey the state constitution allowed unmarried women who owned property to vote between 1797 and 1807. After that New Jersey restricted voting rights, as in most U.S. states, to adult white males. In France, Bonaparte actually restricted women's rights more narrowly than before 1789.

Slaves also played a part in several of these revolutions, most prominently in Haiti and Kongo, but also in the birth of the United States and in Spanish America. The revolutions produced abolition of slavery in Haiti and most parts of Spanish America. In the United States, some northern states abolished slavery after the revolution, but it took the Civil War to achieve this on the national scale. France abolished slavery but then Bonaparte reinstated it, and it lasted until 1848 in the French Empire. In Kongo, slavery survived until the kingdom ended in the 1850s.

The American Revolution and those in Spanish America also had important implications for Amerindians. Both Britain by 1763, and Spain long before, had imposed constraints on the exploitation of Amerindians, in particular checking the seizure of Amerindian lands. The revolutions lifted most of those constraints, inviting the displacement of Amerindians by settlers of European descent. In the Unites States, settlers poured westward into the Midwest and, after 1810 or so, into the Deep South—sometimes bringing slaves as well. In Mexico and most of South America, for half a century (ca. 1820–1870) the newly independent states were too weak militarily to impose their laws on most Amerindian communities, but by the late nineteenth century the legacy of the revolutions in Spanish America and Brazil proved deeply unfortunate for surviving Amerindian communities.

The Atlantic revolutions helped to reshuffle fortunes in a geopolitical sense too. The big winners eventually proved to be Britain, France, and the United States, which in the nineteenth and twentieth centuries would play enlarged roles in international politics. The biggest losers were Spain and Kongo, both of which emerged weaker than before.

Revolutions as Experience

The Atlantic revolutions, like most revolutions, had two more important things in common. First, the outcomes just described were never inevitable, and they rarely resembled what revolutionaries intended. They all took place in fluid situations in which old beliefs, customs, institutions—and usually treasuries and armies—grew weaker. People began to imagine new futures of all sorts, but not necessarily the futures they got. In Kongo, Beatriz Kimpa Vita did not get a united Kongo but a weakened one. Abigail Adams and Olympe de Gouges hoped for political rights for women, but did not get them. Bolívar wanted a united South America, not a handful of unstable republics.

The Atlantic revolutions were also miserable experiences for most people. Although many people felt hope, liberation, and exhilaration, many also felt fear, anxiety, betrayal, and worse. Mass executions, massacres, torture, as well as the more routine sufferings of war, famine, and disease, abounded. While history is rightly concerned with causes and consequences of major events, it is well to remember, at least from time to time, what it was like to live through them.

Conclusion

From 1640 to 1830, the Atlantic world took a new and different path. It experienced an especially rapid expansion of commerce, faster than it had before and faster than anywhere else in the world at the time. This change brought new pressures from new social groups that upset political arrangements all around the Atlantic. Every revolution had its own particular causes, of course, but they all owed something to the economic and social changes common around the Atlantic.

In Britain, the United States, and Spanish America, these revolutions led to a decentralization or disappearance of royal power, greater self-rule, and more representative political institutions such as legislatures or parliaments. Even where such formal institutions did not develop, as in Kongo, royal power weakened and merchant groups, typically Kongolese slave traders, won greater political voice. In France and Haiti, the revolutions brought a temporary decentralization of power, followed by dictatorship.

The extension of self-rule in the Atlantic revolutions did not go so far as to include women; nor Amerindians in their homelands. The revolutions in Spanish America led to the abolition of slavery, but former slaves remained marginal citizens with limited, if any, political rights. And in the United States, slavery long outlasted the revolution.

In the long run, however, the trend established by the ideas, principles, and rhetoric of the Atlantic revolutions led to more open, equal, and democratic societies, both around the Atlantic and eventually in many countries around the world. In cases it took centuries before women, Amerindians, and people of African descent in the Americas enjoyed legal equality with other citizens. That it happened at all is testament to the strength of ideals voiced by the makers of revolution in Kongo, Britain, the United States, France, Haiti, and Spanish America.

‖‖

Chapter Review

KEY TERMS

Kongo monarchy p. 792

Beatriz Kimpa Vita p. 794

rising merchant classes p. 795

Parliament p. 796

Glorious Revolution p. 798

Pontiac's War p. 801

American Revolution p. 802

French Revolution p. 805

Jacobins p. 810

Napoleon Bonaparte p. 811

Toussaint L'Ouverture p. 815

Haitian Revolution p. 816

Bourbon Reforms p. 818

Túpac Amaru II p. 819

Simón Bolívar p. 821

political decentralization p. 823

REVIEW QUESTIONS

1. What liberties did the rising merchant classes seek during this period?

2. On what principle did the legitimacy and power of Kongo kings rest?

3. In what ways was the fragmentation of power in Kongo linked to its Atlantic connections?

4. What were the main sources of conflict between Charles I and Parliament?

5. What political and religious arrangements did the British Civil Wars and Revolution cement?

6. Describe the disagreements between American colonists and the British government over land access and taxes.

7. What principles did the American Constitution include, and whose rights did it exclude?

8. Explain the intellectual and socioeconomic changes that contributed to the start of the French Revolution.

9. Why and how did the French Revolution enter a violent phase?

10. What features did the Haitian Revolution share with the American and French Revolutions, and what feature was different?

11. How did Toussaint L'Ouverture fend off British and French armies during the Haitian Revolution?

12. Whom did the Bourbon Reforms irritate, and why?

13. How did Napoleon Bonaparte's takeover of Spain contribute to Spain's loss of control over most of its colonies in the Americas?

14. What were the common roots and interconnections of the Atlantic revolutions?

15. What were the effects of the Atlantic revolutions for women, slaves, and Amerindians?

Go to INQUIZITIVE

to see what you've learned—and learn what you've missed—with personalized feedback along the way.

Fossil Fuels and Mass Production

INDUSTRIAL REVOLUTIONS AROUND THE WORLD

1780 to 1914

FOCUS QUESTIONS

1. In what ways was the Industrial Revolution an energy revolution?

2. Why did England experience the first Industrial Revolution?

3. How did the aims and technologies of industrialization spread across the globe?

4. What were the important global effects of the industrial revolutions?

The world is too much with us; late and soon,
Getting and spending, we lay waste our powers;—
Little we see in Nature that is ours;
We have given our hearts away, a sordid boon!

—William Wordsworth, ca. 1802

[The steam engine] has armed the feeble hand of man with a power to which no limits can be assigned; completed the dominion of mind over the most refractory qualities of matter; and laid a sure foundation for all those future miracles of mechanical power which are to aid and reward the labours of after generations.

—Sir John Sinclair, 1825

The first four lines of Wordsworth's sonnet express regret about the changes brought by Britain's **Industrial Revolution**. He felt people had become overly concerned with money and had spoiled nature's beauty. Sinclair, in contrast, praised the potential of industrial technology and brimmed with confidence in benefits to come. Wordsworth (1770–1850) and Sinclair (1754–1835) were contemporaries and lived only a few miles apart—the former in England and the latter in Scotland. Together, they capture some of the key features of the British Industrial Revolution: it shattered longstanding limits on production and wealth, while fundamentally changing society and nature. It was the most significant revolution in modern history.

The term *Industrial Revolution* entered the English language in the 1880s and refers to two main changes in manufacturing methods. The first was the transition from muscle and hand tools to machinery driven by inanimate power—at first water power and then coal-burning steam engines. The second change was the transition from household- or workshop-scale production to factory-scale production. What made these transitions truly revolutionary was steam power, which vastly expanded the levels of production and consumption a society could achieve. What made steam power work was the energy locked up in coal.

The Industrial Revolution began in the eighteenth century, roughly 250 years ago, and is still under way. No other 250-year period in world history can rival this one for the scale and scope of the transformations it has brought. In the process of transforming many parts of the world, the Industrial Revolution tightened many of the connections of the Global web.

The term *Industrial Revolution* is sometimes

CHRONOLOGY

1733 "Flying shuttle" is introduced in Britain

1769–1785 James Watt registers six patents on steam engines

1770s First steamships are built in France

1780s Water-powered loom is developed

1790 Cotton mill makes use of steam engine for first time in Britain

1791 Alexander Hamilton writes tract supporting tariffs

1794 Cotton gin is patented

1804 First locomotives go into use in coal mines in Britain

1825 First railway carrying passengers and general freight operates in Britain

1838 Steam-powered vessels begin scheduled Atlantic crossings

1840s Long-distance telegraph is patented

1848 Worker uprisings in Milan, Berlin, Vienna; Communist Manifesto is published

1853 American fleet invades Japan; Lowell girls successfully lobby for shorter work day

1853–1856 Crimean War

1867–1868 Meiji Restoration

1871 German unification

1872 Compulsory education for girls and boys is introduced in Japan

1875 German Social Democratic Party is founded

1879 French socialist party is founded; Canada launches National Policy to promote industry

1882 Japan's first modern cotton mill is set up

1886 Canada's first transcontinental railway opens

1889 Hull House is set up in Chicago

1894–1895 Sino-Japanese War

1900 British Labour Party is founded

1901 Japanese Social Democratic Party is founded

1903 Trans-Siberian Railway opens

1905 Revolution of 1905 in Russia

used only for the first century or so, from about 1770 to about 1870, and sometimes only for the case of Britain. This chapter, however, deals with the origins and course of industrial revolutions globally up to 1914, emphasizing in particular the experiences of Britain, Germany, the United States, Russia, and Japan. In following the story to 1914, this chapter includes what historians sometimes call the Second Industrial Revolution. In some cases—notably the United States, Britain, and Germany—after 1870 new industrial techniques dramatically improved the efficiency and scale of production of steel, chemicals, oil, and electricity. This surge of technological change relied more heavily on science and educated engineers than did the early Industrial Revolution. A large proportion of the important technologies of today—automobiles, aircraft, turbines—made their debut between 1870 and 1914 in the Second Industrial Revolution.

The Industrial Revolution began in Britain; but as it spread, it had global consequences. It transformed economies through the production of cheap, mass-produced goods, and it vaulted Britain, a small island nation, to the first rank of economic powers for the entire nineteenth century. It transformed societies through the formation of a new urban class of factory workers and the expansion of a middle class of accountants, lawyers, teachers, secretaries, and factory managers. It transformed politics by creating a newly rich class of entrepreneurs who eventually claimed a share of political power in accordance with their wealth. It also led to groups of workers claiming a share of power through union activism and politics, although that happened more slowly. It transformed the environment too, by generating unprecedented quantities of air and water pollution from its factories, and by equipping people with powerful new tools that made it more profitable than ever before to dig new mines, turn forests into cotton fields, or kill 30 million North American bison for their hides.

The Industrial Revolution was the most momentous change in human history since the Neolithic Revolution some 10,000 years ago. The Neolithic Revolution—the domestication of plants and animals and the advent of farming—opened the way to dense settled populations, cities, hierarchical societies, and eventually states. The Industrial Revolution opened the way to a high-energy society based on fossil fuels such as coal or oil. Over decades, the use of fossil fuels in industry and transport boosted economic growth so that it usually outpaced population growth, enriching at least a segment of every society around the world. It opened the way to greater inequality, as some people could now amass wealth on a scale unavailable even to pharaohs and emperors in previous times. It opened the way to fossil-fuel combustion and carbon emissions to the atmosphere in quantities sufficient to change the Earth's climate. And it opened the way to outcomes we haven't yet seen or imagined, because industrialization is still ongoing.

Although both the Neolithic Revolution and the Industrial Revolution were momentous turning points in world history, they were very different. For one thing, people independently transitioned from hunting and foraging to farming in at least seven places around the globe, and with different sets of crops and animals in each case. In contrast, there was only one independent transition from agrarian to industrial society, in Britain. Every subsequent transition has drawn directly or indirectly upon the British experience. By the time of the Industrial Revolution, unlike the situation in 9000 BCE, the world was so bound together by the connections of the Global web that one transition was enough: sooner or later, the example of the British Industrial Revolution influenced every corner of the world.

Compared to the Neolithic Revolution, industrialization spread at a lightning pace. What germinated in British soil could not, however, simply be transplanted to other lands. In every case geography, culture, legal systems, and much else were different from Britain's. Rather, the ambition to imitate Britain's Industrial Revolution spread to many other peoples, some of whom managed to pull off their own industrial revolutions.

The interconnectedness of the Global web made the ambition to imitate Britain an urgent one from a business point of view. Once Britain could mass-produce inexpensive goods, the increasingly unified world economy created ruthless competition for businesses everywhere else. They needed to modernize and mechanize quickly to survive. There was a geopolitical urgency to industrialization too. As British society and the British state quickly grew in wealth and power after 1800, some people in other societies recognized that they needed to follow suit to avoid domination. This recognition created enormous internal stresses within societies and states, as reformers eagerly sought to industrialize their societies while traditionalists fought to preserve the old ways that, as they saw it, had served their societies so well for so long.

The circuits of the Global web proved highly efficient in transmitting the desire to industrialize. They proved reasonably efficient in transmitting specific technologies, whether power looms or locomotives, from one setting to another. But the underlying knowledge of how to build and maintain machinery, or how to manage a factory and a supply chain, traveled less well. And the interlocking social, political, economic, and technological systems that enabled industrialization to develop, grow, and survive amid the social tensions it provoked—those systems developed only here and there. Some countries, such as the United States or Japan, built such interlocking systems fairly quickly and rode the wave of industrialization with a success that surprised all observers. Other countries, such as Egypt, tried and failed. A few countries, mainly those with minimal traditions of formal education and meager natural resources, did not try at all.

The industrial revolutions changed the nature of older global linkages, especially in terms of economic specializations and economic power. More than ever before, some regions specialized in raw material production—cotton, iron ore, leather—while others concentrated on making these raw materials into shirts, ships, and shoes. By and large, those regions focused on raw material production found themselves poor and weak in relation to those that performed the more skilled, complex, and profitable tasks of industrial production.

So the industrial revolutions of the period 1780–1914 created a more differentiated world, but also a more unified one. It became more differentiated because social inequality within societies, and economic and military gaps between societies, grew spectacularly, and they continue to grow to this day. But it also became more unified because the connections among people, institutions, and societies grew thicker than ever before, thanks to new technologies of transport and communications, new market linkages, and much else brought about by industrialization, patchy though it was.

An Energy Revolution

In every case around the world, industrial revolutions featured textiles and metallurgy above all else. In most societies, spinning thread and weaving cloth had long occupied many peasant women and girls. Men also wove, especially in the slack months of the agricultural calendar. Other handicrafts, such as leather working or furniture making, were typically male pursuits, followed both in village households and in town workshops. This local, small-scale manufacturing was conducted with muscle power or occasionally with help from a watermill or windmill. Many of these businesses— leather working or beer brewing, for example—could not scale up to factory mass production easily.

But **textiles and metallurgy** could scale up. Mills, forges, and factories, in which relatively unskilled laborers worked at machines powered by flowing water or by steam engines, suited the tasks of making cloth and iron. So these industries were in the vanguard of industrialization. By 1870, with the Second Industrial Revolution, factory-scale production was successfully applied to a wider range of activities, creating new key industries such as steel, chemicals, and electricity. To scale up, almost every industry required inputs of energy far beyond what human and animal muscle could provide. So underlying the newly mechanized industries lay a special resource vital to the British Industrial Revolution and important to all of them: coal.

Coal and Steam

At its heart, the Industrial Revolution was an energy revolution. At first, the textile industry in Britain scaled up to factory production with waterwheels that conveyed the energy of flowing water to power looms. Steam engines weren't efficient enough yet. But over time, the best riverside locations for siting water-powered mills were taken and steam engines improved. So by the 1830s, new mills typically used steam power.

Steam power came from **coal**. The central feature of the energy revolution was the development of new ways to use the chemical energy contained in coal and, later, in other fossil fuels such as oil or natural gas. The use of fossil fuels for heat energy wasn't new. In north China during the Song dynasty (960–1279), for example, coal had fueled a metallurgical industry that flourished for over a century. In the Dutch lands from the fourteenth century onward, people used peat (semi-fossilized remains of bog moss) to fuel brewing, salt making, sugar refining, and other energy-intensive pursuits. From the sixteenth century, Londoners used coal for home heating and for enterprises such as glass making that needed heat energy.

Steam Power   **Steam engines**, however, could convert the chemical energy of fossil fuels into mechanical energy rather than simply into heat energy. They used coal fires to heat water into steam. The expansion of hot steam, and its contraction as it cooled, served as the motor force behind pistons, shafts, and belts that carried power to looms, pumps, or wheels. Coal worked its transformations only because of steam engines.

For centuries, people in Ptolemaic Egypt, the Ottoman Empire, Italy, France, and possibly China as well, had experimented with rudimentary steam engines, but they were only curiosities. In eighteenth-century Britain, which had a developed coal industry already, steam engines proved more useful. The first steam engines built there were so fuel-hungry that they could only be used at the mines themselves, where scraps of coal lay around unused. Only Britain had enough coal mines, and a strong enough market for coal, to make it worthwhile to improve steam engines. Between 1712, when Thomas

Steam Engines James Watt's new, more efficient steam engine, depicted here in a technical illustration, used the pressure generated from steam to drive a series of pistons and shafts, which in turn could operate machines in factories and mines.

Newcomen revealed an early model, and 1812, steam engines mainly worked to pump water out of coal pits. That made mining easier and coal cheaper, and in turn motivated people to tinker with steam engines. During those same years, engineers introduced many small improvements to steam engines, making them 10 times more fuel efficient.

The most famous of these engineers was **James Watt** (1736–1819), a Scot born into an educated family and trained to make mathematical instruments. While employed to maintain instruments at the University of Glasgow, he registered six patents on steam engines between 1769 and 1785. Watt had no head for business, but he found partners who did. Together, they designed, built, and marketed much more efficient steam engines starting in the 1780s. They also sued everyone else who built good steam engines until their key patent ran out in 1800.

The first cotton mill to make use of a steam engine opened in Manchester, England, in 1790. Water power still remained more efficient for most factories until the 1830s, but by 1870 steam engines reigned supreme and water power was effectively extinct in British manufacturing.

The Power of Fossil Fuels

This shift in Britain represented the beginning of a global energy transition to fossil fuels. The Neolithic Revolution had allowed people to harvest perhaps 10 to 100 times as much energy, in the form of edible plants, as they could when foraging and hunting. Farming allowed more people to exist, but most of them had to work harder to get enough to eat than did hunters and foragers. Despite the expanded energy harvest, energy regimes based on the annual conversion of sunshine into plant tissues kept almost everyone poor. But coal, and fossil fuels generally, made it possible for the first time ever for more than a tiny fraction of people to avoid poverty.

Coal is the residue of ancient plants, the equivalent of solid sunshine. Burning it provided access to accumulated stocks of energy, the bounty of about 500 million years of photosynthesis. Machines that could transform coal's energy into motor power burst the boundaries of the old economy, permitting the creation and accumulation of previously unimaginable wealth—as Sinclair foresaw. Since about 1870, humankind has obtained more energy annually from coal than all the green plants on Earth could capture from the sun through photosynthesis.

In short, fossil fuels, combined with machinery and know-how, enabled industrial production far faster and far greater than even the hardest workers could manage using only human or animal muscle. This ended the necessity of mass poverty, to which all previous societies were condemned. That was the most important social consequence of the Industrial Revolution.

But the energy in coal scarcely made everyone rich. The wealth created by burning vast quantities of fossil fuels in order to make goods more efficiently normally went only to some people, especially in the early decades of industrialization. So a second major consequence of the adoption of coal, and of the industrial revolutions more generally, was an expansion of inequality. This combination—simultaneous increases in both wealth and inequality—is routine in world economic history, but rarely did it come so suddenly as during the Industrial Revolution.

The Industrial Revolution in Britain

England, specifically the north of England, was the birthplace of the Industrial Revolution. Why not in Europe's centers of textile manufacturing such as Flanders (in today's Belgium) or northern Italy? Or the textile districts of India, such as Gujarat or Bengal? Or Ottoman Egypt? Or China's manufacturing heartlands? England in the seventeenth century was still a backwater within Europe. It was among the least urbanized lands, and innovations in its economy often required importing Dutch or Italian expertise. Why was England the site of this economic revolution?

Why England?

A short answer is: a fateful coincidence. England by 1700 had cheap coal and expensive labor. So it made more economic sense in England than anywhere else to find ways to use less labor and more coal in order to create goods. A fuller answer involves trends in English agriculture, urbanization, transport, and public policy—and it begins with farming.

England underwent a gradual agricultural modernization after 1650. Technical improvements doubled cereal yields per acre between 1650 and 1900. By the 1750s, England was exporting about 7 percent of its grain harvest. More efficient farming also fed urbanization. Fewer people were needed as farmworkers. In human terms, this often led to underemployment and hunger in villages. In economic terms, it meant labor was freed to work in non-agricultural sectors. Young people streamed from farms into cities, seeking work. England was urbanizing faster than anywhere else in the world for two centuries after 1650. Industrialization did not launch England's spurt in urbanization; it sped up a trend already in motion.

Urbanization and industrialization each promoted the other. Cities, as always, served as hothouses of information exchange and innovation. Industrialization rested on technical advances in machinery, and those happened more often when mechanically inclined people with restless minds could easily find one another, share ideas, and either work together or compete with one another. Industrialization fostered urbanization, but the connectivity of city life also fostered industrialization.

Improved Transportation Infrastructure Improvements in rural transport also spurred industrialization. The growth of towns and the increase in farm production

Water Transportation A painting from the nineteenth century shows construction of a canal in southwest England. Canals joined Britain's inland waterways into a single system, enabling raw materials, manufactured goods, and people to travel much more efficiently around the country.

required better roads and canals to move more food to cities. Firewood, bales of wool, and other bulky items could find bigger markets if better transport links existed. So landowners and merchants saw it in their interest to pay people to build and maintain roads and canals. Coal use also provided incentive to dig canals: if moved in carts pulled by animals, coal's price doubled within 10 miles, even on the best roads.

Before 1750, Britain had few good roads. In 1703, the ruts and potholes along a 50-mile stretch of road out of London caused the horse-drawn carriage of future Habsburg emperor Charles VI, at that time merely a king of Spain, to overturn 12 times. The young king survived.

After 1750, British and immigrant Irish laborers constructed thousands of miles of new canals and roads. Between 1750 and 1850, they quadrupled the extent of Britain's navigable inland waterways. By 1770, Britain had 15,000 miles (25,000 km) of turnpikes, or privately maintained roads, and almost everyone lived within a day's walk of one. What had been a four-day ride between London and Holyhead before 1787 took little more than one day by 1837. This infrastructure development, roughly analogous to what Song China (960–1279) had done with its canals, dramatically increased the connectivity of Britain. It became one of the most internally integrated parts of the Global web—as Song China had been within the Old World web. By 1820, even before railroads, the dense transport network moved people, goods, and information more swiftly around Great Britain than almost anywhere else.

The government showed unusual enthusiasm for spending on infrastructure. After the British Revolution (1640–1689), the English nobility and merchant elite who dominated Parliament gradually grew accustomed to taxing itself and empowering government ministers to attend to the national interest. That occasionally included building a turnpike or a canal across landowners' property against their wishes. Moreover, in an effort to pacify rebellious Scots, the British government invested in military road and bridge building throughout Scotland in the 1730s and 1740s.

Protectionist Tariffs The British state took other steps that contributed to the Industrial Revolution, if sometimes in unforeseen ways. Parliament imposed tariffs on imported cloth from India and erected other tariff barriers to protect British manufacturers. The government clarified property rights and patent laws. After the 1790s, innovators could patent not just new inventions but also improvements to existing ones. In addition, during decades of warfare against revolutionary France (1793–1815), the government became an important customer for large-scale production runs of certain manufactures, such as military uniforms and weaponry. James Watt drew on changes in cannon design to make key improvements in steam engines. So British government policy on transport infrastructure, tariffs, intellectual property rights, and patent law—and its frequent wars—helped promote the Industrial Revolution without the intention of revolutionizing anything.

Labor Costs and Technological Change None of these changes would have brought on the Industrial Revolution had it not been for low-lying coal and high wages. After 1680, wages in England climbed, then stagnated from 1700 to 1740, then climbed again. By 1780, wage labor in England was more expensive than just about anywhere else in Europe—or the world. High labor costs created persistent incentives for employers to find ways to substitute machinery for labor.

As a result, almost every manufacturing process in England underwent labor-saving technological changes, which often, in turn, inspired more technological change. The textile industry provides the best examples. The "flying shuttle," introduced in 1733, doubled the productivity of weavers, who now wanted more cotton yarn than hand-spinners could make. This created pressure to invent a more efficient spinning process, which happened in the 1760s with the "spinning jenny" and in the 1770s with the "spinning mule." One person operating a "mule" in 1830 could spin as much cotton into thread as 350 skilled women working by hand with spinning wheels. With spinning machines churning out yarn and thread by the mile, incentives now grew to make weaving even more efficient. Tinkerers developed a water-powered loom in the 1780s, and despite active opposition from skilled weavers, by 1800 some 2,000 power looms were installed in Britain. By 1857, there were 250,000 of them—weaving more cloth than tens of millions of hand-weavers could make.

Other industries, from iron making to lens grinding, underwent technological change, motivated by the entrepreneurial desire to save on labor costs. Thousands of men, and some women, learned the intricacies of the new machinery, tinkered with it, and found ways to make improvements.

This blend of circumstances and policies might have been enough to start the Industrial Revolution in Britain, but only coal kept it alive. Many places had coal, but Britain had large quantities of cheap, transportable coal that lay near riverbanks and natural harbors.

British Coal

As we've seen, the first important industrial use of coal was in the mines themselves. Once the easiest surface deposits of coal had been exploited, what remained lay underground in pits where water collected rapidly unless pumps outworked the rain. Coal-powered steam pumps working night and day prevented the Industrial Revolution from drowning in infancy. This was the only major technical improvement in mining between 1780 and 1914. It remained hard labor throughout. A vigorous coal miner scraped 200 to 300 tons per year from the earth.

Coal enabled British manufacturing to escape its former constraints. By 1700 if not before, brewing, glass making, brick making, metal smelting, and tile making had all switched from firewood to coal except in a few remaining well-wooded parts of Britain. Half of England's energy use came from coal, a situation unique in the world. After 1700, British coal use rose briskly, from 3 million tons annually to 30 million in 1830.

Using coal enabled Britain to keep less land in forest. The 5 million tons of coal burned in 1750 took the place of fuelwood that would have required forests covering one-third of Britain's surface area. By 1820, if all the British Isles had been forested, it would have yielded fuelwood energy equal to that year's coal use. Several Britains covered in forest could not have yielded as much fuelwood energy as the 125 million tons of coal burned in 1870. Britain's coal deposits were in effect a subterranean forest, providing a resource equivalent to extra land.

Coal substituted for labor as well as for wood. In 1840, steam engines in Britain did the work of about 1 million adult men. In 1880, the energy obtained from the coal they produced performed work equal to that of 100 million adult men. At the time, Britain's total population was 34 million, of whom maybe 8 million were adult men. It took about half a million men, women, and children to dig out the necessary coal.

Until the 1830s, few recognized what coal was doing to Britain. The brilliant economists Adam Smith, Thomas Malthus, and David Ricardo all supposed that economic growth could never last long because the supply of natural resources (they termed it *land*) was limited. By the 1860s, however, everyone could see what was happening. As the economist W. S. Jevons put it in 1865: "Coal in truth stands not beside, but entirely above, all other commodities. It is the material source of the energy of the country—the universal aid—the factor in everything we do. With coal almost any feat is possible; without it we are thrown back into the laborious poverty of early times." Jevons put his finger on it. Coal, and the ability to convert its energy into motion that could do work and make things, lay at the heart of Britain's Industrial Revolution.

British Industries

The power of coal and steam engines transformed almost every part of British industry in the decades after 1830. Of these, the most important to British history, and to world history, were cotton, iron, and transport—specifically, the advent of railroads and steamships.

Cotton A large part of the work that coal did was powering machines that made cotton cloth. In 1700, Britain hardly spun any cotton and imported finished cloth from India. British cotton was uncompetitive with India's because British wages were

Textile Machinery The "spinning jenny" *(left)* sped up the process of making yarn or cotton thread. The "spinning mule" *(right)* accelerated production far more by using water to power hundreds of spindles at once. Substituting machinery for labor was central to the British Industrial Revolution.

too high and skills too low, and because raw cotton had to be imported since the plant would not grow in Britain's climate. British weavers, who made mainly woolens and linens, objected to the foreign cotton cloth. To protect the woolen industry and its weavers, Parliament restricted the import of Indian woven cotton cloth, although not raw cotton. That policy inadvertently helped English cotton manufacturers by eliminating Indian competition.

The tariff gave entrepreneurs an incentive to find ways to weave more cotton in Britain and to adopt the new devices—flying shuttle, power loom—that would reduce labor costs. In a few decades, British cotton manufacturing became internationally competitive: by 1810, cotton cloth accounted for nearly half of British exports. By 1830, cotton mills employed nearly half a million workers in Britain and accounted for about 8 percent of the national economy. Overall, between 1770 and 1840, British imports of raw cotton climbed 100-fold and the cost of cotton clothing fell by 85 percent. The cotton industry became increasingly steam-powered after 1830 and continued to occupy a central place in Britain's industrial landscape.

Iron The energy in coal had an even greater impact on the iron industry, which became as important as cotton to Britain's economy and far more important to British military power. Iron making was fuel-intensive. It took 10 acres (4 hectares) of English woodland to make enough fuel to make a ton of iron in the eighteenth century. Fuel constraints made the industry uncompetitive against imported iron from Sweden and Russia, where fuelwood was far cheaper. Coal, together with some technical improvements that made it easier to remove impurities in the iron-making process, revolutionized the British iron industry.

In the century after 1788, British iron production climbed 130-fold, and Britain, instead of importing iron, became Europe's largest producer and the world's largest exporter. Massive iron foundries sprang up near coalfields. Iron replaced wood as the key material in construction of everything from tools to bridges to ships. By 1815, with its flourishing iron industry, Britain produced millions of guns annually and all the cannon needed for the world's biggest navy. By 1890, British shipyards built naval vessels for several countries and some 80 percent of the world's seagoing ships of all sorts.

Railways The iron and coal industries gave rise to locomotives and **railways**, another key sector of the British Industrial Revolution. The first locomotives were used underground in coal mines, in 1804. The first railway to carry passengers and general freight opened in 1825. A railway line between the port of Liverpool and the cotton-manufacturing center of Manchester opened in 1830. Newspapers reported in detail on this maiden voyage, not least because the first train to make the journey ran over a member of Parliament, killing him. Despite this inauspicious debut, the Liverpool and Manchester railway quickly proved a commercial bonanza, carrying half a million passengers in its first full year of operation, and many thousands of tons of cotton and coal. A frenzy of railway construction followed, undertaken by private companies employing tens of thousands of poor men with picks, hammers, and shovels, so that Britain quadrupled its total railway track between 1850 and 1880. Railways linked the country together more thoroughly than canals ever could, making Britain the world's most interconnected country, the thickest patch of the Global web.

Steamships Meanwhile, seaborne navigation tightened Britain's links to the rest of the world. Steamships were first built in France in the 1770s. The first to become a commercial success plied North American waters—the Hudson River in 1807 and the St. Lawrence in 1809. In the next few decades, steamships came to rival and then replace most sailing ships on rivers and in coastal waters.

Oceanic steam navigation took longer to take hold because it required carrying so much coal. Scheduled Atlantic crossings with steam-powered vessels began in 1838. Sailing vessels still dominated the routes between Britain and Asia until the opening of the Suez Canal (in Egypt) in 1869, because steaming around Africa required too much expenditure on coal. The Suez Canal shortened the route between Britain and India by about 4,000 miles (6,400 km), making it practical for steamships. By 1870, new ocean-going ships were usually steam-powered. Only on the longest routes—between Britain and China, for example—did sailing ships still out-compete steam vessels into the 1890s.

Steamships lowered freight rates at sea, as railways did on land. Between 1840 and 1910, British seaborne freight costs fell by 70 percent, the result mainly of the switch to steamships and continuing technical improvements such as the screw propeller, in regular use by the 1860s. Railways and steamships, built of iron—iron that was made with coal—knitted Britain together and tied it ever tighter to the rest of the world.

British Society

Industrialization brought a social revolution to Britain. In 1750, most of the work done in Britain, as in most societies, was farm work, and most people lived in villages. By 1850, half the British population of 27 million lived in cities and millions worked in coal mines, textile mills, iron foundries, or factories.

The conditions of life and work in the new industrial cities took a toll on the health of factory workers. Titus Rowbotham, for example, went to work in Manchester's cotton mills at age 18. In 1801, looking back on his life, he said of textile mill workers like himself: "Their intellect is enfeebled.... They are more like grown up children. ... The long hours of labour, the high temperatures of the factories, produce lassitude and excessive exhaustion. The operatives... seek to sustain life by the excitement of drink."

Labor in coal mines made factory work look like leisure. Child labor was commonplace in the tight spaces underground. Sally Fletcher, age 8, testified to a government committee in 1841 that she had worked in a coal pit since age 5 and had never been to school. "I cannot read or write.... I go to work between six and seven o'clock in the morning.... I sometimes go home at three o'clock. Sometimes six." Her job was pushing small wagonloads of coal along a 400-yard underground passage. Most mine work was done by people younger than 30. Few miners could still work by age 40. On-the-job accidents and lung diseases from the long-term effects of breathing coal dust ended many a working life. One flood in a coal mine in 1838 drowned 26 mineworkers, the eldest of whom was 17 and the youngest 7 years old.

Child Labor As a lithograph from 1844 demonstrates, British mine owners relied on the small bodies of children to transport coal through extremely narrow tunnels underground. Children could spend as many as 12 hours a day, 6 days a week, underground.

The Working Classes The new forms of work in mines and factories created new social classes in Britain. Over a generation or two, millions who toiled at looms and lathes, or worked as household servants, gradually came to see themselves as members of a vast **working class**, amounting to about 40 to 45 percent of the English population by 1850. Unlike farmworkers, they worked shifts defined by the clock, not the light of the sun. At work they were subject to the discipline of bosses, not their parents or older siblings. The din, drudgery, and danger of factory or mine work dominated their lives for 10, 12, or 14 hours a day. They lived and worked in crowds. Manchester in the 1840s had a population density higher than any big city in the world today except Dhaka (Bangladesh). Its working-class districts were a warren of dingy alleys and open sewers.

The term *working class* might better be *working classes* because a person's condition and prospects could vary. Fortunate working-class men learned a skill that ensured employment and a wage sufficient to support a family. With luck, some could rise to positions of management, overseeing the work of others. Women typically held poorer-paying jobs with fewer prospects of advancement. The most common job for women in nineteenth-century Britain was domestic service, doing housework and child care for someone else, but many worked in factories or mines too. Daughters expected to contribute their wages to their parents' household. If they married, they might quit factory work. If they became mothers, they usually did quit.

The least fortunate members of the working classes rarely found work and lived on city streets, slept under bridges, dressed in rags, and scrounged for food. In London, thousands of sharp-eyed, nimble-fingered, hungry children, called mudlarks, lived by scavenging buttons, nails, and other saleable items from city sewers and the muddy banks of the river Thames. Orphans and widows often could survive only by stealing or by selling their bodies for sex.

Britain's working classes lived and worked on the verge of disaster. If they annoyed an overseer, they might lose their job—which meant going hungry. Their jobs were dangerous. Thousands lost fingers, hands, or limbs to power machinery or mine accidents, ending their working lives. Many others, especially miners, lost their lives on the job in explosions, cave-ins, or floods. Like everyone, rich or poor, they also worried about lethal diseases—much more dangerous than anything else in their lives.

You might wonder why anyone agreed to work in factories or mines in industrial Britain. The answer is that millions of young people had no better option. Farms now needed fewer workers. Spinning and weaving within the home was hopeless in the face of factory competition. Teenage girls could become domestic servants; boys could join the army or the navy. They could gamble on life in Canada, Jamaica, or Australia as indentured servants. But these and other options looked no better to most young people than a hard life in the factories or mines.

The Middle Classes A notch above the working classes in industrial Britain's evolving social hierarchy stood a lower middle class, also growing, some 10 to 15 percent of the population by 1850. Its members were shop clerks, nurses, teachers, pharmacists—jobs for which at least some education was required. Their work included little dirt or danger, but their wages remained modest. Women in these jobs usually quit upon marriage or motherhood. These families typically rented rather than owned their homes but might have books and even a piano in them.

Industrial Britain also generated a more prosperous upper middle class. Factories and mines, if large enough, required managers and professionals. Accountants, engineers, purchasing agents, lawyers—these and other growing professions permitted hundreds of thousands of men (and a few thousand women) to earn enough for a comfortable life in the new industrial society. These men could expect to own their homes, pay fees to educate their children, support small-scale charities, and enjoy deference, at least outwardly, from members of the working classes. Their wives did not need paid work. They could expect to manage a house with domestic servants and might devote their time to civic causes, music and art, their church and their children—unless they assigned all child care to servants. The prosperous middle classes also included middling entrepreneurs, who might own a single mill or small factory. They rejoiced in a good year and feared bankruptcy in a bad one. These middling entrepreneurs were usually but not always men: about 10 percent of British businesses were owned by women between 1780 and 1850. That figure included widows who took over the business affairs of dead husbands, and women who owned small bakeries or butcher shops rather than mills or factories.

Industrialists Higher up the social pyramid of industrial Britain stood a new class of rich factory and mine owners. Some came from modest origins, such as John Rylands (1801–1888), born in a village near Manchester and recipient of a grade school education. He learned the weaver's trade and soon founded a textile manufacturing company with his brother and father. Rylands, who allegedly worked 19-hour days, became the first cotton millionaire in Manchester and, despite giving substantial sums to charities, died very rich. Wealth did not insulate him from personal tragedy, though: he buried all of his seven children. Manchester was an unhealthy city, even for its richest citizens. More typical of this new class—in his social origins—was Joseph Chamberlain (1836–1914). His father was a businessman who could afford to educate his son to age 16, at which point Joseph became an apprentice in his father's warehouses. But at age 18 he moved to Birmingham, started work in his uncle's brass screw–manufacturing business, became a partner, and at age 37 retired immensely wealthy and launched a career in politics, fighting for social reforms.

The traditional uppermost elite in British society, the landed aristocracy, often resented the wealth of industrialists such as Rylands or Chamberlain. But times were changing, and new money was slowly taking over. Aristocrats who found themselves strapped for money often chose to marry a son or daughter into a prosperous industrial family to restore their fortunes.

Family Life Industrialization changed family life as well as social structure in Britain, particularly the condition of young people. In 1820, more than half of Britain's cotton workers were teenagers. In 1842, one-third of mineworkers were teenagers. Factory and mine bosses preferred young workers, who were easier to train and—in most cases—easier to control. Some textile work required fine motor skills and small hands, for which employers preferred girls. When young people went to work in factories and mines, they partly escaped the authority of their parents. During working hours they became subject to the authority of male bosses, which women sometimes found hazardous. In their scant free time, young industrial workers became freer from parental supervision than village youths could expect to be.

If they held a job, people could marry young. Age at first marriage for British men dipped to about 26, and for women fell from about 26 in the early eighteenth century to about 23 in the mid-nineteenth, and lower still in the industrial cities. Despite younger marriage, out-of-wedlock births became far more common in the industrial towns than in rural villages—a reflection of the greater independence of industrial youth from parental supervision.

Environmental Impacts and Health

In 1837, the German chemist Justus von Liebig visited England. He described the country between Leeds and Manchester as "one big smoking chimney." Soot and cinder blanketed the iron-making region north of Birmingham by 1840, earning it the name "the black country." In London, a million chimneys spewed sulfur dioxide and soot into the air. In Manchester in 1900, the pH of rain averaged 3.5—somewhere between the acidity of tomato juice and that of wine. A perpetual haze of coal smoke enveloped all the industrial towns. Just as the sun famously never set on the British Empire, it never really rose on countless alleys and tenements. Lung diseases became common complaints, especially among miners and millworkers who breathed coal or cotton dust day and night. By one modern estimate, health problems provoked by air pollution around 1900 reduced Britain's total economic output by one-quarter.

Water quality was no better. Rivers and canals everywhere served as industrial sewers. The water of the river Calder made a "tolerably good ink" in 1864, according to a government commission. Another commission, in 1869, described a river flowing through Manchester as:

> ...caked over with a thick scum of dirty froth, looking like a solid, sooty crusted surface.... Wherever a yard or two of the scum was cleared away, the whole surface was seen simmering and sparkling with a continual effervescence of smaller bubbles ...showing that the whole river was fermenting and generating gas. The air was filled with the stench of this gaseous emanation many yards away. The temperature of the water was 76 F, and that of the air 54 F.

For a few generations, industrialization had catastrophic effects on British health. In the "black country," average life expectancy fell by six years between 1820 and 1840. While the industrial working classes grew in number, they shrank in stature. Between 1800 and 1850, army recruits and prisoners—the only populations systematically measured—lost an average of 1 inch in height. The average male in 1850 stood 5′4″ (163 cm) and the average female 5′0″ (152 cm). The shortest came from industrial cities, and the tallest from the counties farthest from the centers of industry. Some combination of poor nutrition, heavy work, and frequent disease accounted for the stunted stature of industrial workers.

Air Pollution The toxic smoke of copper foundries fills the sky above the copper-producing region of Cornwall in southwest England in this late-nineteenth-century engraving. Air pollution was a feature of life throughout industrial Britain, leading to widespread respiratory illness and other health problems.

After 1850, these grim conditions gradually improved. Industrial workers' wages began to inch upward. Life expectancy in Britain lengthened, and after 1870 it never again dipped below 40 years. Health improved more quickly after 1890 through improved medical understanding of infectious disease. By 1900, the Industrial Revolution had clearly improved the average health and well-being of the British population, now 38 million, nearly four times its size in 1800. Twenty-year-old army recruits in 1900 averaged nearly 5′6″ in height (167 cm) and 130 lbs (60 kg).

The Industrial Revolution enriched and empowered Britain. It made Britain the "workshop of the world." Britain's manufacturing exports in 1840 stood at about 50 times their level as of 1700. Efficient production of coal, cotton, or iron underpinned hundreds of huge personal fortunes. And the Industrial Revolution enabled Britain to construct a military machine that helped make a little island into a great power. The rest of the world took notice.

Industrial Revolutions around the Globe

Britain strove to keep the Industrial Revolution to itself. Parliament passed laws making it illegal for people who knew industrial secrets to go abroad. Authorities vigorously hunted down foreign industrial spies, hundreds of whom prowled British factory towns. The government tried hard to enforce intellectual property rules. But nothing worked. Industrial secrets leapt to the European continent and beyond.

The technologies and organizational techniques of industrialization first escaped to continental Europe. Thousands of European towns had supported small-scale handicraft production of textiles since medieval times. As in Britain, by 1800 water power provided the primary energy source for new mills and factories on the Continent.

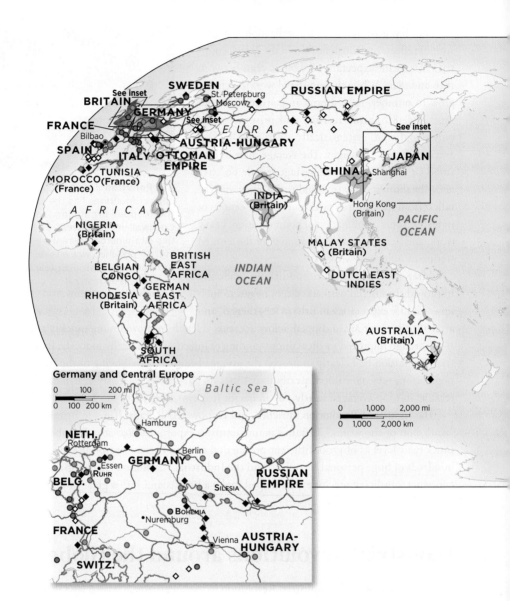

Clusters of textile mills sprang up where ambitious entrepreneurs found suitable rivers for water power, undercutting household-scale spinning and weaving.

But quickly coal became king in much of continental Europe as it had in Britain. A long carboniferous crescent, as important for the early industrial age as the Fertile Crescent had been for the early history of agriculture, underlay parts of Britain, northern France, Belgium, Germany, the Czech lands (Bohemia), and what is now southern Poland (Silesia). By 1820, northern France and Belgium had developed steam-powered

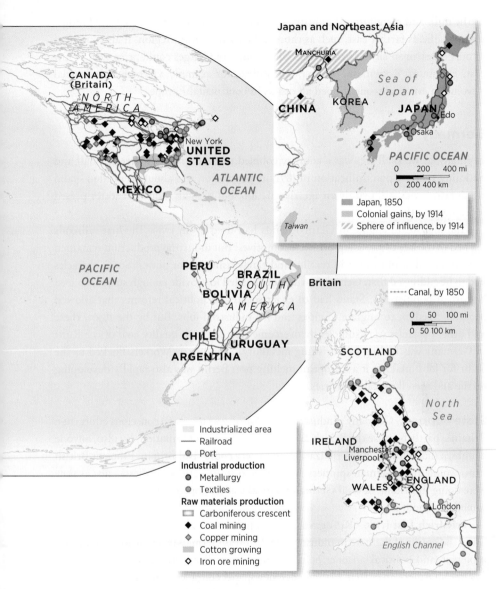

The Global Impact of Industrialization, ca. 1914 Industrialization gave rise to a global economy that was both more geographically differentiated than before—into zones of industrial production and zones of raw material production—and also more tightly knitted together through long-distance trade. Cotton mills, steel mills, and factories as of 1914 were concentrated in Japan, Europe (including Britain), and eastern North America, but the raw materials necessary for industrial production were scattered among all the continents. Railroads, ports, and ocean-going ships handled enormous quantities of raw materials to keep factories and mills supplied. In Europe's case, one crucial raw material—coal—came from one of the world's giant coalfields, the carboniferous crescent, stretching from Scotland to Silesia.

textile mills and metallurgical industries. Businessmen soon brought coal-fired industry to coalfields farther east, such as those in Germany's Ruhr region. It also sprouted in port cities, or in cities astride rivers where ships and barges could bring coal at low cost: Hamburg, Rotterdam, Vienna, and Bilbao, for example. Germany's Industrial Revolution eventually outstripped all others in continental Europe.

Germany

Germany, as we shall see, was a country cobbled together from a welter of small and middling states. Upon unification in 1871, its population was about 40 million—and rising fast. It was still mainly an agrarian nation, but with an industrial sector poised for rapid growth.

The first steam engine in German lands had fired up in 1789. The first railroads opened in the late 1830s, using British locomotives. But industrial production remained tiny for decades, most of it in textiles and rarely using steam power. Some obstacles had to be addressed first. German agriculture needed to provide enough surplus to feed big urban populations. States had to enact social and political reforms that allowed peasants freedom to migrate to cities and fill industrial jobs. But by the 1850s, these and other obstacles were sufficiently overcome that the high-quality coal of the Ruhr in Germany was fueling a flourishing metallurgical industry. Workers flocked to the Ruhr for jobs, making it a European melting pot. Berlin was also rapidly developing textile and metallurgical industries.

State Support   Germany's Industrial Revolution was more of a conscious effort than Britain's, partly because the British example inspired urgent imitation. By 1850, anyone could see that without industrialization no society could rival Britain. Efficient British firms would drive German spinners, weavers, and smiths out of business—just as they were doing in Britain. Several German political leaders hoped to use state power to do something about it.

Friedrich List (1789–1846) gave German politicians an intellectual blueprint for using the power of the state to industrialize. List was German by birth, an accountant, professor, and political prisoner before emigrating to Pennsylvania in 1825. There he became an American citizen, a landowner, newspaper editor, coal merchant, and author of a book praising the protectionist trade policies of the U.S. government. Returning to Germany in 1833, List wrote newspaper articles and books urging that German states form a customs union, protect their industries against foreign competition, and build railroads. List's ideas proved one of the world's most influential guides on how to industrialize a country.

The German state after unification in 1871 made strong contributions to the country's rapid industrialization. It invested in technical education. It funded research institutes, especially in physics and chemistry, to bolster the science behind industry. By 1900, this expenditure had repaid the investment handsomely, and by many accounts Germany led the world in scientific research and the application of science to industry. Germany also put up tariffs from the early 1870s to keep out foreign competition. It built transport infrastructure—mainly railways (partly state-owned), ports, roads, and a few new canals—helping to create a unified national market. In 1850, Berlin had still imported its coal by ship and canal-barge from Britain. By 1880, the city's coal all came from Silesia by rail.

Bismarck and Labor Politics Like other industrializing countries, Germany developed a working class and a labor movement representing their interests. German labor unions at first represented workers from single industries, such as the cigar-workers union that formed in 1865. The unions joined their efforts to support industrial workers in a political party known by its German initials, the SPD (Social Democratic Party), born in 1875. More radical workers—a tiny minority of the whole—supported the revolutionary ideals of the German journalist Karl Marx, whose powerful pamphlet, the **Communist Manifesto**, co-authored with Friedrich Engels, was published in 1848. Presenting class struggle as the motor of history, Marx and Engels called on the workers of all countries to unite to overthrow the ruling class of entrepreneurs and their allies in government and the professions. The idea of communist revolution remained unpopular until the 1870s, attaining major importance only with the Russian Revolution of 1917. But the strength of the SPD worried the German chancellor and aristocrat Otto von Bismarck.

Under Bismarck, the German state used carrot and stick to promote labor peace in pursuit of industrial strength. The state provided, or obliged employers to provide, pensions, health insurance, and unemployment benefits for workers—the first country in the world to do so. Bismarck also encouraged employers to compromise with laborers on wages and working conditions. Employers at first complained that such compromises would undermine their international competitiveness, but time and protective tariffs soothed their fears. At the same time, Bismarck banned the SPD and labor union activity in his anti-socialist laws of 1878. As a result, the German labor movement remained modest until the 1890s, when the anti-socialist laws were repealed and unionization skyrocketed. By 1904, fully 1 million German workers had joined unions, and by 1913, some 2.5 million—the metalworkers union alone had half a million members.

Bismarck's program of state-supported industrialization worked. Between 1850 and 1913, the per capita size of the economy in the German lands tripled, while industrial growth quintupled. Cities sprouted from next to nothing. Essen, in the Ruhr, was a big village of 3,000 people in 1831, and in 1913 an industrial city of 300,000. The major surge in German industrialization came after unification in 1871, with heavy industry in the vanguard. Iron ore production jumped ninefold between 1870 and 1913, while coal output quintupled. Germany's total railway mileage, still smaller than Britain's in

German Industrialization Workers in the Krupp factory in Essen ca. 1900 inspect the steel train wheels that the factory manufactured. The steel industry and the expansion of the German railway network allowed it to rival Britain for industrial dominance.

1870, was double its rival's by 1910. The growth of railways created a huge and reliable market for Germany's iron and steel industries.

The German version of industrial revolution favored giant firms. In 1870, almost all German industrial workers still toiled in tiny enterprises, no bigger than a family. But soon large firms came to account for nearly half of industrial employment. By 1913, Krupp, an iron, steel, and weapons manufacturer in Essen, employed 77,000 people. Siemens, an engineering firm based in Berlin and Nuremberg, employed 57,000 people.

The United States and Canada

The United States at its birth was an agrarian country, with 95 percent of its population living on the land. Many of its leaders preferred it that way, but not **Alexander Hamilton** (ca. 1755–1804). As secretary of the Treasury in 1791, Hamilton wrote a tract advising that the new nation should protect its small and inefficient manufacturers from foreign—mainly British—competition. Tariffs would, he claimed, enable American manufacturers to survive and grow, taking advantage of an ever-larger domestic market. Hamilton's vision served as the chief inspiration for U.S. trade policy for more than a century, during which time the United States became an industrial powerhouse. Hamilton's program also served as an inspiration for Friedrich List's ideas.

A nation of only small-scale industry in 1790, the United States had, as Hamilton saw, strong growth potential. It had plentiful timber, good soil, coal, iron ores, and other minerals. Its population was among the fastest-growing in the world: from 4 million in 1790, it leapt to 17 million in 1840 and 63 million by 1890.

High wages (by international standards of the time) throughout the U.S. economy strengthened the economic logic of both slavery, prevalent in the southern states, and labor-saving machinery. To get labor-saving technology, American businesses and officials tried to lure British craftsmen versed in the secrets of the textile and iron-working industries to break British law and bring their knowledge to America. Samuel Slater had worked in the textile business for years when he left England for Rhode Island in 1789. Rather than risk arrest for carrying plans of the latest textile mill technology, he committed it all to memory. He set up a cotton mill for the merchant family that had founded Brown University but felt ill-treated and soon set up his own. In the following decades, thousands of others emigrating to the United States brought British industrial technology with them.

American entrepreneurs such as Francis Cabot Lowell also went to Britain to learn what they could. A Bostonian with an inherited fortune, he traveled to Manchester and Scotland in search of the secrets of cotton manufacturing. He learned enough—how to build a power loom using water or steam power—to set up a large-scale cotton mill in Waltham, Massachusetts.

Not all of the imported expertise for U.S. industrialization came from Britain. One of the nation's first large-scale factories was the gunpowder works established by refugees from the French Revolution, the du Pont family. Pierre du Pont, a watchmaker's son, had done stints in Parisian prisons in the 1790s. Du Pont fled revolutionary France with his family, emigrating to the United States in 1799. One of his sons founded a gunpowder factory in 1803 using water power from Delaware's Brandywine River and chemistry expertise he brought from France.

The American System The U.S. weapons industry was especially important to world history. Together with clock making, the arms industry developed the practice of manufacturing with interchangeable parts. Instead of a single craftsman making an entire musket or grandfather clock, this system relied on semi-skilled workers using machine tools to mass-produce components that other workers could assemble into a final product. This method, pioneered in British naval shipbuilding, required less skill, lowered production costs, and—crucially for weapons—eased repair. All musket triggers, for example, were so close to identical that a musket with a broken trigger was not junk; it just needed a new trigger. The virtues of the system of interchangeable parts in weapons manufacture became clear during the War of 1812 with Britain, and the principle was widely followed throughout U.S. industries by 1850. Guns and clocks, and eventually almost everything else, were not designed to last, but instead to be cheap to make and easy to fix. The use of interchangeable parts in mechanized production was often called "the American system" of manufacturing.

Southern Cotton, Northern Textiles, and American Slavery Americans also developed technologies beyond those they acquired from overseas. Perhaps most important were the cotton gin and the telegraph. The **cotton gin** (short for "engine"), patented in 1794, was a device that helped remove the seeds from cotton fiber, making it ready to spin. It eliminated a bottleneck in cotton manufacture and was crucial for the rise of mechanized cotton production in the United States as well as in Britain. It was equally crucial in spreading cotton cultivation and slavery in the U.S. South—the cotton industry could not flourish without abundant raw cotton. Samuel Morse patented the long-distance telegraph in the 1840s. It helped tie the country together by sending information at the speed of electricity from telegraph office to telegraph office. Such near-instant communication suited the needs of railroads and eventually became an important military technology as well. In the 1850s alone, Americans registered 28,000 patents for inventions.

By 1830, the United States had a robust textile industry based in New England. Francis Cabot Lowell had opened his first mill in Waltham in 1814, followed by several more in Lowell, Massachusetts, outside of Boston. At first the American textile industry relied on water power, but, like Britain's, it gradually shifted to coal and steam. Also like Britain's, it relied heavily on female labor, and on cotton grown—before the Civil War—on slave plantations in the southern states. In 1860, about 70 percent of the 4 million enslaved African Americans worked on cotton plantations producing the raw material for New England's—and Europe's—cotton industry.

Industry and Government Support   Meanwhile, the U.S. metallurgical industry churned out rails, locomotives, and guns, among other goods. The iron industry began to take off in the 1840s in Pennsylvania, where high-quality coal was abundant. Coal output jumped 13-fold and iron ore 16-fold between 1870 and 1913. Immigrants from Europe flocked to American coal mines, iron foundries, and by 1880 big steel mills in cities such as Pittsburgh and Cleveland. Led by iron, steel, and railroads, total U.S. industrial output leapt 8-fold in the years 1870–1913. The United States and Germany were the tigers of the world economy in those decades, fed by their industrial revolutions.

The U.S. government took deliberate steps to advance its Industrial Revolution, although not as directly as the state in Bismarck's Germany. Tariffs protected young and inefficient industries from foreign competition. Cotton cloth, for example, received tariff protection in 1816. The patent system and legal system rewarded innovation and investment—as in Britain. The law provided for a limited liability corporation, widespread among U.S. states by 1860, which enabled investors to pool their resources without fear of becoming liable for a company's debts. The Congress and the Patent Office supported Morse financially while he was improving the telegraph. The federal government gave millions of acres of public land to railroad companies and, beginning in 1862, to the states to encourage the creation of agricultural, technical, and engineering colleges and universities.

Economies of Scale   The most distinctive feature of the American Industrial Revolution was its exploitation of economies of scale. After the Erie Canal opened in 1825 and railroads crisscrossed the country by 1870, the United States was sufficiently connected that it essentially formed one big, fast-growing national market. U.S. industries got very good at mass production of cheap goods. Several million American families could afford to buy clothing, furniture, and tools made in factories. That prosperity, a result of both high wages by the standards of the time and a thriving middle class, helped to enlarge the market and reward manufacturers in their quests for economies of scale.

The size of the U.S. market and the scale of production also favored bigger business organizations. American entrepreneurs, like their counterparts in Germany and Japan, created gigantic companies and conglomerates that employed tens of thousands of people. At one point in nineteenth century, the DuPont company employed 10 percent of the population of the state of Delaware. By 1890, the United States had surpassed Britain in total industrial production to become the global leader, the result mainly of the size of its domestic market.

Canada Industrialization came more slowly to Canada than to the United States. For most of the nineteenth century, Canadians imported most of their industrial goods from either the United States or Britain. Until Confederation in 1867, Canada was a set of British colonies largely governed from London. Britain sought to keep its edge in industrial production, and so Canada had few manufacturing enterprises. But after 1867, Canada—with about 3.5 million people and abundant natural resources—acquired more authority over its own affairs. It soon launched a **National Policy** (1879) intended to promote industry. Tariffs on foreign goods boosted enterprises such as textiles, shoe-making, pulp and paper, meatpacking, and steel, mainly in Quebec and Ontario. Nova Scotia also developed coal, steel, and shipbuilding. A political emphasis on railroad building—Canada's first transcontinental railroad opened in 1886—helped inspire rail and locomotive works, as well as iron ore and coal mining.

A growing labor supply, as well as abundant raw materials and prudent national policy, also helped Canada to industrialize. By 1890, its population was climbing fast, the result of slowed emigration of Canadians to the United States combined with booming immigration from Britain, continental Europe, and—to British Columbia—from

Chinese Labor in Canada Chinese workers build the tracks of the Canadian Pacific Railway. In 1882 alone some six thousand Chinese arrived to work on the Canadian Pacific in British Columbia.

China. Many immigrants settled in industrial centers, as did many native-born farm youths. By 1910, when the national population reached about 7 million, some 3 million lived in cities and towns, and half a million worked in industry. Many Canadian industries exported to the much larger market in the United States; some were branch plants of U.S.-owned firms. Canada was well on its way to becoming an industrial society, deeply integrated with the United States as well as Britain.

Russia

Like the United States and Canada, Russia had natural resources well suited to launching an industrial revolution. It had abundant coal and iron. During the nineteenth century, it conquered Central Asian lands that would prove suitable for growing cotton. Russia's social base, however, was less promising. Part of Russia's elite was attuned to western European trends and accustomed to borrowing ideas from abroad. But the rest of the population was poorly prepared to support industrialization—partly because it was too poor to buy much. Unlike in Britain or the United States, the middle class, and the market for anything beyond basic goods, was small.

As of 1860, some two-thirds of Russia's roughly 70 million people were serfs, some owned by the state and others bound to lands owned by the nobility. Most had only rudimentary education, if any. Few were legally free to migrate to cities or jobs. Russia's largest industrial cluster was around the city of Łódź (pronounced Woodge) in Russian-controlled Poland. The city hosted hundreds of small textile mills in 1850, most of them owned by German businessmen. At that time, almost no one imagined that a Russian Industrial Revolution was either possible or desirable.

Russia's existing industrial plant was old and small. The weapons industry, developed originally under Ivan the Terrible and Peter the Great, was antiquated by the 1850s. The country had only one real railroad line, opened in 1851 between Moscow and St. Petersburg. Despite longstanding efforts to import technology and expertise from abroad, which included an offer to James Watt to move to Russia, the Russian Empire in 1850 remained overwhelmingly agrarian.

Then Russia lost a war in humiliating fashion. Russia's military performed embarrassingly in the Crimean War (1853–1856) against the Ottoman Empire, France, and Britain. The defeat clarified matters for Russian elites: they needed to reform and strengthen their country in a hurry. Their anxieties made more of them sympathetic to new ideas such as the abolition of serfdom (see Chapter 23) and the industrialization of Russia.

The ambition to industrialize faced many obstacles. Before 1880, the country lacked engineers, compared to Britain or Germany, and technical training was rare. The legal system made it awkward to create businesses. Transport infrastructure was creaky. By 1880, it still had only about 13,000 miles (21,000 km) of railroad—about one-seventh the U.S. total. But in the 1880s and especially the 1890s, Russian industrialization gathered steam. Industrial output expanded at 8 percent per year in the 1890s, and the rail network more than doubled between 1880 and 1905. Russia was late getting started by the standards of Germany or the United States, let alone Britain, but it made up ground fast. From low levels in 1870, Russian coal output climbed 40-fold by 1913 and industrial production 9-fold.

The crowning achievement of Russia's Industrial Revolution was the opening of the **Trans-Siberian Railway** in 1903, financed mainly by the state. Construction began in 1891 and required 90,000 laborers, many of them convicts, army conscripts, or migrants from Korea and China. When finished, the iron road crossed bogs, mountains, and hundreds of rivers over about 5,700 miles (9,000 km) from Moscow to the Pacific Ocean. The railroad opened much of Siberia and its natural resources to Russian settlement and use.

Government Support   The Russian Industrial Revolution was very much a revolution from above. It could scarcely have succeeded without determined government support, stronger than that in the United States or Germany. That support resulted largely from the efforts of **Sergei Witte** (1849–1915). Born into a noble family, Witte aspired to an academic career in mathematics. Instead, he made his early mark in railroad management and entered government service in 1888. In a political career spanning nearly three decades, and inspired in part by Friedrich List's ideas, Witte promoted railroad building and the creation of technical schools, together with tariffs to protect Russian industry. Guided by Witte, the Russian government welcomed foreign investment (except on the Trans-Siberian project) and technical experts, financed the sale of Russian industrial goods to neighboring countries without much industry (such as China and Iran), and fostered heavy industry by purchasing locomotives, rails, and military hardware. No one else in Russia—or for that matter in Germany, Japan, the United States, or Britain—played a larger role in advancing industrialization than Witte.

Japan

Japan blazed its own trail to industrialization. It involved more labor and less machinery, because in Japan labor was cheap and, initially, machines and mechanical expertise were scarce. As much or more than the Russian, American, and German cases, the Japanese Industrial Revolution was nourished by state support.

Like Russia, Japan in 1850 seemed an unlikely candidate for industrialization. Its economy remained agrarian, although Japan was unusually urbanized: perhaps 10 percent of Japanese lived in cities in 1700, and 20 percent—of about 34 million—by 1870. With its countryside crowded after 1720 or so, couples tried hard to limit their family size, and population growth proceeded slowly for about five generations. Japan had some accessible coal, but not much iron ore. Japan seemed to lack the incentive and most of the wherewithal for an industrial revolution, although its highly productive agriculture could feed cities.

Meiji Reforms   But in 1853 Japan received a shock when a well-armed American fleet steamed into Edo (Tokyo) Bay and demanded diplomatic relations, a commercial treaty, and the rights to build a coaling station. The government—the Tokugawa shoguns in power since 1603—had for 200 years sought to minimize contact with the rest of the world. Now some of the elite realized that their national security was at risk and Japan's power inadequate. This provided motivation for reforms, just as the defeat in the Crimean War did for Russia. The efforts of the Tokugawa deepened divisions, and a civil war in 1867–1868 brought the **Meiji Restoration**, which reinstated rule by emperors. A new elite took power in Meiji Japan (1868–1912) that was committed to pursuing the knowledge and technologies that made foreigners so threatening. Occasional bombardments of Japanese ports by British, French, Dutch, and American naval ships seeking better trade deals emphasized to the leaders of Meiji Japan the urgency of strengthening the country.

Japan's population was unusually literate and accustomed to hierarchy, group loyalty, and discipline. Millions of women were used to long hours spinning thread in their homes. Japan had the makings of a productive working class. But it needed efficient technology, which the government set out to acquire. Japan's coastal shipping routes and longstanding commercial traditions allowed the makings of a national market by 1868. That appealed to ambitious entrepreneurs who were eager to build industrial enterprises.

No one was more ambitious than **Eiichi Shibusawa**. He was born in 1840 to a prosperous farm family and studied Confucian classics. After an eye-opening trip to view efficient, modern factories in France, he came home during the chaotic fall of the Tokugawa. Called to government service in the Ministry of Finance, he used his office to help start hundreds of companies in textiles, shipping, sugar refining, beer brewing, paper manufacture, hotels, banking, insurance, and railroads. Shibusawa moved among elite businessmen and high government officials who showed remarkable determination to bring an industrial revolution to Japan. They sometimes differed on the means, but rarely on the end: a prosperous, strong, industrial Japan. Most also hoped to get richer in the process.

Textiles and Heavy Industry   As in Britain, Germany, and the United States, textiles led the way in Japanese industrialization. In 1870, Japan was importing vast amounts of cloth from British factories, which produced cheaper and better cottons than could Japanese households. Then in 1877 a Japanese student at the University of London agreed to the suggestion from a total stranger—Shibusawa—that for the sake of Japan he should abandon his study of economics and instead learn the cotton business. So Takeo Yamanobe headed to Manchester, learned all he could, and in

1882 came home to help Shibusawa set up Japan's first modern cotton mill, in Osaka. It soon prospered, drawing imitators into the business. By 1890, Japan was producing almost all its cloth in its own factories and had begun exporting to neighboring countries. Its factories generally worked differently from those in Europe, often using human muscle to power machinery instead of steam engines—because labor was cheap.

The biggest industrial sector in Meiji Japan by employment was textiles, but Japan's place in the world depended more on heavy industry. Meiji reformers regarded iron, steel, shipbuilding, chemicals, mining, and railroads as too important to be left to the private sector. The state guided, and often initiated, the industrial revolution in these sectors, while leaving textiles to the market.

Acquiring industrial expertise became a top priority. At any given time in the 1870s and 1880s, some 2,000 foreign engineers, mechanics, or technicians were working in Japan, sharing their knowledge. Japan also sent students overseas to learn, as Yamanobe had done in London and Manchester. Between

Japanese Textiles By the end of the nineteenth century, industrial methods of textile production overtook traditional Japanese methods. An 1872 illustration depicts the spinning floor in a silk factory, combining the methods of manual and machine labor.

1868 and 1900, some 11,000 Japanese students, almost all male—the first large-scale study-abroad initiative in world history—went to the United States, Germany, and Britain, mainly to master the latest industrial techniques and technologies. Japan also imported foreign technology directly and encouraged engineers to build similar, perhaps better, models, adapted to Japanese conditions.

The Meiji reformers also changed Japanese conditions to fit a more industrial society. They imposed compulsory education for girls and boys in 1872 and adopted patent law in 1885, prompting inventors to improve machinery. They founded engineering schools and sponsored industrial exhibitions. They adopted the metric system of measure, the 24-hour day, and a Westernized calendar.

Military Considerations As in Germany and Russia, military considerations played a major role in the government's choices. Japan, its leaders came to believe, needed a modern military to deter powerful countries such as Britain or the United States that otherwise might conquer it. A modern military required immense quantities of iron and steel. The Meiji state supported shipbuilding, mines, railroads, steel, and armaments with subsidies, credit, and tax breaks. At times it also unleashed police or army violence against disgruntled laborers and peasants—whose taxes helped finance

The Metallic Web

1800–1920

IN 1800, THE FASTEST ANYONE could move was atop a galloping horse at about 30 mph (48 kph)—and that only for a couple of minutes. Horse travel averaged about 5 mph (8 kph). Boats or ships traveled at the speed the wind propelled them, which at times meant no movement at all. It might take 6 to 18 months for messages to get back and forth between Java and Amsterdam.

Between 1800 and 1844, three new technologies sped up global movement: the railway, steamship, and telegraph. Metallic webs soon spanned the globe: steel railway track, copper telegraph wires and undersea cables, and iron steamships. Telegraph messages from Java to Amsterdam and back took a few hours. Overland journeys from New York to San Francisco in 1850 took 6 months, but by 1870 only one week by rail. Transatlantic crossings by sail in 1800 had taken about a month on average; by 1880, steamships took a week.

The metallic web made the world feel smaller. The isochronic areas shaded on the map show, for instance, the broad swathe of Eurasia reachable from London in five days. Even those millions around the world who as late as 1900 had never seen a locomotive, steamship, or telegraph wire—mainly villagers in the areas shaded purple in South America, Africa, and Asia—found their lives changed by people, businesses, and governments who used these technologies every day.

KEY

—	Railway
—	Shipping lane
—	Undersea cable
•	20 largest cities
○	Other city
Lima ○	Port

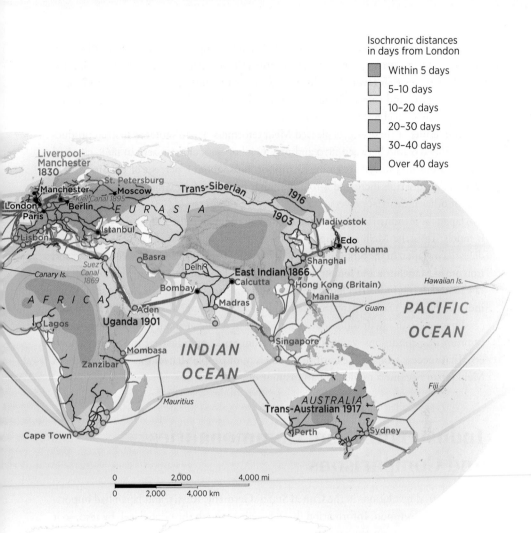

Isochronic distances
in days from London

- Within 5 days
- 5–10 days
- 10–20 days
- 20–30 days
- 30–40 days
- Over 40 days

Liverpool-
Manchester
1830

Manchester
London
Paris
Berlin
St. Petersburg
Moscow
Kiel Canal 1895
EURASIA
Trans-Siberian
1916
1903
Vladivostok
Lisbon
Istanbul
Basra
Suez
Canal
1869
Delhi
East Indian 1866
Calcutta
Bombay
Edo
Yokohama
Shanghai
Hong Kong (Britain)
Manila
Hawaiian Is.
Canary Is.
AFRICA
Aden
Madras
Guam
PACIFIC
OCEAN
Lagos
Uganda 1901
Singapore
Mombasa
INDIAN
Zanzibar
OCEAN
Fiji
Mauritius
AUSTRALIA
Trans-Australian 1917
Cape Town
Perth
Sydney

0   2,000   4,000 mi
0   2,000   4,000 km

Questions for Analysis

*Based on this feature and your chapter reading, consider the
following questions:*

1. What parts of the world remained least globally
    connected in 1900, to judge by the isochronic regions
    and the railway networks?

2. Within Africa and Asia, South Africa and India had
    unusually dense rail networks. Why?

industrialization and whose irrigated ricefields increasingly suffered from deadly water pollution. Firms nurtured their political connections to get their share of state support, an arrangement that favored big businesses like Mitsubishi and Kawasaki, both originally shipping and shipbuilding companies. By 1890, both were giant conglomerates owning mines, steel mills, and factories.

The results of these efforts pleased Meiji reformers. Japan's total industrial production climbed 6-fold between 1870 and 1913. Coal output, close to zero in 1868, climbed 20-fold from 1883 to 1913, reaching 21 million tons (about 8 percent of Britain's total). Iron ore production increased 4-fold over that period but remained tiny compared to that of other industrial powers.

Japan, as it industrialized, needed ever more raw materials, and nature hadn't given it much. Thus the Meiji state undertook imperial conquests at the expense of China, defeated by Japan in the Sino-Japanese War of 1894–1895. Japan secured access to coal and iron ore in Manchuria and sought to promote cotton farming in Taiwan. Shortages of key raw materials put industrial Japan on the road to overseas imperialism; at the same time, industrialization made Japan strong enough to win an imperialist war against China.

By 1914, Japan's swift industrialization, a case of deliberate policy triumphing despite unpromising conditions, vaulted it into the front ranks of industrial and military powers. That success aroused the curiosity, and envy, of people all over the world for whom Meiji Japan became a model and an inspiration.

Industrialization: Commonalities and Comparisons

The industrial revolutions in the United States, Germany, Russia, and Japan had important things in common. Information flowed easily through the Global web by 1850, so it was easy to learn from the prior British example. All four countries rejected free trade and a fully free market in favor of protection of their industries and government promotion of transport infrastructure. Their leaders were well acquainted with the ideas of Alexander Hamilton and Friedrich List, and adapted them to their own circumstances. The Russian and Japanese governments, late to start pushing industrialization, took the most active roles. Each of the four countries benefited from a large domestic market, providing manufacturers with potential economies of scale. Good transport systems and integrated national markets were a requirement for large-scale industrialization. And it helped to have additional accessible markets—for example, in the form of overseas empire or neighbors with few efficient industries of their own.

All four countries also shared a reliance on military industry. The first large-scale industrial system of interchangeable parts came in American armories charged with military production during the War of 1812. The first high-precision mass production

Coal Output, 1820–1900 (in million tons)

	BRITAIN	GERMANY	FRANCE	RUSSIA	JAPAN	UNITED STATES	CANADA
1820	~25	1	1	n/a	n/a	0.3	n/a
1840	43	4	3	n/a	n/a	2	n/a
1860	88	19	8	0.3	n/a	18	0.3
1880	149	59	19	3	0.8	72	1
1900	229	150	33	16	7	245	5

Sources: B. R. Mitchell, *International Historical Statistics: Europe, 1750–2005* (2007), 464–66; *Africa, Asia & Oceania, 1750–2005* (2007), 375; *The Americas, 1750–2005* (2007), 327–28.

Iron Ore Output, 1840–1900 (in million tons)

	BRITAIN	GERMANY	FRANCE	RUSSIA	JAPAN	UNITED STATES	CANADA
1840	n/a	0.4	1	n/a	n/a	n/a	n/a
1860	8	1	3	n/a	n/a	n/a	n/a
1880	18	5	3	n/a	0.2	7	n/a
1900	14	13	5	6	0.3	28	0.1

Sources: B. R. Mitchell, *International Historical Statistics: Europe, 1750–2005* (2007), 490–91; *Africa, Asia & Oceania, 1750–2005* (2007), 397; *The Americas, 1750–2005* (2007), 341.

took place in Portsmouth, England, in a factory designed during the Napoleonic Wars to produce hundreds of thousands of standardized pulleys for naval ships. What motivated the Englishman Henry Bessemer to find a new way to make steel in the 1850s was the problem of making big artillery pieces more durable. German steel making, especially that undertaken by Krupp's firm, was first devoted to tableware but by 1865 to weaponry. The programs of industrialization in Russia and Japan, at least the large sectors devoted to metallurgy, were calculated to make their countries militarily strong.

The tables above show the growth of heavy industry in various countries worldwide. Note the early start but modest growth in France; the surge in the United States after 1860 and in Russia after 1880; and the general dominance of the United States, Britain, and Germany.

De-industrialization

All these industrial revolutions sparked a related process: **de-industrialization**, the disappearance of old handicraft industries that could not compete for long with mechanized production. It too began in Britain. Hand-weavers, for example, working at home,

Handicraft Industry A mid-nineteenth-century watercolor shows a South Asian woman spinning thread by hand, one of the traditional crafts that was threatened world-wide by industrialization.

eventually had to find other work after steam-powered textile mills were up and running. Village smiths, whose hoes and horseshoes could not compete with those churned out by iron foundries in Birmingham, had to do the same. Industrial cities put village industries out of business. This also happened in France, Belgium, and Germany after factory systems took root there, taking decades in each case.

Soon de-industrialization was a near-global trend. By 1830, millions of spinners, weavers, and metalsmiths working in China, India, Iran, or Algeria were feeling the impact of British factory competition. A Bengali widow in 1828 reported that she had taken up spinning when her husband died but her business quickly evaporated. She said that previously:

> ...weavers would come to my doorstep to buy the yarn...and they would immediately advance as much cash money as I wanted. As a result, we did not have any anxiety about food and clothing....Now...the weavers have stopped coming to my doorstep to buy my yarn, [and] even when I send it to the [market] they will not buy it at one-fourth the former price....I...have learned that the weavers are using English yarn now....When I examined the yarn I found it better than mine.

She was not alone in her misfortune. In 1835, the governor-general of British India wrote: "the bones of the cotton weavers are bleaching the plains of India."

Misfortune befell spinners and hand-weavers wherever factory cloth could be sold. Isfahan, in Iran, in 1890 had only 10 percent as many silk looms as in 1830 because British cotton took market share from Iranian silk. Spinners and weavers from China to Chile faced similar challenges. The table opposite shows some of the geographical relocation of industry in the nineteenth century.

By the mid-nineteenth century, Britain's factories produced so much so cheaply—and often of such good quality—that handicraft industries worldwide met the same fate as Indian and Iranian textiles. British-made iron, steel, pottery, and even coal were competitive on every continent. The innovations of the Industrial Revolution conferred an enormous advantage on British industries, especially those that were energy- or knowledge-intensive. By 1870, industries in the United States and continental Europe came to share that advantage, contributing to more de-industrialization. Industrialization not only changed peasants into workers in Britain, Germany, Russia, or Japan; in much of the world it changed handicraft workers into peasants or paupers.

Economic Shifts and Political Power in the Global Web

The efficiency of modern industrial production and transport launched a geographical reorganization of the world's economy. Lands with limited prospects for industrialization came to specialize more in primary products, mainly food and fiber crops. The slave states in the U.S. South before the Civil War, for example, deepened their commitment to cotton production in response to the demand for raw cotton from British and New England mills. After the Civil War, despite the abolition of slavery, the trend toward cotton strengthened in the southern states. Egypt, India, and China by 1900 produced more raw cotton and less cotton cloth than they had in 1800. Australia and Argentina found niches producing wheat, wool, and leather, although each developed some light industry too. The advent of refrigerated shipping in the 1870s enabled the North American plains, the Argentine pampas, and other grasslands to specialize in beef, transported by rail and ship to distant markets.

The rails and steam that stood at the center of the industrial revolutions helped to knit the world economy into a tighter web than ever before. In the early modern centuries, as we've seen, certain goods such as silver, spices, and sugar were traded across oceans. Bulk goods, with few exceptions, did not reward the cost of long-distance transport. But by the 1840s that was changing fast. Cheap cloth, grain, timber, and coal could now yield profit if carried by steam-propelled trains or ships. Ever-larger spaces functioned more or less as single markets—where tariffs permitted.

Industrialization also changed the distribution of military and political power around the world. Britain, already on its way to becoming a great power before its Industrial Revolution, became the world's strongest power by 1840. It used its leverage to force weaker countries to lower tariffs on British goods and to expand

Approximate Share of Global Industrial Production, 1800–1900

	BRITAIN + EUROPE	CHINA + INDIA
1800	25%	50%
1850	37%	30%
1900	60%	12%

Source: Elaborated from Kaoru Sugihara, "Global Industrialization: A Multipolar Perspective," in *The Cambridge World History*, eds. J. R. McNeill and Kenneth Pomeranz, Vol. 7 (2015), 123.

CONSIDERING THE EVIDENCE

Rage against the Machines

The capitalists who owned textile mills and the laborers who worked in them often disagreed about the benefits of steam power. Capitalists claimed the machines made life easier for workers by saving them from the time and labor of monotonous tasks; workers focused on how machines reduced the number of available jobs. Great Britain and other states initially defended the interests of the less numerous capitalists against the demands of the much larger population of workers. Without a sympathetic ear in government, some workers organized violent riots to destroy the machines that threatened their livelihoods. In the following excerpt from a newspaper in Leeds (near Manchester, England), an anonymous contributor describes a confrontation in 1812 between a "furious mob" and mill owners who had recently adopted steam power.

Middleton, April 22, 1812.
On Monday ... afternoon, the Mills of Messrs. Daniel Burton and Sons ... about five miles from Manchester, were attacked by a furious mob, not from any dislike personally to the proprietors, ... but from using a species of looms worked by *power*, as it is called, that is by steam, and by the use of which manual labour is materially diminished.... Mr. Emanuel Burton and [about 50] men ... posted themselves in the works, determined to resist any attacks.... After breaking the windows, the mob fired several shots into the Factory, and endeavoured to force an entrance; in this they did not succeed, and Mr. Burton and his party fired about 50 blank cartridges ... to intimidate and disperse [the mob] ...; but [they] found [it] necessary to fire upon them with ball, when five of the rioters were shot dead, and a number were desperately wounded, two ... have died of their wounds. Seeing their companions

its overseas empire. Germany too, after unification (1871), emerged as a great power within Europe and, by the late 1880s, as an imperial power in Africa and the Pacific. France, although early to begin industrialization, could not keep pace with Britain and Germany, and by the 1870s no longer matched them in military power. The United States and Russia accelerated their overland expansions with their newfound industrial might, and in the U.S. case took up overseas empire after 1898 as well. As we've seen, Japan's Industrial Revolution thrust that nation into the East Asian mainland as an imperial power from the 1890s.

Meanwhile, Mughal India vanished and Qing China languished. Their militaries, still formidable in the mid-eighteenth century, by 1840 proved helpless in the face of British gunboats and artillery. Britain controlled India by 1860 and, together with other industrial powers, parts of China as well. After 1870, peoples without industrial weaponry generally soon lost their independence—and some disappeared altogether.

fall around them, the assailants became panic-struck, and ... they dispersed.

... Early on Tuesday morning a much more numerous mob ... assembled.... Finding that a detachment of the Scotch Grevs [a cavalry regiment of the British Army] had been brought to protect the works, the mob ... burnt [Mr. Emanuel Burton's mansion] to the ground.

Encouraged by their success, they repaired to [the mill], when an engagement between the mob and the cavalry took place, [four rioters were] shot dead upon the field, besides a great number wounded, and 17 of the most active of the insurgents taken prisoners.... It was observed that all the rioters were strangers at Middleton, and that [Middleton's] labouring classes ... took no part in the engagements.... This simple narrative of facts cannot be read without mixed emotions of horror and regret. For many years the military of this country have been solely employed against our foreign enemies; but now, unfortunately, they are under the necessity of acting against their own misled countrymen, and the tranquillity of the country is only imperfectly preserved even at the point of the bayonet!

Questions for Analysis

1. Why do you think the narrator needed to explain what "steam power" was and why it made people angry in 1812?

2. Does the narrator seem to have more sympathy for the "labouring classes" or the mill owners?

3. Why would the British government give a military regiment (which was accustomed to fighting foreign wars) an assignment to defend the private property of a mill owner?

Source: "Riots," Leeds Mercury, 25 Apr. 1812, in British Library Newspapers.

Rarely in world history had so much political and military power concentrated in so few spots. Now, in the nineteenth century, those who had pulled off industrial revolutions found themselves far more formidable than those who hadn't, and usually converted their advantages into conquest and empire. We will examine this theme more closely in Chapter 24.

Social Contracts and Industrial Society

The energy revolution and economic transformation that industrial societies experienced deepened their inequalities. This cast new doubt on the social contracts on which those societies had formerly operated. Social contracts—the phrase was popularized by the French Enlightenment thinker Jean-Jacques Rousseau—are not real contracts. They are shared understandings of what is fair in terms of the distribution of wealth, income, and opportunity. They always reflect the distribution of political power and are reinforced by laws, customs, and policies.

The social contract of industrial society had to incorporate the new urban and professional upper middle classes into ruling elites that formerly had comprised aristocrats, landowners, and big merchants. Between 1830 and 1900 in every industrialized country, the upper middle classes obtained rights to vote and hold public office, to join prestigious schools and clubs—in short, to acquire substantial political power and social standing.

It was harder for industrializing societies to agree on the proper standing of the working classes. The older elites included a few people who sympathized with workers, but most people in the upper classes were reluctant to share power, or even the right to vote, with people they considered their social and cultural inferiors. Also, workers could never unify behind a single set of aims. Some advocated for individual self-improvement, emphasizing the virtues of sobriety, hard work, and thrift. Others despaired of achieving improvement in this world and placed their hopes in a better life to come in the next. Many, however, came to think that political action provided their best hope.

Reform In political terms, workers were divided on the question of reform or revolution. Reform, meaning working within established institutions to achieve gradual improvements in working conditions and political rights, rested on the belief that progress was possible. In Europe, this outlook drew strength from Enlightenment ideology. Some of the poor, and as we've seen some middle-class observers such as Marx and Engels, rejected reform as a strategy for workers and advocated revolution. Workers' resentments sometimes boiled over into riots or rebellions. French workers took major roles in uprisings in 1830, 1848, and 1871. Workers in Milan, Berlin, Vienna, and other cities joined in revolutions in 1848—chaotic events that involved unstable coalitions with many agendas. In Russia, urban workers played a central role in an insurrection called the Revolution of 1905. But most attempts at revolution failed, sometimes in rivers of blood, and none managed to put the working class in power.

Reform efforts were more successful than revolution in renegotiating social contracts to the advantage of the working classes. There were several keys to the success of labor reform movements: the level of organization, the strength of alliances with the middle classes, and the continuing threat of revolution or economic disruption.

Labor Activism The most important key to the success of working-class reform was organization. Where they created labor unions, workers could negotiate more effectively with employers and put pressure on politicians. In 1824, the British Parliament repealed the Combination Acts that prohibited unions and strikes. In the ensuing decades, trade unions successfully drove parliamentary reforms of working conditions and the use of child labor. The unions also supported efforts to expand suffrage to all adult males.

The main weapon available to workers was the threat of a strike. In certain industries, such as coal or railroads, workers had particular power. In 1877, for example, U.S. railroad workers went on strike in response to reduced wages. State governors called out militias and violence broke out in several cities, obliging the federal government to send in the army. The strikers returned to work, but the railroad companies soon offered pensions and better wages in hopes of preventing further strikes. On a much larger scale, in 1912 nearly 1 million British coal miners struck for a minimum wage. Because factories, railroads, and the navy could not operate without coal, the miners had real power; after 37 days, the national government intervened and the miners got a minimum wage.

Alliances Another key to the success of labor reform was alliances with sympathetic members of the ruling elites or middle-class reformers. Every industrial country included people who were appalled at the squalor of urban working-class neighborhoods and the greed of many factory owners. In Britain, for example, Joseph Chamberlain, the industrial millionaire who turned to politics, became mayor of Birmingham and worked to deliver better schools, public libraries, clean water, streetlights, and other improvements to the entire city, including its working-class tenements. Others, such as the intellectuals Beatrice Webb and Sidney Webb and their colleagues in the Fabian Society (est. 1884), supported public education, shorter working hours, a minimum wage, and nationalized health care. Bismarck, as we've seen, agreed to provide health insurance and other benefits to German workers.

In Chicago, Jane Addams and other educated, well-to-do women set up Hull House in 1889 as a center for research into the plight of the city's poor, especially women and children, and advocated for improved education, housing, health care, and working conditions. By 1913, the United States had 413 **settlement houses**, as these institutions were

Settlement Houses Chicago children pose for a photograph outside Jane Addams's Hull House in 1908. Settlement houses like Hull House pioneered new methods of social work among the urban poor.

called. In Japan, middle-class reformers such as the professor Kanai En called attention to the widening social gulf, lamenting that "since the coming of factory organization . . . there is an estrangement between managers and workers." They supported legislation, passed in 1911, that outlawed labor for those under age 12 and shortened the working day to 12 hours for women and children over age 12. These reform efforts were all linked to one another. Bismarck's program influenced the Fabian Society. Hull House, based on a London settlement house called Toynbee Hall, was itself the model for a settlement house in Tokyo set up by American and Japanese women in 1919. Russian reformers established a settlement house in Moscow in 1905.

Expanding Suffrage Some of these allies of the working class, and many workers too, called themselves liberals or socialists. Roughly speaking, liberals favored individual freedoms, constitutional checks on rulers, and often some legal protections for society's most vulnerable members. At the core of liberal movements and political parties were the urban middle classes. **Socialists** placed stronger emphasis on empowering the working classes—in some cases through cooperatives and unions, in others through workers' ownership of factories, farms, and mines. Both liberals and socialists generally wanted to end aristocratic privileges, curtail religion in public life, and broaden political participation. Most sought to reform, rather than smash, existing political systems.

An important focus of political reform was expanding the right to vote. Workers in the early decades of industrialization were not allowed to vote. But through the allied efforts of workers and middle-class liberals, universal male franchise became law in France in 1848, in Germany in 1871, and in Japan in 1925. In Britain it came in steps between 1868 and 1918. In the United States, adult white males could generally vote by 1856, with exceptions in particular states. African American men generally could not vote until ratification of a constitutional amendment in 1868; even then, their voting rights were often denied in the southern states for another century.

Everywhere that workers were winning the right to vote, they and their middle-class allies formed new political parties focused on advancing the welfare of the working classes. The German Social Democratic Party (SPD) was founded in 1875, the French socialist party in 1879, the British Labour Party in 1900, and a Japanese Social Democratic Party in 1901. By 1910, they were all important forces in the day-to-day politics of their countries, part of the political system. The United States, in contrast, never developed a successful political party explicitly devoted to the interests of workers. The main workers' party in Russia, the Russian Social Democratic Workers' Party, founded in 1898, did not seek reform within the Russian political system but, instead, strove to overthrow it.

Women and Youth In Britain, the United States, and elsewhere, women launched suffrage movements in the nineteenth century, but they achieved few political rights until the twentieth. But with industrialization, wage work in factories set apart from the home altered the fabric of women's lives. They now had a little money to spend, and sometimes a wider network of friends in their co-workers, usually other women much like themselves, to whom they could turn in time of need. Women also organized to advance their own interests in response to new pressures brought by industrialization. In the early years in Lowell's mills, for example, young women made what for the time were good wages and were offered free evening educational classes. By the late 1830s, however, Lowell's mills slashed wages to match competition from other entrepreneurs. The Lowell girls, as they were known, resisted by going on strike and organizing a union. By 1853, they managed to convince the mill owners to reduce the work day to 11 hours.

In Japan, teenage girls made up most of the labor force in textile mills and worked in miserable conditions. They often lived in dingy dormitories and labored long hours for little pay. Women coal miners, usually older and married to male miners, fared worse. One observer commented: "Returning black and grimy from a day's work in the pits with their husbands, they immediately had to start preparing meals...[and] nursing their babies.... [N]o man would be found helping with what were designated as women's tasks."

In the early Meiji years, activists sought a new social contract for women. They argued that the new Japan needed educated, independent women in order to compete in the international arena. Their main impact came in 1872, when four years of compulsory education was required for girls as well as boys. But by the 1890s, the Meiji state had banned women from all political activity and passed new legislation confining them to traditional roles, summarized in the slogan "good wife, wise mother." The most successful women's organization in Meiji Japan, the Patriotic Women's Society established by Okumura Ioko, which had half a million members by 1905, worked to prepare soldiers for overseas deployments and console families whose sons never returned from war. That suited the Meiji state perfectly.

For working-class teenagers and children of both sexes, the industrial revolutions brought more independence from family supervision and, for some, the first formal schooling. They spent more of their time with other youths, whether on the streets, in cotton mills, or in schools. In every industrial city, unemployed children roamed the streets while their parents toiled in factories. Many children worked long hours in mills or mines. Increasingly, some attended school. Industrial societies from France to Japan to Canada created systems of public education between 1830 and 1880, changing the nature of childhood. In many cases, education for girls came later than for boys. In most Catholic countries, girls' education was entrusted to nuns rather than public employees. In addition to reading, writing, and arithmetic, schools taught the young to accept adult discipline, preparing them for life in the workplace.

More time spent together with their age-mates led the young in industrial cities to create their own culture—and led dismayed adults to try to shape it. British boys in growing numbers turned to sports such as soccer. In nineteenth-century Britain, and other countries too, young men in many working-class trades—masons, carpenters, smiths, tailors—regularly took to the road, tramping from town to town, looking for work, singing songs, forging bonds of youth before settling into full adulthood. In many cities teenage gangs sprang up. Concerned adults organized wholesome organizations and clubs, such as the YMCA and YWCA, founded in London in 1844 and 1855, respectively, or the Girls Club Union, begun in London in 1880. Churches of every denomination began creating youth groups starting in the 1880s. The industrial revolutions forced renegotiation of social contracts between generations and within families as well as within societies.

Industrialization and the Global Environment

The industrial revolutions altered nature as well as human society. In the industrialized lands, the sharpest impacts came in the form of air and water pollution, as we saw in Britain. The iron and steel centers of the Ruhr or Pittsburgh or Osaka (Japan), and hundreds of other cities, were also enveloped in smoky haze day and night. Their rivers became toxic currents contaminated by chemicals from dyeworks, bacteria from meat-packing plants, and coal soot raining down from chimneys and smokestacks. Efforts at pollution control remained rare until the twentieth century, although filtration, which turned dirty water into drinkable water, made considerable progress in industrial cities between 1850 and 1920 and sharply reduced the burden of disease.

The environmental impacts of the industrial revolutions were not confined to industrialized landscapes. They were global, transmitted via long-distance trade in commodities. The fibers, minerals, and lubricants needed for industry often came from far afield. Demand for whale oil, a good lubricant for machinery, inspired a global hunt that by 1870 had brought sperm whales and right whales to the edge of extinction. The suitability of bison hide as leather belting in textile mills helped drive the North American bison hunt that reduced herds of 30 million to a total of about 1,000 animals between the 1830s and 1880s. Farmers in New Zealand burned ancient forests to make room for sheep pasture to provide wool for Britain's textile mills. To feed cotton mills, huge swathes of forest in the U.S. South were converted into cotton plantations. To provide lead for British industries, Spanish miners gouged ore from mountains in the southeastern province of Almería. These were all ecological changes brought about by industrialization and its long-distance commodity trade links.

Last, but perhaps most important in the long run, the burning of hundreds of millions of tons of coal added more greenhouse gases to the atmosphere. This had no discernible effect on climate during the nineteenth century, and no one was concerned by it at the time. But these greenhouse gas emissions began, in a small way, the process of destabilizing climate that is still ongoing today. Some of the carbon dioxide from the chimneys of early coal-burning factories in 1830 remains in the atmosphere nearly 200 years later, warming the Earth. Some of it is now in the oceans, raising their acidity.

Conclusion

Here's an indication of how extraordinary the British Industrial Revolution was: in 1845, raw cotton grown in India was carried by ox-carts to ports, put on ships to sail around Africa to Britain, there spun into thread, woven into cloth, put back onto ships to sail around Africa again to ports in India, off-loaded and carried to Indian markets—and that cloth would be better and cheaper than cloth made in Indian villages.

The industrial revolutions in Europe, North America, and Japan shook up the world in several ways. They freed societies from the old constraints and near-universal poverty of an energy regime based on muscle and wood, as steam engines enabled conversion of the chemical energy in coal into motion and power. They re-ordered social relations by creating industrial working classes and expanding the middle classes. The industrial revolutions altered family dynamics. They created new inequalities of unprecedented size within societies. They also reshuffled international relations, creating a handful of great powers in Europe, North America, and Japan out of formerly small or peripheral states. And they recast the ongoing relationships between human societies and the natural world, accelerating the use of resources such as iron, lead, or copper ores and fibers such as cotton or wool, and pouring out pollution—including greenhouse gases such as carbon dioxide.

All these changes are still with us. By 1900, they shaped the lives of almost everyone in industrial countries, affecting work, consumption, social groupings, travel habits, and much else. Today, lives everywhere, even in remote villages, are shaped by the industrial revolutions of the years 1780–1914.

Chapter Review

KEY TERMS

Industrial Revolution p. 831

textiles and metallurgy p. 834

coal p. 835

steam engine p. 836

James Watt p. 836

railways p. 842

working class p. 844

Friedrich List p. 850

Communist Manifesto p. 851

Alexander Hamilton p. 852

cotton gin p. 853

National Policy p. 855

Trans-Siberian Railway p. 857

Sergei Witte p. 857

Meiji Restoration p. 858

Eiichi Shibusawa p. 858

de-industrialization p. 863

settlement houses p. 869

socialists p. 870

REVIEW QUESTIONS

1. What two main changes in manufacturing methods define the Industrial Revolution?

2. What were the key industries of the Industrial Revolution, and why were they well suited to new manufacturing methods?

3. What combination of fuel and technology made up the energy revolution at the heart of the Industrial Revolution?

4. How did expensive labor and plentiful coal in Britain contribute to the start of the Industrial Revolution?

5. How did energy from coal change the cotton and iron industries in Britain?

6. Describe each tier of the social hierarchy of industrial Britain.

7. What measures did the German state introduce to spur industrialization?

8. Why was the U.S. weapons industry especially important to world history?

9. What obstacles to industrialization did Russia face, and how did it overcome them?

10. What was the role of the Meiji government in Japan's industrialization?

11. Why, after transport and communication technologies changed slowly for millennia, did the technologies of the metallic web come in a cluster between 1800 and 1850?

12. Compare and contrast the level of state involvement in industrialization in Britain, the United States, Germany, Russia, and Japan.

13. What important features did the industrial revolutions in the United States, Germany, Russia, and Japan have in common?

14. How did the Industrial Revolution lead to de-industrialization among handicraft industries?

15. In what ways did industrialization change military and political power around the world?

16. What were the most important keys to working-class labor reform, and what was the main alternative to reform?

17. Identify and describe the main environmental impacts of industrialization and long-distance commodity trade.

Go to INQUIZITIVE

to see what you've learned—and learn what you've missed—with personalized feedback along the way.

23

Two Liberations

THE VITAL REVOLUTION AND THE ABOLITIONS OF SLAVERY AND SERFDOM

1750 to 1950

FOCUS QUESTIONS

1. What made the Vital Revolution such a dramatic departure in human history?
2. What major developments contributed to the abolition of slavery in the nineteenth century?
3. How did the abolition of serfdom come about?
4. What brought the use of indentured labor to an end?

C hristine of Mecklenburg-Güstrow was born in 1663, one of 11 children, to a noble family in a reasonably healthy part of Germany. The daughter of a duke, she married a count when she was 19 and gave birth to twins almost exactly 8 months later. Both twins died the day they were born. Over the next 22 years, Christine bore 21 more children (she had four pairs of twins). Of her 23 children, 12 died before age 5. Of those who made it to age 5, all survived to age 38 and four saw their 70th birthdays. Christine herself succumbed in 1749 at age 85. Seventeen of her children had already died.

Christine was unusual for her time. She was a noblewoman, she married young, she lived long, and she bore about four times as many children as the average woman of that era. But she was far from unique. England's Queen Anne, born two years after

CHRONOLOGY

1670s Objections to slavery arise in Quaker community in Barbados

late 17th century Kangxi emperor requires smallpox inoculation in imperial lineage

1758 Philadelphia chapter of Quakers formally denounces slavery

1773–1774 Emelian Pugachev's rebellion in Russia

1787 Thomas Clarkson, Quakers, and evangelicals form abolitionist committee in Britain

1798 Edward Jenner publishes account of cowpox experiment

1800–1860 Slave population in American South quintuples

1801 Toussaint L'Ouverture abolishes slavery in Haiti

1802–1805 Spanish Empire establishes vaccination program

1807 Britain bans slave trade; Prussia ends serfdom

1808 United States bans slave trade

1812 José Aponte leads slave revolt in Cuba

1817 Cholera begins to spread worldwide; Spain bans slave trade

1823 Jack Gladstone leads Demerara revolt; Anti-Slavery Society forms in Britain

1831 Samuel Sharpe leads slave revolt in Jamaica; autobiography of Mary Prince is published

1834 Britain abolishes slavery

1835 Malê revolt in Brazil

1845–1847 Famine kills 12 to 15 percent of Ireland's population

Christine, made every effort to provide the realm with an heir. She had 18 pregnancies that led to 5 births. Only one of her babies reached age 2, and the survivor died at age 19. She had the benefit of the best diet and medical care available in her era—as did Christine.

Even though she was unusual in some ways, Christine's career as a mother tells us a few things about health history in her day. Despite being prosperous and reliably well fed, more than half of her children died young, probably all victims of disease. Even a family as comfortable as hers could not consistently keep children healthy and alive. That was equally true in Mecklenburg, Mozambique, and Mongolia—and the London of Queen Anne. In most of the world, just as it took two adults to generate a birth, it took on average two births to make an adult.

Christine's family story also shows us that people who made it past age 5 had a good chance of making it to 40. After age 40, life grew more precarious quickly. Even though life expectancy at birth was only about 25 or 30 years, people age 10 to 40 stood the lowest risk of dying—on average. Warfare and childbirth could raise the risk of death for people in the prime of life. But in general, death stalked the very young and those over age 40.

A lot has changed since Christine's day. Consider this: for the first 10,000 generations in human history, the average life expectancy of *Homo sapiens* populations was about 25 years. In the last 10 generations since Christine's death (1749), it has nearly tripled. It now stands a little above 72 years—slightly higher for women and lower for men. Japanese people can expect to live the longest, on average about 85 years, and people in the Central African Republic the shortest, about 53 years. This lengthening of life expectancy has brought a new inequality around the world. In Christine's day, life expectancy in the least healthy lands might have stood around 25, and in the healthiest around 35. Now the gap between richest and poorest countries is 32 years of life expectancy, three times longer—although in percentage terms the gap remains about 40 percent. The gaps between the richest and poorest within societies today are much smaller—roughly 2 to 10 years, depending on the country and the particular measure. Whether these gaps have grown or shrunk since Christine's day is unclear.

So industrialization, the focus of the previous chapter, was far from the only process at work changing the world after 1750. This chapter takes up two broad themes, each of which had some links to industrialization but both of which were, in their own right, major historical forces shaping the modern world.

The first of these is sometimes called the Vital Revolution, because it deals with basic biological facts of life such as disease, health, and longevity. On average, human health and life expectancy improved steadily after 1750. For ordinary people, this change might have been the most important revolution of them all, even if at the time no one noticed it—because it was slow and incremental. It is a curious paradox that the most important processes changing the lives of ordinary people might go unnoticed. It is also testimony to the advantages of hindsight—of historical perspective.

The second of these important historical shifts was the decline of forced labor—a broad category. Forced labor ranged from chattel slavery, a lifetime status as human property in which people were bought and sold and their children were slaves by birth, to milder forms of bonded status that were temporary and not heritable. In some systems of forced labor, especially in Africa, the Islamic world, and Brazil, manumission—the granting of freedom—was more common than in others. In eastern Europe, serfs were bound to labor for the lords who owned the land they worked; serfs could also be their masters' legal property. In some cases, such as in the Americas and the Arab lands, forced labor carried with it a strong racial component, as we will see. In the rest of the world, that was less often the case. This chapter will focus on slaves and serfs, but even these categories were broad

1848 France's final abolition of slavery

ca. 1850 Germ theory of disease develops; sanitation reform begins

1850–1880 Migrant flows of indentured labor peak

1853 Britain requires smallpox vaccination for all children

1861 Emancipation of serfs in Russia

1865 United States abolishes slavery

1870s Slave imports peak in Egypt

1873 Puerto Rico abolishes slavery

1886 Cuba abolishes slavery

1888 Brazil abolishes slavery

1890s Cattle disease kills almost all herds in East and southern Africa

1902–1904 Cholera kills 200,000 people in the Philippines

1910 China abolishes slavery

1918 Flu pandemic kills 50 to 100 million people

1924 Turkish Republic abolishes slavery

1928 Iran abolishes slavery

Justification of Slavery
Europeans who wanted to defend chattel slavery often relied on images of Africans as childlike, savage, or otherwise mentally and psychologically unfit for freedom—as in this 1833 American cartoon, which is critical of abolitionists.

and variable: there could be a world of difference between the lives of a slave cutting Cuba's sugar cane and another weaving Central Asia's carpets.

Between the 1790s and 1920s, slavery as a legal institution in all its variety almost disappeared around the world. And between 1800 and 1870, the eastern European practice of serfdom vanished, and other forms of forced labor elsewhere waned. New labor arrangements and new hierarchies took the place of slavery and serfdom. Unlike the Vital Revolution, this historical shift was easily visible to contemporaries—because it was sudden, controversial, and contested.

These two fundamental changes help mark the modern world off from what came before. Until 1750, for all of human history, life expectancy at birth in every society was less than 30 years, and a third or a half of all babies born did not make it to their fifth birthday. That was the normal human condition. But in the nineteenth century, and more conspicuously in the twentieth, that changed. More people survived infancy and more lived to ripe old age. In broad terms, since 1750 life expectancy has tripled in the healthiest societies and doubled in the least healthy.

Until recently, forced labor was also a normal part of the human condition, although perhaps only for the last 5,000 years or so. Just about every agricultural society had one or another form of forced labor. Just about every agrarian culture regarded forced labor as acceptable, natural, and normal. Then, at the end of the eighteenth century, that attitude began to change. People who were held in bondage increasingly found allies elsewhere who opposed slavery or serfdom, and together they forced an end to legal forced labor—even if illegal forced labor survives in the shadows of the world economy to this day.

One can judge the improvements in health and longevity, and the abolition of forced labor, as human triumphs and important examples of progress in modern world history. One can also judge the remaining inequalities in health and longevity, and the lingering legacies of slavery and serfdom, as continuing injustices. The study of world history enables each of us to assess these issues and arrive at informed conclusions.

The Vital Revolution

Like the Industrial Revolution, the **Vital Revolution** was a gradual development with no clear starting date. It began earlier in some places (such as France and Sweden) than in others (such as China and Japan). It could be temporarily reversed: in many cities of Britain, as we've seen, health worsened with industrialization. But whenever it began, within a century it brought a giant change in the human condition.

Just as the Old Regime preceded the French Revolution, what we can call a **biological old regime** preceded the Vital Revolution. It was broadly similar around the world. For most people, life was nasty, sickly, and short. Rich and poor alike were preoccupied with their health and, particularly in the case of women, with the health of their families. And there was a lot to fret about. Poor people had to worry about not getting enough to eat, and everyone had to face the risks of many dangerous diseases, few of which anyone could prevent or treat effectively. It is hard for those of us who have grown up with vaccines, antibiotics, and other powerful tools of modern medicine to imagine the insecurity of life and health under the biological old regime. But let's try.

The Biological Old Regime: Health and Nutrition before 1800

Before 1800, everywhere from China to Chile and Iceland to India, most people were sick much of the time. The crowd diseases, such as smallpox, measles, or mumps, were the most dangerous. They all had spread widely around the world by 1700. Wherever populations were dense enough and large enough to sustain them, they appeared as endemic diseases, always present and afflicting mainly babies and toddlers. Older people had already encountered and survived them, developing disease resistance in the process. Sometimes, however, such as in more isolated places, the crowd diseases appeared as epidemics, which arrived suddenly, from afar, and could affect people of all ages. Smallpox and measles were the worst of the crowd diseases. Both were breath-borne and spread easily from person to person. Both were extremely dangerous to people who had never had them before. In Iceland in 1707, for example, smallpox returned after a 35-year absence and killed about 30 percent of the population—most of them younger than age 35. Other important crowd diseases, although less lethal than smallpox or measles, included influenza and whooping cough (pertussis).

Many other infections besides the crowd diseases caused misery. Gastrointestinal infections raged wherever people lived in settled communities, and these illnesses were often fatal to babies. Typhoid was one such disease, usually spread by bacteria in contaminated water. In warm weather—and in many places it was always warm enough for typhoid—it could rip through a community, killing up to 10 percent. Cholera, another mainly water-borne disease, was more deadly. Before 1800 it probably existed only in South Asia, but after the 1810s cholera occasionally attacked communities around the world. Where wastewater and drinking water were not carefully kept apart, which before 1800 was almost everywhere, water-borne diseases took a dreadful toll.

At-Risk Populations   Cities were especially unhealthy. In 1608 a Chinese observer described Beijing, then the world's biggest city, writing:

> The houses in the capital are so closely crowded together that there is no spare space, and in the markets there is much excrement and filth. People ... live together in disorderly confusion, and there are many flies and gnats. Whenever it becomes hot it is almost intolerable. A little steady rain has only to fall and there is trouble from flooding. Therefore malarial fevers, diarrhea and epidemics follow each other without stopping.

European cities were no better. In the early eighteenth century, Tsar Peter the Great's family lived mainly in Moscow and the new city of St. Petersburg. Of his 14 children, 11 died before age seven. London between 1550 and 1800 recorded more deaths than births every year. Only a steady inflow of thousands of migrants each year kept the city going. Every sizeable city had a similar murderous effect due to its intense disease environment. As a German physician put it in 1796, cities were the "open graves of humankind." Before 1800, only about 3 percent of humankind lived in cities. The proportion could not have been much higher without the human race dwindling toward extinction—because urban conditions before 1850 inflicted such a harsh penalty.

Children whose immune systems had not yet been strengthened by surviving infections faced particularly daunting risks, as Christine's misfortunes in motherhood attest. The most dangerous age for babies began the day they were weaned of breast milk, which carried some immunity protection loaned, so to speak, by mothers. Children were also especially likely to suffer from diarrhea and gastrointestinal ailments, as they are today. The wide range of lethal diseases was the main reason that 35 to 50 percent of children around the world did not live to age five.

In some cultures, the risks babies faced also included infanticide. Unwed mothers often abandoned or drowned their babies. Families sometimes did the same when they judged that the addition of a new child was disadvantageous. The best-documented case is probably Qing China, where in the eighteenth century infanticide (already practiced for more than 1,500 years in China) was commonplace. In some parts of the country, such as the lower and middle Yangzi, infanticide claimed about half of all newborns. Girls were especially vulnerable. Across the empire, roughly 20 to 25 percent of baby girls were deliberately killed before their first birthday. Even the imperial lineage, among the most prosperous segments in Qing society, killed about 10 percent of their baby girls. In Chinese families, elders decided when young people should marry, when they should have children, how many children there should be, and whether or not to kill unexpected babies. They left less to chance than families in most other parts of the world.

Adult women faced at least one health danger that children and men did not: childbirth. The evolution long ago of our big brains and big heads came at a price that mothers pay. Before 1800, about 1 to 3 percent (reliable figures are scarce) of births killed the mother via hemorrhage or infection. By 1880, the risks of childbirth began to diminish in Finland, the country for which we have the earliest systematic data, and by 1940 just about everywhere else. The biggest cause of this improvement was the recognition that those assisting with births—midwives, nurses, and doctors—should wash their hands. Today, worldwide, about 0.2 percent of births are fatal to mothers, but in Africa it is 0.5 percent while in Australia and New Zealand about 0.007 percent.

Malnutrition and Famine The health risks of the biological old regime included malnutrition and starvation. As we have seen, during the worst decades of the Little Ice Age in the seventeenth century, cold

Childhood Illness A Chinese painting from around 1800 shows a little girl covered in the distinctive sores of smallpox, one of the common crowd diseases often contracted in infancy or early childhood.

and drought ruined many a harvest. Even in less challenging times, bad weather sometimes destroyed crops. In India, where a bad monsoon meant crop failure, a drought during the years 1630–1632 cost at least 3 million lives in the area around Gujarat. Over the next 200 years, sizeable killing famines appeared somewhere in India about once a decade, on average. As late as 1845–1847, a famine killed 12 to 15 percent of Ireland's population. Because most people around the world lived close to the bone, even modest shortfalls—the sort that came one in every three or five years—usually brought hunger.

Peoples who lived from herding, or otherwise depended on animals, suffered hunger and malnutrition too. When drought dried up pastures, then cattle, sheep, and other grazing animals died in droves, depriving people of milk, cheese, and meat. Without animals, herders found it difficult to trade for other foodstuffs. Animal epidemics (called epizootics) could have the same deadly effect as drought. Where farming involved plows pulled by oxen, horses, or water buffalo, as in most of Eurasia, the loss of animal traction paralyzed plowing. The worst episode we know about came in the 1890s, when a cattle disease wiped out 80 to 95 percent of the herds in East and southern Africa. The result was starvation that killed as much as one-third of the population of Ethiopia and twice that proportion among the cattle-keeping Maasai of East Africa.

Famine meant different things for different people, of course. The rich and powerful could usually find a way to get the food they needed—by buying or seizing it. Ordinary families had to ration food, which brought painful decisions. All else equal, women survive food deprivation slightly better than men, but all else was often not equal within families. In most cultures, parents preferred to feed boys over girls when they could not feed everyone. In Africa and China, where the prestige of the elderly was high, grandparents might eat more and younger people less when there was not enough for everyone. Babies and toddlers were often the first to suffer malnutrition. Parents knew that their older children were more valuable, not only because they were already more useful around the home but also because they were likelier to survive. So if families faced the cruel choice of feeding only some children, it made sense to feed the older ones.

Malnourished people suffered more from diseases because a consistently poor diet had weakened their immune systems. So, in the biological old regime, disease and hunger often went hand-in-hand, and death was front and center in life.

Improving Global Health

After 1750 or so, health started to improve and life spans lengthened. To understand how this happened, let's first review the facts on the macro scale, beginning with global population. As the table below shows, global population grew just about everywhere after 1650. The increase started slowly at less than 0.1 percent per year; but by 1750 in some places, such as China, it had gathered pace. Between 1850 and 1950, global population doubled, meaning it had achieved an annual growth rate of 0.7 percent.

Declining Mortality Global population was increasing because people lived longer as death rates fell. The largest component of the drop in death rates was declining

---

Estimated World Population, 1650–1950

YEAR	GLOBAL POPULATION	URBAN POPULATION	PERCENTAGE OF GLOBAL POPULATION IN EURASIA	PERCENTAGE IN AFRICA	PERCENTAGE IN AMERICAS	LIFE EXPECTANCY AT BIRTH (GLOBAL AVERAGE IN YEARS)
1650	630 million	15 million	80%	16%	1–2%	[no data]
1750	770 million	20 million	83%	13%	2–3%	approx. 27
1850	1.2 billion	100 million	84%	8%	5%	[no data]
1950	2.5 billion	800 million	77%	9%	13%	approx. 45

infant and child mortality. Crisis mortality (from famines or epidemics) also fell sharply, although this happy trend contributed less to the bigger demographic picture. A still smaller reason behind the overall trend was that fertility rates in some places increased a bit, mainly because people married a year or two younger.

Overall mortality, and especially infant and child mortality, fell in part because of better nutrition. That improvement came to some degree from the Columbian Exchange, in which people brought crops from one continent to another. Potatoes in northern Europe, maize in Atlantic Africa, and wheat in Canada or Argentina: each of these introduced crops, well suited to their new locations, raised farming output. Refined techniques, such as the adoption of crop rotations that restored nitrogen to soils, boosted farm yields in western Europe and elsewhere. Moreover, the worst of the Little Ice Age had passed by 1750, so bad weather brought killer famines less often. Last, the distribution of food improved in many places, thanks to better transport networks and in Qing China to government policies. The Qing maintained state granaries, which absorbed roughly 5 percent of their empire's annual harvest. These enabled the government to distribute grain wherever it might be needed. All these developments helped to check the ravages of hunger and reduce the frequency of starvation after 1750.

The death toll from disease began to fall after about 1730. Better nutrition and healthier immune systems contributed to this outcome, but a larger factor was an accidental by-product of the microbial unification of the world, an effect of the interactions in the Global web. After a few centuries of more frequent contact among the various parts of the world (ca. 1500–1750), pathogens had gotten pretty much everywhere they could easily go and had become endemic just about everywhere they could. As a result, big epidemics—and crisis mortality—gradually became less common. In northern Europe, for example, between 1680 and 1780 mortality crises almost disappeared—a big change in what people could expect in life. Plague disappeared from Europe, making its final appearance in Russia in the 1770s. Other diseases that formerly had killed adults and children alike as epidemics became endemic and only killed small children. The average life got a little healthier and longer.

Control of Smallpox Some of the reduced burden of disease was not accidental but the result of conscious efforts such as **smallpox inoculation**: deliberately putting a tiny bit of infected scab into a cut or scratch on the skin. In most cases, inoculation brought on a mild case of smallpox yet conferred lifetime immunity. In about 2 percent of cases, inoculation proved fatal; but those odds easily beat taking one's chances with the disease. The earliest good evidence for inoculation comes from sixteenth-century China. In the late seventeenth century, one of the Qing rulers, the Kangxi emperor, began to require inoculation against smallpox in the imperial lineage. When inoculation became routine in the imperial families, infant and child mortality fell from about 40 percent (before 1740) to about 10 percent (by 1830). Smallpox inoculation grew in popularity among ordinary people too, helping to account for the doubling of the Qing Empire's population between about 1720 and 1820.

By the mid-eighteenth century, many people in Eurasia and Africa had learned about inoculation. It was practiced in Mughal India and the Ottoman Empire, although to what extent is unclear. Some Africans inoculated against smallpox too. In early eighteenth-century Boston, an enslaved African named Onesimus explained to his legal owner, the prominent Puritan preacher Cotton Mather, that he had undergone inoculation and that many Africans did so. In Mather's version of Onesimus's words, "People take Juice of Small-Pox; and Cutty-skin, and Putt in a Drop." By 1800, smallpox inoculation of babies helped to lengthen lives, reduce mortality, and raise population in many lands. The interconnectedness of the world after 1500 helped smallpox inoculation to spread widely.

After 1796, an even better method of smallpox control came to light. In that year an English dairymaid, Sarah Nelmes, consulted a country doctor, Edward Jenner, about a rash on her hands. Jenner, a university graduate trained in medicine, thought she had cowpox, a mild cattle disease. He had heard that people who milked cows rarely got smallpox, and Sarah Nelmes's hands gave him the opportunity to conduct an experiment. He scraped pus from her rash and put a drop into two scratches he made on an eight-year-old boy. The boy felt poorly for a couple of days, then recovered quickly. Jenner, himself a smallpox survivor, next infected the boy with smallpox and exulted when no symptoms appeared. Jenner repeated the experiment on others and then in 1798 published an account of his work. Today, Jenner's medical ethics would earn a prison sentence, but the British government in 1802 awarded him a princely sum for his experiment.

Jenner's experiment gave rise to the first vaccination programs in history. Vaccination, using cowpox virus, was less risky than inoculation, which used real smallpox virus. In 1853, Britain made vaccination against smallpox mandatory for all children.

The spread of inoculation and then vaccination spelled the beginning of the end

Jenner's Smallpox Vaccine Anti-vaccination sentiment in Europe is evident in this British cartoon from 1802, which found absurd the notion that anything found in cattle could give patients immunity to a human disease.

The Cow Pock _ or _ the Wonderful Effects of the New Inoculation! _ vide _ the Publications of ye Anti Vaccine Society.

for the smallpox virus, the greatest killer of human beings ever known. The growing interconnectedness of the Global web spread vaccination around the world faster than inoculation had done. In the Spanish Empire between 1802 and 1805—only a few years after Jenner published his results—authorities established a vaccination program that saved millions of lives. The decline of smallpox between 1750 and 1900 played a large role in lengthening life expectancy and reducing the fear of disease in general. In 1978, smallpox was eradicated, the first such success in human history.

Sanitation Reform Sanitary improvements after 1850 had a parallel effect to the spread of smallpox vaccination. In cities especially, clean water had always been scarce, and dirty water killed millions. By the second half of the nineteenth century, scientists and doctors in western Europe figured out the role of bacteria in many infections, developing what is sometimes called the **germ theory of disease**, and successfully lobbied for waterworks that carefully separated wastewater from drinking water. These measures were expensive, and public officials often resisted on the grounds of cost. But the results, in the form of reduced death and illness from typhoid and cholera between 1880 and 1930, were so spectacular that the news spread almost everywhere. Chicago, for example, lost 6 percent of its population to cholera in 1854 and suffered repeated typhoid epidemics in the 1880s. But by 1920, water-borne disease killed almost no one in Chicago. Just about every city in western Europe, the United States, Canada, and Japan paid the price for cleaner water in money so as no longer to pay the price of dirty water in lives.

Sanitation reform did not spread uniformly. Some cities continued to run the risks of water-borne disease, partly for reasons of cost. Cities without access to banks and lenders simply could not pay for waterworks. In addition, many people did not subscribe to the novel germ theory of disease, without which there is no obvious logic to paying for sanitary measures and waterworks. So the spread of effective sanitation around the world took more than a century—and indeed is still incomplete.

The control of smallpox and the emergence of sanitation were the most important steps in checking the ravages of disease between 1750 and 1950. But there were many more. The germ theory opened the door to research on the specific organisms—pathogens—behind infections. Medical research and public health programs after 1890 led to successes in reducing the impact of tuberculosis, yellow fever, polio, and several other killers (1885–1960). All these developments saved lives, improved health, and set the stage for a golden age of health and longevity after 1950—a subject for a later chapter.

Sanitation Reform An 1880 diagram illustrates a design for an elaborate new water supply and waste management system under the streets of Paris. By increasing access to fresh drinking water and separating fresh water from wastewater, it dramatically reduced deaths from water-borne illnesses.

Counter-Trends: Cholera and the 1918 Flu

Two great exceptions bucked this happy trend. One was the globalization of cholera after 1817, and the other was the great influenza pandemic of 1918. Both show how the tightening of the Global web brought hardships as well as benefits in health. That tightening converted many infections into endemic, childhood diseases through the microbial unification of the world, which on balance was an improvement for humankind. But it also unleashed searing pandemics—worldwide epidemics—which now spread faster and farther than ever before.

Cholera Cholera escaped South Asia in 1817. It is a bacterium, transmitted from person to person via contaminated water or, more rarely, food. Untreated, it can kill half of those who contract it. Its course is swift, with only a few hours between first symptoms and death. This speed, combined with gruesome symptoms, inspired particular dread. People fled at the rumor of cholera. Authorities put up quarantines, forbidding entry into cities or countries, when they suspected cholera among travelers. But in 1817 cholera made it to Russia and in 1820 to southern China and Java. In the following decades it traveled all over the world, killing tens of millions and hitting cities especially hard.

Faster and more frequent travel changed cholera from a local to a global scourge. It was an occasional companion of South Asian Muslims making the annual *hajj* in the nineteenth century; in 1863, it killed 30,000 pilgrims in Mecca. Once British soldiers took control of parts of India in the 1760s, they carried cholera to ports around the British Empire. For example, Quebec City, in British Canada, suffered frequent cholera epidemics between 1832 and 1854 generally brought by soldiers and sailors re-located from India. After 1850, cholera gradually came under control wherever efficient sanitation was practiced. But elsewhere its destruction continued, claiming 270,000 in Russia in 1892 and 200,000 in the Philippines in the years 1902–1904. By 1925, however, public health authorities and sanitation infrastructure had cholera in check. At the same time that faster transport was spreading cholera to all inhabited continents, better water sanitation—wherever such expensive investments were made—was stopping its ravages.

Influenza Influenza was harder to control. It is a virus, or a series of viruses, in circulation among pigs, birds, humans, and a few other species. It spreads via coughs, sneezes, and contact. Usually, the flu was an inconvenience and killed well under 0.1 percent of those who contracted it. But it mutates quickly, and from time to time produces a new and deadly strain. This is what happened in 1918.

In late 1917 a new strain evolved somewhere, perhaps on the farms of the American Midwest, perhaps in China, perhaps near the battlefields of World War I in western Europe—there is as yet no clear evidence for its origin. Unlike most forms of the flu, the **1918 flu pandemic** was most severe among people in the prime of life. It killed

Influenza in 1918 Volunteer nurses tend invalids in a makeshift flu ward at a concert hall in Oakland, California, in 1918. So many people worldwide contracted the illness that it was not possible to care for them in standard medical facilities.

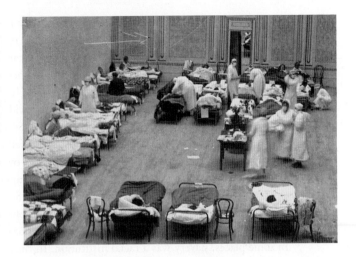

primarily people between ages 15 and 40, and so it was especially dangerous in communities such as universities and armies. Pregnant women were the most vulnerable of all.

When millions of soldiers dispersed in late 1918 at the end of World War I, they carried the flu all over the world. About 500 million people suffered from it, and 50 to 100 million died—roughly 3 to 6 percent of the global population. In India alone it killed about 15 million, about 5 percent of the total population. On some Pacific islands, it killed 10 percent or more. In Samoa, for example, it killed 22 percent of the population within two months. It killed a little under 1 percent of the people in the United States (some 675,000) and Canada (50,000). Japan imposed rigorous quarantines and kept mortality to 390,000 (about 0.7 percent of the population). After peaking in late 1918, the flu died out within months for reasons that remain unclear.

Cholera outbreaks and the 1918 flu pandemic were deadly exceptions to the general rule. They were both diseases of globalization in the sense that improved transport and stronger interconnections eased their spread. But the stronger trend was the Vital Revolution, in which mortality fell and lives lengthened. The Vital Revolution, too, spread around the world, through the Global web's circuits of information about crops, inoculation, vaccination, sanitation, and other practices that either improved nutrition or limited the toll of infectious diseases. That is the main reason why people on average now live nearly three times as long as their ancestors did before 1800.

The Abolitions of Slavery and Serfdom

Forced labor is an old human tradition. Legal codes designating some people as the property of others go back to ancient Mesopotamia. The Greek philosopher Aristotle thought that some people are by nature slaves and others free. Ibn Sina (Avicenna), the great physician and philosopher of eleventh-century Persia, held a similar view, extolling the wisdom of God (Allah) who had "placed, in regions of great heat or great cold, peoples who were by their very nature slaves, and incapable of higher things—for there must be masters and slaves." The English philosopher-statesman Thomas More, imagining the ideal society in his novel *Utopia* (published in 1515), depicted each family with two slaves. Slavery and other forms of bondage were widespread until 250 years ago, and few people viewed slavery as immoral or unnatural. Strange as it may seem today, many former slaves worked on slaving ships transporting fellow Africans to plantations in the Americas. In the Caribbean, many former slaves owned slaves themselves. In Russia, serfs who had escaped to freedom sometimes bought serfs. In some societies, forced labor was rare. In others, including those in Korea, Southeast Asia, Central Asia, the Ottoman lands, Russia, West Africa, Brazil, the Caribbean, and the United States, among many others, slavery or other forms of unfree labor were common.

In some places, slavery was a racial institution. In the Americas after 1492, slaves were almost all of African or Amerindian descent, or at least partly so, and slaveholders usually of European descent. There were also many free blacks in Brazil, the Caribbean, and the United States, but they were often subject to discriminations derived from prevailing concepts connecting race and slavery. A similar racial outlook had taken hold even earlier in North Africa and Southwest Asia. As we've seen, Arabs imported slaves from sub-Saharan Africa and came to associate black skin with slavery, notwithstanding the presence in these lands of slaves imported from southern and eastern Europe. But elsewhere slavery and other forced labor regimes had little or nothing to do with concepts of race. In Russia, both masters and serfs were normally Russian. In Korea, both slaves and masters were Korean. And in sub-Saharan Africa, slaves and slave owners were equally African.

Masters and slaves in Africa and Asia often came from different ethnic or religious groups. In Central Asia, slave owners were generally Muslims and speakers of Turkic languages, while many if not most slaves were Hindus from India. In China, slaves often came from Muslim groups in Central Asia or from Vietnam. In maritime Southeast Asia, slaves were usually taken on one island and sold on another, so masters and slaves often differed in language or religion. In nineteenth-century Ethiopia, Christians generally enslaved Muslim war captives, and Muslims typically enslaved Christians. These differences—in ethnicity, language, religion, or race—helped slave owners and their supporters to believe that slavery was part of the natural order of things. But in Russia and Korea, where such differences between master and serf or slave did not exist, the commitment of both society and state to forced labor was no weaker.

Unfree labor and its abolition bore a complex relationship to the processes of globalization and industrialization. Recall that globalization both extended the ravages of some diseases and at the same time encouraged the spread of practices that led to longer and healthier lives—the Vital Revolution. A similar paradox exists with slavery: the

Global web eased the spread of the trade in human beings, but then it also propelled ideas, information, attitudes, and practices that curtailed slavery. To make sense of the paradox, we need to zoom in.

The Expansion of Slavery and Forced Labor, 1750–1850

Industrialization, as we saw in Chapter 22, quickened the demand for fibers, ores, and lubricants needed in factories. Clever entrepreneurs saw reward in expanding operations in the mines, forests, and plantations that produced cotton, copper, palm oil, and a hundred other raw materials. To do so they usually needed more labor, which they sometimes hired for wages and in other cases bought in the form of slaves. During the first roughly 75 years of industrialization, until about 1850, market-savvy landowners and businessmen had strong incentives to deepen their reliance on forced labor.

The Americas In the American South, between 1800 and 1860 the slave population quintupled to 4 million. This was the largest enslaved population in any single polity in modern world history, although much smaller than that of the Roman Empire. Slaves accounted for about 12 percent of the U.S. population in 1860, and for about 45 percent in the South. While slaves worked in many different trades, the biggest reason for the expansion of U.S. slavery lay in the growing appetite for raw cotton in the textile mills of New England and Britain. Slave labor also underpinned the production of tobacco in Virginia and Maryland, rice in South Carolina and Georgia, and sugar in Louisiana. But cotton, grown from Georgia to Texas, stood at the heart of the slave economy of the United States.

Elsewhere in the Americas, a similar expansion of slavery took place after 1780. Sugar, tobacco, cotton, and coffee were the main plantation crops in the Caribbean and Brazil. As we saw in Chapter 21, the French colony of St. Domingue had nearly half a million slaves in 1790. The British Caribbean colonies—Jamaica, Barbados, and several others—by 1830 had 1.5 million slaves. In Cuba, the enslaved population grew from 30,000 to 290,000 between 1750 and 1870. In 1840, more than 2.5 million Brazilians, about 20 percent of the total population, were slaves. As in the United States, they were almost all African or of at least partially African descent. They worked in every sphere from whaling to mining and on plantations. They also worked in cities—cooking, washing clothes, laying bricks, tanning

African Chattel Slavery There were 4 million enslaved people of African descent living in the states of the American South before the U.S. Civil War. A mid-nineteenth-century photograph shows enslaved men, women, and children picking cotton on a plantation.

leather, and at other tasks, many of them dirty or dangerous. In contrast to the United States, where the sex ratio in the slave population was about even by the nineteenth century, it remained primarily male in the Caribbean and Brazil, where imports rather than natural increase accounted for growth, and slave purchasers selected males specifically for plantation work.

Other Regions   The eighteenth- and nineteenth-century expansion of forced labor was no less remarkable outside the Americas. In Southeast Asia, growers of sugar, peppers, and other goods used slave labor on an expanding scale, contributing to a boom in slave raiding and slave trading in the islands of Indonesia between 1770 and 1840. Slavery surged on several Indian Ocean islands, such as Mauritius and Réunion, where after 1780 French planters increasingly bought slaves from East Africa for newly created sugar and cotton plantations. Unfree labor, long commonplace in Africa, expanded after 1780 as powerful men took advantage of new opportunities, first in South Africa and then, by 1850 or so, in West and East Africa too. In both latter regions, new plantation economies emerged using slave labor, notably for palm oil in the Niger delta and cloves in Zanzibar. On the Arabian shores of the Persian Gulf as well, slavery increased sharply after 1820. Here the rise of export industries of dried dates and pearls led to heightened demand for slaves, most of whom came from East Africa on ships owned by merchants based in Oman or Zanzibar. Egypt, which turned to cotton production increasingly after 1805, experienced an upsurge in slavery too; its slave imports peaked in the 1870s. Precise numbers are lacking for Southeast Asia, the Indian Ocean islands, and Africa, but a reasonable guess is that among them the enslaved population reached 10 to 15 million as of 1850.

Slavery or bonded labor as a legal category and common practice existed elsewhere in the nineteenth century too—in Central Asian khanates, the Ottoman Empire, India, and on a modest scale in China and Korea. In the Russian Empire, the numbers of serfs also increased as a result of population growth. As we shall see, Russia's forced laborers numbered about 50 million in 1860, some 70 percent of the total population.

By and large, slavery and forced labor flourished only in certain circumstances. One was where labor was scarce and opportunities to make money beckoned to powerful people. They could profit from mines or plantations only if they could amass enough labor. Another circumstance conducive to slavery was where warfare yielded abundant captives. If numerous, such captives were cheap and could profitably be put to work at almost anything. Such situations were common enough around the world before 1800, and they grew more common as markets developed for fibers, ores, sugar, coffee, dates, and in the Russian case, grain. The evolution of the global economy ensured a market for any healthy captive. That is why slavery and other forms of forced labor were expanding in the first half of the nineteenth century.

During the nineteenth century, as before, a large share of slaves and forced laborers were female. In Africa, Ottoman lands, Central Asia, and probably China, they were the majority. Their labors included household chores such as cooking, cleaning, and

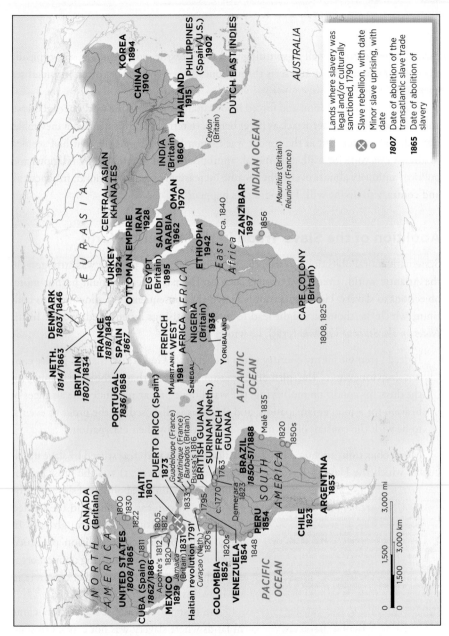

Resistance to Slavery and Abolition of Slavery, ca. 1750–1950 Slavery was legal and commonplace across much of the world in 1750. In the Atlantic world, slave uprisings became more frequent after the rebellion in Haiti (1791–1804), weakening the support for slavery in Europe and the Americas. Beginning with Denmark in 1803, the European nations whose merchants—together with those of Brazil, Cuba, and the United States—conducted the transatlantic slave trade, made it illegal. The abolition of legal slavery began soon after in the Atlantic world and was complete by 1888. Partly through pressures applied by Britain, legal slavery was abolished throughout Asia and Africa later in the nineteenth and twentieth centuries.

caring for children, as well as spinning and other textile work. And, as was typically the case for women slaves and serfs throughout history, their duties often included sex with their masters.

Even as slavery, serfdom, and forced labor expanded around the world between 1750 and 1850, they came under attack as never before. In retrospect, this may seem inevitable, normal, and proper. But at the time it was extraordinary. A practice that had seemed to almost everyone for millennia moral, appropriate, and sanctioned by religious and political authority almost overnight became increasingly seen as immoral, impractical, and contrary to divine will. How did this happen?

Abolition of the Slave Trade in the Atlantic World

Systematic moral objections to slavery originated where the practice was strongest, in the Atlantic world. Even slave owners such as Thomas Jefferson could harbor moral objections to slavery. He most certainly feared the consequences of allowing it to continue, which, he thought, might lead to violent uprisings by enslaved people. In his *Notes on the State of Virginia* (1785), he wrote:

> Indeed I tremble for my country when I reflect that God is just: that his justice cannot sleep for ever.... The spirit of the master is abating, that of the slave rising from the dust, his condition mollifying, the way I hope preparing, under the auspices of heaven, for a total emancipation, and that this is disposed, in the order of events, to be with the consent of the masters, rather than by their extirpation.

Moral objections anchored in Christianity, together with fear stirred by slave uprisings of which the Haitian Revolution (discussed in Chapter 21) was the most prominent, help explain the abolition of slavery in the Americas. In two cases, Haiti and the United States, abolition triumphed through war. In Britain and other cases, abolition prevailed politically—as a result of shifting opinion organized through political parties. Let's zoom in to see how this transformation happened.

The first movements for abolition came in lands where slavery was not central to society: the northern United States, Britain, and France. But in all three of those lands, profits from slavery and the transatlantic slave trade were economically significant and supported a segment of society with much to lose if slavery vanished. And in all three, information about the horrors of the slave trade and slavery was

RUN away from the subscriber in *Albemarle*, a Mulatto slave called *Sandy*, about 35 years of age, his stature is rather low, inclining to corpulence, and his complexion light; he is a shoemaker by trade, in which he uses his left hand principally, can do coarse carpenters work, and is something of a horse jockey; he is greatly addicted to drink, and when drunk is insolent and disorderly, in his conversation he swears much, and in his behaviour is artful and knavish. He took with him a white horse, much scarred with traces, of which it is expected he will endeavour to dispose; he also carried his shoemakers tools, and will probably endeavour to get employment that way. Whoever conveys the said slave to me, in *Albemarle*, shall have 40 s. reward, if taken up within the county, 4 l. if elsewhere within the colony, and 10 l. if in any other colony. from
THOMAS JEFFERSON.

American Slave Owners Many of the United States' founders owned large numbers of enslaved people despite their stated moral opposition to the institution of slavery. Thomas Jefferson, who owned over 600 enslaved people throughout his life, circulated this advertisement for a runaway slave in colonial Virginia.

readily available by 1750. Antislavery activists in Britain and America, and to a lesser extent those in France and elsewhere, were regularly in touch with one another through correspondence, by reading one another's published writings, and occasionally in person. They were all familiar with the arguments against slavery voiced by thinkers of the Enlightenment, such as the Baron de Montesquieu, who extolled liberty and condemned slavery as bad both for slaves and for slave owners.

Quaker Opposition The organized antislavery movement began among **Quakers**, a small Protestant sect originating in seventeenth-century England. Quakers defied social convention, avoided alcohol and fine clothes, refused military service, and were regarded as peculiar by everyone else. Many Quakers, like other religious minorities, were conspicuously successful in business. Before 1750, many of them in North America owned slaves and some were slave traders. But within the Quaker community religious and moral objection to slavery emerged, first in Barbados in the 1670s, and more prominently in England and colonial America by the 1750s. Quakers regarded all warfare as immoral, and so trading or owning slaves captured in African wars ran contrary to their principles. Moreover, their interpretation of Christianity stressed humility, simplicity, and the fundamental equality of all human beings. This view of the moral duties of Quakers gradually won out among the Philadelphia chapter—by far the biggest in North America—which formally denounced slavery in 1758. Several Philadelphia Quakers visited London to convince their brethren of the Christian duty to end slave trading and slavery. By 1774, all Quaker meetings (as their communities are called) in Britain and North America had agreed that one could not both be a Quaker and also own slaves. In 1790, Quakers petitioned Congress—in vain—for an end to slavery throughout the United States.

British Abolition of the Slave Trade Quakers and their allies proved more effective in Britain. Although Britain had few slaves, it was deeply invested in slavery. British merchants ran the biggest slave trade in the world in the late eighteenth century. Britain's empire included Caribbean slave plantation colonies—Barbados, Jamaica, and others—exports from which were worth five times those of all British North American colonies combined in 1773. The Church of England owned slaves in the Caribbean. Adam Smith, author of *The Wealth of Nations*—a defense of free markets—lamented in 1763 that although wage labor would be more efficient, "the love of dominion and authority over others will

British Abolitionism The abolitionist ceramics entrepreneur Josiah Wedgwood manufactured medallions bearing an image of a manacled enslaved man and the phrase "Am I Not a Man and a Brother?" This iconography became closely associated with the abolitionist cause in Britain and the United States.

probably make [slavery] perpetuall." Smith was wrong on both counts as regards the British Empire: slavery remained more efficient than wage labor until abolished, and it proved anything but perpetual.

Clarkson and Wilberforce   Quakers started the British antislavery movement. Barred from serving in Parliament because they were not Anglicans, to change any laws they needed allies and spokesmen from within the Anglican elite. They found one in **Thomas Clarkson**, who in 1785, as a 25-year-old fresh out of Cambridge University, entered a Latin essay contest with no loftier intention than winning a prize. But the contest's question was about the justice of slavery, and Clarkson, a good student, read everything he could find on the subject, won the prize, and in the process came to the conclusion that slavery was un-Christian. From the evangelical wing of the Anglican Church himself, Clarkson became a tireless pamphleteer, researcher, and activist in the cause, sometimes risking his life on the docks of port towns to gather information about the British slave trade. Clarkson and friends, mostly Quakers and evangelicals, formed an abolitionist committee in 1787 and decided to focus their efforts on legal reform, in Parliament, and to target the slave trade first, leaving slavery itself for later.

Clarkson helped recruit a sitting member of Parliament to the cause in 1787. William Wilberforce was sickly and half blind, but rich and well connected. He also had attended Cambridge University, where he specialized in gambling and drinking before becoming an evangelical Christian. At Cambridge he became close friends with William Pitt, who in 1783—at age 24— had become prime minister. Wilberforce, the same age as Pitt and a year older than Clarkson, became the parliamentary voice of antislavery, denouncing the slave trade as contrary to God's will and a source of moral corruption. By some accounts, including Pitt's, he was the silkiest public speaker in Britain.

The movement organized by Clarkson, Wilberforce, and their colleagues took shape in the late 1780s. With zeal and stamina, they documented and publicized both the cruelties of the slave trade and the debauchery of slave traders and their crews.

Olaudah Equiano A detail of the frontispiece of Olaudah Equiano's eighteenth-century account of his life. Equiano's antislavery activism as a freedman in the Atlantic world played an important role in rallying support for abolitionism.

Cugoano and Equiano   Former slaves such as Ottobah Cugoano and Olaudah Equiano added their voices to the anti–slave trade movement at the same time. About a dozen of them formed the **Sons of Africa**, an abolitionist committee in London closely allied with that of Clarkson and Wilberforce. Cugoano had been born in West Africa, captured as a young teenager, and shipped to the British Caribbean, where he worked on a plantation for two years before a master brought him to England. While it is unclear whether or not Equiano was born in West Africa (as he wrote in his autobiography), he worked as an enslaved and later as a free man, traveling all over the Atlantic world as a sailor before settling in England. Both men wrote detailed accounts of their experiences, helping to convince readers of the moral depravity and injustice of slavery and especially the slave trade. Their descriptions of slave ordeals had an air of authenticity about them that the youthful, privileged, and white-skinned Wilberforce and Clarkson could never provide.

Action in Parliament In 1787, both the antislavery and proslavery factions in Parliament held about 40 seats. They debated the humanity of Africans, whether slavery was supported in the Bible, and the economic value of the institution. Opponents of the slave trade published reams of moral argument and statistical data, distributed pamphlets, organized mass petitions to Parliament, and raised funds. They penned plays, novels, and especially poems against the slave trade. They presented more than 100 petitions against the slave trade to Parliament, signed by about 12 percent of Britain's population. They persuaded Pitt, as prime minister, to denounce the slave trade in Parliament. They pointed out that Denmark ended its slave trade in 1803. Within two decades they achieved a shift in public opinion against the slave trade. All this was necessary, but it was not enough: every attempt to pass a law banning the slave trade failed—until 1807.

Then Wilberforce, by now a veteran of 23 years of parliamentary intrigues, took advantage of changed political circumstances to press for abolition of the slave trade. A weak, coalition government that needed abolitionist votes took office in 1806. With the help of its topmost ministers, Wilberforce framed abolition of the slave trade as a patriotic measure that would hurt Napoleon Bonaparte's effort to re-establish profitable French Caribbean colonies after the Haitian Revolution. In 1807 he shepherded an abolition bill through Parliament, carrying the House of Commons by a vote of 283–16.

Banning the British slave trade was a dramatic beginning of the end for slavery. By this time in the Caribbean, except on Barbados, the slave population did not reproduce itself biologically, so without the transatlantic slave trade slavery could not long continue there. Wilberforce and his colleagues expected that with their legislative victory, slavery in the British realm would fade away.

Other Slave Trade Abolitions Other countries around the Atlantic soon followed the British example. The U.S. government made slave imports illegal in 1808, the first year permitted by the Constitution. That act carried different implications, however, because it did not endanger slavery in the United States. Slave populations in the United States since about 1730 had grown by natural increase (more births than deaths), which meant that slavery could persist there without the transatlantic slave trade. Indeed, as we saw above, the enslaved population expanded for 50 years after 1808 in the United States.

Nevertheless, the British abolition established a precedent. In the next 20 years, the Netherlands—a minor participant in the slave trade—and France both prohibited slave trading. Spain announced abolition of its slave trade in 1817 but did not enforce it until 1867. Britain began to use its navy, the world's largest, to intercept slave ships on the high seas and return captives to Africa, usually to Sierra Leone, a British colony established largely for this purpose. Some 100,000 Africans disembarked in Sierra Leone this way. The re-captives, as they were called, had come from all over Atlantic Africa, spoke dozens of different languages, and had to forge a new society in Sierra Leone. The tiny Haitian navy between 1811 and 1819 also captured three slave ships and liberated more than 800 people.

The strength of the slave markets in Cuba and Brazil kept the slave trade alive after 1830. Both markets still imported thousands of Africans annually—in Brazil's case, up to 60,000. A large share of these came from Yorubaland in West Africa, where frequent warfare during the decline of the Oyo Empire resulted in streams of captives sold into the Atlantic trade. This surge in the slave trade, however, helped lead to its demise.

The large and growing concentrations of Yoruba-speakers in both Cuba and Brazil led to an upsurge in slave revolts. One, in Cuba in 1812, was led by **José Aponte**, a Yoruba-speaking free black, an artist, and a former militia officer whose scrapbook, found by police, contained homages to both Toussaint L'Ouverture and George Washington. After 1825, Cuban elites increasingly questioned the slave trade, alarmed by the frequency of revolts. They also feared the introduction of epidemics from Africa, the "Africanization" of Cuba's population, and the patrols of the British Royal Navy. Spanish slavers and some Cuban planters resisted for a while, but Cuba's slave trade wound down in the 1850s and became illegal in 1867.

In Brazil, where the scale of the slave trade was much larger than in Cuba, it ended sooner, in the years 1850–1851. Uprisings averaged about one per year from 1810 to 1830, and climaxed in the Malê revolt in 1835, involving some 600 slaves—mostly Yoruba speakers. Fear of further revolts played a role in shifting elite opinion. So did attacks on Brazilian and Portuguese slavers by the British Royal Navy. As in Cuba, intellectual and political elites gradually became convinced that the slave trade was bad business and banned it. Like Wilberforce, they anticipated that without the slave trade, slavery would die out.

Abolition of Slavery in the Atlantic World, to 1832

The abolition of slavery in the Atlantic world, as opposed to the slave trade, came later and involved not only legislation but two major wars. The first of these, the Haitian Revolution of 1791–1804 (see Chapter 21), brought the first large-scale abolition of slavery and raised hopes for abolition throughout the Atlantic world. The second, the

American Civil War (1861–1865), put an end to slavery in the largest slave society of the Atlantic—and made it clear to all that slavery's days were numbered.

Even before the Haitian Revolution, movements for the abolition of slavery met with some minor successes in the Atlantic world. Since 1606, it had been legal in Scotland for mine owners to hold miners—fellow Scots—in lifelong bondage. If they ran away, they were subject to "torture in the irons provided only for colliers and witches and notorious malefactors." But in 1775, Scotland banned enslavement of new recruits to the coal mines. In 1777, during the American Revolution, Vermont banned slavery, and Massachusetts did so in 1783. Other New England states followed suit. In 1780, Pennsylvania enacted a gradual abolition that finally brought slavery to an end in the state in 1847. These acts of abolition did not resonate loudly because none of these places had many slaves.

Slave Uprisings and Their Political Consequences St. Domingue, in contrast, had nearly half a million slaves when the Haitian Revolution erupted in 1791. Toussaint L'Ouverture, who had been both a slave and a slave owner himself, formally abolished slavery in 1801. The destruction of slavery in Haiti showed slaves throughout the Atlantic that they could conceivably free themselves. It convinced slave owners everywhere that they courted economic ruin and vengeful massacres if slavery ended through revolution rather than legal abolition. The Haitian Revolution, because of its scale and violence, resonated throughout the circuits of the Atlantic world, an inspiration to some and a terror to others.

While former slaves were ending slavery in Haiti, the revolutionary French government in Paris decided in 1794 to end the institution everywhere in the French Empire. French antislavery activism, a modest movement compared to that in Britain, had less to do with the 1794 abolition than did fears that the uprising in Haiti might spread to nearby French colonies such as Guadeloupe, Martinique, and French Guiana. But principle supported political calculation: slavery, after all, was clearly incompatible with the "rights of man" and other ideals of the French Revolution. The 1794 abolition, however, proved incomplete and fleeting. It was never implemented in Martinique, Senegal, or France's Indian Ocean colonies. And in 1802, Bonaparte reinstated slavery throughout the French Empire and would have restored it to Haiti had his army there not been defeated. He restored slavery, using force where necessary, to prevent French Caribbean planters from surrendering their islands to Britain, his archenemy, which they seemed ready to do in order to preserve slavery. And he did it to please his wife, Josephine, and her family, who were slave owners from Martinique.

Bonaparte could not stop the momentum of Atlantic abolition. The Haitian Revolution inspired slaves elsewhere to test their chains in a series of uprisings. In addition to the revolts in Cuba and Brazil—word of which also ricocheted around the Atlantic— several broke out in British slave colonies. One took place in 1816 on Barbados, led by an enslaved African known as Bussa. A larger one occurred at Demerara, in British

Slave Revolts A lithograph shows a Jamaican plantation set on fire during the major slave revolt that Samuel Sharpe led in the British colony in the years 1831–1832.

Guiana, a sugar colony, acquired from the Dutch in 1814. For a few days in 1823, some 10,000 slaves there resisted their masters, following the call to freedom issued by one **Jack Gladstone**. Gladstone and his father, an African-born slave named Quamina, had learned of discussions of emancipation in Britain. Both were literate and, as carpenters and coopers, relatively privileged slaves. Quamina was a deacon in the local church and by all accounts deeply pious. Jack Gladstone (his surname was that of his master, the father of a future British prime minister, William Gladstone) believed that legal abolition had already passed in London and that the Demerara planters were conspiring to hide the fact. This conviction lay behind his call to freedom and what was until then the largest slave revolt in the British Empire.

A still larger revolt caught fire in Jamaica in 1831, involving perhaps 60,000 slaves, one-fifth of Jamaica's total. It too was led by a slave preacher, Samuel Sharpe, a deacon in the Baptist church; thus the revolt is sometimes called the Baptist War. Sharpe's lieutenants were mainly from the slave elite—smiths, masons, coopers, and coachmen. They were all born in the West Indies. As at Demerara, rumors of emancipation swirled around Jamaica, leading to the false belief that London's Parliament had already voted for slavery's abolition. Sharpe called for a slave strike during the sugar harvest season, which led to widespread burning of the crop. In sporadic violence, 14 whites and several hundred slaves were killed. Planters managed to suppress the rising with decisive help from maroons—former slaves who had escaped to Jamaica's mountains—and the Jamaica garrisons of the British Army.

The growing frequency and size of slave revolts in the British West Indies quickened the debate on abolition of slavery in Britain. The planter lobby wished to see the activities of missionaries curtailed, because rebel leaders in Demerara and Jamaica were educated Christians, schooled by missionaries. In Jamaica, proslavery factions attacked missionaries and burned several mission churches. The effect was to reduce political support for slavery within Britain. The fact that very few whites had been killed in these uprisings, unlike in Haiti, supported the argument of abolitionists that freed slaves would be capable of restraint and would not massacre their former tormentors. They were proved right.

Abolitions of Atlantic Slavery, 1833–1888

The first truly large legislated abolition of slavery came in the British Empire. The groups that had lobbied for abolition of the slave trade mostly disbanded after 1807. Few favored a swift end to slavery. Even Wilberforce in 1807 wrote that slaves were unready for freedom and "To grant it to them immediately, would be to insure not only their masters ruin but their own." Instead, Wilberforce and his circle thought slavemasters should improve conditions on plantations and provide Christian instruction to prepare for an eventual end to slavery, which in the absence of the slave trade time alone would bring.

Once again, events changed opinion. The Demerara revolt in 1823 in British Guiana created new support for the immediate abolition of British slavery. Over the next eight years, abolitionists, once again led by religious minorities such as Methodists, Congregationalists, Baptists, and Quakers, printed and circulated nearly 3 million antislavery tracts. They—Clarkson, Wilberforce, and a younger generation more inclined to push for immediate abolition—formed the Anti-Slavery Society in 1823 and beginning in 1825 sponsored a monthly periodical, *The Anti-Slavery Reporter*. They helped prepare and publish, in 1831, the autobiography of Mary Prince, born into slavery in Bermuda and sold several times in the British Caribbean. The book sold out three printings in its first year. In the years 1828–1830, some 5,000 petitions asked Parliament to end slavery. Over 98 percent of Britain's 233,000 Methodists signed at least one. News of the 1831–1832 slave revolt in Jamaica (the Baptist War) and the proslavery attacks on churches there strengthened support for immediate abolition. About 20 percent of Britain's entire adult male population signed the petitions of 1833. The petitions also included one that was half a mile long with the names of 350,000 women on it. Women could not vote in Britain, but they could sign petitions.

The antislavery faction in the House of Commons expanded when non-Anglicans became eligible to sit in Parliament in 1828. Two years later, an election brought to power the Whig Party, keen on reforms of many sorts, including abolition. In 1832, the Whigs succeeded in broadening the franchise to include some of the upper middle class, and then won a large majority in another election. They used the victory to pass the **Slavery Abolition Act**, which took effect in 1834. As with the abolition of Britain's slave trade in 1807, sustained agitation, a shift in public opinion pushed along by slave uprisings, and a political realignment in Parliament combined to bring about the legislation that ended slavery in the British Empire.

The terms of slavery's abolition included a large payment to slave owners by their government. Moreover, the abolition would be gradual. Until 1838, former slaves still owed services to their former masters, which left many former slaves disappointed. But as of 1838, all slaves in the British West Indies, Mauritius, and British territories elsewhere (except India, Ceylon, and the tiny South Atlantic island of St. Helena) were free, a little under 1 million people. British India officially ended slavery in 1860.

Abolition within the British Empire inspired abolitionists elsewhere. In the northern United States, abolition gathered momentum in the 1830s, at the same time that slavery was growing entrenched in the cotton South. An antislavery society formed in 1833. Abolitionists such as William Lloyd Garrison offered moral, religious, and economic arguments in countless lectures, pamphlets, and editorials, drawing freely on the works of British abolitionists. Former slaves such as Frederick Douglass did the same, with the added weight of firsthand knowledge of slavery's grim realities as he had lived them in Maryland before his escape to freedom in 1838. The 1852 publication of Harriet Beecher Stowe's melodramatic novel *Uncle Tom's Cabin*, which sold more copies in the United States than any book other than the Bible, won sympathy for slaves—and support for abolition. The formation of the Republican Party in 1854 was motivated by opposition to the expansion of slavery into the western territories. Abolitionists and slave owners both realized that if freedom was the rule in the new states entering the union, then over time Congress would become more antislavery and abolition would prevail. The new party won the 1860 election, putting Abraham Lincoln in the White House without carrying any southern states. Abolitionism in the United States proved influential enough to threaten restrictions on slavery that seemed, to slaveholders and their supporters, dangerous to the institution and their prosperity.

In the end, it required an all-consuming war between North and South to end slavery in the United States. When 11 southern states seceded in the wake of Lincoln's election, the president resolved to go to war to keep the union intact. In the Civil War (1861–1865), the North enjoyed a preponderance of resources and military manpower, and after four years of grinding combat, prevailed. Meanwhile, hundreds of thousands of slaves ran off either to the North or to the Union Army encampments, in effect liberating themselves. Lincoln in 1863 issued the Emancipation Proclamation, a military order that declared slaves in rebel-held territory free. Complete abolition came only with the war's conclusion and the **Thirteenth Amendment** to the Constitution, both in 1865. Altogether, some 600,000 soldiers died in the Civil War, liberating 4 million people—the single largest slave emancipation in world history.

The end was now near for Atlantic slavery, which remained mainly in some Caribbean sugar islands and Brazil. The success of beet sugar—5 percent of the world's sugar market in 1840 and 50 percent in 1880—weakened sugarcane planters everywhere by cutting their sales. Dutch Caribbean colonies—Surinam and Curaçao the largest—abolished slavery in 1863. An abolition society formed in 1858 in Puerto Rico, still a Spanish colony. An uprising there in 1868 included abolition among its goals. Shifts in Spanish politics led to the abolition of slavery in Puerto Rico in 1873, freeing 30,000 people over the next three years. Cuba, which had some 370,000 slaves (27 percent of the island's population), did the same in 1886, ending the long history of slavery in the Spanish Empire.

Brazil was the second-largest slave society in the Americas after the United States. By 1800, slaves worked in many economic sectors, including mines, manufacturing, and domestic services as well as on plantations. So a broad coalition of slave owners defended slavery. But by 1850, rapid immigration of poor Europeans was making wage labor increasingly practical for slave owners. It made business sense to manumit (grant freedom to) their slaves, especially the old, sick, or injured, and to hire labor instead. So by the 1880s they put up little resistance to abolition, which finally arrived in Brazil in 1888, freeing about 1.7 million slaves, or 17 percent of the overall population.

Abolitions of Slavery beyond the Atlantic

The Atlantic world by the late eighteenth century was by headcount the world capital of slavery and slaving, but it was not the only region where bonded labor, after prevailing for centuries, now came under assault. Abolitionism went global, an example of an idea spreading around the web, crossing cultures, and effecting changes on every continent.

In many cases, the abolition of slavery struck local elites as desirable, even necessary, to make their countries modern and competitive. The example of abolition by Britain, the world's most powerful country by 1850, was highly influential. In cases such as Cuba and Brazil, the rapid growth of population, which reduced labor shortages and thereby undercut the economic logic of slavery, swayed elites. With enough potential laborers, wages would be low enough to keep mines and plantations profitable. In this way, the trends of the Vital Revolution, outlined in the first section of this chapter, helped to advance the cause of abolition.

Slavery was abolished on the Pacific coasts of Spanish America beginning in newly independent Chile, which had very few slaves, in 1823. Peru, where African slavery had been important in mining and agriculture for more than two centuries, enacted abolition in 1854. France re-abolished slavery in its empire in 1848, within weeks after a revolution overthrew a monarchy and established a republic led by reformers hostile to slavery. Some 250,000 people in the Caribbean, Senegal, and the Indian Ocean sugar islands gained their freedom, but not all instantly. As in the British and Dutch cases, liberation in the French Empire came gradually, and some legal labor obligations to former masters remained in effect for a few years. In East Asia, Korea—where slavery had once been a major institution—joined the trend in 1894. China, where slavery had existed for many centuries but was never important, officially abolished it in 1910. Thailand did so in 1915.

In the Ottoman Empire, slavery had long been a crucial social institution. The status of slave is recognized in the Qu'ran and Islamic law, which stipulates that slave status cannot be inherited and Muslims cannot be enslaved. Outside pressure made a

Ottoman Slavery This engraving, the work of a British artist, depicts a nineteenth-century Ottoman domestic scene with several domestic workers and concubines who were likely to have been enslaved.

difference here. After about 1850, Britain in particular used its influence to induce the Ottoman sultans to restrict the import of slaves, most of whom were women—concubines, servants, or textile workers. The Royal Navy intercepted slave ships sailing from East Africa, reducing slave imports and slave populations in Ottoman lands. The Ottoman sultans could not, however, formally abolish slavery. As caliphs—successors to the Prophet Muhammad—they had the duty to prevent revisions to the divine word of Allah. After the fall of the Ottoman Empire, the Turkish Republic formally banned slavery in 1924. In Iran, rulers responding to British pressure abolished slavery in 1928.

In Africa, European pressure was even more direct. African slavery had expanded notably after 1850: British suppression of the Atlantic slave trade lowered slave prices within Africa, as we've seen, and made it economically attractive to African entrepreneurs to create new plantations, raising peanuts, cloves, or palm oil using slave labor. In the West African Sahel, a series of wars launched by Muslim reformers, who felt that African rulers did not fully abide by the rules of Islam, generated streams of captives. The enslavement of many thousands of these captives, in places such as what is now northern Nigeria, raised the slave proportion of the total population to a third or a half. By some estimates, after 1850 there were more slaves in Africa than in all the Americas, which then had about 7 to 8 million.

In the next few decades, as we shall see in Chapter 24, almost all of Africa fell under European colonial rule. Christian missionaries flocked in and, as in the British West Indies early in the nineteenth century, began to agitate against the evils of slavery and slave trades. This agitation normally struck African elites as unwelcome, presumptuous, and culturally ignorant. For them, as for so many people for so long, slavery was normal and natural. In the early decades of colonialism in Africa, European authorities often went along with slavery, even if they did not like it and missionaries hated it. In most parts of the continent, they could only rule with the help of Africa's slave-owning elites, and the continuation of slavery was one of the prices they were willing to pay for that cooperation. Moreover, colonial authorities often judged that slavery within Africa was not so oppressive—an argument advanced by African slave traders and slave owners themselves. In any case, the authorities made an uneasy truce with slavery for a while.

Enslaved Africans, however, often took a different view. Many sought to liberate themselves by running away, often to Christian missions. In the 1890s, this movement became a torrent in West Africa. Their escapes, in some respects parallel to the actions of southern slaves fleeing to Union Army camps during the American Civil War, weakened the elites

CONSIDERING THE EVIDENCE

Demanding Freedom and Dignity in West Africa

After abolition, enslaved men and women often had to take the initiative to demand their freedom. For example, Abina Mansah gained her freedom by leaving the household where she was enslaved in the Gold Coast Protectorate of Great Britain (now part of Ghana). She had been captured as a young girl during a war between her people and the Asante kingdom. A few years later, a man named Yowahwah bought her to be his wife. When they visited the Gold Coast together on business in 1876, Yowahwah secretly sold her to a man named Quamina Eddoo. Abina only became aware that she had been sold after Eddoo demanded that she marry one of his other dependents. This deception and disregard for her dignity as a married woman convinced her to flee and seek assistance from British colonial courts. Leaving Eddoo's household freed her from those who treated her as a slave; but she also decided to press charges against Eddoo for purchasing her. The trial transcript reveals what slavery and freedom meant to her and other enslaved women in West Africa as they asserted their new status after abolition.

Yowahwah brought me [to Gold Coast] from [Asante]. I was his wife.... [H]e handed me over to [be with Eddoo], and said that he was going back and would return.

About ten days after, [Eddoo] gave me two cloths and told me that he had given me in marriage to one of his house people.... I asked him how ... he had given me in marriage to one of his people. On this I thought that I had been sold and I ran away.... The defendant [Eddoo] said that if I did not consent to be married ... he would tie me up and flog me.... If the defendant had not given me in marriage, I could not have formed any idea that he had purchased me.... I thought I was a slave, because when I went for water or firewood I was not paid.

...

I did not know that I was free.... I heard that [the colonial government] had said we were all free. Yet I had been sold and I had no will of my own and I could not look after my body and health: that I am a slave and I would therefore come and complain.

...

If [Eddoo's sister] said to me "go for firewood" and I said "I won't go," she said "If you don't you will be tied and flogged," and I said "Now all are free. I also am free. I claim freedom." That was why I ran away.... [Eddoo's sister said:] "You are your master's slave." [W]hen she said this I sat down and said I did not like this and I made up my mind to come away.

Questions for Analysis

1. What are the different reasons Abina Mansah gives for why she ran away?

2. Why did Abina equate freedom with the ability to "look after my body and health"?

3. How did people who had been enslaved assert their dignity, despite the servile status that slaveholders and others forced upon them?

Source: Trevor Getz, *Abina and the Important Men*, 2nd ed. (Oxford, England, 2015).

Formal Abolitions of Slavery	
JURISDICTION	DATE
Vermont	1777
Massachusetts	1783
Chile	1823
New York	1827
Mexico	1829
British Empire	1834
Danish West Indies	1846
French Empire	1848
Colombia	1852
Argentina	1853
Peru	1854
Venezuela	1854
Portuguese Empire	1858
Dutch Empire	1863
United States	1865
Cuba	1886
Brazil	1888
Korea	1894
Zanzibar	1897
China	1910
Thailand	1915
Iran	1928
Northern Nigeria	1936
Ethiopia	1942
Saudi Arabia	1962
Mauritania	1981

Note: These represent final, formal abolitions. In some cases, such as the French Empire, slavery was abolished, reinstated, and abolished again. In many cases, abolition was a drawn-out process involving gradual steps.

on whom colonial authorities intended to rely. So, making a calculated decision that went hand-in-hand with their moral views, both British and French colonial rulers changed their allegiances and began to support former slaves, especially those who embraced Christianity, and to pressure African elites to abandon slavery. This was a case of simultaneous abolition from below and above. Formal, legal abolitions began in 1905. The biggest took place in northern Nigeria in 1936, where about 1 to 2 million slaves became officially free; and in Ethiopia in 1942, when roughly 3 million were liberated.

As everywhere, the passing of laws did not instantly end an age-old institution. Slavery persisted illegally in many parts of Africa. It was abolished in what is now Mauritania when that was officially French territory but survived well enough that independent Mauritania abolished it again in 1981. The table at left indicates the date of legal abolition in 26 jurisdictions around the world.

The largest abolition took place in the United States, freeing 4 million slaves. The next largest was Ethiopia and then either northern Nigeria or Brazil—the numbers are too unreliable to be sure. In total, the many acts of abolition of slavery freed about 15 to 25 million people.

Abolition of Serfdom

The largest of all labor liberations took place in Russia. In 1861 and the years following, the Russian state freed 23 million serfs held by landlords, 25 million state peasants owned by the imperial government, and nearly 2 million crown peasants owned by the tsar's family. Together, they accounted for more than two-thirds of Russia's population of roughly 74 million people. This momentous event followed on prior abolitions of serfdom in central and eastern Europe, all much smaller than Russia's.

Serfdom and Reform in Eastern Europe and Russia

Serfdom in Europe had a long history, existing in one form or another for 1,500 years. In Europe east of the Elbe River, it became widespread in the fifteenth and sixteenth centuries, when markets for grain developed and landlords wanted to secure labor for their expanding agricultural estates. Serfdom consisted of a package of legal obligations that peasants—serfs—were by law and custom obliged to furnish to lords. The package usually included obligatory labor on the lords' estates, and often delivery of produce to lords' households, fees for using the lords' grinding mills, and permission from lords to marry, leave an estate, or take up a trade. In many cases, serfs were in effect owned by lords. In others, serfs were legally bound to land owned by lords, which for serfs amounted to much the same thing. In some cases, serfs paid money in place of furnishing labor to lords.

By and large, forms of serfdom were milder in the Habsburg lands and Prussia, and harsher in Poland-Lithuania and Russia. Serfs in the latter lands had no legal recourse against exploitation, were subject to brutal punishments, and differed little in status from chattel slaves. Individuals or families could be bought and sold—whole villages of serfs could be bought and sold. Lords routinely used enserfed women for sex. In fact, in Russia, serfs differed from slaves mainly in that serfs were required to pay taxes and serve in the army. That inspired some of them to sell themselves into slavery until, in 1723, slavery was abolished in Russia to prevent that escape route from serfdom. In Prussia, the Habsburg lands, Poland, and Russia, the landlord class, church, and state all supported serfdom until at least 1750; and while they did, there was little serfs could do to improve their condition, let alone end serfdom.

The Abolition of Serfdom in Eastern Europe and Russia, ca. 1800–1861 The abolition of serfdom freed tens of millions of peasants, beginning in German lands and moving eastward to Russia and Romania. The largest of all abolitions of legal forced labor in world history occurred in Russia.

The Impact of the Enlightenment and the French Revolution In the late eighteenth century, the ideals of the Enlightenment undermined the agreement of lords, church, and state about serfdom. Voltaire, Kant, Adam Smith, and other influential writers denounced the institution as inhumane, contrary to the principle of liberty, and inefficient besides. Monarchs in Prussia, the Habsburg Empire, and Russia by 1780 tended to agree with the intellectual challenge to serfdom and changed their minds about its legitimacy. But they did little about it, bowing instead to the interests of landlords.

The Enlightenment changed some minds, but it took the French Revolution to change the politics of serfdom in eastern Europe. French armies under Bonaparte proclaimed an end to serfdom wherever they found it. In the case of Prussia, disastrous defeats at the hands of Bonaparte's free peasant armies in 1807 inspired the king to abolish serfdom in hopes of modernizing his country—and converting Prussia's serfs into more motivated peasant soldiers. Some 25 tiny German principalities abolished serfdom between 1807 and 1852. The Habsburg lands did so between 1848 and 1853.

Russia In Russia, the morality and utility of serfdom had also come into question. In her memoirs, the tsarina Catherine the Great (r. 1762–1796) wrote that serfdom was both immoral and inefficient, even while she extended its domain by awarding serfs to loyal nobles. By the 1790s, a few courageous intellectuals such as Aleksandr Radischev had begun to denounce it (he likened serfdom to Caribbean slavery), risking exile or prison. Like their counterparts elsewhere, educated Russians absorbed Enlightenment ideals of liberty and equality, and gradually came to see serfdom as a backward institution that dragged their country down. But landowners usually did not see how they could manage their estates without it: they considered serfdom an inevitable evil. As with slavery, moral opposition was necessary for the abolition of serfdom, but far from sufficient to get it done.

The Russian reformers were aware of the ongoing saga of abolition of forced labor in the Atlantic world. Some, like Radischev, saw resemblances between serfdom and slavery. In the early nineteenth century, Russian emperors often used the word for slave (*rab*) to describe serfs. The novelist Ivan Turgenev referred to serfs, whom he often depicted in a favorable light in his short stories, as "our own blacks." Many in Russia's elite were moved by the gripping scenes in Harriet Beecher Stowe's *Uncle Tom's Cabin* (1852), which was translated into Russian in 1857 and struck a chord with many readers. The Atlantic examples of abolition, often in the background of debate, did not make the issue of emancipation any easier for Russians, but perhaps made it a little more urgent.

As often happens, war made matters more urgent still. Back in 1812, Russia's army, with help from winter and typhus, had expelled Bonaparte's army of 600,000 soldiers. In contrast, during the Crimean War (1853–1856), Russia could not defeat 60,000 British and French soldiers encamped on the Crimean Peninsula (which juts into the Black Sea). The great Russian novelist Leo Tolstoy, who served as an officer in the Crimea, wrote that Russia did "not have an army but a mob of oppressed disciplined slaves." Defeat in the Crimea and the performance of an army composed mainly of serfs convinced Tolstoy and thousands of others that his country was administratively, technologically, and economically backward compared to Britain and France.

Alexander II and Memories of Pugachev A new tsar, **Alexander II**, came to power in 1855 determined to enact reforms that would modernize Russia and restore it to the first rank of European powers. Among his top priorities was military reform—in particular, providing the army with more educated, patriotic conscripts than could be found among the serf population. He especially wanted a reserve system such as several European countries had devised, in which soldiers in peacetime would go home but could be called up quickly when war broke out. This was far cheaper than maintaining a full-size standing army in peace and war. But no Russian tsar wanted serfs with military skills on the loose in their home villages, and for good reason. To get a cheaper and better army, Alexander would have to get rid of serfdom.

Alexander and Russian reformers rightly feared serfs with military skills. Just as in the Atlantic world, uprisings of the oppressed in Russia caused shudders among the elite. Just as every slaveholder in the early nineteenth-century Atlantic world knew of the Haitian Revolution and its furious violence, so every Russian lord was aware of the vast rising in the years 1773–1774 led by a Cossack named Emelian Pugachev. In the middle of a war against the Ottoman Empire, Pugachev, a low-ranking army officer, led a ragtag rebel army of tens of thousands of Cossacks and serfs on a sustained rampage. They looted estates and took important cities such as Kazan on the Volga River, promising freedom to all serfs and death to landlords—of whom they killed about 3,000. It took all that the Russian state could do to defeat Pugachev, who was betrayed by associates and executed in 1775.

Fears of another Pugachev were stoked every year by news of serf uprisings somewhere in Russia. The office responsible for Russia's internal security recorded 712 revolts between 1826 and 1854, or roughly one every two weeks. As with the abolition of slavery in the Caribbean, fear of uprisings provided a strong motive for abolition of serfdom.

The Politics of Russian Abolition

For Alexander II and reform-minded Russians, the problem of abolition was practical: how to enact it without alienating either the serf owners or the serfs. In this respect as well, the situation paralleled that of the abolition of slavery. Even those masters who wanted to do away with serfdom felt they were riding the tiger: it was dangerous either to stay on or to get off.

In 1856, Alexander II convened a committee of serf owners, men from the landholding elite, to craft a program of **emancipation for serfs**. Invoking the ghost of Pugachev, he stated in his instructions that "the existing condition of owning souls [serfs] cannot

Emancipation of the Serfs Alexander II's proclamation announcing the emancipation of the serfs was read aloud in churches throughout Russia in March 1861. This illustration shows a crowd listening to the proclamation at the Dormition Cathedral in Moscow.

remain unchanged. It is better to begin to destroy serfdom from above than to wait until that time when it begins to destroy itself from below. I ask you, gentlemen, to figure out how all this can be carried to completion." After five years, the committee produced recommendations that underlay the 1861 statute of emancipation of the serfs, a 360-page small-print document. The tsar was so worried that the terms of liberation might disappoint the serfs that he arranged for it to be read out on the first day of Lent, when Orthodox Christians are expected to abstain from alcohol. In theory, it allowed former serfs to own property, engage in trade, move freely, marry as they pleased, sue in courts, and vote in newly created local elections.

But the landlords who crafted the statute had not neglected their own interests. The government paid them handsomely for the loss of their serfs and some of their land. The emancipation provided former serfs with some land but required them to pay for it—except the few who accepted tiny plots called paupers' allotments. Since they had no money, serfs in effect had to buy land on credit from the state by paying a "redemption tax" over the next 50 years. Until they met their payments, former serfs faced many restrictions on their freedom and often remained tied to their village. In many cases, the restrictions lasted the rest of their lives. The landlords kept about two-thirds of the land—usually, the best. As with the abolitions of slavery, the fine print in the deal did not live up to the hopes of those liberated, because legal constraints and obligations lingered on for many years. Peasant unrest remained a feature of Russian rural life in the decades following the abolition of serfdom.

But the mere fact of liberation, of slaves and serfs—some 60 to 80 million people in all, most of them Russian, but many either African or of African ancestry—carries world-historical importance. Thousands of years after forced labor became widespread, enshrined in law codes, and routinely judged normal, natural, and divinely sanctioned, it was prohibited almost everywhere.

Indentured labor

Temporary labor bondage, however, persisted. In 1840, shortly after the abolition of slavery in the British Empire, a future prime minister, Lord John Russell, wrote that the growing business of **indentured labor** was in danger of becoming "a new system of slavery." Indentured labor systems had existed for a long time. In the Atlantic world from the seventeenth century through to the 1830s, some 450,000 indentured laborers came from Europe to work in the Americas. Some early ones worked on sugar plantations in the Caribbean, until replaced by African slaves. Others worked as domestics, artisans, or farm laborers. A second and larger stream of indentured laborers, mainly from India and China, arose in the nineteenth century. It began as a trickle in response to the end of the slave trade and rose to a torrent with the end of slavery.

Russell's remark notwithstanding, the legal terms of indentured labor were not the same as those of slavery. The main differences were that indenture was a voluntary arrangement and applied for a fixed number of years, usually between two and eight. But often trickery or coercion lay behind an indenture contract. Unworldly villagers in India or China fell for sunny promises made by labor recruiters. And until their contract expired, indentured laborers often faced some of the same hardships that slaves or serfs endured: they could not leave their employment, or marry, without permission from their employers, and they often faced corporal punishment if they failed to satisfy their bosses. Indentured laborers, unlike almost all slaves or serfs, drew a wage, although a lower one than planters or mining companies would have had to pay without indenture—which is why the system existed.

Indentured Migrants

Between 1830 and 1920, about 2 million indentured laborers left India and China for hard work as plantation laborers or miners in the Caribbean, Peru, Hawaii, Mauritius, South Africa, or Southeast Asia. Smaller flows came from Japan, several Pacific islands, and parts of Africa. Some Europeans, mainly Portuguese, also signed up as indentured laborers. Indians accounted for the majority, about 1.4 million—much more than that if one adds in more local migrations to nearby Ceylon, Burma, or Malaya. Chinese indentured migrants numbered about 500,000. Pacific Islanders and Africans each accounted for about 100,000. Most of the Africans were taken from the re-captives in Sierra Leone. Some of them, in fact, never made it to Sierra Leone, but were rescued from a slave ship in the Atlantic only to be indentured for labor in the Caribbean. Japanese indentured migrants numbered about 85,000; and Europeans 56,000. The flows, boosted by each famine or war in Asia, peaked between 1850 and 1880.

The chief destinations for Indians were sugar plantations in Mauritius, the Caribbean, South Africa, and Fiji (the Pacific archipelago) and for Chinese, the plantations of Cuba or the mines of Peru. For Japanese, the likeliest destinations were plantations in Hawaii and Peru.

Most indentured laborers were men, about 95 percent in the case of Chinese, maybe 75 percent for Indians. The first indentured Japanese in Peru, a shipload of 790 who arrived in 1899, were all men, destined for sugar cane plantations. Single men, if they stayed after their indenture expired, usually married local women if they married at all.

Indentured Labor After the abolition of slavery, unfree labor still contributed to the global movement of peoples—such as these Indian indentured workers in British Jamaica (left) and Chinese indentured workers in Spanish Cuba (right).

Crossing the oceans in sailing ships with hundreds of other labor migrants was risky. Voyages typically took from one to six months. The death rate for the roughly 150,000 Chinese shipped to Cuba (1847–1873) averaged about 3 percent. For Indians sailing to the Caribbean, it was about 2 percent. Meanwhile, during the last decades of the transatlantic slave trade (1811–1867), mortality in the Middle Passage was 6 percent. (For reference, the death rate for free people traveling from Britain to New York in these decades was 1 percent, and the annual risk of death on the roads of the United States today is about 0.01 percent.) All the death rates for indentured migrant voyages fell with time, so that after 1880 all averaged under 1 percent.

Many of these indentured migrant laborers, especially the Indians, returned home. About one-third of Indians who went to Jamaica, Surinam, or Mauritius went home after their term was up. And more than two-thirds of those who went to Thailand or Malaya did so. Many indenture contracts included promise of a return trip. But even for those whose arrangements did not include that promise, it was often possible eventually to earn enough money for the passage home. By the late nineteenth century, information about global travel was more abundant than before, and its price lower, making return voyages for indentured laborers likelier.

The End of Indentured Labor

Indentured labor, although not the same as slavery, served the same purpose. It kept the plantations and mines formerly worked by slaves in business. It disappeared, gradually, because mines and plantations could increasingly find enough cheap labor on the free market. After 1870, tens of millions of free people—Europeans, Indians, and Chinese predominantly—left home to cross the oceans in search of employment. Accelerating population growth brought more youths into labor markets. Their sheer numbers reduced labor shortages and lowered free-market wages to the point where indentured labor no longer made economic sense for anyone even in the less thickly populated regions. By 1914 it was, for all intents and purposes, finished. And with it, a long era in human history in which unfree labor was legal and commonplace came—almost—to an end.

Unfortunately, one has to include "almost." Legal slavery lasted in a few countries—Saudi Arabia, Ethiopia, Mauritania, for example—well into the twentieth century. Colonial rulers in Africa—the same ones who had legally abolished slavery in many cases—in the 1920s and 1930s organized temporary forced labor brigades for work in mines, plantations, or on railroads. Certain totalitarian regimes—Nazi Germany, Soviet Russia, among others—re-established slave labor by other names for a few years or decades. As we will see, about 18 million people worked in Soviet forced labor camps between 1929 and 1953. North Korea uses 200,000 slave laborers in its manufacturing and agricultural economy today. And various forms of illegal slavery persist, involving millions of people. Dozens of countries traffic in sex slaves, typically young women lured by false promises of good wages far from home.

Conclusion

Over the period 1750–1950, humankind underwent two great liberations. The first liberation was from a biological old regime that had featured frequent disease, famine, and early death. As a result of scientific advances, deliberate policies, and some good fortune, the biological old regime was banished in a Vital Revolution that saw life expectancy lengthen and child mortality shrink dramatically. By 1950, far fewer parents had to bury most of their children as Charlotte of Mecklenburg, Queen Anne, Peter the Great—and millions of anonymous mothers and fathers—had done. For the fabric of ordinary people's lives, this stands among the biggest changes in modern history, although the benefits of the Vital Revolution remain unequally distributed. The revolution might continue, but it might also prove reversible: there is no guarantee we can always keep infectious diseases in check.

The second great liberation involved less fortune and more human will. The various abolitions of slavery and serfdom around the world, from 1777 to 1981, represent another sea change. Serfdom had existed for centuries, and slavery for millennia. Until the end of the eighteenth century, few voices objected to forced labor, even if many slaves and serfs objected vehemently to their own exploitation. In some cases, former slaves became slave owners themselves. But then, starting in the 1770s and 1780s, a groundswell of dissent began to build. It rose up in eastern Europe against serfdom as it was mounting in the Atlantic world against slavery. Slavery's abolition rested in part on the skill and commitment of antislavery activists. But it also rested on the actions of slaves themselves, who launched rebellions that in one case—Haiti—directly forced the end of slavery and in others such as Brazil, Cuba, and the British Caribbean, helped tip the political balance against slavery. Serfs too, with their frequent uprisings, hastened the abolition of serfdom in Russia.

Looking more deeply, one can see other forces at work in the end of forced labor. One was the general rise in population that gathered pace after 1750, the result of the early stages of the Vital Revolution. Forced labor in most contexts made economic sense when and where labor was scarce and therefore, in a free market situation, expensive. Slavery and serfdom kept labor costs low. At great cost in human suffering, they made plantations and other enterprises profitable. When population grew, labor at free market prices grew cheaper, undermining the economic logic of forced labor. Bear in mind this was not central in some important cases, such as the British West Indies, where population was not growing and slavery remained, up to the day of abolition, economically rewarding for employers. Nor was it relevant in the United States, where slavery remained profitable and a massive war was required to abolish it.

A second force at work was intellectual. Enlightenment thinkers after 1750 increasingly advanced ideals of liberty and attacked slavery and serfdom as unjust and inefficient. Their ideas won many followers in influential circles from Brazil to Britain to Russia. At the same time, religious thinking shifted against slavery—less so against serfdom. While for centuries established churches had supported slavery, in the eighteenth century a few branches of Protestantism came to see slavery as a moral evil and repugnant to God. Quakers, Methodists, and evangelical Anglicans stood in the forefront of antislavery in Britain and the United States, and used their networks to promote abolition.

Another influential force was the prestige of British example. In the nineteenth century, thanks mainly to the power conferred on it by the Industrial Revolution, Britain enjoyed an influence all out of proportion to its size. When it threw its weight behind antislavery, that commitment reverberated around the world. The tightened webs—which British steamships, railroads, and telegraph lines helped tighten even more—ensured that millions on every continent knew the moral and economic arguments against slavery. Many of them gradually found themselves persuaded. Others, whose minds were less susceptible to gentle suasion, knew by 1820 that the British Royal Navy would punish them for slave trading and, by about 1870, that British foreign policy would penalize them for maintaining slavery.

All these broad currents—population growth, shifting intellectual currents, and the weight of British example—depended on the tightening links in the Global web forged over the course of the eighteenth through the nineteenth centuries. The spread of inoculation, sanitation, and vaccination occurred as speedily as it did only because millions learned quickly about the success of these practices and changed their behavior accordingly. So too with the spread of ideas opposed to slavery and serfdom, and for that matter, of information about slave or serf uprisings. Globalization has its dark sides, many of them noted in this book. But globalization also contributed to the Vital Revolution and the decline of regimes of forced labor.

The twin liberations were linked, momentous, and simultaneous. The growth of population resulting from the Vital Revolution reduced the economic logic of forced labor. The end of the deliberate deprivations of slavery and serfdom helped improve health and longevity for tens of millions. The two liberations were part of a new era of revolutions in which big changes happened faster and more globally. The Industrial Revolution, Vital Revolution, and abolition of forced labor took a century or two to affect the whole world—a blink of the eye compared to the spread of domestication, cities, writing, or gunpowder in previous eras.

Chapter Review

KEY TERMS

Vital Revolution p. 879

biological old regime p. 879

smallpox inoculation p. 883

germ theory of disease p. 885

1918 flu pandemic p. 886

Quakers p. 893

Thomas Clarkson p. 894

Sons of Africa p. 894

José Aponte p. 896

Jack Gladstone p. 898

Slavery Abolition Act p. 899

Thirteenth Amendment p. 900

Alexander II p. 907

emancipation for serfs p. 907

indentured labor p. 908

REVIEW QUESTIONS

1. What health risks, including specific risks for women and children, characterized the biological old regime?

2. What accidental and deliberate changes caused the death toll from disease to drop after 1750 or so?

3. What do cholera and the 1918 flu pandemic demonstrate about globalization and disease?

4. Explain the link between race and slavery, and discuss where this connection was most prominent.

5. Why and where did slavery expand between 1750 and 1850?

6. Why did the 1807 British ban of the slave trade endanger slavery more than the 1808 U.S. ban?

7. Describe the key driving forces of the abolition of the slave trade in Britain, the United States, Cuba, and Brazil.

8. What was the broader impact of the Haitian Revolution on abolishing slavery?

9. Compare and contrast the main reasons for the abolition of slavery in the British Empire, the United States, the Caribbean sugar islands, and Brazil.

10. Why did elites outside of the Atlantic world find the abolition of slavery appealing?

11. Why did African slavery expand after 1850?

12. Identify the links among the Crimean War, Alexander II's military reforms, and the emancipation of the serfs.

13. What did the abolition of serfdom mean for former serfs?

14. Who constituted the second and larger stream of indentured laborers, and where were they mainly working?

15. Explain the chief forces that caused the decline of forced labor during this period.

16. Identify the links between the Vital Revolution and the decline of forced labor.

Go to INQUIZITIVE

to see what you've learned—and learn what you've missed—with personalized feedback along the way.

Nationalism and Imperialism

TIGHTENING THE GLOBAL WEB

1800 to 1930

FOCUS QUESTIONS

1. In what ways did nationalism prove a powerful force in the modern world?

2. What made imperialism such a powerful force in the nineteenth and twentieth centuries?

3. What were the most important land empires during this period?

4. What global effects did nationalism and imperialism have?

I n 1890, on the Makonde plateau in what is now southern Tanzania, in East Africa, there lived a merchant-prince and slave trader named Machemba. Leader of a people known as the Yao, he was among a handful of African and Afro-Arab warlords prospering from a growing trade in slaves and ivory that linked the East African hinterland to its seacoast and beyond to distant markets in Arabia, India, and Europe. Germany had just laid claim to a big slice of East Africa—Tanganyika—and needed cooperative African leaders who would support German authority. Hermann von Wissman, a distinguished German army officer who had spent several years in Africa, invited Machemba to do so. Machemba had his own ideas:

CHRONOLOGY

....

1795 France makes *La Marseillaise* its national anthem

1818 Hongi Hika begins importing guns and potatoes to New Zealand

1819 British found Singapore

1829 Establishment of Serbia

1830s Abdelkadir leads Algerian uprising

1832 Establishment of Greece

ca. 1840 Peak of Comanche Empire's economic and military strength

1847 French capture and exile Abdelkadir

1858 Start of the British Raj

1859 Charles Darwin publishes *The Origin of Species*

1860s Italian unification

1867 Canadian Confederation; Kingdom of Hungary is granted limited independence

1871 Algerian uprising

1876–1878 Major famine in India

1878 Establishment of Romania and Bulgaria

1884–1885 Berlin Conference partitions Africa

1888–1892 Drought and famine in Ethiopia kill half of population

1889 Adoption of Meiji constitution; rinderpest arrives in East Africa

1894–1895 Japan defeats China in war and takes Taiwan

1896 Menelik II's army defeats Italians at Adowa

I have listened to your words but can find no reason why I should obey you. I would rather die first. . . . If it should be friendship that you desire, then I am ready for it, today and always; but to be your subject, that I cannot be. If it should be war you desire, then I am ready, but never to be your subject. I do not fall at your feet, for you are God's creature just as I am. . . . I am Sultan here in my land. You are Sultan there in yours. Yet listen, I do not say that you should obey me: for I know that you are a free man. As for me, I will not come to you, and if you are strong enough, then come and fetch me.

Disappointed but not surprised, von Wissman came to fetch Machemba. The Germans assembled an army of Africans, some from as far away as Zululand (South Africa) and Sudan, trained and equipped by German veterans of European wars. It took nine years to defeat Machemba and a few more to subdue all of Tanganyika.

Machemba, in his defiance, had not appreciated that von Wissman had behind him the resources of an industrialized country of 50 million people. Even when he learned the full measure of German power, there was little he could do to preserve his own independence. For his part, von Wissman didn't know much about Machemba and the Yao, who proved to be resourceful guerrilla fighters. But when he learned, there was plenty he could do to them.

Encounters of this sort, featuring unequal levels of knowledge about the world and unequal resources, became especially frequent in the nineteenth century. Thanks mainly to industrialization, some societies and states, including Germany, were in a position to use overwhelming power thousands of miles from home. It proved a temptation hard to resist.

Between 1826 and 1919, about a quarter of the

Earth's land surface changed hands politically. People inspired by the ideologies of **nationalism** and imperialism, and in most cases empowered by industrialization, helped to re-draw the political map of the world through violence and negotiation. These ideologies, in effect, made some peoples and states stronger and others weaker, rearranging the world political order.

Nationalism and imperialism were the most powerful ideologies changing world politics between 1800 and 1930. Other important political ideas, such as democracy, socialism, or pan-Islamism (the belief that Islam should be politically unified), had less global consequences. Nationalism and imperialism loomed so large because they traveled well from one cultural setting to the next. People on every continent found the idea of nationhood appealing. And most people in powerful societies approved of imperialism too.

1898 Spanish-American War; United States takes Spain's colonies and annexes Hawaii

1899 Rudyard Kipling publishes "The White Man's Burden"

1900 Australian Federation

By 1910 All local Indonesian rulers submit to the Dutch

1910 Japan annexes Korea

1912 Italy takes Libya from Ottoman Empire

1918 Collapse of Habsburg Empire; Aladura churches in Nigeria take shape

1930s Development of Yamato race theory

This chapter begins with an assessment of nationalism, explaining the concept, where it mattered, why it arose when it did, and what difference it made. It then considers imperialism, outlining why it reached such heights during the nineteenth century, what forms it took, and where it mattered most. As we shall see, nationalism and imperialism sometimes overlapped in mutually reinforcing ways, and sometimes worked at cross purposes. Both encouraged people to emphasize their differences, but both brought peoples into closer interactions and tighter webs.

Nationalism and Nation-States

Nationalism—perhaps the single most powerful ideological force in modern centuries—is stubbornly difficult to define. It is a set of ideas, beliefs, and attitudes that exalts the virtues of a community claiming distinctive characteristics and, in most cases, a bounded territory. The characteristics that provide solidarity can be shared language and culture, shared ethnicity and ancestry, or shared political and civic values—or some combination of them.

Scholars often distinguish between ethnic nationalism and civic nationalism. The first refers to groups, such as Japanese, that get their sense of solidarity from a common language, ethnic identity, or ancestry. The claim to common ancestry can be, and usually is, fanciful. But if people believe it, the effect is the same as if it were true. The second, civic nationalism, refers to nations whose sense of solidarity comes instead from common acceptance of a set of institutions and political values. The United States is a good example: the ideals articulated in the Declaration of Independence and the U.S. Constitution, though never fully realized in American society, remain an inspiration and a source of identity for the nation. In practice, ethnic nationalism and civic nationalism often overlap.

Nationalism begins with human biology but doesn't end there. A craving to belong to a group is one of the deepest human desires. Our fellow apes seem to feel it too. In the long hominin and human career, this desire conferred strong advantages. People could forage, hunt, and defend themselves better as groups than as lone individuals. Over hundreds of thousands of years, our brains evolved to make us long to belong to groups.

But human biology has no bearing on just which groups we wish to belong to. It could be a hunter-forager band, a high school debate team, or the community of Green Bay Packer fans known as Cheeseheads. Membership in all these groups and millions of others, however large or small and whatever their practical advantages, delivers psychic rewards. For some people at least, nationalism offers a satisfying sense of solidarity with a large community, enabling people to feel part of something greater than their family or village. We humans are pre-adapted to be receptive to group identities such as nationalism.

Modern nationalism, especially ethnic nationalism, has a strange relationship to history. It rests on simplifying myths. Nationalists typically emphasize glorious, ancient, and unified pasts—air-brushed pasts. Modern Mongolian nationalism harkens back to the Eurasian conqueror Genghis Khan, overlooking his gory massacres. Mexican nationalism invokes the Aztecs, overlooking their ruthless rule over the ancestors of millions of today's Mexicans. As the French scholar Ernst Renan wrote in 1882, "Forgetting, I would go so far as to say historical error, is a crucial factor in the creation of a nation."

Nationalism prospered in some circumstances more than others. Ethnic nationalism arose most easily where ethnic, linguistic, cultural, and religious diversity was minimal and a unified state already existed. Nineteenth-century Japan is a good example. Nationalism also developed where ethnic minorities in multiethnic states felt persecuted: Poles in the Russian Empire or Afrikaners in South Africa. The idea—whether accurate or not—of a peasantry deeply rooted in the ancestral soil, as in modern Korea or France, also helped foster ethnic nationalism. People who felt their nation was specially chosen for some divine purpose or that their nation was unfairly victimized—or both—also found nationalism appealing.

Another circumstance that favored the development of nationalism was urbanization. As we've seen, cities grew larger and more numerous during the nineteenth century, especially in industrializing countries. Tens of millions of people uprooted from villages felt the need to belong to a community, and so were all the more receptive to nationalistic messages. Those messages might take the form of journalism, heroic novels, poetry, or painting—or stirring patriotic music adopted as national anthems. France in 1795 designated *La Marseillaise* as a national anthem, launching an international trend. Vietnam chose one in 1802, Argentina in 1813, Peru in 1821, and Japan in 1888. The United States adopted its national anthem in 1931. City populations, because clustered together, were easier to reach with nationalist music, art, or journalism.

Nationalism's adherents generally wanted a state whose borders matched those of an ethnic or linguistic group, whether Germans or Koreans or Bengalis. They often claimed that any state with borders that did not correspond to a nation—a multinational state—was illegitimate. Their ambitions almost always required some political re-engineering: nationalism served to unite peoples into a single nation-state in some cases and in others to grind multicultural empires into pieces. Let's look at some examples.

France

Many scholars think France provides the earliest example of genuine nationalism. While France became a kingdom over the span of many centuries, only its elite felt French before the 1790s. The masses generally felt attachments to their family, village, region, religion, and perhaps to their king. But in the course of the French Revolution and especially Napoleon Bonaparte's foreign wars, more and more people within France came to feel increasingly French. Some were moved by the ideals of the Revolution—liberty, equality, and fraternity (perhaps better translated as solidarity). When the French established a republic that supposedly represented the will of the people, many of them felt they had laid the foundation for a better political community.

In the 1790s, leaders of the French Revolution tried to drum a sense of French-ness into the uneducated peasantry—80 percent of the population. One tactic was requiring the use of standard (Parisian) French throughout the country, a policy employed off and on ever after. Another tactic, used only in the desperate 1790s, was killing people who declined to identify themselves with the French nation.

French Nationalism An 1880 lithograph shows the Place de la Bastille in central Paris decorated with French flags in honor of France's July 14 national holiday. A national day, imagery connected with a national flag, and national history grounded in pivotal founding events such as the storming of the Bastille are all characteristic nationalist symbols.

Two decades of warfare, from 1792 to 1815, helped forge a French nation. Military service in a national army made soldiers feel French. Supporters of the Revolution and Bonaparte devised symbols, ceremonies, and rituals to convey the meaning of French identity to people who could not read: a national flag to match the anthem, for example, or parades and funerals for heroes of the French nation. Army service exposed young men to standard French, no matter which tongue they spoke at home.

After the final defeat of Bonaparte in 1815, subsequent rulers of France, even monarchists who hated everything else about the French Revolution, cultivated nationalism. Throughout the nineteenth century, French elites hammered home the nationalist message, using the newly created countrywide public school system, the army, and the press to deepen the popular sense of French national identity. After 1871, the government, now called the Third Republic, tried again to impose a standard French language on the country. Ordinary French citizens learned to feel that theirs was a special nation, committed to political ideals such as liberty and equality. They were also taught to consider themselves blood descendants of the formidable ancient Gauls, in whom various admirable traits were conveniently found. At the same time, they identified with the glorious legacies of the Romans and Charlemagne, and the more recent glory of Bonaparte. French nationalism was, and is, mainly civic nationalism, based on the ideals of the French Revolution; but it also has had, and still has, an ethnic basis for many French people.

Japan

Japanese nationalism was based mainly on a sense of ethnic solidarity. It had deep roots, but it matured in the late nineteenth century when Japanese leaders worried, with ample reason, that their country might be overrun and colonized by Britain or another industrial power. They made a concerted effort to industrialize, as we've seen, and to foster nationalism and a sense of Japanese exceptionalism. They calculated that these efforts would rally the masses to make sacrifices for the state, which they believed was essential to Japan's continued independence.

Around 1875, Japanese leaders started promoting the fiction of common ancestry among all Japanese. By the 1930s it had developed as **Yamato race theory**, according to which the Japanese were descended from an ancient ancestral people and were different from, and better than, Koreans, Chinese, and other neighbors. Japanese nationalism also had a strong religious component: the elite in Japan typically embraced the ancient Japanese rituals called Shinto in preference to imported religions such as Buddhism. The state supported Shinto shrines and encouraged worship of the emperor as divine. The Meiji constitution, adopted in 1889, instructed Japanese people that their first allegiance was to the state. Japan's nationalists emphasized the respects in which the country was unique, and especially how it was different from—and, as they saw it, more disciplined, energetic, and warlike than—China.

Japanese Nationalism
Japanese efforts to support Shinto as the national religion resulted in the persecution of Buddhists. An 1874 illustration shows Shinto priests burning Buddhist scriptures, over the tears and protests of a Buddhist monk.

As elsewhere, public education in Japan helped get the message to the masses. After 1870, an older tradition of Confucian learning taught to a few was replaced by a more practical, and nationalistic, curriculum, and by 1900 almost every Japanese boy and girl attended school. University students had to swear an oath promising to "offer [myself] courageously to the state." Urbanization and increasing literacy also helped nationalism to take root.

Japan's nationalism emphasized military virtues. By 1890, sailors and soldiers were instructed to see Japan as a "sacred nation protected by the gods." Civilians were encouraged to revere the armed forces as embodiments of the warrior spirit of the Yamato race. As we will see, after Japan's defeat in World War II, the character of its nationalism underwent a radical makeover, dropping militarism in favor of a narrative of victimization and pride in economic progress.

Canada

Canadian nationalism, in contrast, had (and has) no ethnic basis and little military emphasis. In 1800, what is now Canada was a handful of British colonies with two distinct ethnic and religious populations. In Quebec, especially in the countryside, almost everyone spoke French and followed the Catholic religion, a consequence of French colonization and settlement dating back to 1608. In what are now the Maritime provinces and Ontario, people mainly spoke English and were mainly Protestants. The process of building a Canadian identity and nation took shape with Confederation in 1867, the fusing of the various colonies into a self-governing country through negotiations and an act of the British Parliament. The British North America Act reserved Canadian military and foreign affairs for Britain to control but left domestic matters to Canadians.

First Nations and Assimilation The biggest challenge in creating a Canadian nation was reconciling differences between the Anglophone and Francophone communities—something Canada is still working on. Few Canadians had any intention of including First Nations, as the indigenous Amerindians of Canada are now called, in their political community—unless the First Nations first abandoned their culture. For two centuries after European settlement, Canada's First Nations had slowly lost land in the east but lived alongside Euro-Canadians as trading partners. Wars between France and Britain in North America, especially between 1756 and 1815, featured Amerindian involvement, which in every case turned out badly for Canada's First Nations. After those wars ceased, First Nations seemed more like obstacles to expanded Euro-Canadian settlement than potential allies and trading partners.

By 1870, Amerindian numbers in Canada had been reduced to a few tens of thousands through loss of land, searing epidemics in the 1780s and 1830s, and the near extinction of the buffalo, a major food source in western Canada. Through treaties in the 1870s, Canada confined the lands available to First Nations to "reserves" that usually did not include good farmland. First Nations leaders accepted these treaties, in effect making them wards of the Canadian state, in order to obtain medicines, manufactured goods, and education for the young. A program of residential schools, often run by Catholic or Protestant churches, aimed to assimilate First Nations into Canadian Anglophone or Francophone culture. Many members of First Nations did assimilate; 6,000 volunteered for the armed forces in World War I. Those who didn't assimilate remained, in effect, outside the Canadian nation.

The great champion of Confederation and Canadian nationalism was a Scottish-born lawyer, John A. MacDonald, who after 1867 served 19 years as prime minister. Despite a weakness for whiskey and bribes, he energetically sought to forge a nation from the newly confederated parts of Canada. He encouraged railroad building on a transcontinental scale and pursued a form of economic nationalism, trying to keep American imports to a minimum, to build a truly national economy. He favored the settlement of western farmlands as far as the Pacific. When some 350 Métis—French-speaking people of partly Amerindian descent in Manitoba and Saskatchewan—decided they didn't want to be part of Canada, in what is called the North-West Rebellion (1885), MacDonald sent Canadian militia to crush them. He then insisted on the execution of Louis Riel, the charismatic Métis leader. By 1905, western and prairie regions had been organized into Canadian provinces, and the country stretched from the Atlantic to the Pacific.

Canadian Nationalism and Foreign Relations The unintentional help of the colossus to the south helped make the idea of Canada work. Part of nationalism's appeal rested on popular fears that the United States might try to conquer Canada, using the giant army that had won the U.S. Civil War in 1865. Ragtag bands of Irish Americans called Fenians, mainly Civil War veterans, burned to right the wrongs Britain had done to Ireland: they invaded British Canada twice in 1866 and killed several Canadian militiamen. The U.S. purchase of Alaska (1867) only added to Canadian concerns. Invasion fears subsided after 1871, when a hapless group of 35 Fenians misjudged the location of the border and attacked northern Minnesota by mistake.

But realistic anxieties about American economic and cultural power persisted, strengthening a sense of national solidarity among Canadians. In addition, many Canadians, Francophones especially, resented the power—in military and foreign relations—that politicians in London still exercised over them after Confederation. So Canadian nationalism was—paradoxically enough—based on fears and resentments directed at the United States and Britain, Canada's closest cultural cousins and political allies. It was and is for the most part a civic nationalism crafted to overcome the ethnic and religious diversity characteristic of Canada from the outset.

Germany

German nationalism, like Canadian, served to weld together a country. German nationalists fused many smaller political units together to make a new country, but at the same time they set Germany off from the larger cultural unit of German-speakers. Most Austrians and Swiss also spoke varieties of German, but they remained outside of Germany.

Like Japanese nationalism, German nationalism emphasized ethnic and linguistic solidarity. The notion of a common language involved more wishful thinking than it did in Japan. In the eighteenth century, despite a common literary language, the many varieties of spoken German were often mutually unintelligible. As late as 1800, few people thought there should be a country called Germany.

But when Bonaparte destroyed the Holy Roman Empire in 1806, he united several little German duchies and principalities into a rickety political structure called the Confederation of the Rhine. He then demanded soldiers and taxes from them, arousing fierce resentment and helping German-speakers to see their collective interest and identity more clearly. Parallel efforts following conquests by Bonaparte in Spain, Italy, the Netherlands, and elsewhere helped to inspire nationalisms elsewhere in Europe. After Bonaparte's final defeat in 1815, some Germans tried and failed to unite Germany politically. But they did manage to establish a customs union called the *zollverein*—basically a free-trade zone—that gradually tightened the economic bonds among its members.

German cultural nationalism prospered too. Literature, music, and painting extolled the supposed special merits of German-ness, such as the canvas by Philipp Veit that presents Germany in the form of a medieval woman. German scholars and schoolmasters found inspiration in the hardihood and virtue of the wild Germanic tribes described by the ancient Roman author Tacitus, and they encouraged modern Germans to see themselves as a single people, descendants of the ancient tribes. As in Japan, in Germany some nationalists by 1880 understood German ethnicity as a matter

German Nationalism Philipp Veit's *Germania* (1848) imagined the German nation in the form of a beautiful woman in supposed medieval dress—appealing to a myth of a common ethnic German identity that stretched back centuries.

of race. They argued that Germans stood superior to all other "races"—a view that, as we shall see, attracted more followers after 1918.

Bismarck and German Unification The development of German nationalism and the political unification of Germany went hand in hand. Uprisings against princes and kings in 1848 briefly led to an all-German parliament and an effort by some of the urban middle classes to create a united German republic or at least a constitutional monarchy. Although the revolution failed and the principalities, dukedoms, and kingdoms of the German Confederation survived, the prospect of a united German nation proved inspirational. Soon the chancellor of Prussia (a kingdom and the biggest part of Germany) saw a way to make nationalism serve his ends. In a series of small wars and one-sided negotiations from Prussia's position of strength, the Prussian aristocrat Otto von Bismarck fused patches of predominantly German-speaking lands to Prussia, creating a politically unified country by 1871. Bismarck deliberately left German-speaking Austria out of this union to ensure that his Prussia would dominate Germany. Ironically, in the process of unification Germany acquired minority populations who spoke Polish, Lithuanian, Danish, or French. They did not feel at all German, although with time many of their children did.

At every step, Bismarck encouraged the development of a German national identity, using the same tools—schools, army, press—as in France or Japan. As in Japan, industrialization and urbanization helped put more people within reach of messages urging them to think of themselves as German rather than as, for example, Swabian or Silesian. Bismarck's version of German nationalism emphasized military virtues and promoted the army and navy as symbols of national strength. He and his successors encouraged Germans to think in terms of national greatness and geopolitical strength, which many Germans eagerly embraced until it brought their country to ruin in two world wars.

Nationalism as a Source of State Power

As these four examples show, there were many routes to nationalism and to a nation-state. Where ethnic, linguistic, and religious divisions were weak, and where a unified state already existed, as in Japan, nationalism was an easier project than in France, where nationalism was born of revolution and war. In Germany and Canada, deep

Catholic-Protestant divisions proved an obstacle, and nationalist leaders such as Bismarck and MacDonald had to deploy formidable political skills to create a nation-state out of smaller units.

Nationalism could confer great power upon states. If people accepted the notion that they were, say, French, then a government of the French people could get tax revenues and military conscripts with less resistance than if people did not agree they were French. Nationalism helped justify bigger military budgets. Nationalism could discourage workers from calling strikes that would weaken the state. It could prepare people psychologically to let the state manage schooling of the young or use private property for railroad-building programs—both of which (schools and railroads) helped governments foster nationalism even more. Nationalism, in short, could make states much stronger, both with respect to their own citizens and with respect to foreign countries. It reduced the difficulties of governing—as long as the state's citizens felt that they belonged to one nation and that the state championed the interests of the nation.

Nationalism and Multiethnic Empires

Nationalism could also weaken states. The best examples were big multiethnic polities of the nineteenth century such as the Habsburg, Russian, or Ottoman empires. These **multiethnic empires** all included many linguistic and religious groups, as well as millions of people who might be just as comfortable speaking Czech as German or equally comfortable in Turkish and Greek. Nationalists, although often educated and multilingual themselves, wanted people to declare themselves as members of one or another nation, and wanted separate states for each nation—or at least a state for their own nation.

The Habsburg Empire   The Habsburg Empire, dominated by German-speaking Austrians, comprised many ethnic minorities, including Hungarians, Czechs, Slovaks, Poles, Italians, Romanians, Serbs, and Croats, among others. Its multiethnic character made it especially vulnerable to nationalist divisions. After 1815, many members of these groups gradually concluded that they should be recognized as nations. They did not necessarily want to be fully independent but sought autonomy within the Habsburg framework, which the rulers—themselves mostly German-speaking Austrians—were slow to offer. So the minorities increasingly considered the imperial state an unjust yoke. Nationalist uprisings peppered the empire from 1848 onward. The Habsburgs responded with repression and attempts to impose the German language in schools and for all official business, provoking more unrest.

Eventually, the Habsburgs relented and allowed more cultural expression and some political autonomy among certain minorities. In 1867, the historic Kingdom of Hungary was granted independence except in military matters and foreign policy—a similar status to the one Canada achieved within the British Empire in the same year. The arrangement for Hungary incited other minorities who felt their nationality was just as worthy of special status. To compound matters, once Hungarians acquired power over their internal affairs, they ruthlessly repressed Romanians, Croats, and other minorities in their part of the empire. Until its collapse in 1918, the Habsburg Empire struggled to contain minority nationalisms.

The Russian Empire   The Russian Empire faced a similar problem. Although most of its subjects spoke Russian and adhered to the Russian Orthodox faith, it had a dozen or more sizeable ethno-linguistic groups and some religious minorities. Poland, as we have seen, was partitioned during the eighteenth century among Prussia, the Habsburg Empire, and Russia, leaving Poles with no country of their own. That circumstance led to a robust nationalism, at least among urban and educated Poles, creating a recurrent problem for Russia. Bonaparte's armies had established a short-lived puppet Polish state, the Duchy of Warsaw. With Bonaparte's defeat, most of it was taken over by Russia. Polish nationalism inspired major rebellions in the years 1830–1831 and 1863–1864. Russian authorities tried to prevent the rise of Polish, Lithuanian, Ukrainian, and other nationalisms, often forbidding the use of these languages. Such repressive measures, part of a general program of Russification, typically inflamed minority nationalist sentiment still further.

In Russia, religious divisions often strengthened minority nationalisms. In the first census (1897), some 70 percent of the tsar's subjects were counted as Russian Orthodox, which left roughly 40 million followers of minority religions. For most Poles, Catholicism was a sacred point of pride. In Finland and the Baltic provinces, Lutheranism was woven into people's sense of identity, as was the Armenian Apostolic Church for Armenians. In the western parts of the empire, the census showed Russia with more than 5 million Jews, few of whom identified strongly with the empire. The Caucasus and Central Asia were home to 14 million Muslims, who firmly resisted efforts at conversion to Russian Orthodoxy. The Russian Empire's promotion of Orthodoxy, which included banning several other religions, added to the irritation of religious minorities, providing them another reason to feel Polish or Estonian or Armenian. As in the Habsburg Empire, in Russia the imperial state never found a way to subdue surging minority nationalisms.

The Ottoman Empire   The multicultural and multiethnic Ottoman Empire also suffered from the rise of nationalisms. As in Russia, religious identities and national ones often bolstered one another. Muslims accounted for the great majority of Ottoman subjects—about 75 percent in 1906, the first year for which good census data exist. Some 14 percent were officially Greek Orthodox in religion, although not necessarily Greek in language or nationality. In the nineteenth century, Greeks, Serbs, Romanians, Bulgarians, and other linguistic and religious minorities of the empire grew more restive, convinced that they constituted nations. They each had their own increasingly national form of Orthodox Christianity, with priests and bishops who occasionally stirred up nationalist sentiments. From the beginning of the nineteenth century, the Ottomans faced one rebellion after another in the Balkans, often led by university graduates who had lived in France or Germany and who pined for national independence.

Although nationalist consciousness was mainly an elite concern, armed rebellions helped establish new nation-states such as Serbia (1829), Greece (1832), Romania (1878), and Bulgaria (1878). All were mainly Orthodox in religion, but with substantial Muslim minorities. All were keenly nationalistic at birth, eager to expand their territories so as to embrace all their "unredeemed brethren"—to use the language of the time. Arab nationalism was a worrisome sleeping giant for Ottoman authorities, because so much Ottoman territory—the Levant, the Arabian Peninsula, and much of what is now Iraq—was inhabited by Arabic-speakers. But into the early twentieth century, only a few intellectuals and merchants had developed much sense of Arab national identity.

Nationalism in the Ottoman Empire This evocative painting by the French Romantic artist Eugène Delacroix shows Greek rebels—including women and children—being massacred by Ottoman troops during the Greek War of Independence. The pathos of the image invites the viewer to sympathize with the Greek nationalist cause.

In the early twentieth century, the Ottoman state increasingly turned to a policy of Turkification, broadly parallel to Russification. All branches of government were increasingly required to use only the Turkish language. Muslim minorities, such as Arabs and Kurds, were urged to consider themselves Turks. (Kurds were an ethno-linguistic group living in what is now southeastern Turkey, northeastern Syria, northern Iraq, and northwestern Iran.) Christian minorities, such as Armenians and Greeks living in Ottoman lands, were encouraged to convert to Islam and speak Turkish. Turkification brought scanty results and irritated many of those who were its targets—again, roughly parallel to Russification.

Minority Nationalisms The Russian and Ottoman empires became masters at meddling in one another's affairs by means of minority nationalism. Russia encouraged Greek, Serbian, and Bulgarian nationalisms, supporting publications, welcoming exiles, or supplying weapons for uprisings. To some extent, this policy rested on a shared Orthodox Christianity, but often it emerged from Russian geopolitical calculation. Russia's leaders hoped that vigorous minority nationalisms would weaken their historical foe. In turn, the Ottomans, especially after 1908, promoted nationalisms, and Muslim identity, among peoples of the Russian Empire in the Caucasus region and Central Asia. Britain and France, and eventually Germany too, meddled in Ottoman and Russian ethnic politics, at times encouraging nationalism among minorities. Nationalism provided a new weapon for geopolitical struggles, one that undermined multinational empires but not nation-states.

Minority nationalisms also made it difficult for multinational empires to allow subjects more political voice. The emperors and elites in the Habsburg, Russian, and Ottoman empires feared—quite reasonably—that permitting more representative institutions would inflame ethnic passions and weaken their own grip on power. So they experimented with political reform, but only tentatively, and overall held fast to the principle of autocracy. Nation-states, in contrast, could, and did, enhance their popularity and legitimacy by allowing more citizen representation in politics—for example, by allowing more people to vote. In this way too, nationalism strengthened the hand of the state in Germany, France, and Japan, but weakened it in the multinational empires.

Imperialism

Empires were once widespread and widely regarded as normal and natural. They go back at least 44 centuries to Sargon of Akkad in ancient Mesopotamia. For most of those millennia, empires were built mainly by land. They could be large, like the fourteenth-century Mongol or the fifteenth-century Inka empires, but they usually comprised contiguous territories. Only a few, like South India's Chola kingdom in the eleventh century, also had a significant seaborne element.

But in the sixteenth and seventeenth centuries, as we have seen, truly oceanic empires emerged with the Iberian conquests in the Americas. By 1700, the Atlantic European states—Portugal, Spain, France, the Netherlands, and Britain—all had substantial seaborne empires, held together by commerce and naval power. This marked the beginning of a new era in the long history of empire, one in which naval power and commercial dominance mattered as much as armies.

European overseas empires in 1830 covered about 6 percent of the Earth's land surface and held about 18 percent of its population. Over the next century, a surge of imperialism, mainly on the part of western Europeans and Japanese, changed the world's map as well as its politics, economy, and much else. By 1914, European and Japanese overseas empires controlled about 39 percent of the Earth's land surface and about 33 percent of its population.

While empire was common enough before 1800, by 1900 it reached almost everywhere. Seaborne empires on which the sun never set now spanned the globe. Imperialism after 1870 was so pervasive, and different enough from what had come before, that historians often call it the **new imperialism**. They might better call it industrial-strength imperialism, because what made it so pervasive and different was, first and foremost, the industrialization of some parts of the world—western Europe, Japan, the United

States—but not others. That created huge gaps in power and wealth, a situation that invited imperialist attitudes and actions.

Technologies and Imperialism

Just as the Americas were breaking free of European control (1776–1830), several European states, Britain and France foremost among them, were growing more powerful through the effects of industrialization and nationalism.

Industrial societies developed new technologies useful for building empires. Steamships, at first small, shallow-draft gunboats, proved excellent at projecting military power on coasts and up navigable rivers. They first saw duty putting down rebellions along the St. Lawrence River in Canada

Military Technology British Marines stationed in South Africa at the end of the nineteenth century demonstrate the use of a state-of-the-art Maxim machine gun, which proved effective in wars of imperial conquest in Africa, including Hermann von Wissman's campaign to establish German rule in East Africa.

in 1837. Over the next 50 years, others chugged up and down rivers such as the Niger, Ganges, Mekong, and Yangzi, helping Europeans to trade and negotiate treaties on favorable terms. Steam-powered gunboats on the Waikato River gave British forces a major advantage in wars with Maori that led to the entrenchment of British rule in New Zealand. Big steam-powered ocean-going ships became practical in the 1870s, which cut transport times and permitted "sailing" routes independent of prevailing winds. That made it much easier for industrial powers to project military force overseas.

At least as important as industrial sea power were new, improved, and cheaper guns. Over the course of the nineteenth century, European and U.S. gun manufacturers multiplied the killing power of their products, ranging from pocket-sized pistols to large artillery pieces. This opened a chasm between the effectiveness of their armies and those of peoples without modern guns. While the Zulu of South Africa, the Maori of New Zealand, or the Lakota Sioux in North America could trade for guns, and learned to repair them, they did not have the capacity to mass-produce them. They could win occasional battles against industrial states, but not wars. As the British writer Hilaire Belloc put it in 1898, referring to an early version of a machine gun:

Whatever happens, we have got
The Maxim gun, and they have not.

The couplet captured the gulf in military technology between the armies of imperialists and the forces arrayed against them in Africa or Asia.

Other new technologies further widened that gulf. The telegraph, in use from the 1840s, radically cut the time needed to transmit messages over long distance. After 1870, the British government could exchange messages with its representatives in India in five hours instead of five months. Over the next 30 years, Britain laid submarine telegraph cables across the world's oceans, linking its empire in a communications web far superior to anything available to anyone else. Aspiring imperial powers tried to imitate Britain's network. For military and commercial purposes, the telegraph was a crucial tool of imperialism.

So was a growing ability to check the ravages of malaria through the mass production of a drug, quinine. Use of quinine, extracted from the bark of a tropical tree called cinchona, dates back centuries. Malaria had long menaced people from malaria-free zones who tried to visit, let alone conquer and occupy, most of Africa, South Asia, and Southeast Asia. People born and raised in malarial lands usually carried strong resistance to the disease. But quinine, mass-produced by the 1850s, could make anyone resistant. Chemical industries capable of mass-producing quinine, together with ships, guns, and telegraph networks, were all part of the surge in power that industrialization afforded to a handful of societies in the nineteenth century.

Nationalism in Support of Imperialism

If industrialization provided new hardware suited to empire building, nationalism offered new popular support. Nationalism contributed to the capacity of states such as Britain, France, Japan, and Germany to indulge in imperialism. The same held for Italy, unified by committed nationalists by 1870, and eagerly imperialist by the 1890s. All cases of imperialism enabled by modern industry were supported by populations fired by nationalism.

This support often took the form of an ideology that explicitly justified imperialism. The French developed the *mission civilisatrice* ("civilizing mission") according to which it was France's special destiny to bring civilization—Christianity, sanitation, antislavery, self-discipline, and so forth—to peoples of the world who lacked it. Such an outlook helped to legitimize the human and financial costs of conquests. Every other imperial power created some version of the same self-serving ideology, according to which their nation must shoulder the moral obligation—rarely met in practice—to lift up downtrodden and often darker-skinned masses in Africa or Asia through imperial rule.

Nationalism bolstered imperialism in another important way: through the geopolitical logic of imperial rivalry. From about 1500 onward, European states had competed with one another overseas, mainly in the Americas. Now, in the nineteenth century, with growing global connections, they did so everywhere else—in Africa, Asia, and the archipelagoes of the Pacific. European statesmen came to think in terms of global competition. With nationalistic journalists, business lobbies, and religious establishments all urging action lest their country be left behind, governments sometimes leapt into imperial ventures without much idea of what they were getting into.

This particular motive, geopolitical rivalry, proved strong in the case of Germany, which had no tradition of overseas empire when Bismarck came to power over the newly

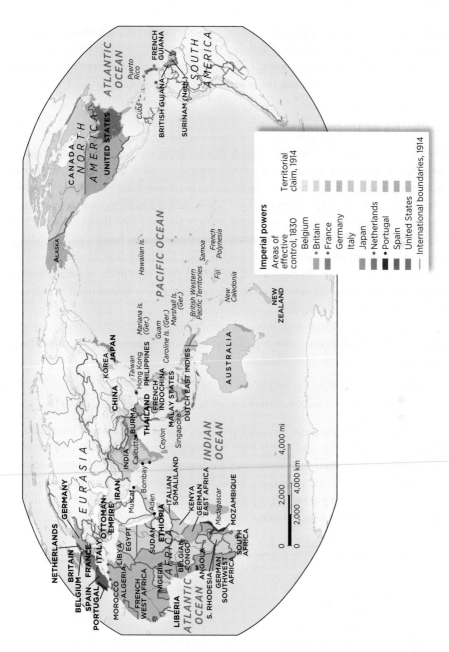

Colonial Empires in 1830 and 1914 Between 1830 and 1914, European powers, the United States, and Japan acquired the capacity to extend or create colonial empires. That capacity depended largely on industrial strength and the ability to mass-produce weaponry, steamships, quinine, and other tools of empire. Africa and both South and Southeast Asia were colonized by European powers. Japan took Korea and Taiwan, while the United States acquired Alaska, Hawaii, Puerto Rico, and the Philippines.

unified state in 1871. By the 1880s, Germany, pushed by nationalistic lobbies, competed for influence and territory in Africa and the Pacific, plunging into imperial ventures for fear that its rivals were getting ahead. Russia and Britain waded deeper into Central Asia after 1870 mainly to prevent the other from dominating it.

Cultures of Imperialism

Nationalism and imperialism fed off each other. Nationalistic feeling made it easier for people to support imperialism; but at the same time, successful imperialism made many people feel more nationalistic. The British in particular developed a sense of themselves as an imperial people, fit to rule over others, and gradually wove that self-image into their culture. In the later nineteenth century and well into the twentieth, they created celebratory literature, theater, music, public ceremonies, honors, and medals—in short, a **culture of imperialism**. It helped them feel more British, as opposed to merely English, Scottish, Welsh, or Irish. It helped them take pride in their country, as opposed to focusing on their social class or religion. And it helped them to support a more nationalistic British policy.

In the 1870s, the British even invented a new word for a particularly pushy foreign policy based on faith in one's own superiority: jingoism. It came from a popular ditty sung in pubs, the refrain to which went:

> We don't want to fight but by Jingo if we do
> We've got the ships, we've got the men, we've got the money too...

Rudyard Kipling was an influential exponent of this British culture of imperialism. His poetry, short stories, and novels were extremely popular in his day, and are still read—and made into movies—more than a century later. Kipling, who was born in India and spent much of his life there, wholeheartedly endorsed British imperialism. He emphasized the duty of racially superior peoples (as he saw it) to rule the rest in his 1899 poem "The White Man's Burden," which begins this way:

> Take up the White Man's burden—
> Send forth the best ye breed—
> Go bind your sons to exile
> To serve your captives' need
> To wait in heavy harness
> On fluttered folk and wild—
> Your new-caught, sullen peoples,
> Half devil and half child.

The culture of imperialism and confidence in national fitness to rule over others developed as strongly in Britain as anywhere. But to a lesser extent it existed by the 1880s in the United States, France, Germany, Italy—and was developing rapidly in Japan.

Social Darwinism and Pseudo-Scientific Racism The European, U.S., and to some extent Japanese cultures of imperialism drew strength from three particular late-nineteenth-century trends. One was pseudo-scientific racism. In 1859, Charles Darwin published his masterwork on biological evolution through natural selection, *The Origin of Species,* with its emphasis on competition and the survival of the fittest. Others soon extended his concepts to subsets of the human species in a doctrine now called **social Darwinism**, which held that some people—usually either nationalities or "races," but sometimes socioeconomic classes—were more fit, in Darwin's sense, than others. If Europeans, and their biological descendants in North America, South America, South Africa, Australia, and New Zealand, were economically and militarily successful, the thinking ran, it was ultimately because they were a superior breed of human, fit and foreordained to rule over the world. Sometimes Europeans, and their descendants around the world, applied this notion to white people in general, understood as an inherently superior "race." But especially in Germany and Britain, the notion of a superior breed of human suited for imperial rule was often applied to a nationality understood to be a "race." Cecil Rhodes, the English business magnate and politician who made a fortune in South Africa, put it confidently in 1877:

The first step towards lightening

The White Man's Burden

is through teaching the virtues of cleanliness.

Pears' Soap

Popular Imperialism In the late nineteenth century, British advertising and popular culture often appealed to imperialist and nationalist imagery. This advertisement references Kipling's poem "The White Man's Burden" and the idea of the civilizing mission in order to sell soap.

> I contend that we are the finest race in the world and that the more of the world we inhabit the better it is for the human race.... Africa is still lying ready for us it is our duty to take it.... It is our duty to seize every opportunity of acquiring more territory and we should keep this one idea steadily before our eyes that more territory simply means more of the Anglo-Saxon race, more of the best, the most human, most honorable race the world possesses.

The social Darwinist perspective and pseudo-scientific racism proved especially popular in Germany, the United States, Britain, and the British dominions of Australia, New Zealand, South Africa, and Canada. The supposedly unfit breeds of humankind included all Africans, Asians, and Amerindians, and usually several sorts of Europeans as well, such as the Irish, Slavs, Greeks, Italians, Spaniards, and Jews, among others.

At the same time, Japanese intellectuals developed their own version of social Darwinism. A prolific professor and colonial official, Nitobe Inazo, who had studied at

U.S. and German universities, justified Japanese imperialism by arguing that Koreans were not suited to self-government and it was Japan's responsibility to bring modern civilization to Korea. Japanese intellectuals adapted social Darwinism to encourage the belief that the Japanese were a distinct biological race, inherently superior to Koreans and Chinese—if not everyone else too.

Disdain for other peoples is of course routine in world history. Chinese and Mongols typically considered one another inferior, as did French and Germans. Rival religious groups regularly vilified one another. What was different about social Darwinism was its resort to science for supposed proof of the notion that humankind is composed of biologically distinct races, of which some are better than others. That gave pseudo-scientific racism an impressive intellectual basis for nearly a century, but in the end made it brittle because it was susceptible to scientific disproof via genetics. Racism flourishes on every continent today, but it no longer appeals to science.

Concepts of Manliness and Muscular Christianity Beyond social Darwinism, the culture of imperialism also drew upon anxieties about manliness. In industrializing and urbanizing societies such as Japan, Britain, Germany, France, and the United States, some people came to think men were growing soft, losing their resourcefulness and hardihood. It seemed less worrisome if women lacked these qualities because they were not considered suitably feminine virtues. Physically challenging duties in the great outdoors might prevent the enfeeblement of males, and so conquest and empire were, so to speak, a cure for this societal disease. The U.S. president Theodore Roosevelt was among the more eloquent spokesmen for this anxious view, and he dedicated himself to restoring to American men a suitable vigor and valor.

Curing a loss of manliness could go hand in hand with advancing the cause of one's preferred religion. The culture of imperialism also drew upon developments within European and North American Christianity in the nineteenth century—specifically, the advent of what was called muscular Christianity. The phrase became commonplace by the 1870s, embraced by Protestants and Catholics alike as an ideal. Roosevelt was one among many advocates in the United States. Britons, Germans, and French had their own versions. The best places to exhibit muscular Christianity were in distant, physically challenging lands such as Africa, where, amid hardships, certain disciplined, forceful, and energetic men might spread the gospel. Christian missionary societies enjoyed unprecedented support in the late nineteenth century, typically working within the frameworks of one or another empire. New ones, such as France's Pères Blancs ("White Fathers"), were founded to focus on Africa. Muscular Christianity wasn't confined to missionaries. Soldiers could exemplify it too. A British author in 1901 delighted in "the Englishman going through the world with rifle in one hand and Bible in the other."

Some Intellectual Responses The culture of imperialism provoked a variety of intellectual responses in Africa and Asia, including everything from self-doubt to defiance. An anti-colonial politician from the Dutch East Indies, E.F.E. Douwes Dek-ker (also known as Setyabudi), noted the psychological impacts of the culture of impe-rialism in 1912: "There is nothing we need so much as self-assurance . . . we must feel . . . a strong sense of our own worth, a realization that we are not inferior to anybody." In an assessment of imperialism written in 1950, Aimé Césaire, a poet and essayist from Martinique, wrote of colonized people around the world: "I am talking about millions of men in whom fear has been cunningly instilled, who have been taught to have an inferiority complex, to tremble, kneel, despair." As we shall see in Chapter 28, colonized peoples in the course of the twentieth century rebuked the culture of imperialism in winning independence.

Industrialization, nationalism, and cultures of imperialism, in varying mixtures, created strong coalitions in favor of imperialism in western Europe and Japan, and a modest one in the United States. But the main incentive for the so-called new impe-rialism was simply that by 1870, for a handful of countries, Britain first and foremost, industrialization made imperialism increasingly cheap and easy. Thus it was both more practical and tempting.

The British in India, 1818–1914

Britain, with its former American colonies having become an independent nation by 1783, focused its imperial efforts primarily on South Asia—all of which was generally called India. British influence in India remained largely in the hands of the East India Company, or EIC, which held a monopoly on external trade and maintained its own armed forces. The EIC had conquered small parts of India beginning in the 1750s, even before Britain's Industrial Revolution. In the early nineteenth century, it acquired much more territory and power through war and diplomacy, leaving it in control of most of India by 1818. Meanwhile, the British Crown took Ceylon in 1815 and parts of Burma starting in 1824, among other territories. Then, after a major uprising and civil war in India in 1857–1858 (discussed in the next chapter), the British state terminated the once-mighty Mughal Empire and the EIC, and in 1858 claimed control over most of India. Nearly 600 "princely states" remained, which had formerly paid tribute to either the Mughals or the EIC. They were all militarily weak, and their rulers had to bend to British wishes on every important matter, even though Britain did not rule them directly.

The princes, variously called *rajputs, maharajas, nawabs, sultans,* or *emirs,* were part of the local elite through which Britain ruled. In 1880, the ratio of Briton to Indian in India was only about 1:250,000. The large standing army of British India consisted overwhelmingly of Indians, called *sepoys,* who enforced British rule and fought overseas for the British. So, of necessity, British rule relied on the cooperation of Indian elites, including princes, big landowners, and the religious authorities of both Hinduism and Islam. For these men (and they were all men), British rule—sometimes called the

British Rule in India Sikh infantrymen in the British Army pose for a portrait during the Indian Rebellion of 1857–1858. Sikhs remained loyal to Britain during the rebellion—one of the many divisions between minority ethnic and religious groups that Britain exploited in order to consolidate power in India.

British Raj—offered many advantages, helping to firm up their authority, including the property rights of landowners. But it brought frustrations too, as when, despite their distinguished ancestry, great wealth, or deep learning, they were treated as inferior beings by—as they saw it—ignorant commoners without princely blood whose only distinction was being British.

Imperial Strategy: Divide and Rule In addition to finding willing partners among the elite, British rule relied on divisions in South Asian societies. All imperial states practiced the policy of divide and rule; five aspects of India's diversity made this policy especially effective there. First, India had been politically fragmented since the decline of the Mughal Empire in the early eighteenth century. Second, India, although mainly Hindu in religion, had large Muslim, Buddhist, and Sikh minorities. Third, within the Hindu majority, longstanding caste identities discouraged people from making common cause. Fourth, Indians spoke hundreds of different languages and wrote in several different scripts. And fifth, British authorities recognized certain groups in India as "martial races," such as Sikhs or the hill peoples of Nepal called Gurkhas, suitable for army and police work. Men from the "martial races" were encouraged to see themselves as better than others and to sign up for duty controlling other Indians on behalf of the British Raj. Only by exploiting these divisions could Britain rule some 250 million Indians.

Economic Effects British rule in India had modest economic effect on the bulk of the people. Roughly 80 percent raised rice or wheat for their families and village markets. Their yields were among the world's lowest; their risk of crop failure and famine, usually from droughts, among the world's highest. British rule affected their routines only rarely before 1914. The biggest exception came during a major famine in the years

1876–1878, when colonial policy prioritized grain exports over relief efforts, contributing to the death of 5 to 6 million Indians.

British rule made a much bigger difference for those Indians in cities, or connected to export agriculture, and for the long-term direction of India's economy as a whole. Beginning in the 1840s, British engineers laid out thousands of miles of railroads and upgraded port facilities. The new infrastructure helped to extend the domain of market relations into Indian society. Together with British efforts to standardize law through-out India, and the spread of English as a common language, the new infrastructure promoted market integration within India and the integration of Indian markets with those elsewhere in the British Empire. Many Indian merchants and landowners took advantage of these market opportunities. The politician Jawaharlal Nehru expressed the ambivalence that many other Indians felt about the infrastructure acquired under the Raj: "I am all in favor of . . . the latest methods of transport, but . . . as I rushed across the Indian plains, the railway, that life-giver, has almost seemed to me like iron bands confining and imprisoning India." Overall, the Indian economy grew slowly under British rule.

The biggest change in economic life under the Raj came as a result of the policy of free trade, both within the empire and with the world at large. That proved dev-astating in the short run for Indian weavers and cloth manufacturers, who could not compete against the mass production of British factories. For decades, India's economy shifted in the direction of raw material production, typically of fibers such as cotton and jute—jute fiber is used to make burlap bags for transporting commodities such as rice and cotton. By the 1870s, however, Indian and British businessmen in the leading cities of Bombay and Calcutta (now Mumbai and Kolkata) began to build textile mills; and for a while, until the rise of the Japanese cotton industry by 1900, they did very well selling to China. Jamsetji Tata, for example, from the Parsi religious minority in Gujarat, made a fortune in cotton exports, and in 1907 his descendants started India's most successful steel business. This pattern, in which some found ways to profit hand-somely from the changes brought by imperialism while the bulk of the population did not, proved characteristic of modern empires as a whole.

For its economic contributions, its military manpower, and its strategic position in the Indian Ocean world, India remained the jewel in the crown of the British Empire. How Indians responded politically to British rule, and ultimately overthrew it in 1947, is a story taken up in Chapters 25 and 28.

The French in Algeria, 1830–1914

Algeria was as important to France as India was to Britain. Located in the Maghreb region of North Africa, Algeria was overwhelmingly Sunni Muslim in religion and mainly Arabic-speaking. It had been a loosely governed part of the Ottoman Empire since the sixteenth century, dominated by local authorities called *deys*. Several of the

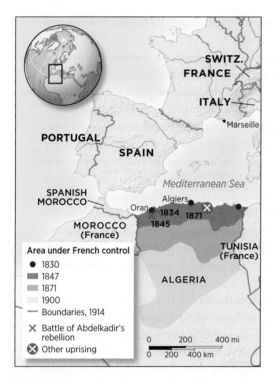

French Expansion in North Africa, 1830–1914 Beginning in 1830, Algeria was conquered by France and became its most important overseas possession. Algerians resisted militarily in the 1830s and 1840s, and again in an uprising in 1871. But French power advanced steadily southward, extending well into the Sahara desert by 1900.

deys practiced piracy and the ransoming of Christian captives, attracting attention from French officials. Disputes over debts and ransoms, and an alleged insult to a French diplomat in Algiers, triggered a French assault on Algeria beginning in 1830. In the coming decades, Algeria became—officially—part of France, although in all but name it was a colony. Boatloads of European settlers, Italian and Spanish as well as French, flooded in. The French army pushed the locals off the best lands, sometimes with ruthless violence, turning them over to settlers—called *colons* in French North Africa. The big cities, such as Algiers and Oran, soon had more *colons* than Muslim Algerians. The indigenous Algerian population, only about 1.5 million in 1830, fell during the early years of French rule, the result of dispossession, disease, and violence. It recovered, to about 3 million in 1862 and 4 million in 1900. The *colons* numbered 650,000 by 1900.

The French conquest initially provoked violent rebellions. The biggest, led by a Sufi scholar named **Abdelkadir**, took control of most of Algeria in the 1830s. But when the full force of the French military was brought to bear, Abdelkadir's uprising ended in his capture and exile in 1847. Another rebellion in 1871 lasted a few months, after which French rule remained secure, although punctuated by small-scale violence, until the 1950s.

Colons **and French Rule** With hundreds of thousands of *colons* living in the cities and on the best lands, French rule relied less on a cooperative indigenous elite than did British control in India. Nevertheless, cultivating cooperation was a useful imperial strategy everywhere, and the French worked hard at it. They claimed to be civilizing Algeria and encouraged Algerians to embrace French language and culture, and to accept Christianity. Those who did so could become French citizens. Many learned French, but only about 3,000 abandoned Islam to take this path.

Like every other imperial power, the French in Algeria followed the strategy of divide and rule. Dealing with an overwhelmingly Muslim population, the French exploited distinctions based on language between Arabic-speakers (about 75 percent) and Berber-speakers (25 percent). Berber is a language, or set of languages, long spoken in North Africa, but since the arrival of Arabs in the eighth century mainly confined to mountainous areas. The French also played up more local tribal identities among both Arabs and Berbers, and, like the British in India, recruited some groups reputed to be warlike—such as the highlanders known as Zwawa or Zouaves—for army and police duty. This strategy of divide and rule helped France to maintain control until 1962.

Economic Impact The economic impact of French imperialism in Algeria was considerable. The *colons* by and large did better than they could have hoped for had they stayed in Europe. A few Algerians who worked with the French also found rewarding niches in the new imperial economy. The majority of Algerians found little or no economic benefit in French rule, especially the peasants and herders who lost their land and the textile producers suddenly put in direct competition with power looms in French industrial cities. The size of Algeria's economy grew considerably under French rule, but the redistribution of land and wealth away from Muslim Algerians and toward *colons* was more conspicuous—and accounts for the vigor of Abdelkadir's resistance and Algerians' later efforts to overthrow colonial rule, discussed in Chapter 28.

Forms of Imperialism: Settler Colonies

Algeria and India exemplify an important contrast in modern imperialism: colonies with settlers and those without. Algeria was a **settler colony**. Its European population varied between 10 percent and 30 percent of the total. French policy put settler interests foremost, but not always fully to their satisfaction. The *colons* often wanted yet more land and more restrictions placed on Muslim Algerians. The authorities in Paris, and French officials in Algeria, did not always agree with the *colons*. The situation resembled that in British North America before the American Revolution, when colonists wanted to take more Amerindian land and officials in London did not fully cooperate. Settler colonies always featured conflicts over land, and consequently more violence, than those without settlers. In addition to Algeria, the best examples of settler colonies—after the independence of the Americas—include Australia, New Zealand, South Africa, and to a lesser extent Morocco, Kenya, and Southern Rhodesia (now Zimbabwe). Japan's colonial empire, discussed below, also featured partial settler colonies.

Australia, New Zealand, and Canada were settler colonies, but with a big difference. Unlike the situation in Africa or East Asia, in these lands the indigenous populations were, as we've seen, drastically reduced in numbers by disease and violence. They were driven off not just the best lands, but almost all productive lands, and in the nineteenth century they were swamped demographically by European settlers. With such a small proportion of indigenous people left in the population in these colonies, almost everyone, except the French in Quebec, traced their ancestry to Britain and had kinfolk there. These ties enabled Australia, New Zealand and Canada to negotiate more and more self-government and autonomy, beginning in the 1840s. Canada, as we saw earlier in this chapter, won substantial independence at Confederation in 1867. Australia achieved much the same in 1900, when several colonies united in what Australians call Federation. Both Canada and Australia became fully self-governing in 1931. New Zealand's transition from colony to nation had many little steps, spanning the period 1852–1947, and nothing comparable to Confederation or Federation. These were settler colonies that, in the heyday of imperialism, stopped being colonies—but only because their populations had become predominantly British and therefore were judged capable of self-rule by British authorities in London.

India, in contrast, attracted very few European settlers. Malaria and other dangerous diseases discouraged migration, and so did the absence of free land. Other destinations, especially North America, appealed more to potential migrants. The British presence in India, therefore, was mainly administrative and military. Almost no expropriation of land took place. During the period of industrial imperialism, roughly 1850–1960, the majority of colonies around the world were, like India, exploited economically but scarcely settled by colonizing populations.

After 1870, the European powers extended their imperial reach in Africa and Asia. Their motives included the hope they might grab territory with minerals or other resources useful to industry, the geopolitical ambition to seize colonies so as to deny them to their rivals, and the desire to spread what they regarded as the best culture and religion—their own—to other peoples. Colonization often happened quickly, without much knowledge about the peoples or lands in question, especially in Africa.

The Partition and Conquest of Africa, 1874–1914

In 1870, sub-Saharan Africa remained extremely diverse politically. Many people lived in kin groups without any state ruling them. Some lived in small statelets, others in full-blown states with kings, taxes, and armies. A few lived in small imperial states, such as the Zulu kingdom in South Africa. The only places not under African control were southernmost South Africa, British since 1815; the thinly administered Portuguese colonies of Angola and Mozambique; and a few small coastal outposts.

The Berlin Conference Between 1874 and 1890, six European powers carried out the **partition of Africa** among themselves. At first it was a haphazard process in which European states would unilaterally claim chunks of African territory, often merely to prevent a rival from seizing it. But in the years 1884–1885 at Bismarck's insistence, European diplomats gathered at the so-called Berlin Conference and agreed on who should get which territories. They also agreed to ban trading in slaves, guns, and alcohol in their territories. The first agreement held up better than the second.

Military Conquest and Cattle Disease

Once these six powers had carved up Africa on the map, they set about conquering it on the ground. For centuries African militaries, combined with a lethal disease environment, had kept outsiders at bay except in the far north and far south of the continent. From the 1870s, however, armies working for European states increasingly fared well in battle in Africa. Improved medicine and guns—and in the case of Britain, the availability of Indian troops—all helped to change the military balance. The bigger

Berlin Conference An 1885 French cartoon shows delegates to the Berlin Conference expressing surprise as the German chancellor, Otto von Bismarck, slices a cake—representing the cavalier way in which Bismarck proposed to carve up the continent of Africa among the European powers.

African states might win major battles now and again, as the Zulu kingdom (1879) and Ethiopia (1896) did, but the tide had turned very quickly in favor of Europe's armies. Those armies were led, trained, and equipped by Europeans. The rank-and-file soldiers were overwhelmingly Africans. So, in a sense, African soldiers in the service of European states conquered Africa. It took until about 1914.

As in the conquest of the Americas centuries before, European imperialists in late nineteenth-century Africa had an extraordinarily powerful ally in the form of disease—in this case, a cattle disease. Rinderpest broke loose in Asia in the 1860s and 1870s and arrived in East Africa from India in 1889. Over the next 12 to 15 years, in many regions it killed as much as 95 percent of the cattle and goats, sheep, and wildlife too. The plague extended from the savannas of East and southern Africa to the Sahel in West Africa. Cattle were the main form of wealth in these lands and a major source of food. Millions of Africans starved to death in the 1890s. In the pastoral and farming societies of East and southern Africa, men had to accumulate cattle before they could hope to marry. With rinderpest rippling throughout the continent, this became a forlorn hope. For some young men, serving as a soldier and helping to conquer Africa on behalf of colonial armies was the best remaining option.

The rinderpest plague stands among the greatest disasters in modern African history. It made European conquest much easier, as Lord Frederick Lugard, a leading British empire builder, recognized: "[Rinderpest] has favored our enterprise. Powerful and warlike as the pastoral tribes are, their pride has been humbled and our progress facilitated by this awful visitation." Indeed, one wonders: Would European societies have willingly paid the price in blood and treasure for colonization that African resistance—without rinderpest—would have exacted?

Even as rinderpest sapped the will and capacity of Africans to resist conquest, armed resistance and rebellions flickered on and off for two decades. In the West African Sahel, local rulers fought off French authority until 1898. In what is now Zimbabwe, armed resistance to British rule lasted until 1897. In German Southwest Africa (Namibia today) in the years 1904–1905, rebellion brought especially vicious responses—sometimes labeled genocide—almost obliterating a people called the Herero. As we will see, in Ethiopia, African armies succeeded in fending off colonialism. Elsewhere in Africa, however, by 1914, armed resistance had faded away, and opposition to colonialism took other forms.

Colonial Africa to 1930

These victorious powers set up cheap and flimsy colonial states in Africa. Governments in Europe did not wish to invest in infrastructure, education, or almost anything else for Africans. Neither did private businesses, except where mining was involved. So, until the late 1940s, African colonies did not get much in the way of roads or railroads, except lines connecting mines to ports. They got only rudimentary schools, generally run by missionaries. At times, colonial officials restricted the educational work of missionaries, fearing it would raise the hopes and skills of Africans so much that they would become harder to rule. The colonial court systems were also threadbare, with the administration of justice entrusted to favored African elders.

Imperial power in colonial Africa worked through local elites. The strategy was generally to find cooperative Africans and enhance their authority. This normally meant empowering male elders, making them responsible for organizing labor brigades, tax collection, and military conscription, and rewarding them when they did so. Machemba, the Yao leader in Tanganyika with whom this chapter began, refused just such an offer.

Colonial rule also relied on large lineage and language groups, labeled tribes. By assigning tribal identity to everyone, whether or not they considered themselves Xhosa, Masai, Hausa, and so forth, colonial administrators emphasized social divisions, making colonial rule easier. Such identities existed to some extent before colonial rule in Africa; but because they suited administrative needs, colonial rulers tried and generally succeeded in strengthening them. In particular, colonial authorities found it useful to recruit soldiers and police from among those groups they regarded as "martial tribes," such as Bambara-speakers in what is now Mali or Kamba in east-central Kenya. This recruitment policy encouraged some—males, at least—to prize their distinction from non-martial, lesser peoples.

Economic Exploitation The economic approach of the imperial powers, at least until the 1930s, was ruthlessly extractive. They intended to make money from mining or commercial agriculture. Each colony was to pay for its own administration and ideally contribute revenue to its colonizer. Monetized, taxable economic activity such as commercial farming helped attain this goal; subsistence farming or herding did not. In West Africa, colonial rulers encouraged cocoa, palm oil, peanuts, cotton, and other cash crops. In South Africa and the copper belt of central Africa, colonial authorities invited private companies to develop mining and offered to provide migrant workers for the mines by organizing labor recruitment drives. In South Africa, that sometimes required recruiting young men from hundreds of miles away, housing them in barracks, and policing them carefully.

In the Congo, where Belgium's King Leopold II claimed a personal fiefdom, economic extraction took a notoriously brutal form. Private companies paid the king for the right to harvest rubber from the forests, with no constraints on how they did it. They relied on forced labor and created a police force encouraged to kill men who refused to collect rubber. Sometimes they held women hostage until their husbands brought in enough rubber. In one case, 55 women were hanged because their husbands did not meet a production quota. The Belgian parliament considered the abuses sufficient to take control of the Congo away from the king in 1908.

Supporters of imperialism cloaked this economic exploitation in altruism. Confident in the righteousness of their religion and the superiority of their culture, colonial rulers convinced themselves and their publics back home that imperialism was good for Africans and Asians. Britain's Secretary of State for Colonies in 1897, Joseph Chamberlain (the former Birmingham industrialist we encountered earlier), gave voice to this conviction: "We now feel that our rule over these territories [British colonies in Africa and Asia] can only be justified if we can show that it adds to the happiness and prosperity of the people, and I maintain that our rule does." Chamberlain, and tens of millions of others in Europe, sincerely believed in the uplifting effect of colonial rule. A minority of Africans agreed.

Christianity in Africa Many Europeans counted Christianity as a blessing conferred by colonial rule. As we've seen, Christianity had ancient roots in Ethiopia and won many converts in Portuguese-influenced Angola after 1500. But elsewhere in Africa it figured little, if at all. In 1900, about 6 to 9 million Africans, of a total population of 80 to 90 million, considered themselves Christians. By 1930, missionary work and the spread of hundreds of independent African churches had boosted the Christian population to about 20 million. (Today, African Christians number about 400 million.)

By 1910, some 10,000 Christian missionaries—Catholics and at least 10 varieties of Protestants—were at work in Africa. Their most lasting impact came through mission schools, which appealed to many Africans who wanted to learn to read and write, and perhaps get a post in the colonial bureaucracy. Instruction in literacy came with instruction in Christianity. Slaves, women, poor men, refugees from wars, and the young were especially likely to embrace Christianity. In most African societies, young men had to prove themselves before they could hope to marry and take fully adult roles, while older and richer men could marry several women. Christian missionaries denounced polygamy and, through literacy, offered the hope of rapid advancement to younger men. For young women who preferred to marry someone of their own generation, it offered hope too. In some respects, the success of mission Christianity was a youth revolt against the authority of African male elders.

Many Africans joined independent churches outside of missionary control. Interactions with missionaries under colonialism inspired novel versions of Christianity. Some independent churches accepted polygamy, which mission churches never could. Some promised to counter the evils of witchcraft and sorcery, in which most Africans believed, whereas mission churches denied such malevolent powers existed. Some offered rewarding roles for women as spiritual leaders and faith healers. And all emphasized certain sides of the Christian tradition that spoke to millions of Africans, such as healing the sick. In some respects, the success of independent churches was a revolt against missionary control over Christianity and against colonialism in general. The most successful independent churches developed in Nigeria, South Africa, and the Belgian Congo.

The Aladura churches in Nigeria took shape during the 1918 influenza epidemic. A young Anglican schoolteacher, Sophie Odunlami, had a vision in which God told her that faith alone could heal the sick. She and others began to preach against traditional African religions, polygamy, and European medicine, claiming healing powers through God and blessed water. Within a decade, they gathered disciples and thousands of followers who set up churches.

In South Africa, the most popular independent churches were those called Zionist. They followed the teachings of faith healers from Zion, Illinois (a northern suburb of Chicago), notably John Lake. Lake moved to South Africa in 1908 to escape the wrath of parishioners after an attempted exorcism left two dead. His preaching skills brought him followers who quickly organized several Zionist churches. Migrant workers in

Missionaries in Africa
A German nun teaches reading and writing to children enrolled at a mission school in South Africa in this 1912 photo. Mission schools were one of the most visible presences of Christianity—and of European power and cultural influence—in colonial Africa.

South Africa's mines carried African Zionist faith and practices back to their home villages all over southern Africa.

The most enduring of the independent African churches arose in the Belgian Congo. **Simon Kimbangu**, raised at a Baptist mission in western Congo, felt called as a prophet in 1921, and followers credited him with many healing miracles at a time when epidemics were ravaging central Africa. His popular preaching quickly aroused suspicions among Belgian authorities, who imprisoned him for the last 30 years of his life. But disciples spread his message of faith healing, non-violence, monogamy, and sobriety—and added the notions of Kimbangu's divinity and the injustice of Belgian rule. By the end of the colonial era in 1960, half a million people had embraced Kimbanguism (as do roughly 20 million today). Independent churches—the Africanization of Christianity in the context of the partial Christianization of Africa—constituted the most important and enduring cultural response to colonialism in Africa.

Islam in Africa Islam, like Christianity, prospered as a result of colonial rule. As we've seen, Islam also had deep roots in the northern half of Africa. Colonial rulers often found prestigious Muslim clerics useful in their efforts to control subject populations. French authorities in Senegal supported Malik Sy, who in 1902 set up a *zawiya* (as Islamic schools are called in West Africa) and urged his fellow Muslims to accept French rule and to serve in the French army. Colonial rule inadvertently promoted Islam. Village families often could not pay taxes demanded by colonial authorities and sent their young men to towns, mines, or plantations where they could earn a wage. In these new and unfamiliar settings, Islamic brotherhoods often offered these youths community and hospitality. Muslim clerics in West Africa who needed workers for their peanut farms employed many such young men, who often became disciples as well as laborers. They brought back Islamic practices with them when they returned to their native villages. In these ways, colonial rulers, although intending nothing of the sort, expanded the domain of Islam especially in West Africa.

Colonial rule changed African religious life as much or more than it did African economic life. While Africans had long been receptive to innovation in spiritual matters, now they had a wider range of examples to choose from. Selective borrowing led to great creativity and novelty, as well as to the spread of established forms of both Christianity and Islam.

European Imperialism in Southeast Asia and the Pacific

Europe's imperial powers fastened colonial rule on Southeast Asia and the Pacific Islands at the same time that they partitioned Africa. The Dutch East India Company (VOC) had dominated island Southeast Asia since the sixteenth century. The trading company went bankrupt by 1800. The Dutch monarchy then stepped in and tried to tighten its grip on the archipelago (now Indonesia). That required repeated warfare from the 1820s to 1910, by which time all local Indonesian (the term came into use in the 1880s) rulers had submitted to the Dutch. Export trade in spices and plantation crops formed the basis of the Dutch colonial economy. Meanwhile, in 1819 the British founded Singapore, a port at the southern tip of the Malay Peninsula. They gradually took over large parts of Malaya, which had the world's best tin deposits and was well suited to rubber tree plantations—both tin and rubber were important to British industrial production. Islam had been the majority religion in these lands since the sixteenth century; neither the Dutch nor the British tried hard to convert Indonesians or Malays to Christianity.

The French conquered much of mainland Southeast Asia starting in 1858. Initially intending only to protect French Catholic missionaries from persecution by Vietnam's Nguyễn dynasty, French armies, with gunboats and industrial weaponry, soon claimed the kingdoms of Vietnam, Cambodia, and Laos—all formerly in the orbit of China. Vietnam became a principal rice exporter and eventually home to rubber plantations too. Many of its elite families, who had long served Vietnamese monarchs, nimbly pivoted to work with French authorities. Few French migrated to Southeast Asia; in 1913 in Vietnam, the French were outnumbered about 700:1 by locals.

Most Vietnamese were Buddhists. The Catholic Church, which had been present for 200 years and the spiritual home of perhaps 3 to 5 percent of Vietnamese, proved a valuable ally: most Vietnamese Catholics welcomed French rule. France rewarded them, and the Church, with land grants and other favors. In mainland Southeast Asia, only Thailand (or Siam, as it was then) remained outside of European empires. Its kings carefully played off the French against the British and preserved a precarious independence.

In the Pacific, the French, Germans, and British claimed several archipelagoes in the late nineteenth century. Islanders could not resist effectively. Their populations were too small and, in most cases, falling fast due to introduced infections. Their stone and wood weapons, supplemented by a few imported muskets, were no match for what European navies could bring to bear. So European rule came swiftly. France used New Caledonia as a dumping ground for convicts and political prisoners after 1864. British Fiji and German Samoa became plantation islands. None of these islands mattered economically to their colonizers. But in an age when navies needed coal to power their warships, Pacific ports carried strategic value as **coaling stations**. Whatever their value, the cost of controlling Pacific islands was so low by European standards that using them to park coal or grow coconuts was reason enough to keep them. Missionaries met greater success here winning converts to Christianity than they had in Southeast Asia, partly because there was no Islam to contend with.

Imperial Latecomers: Italy, Japan, and the United States

Italy, unified only in the 1860s, was a latecomer to overseas imperialism. By the 1880s, boatloads of poor Italians migrated every year to the United States, Brazil, or Argentina. Italian nationalists hoped to build an empire of settlement in Africa, where Italian emigrants could contribute to Italy's strength. Ambitious statesmen found it irresistible to bring up the Roman Empire as an example to follow, and to exhort Italians to greatness through conquest. Italy first tried to get hold of Tunisia in North Africa but lost out to France. It did manage to obtain part of Somalia in the 1880s.

But that hardly signaled greatness worthy of descendants of the Caesars. Taking advantage of drought, rinderpest, and a resulting famine that killed about half of Ethiopia's 7 million people (1888–1892), Italy launched an invasion of Ethiopia in 1896. At the Battle of Adowa, Ethiopian armies killed or captured three-quarters of the Italian force, securing Ethiopia's independence for the next 40 years. Italy managed to take Libya from the Ottoman Empire in 1912 with the help of the first aerial bombing campaigns in world history. Italy's empire was small, thinly populated, of little economic value, and controversial within Italy.

Japan and the United States were also latecomers to overseas empire. Both had some background in territorial expansion. Japan in the eighteenth and nineteenth centuries had conquered and settled the northern island of Hokkaido, at the expense of the indigenous Ainu people. The United States from its inception had expanded westward across the continent, at the expense of Amerindians. Both had become industrial powers with modern weaponry, increasingly nationalistic populations, and vocal lobbies eager for imperial ventures. In the 1890s, both became seaborne empires, although on far smaller scales than Britain or France, exploiting the regional military superiority they enjoyed by industrializing earlier than their neighbors.

Japanese imperialists began calling for expansion in the mid-1870s, believing that to fend off foreign imperialists Japan had to become imperialist itself. Their opportunity came when Japan defeated China in war in the years 1894–1895, took over Taiwan, and began to play a larger role in Korea. Japan's expansion brought on the 1904–1905

Russo-Japanese War
A Japanese illustration celebrates a military victory by Japanese troops against Russian opponents in 1904. Winning the Russo-Japanese War enabled Japan to consolidate its presence as an empire in the Pacific.

Russo-Japanese War, which ended with the Russian navy at the bottom of the sea. When Japan fully annexed Korea in 1910, it ruled a seaborne empire with a population only somewhat smaller than that of the home islands.

Japan's government encouraged emigration to its colonies. Taiwan, under Japanese rule until 1945, was partly a settler colony: some 5 to 10 percent of the total population was Japanese. Only a few hundred thousand Japanese moved to Korea, accounting for roughly 1 percent of the peninsula's population. But Japanese settlers took over half the farmland by the 1930s and obliged Korean farmers to work as tenants, giving Korea a key feature of settler colonies. Japan also resorted freely to deadly military force to suppress political resistance in Korea, especially in the years 1919–1920.

The United States became an overseas imperialist power in 1898. Ever since the Monroe Doctrine in 1823, the United States had tried to discourage European imperial powers from extending their sway in the hemisphere. In 1898, it intervened in a Cuban nationalist rebellion against Spain, which expanded into the Spanish-American War. Victorious, the United States took over Spain's colonies in the Philippines, Puerto Rico, Guam, and—briefly—Cuba, meanwhile annexing the Hawaiian Islands, partly to secure the ocean route to the Philippines. The newly acquired territories and populations were small compared to the continental United States and, in the Philippines, where a nationalist guerrilla resistance lasted until 1903, cost considerable blood and treasure to keep. Suppressing the Filipino insurrection cost the U.S. army 10 times as many lives as did the Spanish-American War. Overseas imperialism delivered no conspicuous advantages to the United States except naval outposts, and as in Italy it was controversial domestically. The new overseas empire thrust the United States into world affairs as never before.

Land Empires

It is customary to use the word *imperialism* in modern history for empires that stretched overseas, but empires existed on land as well. One could use the term *empire* for nineteenth-century Canada, the United States, Brazil, and Argentina: they were all new countries, and they used industrial technologies and nationalist ideologies to support westward extension of their rule over Amerindian peoples. Indeed, even an Amerindian people, the Comanche, used rifles, an industrial technology, to help build a **land empire** in North America. In Africa, Ethiopians used modern firearms, combined with a growing sense of nationalism, to create a land empire of their own. The biggest land empire was Russia's.

Russia: The World's Biggest Land Empire

Through war or diplomacy in the eighteenth century, Russia had already acquired what are now called the Baltic States—Estonia, Latvia, Lithuania—as well as Crimea, parts

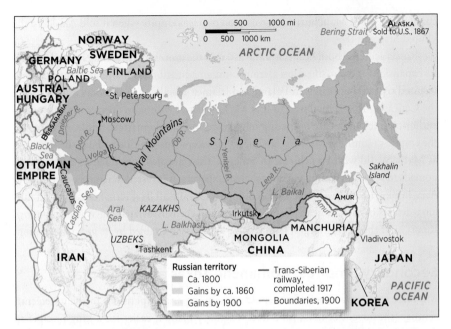

Russia's Land Empire, 1800–1900 Russia had built an empire in thinly populated Siberia beginning in the sixteenth century. During the nineteenth century, it began to use the tools of industrial imperialism to expand into the Caucasus region and Central Asia at the expense mainly of Islamic khanates. This brought millions of Muslim subjects into the Russian Empire. As the Trans-Siberian Railway progressed eastward, Russia was also able to tighten its hold on southern Siberia and eventually the Pacific coast, which in the years 1904–1905 brought conflict with Japan.

of Poland, and Ukraine. In 1809, it acquired Finland in a peace treaty. Emerging victorious in war against Napoleon Bonaparte, Russia accelerated its territorial expansion. Between 1812 and 1864, it conquered territories in the Caucasus—the region between the Black Sea and Caspian Sea—populated by diverse ethnic groups such as Georgians, Armenians, Circassians, and Chechens. In the Baltics, Poland, and the Caucasus, the Russian state tried hard to spread Russian language, culture, and the Russian Orthodox religion—policies called Russification. It banned the use of Polish, for example, in schools and offices, and converted some Catholic churches into Russian Orthodox ones. Growing Russian nationalism spurred the belief, in elite circles, that it was Russia's destiny to rule over lesser peoples on its periphery.

Between 1860 and 1885, the tsar's armies also conquered vast swathes of steppe and desert in Central Asia. Like other imperialists, they exploited advantages conferred by modern rifles, telegraph systems, and a growing railroad network. Dotted by oases, the region was inhabited by Muslim and mainly Turkic-speaking groups such as Uzbeks and Kazakhs. Russia also tightened its grip on Siberia with the construction of the Trans-Siberian Railway beginning in the 1890s and added territories along the Pacific coast northeast of Manchuria. It gave up on overseas empire when it sold Alaska to the United States in 1867.

Russia acquired both headaches and assets in the process of extending its land empire. Its expansion, and Russification attempts, inflamed nationalism among minorities and inspired repeated uprisings in Poland and Islamist rebellions in the Caucasus. Outside the Caucasus, Russia managed to find Muslim clerics willing to operate under Russian authority. They took care of meting out justice and family matters, while encouraging the empire's 14 million Muslims (as of 1897) to accept Russian rule and pay their taxes—as Malik Sy did with French rule in Senegal. The state also continued its efforts to get nomads to settle down and become reliable taxpayers. It invested in irrigation in Central Asia, hoping to create a viable cotton industry. Despite all its internal tensions and military defeats in the Crimean War (1853–1856) and the Russo-Japanese War (1904–1905), Russia built the world's largest land empire—after 1880 enabled by its industrialization.

Secondary Empires: Comanche Texas and Ethiopia

Any state with weaker neighbors could take up imperial expansion. In the nineteenth century, the advent of mass-produced weaponry made it easier for a king or chief to monopolize military power in his neighborhood and use it to build a regional empire. The phenomenon is sometimes known as secondary empire, because a key source of power undergirding this imperialism was not internal, but acquired from abroad—usually from armaments factories in Europe or the United States.

Comanche Texas, 1730–1870   Between 1730 and 1850, a Comanche empire flourished on what is now the southern plains of the United States—roughly central and west Texas, plus bits of Oklahoma, Kansas, Colorado, and New Mexico. The Comanche, one of many Amerindian peoples called Plains Indians, based their political power on access to horses and guns. They were recent migrants to the plains, having arrived in the seventeenth century from what is now Utah and western Colorado at more or less the same time that horses galloped onto the scene. Horses had revolutionized North American plains life starting around 1680. Spanish traders introduced horses via New Mexico, and the Comanche quickly mastered the arts of riding and raising horses. With the mobility that horses gave them, the Comanche became more efficient bison hunters—and more effective fighters against their neighbors.

The Comanche numbered about 40,000 people in 1780, with herds of about 300,000 horses. Smallpox in the period 1779–1782 halved their number, but they rebounded quickly by capturing women and children from neighboring Amerindian peoples and assimilating them into Comanche society. Although few in number by the standards of imperial peoples, the Comanche were lords of the vast grassland of the southern plains.

The **Comanche Empire**'s political success rested on guns as well as horses. Spanish authorities in Mexico prohibited the trade of guns northward to Amerindian peoples, but the French based in Louisiana did not; nor did the Americans who bought Louisiana from France in 1803. The Comanche secured a near-monopoly position in the gun trade on the southern plains, allowing them to exert military power unmatched in their neighborhood. They seized captives from the agricultural peoples in New Mexico. After 1820, when Mexico was becoming independent from Spain, the Comanche raided deep into Mexico, taking horses, mules, and women and children to keep or sell as slaves.

Successful raiding over broad territories enabled the Comanche to trade profitably. They sold people, horses, and mules from Mexico to Amerindians of the central plains (today's Kansas and Nebraska) or to white Americans in the Louisiana Territory. The Comanche traders came to know which markets preferred which kinds of horses and who would pay the most for captives. They exploited their mobility to acquire broader market knowledge and prospered as a result.

They occasionally captured white children and raised them as Comanche. In 1836 in east Texas, Comanche raiders seized 10-year-old Cynthia Ann Parker, who gradually became Comanche. She married Peta Nocona,

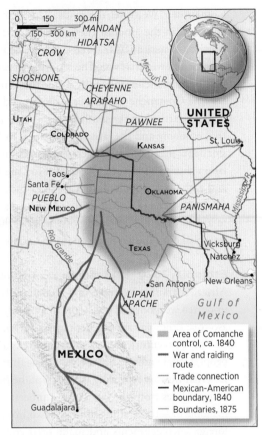

The Comanche Empire, ca. 1800–1850 After 1780, horses and guns gave the Comanche advantages over their neighbors. They mounted raids deep into Mexico, especially during the period 1820–1845, and maintained long-distance trade with several other Amerindian peoples and with white Americans along the Mississippi River. The Comanche way of life ended between 1850 and 1875, defeated by U.S. forces and repeated epidemics.

leader of the Nokoni band and one of the most successful of Comanche war captains in the 1850s. Among their children was the last independent Comanche leader, Quanah Parker.

Comanche economic and military strength peaked around 1840. They demanded tribute and attacked anyone who did not pay. Most people gave the Comanche what they wanted most of the time. By 1840, 10 to 25 percent of Comanche people had been kidnapped from Mexico and assimilated as adopted children, wives, or slaves. In 1846, the Mexican authorities in the northern state of Chihuahua complained of the

Comanche: "We travel the roads...at their whim; we cultivate the land where they wish and in the amount they wish." Comanche attacks in the years preceding the Mexican-American War (1846–1848) made it easier for U.S. forces to drive deep into Mexico and win that war. The resulting treaty cost Mexico nearly half its territory and put the Comanche lands fully inside the United States—a great misfortune for them.

The Comanche Empire came to an end for several reasons, the most important being the arrival on the southern plains after 1848 of the U.S. army backed by an industrial economy and the largest population in North America. Suffering from repeated smallpox, measles, and cholera epidemics and military defeats, the Comanche population slipped to about 20,000 by 1850. The Comanche struggled against U.S. forces and emboldened Amerindian enemies such as the Osage. After the U.S. Civil War (1861–1865), the U.S. army, battle hardened and well supplied, reduced the Comanche to a shadow of their former glory. In 1875, the last of the remaining 3,000 Comanche straggled onto Indian reservations in Oklahoma, led by Quanah Parker.

Ethiopia, 1870–1913 Ethiopia, a land of mountains and deserts in northeastern Africa, is another example of a secondary land empire built on monopoly access to imported weaponry. It was home to a mainly Christian population with a literate elite aware of Ethiopia's ancient heritage as the land of Aksum, an empire of the fourth century CE. For centuries before 1850, however, Ethiopia had been disunited, and its various peoples fought among themselves and against Muslim sultanates in neighboring lands. External threats, especially from Egypt, helped Ethiopians unite across linguistic and cultural lines from the late 1850s, a process begun by a warlord who united much of Ethiopia by force. Calling himself Tewodros II, he and his successors sought to prevent foreign encroachments and make their country more formidable—much as Japan's leaders were doing after the Meiji Restoration. The surest route, in Ethiopia as in Japan, was judicious borrowing of techniques and technologies of power from elsewhere. In the 1870s, a successor of Tewodros managed to get large quantities of modern British weapons, which he used to subdue all rivals within Ethiopia, fend off an Egyptian attack, and assault his nearest neighbors. Ethiopia was becoming an empire.

The master empire builder of Ethiopia was **Menelik II**. He took the throne in 1889 when the reigning emperor was killed in battle. Menelik claimed descent from King Solomon and the Queen of Sheba (of Old Testament fame) and maintained he was the rightful heir of the ancient emperors of Aksum. Through diplomacy and force, he increasingly brought the various peoples in and around Ethiopia (Amharic- and Oromo-speakers were the biggest groups) into a single imperial state. Aware of the partition of Africa under way in the late 1880s, he was determined to keep newly enlarged Ethiopia under Ethiopian—and his—rule.

Menelik adapted foreign techniques and technologies that bolstered his own power. In the early 1890s, as rinderpest was ravaging the pastoral societies in and around Ethiopia—Menelik himself lost 250,000 head of cattle—he forged a friendship with a Russian cavalry officer sent by the tsar to build a Russian-Ethiopian bond. Nikolai Leontiev brought advisors and weapons for Menelik's army, including 30,000 modern rifles and a few dozen artillery pieces. Menelik's army even acquired a few machine guns. With this armament, Menelik's forces sliced to ribbons the Italian army of 18,000 men at Adowa in 1896.

Menelik continued to exploit his access to foreign weaponry and skills after scattering the Italians. He campaigned against any neighbor bold enough to resist his armies, which now numbered a few hundred thousand men. His conquests to the south and east doubled the size of Ethiopia and left longstanding memories of atrocities and enslavement. Menelik was grateful enough to his Russian friend that he created a new titled rank in Ethiopia and made Leontiev a count.

While in some respects an old-fashioned conqueror, Menelik II was also a relentless modernizer. Starting in 1894, he worked to bring Ethiopia its first railroad line. He introduced electricity and a telegraph and tele-

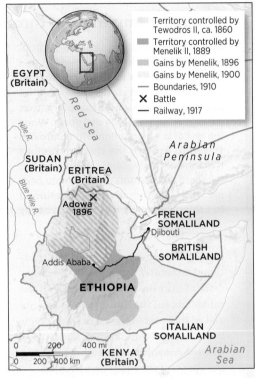

The Expansion of Ethiopia, 1850–1910 Access to modern weaponry underpinned the imperial expansion of Ethiopia in the late nineteenth century, achieved at the expense of neighboring Muslim peoples. Under Menelik II, the Ethiopian military destroyed an Italian army of invasion in 1896, one of the few resounding defeats delivered to European imperial armies during this period.

phone system. In addition to foreign technologies, Menelik borrowed foreign institutions that he thought would make Ethiopia stronger. He started public schools, a postal service, and a formal bureaucracy including a judiciary using the principle of jury trials.

By the time of Menelik's death in 1913, Ethiopia stood alone as a fully independent polity in Africa. He had ruled for a quarter-century over an empire the size of Texas, made possible by the judicious introduction of foreign technologies and skills.

Other Secondary Empires

Secondary empires of the sort built in Ethiopia and Texas were many but fleeting. The Maori leader Hongi Hika in New Zealand studied European military and agricultural methods before importing guns and potatoes to New Zealand's North Island in 1818.

CONSIDERING THE EVIDENCE

Ethiopian Imperialism through Russian Eyes

Alexander Bulatovich first arrived in Ethiopia in 1896, as part of the Russian Red Cross. The medical mission was charged with offering aid during the conflict between Italians and Ethiopians that culminated in the Battle of Adowa. When the rest of the delegation left, Bulatovich stayed to explore the western regions that Ethiopia had recently conquered and to record the customs of the Oromo people who lived there. When he returned to Ethiopia again the following year as part of Russia's diplomatic delegation, he joined several thousand Ethiopian soldiers on a military expedition to claim territory between the Nile River and the Red Sea. Emperor Menelik had claimed this region to preempt British and French claims, but it was much farther than Ethiopia had previously extended its reach. In Bulatovich's journal of the expedition, published in 1900, he wrote the following introduction to justify Ethiopia's conquests.

Menelik is only carrying out the traditional mission of Ethiopia as the propagator of culture and the unifier of all the inhabitants of the Ethiopian Mountains and of the related tribes in their neighborhood, and only makes a new step toward consolidating and developing the power of the black empire....

[W]e Russians cannot help sympathizing with his intentions, not only because of political considerations, but also for purely human reasons. It is well known to what consequences conquests of wild tribes by Europeans lead. Too great a difference in the degree of culture between the conquered people and their conquerors has always led to the enslavement, corruption, and degeneration of the weaker race. The natives of America degenerated and have almost ceased to exist. The natives of India were corrupted and deprived of

He used the guns to defeat rivals who had none, capturing slaves whom he put to work raising potatoes for his armies. For a decade, he ruled a secondary empire. On a larger scale, the Albanian Mehmet Ali created a secondary empire in Egypt, wresting it from Ottoman control in the early nineteenth century and using European weaponry and military technique to extend Egyptian power south into Sudan.

Secondary empires of a sort had existed long before the nineteenth century, but with industrialization they became easier to create. The gap in formidability between those with modern guns and those without was huge, and modern guns came from only a few places. The Global web enabled transfers of guns and relevant military skills from Britain and Russia to Ethiopia or from French Louisiana and the United States to Comanche Texas. But the world was not yet so well connected that everybody in and around Ethiopia and Texas had similar access to the tools of power. So ambitious, individuality. The black tribes of Africa became the slaves of the whites.

Clashes between nations more or less close to one another in culture bring completely different results.

For the Abyssinians [Ethiopians], the Egyptian, Arab, and, finally, European civilization which they have gradually adopted has not been pernicious: borrowing the fruits of these civilizations, and in turn conquering and annexing neighboring tribes and passing on to them her culture, Abyssinia [Ethiopia] did not obliterate from the face of the earth, did not destroy the uniqueness of any one of the conquered tribes, but rather gave them all the possibility of preserving their individual characteristics.

Thus Christian Abyssinia [Ethiopia] plays an important role in world progress as a transmission point of European civilization to wild central African peoples.

The high civilizing mission of Abyssinia [Ethiopia], its centuries-old, almost uninterrupted struggle for faith and freedom against the surrounding Moslems [Muslims], the nearness of her people to the Russian people in creed, won for her the favor of the Russian people.

Questions for Analysis

1. What "political considerations" and "human reasons" motivated the Russians to support Ethiopia's imperial expansion?

2. Why does Bulatovich think Ethiopians are better than Europeans at transmitting "European civilization" to Africans?

3. How does Bulatovich's description of Ethiopia's "role in world progress" reveal European stereotypes about Africa?

Source: Alexander Bulatovich, *Ethiopia through Russian Eyes: Country in Transition*, trans. Richard Seltzer (Lawrenceville, NJ, 2000). Published in print by Red Sea Press.

skilled, and lucky warlords could monopolize that access in their own neighborhoods and build secondary empires—at least for a while. Most secondary empires vanished within years or decades, destroyed by their neighbors, by internal rifts, or swallowed up by larger empires.

Nationalism, Imperialism, and the Global Web

Nationalism and imperialism further tightened the Global web. Nationalism, often sparked by conflict, was infectious and spread along the circuits of the Global web. Its emergence thickened the web—for example, by inspiring people in Japan to pay more attention to military practices in Germany.

Imperialism, for its part, contributed to the more rapid exchange of goods, and the extension of market relations, into places such as central Africa or Samoa, where they had been weak. It helped spread versions of Christianity in colonized lands. And in parts of Africa and Southeast Asia, it—unintentionally—helped extend the realm of Islam, the religion that appealed most to people who opposed European empire. Most conspicuously, imperialism brought political consolidation. Its forces crushed hundreds of smaller polities around the world, replacing them with a few empires. Imperialism and nationalism made the world a smaller, more tightly interactive, place.

While nationalism and imperialism brought the world into tighter interaction, they also deepened the differences among peoples in two respects. The first was economic status. The imperial powers, already growing rich through industrialization, enriched themselves further through the economic policies of imperialism—although by just how much is controversial among scholars.

Second, imperialism and nationalism emphasized differences among peoples and religions. As ideologies, nationalism sometimes and imperialism always supported racialist outlooks that divided humankind into several "races" arranged in hierarchies based on either skin color or ethnicity. In racial hierarchies, whites deemed darker-skinned people to be inherently inferior. Imperial strategy fostered division to make subject populations easier to rule, underscoring distinctions, perhaps inventing them. Nationalism had contradictory effects: nationalists invited people to bury their class or religious differences and to prize solidarity as a Japanese, Canadian, or Italian nation; but at the same time, they divided humankind into hundreds of nationalities and often claimed these were biological categories and unchangeable. With respect to religion, both nationalism and imperialism showed contradictory effects: while helping to spread Christianity and Islam, they also helped to splinter both religions. Christianity in Nigeria or Vietnam took on local flavoring. Local religion and culture colored Islam too, as it spread in West Africa or Indonesia under European imperial rule. So nationalism and imperialism bound the world more tightly into a global web; but at the same time, they both emphasized differences within the human species.

Conclusion

The ideas and practices of both nationalism and imperialism reshaped the world between 1800 and 1930. Nationalism took root first in revolutionary France but spread easily to other lands. It helped to forge nation-states and to weaken multiethnic empires. Together with industrialization, it combined to make some countries, such as Britain, France, Germany, Japan, and the United States, much stronger. They used that strength to expand, or to create, overseas empires at the expense of less powerful societies in Africa, Asia, and the Pacific.

Sometimes imperialism took the form of settler colonies in which migrants from Europe or Japan put down roots in conquered lands, as in Algeria or Taiwan. But more often settlers were few and colonial rule more narrowly focused on economic extraction and religious conversion. The empires of the nineteenth and early twentieth centuries often had profound economic and cultural effects. Among the unintended effects was the emergence of many new examples of nationalism among the colonized peoples. Their political ambitions, as later chapters will explain, made imperialism too costly to sustain.

Chapter Review

KEY TERMS

nationalism p. 917

La Marseillaise p. 918

Yamato race theory p. 920

multiethnic empires p. 925

new imperialism p. 928

culture of imperialism p. 932

social Darwinism p. 933

British Raj p. 936

Abdelkadir p. 938

settler colony p. 939

partition of Africa p. 940

Simon Kimbangu p. 945

coaling stations p. 946

land empire p. 948

Comanche Empire p. 950

Menelik II p. 952

REVIEW QUESTIONS

1. Identify the circumstances that contributed to the rise of nationalism, and explain the difference between ethnic nationalism and civic nationalism.

2. Compare and contrast the emphases of French, Japanese, Canadian, and German nationalisms.

3. In what ways did nationalism confer power upon states?

4. How did nationalism contribute to the weakening of the Habsburg, Russian, and Ottoman empires?

5. What were the key reasons that imperialism after 1870 was so pervasive and different from the empire building that came before?

6. Name the industrial technologies that contributed to the rise of the new imperialism, and describe their contributions.

7. On what three trends did Europe, the United States, and Japan base their cultures of imperialism?

8. Identify the similarities between British control in India and French rule in Algeria, and explain the main difference between the two.

9. What was the main difference between settler colonialism in Australia, Canada, and New Zealand and that in Africa and East Asia?

10. How did rinderpest facilitate the European conquest of Africa?

11. In what ways did colonial rule in Africa rely on local elites and the assignment of tribal identities?

12. To whom did missionary Christianity appeal in Africa, and why?

13. What products formed the basis of the Dutch, British, and French colonial economies in Southeast Asia?

14. Discuss the main reasons for Italian, Japanese, and U.S. late imperial expansion.

15. On what techniques and technologies did the political success of the Comanche and Ethiopian empires depend?

16. In what significant ways did nationalism and imperialism tighten global connections, and in what ways did they deepen global divisions?

Go to INQUIZITIVE

to see what you've learned—and learn what you've missed—with personalized feedback along the way.

25

Making the Modern World

CONFRONTING INDUSTRIALIZATION, NATIONALISM, AND IMPERIALISM

1850 to 1920

FOCUS QUESTIONS

1. How were millenarian movements responses to the pressures of state power?
2. How did the Taiping and Indian rebellions reflect the impact of global connections?
3. What mix of global and local forces fueled the Chinese and Mexican revolutions?

In April 1856 a teenage girl named Nongqawuse, of the Xhosa people in South Africa, was on duty chasing birds from maize fields down by the Gxarha River. As she explained it, she saw two strangers who instructed her to tell her people they must kill all their cattle and destroy all their crops. The cattle and crops were impure, the strangers said, having been raised by the Xhosa people, who practiced witchcraft. She also heard them say that if the Xhosa did this, new cattle would spring up from the Earth, fresh maize would burst forth, and the ancestors of the Xhosa would return from the dead. Joy and justice would prevail in the land.

959

CHRONOLOGY

1813 British state strips East India Company of its trade monopoly

1821 Mexico wins independence from Spain

1839–1842 First Opium War

1842 Treaty of Nanjing

1848 Mexico loses territory to the United States

1850–1864 Taiping Rebellion

1856–1860 Second Opium War

1857–1858 Indian Rebellion

1869–1870 Development of Ghost Dance among northern Nevada Paiute

1876–1910 Porfiriato

1877–1878 Drought in Brazil; famine in China

1879 Japan takes Ryukyu Islands

1885 French seize Vietnam

1887 Dawes Act opens Amerindian land to white settlers

1889 Wovoka has first prophetic vision; Brazil becomes a republic

1890 Massacre of Wounded Knee

1894–1895 Sino-Japanese War

1897 Brazilian army defeats Canudos rebellion

1899–1900 Boxer Rebellion in northern China

1899–1902 Boer War in South Africa

1905 Revolution of 1905 in Russia

1905–1911 Revolution in Iran

It was a difficult time for the Xhosa. They were engaged in frequent wars with their neighbors, including the British-run Cape Colony, which was swelling daily with new settlers from Britain. The Xhosa leader, Sarhili, a man of considerable diplomatic talents and now at the height of his powers, was hard-pressed to maintain Xhosa independence. To make matters worse, a terrible cattle plague had struck—a disaster for a cattle-keeping people like the Xhosa. Many of them were desperate for relief and eager for good news.

At first no one believed Nongqawuse, even though for the Xhosa it was not unusual for spirits to appear from time to time and offer prophecies. Young girls' words did not count for much in Xhosaland. But she told her uncle, Mhlakaza, who went with her to meet the strangers and heard their message for himself. Mhlakaza had once worked for an Anglican archdeacon, and he embraced Anglican ideas of redemption and resurrection. Now he convinced King Sarhili to visit the Gxarha. The king heard the voices, accepted the prophecy, and arranged for the slaughter of his vast herds of cattle. He instructed his followers, some of whom had also gone to hear the strangers' voices, to do the same. Most of them did so, and then keenly awaited the day when the new cattle would come and their ancestors would arise.

Over the next two years, the Xhosa killed about 400,000 of their cattle. They dug up their maize crop. And then they starved. No replacement cattle came, no new maize sprouted, and the ancestors did not return to help them oust their enemies. The Xhosa population fell from about 105,000 to 27,000. They lost much of their land too. The Cape Colony's governor, the brilliant and ruthless Sir George Grey, urged British settlers to help themselves to Xhosa land, spelling the end of Xhosa independence. After 1858, they were a subject people in British South Africa.

The Xhosa were one of many peoples in the nineteenth century struggling to make sense of a confusing world. For many, as for the Xhosa, the extraordinary power of modern imperialism cost them land and liberty. For others, the newly unleashed force of nationalism upset their lives, making them feel like foreigners in their own

1908 Cixi and Guangxu die; Young Turk Revolution

1910–1911 Chinese Revolution

1913 Yuan Shikai forces Sun Yatsen into exile

land. For still others, the overnight economic changes brought on by industrialization and new competition turned their worlds upside down and dimmed their future prospects.

All these forces, and others too, worked together to confuse, irritate, and arouse millions of people around the world. Old truths came into question. Old ways no longer worked. Young people tuned out the old, seeking new opportunities and new forms of truth. The disruption, disorientation, and dissatisfaction drove many of the millions to seek spiritual solutions, like the Xhosa. Others took up arms. Some did both at once. Some wished to embrace nationalism and industrialization—in short, to compete with the imperial powers at their own game. Others rejected such a course, hoping instead to strengthen their communities without imitating foreign ways. The growing power of industrial societies made these choices increasingly urgent after 1850.

This chapter explores several responses to the pressures people came to feel during the nineteenth century. First, we'll consider a pair of small-scale **millenarian movements**—religious movements in which people expect spiritual or divine intervention to bring about a better world. We'll see how some Amerindians in the United States tried to cope with their problems by calling for spiritual aid through the Ghost Dance. Then we'll move to Brazil, to the town of Canudos, where destitute people tried to set up their own new community according to Catholic principles as they understood them. These were religious responses with political meanings, involving tens of thousands of people.

Next we'll turn to a pair of giant rebellions that involved tens of millions of people. The Taiping Rebellion (1850–1864), also a millenarian movement in some respects, shook Qing China to its foundations, a cataclysm from which the dynasty never recovered. The Indian Rebellion (1857–1858) destroyed both the Mughal Empire and the East India Company, brought more direct British rule over more of the subcontinent, and stimulated the first stirrings of Indian nationalism.

Finally, we'll look at a pair of revolutions that occurred between 1910 and 1920, one in China and the other in Mexico. Both of these succeeded in overthrowing a ruling elite in the name of liberty and justice, and of creating nations strong enough to resist foreign encroachments.

Millenarian movements, rebellions, and revolutions happen from time to time. This book has touched on several already. But they came thicker and faster in the late nineteenth and early twentieth centuries, because the pace and prevalence of change was so great, and because the changes so unsettled populations across the globe. These three pairs of millenarian movements, rebellions, and revolutions represent a sampling of ways in which peoples confronted, and participated in, the disruptive changes of the period from 1850 to 1920.

Millenarian Visions: The Ghost Dance and Canudos

Among the many responses to the pressures of imperialism and intrusive state power were efforts to enlist spiritual forces against unwelcome change. These efforts took many forms, but a common one was millenarian movements.

The Ghost Dance in the North American West

The nineteenth century brought hard and bewildering times to the Amerindian peoples of North America. They were defeated in wars by the U.S. Army and decimated by disease. In the first half of the century, native peoples of the eastern United States were pushed westward or confined to small reservations.

After 1850, those of the western part of the country met similar fates. On their home ground in the Great Plains, Rocky Mountains, and the Great Basin, Amerindians had to deal with vast disruptions to their ways of life. Fur traders offered access to novel goods such as guns and hard liquor. Epidemics raged as never before. Hunters—including many who were Amerindians themselves—obliterated the once vast bison herds in order to sell hides, leaving the Plains Indians without their main source of food and clothing. The U.S. government kept breaking promises and treaties, turning over more and more Amerindian land to white American settlers. After the end of the U.S. Civil War in 1865, these disorienting trends grew stronger. In 1887, the Dawes Act opened the vast preponderance of remaining Amerindian land to white settlers. Amerindians had to face more soldiers, settlers, and railroads; restriction to reservations; and efforts by the federal government to "Americanize" their children through special schools and conversion to Christianity.

The disruptions of Amerindian life invited intellectual and religious creativity in response. The Amerindians of the Great Basin and northern Rockies had long had a prophetic tradition which, from the 1830s onward, acquired some Christian overtones through contact with white Americans and Iroquois missionaries from upstate New York.

This prophetic tradition took a new direction among the Paiute in northern Nevada in the years 1869–1870. In a vision, a prophet sometimes known as Wodziwob

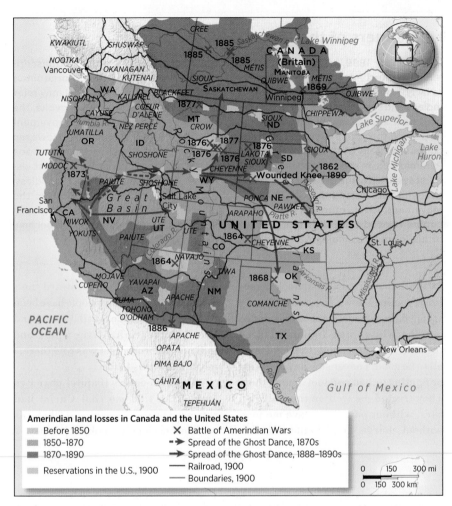

Amerindian North America: Devastation and Response, 1850–1900 The centuries-long displacement and destruction of Amerindian communities continued during the late nineteenth century in the United States and Canada. Land losses accelerated, as Amerindians lacked the military and demographic power to fight off the U.S. Army and prevent further expansion by land-hungry American settlers, whose numbers swelled, especially along railroad lines. The popularity of the Ghost Dance among several Amerindian peoples reflects the desperate position they shared.

("Gray-hair") foresaw that if people followed certain ceremonies, spirits would respond: the vanished game would return, and the recently departed (of whom there were many after an 1867 typhoid epidemic) would return to life amid joy and plenty. By some accounts, his vision included the idea that the Earth would swallow up the whites whose arrival had brought such misery.

CONSIDERING THE EVIDENCE

Messengers of the Ghost Dance

In November 1889, a Cheyenne Amerindian named Porcupine traveled by railway, wagon, and foot to "meet other Indians and see other countries." Beginning near Fort Washakie in Wyoming, he passed through Indian and Mormon communities in Utah before reaching Pyramid Lake in western Nevada, where he stayed with the Paiute communities who had started the Ghost Dance movement. After returning home, Porcupine related the following account of his journey to Major Carroll of the U.S. Army, who transmitted a transcription to the Indian Office. Porcupine's description of meeting Christ may refer to an actual meeting with Wovoka, the prophet of the Ghost Dance movement who lived near Pyramid Lake. However, it also resembles a story from the Book of Mormon that claims Jesus Christ visited America after his death. Regardless, Porcupine's account emphasizes the diversity of Amerindians who embraced the Ghost Dance movement and became its messengers.

All the Indians from the Bannock agency [in Wyoming] down to where I finally stopped [in Nevada] danced this dance. ... [T]he whites and Indians danced together.... The people there seemed all to be good. I never saw any drinking or fighting or bad conduct among them. They treated me well on the [railway] cars, without pay. They gave me food without charge, and I found that this was a habit among them toward their neighbors.... I and my people have been living in ignorance until I went and found out the truth. All the whites and Indians are brothers, I was told there. I never knew this before....

The Fish-eaters [Paiute] near Pyramid Lake told me that Christ had appeared on earth again.... [T]hat was why unconsciously I took my journey....

The **Ghost Dance**, as this spiritual movement is called, featured a ceremony built around a circular dance common among Amerindians of the West. Men, women, and children held hands, sang, and sidestep-shuffled gently clockwise to a drumbeat. They performed this spirit dance at night, for long hours, five nights in a row, to invoke the help of powerful spirits. The ritual dance spread to nearby California and Oregon. But the prophecy failed to come true, and the preaching and spirit dancing died out in these lands by 1873. It survived and spread in southern Idaho and Utah, where Mormon influence reinforced the prophetic tradition of local Amerindians.

Mormons had migrated westward to Utah in the 1840s, bringing a religion that emphasized prophecy. Mormon belief had a special role for Amerindian prophecy: as Mormons saw it, one of the lost tribes of ancient Israel had come to North America, and Amerindians were their descendants. Parts of Mormon doctrine appealed to many

Christ had summoned myself and others from . . . fifteen or sixteen different tribes. There were more different languages than I ever heard before and I did not understand any of them. . . .

Just after dark some of the Indians told me that the Christ . . . was arrived. . . . [H]e commenced our dance, everybody joining in, the Christ singing while we danced. . . .

He told us also that all our dead were to be resurrected . . . ; that we must tell all the people we meet about these things. He spoke to us about fighting, and said that was bad, and we must keep from it; . . . and we must all be friends with one another. He said that in the fall of the year the youth of all the good people would be renewed, so that nobody would be more than 40 years old. . . . He said if we were all good he would send

people [to] heal all our wounds and sickness by mere touch, and that we would live forever. He told us not to quarrel, or fight, nor strike each other, nor shoot one another; that the whites and Indians were to be all one people. He said if any man disobeyed what he ordered, his tribe would be wiped from the face of the earth.

Questions for Analysis

1. What did Porcupine find appealing about the Ghost Dance movement?
2. How did the teachings of the Ghost Dance movement, as described above, promote a shared Amerindian identity?
3. What features did the Ghost Dance movement share with other millenarian movements discussed in this chapter?

Source: "Porcupine's Account of the Messiah," in James Mooney, "The Ghost Dance Religion and the Sioux Outbreak of 1890" in J. W. Powell, ed., 14th Annual Report Part II, Bureau of Ethnology, Smithsonian Institution (Washington, DC, 1896).

Amerindians, and the Ghost Dance prophecies resonated with many Mormons who also looked forward to the restoration of justice and faith. Both groups felt, with justification, persecuted by the U.S. government. Although almost hidden from view, the Ghost Dance survived through the 1870s and 1880s, mainly among Amerindians in touch with Mormon communities.

Wovoka's Prophecy Then in 1889 Wovoka, a Paiute like Wodziwob, had his first prophetic vision. Having lived for 20 years with a white ranching family of devout Presbyterians, his visions had strong overtones of messianic Christianity. Wovoka believed he had gone to heaven, where everyone he saw was healthy and forever young, enjoying their favorite pastimes. His reputation as a healer and spiritual specialist who could end droughts helped earn Wovoka an audience. In the years 1889–1890, he preached that if

Ghost Dance In 1890, the leading American magazine, *Harper's Weekly*, published artist Frederic Remington's impression of Lakota Sioux people from the Dakota Territory performing the circle dance ritual that was central to the Ghost Dance movement. Remington based his drawing on sketches from firsthand observers, but he never saw the Ghost Dance himself.

Amerindians conducted themselves peacefully and honestly, and performed the spirit dance, then the joyful prophecy would come true.

Wovoka's prophecy passed from one people to another. In some versions of the prophecy, white people would be swallowed up by the Earth or drowned in a flood. In others, they and Amerindians would live together in peace and health. At some point, Wovoka added the promise that Jesus Christ would return in 1892 to oversee peace on Earth, working through the American president and through Wovoka himself.

Everywhere, the prophecy included the instruction to perform the circle dance for five days and nights. The community dance helped people feel that they were doing something constructive to heal their broken world. It also expressed a growing sense of Indian-ness across tribal lines, a new—we might say nationalist—identity for thousands of people who had formerly seen themselves as Paiute, Shoshone, Ute, Blackfeet, Arapaho, and so forth. The common experience of catastrophic disease, loss of land, and other misfortunes helped the various Amerindian peoples of the West feel more "Indian." The spirit dance expressed this growing new identity.

Wounded Knee Among the peoples attracted by Wovoka's prophecy were the Lakota Sioux of the Dakota Territory. Their devotion to the spirit dance worried some local U.S. officials, who called it the Ghost Dance. They summoned support from the U.S. Army. A confrontation just after Christmas in 1890 turned violent, resulting in the deaths of 25 members of the U.S. 7th cavalry and 153 Lakota Sioux, most of whom were women and children. The event, known as the massacre of Wounded Knee, came just short of two years after Wovoka's original vision. It cast a dark shadow over the Ghost Dance movement.

But the Ghost Dance did not die in 1890. It continued to appeal to some Amerindians as a means of meeting up with their dead friends and kin, and as a means of expressing their Indian-ness in an increasingly white world. Amerindians from Oklahoma to

Saskatchewan continued to practice the faith and its rituals well into the twentieth century, often secretly. They were trying to revitalize their vanished world.

Canudos in Northeastern Brazil

While the Ghost Dance movement was sweeping the U.S. West, another religious revitalization movement was washing over the northeast of Brazil. It flourished in the thinly populated backcountry called the Sertão, a scrubby land of cattle ranches and erratic rainfall. Its leader was Antônio Maciel.

Maciel was born in 1830 to a moderately prosperous family. But his mother died young, his father took to the bottle, and Antônio left home to live with his grandfather, a schoolteacher. While in his twenties he married and began work as a teacher. In his mid-thirties, his marriage failed, his career fizzled, and he began to wander the countryside. He dressed in a simple robe, wore a beard and long hair, and reminded some people of paintings of Jesus Christ. Everywhere he went, he repaired churches and cemetery walls.

Gradually he became known for his soaring sermons. Listeners felt as if they were "flying up to the clouds" when he spoke about the path to redemption and salvation. He emphasized that the correct path was one of frugality, sobriety, and modesty. People began to call him **Antônio Conselheiro** ("Anthony the Counselor") for the sage advice he dispensed. Listeners started to follow him from village to village.

Antônio Conselheiro's Quest for Justice In 1877 and 1878, northeastern Brazil was hit by a searing drought caused by one of the biggest El Niños in recent centuries. (El Niños are periodic shifts in Pacific equatorial currents associated with both droughts and floods around the world.) Several hundred thousand people died of starvation as crops failed and livestock died. Antônio Conselheiro attracted still more followers among the destitute refugees, who were drawn to his message of social justice and salvation for the righteous poor. His preaching came to include attacks on Protestantism, which was rare in Brazil, alcohol and prostitution, and the evils of slavery. The drought led many slave owners in northeastern Brazil to free their slaves, turning them loose in desperate times with no means of support. A large proportion of Antônio Conselheiro's followers came from their ranks.

In 1893, after 20 years of wandering, Antônio Conselheiro settled down. He chose a mud-hut town, Canudos, in the middle of nowhere. Brazil had abolished slavery (1888) and become a republic (1889). The new state was anti-clerical and claimed the right to recognize civil (as opposed to church) marriages. Antônio Conselheiro took vigorous exception to this claim and started to denounce the injustice of the state prominently in his outdoor sermons. He tossed tax edicts onto a bonfire. He encouraged his followers—by 1897 some 20,000 people, mainly women—to form a just community, unconstrained by the new godless laws. He wanted to withdraw from the world of injustice and corruption, but in so doing he was now challenging the Brazilian state. He also promised his admirers that in 1900 Jesus Christ would return to bring about the Kingdom of Heaven on Earth.

The Brazilian Army attacked Canudos three times, and three times it failed. Former slaves, servants, and hungry farmworkers with rusty weaponry and no training defended Canudos against three assaults. But in 1897, on a fourth attempt, made with tens of thousands of soldiers, machine guns, and field artillery, the army prevailed. All those captured were promptly killed. Antônio Conselheiro had already died—of dysentery.

Tens of thousands of poor, hungry, illiterate Brazilians, hammered by drought, found hope in the message of Antônio Conselheiro, just as thousands of Amerindians in the U.S. West put their faith in the Ghost Dance. For both groups, as for the Xhosa in South Africa, the world in the late nineteenth century seemed to be spinning out of control. Nature seemed especially unruly. Powerful people seemed to be conspiring against them. They needed something powerful of their own to restore justice to the world and make life more rewarding. Millenarian faith answered their needs, even if, in the end, it could not protect them against modern armies with industrial weaponry.

Movements such as these cropped up around the world during the age of industrial imperialism in Africa, South Asia, New Zealand, and elsewhere. In hundreds of cases, including the Lakota Sioux, prophets encouraged people to believe that spiritual forces—talismans, amulets, tattoos—could protect them against bullets. They knew they could not match the material power of their enemies. If they were not to give up all hope, they had to place their faith in spiritual power. Yet, whatever its merits, that power could not stop the advances of imperial and national states backed by artillery, machine guns, and railroad networks.

Giant Rebellions, 1850–1864: China and India

The millenarian prophets who judged that the tide was running against their people could only mobilize a few thousand followers. Far bigger rebellions, involving tens of millions of people, also broke out in the middle of the nineteenth century in China and India. Both rebellions showed the growing impact of global connections, although in different ways, shaped by specific cultures, religions, institutions, and personalities.

The Taiping Rebellion, 1850–1864

China in the mid-nineteenth century was ruled by the Qing dynasty, which had taken power from the Ming 200 years before. The Qing had doubled the size of their empire during the eighteenth century and benefited from the stability provided by effective and long-lived emperors. The last of these, the Qianlong emperor, died in 1799. In the years that followed, the sprawling Qing Empire—with its far-flung territories in Mongolia, Central Asia, and Tibet; its numerous religions, languages, and ethnic groups—became increasingly unsettled.

The Plight of the Qing At the time of Qianlong's death, the Qing governed lightly. Tax rates were about a quarter of those in Europe. Most revenues (60 to 70 percent) went to the army, which nonetheless was under-paid and under-equipped. The Qing bureaucracy was thin, with roughly 10,000 paid officials, and relied on the goodwill of local landlords for routine administration. That left the state vulnerable to corruption, which flourished, particularly in the 1790s. It also contributed to the development of a large pool of talented men who had passed the civil service exams but could not get a job in government. Many of them became critics of Qing incompetence and corruption, both of which were displayed when a rural revolt, the White Lotus Rebellion (1796–1804), began in central China. At first a largely Buddhist uprising against state corruption, it ended with Qing army units fighting one another in order to continue to draw pay. That drained the Qing treasury dry.

Economic problems facing the Qing worsened early in the nineteenth century. For most of Chinese history, population growth had raised total output and strengthened states because peasants had carved out new farmland from swamps and mountainsides. But now too little land suitable for farming remained. Farm acreage per capita fell by almost half from 1753 to 1812, and continued population growth led only to hunger. In addition, the highly commercial Chinese economy, which had grown accustomed to large infusions of silver for coinage, suffered when the supply of silver diminished in the early nineteenth century. With the wars of independence in Latin America (1808–1830), world silver production fell by about half. After 1810, silver was flowing out of China to pay for imports. Upkeep of canals, dams, roads, and bridges ebbed. By the 1820s, dredging of silt in the Grand Canal was so neglected that the annual supplies of grain from the south to the capital at Beijing rarely arrived. Military morale sagged as Qing revenues plummeted and corruption soared.

Widespread use of opium compounded the Qing plight. An addictive drug that had been introduced by Arab traders a millennium before, opium had been illegal in China since 1729. But its use climbed sharply after about 1820. The British East India Company served as the major supplier, cultivating and purchasing the drug in Bengal and selling it cheaply in southern China. Aware of the growing addiction problem and the resulting outflow of silver to foreign merchants, Chinese officials tried to restrict opium imports in 1838. The British regarded this as an unjust restriction on free trade and used their navy to defeat China in the First Opium War (1839–1842). The harsh terms of the Treaty of Nanjing ending the war opened several Chinese ports to British trade, obliged China to pay a large cash indemnity to Britain, and ceded Hong Kong "in perpetuity"—among other concessions. The defeat shocked China, and the terms

Foreign Incursions and the Taiping Rebellion, 1842–1860 Qing China suffered great disruptions in the middle of the nineteenth century. In the First Opium War, Britain used superior naval forces to force the Qing to open many seaports to foreign trade and made Hong Kong a British colony (1842). In the Second Opium War, Britain and France obliged the Qing to open many more seaports and riverports to foreign commerce. Meanwhile, in central and southeastern China, the Taiping Rebellion brought violence and destruction on a staggering scale. The Qing never fully recovered.

of the treaty outraged most Chinese who learned of them. The prestige and finances of the Qing were nearing rock bottom. Many Chinese concluded that in order for their country to restore its fortunes, the Qing would have to go.

Jesus's Younger Brother Things soon got a lot worse thanks to Hong Xiuquan. Hong (1814–1864) came from a gentry family that had fallen a few rungs. His great-grandfather had been a Qing official and landowner in the southern coastal region of Guangzhou. His family, part of an ethnic minority in south China called the Hakka ("Guest Families"), still owned land. But Hong needed the support of many relatives and neighbors while he pursued that venerable ambition: to pass the civil service exam and pursue a career in government. After many years of study, Hong, now in his mid-twenties, failed the examination three times.

Such failures were common, but Hong's reaction to disappointment was unique. He read Christian missionary pamphlets and, after a stint as a schoolteacher in his home village, began to study Christian doctrines with an American Baptist missionary, Issachar Roberts, in the port city of Guangzhou. Under Roberts's tutelage, and the influence of dreams, Hong in 1843 concluded that he was a son of God, the younger brother of Jesus, and responsible for realizing the Kingdom of Heaven on Earth. Prominent among his instructions was to rid China of corrupt, foreign rulers—that is, the Qing dynasty, which was originally from Manchuria. Roberts refused to baptize his imaginative pupil, so Hong did it himself.

Hong began to preach a version of Christianity blended with popular spiritual beliefs. He found an audience in the poorest parts of the population—at first, mainly among his fellow Hakka. The economic decline of China and the humiliation of the First Opium War played into his hands. Before long he had inspired a social movement, tinged with Christian lore, dedicated to the overthrow of the Qing, whom he branded as foreign devils. Hong's agenda included the extermination of demon-worship, by which he meant Buddhism and Confucianism. Persecuted by Qing authorities, Hong raised the flag of rebellion in 1850 during a local famine in south China.

Rebellion By 1853, his army had taken cities in the Yangzi valley, the commercial highway of China. They made Nanjing (which means "Southern Capital") their base. Northern thrusts toward Beijing ("Northern Capital") proved unsuccessful—by and large, northerners found Hong's message, soaked as it was in southern culture, unappealing. But for 10 years the Taiping (meaning "Great Peace") controlled much of the Yangzi valley and parts of southern China.

The Taiping had a distinctive program that in ordinary times would have repelled most Chinese. On the social front, they assaulted the traditions of the Chinese family. They proclaimed that women were equal to men, and they banned prostitution, adultery, concubinage, and indeed all sex outside of marriage. Until 1855, they tried to enforce segregation of the sexes. They proscribed alcohol, opium, and tobacco. On the political side, they invited, and soon compelled, peasants to reject private property and contribute all their possessions to a central Taiping treasury. They instructed everyone to regard Qing officials as foreign devils and southerners, Taiping rebels especially, as the only uncorrupted Chinese. As for religion and culture, Hong and his followers preached that Christianity was not an import from abroad but had been born in China. They took a militant line against rival faiths, destroying Buddhist and Confucian temples and texts, and killing priests and sages. They were gentler with Islam, a minor religion in the areas they controlled. They disdained the refinement and learning of Chinese elites.

Despite their puritanical principles, the Taiping leaders indulged in the looting, forced sex, and gratuitous violence of conquest. Taiping leaders organized the kidnapping of women for sex duty. They amassed personal fortunes in looted goods, apparently including solid-gold chamber pots. They readily executed those who disagreed with them, and massacred millions whose loyalties displeased them.

At first, the Qing armies offered scant resistance. In 1856, Britain and France invaded north China, attacked Beijing, and burned the emperor's summer palace. They wanted still greater trading privileges in China and the legalization of opium, which was of considerable importance to Britain's commercial prosperity. Meanwhile, three or four other significant rebellions broke out. Amazingly, the dynasty limped on.

In 1860, Britain and France got the trade concessions they wanted from the Qing, and yet more indemnities, and threw their support behind the dynasty. The Taiping, after all, had banned opium and preached a faith that looked like heresy to European Christians. So Qing armies trained and led by American and British officers began to attack the Taiping. At the same time, local gentry leaders such as Zeng Guofan in

The Taiping Rebellion A massive battle between Taiping and Qing forces in the region of Nanjing, the Heavenly Capital of the Taiping leader, Hong Xiuquan. Qing forces prevailed over the Taiping in part through the effectiveness of regional militia organized by talented leaders such as Zeng Guofan (right).

Hunan raised effective anti-Taiping armies. Now the momentum switched, and the Taiping leaders' quarrels, already murderous, became large-scale purges. Hong died, either from illness or from poison, in 1864. A few months later the Hunan army finally finished off his diehard supporters, massacring the population of Nanjing in 1864.

When after 14 years it was all over, at least 30 million of China's 350 to 400 million people, some 7 to 9 percent of the population, were dead. As usual, epidemics and starvation killed more than combat did. Some provinces along the middle and lower Yangzi lost 70 to 90 percent of their population to death and flight. The Qing survived, tottering, until 1910.

The **Taiping Rebellion** shows the interplay of internal and external forces in China. Many of its underlying causes were linked to China's changing place in the Global web. The sources of Qing economic weakness involved its dependency on imported Latin American silver and its people's growing addiction to opium from British India. Hong's ideology, a curious mix of local beliefs and Christianity imported from the United States, was as persuasive to downtrodden people eager for hope as the prophecies of Nongqawuse, Wokova, or Antônio Conselheiro. Defeat by a distant nation they disdained as barbarian also undercut the legitimacy of the Qing—before 1839, few Chinese officials had a proper appreciation of the power of Britain's Royal Navy and its modern weaponry. The Qing's failings with respect to the economy, opium, and foreign powers made them all the more vulnerable to nationalistic charges that they were not proper Chinese. China, of course, has always had rebellions. But the character and magnitude of the Taiping Rebellion had everything to do with the global processes corroding the Qing Empire.

The Indian Rebellion, 1857–1858

The **Indian Rebellion**—also known as the First War of Independence, Indian Mutiny, Sepoy Rebellion, or Great Rebellion—also showed the impacts of global connections, most obviously of British rule. Before 1857, British rule in India was mainly company rule. Since the 1750s, the British East India Company (EIC) had acquired growing authority in parts of India, especially Bengal in the northeast. The Mughal Empire still nominally ruled north India, but increasingly it served as a façade behind which stood agents of the EIC. By 1803, the EIC—some 600 British merchants and officials protected by an army of 200,000 Indian soldiers—had outmaneuvered or defeated all indigenous powers in India and stood supreme in most of the subcontinent. Until 1813, the company enjoyed a monopoly on trade with India and tried hard to keep interlopers, including missionaries, out. But in 1813, the British state, bending to the wishes of merchant and evangelical groups at home, stripped the EIC of its trade monopoly and lifted the ban on missionaries. The British government took an ever-larger role in India and directly controlled about two-thirds of it by 1857, with the rest either under Company control or under local independent Indian rulers.

Grievances The British—both the EIC and the Crown—enacted reforms that deeply aggrieved the Indian elite through whom Britain governed the country. Among these were changes to the trade and tariff regime that opened up India to foreign competition, including the efficient cotton mills of England. As we've seen, this undercut the business of Indian merchants as well as village spinners and weavers. Reform to the patchwork tax regime awarded the Company most of the revenues from Indian lands and required some landlords to pay tax on lands that had formerly been exempt. A political reform (called the doctrine of lapse) stipulated that any principality without a biological son as heir would henceforth fall to British rule, which meant that sooner or later all of India would be British. In addition, the EIC by means fair and foul annexed chunks of India, leading many princes to suspect that they might be next. In 1856, the Company took over a prosperous polity, Oudh (also spelled Awadh), on the grounds that its ruler was inept and corrupt.

Religion also provided grounds for Indian anxiety and grievance. Christian missionaries proved a particular source of irritation to Indians, all out of proportion to their tiny success in converting Hindus, Muslims, Sikhs, or Jains. Moreover, the EIC army, made up overwhelmingly of Indians, grew restive over call-ups for overseas duty in the Crimean War, Persia, and Burma. High-caste Hindus, who could not cook according to ritual requirements on shipboard, risked their caste status as a result of these deployments. In general, elite Muslims and Hindus felt that they—not Christian foreigners—should rule India.

The spark that ignited the Indian Rebellion came in 1857 in the form of new rifle cartridges introduced in the Bengal Army, the largest of the three separate Indian armies run by the EIC. Annoyed by overseas duty and reductions in pay, the Indian soldiers, called *sepoys*, were already on edge. The Enfield rifle, a big upgrade over the muskets in use before, required cartridges that would slide down the gun barrel for loading. Rumors spread that the grease used for this purpose was animal fat from both pigs and cows.

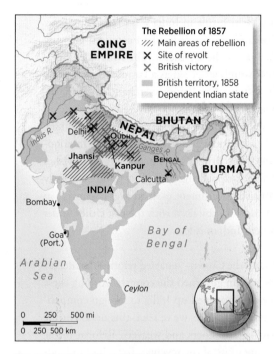

The Rebellion of 1857
/// Main areas of rebellion
✕ Site of revolt
✕ British victory
▨ British territory, 1858
□ Dependent Indian state

The Indian Rebellion, 1857–1858 Large-scale uprisings against British authority took place in the years 1857–1858 in the Ganges plain and in central India. The British-led Indian Army defeated the uprisings militarily, leading to the end of EIC rule and the creation of a British Crown colony of India in 1858. Those states that remained nominally independent had to bow to British wishes on all important matters.

Since soldiers had to bite off the tip of a cartridge before inserting it in their rifle barrel, Muslims feared defilement by pig fat and Hindus feared breaking taboo against beef. In the spring of 1857, soldiers who resisted orders to use these new cartridges were hanged by EIC military officers, setting off a rebellion.

Rebellion The Indian Rebellion of 1857–1858 was an army mutiny combined with a series of local and regional rebellions. It was never a unified movement under a single command. Several garrisons in northern and central India rose in revolt, joined by about a quarter of the Bengal Army. At its height, the rebels controlled much of the Ganges plain for more than a year, and pockets elsewhere in India.

The main goals of the rebellion were the destruction of British rule in India and the restoration of various old regimes. For Muslims, that generally meant returning to the glory days of Mughal power through the person of Bahadur Shah II, the 82-year-old figurehead emperor. Bahadur Shah, who preferred poetry to politics, reluctantly sided with the uprising. For Hindus, the goal was to restore earlier golden ages, when one or another Hindu leader had ruled wisely. Followers of minority religions generally chose not to rebel. Sikhs, for example, proved staunchly loyal to the EIC, preferring it to the prospect of Hindu or Muslim rule.

Local princes were divided too. Several took the opportunity to try to reclaim lost power. One of these was **Lakshmibai**, known as the Queen of Jhansi, a city in north-central India. Married at age 13, she was a widow when the EIC invoked the doctrine of lapse, which she regarded as an unjust seizure of her throne. Age 29 when the rebellion came, she gambled on its success and for a few months ruled Jhansi in defiance of the EIC armies. But soon her capital was under siege, her kingdom captured, and her life lost in combat. She has since become a national hero in India, portrayed in movies, TV shows, and video games.

The Indian Rebellion failed because too many Indians, and especially army units, resisted the call to revolt and stayed loyal to EIC army commanders. Had the armies united in revolt, they would easily have driven the British from India. The rebels hoped in vain that Britain's rivals, France or Russia, might come to their aid.

Aftermath The rebellion and its aftermath featured all the butchery and gore that are customary in warfare. In one notorious episode, an Indian commander, Nana Sahib, an aristocrat well educated in English and French literature, arranged for 200 British women and children to be chopped up and stuffed down a well in Kanpur—the event is famous in Britain as the massacre of Cawnpore. British officers oversaw vengeful reprisals against Indians, killing men, women, and children indiscriminately. These slaughters continued after the rebellion ceased. The greatest legacy of the rebellion was bitterness on all sides.

Lakshmibai The Queen of Jhansi is portrayed wearing white and riding on a white horse, crowned and carrying a crop. All these symbols indicate her status as a hero in the eyes of many Indians for her support of the Indian Rebellion.

The casualties included 11,000 British (most of whom died of disease), several hundred thousand Indians, the Mughal Empire, and the EIC. The rebellion made clear that everything would have to change if Britain were to continue to rule India. India became a Crown colony, and back in Britain Queen Victoria added the title Empress of India. Now Parliament and the India Office in London, represented in India by a viceroy, would rule the country. Hundreds of princely states remained, but all stood subservient to the viceroy. What little remained of the Mughal Empire now vanished into British India, and Bahadur Shah, the last of a line that included great emperors such as Akbar and Aurangzeb, lived out his final years in exile. The EIC lost all its remaining authority. The British Crown took all its assets and liquidated what was left of it in 1874.

Indians often refer to the rebellion as the First War of Independence, emphasizing the attempt to throw off foreign rule and the first stirrings of Indian nationalism. Although Indians fought one another furiously during the rebellion, thereafter the violence, bitterness, and continuing resentments against foreign rule helped them see their common condition more clearly.

In the aftermath, British rule in India, known as the Raj, changed its character in ways that hastened the development of nationalism in India. British authority became more bureaucratic and less personalized. It gave more attention to public works, especially railroads, education, and irrigation. It tried harder to regulate justice and health, and it created an India-wide post and telegraph system. It rewarded the many princes who had stayed loyal by allowing them to exercise modest authority and collect enough tax revenue to live in splendor. In general, the Raj made the experience of being ruled more uniform and less localized. In the long run this helped Indians feel more Indian, as opposed to feeling strictly Muslim or Hindu, or strictly Tamil, Bengali, or Punjabi.

The Indian Rebellion reflected deep distress on the part of many Indians with their situation in the 1850s. The rebels' grievances were different from those that lay behind the Taiping Rebellion in China, and the loss of life far smaller, but at root they had some things in common. One was economic distress resulting from the disruptive impacts of international trade, an example of the blowback from economic globalization. Another was the unintended consequences of Christian missionary activity. A third was resentment against foreign rule.

Resentment against foreign rule took different forms in India and China, but both involved the EIC. Muslim and Hindu elites in India objected to their loss of authority and to the rapid encroachments of the EIC over the previous 100 years. The Taiping resented the foreign origins of China's Qing rulers, in power for 200 years. But part of what led them to despise the Qing was the dynasty's inability to cope with British aggression—specifically, in the First Opium War, which was fought mainly to preserve the Chinese opium market of the EIC. The business interests of the EIC, and the military adventures it inspired, played a role in both of these giant rebellions.

Rebellions as Global and Local

The great rebellions in China and India drew on powerful combinations of macro trends—including nationalism, imperialism, and industrialization—and local institutions, cultures, and leaders. The growing connectivity of the Global web ensured that these were not the only disruptions shaped by the combustible interaction of global and local forces. Pressures from Europe and the United States, as we've seen, helped spur the revolution in Japan known as the Meiji Restoration (1866–1868). Foreign examples of liberal and anti-clerical government helped inspire civil wars in Mexico (1857–1867), in which France intervened. Doctrines of nationalism played central roles in wars of unification of Italy and Germany in the 1860s, and in the deadliest war in South America's history, in which Brazil, Argentina, and Uruguay pummeled Paraguay (1865–1870).

Even the U.S. Civil War (1861–1865), another momentous rebellion, reflected a combination of global trends, in this case including abolitionism, and local causes. The westward—imperial—expansion of the United States provoked the war over slavery. As we've seen, slaveholders and their supporters understood that as new free (non-slave) states joined the Union, they would eventually tip the political balance in Congress in favor of abolition. To counter the effect of expansion into the West, proslavery forces urged imperial expansion into the Caribbean and twice raised private armies in hopes of adding islands such as Cuba as additional slave states. The industrial power and railroad network of the North helped decide the war, keeping the Union intact—at the cost of about 625,000 lives, some 2 percent of the U.S. population. The aftermath of the war featured a more powerful, activist, and nationalist federal government. It amended the Constitution to abolish slavery and extend full political rights to former slaves—although after 1877 most southern states nevertheless sharply curtailed civil and political rights for African Americans. The federal government applied its power to accelerating territorial expansion, including the purchase of Alaska from Russia in 1867; speeding the domination and assimilation of Amerindian peoples; supporting the industrialization of the country; and—by 1898—undertaking overseas imperialism in both the Caribbean and the Pacific.

Meanwhile, the global forces of nationalism, imperialism, and industrialization grew still more influential. Technological advance continued to tighten the world's connections. The first transatlantic telegraph cable came in 1866. The Suez Canal in Egypt, which connected the Indian Ocean world to the Mediterranean Sea, and the first U.S. transcontinental railroad both opened for business in 1869. The flows of information, goods, and people would only quicken. And so social struggles, although as always largely about local concerns, increasingly reflected international and global influences too.

A common pattern emerged in the societies under pressure from Britain and the world's other leading powers. Some reformers in these societies wanted to strengthen their countries by imitating the most powerful foreign examples, while others thought the way to withstand foreign power was to hold tight to their traditions. In Russia, for example, there were so-called Westernizers such as Sergei Witte who, as we've seen, wanted to make Russia strong by adopting techniques and technologies from industrial western Europe. But at the same time so-called Slavophiles, such as the novelist Fyodor Dostoevsky, argued that Russia's strength lay in its unique traditions and culture,

Suez Canal Steamships line up to enter the Suez Canal at around 1890. The canal connecting the Indian Ocean with the Mediterranean Sea was an engineering marvel and a major step toward further tightening of the Global web.

especially the Russian Orthodox Church. Japan faced similar divisions from the 1850s onward, although there the groups that were inclined to adapt foreign examples won decisively in the policy arena. Muslim states such as Egypt or Iran confronted the same issue in their own ways: should they seek to industrialize and encourage a national identity among their populations, or should they try to strengthen their countries by rallying behind the banners of Islam? These divisions fractured many societies and focused political attention on religion, education, economic policy, technology, and other areas that might help peoples and states become stronger in the face of the challenges of the late nineteenth century.

Revolutions, 1870s–1920: China and Mexico

The military defeat of the rebellions in China and India did not resolve the grievances that underlay them. To the contrary, anger and disappointment over the failings of rulers existed widely around the world, particularly wherever imperialism, nationalism, or the difficulty of competing against industrial production affected poor families. In places as different as China, Mexico, Russia, and the Ottoman Empire, millions despaired over their prospects in life and came to resent their governments' failings. For peasants, the main issue was land. Population growth everywhere reduced the land available per family. In some countries, especially those where governments were attempting reform programs, the peasants' tax burdens grew too. Among the educated middle classes, frustration developed at ruling elites that seemed unable to address rising challenges such as the suffering of the peasantry, the lack of opportunity for educated youth, and the growing threat from industrialized and imperialistic states. Observant reformers around the world were concerned by—and often inspired by—the mounting power of Britain, Germany, the United States, or Japan. They wanted their own governments to match that power—typically, by means of military modernization, industrialization, expulsion of foreign missionaries or businesses, and expansion of education. If complacent and corrupt rulers would not rise to the challenge, then the only course was to replace them through revolution.

The Chinese Revolution, 1880s–1910s

After the Taiping Rebellion ended in 1864, matters improved—a little—in China. The intense fighting had laid waste to cities and countryside so that, as one eyewitness put it, "weeds and jungle cover[ed] the land." China's population in 1864, perhaps 350 to 400 million strong, was on average poorer than it had been a century before. In the south and southeast of China, millions gave up on life at home and emigrated to Southeast Asia, the Pacific Islands, and the Americas.

Pressures and Grievances The Qing government never fully recovered its authority. Without much prestige or money, it could not control the provinces, which gave local officials leeway to pursue their own programs. Governors and provincial officials increasingly used the taxes they raised to build their own military forces and undertake their own reform initiatives in education, infrastructure, industry, and military matters.

These efforts in the provinces are sometimes known as China's self-strengthening movement. It owed little to the Qing court, and much to provincial governors. They typically focused on military industries. In Jiangnan province (around Shanghai) and in Wuhan along the central Yangzi River, officials worked with private entrepreneurs to set up iron, steel, and weapons industries. Li Hongzhang, who had made his reputation helping to defeat the Taiping Rebellion, built arsenals, shipyards, a steamship company, a telegraph network, and military academies in eastern China's Hebei province.

These provincial officials were trying to provide the Qing Empire—and themselves—with the tools of modern state power. They saw themselves as following an old saying that originated with Chinese struggles against steppe raiders: "using the barbarians' ways to defend against the barbarians." Now the "barbarians" were not Mongol but European, American, or Japanese. These reformers often wanted to retain Confucian ethics and ideology, or "essence" as they put it, but also acquire the hardware of industrial power.

An illustrative initiative was Li Hongzhang's study abroad program. On the advice of Yung Wing, a Christian convert and the first Chinese graduate of an American university (Yale, Class of 1854), Li sent 113 promising boys to high schools in New England to prepare them for administrative posts in his province—a radically different approach from training them in the Confucian classics. They studied those subjects that fit them for high responsibility: science, technology, engineering, math, languages—and, of course, history. In 1881 the program was discontinued when it appeared the boys had grown too Americanized, taking up baseball among other undignified pursuits. To some Qing officials, it seemed that they were losing their Confucian essence in their effort to acquire foreign practical knowledge.

The urgency of self-strengthening grew with time. For sophisticated Chinese, aware of the antiquity of their culture and the majestic power of earlier dynasties, the role of foreign influence in the late nineteenth century was especially irksome. The treaties signed in 1842 and 1860 after the two Opium Wars gave foreigners special rights, called extra-territoriality, which included exemption from Chinese law. Foreign missionaries roamed the country. Foreign businessmen ran new mines, railroads, and factories. Foreigners controlled the maritime customs houses. Foreign gunboats slithered up and down the Yangzi River, enforcing the privileges of foreigners. In 1879 Japan took the

Ryukyu Islands, which Qing rulers regarded as their own. In 1885 the French seized control of Vietnam, which the Qing considered to be under their protection. By the 1880s, it seemed that at any time Britons, French, Germans, Americans—and, increasingly, Japanese and Russians—might carve up China, as imperialist powers were doing in Africa and Southeast Asia.

The foreign presence was only part of the discouraging situation that set the stage for the **Chinese Revolution**. Opium addiction continued to plague all levels of Chinese society. A terrible famine in the years 1877–1878, caused by the same giant El Niño that brought killing drought to Brazil, cost millions of lives. Japanese silk and Indian tea competed all too well against the Chinese products, undercutting important export trades. More fundamentally, the population kept growing while the available land did not. New crops—maize and sweet potatoes from the Americas—helped somewhat by raising production in areas ill-suited to rice, millet, or wheat. But population growth mainly caused families to grow poorer, more desperate, and more likely to kill their infant girls. Poverty, poor prospects, and a shortage of potential brides encouraged young men to consider radical choices such as banditry, emigration, or rebellion.

The Qing showed few signs of addressing these challenges. Huge indemnities from lost wars and the cost of suppressing rebellions kept their finances in a desperate state. They sometimes supported, but often opposed, the initiatives taken by talented provincial governors such as Li Hongzhang. In any case, the treaties forced upon them in 1842 and 1860 had deprived the Qing of some of the tools—such as tariffs—used by other countries, including Japan and the United States, to help them industrialize.

Patriotic Chinese did not agree on what to do about these pressing problems. For the self-strengtheners such as Li, China needed to adopt modern weaponry, telegraphs, steamships, and railroads. But it became clear that this approach required engineering experts, trained managers, bankers, an industrial labor force, and an educational system to match. You could not get the teeth—modern military might—without the tail of a socially and culturally transformed society, one that undercut the authority of fathers, reduced the subservience of women, de-emphasized family ties, and compromised Confucian principles. For most Chinese, even the keen reformers, that was a painful prospect.

An alternative approach, always popular in difficult times in societies with glorious pasts, was to try to return to tried and true ways. Conservatives recommended banning all things foreign and purifying the commitment to Confucian principles. In most of China, and most of the time at the Qing court, this view prevailed.

Foreign Pressure and Internal Revolt The contrast with Japan brought Chinese observers further discomfort. As we have seen, Japan responded to the shock of foreign aggression with an internal revolution that put in power an elite dedicated to strengthening the nation. With brisk energy and judicious borrowing from foreigners, they had created an industrial economy, a modernized military, and a reformed educational system, and embarked on a program of imperialism. Japan, almost overnight, had become both an inspiring example and a direct threat to China. The Chinese view of Japan as a lesser culture, derivative of China, made Japan's ascendance even more painful.

As Chinese elites struggled with their choices, the urgency of the situation grew. Japan's imperialist actions led Koreans to appeal to China for help, which brought on the Sino-Japanese War (1894–1895). China was trounced, its newly built navy sunk. Humiliated, it had to cede Taiwan to Japan and pay yet another large indemnity. The emperor at the time, 24-year-old Guangxu—the only Chinese emperor to learn English—in practice shared power with his aunt, Cixi, known as the Empress Dowager. In 1898, he embarked on a bold program of reforms. His advisors, inspired by Japan's history, proposed new universities, railroads, and even a constitutional government. But Cixi, an ardent reformer in her younger days, was now a fierce and formidable conservative and a veteran of court intrigue. She engineered a palace coup, confined her nephew to house arrest, and executed reformers who could not escape China.

In the years 1899–1900, an anti-foreign, anti-Christian, and initially anti-Qing uprising by nationalist youths, who called themselves the Righteous and Harmonious Fists, boiled over. Known to foreigners as the Boxers because of their interest in martial arts, they originated during a time of drought and hunger in the northeastern province of Shandong. Their xenophobic movement had a millenarian tinge to it, including a belief that their rituals could make them invulnerable to bullets. They killed Chinese Christians and foreign missionaries. They looted churches and foreign property throughout northern China and killed the German ambassador. After foreign troops guarding embassies and legations killed several Boxers, Cixi in 1900 declared war on all foreign nations involved in China. Within months an international force of eight nations, made up mostly of Japanese and Russian soldiers and ships—and partly funded

Empress Dowager Cixi
The elderly Empress Dowager at court in the 1890s.

by overseas Chinese eager to end Qing rule—invaded China. Twenty thousand foreign troops crushed the Boxers and Qing forces, and imposed yet another heavy indemnity on China. Russia occupied Manchuria, the homeland of the Qing. Cixi and her nephew Guangzu fled Beijing.

The Qing, it seemed in 1901, could sink no further. The futility of fighting foreign ways became clearer after the Boxers' defeat. Advisers convinced even Cixi that radical reform was required if the dynasty—indeed, China—were to survive. Her government sent thousands of students to Japan to observe its modernizing reforms. China abolished the 1,300-year-old civil service examination system, established new schools, including ones for girls, and routed major investment toward military industries.

But it was too little, too late for the Qing. Their incompetence in the face of China's humiliations turned many of their most talented subjects, such as **Sun Yatsen**, into revolutionaries. Sun was born in 1866 to a peasant family in Guangdong. At age 13 he followed an older brother to Hawaii, where he received an English-language education at the same school from which President Obama graduated a century later. Having had little exposure to Confucian study, Sun was fully open to the teachings on offer in Hawaii. He was the most notable of the many young Chinese who were concluding that the Qing could not spearhead reform, and that to save China from foreign domination and enduring weakness required overthrowing the Qing.

Sun Yatsen, Revolutionary   After his schooling in Hawaii, Sun moved to Hong Kong, a British colony, where he studied with missionaries, was baptized an Anglican, and earned a medical degree. Disappointed by Qing weakness, Sun wanted, as he put it in 1894, to see China "do what the Europeans could do." He "tried especially to learn how these countries had grown rich and strong and how they had civilized their people." He thought it especially admirable that in Western countries "the interests of the state and those of commerce flourish together." Building railroads and battleships would not suffice, he thought. China needed to modernize its education system, its agriculture, and its commerce, to address the root of its weakness. His efforts to energize reform by Qing officials, and to gain employment with the government, were rebuffed in 1894. If Qing officials refused to embark on suitably thorough reforms, Sun maintained, it was time for a revolution. He left China in 1895 when the Qing put a price on his head, and did not return for 17 years. Throughout the 1890s and early 1900s, Sun traveled to Southeast Asia, Britain, Canada, the United States, and elsewhere, organizing opposition to Qing rule among overseas Chinese and looking for ideas he could mix into his program for reforming China.

Sun devised a revolutionary credo, his Three Principles. The first was a Chinese nationalist position: the Qing—those Manchu barbarians—must go, and real Chinese must rule China. The second principle was that the imperial monarchy must be replaced by a constitutional republic. This drew on the examples Sun had seen abroad; nothing in Chinese tradition supported this principle. The third was the social

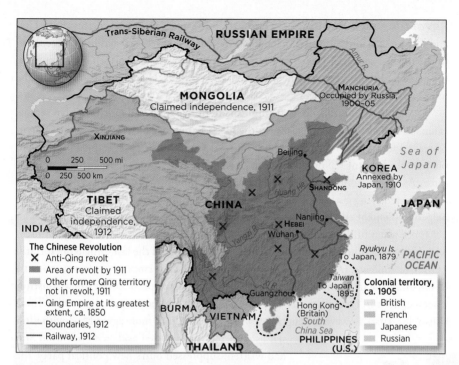

The Chinese Revolution, 1905–1911 Foreign pressures exacerbated internal weaknesses, speeding the decline of the Qing Empire and bringing its final collapse. Foreign powers including Russia, France, and Japan exploited the vacuum of power created by Qing weakness, seizing territories that had long been under Qing sway or even part of the Qing state. Qing subjects in Mongolia and Tibet broke away. Qing failings inspired ethnic Chinese increasingly to see their rulers as incompetent foreigners and led many to support the Chinese Revolution that began in Wuhan in 1910 and ended two and a half centuries of Qing rule by 1911.

principle—influenced by his exposure to European socialism—that everyone should have enough to eat, economic justice should prevail, and peasants should get an education and have a chance to apply their talents. Sun hoped that a China recast along these lines would both recover its proper place in the world and alleviate the suffering of the masses.

For 15 years Sun's efforts at revolution brought only failures. He raised money and recruits, often collaborating with Chinese students in Japan, for rebellions in Guangzhou in 1895, 1900, 1907, and early 1911. All fizzled. But later in 1911, army officers inflamed by nationalist ideas sparked a mutiny in the central city of Wuhan (Hubei province). The uprising spread, and many provinces declared themselves independent of Qing rule. Sun Yatsen, however, was on a fundraising trip in Denver. Now middle-aged, he sensed this was the best chance he would get to change China, and after visiting Europe in hopes of enlisting support, he returned home.

Revolution and Republic, 1911–1916 Sun's assessment was correct. Both Cixi and Guangxu had died in 1908. She had designated a three-year-old boy as successor to the throne, so power passed to a handful of princes. To suppress the army mutiny, the princes chose a talented general named Yuan Shikai. He saw more promise in the mutineers than in the princes.

An ambitious youth from a distinguished family, Yuan had failed the civil service exams twice, then joined the army. In the 1880s he made his mark serving the Qing in Korea. As Qing power waned, he built his own army in the 1890s, trained by German officers. His Beiyang ("Northern") army quickly became China's most effective military force. At Yuan's command, it loyally massacred thousands of hardline Boxers when they rejected Qing authority. In the coming years, Yuan honed the Beiyang Army and helped implement educational and military reforms.

Once given full command to suppress the 1911 mutiny, Yuan decided to join forces with Sun Yatsen and other revolutionaries, and they forced the last Qing emperor, still a child, to abdicate. (A gardener for most of his life, the last emperor—after 2,000 years of imperial rule in China—died in 1967.) Sun was elected president of a new constitutional republic in December 1911. He hoped to reform China along the lines of his Three Principles. Yuan, however, thought a new dynasty would be more agreeable—with himself as emperor. Yuan tossed aside a constitution Sun had written; suppressed Sun's new political party, the Guomindang; arranged for the assassination of many of Sun's associates; and in 1913 drove Sun into exile, in Japan. Various liberations and reforms of 1911 and 1912, including press freedom and representative assemblies, were quickly rescinded. Yuan began to govern like an emperor.

Power in China soon fragmented. Japan made new demands on China in 1915, to which Yuan agreed in return for support of his dynastic dreams. That sparked renewed nationalist outrage and provincial uprisings. Several of Yuan's own Beiyang Army disciples deserted him, and when he died of disease in 1916 at age 56, central rule collapsed. While the republic officially survived in the hands of the Guomindang, China was now fragmented, with dozens of regional warlords competing for power, revenues, and personal survival. Sun Yatsen struggled to unite the country from his base in Guangdong, but he died of disease in 1925 at age 58. Internal warfare continued to plague China for the next 25 years.

Anti-Qing Rebellion A barber cuts off a boy's queue, or braid, following the overthrow of the Qing dynasty in 1911. The Qing had required all men to wear their hair in a long braid, on pain of death. Cutting off the braids came to be seen as a symbol of liberation.

The Qing, in power since 1644, had entered a long death-spiral in the 1790s and were finally undone by military defeat and revolution during the years 1895–1912. Confucian ideology, which had provided a compelling vision of the proper relations among heaven, ruler, and ruled, now stood at a low ebb. Much of the old Qing elite and the Chinese gentry threw their support to the revolution, seeing it as the best bet for the restoration of order and the reconstruction of China. This stood in contrast to elite behavior during the Taiping uprising, when their grandfathers had stood by the dynasty. But in the intervening half-century, the Qing had lost the loyalty of those they most needed.

In the end, the combination of two main challenges undermined the Qing. Population growth and increasing poverty among the peasantry was one, if always slow-moving and rarely commanding urgent official attention. The second challenge was the mounting economic and military strength, and aggression, of industrialized societies, especially Britain, Russia, and Japan. That one was easier to identify and did command urgent attention at the Qing court. But responding to it seemed to require such drastic changes not merely to the state, but to society and family as well, that the Qing policy elite could not agree upon any sustained course of reform. They feared, probably rightly, that enacting radical reforms as the most energetic and imaginative self-strengtheners recommended would provoke widespread rebellion and only hasten the end of the dynasty.

The Mexican Revolution, 1870s–1920

Similar challenges—peasant poverty and unrest combined with inability to fend off foreign power—fueled the **Mexican Revolution**. Like the Chinese Revolution, it was decades in the making. Mexico had won independence from Spain in 1821 but lost the northern third of its territory to the United States in 1848, the result of the Mexican-American War. After independence, its chaotic political life included repeated bouts of civil war, Comanche raids, and in the 1860s a French invasion. After 1876, its politics stabilized owing to the authoritarian rule of Porfirio Díaz. His decades in power, 1876–1910, are called the **Porfiriato**.

The Porfiriato, 1876–1910 Díaz, a theology school dropout from a poor family in Oaxaca, fought in the Mexican-American War as a youth and became a hero of the anti-French struggle in the 1860s. He converted his military prestige into a political career and in 1876 came to power by means of a coup. He stayed in power through intimidation, army support, and rigged elections. His policy consisted of three main initiatives beyond doing whatever was necessary to keep power. First, he restored to the Catholic Church some of the lands and privileges it had lost in recent decades when anti-clerical factions had ruled Mexico. Second, he recruited foreign investment in Mexico, mainly from the United States, Britain, Germany, and France. He awarded tax breaks and other incentives to firms that would own and operate mines, railroads, plantations, and other big enterprises. Third, he endorsed the dispossession of poor peasants whose self-sufficient ways did not contribute to national economic growth, and whose small, communal landholdings got in the way of bigger, more efficient, businesses.

Díaz presided over a rapid growth of inequality in Mexico. On his watch, Mexico's economy grew fast and its richest people prospered mightily. So did many of the foreign firms he invited in. Foreign trade increased ninefold during the Porfiriato, and foreign companies—British, French, and American—built 7,500 miles (12,000 km) of railroads. Investment in mining skyrocketed after Díaz offered tax breaks to foreign companies. It was a good time to be an investor or business leader. But the Porfiriato was a bad time to be poor in Mexico. The standard of living and nutrition for average Mexicans in 1910 was probably lower than in 1810. Wages in the foreign-owned businesses stayed low, and Díaz used armed force to defeat strikes and discourage negotiations for better working conditions.

Peasants, the majority of the population, found less and less land available to them. That trend resulted partly from a rise in population from 9 to 15 million between 1876 and 1910. But mainly it came from land concentration: by 1910, about 80 to 90 percent of Mexican land was owned by 1 percent of the population, mostly of Spanish descent and proud of it. The same elite controlled most irrigation water, which in some arid regions was more precious than land. Education did not provide an exit from poverty: most peasants received little or none, and 70 to 80 percent of the population remained illiterate. Most of them were Amerindians, called *Indios* in Mexico, and spoke indigenous languages such as Mayan or Zapotec rather than Spanish.

The vast and widening social inequality, particularly with respect to land, was the primary grievance behind the Mexican Revolution. Waves of labor strikes and peasant rioting after 1905 demonstrated the levels of discontent. A secondary grievance was nationalist irritation at the generous deals offered to foreign businesses in Mexico. The loss of the north in 1848 and the ejection of the French in the 1860s had bolstered Mexican nationalism. So did awareness among the educated classes of the rising tide of nationalism in Europe and the United States. While Díaz did his best to wrap himself in the cloak of nationalism, and he was skilled at such things, he gave away too much to foreign companies to suit many Mexicans and thus became—like late Qing emperors in China—an object of nationalist frustration and disdain. These two threads, quests for social justice and Mexican nationalism, ran through the Revolution.

Revolution, 1910–1920 The Mexican Revolution started when Díaz said he would retire and scheduled a presidential election for 1910. When various candidates emerged, he changed his mind and jailed the most promising one, Francisco Madero. A previously apolitical northerner, Madero emerged from a wealthy family with interests in ranching, mining, and cotton. He had ties to Diaz's inner circle. But his education in Paris and at the University of California-Berkeley had persuaded him that a less autocratic system

Francisco Madero A mural in present-day Mexico City celebrates the revolutionary leader. Madero appears seated on a horse and carrying a large Mexican flag, surrounded by supporters ranging from peasants to middle-class professionals.

would be better for Mexico—similar to the impact of study abroad in Sun Yatsen's career. After landing in jail, Madero wrote up his political vision, escaped to the United States, and decided to call for the overthrow of the Porfiriato. Insurgencies bubbled up all over Mexico. Díaz, now age 80, chose comfortable exile in Paris.

Those insurgencies included two larger ones driven by grievances of inequality. In Morelos, just south of Mexico City, a peasant, Emiliano Zapata, had been helping villagers retain their land against encroaching sugar plantations. He organized an effective guerrilla war against the big landholders and attracted a large following. Meanwhile, in the ranchlands of the far north, Pancho Villa led another uprising made up mainly of cowboys and bandits like himself, at home on horseback. Villa was a tactical magician at organizing cavalry raids, so much so that the U.S. Army studied his techniques. He also had a fine public relations instinct and made a deal with Hollywood producers to have his exploits filmed. He was well connected with gun runners in the United States who kept his forces supplied. Zapata and Villa both promised land and work to their followers—if they won.

Other insurgent factions were led by urban, middle-class men less flamboyant than Zapata or Villa. But Venustiano Carranza, a politician with a medical education, and Álvaro Obregón, a prosperous chickpea farmer with no education, were the equal of anyone when it came to political guile. They represented more moderate factions, not interested in major redistribution of land or wealth. They favored constitutional government—and focused on crushing their rivals.

Mainly through the backing of Zapata's peasant army, Madero, not yet 38 years old, became president late in 1911. But one of his supporters, Victoriano Huerta, a former military officer, engineered a coup. Huerta arranged for Madero's murder and established a military dictatorship that lasted about a year. But his forces lost out to other factions, and he took the road of exile.

In the coming years, the various factions fought, joined forces, quarreled, and fought again. Their leaders became warlords, leading private armies, making their own rules, enforcing their will where they could. It became hard to tell the revolutionaries from the bandits and vice versa. Rival armies marched this way and that, carrying off food and livestock. The contest was a multisided civil war fought by amateur soldiers with modern armaments. The United States intervened twice, once in Veracruz to help pressure Huerta into resigning, and once in the north to punish Pancho Villa for a raid on a New Mexico town. Germany also got involved, negotiating with most of the warlord factions at one point or another between 1914 and 1918. In early 1917, Germany, wanting the United States too distracted to enter World War I, offered to pay Carranza's government if Mexico would make war on the United States. Mexico turned down the offer.

Outcome and Aftermath By 1920, when the fighting calmed, more than a million Mexicans—6 percent of the population—had been killed. In proportional terms, this came to three times the death toll of the U.S. Civil War. If anyone may be said to have won, it would be the Constitutionalist faction of Carranza and Obregón. They drove out Huerta, murdered Zapata, and bought off Villa, who betrayed his stated principles by accepting a large ranch and pension, which he enjoyed until ambushed and murdered in 1923. Obregón, as the last man standing after Carranza's assassination, became president in 1920, crushed the last Zapata loyalists, and ruled Mexico directly or through a loyal subordinate until assassinated in 1928.

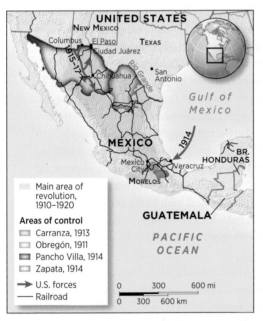

The Revolution remade Mexico. It adopted a new constitution that brought some land reform; more would come in the 1930s. Big estates were broken up and parceled out to indigenous communities, a radical step that resonated throughout the Americas wherever *Indio* and *mestizo* populations were in the majority—for example, in Central America and the Andes. New labor laws provided for a minimum wage, maximum hours,

The Mexican Revolution, 1910–1920 Under the rule of Porfirio Díaz, the average Mexican became poorer. Millions lost control of their farmlands, often to foreign companies that Díaz welcomed. Mexico exploded into revolution and multi-sided civil war in 1910, and the main factions built up regional bases either in the north along the U.S. border or in the highlands south of Mexico City. The largest of the U.S. interventions came first by sea in 1914 and second over land from U.S. states that before 1848 had been part of Mexico.

and—astonishing at the time—paid maternity leave for mothers. The new state stripped the Catholic Church of its lands and privileges, converted churches into public property, and even forbade clerics from wearing their ecclesiastic garb in public. Education was taken from the church and put in the hands of the state. These broad social and economic changes amounted to a fair chunk of the agenda that the followers of Zapata and Villa wanted.

Politically, the constitution and the agreements that ended the fighting guaranteed universal male suffrage and the formal equality of male citizens regardless of wealth or ancestry. It also sharply reduced the economic rights of foreigners, claiming for the state all rights to minerals, oil, and other natural resources. There wasn't much the revolutionary factions could agree on after ousting Díaz, but undermining the church and foreign businesses met with widespread approval.

The Mexican Revolution was both a social and a national revolution. It took until the 1930s before several of the provisions of the new Constitution were put into effect, but eventually the old landed elite lost most of its grip on the country and peasants won access to more land. Although Mexico became a one-party state, its politics after the Revolution included more segments of the population and more representation than during the Porfiriato. The mobilization for revolution and civil war, and anti-foreign sentiments resulting from the two U.S. interventions and Germany's meddling, all sharpened Mexican nationalism. That found expression in popular culture—food, folk dress, songs—and in economic policy, largely directed against the United States. Many Mexicans in 1920 agreed with the statement attributed to the former theology student Porfirio Díaz: "Poor Mexico! So far from God and so close to the United States."

So, although fundamentally about land, the Mexican Revolution became something more than that. It was a succession struggle among warlords, similar to what happened in China after 1911. (Indeed, one might say Mexico had its revolution and warlord period all at once, whereas China did it in stages.) It was a national struggle to reassert the independence of Mexico from foreign influence. It was an anti-clerical struggle to free the country from the grip of the Catholic Church. And, from the point of view of most ordinary people, it was a terrifying, chaotic bloodbath.

Revolutions and Global Forces, 1900–1920

The great revolutions in China and Mexico early in the twentieth century were accompanied by several others that resulted from the macro-scale forces of nationalism, imperialism, and the uneven effects of industrialization. In South Africa between 1899 and 1902, the Boer War, a keenly nationalist uprising against British rule by the Boers—Afrikaans-speaking whites descended from Dutch settlers—led to a settlement in 1910 that, while not called a revolution, in some respects was one. It conceded much more local control and representative government to white South Africans, who quickly stripped black Africans of the right to own most farmland. In Iran, revolutionaries led

Boer War Taking up arms against the British Empire's hold in South Africa, Boer soldiers guard an outpost against British forces during the Boer War, which lasted from 1899 to 1902. The British would gain the upper hand over the Boers in late 1900, though Boer guerrilla warfare continued until the parties agreed on a peace treaty that promised the Boers self-government.

by the merchant classes imposed a constitution, parliament, and elections upon the ruling shahs of the Qajar dynasty between 1905 and 1911. The Qajars had seemed unable to resist Russian and British influence. They were all too willing to grant monopolies to foreign companies, concede control of their finances to foreign bankers, and squander the tax revenue they collected from the commercial classes.

In the neighboring Ottoman Empire, nationalist army officers engineered a coup d'état in 1908 called the **Young Turk Revolution**. The Young Turks considered the imperial government incapable of facing up to foreign encroachments on Ottoman territory. As in Iran, they too constrained a monarch with a constitution. In Russia, frustration with the tsar's inability or unwillingness to address mass poverty and permit wider political participation led to street demonstrations against the government. Although bloodily suppressed, the demonstrations led to constitutional constraints in what is known as the Revolution of 1905. We will return to the Ottoman and Russian cases in the next chapter, because their stories are inseparable from that of World War I.

Each of these revolutions was unique, with its own grievances, coalitions, personalities, and train of events. The Chinese and Mexican revolutions were bigger and bloodier than that of the Young Turks or the Iranian merchants. Yet they all represent the disruptive impacts of nationalism, imperialism, and industrial power upon agrarian peoples.

Conclusion

All of the movements, uprisings, and revolutions in this chapter form important parts of national histories in the United States, Brazil, China, India, Mexico, and South Africa. They occurred in very different settings. They were triggered by things as different as greased rifle cartridges and a young Xhosa girl's prophetic vision. But they all took place within the span of a human lifetime (1856–1920) and shared a few overlapping features.

In a general way, all of them resulted from widespread anxieties about ongoing trends. Changes seemed to be coming too thick and fast. People outside the handful of industrialized countries found reason to fear new technologies and new weapons, powerful strangers from afar, and missionaries with new religions. Economic competition from the other side of the world ruined what had once seemed secure livelihoods. Familiar ways, institutions, and rulers no longer seemed up to the challenges of safeguarding their subjects, keeping order, and preventing hunger. In short, the forces of economic globalization, imperialism, and nationalism, circulating through the Global web, were shaking things up in confusing and threatening ways.

In most cases (Brazil was an exception), the perceived threats to a cherished way of life came in part from foreigners. Sometimes those foreigners were settlers, as in the U.S. West. Sometimes they were Christian missionaries, as in India and China. Sometimes they were representatives of encroaching imperial powers and foreign businesses, as in India, China, and Mexico. The degree to which international influences affected daily life and domestic politics was on the increase, a result of tightening travel, trade, financial, and intellectual links within the Global web.

In many cases, the causes for which so many people died took on religious hues. The followers of prophets such as Nongqawuse, Antônio Conselheiro, Wovoka, or Hong Xiuquan found in their faiths an answer to their fears. Many of the Indian rebels of 1857 couched their battles in terms of Hindu or Islamic revivals. Even the revolution of Sun Yatsen carried religious tinges. Sun's program for nationalist China was inflected by his Christian education. The Mexican Revolution was an exception (on the surface), a case in which the revolutionaries considered the church among their targets. But at the same time the appeal of Zapata and Villa to peasants, servants, and ranch-hands was of a better world to come, a concept that their Catholic upbringing prepared most Mexicans to embrace.

The great rebellions and revolutions heralded an onrushing era of mass politics and mass mobilizations around the world. The forces of nationalism, imperialism, and industrialization—transmitted along the pathways of the Global web—would affect more lives more forcefully, as the next chapter will show.

‖‖

Chapter Review

KEY TERMS

millenarian movements p. 961   **Taiping Rebellion** p. 972
Ghost Dance p. 964   **Indian Rebellion** p. 972
Antônio Conselheiro p. 967   **Lakshmibai** p. 974

REVIEW QUESTIONS

1. Describe the feelings and ideas that the Ghost Dance helped Amerindians to express.

2. Who was drawn to Antônio Conselheiro's message, and why?

3. What shared experiences caused the Xhosa, Amerindians, and Antônio Conselheiro's followers to put their faith in millenarian movements?

4. Explain the external forces that contributed to the Taiping Rebellion.

5. What economic, political, and religious grievances did Indians under British rule have?

6. How did the British Raj change after the Indian Rebellion, and what were the long-term effects of this shift?

7. What common pattern emerged among reformers in societies under pressure from the world's leading powers?

8. During this period, what were the main grievances of peasants and the educated middle classes around the world?

9. Who led the self-strengthening movement in China, and what were its focuses?

10. Identify and discuss the two challenges that ultimately undermined the Qing.

11. What were Porfirio Díaz's three main policy initiatives, who benefited from them, and which groups did they disadvantage?

12. In what ways did Mexico change socially, economically, and politically after the Mexican Revolution?

13. Compare and contrast the aims and frustrations of rebels in South Africa, Iran, the Ottoman Empire, and Russia.

14. What widespread anxieties and changes contributed to revolutions and rebellions around the world during this time?

Go to INQUIZITIVE

to see what you've learned—and learn what you've missed—with personalized feedback along the way.

THE GLOBAL WEB

Since 1870

T he web of connections among societies that helped bring about the revolutions and rebellions discussed in Part 5 grew tighter after 1870. The main engine behind this process was continuing technological change, which sped up and cheapened communication and transport. But several other trends contributed to the growth of the Global web after 1870, such as ideologies that claimed global relevance, the alliance systems of international politics, and the steady march of the English language to its current status as a common world language. All these processes, and others as well, made the contemporary world more interactive than ever before—but in fits and starts rather than at a regular pace.

The Pace of Global Integration

The irregular pace of modern globalization consisted broadly of three phases. The first, from 1870 to 1914, saw rapid extension of links driven above all by new technologies such as railroads, steamships, and telegraphs. The second phase, from 1914 to 1945, showed a mixed record. New technologies such as radio and air travel emerged, speeding flows of information and people. But two world wars and a worldwide economic depression drove several societies to turn inward, fall back on their own resources, and try to be self-sufficient. In economic terms, global integration retreated as flows of international trade and finance slowed. In political and cultural terms, however, there was no retreat. Societies took one another increasingly into account in shaping their own policies and preferences, whether in military matters or music. The third phase, from 1945 to the present, again saw an intensification of the process of globalization, with louder objections to it than ever before. The pace, scale, and scope of international interactions came to exceed those of any previous era especially after about 1980, when computerization and digitization began to take hold.

Key Themes

The next four chapters—Part 6 of the book—look closely at three main themes. First is the prominence of international politics and war. Ordinary people increasingly could not escape involvement in the affairs of states, especially the many states that took part in major wars. These chapters explore World Wars I and II, and the Cold War, the primary conflicts that re-fashioned political, social, and economic life after 1914.

Second is a shift in world power away from Europe. Beginning in the 1490s, Atlantic Europe had slowly attained unusual wealth and power by global standards. With industrialization in the nineteenth century, Europe, North America, and Japan had rapidly attained still greater power expressed in overseas empires. Between 1945 and 1991, the empires of Japan and the European states—including the USSR—crumbled sooner and faster than almost anyone expected. A general re-balancing of world wealth and power took place, and indeed is still in motion. The formerly colonized peoples of Africa and Asia won their independence, and those in several Asian countries—first Japan, but then South Korea, Singapore, Taiwan, and to some extent China—became rich almost overnight. This rise of East Asia is the fastest and most dramatic re-arrangement of the global economy in world history.

The third general theme is the recurrent backlash against global integration. Immediately after World War I, political and ideological movements—fascism and Soviet communism—arose that intensified nationalism and encouraged economies built on self-sufficiency rather than international trade. The global economy became still more protectionist and fragmented during the Great Depression of the 1930s. While international linkages were repaired after World War II, and economic and cultural globalization galloped ahead in the following decades, once again it produced discontent. Politics based on sectarian religion made a comeback, for example, and after about 2010 xenophobic nationalism did too. Many millions also blamed economic globalization for rising inequalities in wealth and income.

Chapter 26 takes up international politics, specifically World War I and its aftermath. It emphasizes not only the war itself, but also some of the political and ideological movements created or advanced by revulsion at the war and its peace settlements: fascism, communism, and anti-colonialism. The chapter also presents suffragism, the campaign to win the vote for women, in the general context of World War I. Chapter 27 continues with the broad political patterns formed during World War II (1937–1945) and the Cold War (1945–1991), explaining the origins, course, and results of both. Chapter 28 focuses on decolonization between 1945 and 1980, and on the extraordinary economic rise of East Asia from about 1950 to the present. These twin developments amount to another basic shift in the geography of power in the global system.

Chapter 29 considers the—equally extraordinary—acceleration of almost every form of globalization since 1980, including international migrations and financial flows. It emphasizes the economy, environment, popular culture, and health and disease, and shows some of the political backlash against globalization. The chapter also explores some unintentional effects of the tight Global web, such as the faster spread of emerging diseases including HIV/AIDS, Ebola, SARS, and COVID-19.

International Politics

WAR, PEACE, AND IDEOLOGIES

1870 to 1940

FOCUS QUESTIONS

1. In what ways was World War I a global event?
2. How did fascism and communism advance in the 1920s and 1930s?
3. Why did anti-colonial movements gain strength after World War I?

> If you could hear, at every jolt, the blood
> Come gargling from the froth-corrupted lungs,
> Obscene as cancer, bitter as the cud
> Of vile, incurable sores on innocent tongues,—
> My friend, you would not tell with such high zest
> To children ardent for some desperate glory,
> The old Lie: *Dulce et decorum est*
> *Pro patria mori.*

Wilfred Owen wrote the poem "Dulce et Decorum Est" during the last months of World War I. An infantry officer in the British Army, Owen had witnessed up close the final agonies of soldiers dying from poison gas attacks. Twice wounded and decorated for valor, Owen was killed in action one week before an armistice ended the war in November 1918. In quoting Horace, an ancient Roman poet, whose message he calls "The old Lie," Owen expresses his disillusionment with the war and his resentment of its proponents. "Pro Patria Mori" was inscribed on the chapel wall of Sandhurst,

Britain's foremost military academy, and familiar to Britain's educated classes. The quotation translates as: "How sweet and suitable it is to die for one's country."

Among the many strands of global politics in modern times, one that stands out is the extreme violence of modern war. The warfare that characterized both world wars (I: 1914–1918, and II: 1937–1945) involved complete mobilizations of the resources and populations of the combatant countries, as well as deadly new technologies, including poison gas in **World War I** and the atomic bomb in World War II. The thorough destruction and mobilization brought by these wars is sometimes called total war.

A second strand is the global scale of politics. The ancient Romans, Mauryans, or Olmecs never worried about peoples on the other side of the world. For them, all politics was local or regional. By the early twentieth century, however, policy makers took into account circumstances and events on distant continents as a matter of course. The interconnectedness of the Global web had reached a point at which decisions made in Paris could quickly trigger uprisings in China.

A third is the increased impact of international politics on ordinary people. Centuries ago, millions of people lived beyond the reach of tax collectors and military recruiters, and they had few dealings with any state. No longer. Since 1914, almost no one has lived free from the demands of states. If your country got into a big war, your life would change, whether you served on the front lines or remained on a family farm. Total war was not the sport of kings, but the concern of all.

A fourth strand is the rise of mass ideological and political movements, including those considered here: fascism, communism, anti-colonialism, and suffragism—the effort to secure voting rights for women. Such movements were not strictly new in the twentieth century, but they became much more common than before. This was the result partly of disillusionment with established

CHRONOLOGY

1869 *The Subjection of Women* is published; Wyoming allows women to vote

1893 New Zealand allows women to vote in national elections

June 28, 1914 Gavrilo Princip kills Austrian archduke

July 1914 Start of World War I

1915 Italy enters World War I; Japan issues The Twenty-one Demands

1915–1916 Gallipoli campaign

Feb.–Dec. 1916 Battle of Verdun

July 1916 Battle of the Somme

Mar. 1917 Tsar Nicholas II abdicates

Mar. 1918 Treaty of Brest-Litovsk

1921 Kronstadt rebellion; Hitler becomes head of Nazi Party; formation of Chinese Communist party

Nov. 7–8, 1917 Bolshevik Revolution

1918–1921 Russian Civil War

Apr. 1919 Amritsar massacre

1918–1919 Global influenza pandemic

1920 League of Nations opens

Apr. 1917 United States enters World War I

1919 Treaty of Versailles is signed; Weimar Republic is established

1922 Start of Mussolini's rule

1939 Germany attacks Poland

Nov. 1918 World War I ends

May 1919 May Fourth Movement

1930 Gandhi leads salt march

1935 Hitler introduces Nuremberg Laws

1927-1928 Stalin consolidates power

1929 Start of Great Depression

1933 Hitler becomes chancellor of Germany

authorities brought on by World War I, partly of new media such as radio that connected audiences with charismatic politicians as never before, and partly of longer-term trends in urbanization and globalization that reached new heights in the twentieth century. Monarchies and empires fell; traditions and certainties melted into air. People everywhere, whether frightened or inspired by the crumbling of old regimes, searched for a new basis for politics. World War I and the peace settlement that followed shaped all of these developments, so that's where this chapter will begin.

World War I and Its Legacies

World War I, despite its name, was mainly a European war, but its repercussions reached every continent. Its unprecedented butchery and unsatisfactory peace settlement gave rise to resentments and ambitions that shaped life for decades—indeed, to this day.

The Great Powers, 1870-1914

Great powers are great because they have more people, money, military force, and unity of purpose than lesser powers. In the nineteenth century, industrialization and the emergence of nationalism created a handful of new great powers, several of them mid-sized European states such as Germany, France, and Britain. They joined multi-cultural empires such as the Ottoman, Russian, and Habsburg—longstanding great powers—atop the greasy pole of international politics. In the years 1914–1918, these powers went to war with one another. Before wading into World War I, let's look briefly at the major participants.

In 1914, the most powerful polity on Earth was the British Empire, thanks to its industry and its navy. Britain's industrial production stood third in the world behind that of the United States and Germany; but counting the industry of the empire—Canada, India, South Africa, Australia—it easily surpassed Germany. Britain's army was tiny, but the British navy was the largest and probably most effective in the world. The British Isles in 1914 had 42 million people, and with the dominions of Canada, Australia, and New Zealand, the empire included 57 million more—most of them British immigrants or their descendants. To some extent, Britain could also rely on the manpower of British India, another 252 million people. Britain's population was, by and large, reliably patriotic, although in the Empire many resented British rule.

By 1914, the United States had the potential to become the world's second most powerful state. Its population of some 100 million was growing fast—by about 2 percent per year. Although about one in every six Americans in 1914 had been born overseas, their loyalty to the state proved reliable when war came. The country produced two-thirds of the world's oil and led the world in coal, iron, and steel production. It had a tiny overseas empire consisting mainly of the Philippines, Hawaii, and Puerto Rico, as well as a small and inexperienced army, but a sizeable and growing navy. Its political elites generally did not like to think of the United States as a great power but rather as a hemispheric power in the Americas. So the United States had the capacity but not the will to function as a great power in 1914.

British Imperial Might A fleet of British battleships maneuvers through the Atlantic in 1914. A new class of battleships called dreadnoughts constituted perhaps the strongest weapon in the British Empire's arsenal, contributing to its status as the world's greatest power at the start of World War I.

If the United States was not the second most powerful state in 1914, then Germany was. Its population of about 67 million was growing by 1.2 percent annually. The majority were enthusiastically patriotic. The sharp divisions between Protestants and Catholics, or among social classes, did not appreciably weaken loyalties to the German fatherland. Its coal, iron, and steel output trailed only that of the United States. Its technological and scientific sophistication was second to none. It had an overseas empire, in Africa and the Pacific, but that added next to nothing to German power. Germany's army and navy were large, well trained, and well equipped, probably the best and second best, respectively, in the world.

A notch below these three, in terms of strength in international politics, stood France and Russia. France had 40 million people and a bit more manpower and resources available in its overseas empire. Its industrial production and its navy came well behind Britain's or Germany's. Russia's strength lay mainly in its size. It had 175 million people and the resources of a giant territory. Its industrial production was growing rapidly, and the recently completed Trans-Siberian Railway gave access to some of the vast mineral supplies of Siberia. But the loyalty of its minority populations was shaky. Russia's Poles, for example, still prized their Polish identity long after the eighteenth-century partitions of their country placed them inside the Russian Empire. Russia's army was big but poorly trained and equipped. Its navy was no better.

A notch below France and Russia stood Austria-Hungary and the Ottoman Empire. Austria-Hungary, as the Habsburg Empire was generally known after 1867, had 48 million people in 1914, but many of them belonged to ethnic or religious minorities and their

Languages of the Army in Austria-Hungary, 1914	
German	25%
Hungarian	18%
Czech	13%
Serbian and Croatian	11%
Polish	9%
Ukrainian	6%
Romanian	6%
Slovak	4%
Slovenian	2%
Italian	2%

Note: Another 4 percent of army recruits spoke other languages.

Source: David Reynolds, *The Long Shadow: The Legacies of the Great War in the Twentieth Century* (2015), 7.

allegiance to the state was tempered. The table at left gives some idea of the ethnic diversity of Austria-Hungary's army. Industrial production was modest—lots of textiles, but not much iron and steel. Austria-Hungary had no overseas empire and virtually no navy, but an effective army despite its mix of languages. The Ottoman Empire in 1914 had recently lost a lot of territory in little wars in the Balkans and North Africa. It had about 19 million people, some 4 million of whom were ethno-religious minorities— mainly Armenians, Arabs, and Greeks, whose loyalty Ottoman elites often rightly distrusted. Ottoman industry produced little military materiel. The army, however, was substantial and partly trained by German officers.

Origins of the War

For more than a century, the question of the origins of World War I has fascinated historians, who still don't agree on an answer. The controversies swirl around the whys of the war, and less around what happened. For the sequence of events to make sense, we have to understand that by 1914 Europe's international system, long in flux, was divided into two big **alliance networks**. One, the Triple Alliance anchored by Germany, included Austria-Hungary and Italy. The other, the Triple Entente, enrolled France, Russia, and Great Britain. The purpose of these alliance networks was to extend Europe's long peace, concluded in 1815 in the aftermath of the Napoleonic Wars. Instead, the alliances drew states into a long, devastating war.

On June 28, 1914, a 20-year-old Serbian nationalist, Gavrilo Princip, shot and killed an Austrian archduke on the streets of Sarajevo. Princip was a member of underground Serbian nationalist organizations eager to liberate Serbs (and other "south Slavs," or "Yugoslavs") from Austro-Hungarian rule. The assassination led to an ultimatum from Austria-Hungary: Serbia must surrender much of its independence or face war. Confident of support from Russia—fellow Slavs who had championed Serbia before—the Serbian government chose war.

In preparing to fight on Serbia's behalf at the end of July 1914, Russia mobilized its vast army against both Austria-Hungary and Germany. Germany, in keeping with its war plans, mobilized its army to attack both Russia to the east and France to the west. When Germany did attack, Great Britain joined the war. By August 4, the two alliance systems—minus Italy, which at first kept out—were at war. In late 1914, the Ottoman Empire joined on the German side; and in 1915, Italy entered the war against Germany and Austria-Hungary despite its treaty commitments to those powers. As wartime coalitions, these two blocs became known as the Central Powers (Germany, Austria-Hungary, the Ottoman Empire) and the Entente or Allied Powers (France, Russia, Britain, Italy). Many smaller nations in Europe joined in too.

So why did the conflict between Serbia and Austria-Hungary bring on a general European war? A short answer includes the cultural climate of nationalism, the political influence of armies in most of the great powers, the rigidity of war plans, and the alliances that bound countries to go to war on one another's behalf. It would also include, more specifically, some key decisions—two above all.

European Alliance Systems and the Ottoman Empire, 1914 Before World War I, the great powers of Europe organized two major alliance systems. One included France, Britain, and Russia. The other enrolled Germany, Austria-Hungary, and Italy. The Ottoman Empire, which lost most of its territories in southeastern Europe between 1830 and 1913, was neutral. When the war began in August 1914, Italy proclaimed neutrality despite its alliances. And by November, the Ottoman Empire, despite its former neutrality, joined with Germany and Austria-Hungary, forming the Central Powers. In 1915, Italy would join the Allies.

First was the choice made by German diplomats to support whatever Austria-Hungary elected to do against Serbia. That made Austria-Hungary's leaders more willing to accept the risk of war with Russia, which they knew might result if they attacked Serbia. Second was Russia's choice to mobilize its army in support of Serbia, which was not a treaty obligation, and, as part of that strategy, to mobilize against Germany and Austria-Hungary. Russian war plans called for such a broad mobilization, but they might have been overridden by a more forceful, attentive, and imaginative tsar. (Nicholas II once described himself as "without will and without character.") These and other fateful decisions might well have been made differently if diplomats and emperors had understood that in the circumstances of 1914, war would bring little glory and much gore.

The Course of the War

Fighting began in August 1914 and continued until November 1918, and in a few places beyond that. Declarations of war were welcomed in some cities by cheering crowds and provoked mass enlistments in most of the countries involved. But joy evaporated fast. In the first months of the war, armies sprinted after one another. Where they met, they discovered the pitiless violence of modern combat. The effect of machine guns on infantry became evident on August 22, 1914, when a French attack against German positions led to the deaths of 27,000 Frenchmen in a matter of hours.

By early 1915, the armies on the western front had settled into lines of trenches. Occasional offensives required men to run across no-man's-land toward enemy trenches amid a hail of bullets and, if all went well, fall upon the enemy. More often, they fell in no-man's-land. On the eastern front, attacks sometimes won a little more ground; but nonetheless the war became one of stalemate and attrition, in which both sides were losing soldiers faster than they could recruit new ones.

Weaponry as well as soldiers soon ran short. Of the combatants in 1914, only Germany, Britain, and France had military-industrial complexes equal to the situation. Mines and munition factories everywhere hummed around the clock to meet the demand for weapons and explosives. Labor supply became a bottleneck. With millions of men in the armed forces, women filled the munitions factories. Germany's Krupp armaments factories employed almost no women in 1914, but by 1917 nearly 30 percent of its workforce of 175,000 was female. The enormous industrial capacity of the United States, despite its official neutrality until 1917, helped ease the situation for the Allies. In general, the Allies had a strong advantage in industrial production, food production, and military manpower.

World War I's chief theaters were in Europe; but from the start, small-scale campaigns took place in Africa among rival colonies. British forces launched bigger campaigns against Ottoman armies in Palestine and Mesopotamia, using mainly Indian

Munitions Factories A photograph of the factory floor at the German Krupp factory in 1917 shows many women workers. Women even operate heavy machinery, which would have been unusual before the war.

troops. Naval actions occurred in the Pacific and off of Argentina, as well as in European waters.

For four years, all efforts to break the stalemate failed. In 1915, the Allies tried to knock the Ottoman Empire out of the war with an attack in Turkey, at Gallipoli, but they succeeded only in opening a new stalemated front. The Allies abandoned the front within a year—a major setback. In 1916, the Germans decided to "bleed France white" with a sustained offensive at Verdun in eastern France. It gained nothing of note and cost both countries rivers of blood. To relieve the pressure at Verdun, the British and French launched an offensive along the Somme River in northern France in July 1916. It cost Britain 20,000 dead on the first day—more Britons than had died in 15 years of wars against Bonaparte.

By 1917, the gambles grew more desperate. Naval power enabled the Allies to blockade the Central Powers. All could see that Germany and Austria-Hungary would slowly starve, because they did not grow enough food—Germany had imported about one-quarter of its calories before 1914. Meanwhile, Britain, which produced only one-third of its food, relied on supplies from the United States, Canada, and Argentina. This situation led the German High Command to open unrestricted submarine warfare everywhere in the Atlantic, attacking neutral shipping in order to starve Britain. Sustained submarine warfare, new with World War I, sank nearly 4 million tons of merchant shipping within six months, from February through July 1917. German leaders understood that submarine attacks would bring the Americans, with all their men and industrial capacity, into the war against them; but they hoped the attacks would weaken Britain fast enough that the Central Powers could win before American forces tipped the balance. But the gamble failed: the attacks drove the United States into the war against the Central Powers in April 1917.

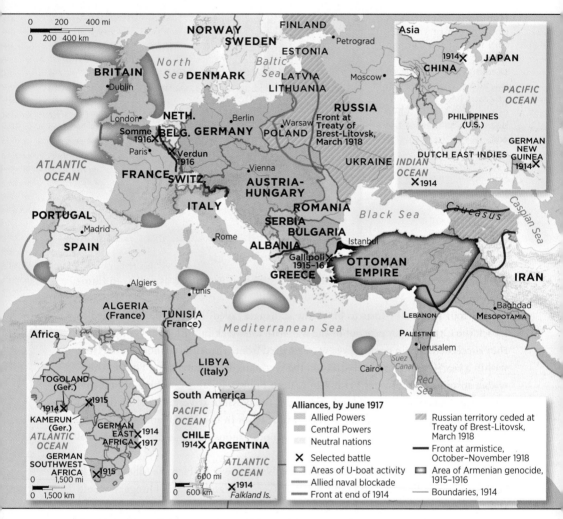

World War I, 1914–1918 World War I was fought mainly in Europe and Ottoman lands in the Middle East, with smaller campaigns on the high seas and in German overseas holdings in Africa, New Guinea, and China. The western front stretched between Switzerland and the shore of the North Sea. The eastern front extended from the Baltic Sea to the Black Sea. Fighting also took place along the Caucasus front, in Ottoman Mesopotamia and Palestine, and in the Balkans. The Allied blockade of the Central Powers, and the German U-boat (submarine) campaigns against Allied and neutral shipping, led to food shortages for civilians behind the lines.

The Russian Revolution of 1917 (see below) gave Germans new reason to hope. By the fall of that year, Russia had stopped fighting. In March 1918, Russia agreed to the Treaty of Brest-Litovsk, surrendering to the Central Powers its 16 westernmost provinces, including 34 percent of its population, half its industry, and 89 percent of its coal mines. The German army now moved 50 divisions to the western front and used its numerical superiority to mount one more gigantic offensive. It almost worked—Britain and France were tottering. But they drew strength from the American forces pouring into Europe in early 1918. The prospect of far more Americans yet to come sapped German morale, as did the Allies' blockade: by 1918, German city-dwellers were living on 1,000 calories a day, half of what an adult body needs to maintain itself. Talk of revolution swirled in the cafés, classrooms, and factory floors of Berlin and Vienna. Strikes broke out. In November, the German top military leadership, aware of the worsening odds against them, decided to quit and negotiated an armistice, ending the war.

The Human Cost

In 51 months of war, the combatants lost about 10 million dead and 21 million wounded, of whom 7 million were maimed for life. On average, about 6,000 men were killed per day. Half of France's male population age 18 to 40 was either killed or wounded. In Austria-Hungary, 90 percent of those mobilized were either killed or wounded. The United States lost 53,000 killed in battle and another 63,000 to disease—some 0.4 percent of males of military age. Canada lost 54,000 killed in combat and a few thousand more to disease—roughly 3 percent of males 18 to 40 years old. The table below shows the human cost to the major combatants.

War Casualties, 1914–1918

COUNTRY	TOTAL MOBILIZED FORCES	KILLED	WOUNDED	PRISONERS AND MISSING	TOTAL CASUALTIES	CASUALTIES AS PERCENTAGE OF FORCES
ALLIED AND ASSOCIATED POWERS						
Russia	12,000,000	1,700,000	4,950,000	2,500,000	9,150,000	76.3
British Empire	8,904,467	908,371	2,090,212	191,652	3,190,235	35.8
France	8,410,000	1,357,800	4,266,000	537,000	6,160,800	73.3
Italy	5,615,000	650,000	947,000	600,000	2,197,000	39.1
United States	4,355,000	116,516	204,002	4,500	325,018	7.1
CENTRAL POWERS						
Germany	11,000,000	1,773,700	4,216,058	1,152,800	7,142,558	64.9
Austria-Hungary	7,800,000	1,200,000	3,620,000	2,200,000	7,020,000	90.0
Ottoman Turkey	2,850,000	325,000	400,000	250,000	975,000	34.2

Source: https://www.pbs.org/greatwar/resources/casdeath_pop.html

Most World War I armies included units drawn from specific regions, so villages and counties could lose almost all their young men in one bloodbath. The Royal Newfoundland Regiment, for example, lost 90 percent of its men (killed or wounded) in a matter of minutes in the Battle of the Somme.

The slaughter broke the morale of the best-trained armies in the world. All except Germany's army mutinied within 35 months. (The American army experienced only six months of combat and did not mutiny.) French soldiers in 1917 baa-ed like sheep going to the slaughter when ordered into an attack. Millions of soldiers suffered mental breakdowns. Few could keep their composure after years living for weeks on end among rats, lice, and mud, regularly enduring artillery bombardments, and, most terrifying of all, occasionally going "over-the-top" into a fusillade of bullets. Since armies were among the most revered institutions in Europe in 1914, the evaporation of military discipline left many soldiers and civilians feeling unmoored.

A cruel irony maximized the carnage. In prior wars, infectious disease had prevented soldiers from massing in their millions long enough to butcher one another on such a scale. By 1914, advances in military medicine enabled armies to stay healthy enough for long enough to kill one another wholesale. In another cruel irony, a global influenza pandemic broke out at the war's end, killing some 50 million people in the years 1918–1919.

The horrors of war extended to civilian populations. In Lebanon, dependent on food imports, one-third of the population starved to death in 1915 when the war interrupted shipping. The Ottoman Turks, suspicious of Armenian loyalties, starved, shot, or bayoneted 1 to 2 million Armenians in 1915–1916 in a genocidal campaign. In German East Africa (today's Tanzania), the war reduced population by 20 percent, mainly through starvation and disease. Atrocities on scales large and small occurred wherever armies occupied enemy territory, as in eastern France or western Russia.

Armenian Genocide Armenian refugees—including several children—flee Ottoman persecution around 1916. The Ottoman state systematically starved or murdered about 1.5 million Armenians during World War I.

Life on the home fronts grew ever grimmer as the war dragged on. Food ran short in Russia, Germany, and Austria-Hungary in particular. Civilians had to work long hours in mines, factories, fields, offices, and hospitals. In many countries, currency inflation ate into workers' wages, leading to hardship and strikes.

Women did the work of men in addition to their own. In Britain, 1.4 million women joined the paid labor force between 1914 and 1917. In Austria-Hungary by 1918, 1 million women had done so. Most of the women laboring in armaments and heavy industry during the war had already been workers before 1914, but now they shifted from textile mills to munitions plants. This was especially true in France and Germany, where total female employment climbed the least during the period 1914–1918. Most of the extra work that women shouldered was on farms. Some armies let some soldiers go on leave during harvest season. But in Germany, France, Austria-Hungary, Serbia, and other countries where almost all able-bodied men and horses were at war, women, children, and the elderly had to assume even the heaviest farm work.

Hundreds of thousands of women volunteered as nurses—some 120,000 in France and 92,000 in Germany. In the United States, about 22,000 did; and 3,000 in Canada. Vera Brittain, a middle-class Englishwoman, put her Oxford education on hold at age 21 to serve as a nurse. Before she returned to her studies, she had spent three hard years amid splintered bodies and shattered minds. She lost her only brother, her fiancé, and her two closest male friends to the war.

German, Austro-Hungarian, and French armies recruited thousands of female prostitutes for regulated army brothels. Unregulated brothels and the demand for prostitutes in general flourished during the war, as millions of men and women were away from the constraints of family and village.

On a small scale, women also served in combat. Bulgaria, Romania, Serbia, and Russia allowed women soldiers to fight. Milunka Savić, who took her brother's place in the Serbian Army, was wounded several times, won a handful of decorations for valor, and on one occasion captured 23 Bulgarian soldiers by herself. In Russia in the summer of 1917, a call for volunteers resulted in 5,000 women joining special battalions, the original purpose of which was to try to shame male soldiers into fighting harder. But two of the women's battalions took part in an offensive in July 1917; and one, the so-called Women's Battalion of Death, led by Maria Bochkareva, a 27-year-old of peasant origins, stormed a German trench line successfully.

The mobilization of women for war work was controversial everywhere. It ran counter to prevailing notions of femininity. Skeptics feared that driving ambulances, doing police work, selling train tickets, or building tanks alongside men would corrupt women's morals. After the war, most of the women who had taken on men's roles left their wartime jobs to return to their former lives.

The Russian Revolution of 1917

In addition to the human casualties, World War I destroyed most of the political structures of Europe and the Middle East. The defeated Central Powers—Germany, Austria-Hungary, and the Ottoman Empire—all crumbled. So did one of the Allies, Russia. The experience of war stoked Europe's nationalisms and made these multicultural and multinational empires less popular than ever. The experience of defeat—which Russia shared with the Central Powers—destroyed them.

The **Russian Revolution of 1917** stands among the largest political legacies of

World War I, partly because Russia was a big country but mainly because it featured an ideology that inspired imitation far and wide. Although it was triggered by World War I, and probably would not have happened without it, the Russian Revolution, like those in China and Mexico discussed in the previous chapter, had deep roots.

Grievances and Reforms After the abolition of serfdom in 1861, Russia remained an agrarian country of 75 million. By 1914, its population had grown to 175 million. For the peasantry, freedom from serfdom did not bring freedom from hunger and hard work. For many educated Russians, the conspicuous strengthening of Britain, France, and Germany as industrial and imperial states led, around the period 1860–1900, to worries that their country was falling behind.

What to do? The answers came down to two broad choices. One, that of the conservatives called Slavophiles, was to return to true Russian ways and shun innovations and reforms. Novelties such as representative government and factories were not suited to Russia, they thought, and would corrode the social cement of Russian Orthodoxy, faith in tsars, and village solidarity. According to others, often called Westernizers, autocracy and the power of the Orthodox Church held Russia back.

These debates grew more urgent in 1881 when a group that called itself The People's Will assassinated Tsar Alexander II. They were one of several tiny groups who sought solutions to Russia's ills through revolution, spurning the path of reform. After his father's assassination, Tsar Alexander III outlawed public discussion of many political topics and drove the revolutionaries underground.

Russia's revolutionaries, although few in number and divided among themselves, figured time was on their side. Some put their faith in the peasantry, noting the egalitarian custom in many Russian villages of periodically re-distributing land, animals, and tools according to every family's needs. Others, under the influence of the ideas of Karl Marx, thought that real revolution could only come from the industrial working class—or as Marxists put it, the proletariat.

The hour seemed to strike in 1905. The government, now headed by Tsar Nicholas II, unleashed the army on unarmed demonstrators in the capital of St. Petersburg, killing more than 100. Instead of being intimidated, workers, peasants, and dissident middle-class groups known as the intelligentsia became more vocal. Demands rang out for more schools, legislative assemblies, and land for peasants. Peasants themselves wanted reduced rents or ownership of the land they worked. Workers wanted better wages and a voice in factory management. Urban workers invented new, city-wide workers' councils, called soviets.

These events, sometimes called the 1905 Revolution, led Nicholas—reluctantly—to make concessions, including an empire-wide legislative assembly, called the Duma, whose members would be elected. The first Duma met in 1906 and called for a radical land reform. To the tsar and his aristocratic landowning counselors, land redistribution seemed to strike at the heart of Russia's political system.

The tsar called upon a brilliant bureaucrat, aristocrat, and scholar of agriculture, Pyotr Stolypin, to manage the Duma's demands. Stolypin tried to stave off peasant resentment with, as he put it, the "wager on the strong." His reforms favored richer peasants, easing their route to greater prosperity and property ownership. He wanted to establish a peasant bulwark against revolution. But a young revolutionary who also worked for the secret police assassinated him in 1911, leaving Russia in less capable hands. Even the most capable hands would have been full, given the pressures facing Russia after the outbreak of World War I.

War, Defeat, and Revolution From the start of the war in 1914, Germany hammered the Russian army. Russia's economy proved unable to produce enough ammunition, artillery, locomotives—even shoes—for the war effort. Russia's soldiers, justifiably, began to think their government was failing them, treating them as mere cannon fodder, while profiteers grew fat from government contracts. Russia mobilized 12 million men, of whom 1.7 million were killed, 5 million wounded, and 2.5 million missing or captured. Only Austria-Hungary's casualty rate was worse.

In this time of crisis, Tsar Nicholas II showed all his many weaknesses. He could not control bickering generals. In late 1915, the tsar went to the front to supervise the conduct of the war personally. That invited Russians to hold him directly responsible for military misfortunes. He ignored mounting economic problems on the home front—notably, inflation of food and fuel prices. The tsar's authority melted away.

Mass demonstrations took place in March 1917 (February by the calendar then in use in Russia). Troops called out to tame the riotous crowds refused to fire. Generals and Duma politicians, agreeing that the tsar had become a liability, forced him to abdicate in favor of his brother, who refused the throne. Russia now had no tsar. The Romanov dynasty, in power for 300 years, was no more.

A handful of Duma politicians now formed a Provisional Government that represented mainly the privileged segments of Russian society. In the capital, now called Petrograd, workers and revolutionaries organized into a soviet and claimed authority. Russia had, in effect, two governments, and thus no government.

Through the spring and summer of 1917, the Provisional Government, headed by the moderate socialist lawyer Alexander Kerensky, made two big mistakes. First, it chose to continue fighting, even ordering an offensive in June that became another retreat by July. Second, it postponed land reform. Millions of peasants took matters into their own hands, seizing control of estates, ousting and sometimes killing landlords. Soldiers from peasant families deserted the battlefront in droves so as not to miss re-distributions of land. Critics of the Provisional Government promised peace, land, and bread—none of which Kerensky could provide.

Lenin Into this chaotic situation came **Vladimir Lenin**. Born in 1870 to a prosperous provincial family, Lenin became a dedicated revolutionary in his teens after the shock of seeing his brother hanged for trying to build an assassin's bomb. An excellent student interested in physics and math, and a fine chess player, Lenin studied law at university but was expelled for taking part in a demonstration. He responded by studying revolutionary writers, especially Marx, on his own. Thanks to his mother's intervention, he was allowed to take university examinations in 1890, despite not having been a student for years. He passed brilliantly and became a provincial lawyer, while devoting every spare minute to preparing for revolution. His activities earned him banishment to Siberia in 1897 and then exile, where he wrote political treatises. He was in Switzerland in early 1917 when the High Command of the German Army decided to provide him with a special train to neutral Finland. From there, he could take his revolutionary skills to Petrograd and undermine the teetering Russian war effort.

Lenin in 1917 was a middle-aged man in a hurry. He belonged to a minority faction of a Marxist party called the Bolsheviks, and because of his theoretical writings and his forceful personality he stood high among them. Most Bolsheviks hoped to take power soon, some of them optimistic it could happen through elections. Lenin wanted revolution now, by whatever means necessary, using the slogan "all power to the soviets." Within those soviets, the Bolshevik faction prevailed, thanks to tight organization and the fervor of its members.

The October Revolution and Early Bolshevik Rule Lenin ordered an armed insurrection. The Bolshevik Revolution was a coup d'état on November 7–8, 1917 (but sometimes called the October Revolution because of the different Russian calendar). Within 10 days, the Bolsheviks controlled Petrograd and Moscow and had begun to squeeze out other revolutionary factions. Within three months, they were governing alone and had set up a secret police and revolutionary courts to identify, and then imprison or murder, those insufficiently loyal to their party.

Bolshevik Revolution Russian soldiers rebelling against the tsar's authority in early 1917 march through the streets of St. Petersburg, carrying a banner that reads "Liberty, Equality, Fraternity" in homage to the French revolutionary slogan.

Their policies, however, won them the loyalty of many Russians. The Bolsheviks made peace with the Central Powers early in 1918. They ratified the peasants' seizures of land. They stripped away the civil rights of priests, landlords, bankers, and others whom they deemed exploiters.

Lenin and many Bolsheviks believed that the Duma, and all democracy, was a sham. The appropriate government for Russia was what they called the dictatorship of the proletariat. In practice, that meant a one-party state led not by proletarian workers but by people like Lenin: long-time professional revolutionaries, some of them brilliant intellectuals, well schooled—if self-educated—in German philosophy, British political economy, and the history of the French Revolution. They saw themselves as "the vanguard of the proletariat" and were so convinced of their historical mission that at times they used armed force against workers and peasants in whose name they claimed to rule. They thought they were "building communism," a social and political system first outlined by Marx that, in theory, was without private property, without exploitation, and in some versions (not Lenin's) without a state.

It took four difficult years for Lenin to consolidate power. In the Russian Civil War (1918–1921), the Bolsheviks—officially called communists by March 1918—created an improvised army to fight opponents of their revolution. Lenin assigned this task to Leon Trotsky, who had planned the coup of 1917. Despite having no military experience, Trotsky built an effective military in the terrible conditions of 1918. He imposed conscription on a war-weary population and hired officers from the old tsarist army against the wishes of almost every Bolshevik. His Red Army prevailed against a loose coalition of counter-revolutionaries backed by foreign powers, including troops from France, Britain, the United States, and—by far the largest contingent—Japan.

By early 1921, Lenin and the Bolsheviks ruled a shattered, bankrupt, and impoverished country now called the Union of Soviet Socialist Republics (USSR). Some 8 to 13 million people had died of violence or disease in the turmoil of the years 1917–1921. Another 2 million emigrated. Industrial production stood at 20 percent of 1914 levels. Hunger stalked the streets. The Bolsheviks concluded that they could not let workers run the factories after all, so they imposed hierarchical management. They requisitioned all the grain they could from the peasantry, who responded with strikes. In March 1921, sailors at a naval base, Kronstadt, renowned for its revolutionary ardor against the tsars, rebelled against Bolshevik rule. The Red Army crushed them at the cost of many thousand lives, demonstrating—for those who needed convincing—that the Bolsheviks would brook no dissent. In the years to come, they would try to destroy the surviving elites of pre-revolutionary Russia, spread their ideology abroad, and make the USSR a powerhouse in world politics.

Versailles and Post-War Partitions

In 1919, representatives of the victorious powers gathered at Versailles outside Paris to hammer out a set of peace treaties. The Allies excluded the defeated Central Powers and communist Russia, which had announced it would not pay the tsars' debts. Edith Wilson, the wife of the American president, Woodrow Wilson, told her husband that the assembled diplomats poring over their maps looked like so many little boys playing a game. The president assured her theirs was a serious business. They were re-drawing the map of east-central Europe and Southwest Asia, dividing up territories, creating countries, marking borders, and defining peoples. In short, they were doing roughly what an earlier generation of European diplomats had done to Africa at the Berlin Conference of 1884–1885.

Re-Making Europe The European powers had carried out the partition of Africa in ignorance, but they undertook the partition of the territories of the Central Powers in a mood of vengeance. French diplomats especially wanted to cripple Germany. The deal imposed on Germany, the **Treaty of Versailles**, explicitly blamed Germany for the outbreak of the war, required Germany to pay huge sums (called reparations) to the victors, and turned some 13 percent of German territory over to either France or newly re-created Poland. It put strict limits on the size of Germany's armed forces. Other treaties, equally vengeful, were signed with Austria, Hungary, Bulgaria, and the Ottoman Empire.

The treaties reflected two other ambitions aside from vengeance. The first was **self-determination**, to use Wilson's preferred phrase. The American president thought that each European nationality ought to rule itself. This would, he hoped, remove an

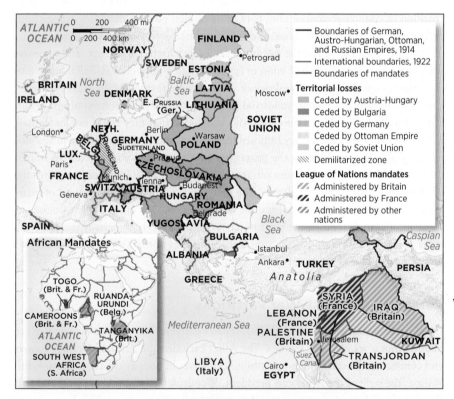

A New Political Geography: Europe, the Middle East, and Africa, 1922 The treaties signed in 1919 and 1920 concluding World War I re-drew the boundaries of Europe, European colonies, and the Ottoman Middle East. New countries arose in east-central Europe and in former Russian, Austro-Hungarian, and German territories. New de facto colonies, as well as the new country of Turkey, were created in former Ottoman lands in the Middle East. The Allied powers devising this new political geography tried to respect ethnic identities in Europe, but not in the Middle East or Africa.

important cause of discontent, helping to ensure future peace. Wilson did not consider Africans and Asians capable of self-rule. Racism of this sort was commonplace in 1919.

The second ambition behind the treaties was, in Wilson's phrase, collective security. He hoped that international institutions might restrain the militarism and nationalism that underlay World War I. So the Allies designed an international body, the League of Nations, to prevent war through arbitration. Based in Geneva, Switzerland, the League opened for business in 1920 and enjoyed modest success in settling international disputes during the 1920s. But in the 1930s it proved helpless in the face of renewed militarism—as we shall see. In a bitter rebuke to Wilson, the U.S. Senate refused to ratify U.S. membership in the League.

World War I and its peace treaties left legacies more durable than the League of Nations. The Romanovs in Russia were not the only longstanding dynasty destroyed. In Germany, when the emperor, Kaiser Wilhelm II, fled the country late in 1918, it ended the reign of the House of Hohenzollern, emperors of Germany since 1871 and kings of Prussia since 1701. In the absence of the monarchy, political factions battled in the streets. In Berlin, a communist uprising was crushed. In Munich, a Soviet-style government briefly came to power. In August 1919, after nine months' painful gestation, Germany brought forth a republic, soon called the Weimar Republic after the town where its first constitutional assembly took place. It struggled to gain legitimacy among Germans. The economy careened from hyperinflation of the currency in 1923 and 1924 to economic depression in 1931. The rise of Adolf Hitler to power in Germany, in 1933, described below, reflected the inadequacies of the Weimar Republic and stands as one of the legacies of World War I.

In Austria-Hungary, the House of Habsburg also lost its throne after 400 years as a major force in Europe. As in Germany, revolution followed defeat in 1918. Reorganization followed along lines set forth in the treaties negotiated in Paris in 1919, which created a series of new countries in place of the multinational Habsburg state. Austria and Hungary became independent countries. Poland was re-created from Habsburg, German, and Russian territory. Another republic, Czechoslovakia, was cobbled together from Habsburg provinces. The southern Slavs were gathered into a new kingdom, Yugoslavia, ruled by a Serbian dynasty. All of these countries were small and comparatively weak. Their borders did not perfectly match ethnic geography—no borders could. Most of them soon became nationalist and authoritarian in character.

Re-Making the Middle East   After 600 years as the ruling family of the Ottoman Empire, the House of Osman also lost its empire as a result of World War I. The result was a dramatic transformation of the Middle East—a term that came into occasional use in the late nineteenth century and became common after 1918. Its precise meaning varies, but in this book it refers to Southwest Asia and Egypt.

After weathering all manner of challenges for centuries, the Ottoman state proved unequal to the demands of industrial warfare in the years 1914–1918. The treaty its representatives signed with the Allies in 1919 amounted to the partition of most of the empire among Britain, France, Italy, and Greece. This outraged many Turks, sparking a nationalist revolution led by an army hero, **Mustafa Kemal**, who as we've seen had played a role in the Young Turk Revolution of 1908. Between 1919 and 1924, Kemal's forces defeated all rivals, repelled a Greek invasion, expelled millions of non-Turks from Anatolia, replaced the Ottoman state with a new Turkish republic, and, most radical of all, abolished the Islamic caliphate.

For more than 1,200 years, caliphs, the earthly leaders of the Islamic faith and the official successors of Muhammad, had guided Muslims. Since 1517, every Ottoman sultan had claimed the mantle of caliph; and for most Sunni Muslims, and therefore most Muslims, the Ottoman claim was legitimate. So it came as a great shock when Kemal's government eliminated the caliphate in 1924.

Kemal and his followers drew the lesson from defeat in World War I that the Ottoman Empire had been backward and inefficient, held down by an antiquated culture steeped in Islamic tradition. So he pushed through reforms in education and law that secularized Turkey, closing Islamic schools and courts. Religious symbols and garb were banned in public. Sisters' inheritances now equaled their brothers', contrary to normal practice under Islamic law. Women acquired more legal rights as individuals rather than as wards of their fathers or husbands. Polygamy was banned and women could initiate divorce. From 1930, women could vote and hold office. The Latin alphabet replaced the Arabic.

This package, often known as the Atatürk Reforms after Kemal's adopted name of Atatürk ("father of the Turks"), was part of a century-long process of reform in Ottoman lands. It was also a legacy of World War I. Kemal's main motivation was to strengthen Turkey as the Meiji reformers had done in Japan. To achieve this, he drew upon the law, culture, and technology of the most formidable states of the day—those of western Europe. Kemal's military record and his success in rallying Turks against

Secularized Turkey A photograph of a Turkish classroom dated to around 1930 shows women students being taught to read and write in the Latin alphabet. Most of the women wear Western dress, and many have their hair uncovered: characteristic signs of Atatürk's program of reform.

foreign invasion gave him the prestige and power to enact far-reaching reforms and harness the nationalism of ethnic Turks.

The territory of the Turkish republic was a mere remnant of the Ottoman Empire. The mainly Arab provinces of the defunct empire, now officially called Mandated Territories of the League of Nations, became de facto colonies of Britain and France. The French got Syria and Lebanon; the British took Palestine, Jordan, and Iraq.

That arrangement stored up trouble for the future. During the war, the British government had promised unspecified land in Ottoman Palestine to Zionist Jews, persuaded by Chaim Weizmann, a Russian immigrant and Zionist leader. A nationalist movement of the Jewish people, Zionism grew up partly in response to anti-Semitism in Europe in the late nineteenth century. Another early organizer, Theodor Herzl, a journalist from Budapest, gave the movement its ideological foundation. The Zionist movement aimed to create a Jewish homeland centered on Jerusalem, despite the presence of tens of thousands of Muslim and Christian Arabs who themselves considered Palestine home. British diplomats had also promised independence to Arabs if they rebelled against the Ottomans. And other British diplomats cut a deal with France, promising to divide the Arab provinces of the Ottoman Empire between them. So when the peacemakers in Paris in 1919 re-drew the map of the Middle East, just about everyone felt betrayed. Their descendants often still do.

The diplomats in Paris re-arranged the political geography of Africa and the Pacific as well as the Middle East. Germany's former African colonies, such as Tanganyika, Togo, Southwest Africa, and others, became League of Nations Mandated Territories administered by Britain, France, Belgium, or South Africa. In the Pacific, former German colonies went to Japan, Britain, Australia, or New Zealand. The local populations in Samoa or New Guinea or Togo were not consulted.

Suffragism to 1939

While the peacemakers at Versailles were discussing the fine points of the right of self-determination of peoples, women reminded them that the female half of humankind did not enjoy that right. As we've seen, Olympe de Gouges, Abigail Adams, and others had advocated women's political rights in the late eighteenth century with little success. Winning the vote—the goal of **suffragism**—and taking part in the direction of one's country was an essential step in women's quest for political equality. It happened in a rush, like the abolitions of slavery, and World War I provided a big push.

Pre-War Suffrage Movements As of 1850, voting was a male preserve in the few countries that permitted it at all. Many voices challenged this arrangement. Their arguments included the notion that denying women the vote was inherently unjust; that women's influence in politics would reduce corruption and war; and, in some cases such as the United States, that woman suffrage, if confined to a preferred class or race, would reduce the influence of poor people, immigrants, or racial minorities who, if they did not already vote, might do so one day.

During the nineteenth century, women in the United Kingdom and the United States built social movements aimed at winning the vote, often allied with supporters of moral causes such as banning prostitution or alcohol. Women in other countries took note: suffragism, like abolitionism, was an international movement, coursing through the Global web. Many who took up the suffragist cause in the United States were abolitionists or Quakers—including Lucretia Mott and Elizabeth Cady Stanton, who in 1848 organized a women's rights gathering in upstate New York, the Seneca Falls Convention. Stanton held that only the vote would make woman "free as man is free." The convention concluded by issuing a Declaration of Sentiments modeled on the Declaration of Independence. The most influential suffragist publication was John Stuart Mill's *The Subjection of Women* (1869), likely written with substantial input from his wife, Harriet Taylor Mill, who had published on suffragism in 1851. The book was translated into dozens of languages and read by suffragists all over the world.

By 1890, suffragists and other reformers in a few countries had achieved some important goals such as limits on working hours or the sale of alcohol, improved city lighting or sanitation, more girls' schools, and a woman's right to own property in her own name. But, despite sustained effort and support from many male politicians, they were not significantly closer to securing women's right to vote in national elections.

In Britain, the movement took on an especially militant character between 1909 and 1914. Suffragists, frustrated with 70 years of meager results, tried mass demonstrations, hunger strikes, and sabotage. They even exploded a bomb at a prime minister's residence. These efforts, organized by a minority wing of British suffragists led by Emmeline Pankhurst and her daughters, failed in their purpose as of 1914.

Early Suffrage When World War I began, about 2 million of the world's roughly 400 million voting-age women could vote, all of them in four small countries. Not counting places such as the state of New Jersey that had provided women the vote and then quickly took it away, the first jurisdiction in the world where women could vote was Wyoming. It was a U.S. territory with only 8,000 people in 1869 when one activist—Esther Hobart Morris—convinced the legislature that women would exert a civilizing influence upon the politics of a wild west territory. Utah followed suit in 1870 when the federal government threatened to ban polygamy, a common practice in the Mormon-dominated territory. Utah's polygamous men granted women the vote to show that the women of Utah were not oppressed. By 1914, women had won the right to vote in state elections in most other western U.S. states.

New Zealand was the first country to pass nationwide legislation enfranchising women. The foremost leader of the suffrage movement in New Zealand was Kate Sheppard, a Scottish immigrant, wife, mother, and formidable organizer in anti-alcohol

Arguments for Suffrage
A California poster in support of women's suffrage from around 1910 suggests that women should be given the vote because they are ready to "clean up" politics by combating bribery, corruption, and social problems.

campaigns. She published persuasive arguments in the same vein as Taylor and Mill, adding the idea that expanding the electorate would reduce vote buying and other forms of corruption. Sheppard presented New Zealand legislators with a petition in favor of enfranchising women signed by a goodly share of the country's adult population. She and her allies, who included several of New Zealand's leading politicians, prevailed in 1893. By 1902, Australia had followed suit. Both New Zealand and Australia were composed substantially of immigrants, with men handily outnumbering women. This made woman suffrage less threatening to them than it did in most other countries. And, as in Wyoming, many men thought women voters might raise the moral tone of public life.

Finland in 1906 and Norway in 1913 allowed women to vote as a result of nationalist campaigns. Finland, part of the Russian Empire since 1815, won substantial autonomy in 1906, including a legislature. To maximize the Finnish voice within what remained a Russian territory, Finnish men agreed that Finnish women should vote. In Norway, the nationalist quest was for independence from Sweden, and once again women's votes seemed politically useful to men hoping to strengthen Norway's claims for independence. These four countries, all small in population, overwhelmingly rural, and far from the centers of world power and intellectual ferment, were the only ones anywhere that allowed women to vote in national elections before World War I.

Elsewhere, resistance to suffragism was too strong. In Catholic countries of southern Europe, for example, and in Islamic lands such as Iran or those of the Ottoman Empire (where few men could vote), the dominant culture led people to suppose that the position of women in society was divinely ordained rather than politically negotiable. Resistance was also entrenched where men—some men, at least—had long ago won voting rights, as in France, the Netherlands, the United States, and the United Kingdom. Political participation had become a ritual of manhood, one that most men felt would undermine feminine virtues if shared with women. In Britain, one of the most active and effective opponents was Mary Augusta Ward, founder in 1908 of the Anti-Suffrage Society. Mrs Humphry Ward, as she preferred to be known, showed astute political skills while arguing—paradoxically—that women were unfit for politics.

Suffrage and the World War In the end, it required major social upheavals— war, invasion, revolution—to splinter the opposition to enfranchising women. World War I provided an opening for suffragist movements, one they were by 1914 fully capable of exploiting.

Between 1914 and 1920, women won the vote in 19 countries, including big and populous ones such as Russia, Poland, Germany, the United Kingdom, Canada, and the United States. Some restrictions applied—so, for example, in the United Kingdom only women over age 30 could vote until 1928, and in the United States the southern states quickly found ways to disenfranchise black women. In Russia, now becoming the communist USSR, women from privileged backgrounds were denied the vote. In Canada, women of Asian or Amerindian (First Nations) background could not vote. But, taken together, more than 100 million women acquired the vote in these seven years. The table at left shows the significance of the era of World War I in the history of women's suffrage up to 1940.

In some countries, including the United Kingdom and the United States, the political winds shifted because women's patriotism and sacrifices for the war effort won them enough goodwill—and undermined notions of their unfitness for public life—to get enfranchisement bills over the top in all-male legislatures. In

When Women Won the Vote (national elections)	
1893	New Zealand
1902	Australia
1906	Finland
1913	Norway
1915	Denmark, Iceland
1917	Russia
1918	Austria, Canada, Germany, Hungary, Latvia, Lithuania, Poland, United Kingdom
1919	Belgium, Luxembourg, Netherlands (and white women in colonial Kenya, Rhodesia)
1920	Albania, Czechoslovakia, United States
1921	Sweden
1922	Ireland
1923	Burma
1924	Mongolia
1928	Guiana
1929	Ecuador
1930	South Africa (white women only)
1931	Spain (revoked 1939)
1932	Brazil, Uruguay, Thailand
1934	Cuba, Turkey
1937	Philippines (U.S. territory)
1938	Bolivia
1939	El Salvador

Source: Jad Adams, *Women and the Vote* (2014), 437–38.

others, such as Germany, Austria, and Russia, when the collapse of autocracy in the years 1917–1918 opened the way to a democratization of politics in general, opposition to women's voting—never organized—quickly crumbled. In all combatant countries, where almost all young men were away from wives and families for months or years, moral reformers hoped that enfranchising women would check the spread of drunkenness and prostitution. In Canada in 1917, a prime minister trying to build support for military conscription pushed through a law allowing the vote to women who were wives, mothers, daughters, or sisters of men in uniform. His reasoning, which proved correct, was that they would favor conscription of other men to join their relatives in the Canadian Army in the trenches of France and Belgium.

So among the legacies of World War I was a giant stride toward the political emancipation of women. By 1920, of countries with constitutional government that allowed regular elections, only France and Italy denied the vote to women. (These countries granted women full suffrage in the 1940s.) Overall, suffragism in the era of World War I was a success. In the coming decades, it would prevail almost everywhere.

The Rise of the United States

In addition to sparking revolutions, shattering empires, and accelerating social and political movements, World War I permanently shifted the global balance of power. In broad terms, it weakened Europe and bolstered the United States. This shift showed up in many spheres, from the size of navies to the pace of industrial innovation. It was most obvious in finance. Britain and France had borrowed heavily from New York bankers and the U.S. government. Anyone seeking big loans in the 1920s now first thought of New York rather than London, Amsterdam, Paris, or Berlin. As the American theologian Reinhold Neibuhr put it in 1930, "We are the first empire of the world to establish our sway without legions. Our legions are dollars."

Bankers aside, Americans proved reluctant to take on the role of the world's leading power. The United States retreated into isolationism in the 1920s, refusing to join the League of Nations, for example. It remained active in the American hemisphere, using its military power freely to intervene in Haiti, Nicaragua, and elsewhere. It kept a world-class navy, equal in size to Britain's. But most Americans preferred to stay out of the world's trouble spots and rely upon broad oceans for U.S. security.

American power—or more precisely, potential power—rested in part on the fact that the United States pumped two-thirds of the world's oil. The centrality of oil to world politics was another legacy of World War I. By the end of the war, trucks, tanks, aircraft, and submarines had become important instruments of military power, and all used oil derivatives as fuel. So did an increasing proportion of surface ships. At the war's end, Lord Curzon, a prominent member of Britain's War Cabinet, said the "Allies floated to victory on a wave of oil." Oil had become essential to modern warfare and a strategic good of the utmost importance—as it remains today.

A further political legacy of World War I was the changed relationship between governments and the governed in many societies. The war dealt a setback to the ideal of restrained government. None of the combatant states trusted the market to provide enough war materiel. All of them relied on government to organize war production to some extent. The German war economy, entirely improvised but carefully controlled by the military, worked miracles in munitions factories, even if it could not adequately feed the civilian population. It made such a favorable impression on Lenin that he used it as his model for Russia once he took power. The combatants only partly demobilized their economies after 1918, keeping government regulation of markets in effect in different ways. World War I advanced a long-term trend, one with several subsequent ebbs and flows, toward bigger government.

The Great Depression

Government direction of economic life surged again in response to the Great Depression of the 1930s, which in some ways was also a legacy of World War I. The Depression began in 1929 with a stock market collapse in the United States. It spread quickly, faster than any previous economic downturn, because of the speed with which information and money now flowed. People tried to pull their money out of banks, many of which failed. Global economic output fell by 15 percent from 1929 to 1932. Agricultural prices fell by as much as 60 percent, and international trade shrank by half. It was the worst economic contraction in twentieth-century world history, by a large margin.

Countries deeply tied into international circuits of finance or dependent on exports were especially hard hit. Unemployment in Germany, which owed large sums in reparations from World War I, reached between 30 and 33 percent; and in the United States and Canada, about 25 percent. Australia and New Zealand, dependent on farm exports, suffered heavily. So did countries relying on mining exports, such as South Africa, Peru, Bolivia, and above all Chile, where total economic output fell by half.

In contrast, countries less tied in to the international circuits and more structured around peasant food production felt far less distress. China, India, and Japan weathered the crisis comparatively well outside of small export sectors. Japan's economic contraction was about 8 percent, India's less, and China's less still. The USSR scarcely took part in international trade or financial flows and thus was unscathed by the Great Depression, although,

Great Depression Unemployed men wait for a hot meal outside a Chicago soup kitchen. In the United States, unemployment during the Depression reached about 25 percent.

as we'll see below, it underwent its own homemade economic crisis in the early 1930s—collectivization.

In the hard-hit countries, families were thrown back on their own resources. Farm families could at least feed themselves. Urban families whose breadwinner lost a job struggled more, selling what they had, scratching out livings as day laborers, peddlers, beggars, or thieves. Families also cut back on reproduction: the global birth rate fell by 5 to 10 percent between 1930 and 1935.

Governments did not know what to do to ease the crisis. The record of successful economic management during World War I made it impossible for them to do nothing, as had been normal in previous—much smaller—global depressions of 1893 or 1873. Some tried to boost their own economies by imposing tariffs on imported goods, which, when many countries did it, only deepened the Depression. Some tried rigorously to balance budgets in hopes of winning reputations for responsible public finance and inspiring investors. The most effective response was increasing public spending, even if it deepened national debt and ran counter to the wisdom of most 1930s economists. At the center of this response was re-armament. Germany and Italy pioneered this path, under leaders who looked forward to a new war that would undo the result of World War I.

Fascism and Communism, 1919–1939

The return to peacetime conditions did not mean the end of turmoil around the world. In 1919, political chaos boiled over in cities throughout Europe and from Winnipeg to Sydney, Buenos Aires to Beijing. New ideologies simmered almost everywhere, with fascism, communism, and anti-colonialism the most important. All were radical in the sense that their followers wished to see thorough changes in the political order. All thrived upon either disgust at the mass butchery of war or the sordid compromises of the 1919 peace—or both.

Fascism to 1939

Fascism was born in Italy during World War I. Italy had joined the war in 1915 on what became the winning side, lured by promises of territory. But in the peace settlement, Italy got precious little and lost some of what was promised by treaty to Kemal's nationalist revolution in Turkey.

To many Italians, this outcome was an outrageous betrayal of the more than 2 million killed, wounded, or missing in the war. They blamed, among others, a weak government, parliamentary institutions, and cultural and business elites. They wanted an Italian state that would be more forceful, nationalistic, imperialistic, and unified— and less hobbled by debate, division, and deliberation. They wanted action, not words. People who saw matters this way found the fascist movement to their taste.

Fascism, whether in Italy or elsewhere, had certain distinctive features. First among them was militant nationalism. Fascists idolized vigor, power, ruthlessness, and war. Their nationalism included a call for regeneration and purification of the nation. Many fascists felt only violence could cleanse their nation of impure elements, which usually included ethnic minorities and immigrants. Fascism also emphasized the cult of the dynamic leader, the man (never a woman) who took bold action and rejected political bickering and backroom deals. Fascists scorned multi-party politics and preferred a one-party state—like Lenin and the Bolsheviks.

Fascist movements tried to make a display of national solidarity and strength through theatrical marches and rallies. They adopted uniforms for party members: blackshirts in Italy, blueshirts in Ireland, brownshirts in Germany. Fascists had their own salutes and catch phrases. Their rallies, often dramatic, emotional affairs, extolled strength and exuded menace toward people judged not genuinely part of the nation. The parties always included youth movements, because the cult of action, vigor, and renewal required young faces.

On the home front, fascists wanted men to wield authority in families and women to keep house and raise strong children. The growing independence of women under wartime conditions often annoyed men—and many women too—who preferred that families live under the authority of an adult male. Fascists wanted men to re-assert that domestic authority. Fascist gender politics was an extreme version of a commonplace outlook around the world in the early twentieth century.

Fascists usually offered an economic program that was critical of both capitalism and communism, proclaiming a third way, sometimes called corporatism, involving substantial state direction but mainly private ownership of property. In any case, they claimed to provide an economy that served all the people, not just bosses or workers. Religious policy differed greatly among fascists. Some were scornful of organized religion. Others allied themselves with the Catholic or Orthodox Church. Fascism never amounted to much outside of Christendom, although Chinese nationalists borrowed some of its elements.

Italian Fascism and Mussolini The mainspring behind Italian fascism was **Benito Mussolini**, born in 1883 in a provincial town. His father was a blacksmith with socialist politics, his mother a pious Catholic and former schoolteacher. Benito did well in school and was certified as an elementary school teacher. But in 1902 he left Italy for Switzerland to avoid army service. He read widely, especially in political philosophy, took part in socialist organizations and strikes, and was arrested now and again in both Switzerland and Italy. He thought of himself as an intellectual, and as of age 30 there was nothing about him to suggest he would become Italy's dictator.

Then came World War I. Unlike most socialists, Mussolini eventually argued for Italy's entry into the bloodbath. He decided that national identity was more important, more natural, than class identity. He volunteered for the army and spent nine months near the trenches, where an accidental explosion left shrapnel in his body. The war years gave Mussolini credentials for political leadership and an audience he otherwise could not have had. In 1919, he formed a paramilitary group in the northern city of Milan that embraced the term *fascist*.

Italy in 1919 was in disarray. Class conflict boiled over into violence between workers and bosses—or thugs hired by bosses—and between peasants and landlords. Fascists claimed to offer a solution, one based on national unity, discipline, and authority. They denounced deliberation and compromise as weakness. In practice they advocated suppressing communists, building up the military, entrusting

Mussolini The Italian fascist leader addresses an enormous crowd in May 1936, delivering a speech in which he proclaims a new Italian empire following Italy's invasion of Ethiopia.

power to a fascist party elite, and grabbing territory from supposed racial inferiors, specifically Slavs in what is now Slovenia and Croatia, and Africans. In 1922, some 30,000 fascists marched on Rome threatening a coup d'état. The king, afraid of civil war, asked Mussolini to form a government.

Mussolini ruled Italy for more than 20 years in an increasingly authoritarian fashion. He excelled at manipulating mass media, including print journalism, his former profession, but also radio and film. He appealed to all those worried about communism, which included most employers. In this respect, the Bolshevik Revolution was indispensable to the rise of Mussolini. He made an effort to appeal to the church and Catholics, and to those upset by women's autonomy—he presented the memory of his pious mother as the ideal for Italian womanhood. Above all, he appealed to the sentiment of Italian nationalism. After 1922, he squashed or co-opted all opposition and increasingly ruled as dictator, through the Fascist Party.

The anxieties that made Mussolini and fascism attractive to millions of Italians existed elsewhere too. Italy's example—a purposeful government that promoted deeds, not bickering—appealed broadly. Mussolini's propagandists did their best to bolster that appeal, trumpeting decisive actions such as draining marshes or building highways and dams.

By 1933, fascist movements had arisen in a dozen or more countries, mainly in Europe. Even countries with longstanding traditions of representative government, such as France and Britain, had fascist movements. The British Union of Fascists claimed tens of thousands of members in the early 1930s, although it never did well in elections. Nor did fascist groups in France. Fascists came to power in Hungary in 1932 and Spain (after winning a bloody civil war) in 1939. Movements that, while not genuinely fascist, found inspiration in Mussolini's Italy took power in Romania, Poland, Greece, and Portugal. Small fascist movements took shape in some Latin American countries such as Chile and Brazil.

German Fascism and Hitler By far the most important case was Germany, where a fascist party emerged in the 1920s and took power in 1933. They were called National Socialists, or Nazis for short. The Nazi Party emerged from the chaotic and violent world of post-war Germany. The Versailles treaty, particularly its war guilt clause and reparations, seemed deeply unjust to most Germans, who felt they had neither caused nor lost World War I. Many found it comforting to believe in the "stab in the back," the idea that traitorous politicians working for Jews or communists or both had sacrificed Germany. One who admired such thinking was the Austrian **Adolf Hitler**.

Hitler was born in 1889 to a modest family—one of six children, three of whom died in infancy. His father was a customs inspector and beekeeper in various small towns along the border between Austria-Hungary and Germany. Hitler's younger brother died in 1900, leaving Hitler sullen and uncooperative, a reaction not so different from Lenin's to the death of his older brother. He quit school at age 16 and went to Vienna, where he was twice rejected for art school. For the next seven years, he eked out a living selling watercolor paintings and sleeping in homeless shelters. In 1913, he moved to Munich in Germany. When World War I began, he volunteered for the German army and served with distinction, chiefly as a messenger, winning an Iron Cross, for which a Jewish officer recommended him. He was wounded in 1916 and temporarily blinded by mustard gas late in 1918. Hitler loved the camaraderie and commitment, and the acceptance, he found in the army.

Outraged by the Versailles treaty, Hitler drifted into politics in 1919 in Munich. He joined a fringe group, the National Socialist Party, one of many hyper-nationalist organizations in Germany. By 1921 he was its leader. He honed a gift for oratory, practicing poses and turns of phrase in front of a mirror. He encouraged the anger and resentment of common people, especially those who felt Germany had been wronged at Versailles. Hitler urged them to believe that Germany's future depended on ridding the country of Jews and communists, and that he alone embodied the will of the people. He promised action, not words—a renewal of German greatness, rather than the squabbling of democracy.

He had a strange charisma, with his frenzied gestures, theatrical poses, and absurd hyperbole. He was a peculiar politician, living simply, avoiding tobacco, alcohol, meat, and the pleasures of the flesh. He was lazy and undisciplined in his work habits, although he went to lengths to project an image of vigor and stamina. For millions of struggling Germans, he seemed like the savior they needed. His early efforts to seize power landed him in jail, and for most of the 1920s he remained a marginal figure in German politics.

Hitler rode to power on a wave of anxiety and anger that grew with Germany's economic setbacks. Hyper-inflation wiped out the value of the currency in the years 1923–1924, so that one needed a wheelbarrow full of banknotes to buy a loaf of bread. Then in 1931 the global depression hit Germany hard.

The Nazi Party started doing well, winning 18 percent of the vote in 1930 and 37 percent in early 1932. Germany's veteran politicians, mainly educated men often from aristocratic backgrounds, thought little of Hitler, a mere Austrian corporal and school dropout. They calculated that they could control him if he became chancellor (more or less prime minister). In early 1933 he took power—because it was offered to him.

In the next few years, he outmaneuvered both the old politicians and all rivals within his party. He co-opted the military, which shared Hitler's contempt for the Versailles treaty restrictions. He gradually purged all institutions of people with insufficient loyalty to himself. He installed Nazis atop all universities, professional societies, and courts, while banning labor unions and political parties other than his own. He was building a total-

Hyper-Inflation Amid the hyper-inflation crisis that hit the Weimar Republic in 1923 and 1924, banknotes became so worthless that children used bundles of them as building blocks.

itarian state—one in which all aspects of life were politicized and displays of loyalty to a dictator and his party were required. It was similar in some respects to what Lenin and his successors had done after the Bolshevik Revolution. But Hitler's consolidation of power was a means to a set of ends very different from Lenin's.

Hitler wanted absolute power in order to return Germany and Germans to great power status. As a first step, that required unshackling the German military from the terms of the Versailles treaty, and Hitler moved to covertly expand the army and create an air force. It also meant gathering into a larger Germany all of the German-speaking peoples, whether they lived in Austria, the Sudetenland (part of Czechoslovakia), or East Prussia (mostly Lithuania at the time). Hitler wanted to purify what he imagined as the German race, which meant killing or exiling those who in German were called *untermenschen*—people he considered lower racial types, such as Jews, Slavs, and Roma (Gypsies). Last, he wanted to smash Bolshevism, which he connected with Jews. He hoped for another great war, one that Germany would win and set terms for the rest of the world. Like most fringe ideologues, he nurtured revenge fantasies.

None of these ambitions were original with Hitler. Most of them were in circulation in Munich, where he settled in 1919, and some of them in the Vienna of his youth. But Hitler gave them both a modest coherence as a political program and an extreme, toxic, and murderous character. In the early and mid-1920s, his views struck most Germans as too crazy for consideration. But by 1932, as we've seen, 37 percent of German voters supported him.

After Hitler became chancellor in 1933, his popular support strengthened. He undertook a large-scale public works and re-armament campaign, which boosted the economy quickly. Workers found jobs more easily—unemployment was eliminated by 1938—and businessmen made bigger profits. Given the frequent hardship Germans had experienced since 1914, Hitler's economic successes won over millions. Most Germans preferred greater prosperity and renewed national pride to the political liberties Hitler took from them. The segments of society that lent him the strongest support were small farmers, artisans, shopkeepers, university students, and youth in general. As long as the economy flourished, most Germans were content with Hitler, and many of them were enraptured by his charisma, accepting his claim to be the authentic voice of the German people.

The business elite adjusted quickly to Hitler and Nazism. Many large industrial firms, such as Krupp and I. G. Farben, looked forward to re-armament or massive public works projects, and donated generously to the Nazi Party. Most employers welcomed Nazi destruction of labor unions. Even some of the refined cultural elite embraced Hitler after he became chancellor. Germany's most distinguished philosopher, Martin Heidegger, joined the Nazi Party in 1933, and as rector (more or less president) of Freiburg University he lavished praise on Hitler. A famous dancer and film star, Leni Riefenstahl, also gushed about Hitler's greatness and made skillful propaganda movies for the Nazi Party.

Despite his genuine popularity among Germans, Hitler and the Nazi Party had plenty of detractors. Most of the political left—socialists and communists—despised him. Many of the more religious Germans, Catholics and Protestants alike, found him too unchristian in his conduct. Some of the old elites regarded him as an uncouth, uneducated upstart who was unfit for the chancellor's office. Hitler ruthlessly repressed his opponents, some of whom were murdered and many more imprisoned.

Hitler ruled for six and a half years before unleashing World War II in Europe. His social program, extremely important to him, included building a classless national German community. He thought it had to be purely German to be strong, which meant purging those deemed un-German. This view lay behind various racial purification efforts such as the Nuremberg Laws of 1935, which deprived German Jews of citizenship and political rights, banned marriage—and sex—between Jews and Germans, and defined Jewish identity as a matter of ancestry, not religion. Hitler also felt strongly that women ought not to compete with men for jobs but should focus on homemaking and child rearing. His laws limited women to 10 percent of the places in universities and offered incentives to marriage and motherhood for women considered truly German. Every marrying couple received as a gift a copy of Hitler's political and philosophical ramblings, dictated from prison in the 1920s and published as *Mein Kampf* (*My Struggle*). Nonetheless, many young women found a career and an escape from humdrum village life by joining the Nazi Party and training as a secretary or a nurse.

In his first six years in power, Hitler delivered on many of his economic promises.

He failed, however, in his ambition to make Germany self-sufficient in food and fuel, which contributed to his decision to seek more *lebensraum* ("living space") for Germans in 1939—by launching an expansionist war.

Communism to 1939

Communists took their cues from Marx and his most influential follower, Lenin. They wanted a political order without private property or capitalism. They entrusted their hopes to hierarchical, disciplined parties that promised revolution and a bright future of equality, harmony, and prosperity. Marx and Lenin touted imagined laws of history assuring the inevitability of such a future. For people raised to believe in a second coming and the arrival of the kingdom of heaven on Earth, **communism** had some familiar features.

As we've seen, Lenin and the Bolsheviks took over Russia during the period 1917–1921, which inspired some people and frightened others around the world. Once the Bolsheviks had consolidated their hold on Russia, they set about spreading communist revolution to other countries, actively supporting tiny communist parties in Europe, China, British India, the United States, and elsewhere. They financed and dominated the Comintern, an international union of communist parties. Thanks in large part to economic downturns, communists in Italy, Germany, Hungary, and elsewhere in Europe attracted followings in the 1920s and 1930s, arousing fears that fed fascism. And to a lesser extent, the success of fascism in Italy, Germany, and elsewhere fed fears that inspired people to join communist parties. Both movements, although enemies, benefited from the other's existence.

Communist and fascist movements typically shared certain elements: a militant and hierarchical party organization, a cult of the leader, a willingness to use violence in politics, an emphasis on youth and the future, for example. Most ominous, both shared the commitment that life would be permanently improved if certain class enemies or national enemies were destroyed.

They differed in important respects too. Communists typically proclaimed equality of the sexes, even if practice was another thing altogether, while fascists claimed either nature or God had subordinated women to men. Fascists could coexist cheerfully with capitalist business and private property, which communists reviled as the root of all evil. Fascism extolled the virtues of war and the solidarity of the nation, whereas communism extolled the virtues of class struggle—specifically of workers against owners and bosses—and the solidarity of the international working class. Fascism found it possible to co-opt churches and coexist with organized religion, whereas communists normally treated religion as an enemy.

Their fortunes differed too. Fascism was an important political movement for a little more than two decades, mainly in Europe. Communism held wider appeal and for a longer period. For 70 years after the Russian Revolution, communism remained an occasional political force in many countries and enjoyed a monopoly on power in a few, the most important of which was the USSR.

Soviet Communism and Stalin In the USSR, the revolutionary regime at first wobbled from crisis to crisis. A power struggle followed Lenin's death in 1924, won by **Josef Stalin** (1878–1953). He was a Georgian from the Caucasus, the son of a hard-drinking cobbler father and a deeply religious mother. A fine student at seminary school, he dropped out and took up radical politics as a teenager. He played small roles in the 1917 revolution. But he caught Lenin's eye as a useful, unflinchingly loyal communist, willing to take on any task. He also had real administrative and organizational gifts. Unlike Hitler and Mussolini, Stalin was hardworking and self-disciplined.

Upon consolidating power in the years 1927–1928 (which involved exiling or murdering senior Bolsheviks), Stalin set to transforming the USSR. He intended to make it—as all communists wanted—a more industrialized country. He wanted a workers' paradise but also a militarily formidable state. Neither goal was easy to attain. To advance these priorities, he put Soviet support for revolution abroad on the back burner. He promoted a "socialism in one country" policy that sat uneasily with the Marxist theory he and all communists had studied. His most revolutionary act came in agriculture.

To squeeze out the investment funds for industrialization, Stalin pushed through collectivization of agriculture from 1929. His agents forcibly gathered private land-holdings into huge farms, run either as collectives or as state farms. The collectives had to turn over quotas of food to the state, which sold it cheaply to industrial workers. Collectivization amounted to taking peasants' land, forcing them into collectives, and seizing much of their grain. Peasants resisted by eating their livestock, destroying machinery, and hiding grain.

Stalin's innovations were more revolutionary than the Russian Revolution of 1917. Let's look first at two areas beyond agriculture: the industrial economy and education. Stalin instituted formal planning of the national economy in 1928. Millions of peasants migrated, some involuntarily, to mines and factories to produce vast quantities of coal, iron, steel, locomotives, and weaponry. In 1931, Stalin proclaimed—correctly, as it happened—that the USSR had only 10 years to become strong enough to defend itself from foreign attack. He spared no effort to build up the armaments industry. After 1934, the economy grew quickly owing to forced industrialization. By the late 1930s, the USSR was the world's third largest industrial economy, after the United States and Germany, an astonishing achievement given its overwhelmingly agrarian character in the late 1920s and the disaster that collectivization brought to agriculture.

Thanks to state schools for all children, social mobility became commonplace in Stalin's USSR. The children of peasants routinely became engineers and doctors, army officers and professors. The number of children in school doubled between 1928 and 1933, despite chaos in parts of the country. The number of high school students climbed from 2 million in 1927 to 12 million in 1939. Stalin intended to create a "proletarian

Gulags *Kulaks* (prosperous peasants) perform heavy manual labor in a Soviet prison camp in 1930. Millions of *kulaks* died in the forced labor camps that Stalin instituted.

intelligentsia," an educated cohort of peasant or worker background—and he did. They proved his most loyal backers.

At the same time, Stalin's program relied on brutal coercion. It did not begin with him. Lenin had unleashed terror without qualms when in power (1918–1922). Ten years later, when peasants resisted collectivization, Stalin ordered the "liquidation" of *kulaks* ("fists," the term used in the USSR to describe prosperous peasants). About 8 million farmers were either killed or sent to forced labor in Siberia in the gulag, a system of slave labor camps scattered in cold and remote parts of the USSR. In 1932 and 1933, poor harvests combined with pitiless requisition of grain led to famines that killed 5 to 7 million peasants, mostly in Ukraine and Kazakhstan.

Stalin responded to these and other misfortunes by unleashing state terror. His secret police, the NKVD, arrested and killed millions. He purged the ranks of the Communist Party and the army, and targeted ethnic Poles and Germans. He murdered most of the remaining heroes of the 1917 revolution and anyone who might supplant him. People whose class origins—children of bankers or aristocrats, for example—made them suspected of disloyalty to the "workers' paradise" were shipped to the gulag. So were people who made jokes about Stalin, people who were denounced by jealous neighbors or by jilted lovers, people who were late to work three times or who stole a hammer from a collective farm. Stalin's terror had a random quality to it. The terror also had a bureaucratic quality. Officials kept records of those whom they shot. In 1937 and 1938, Stalin issued quotas, by district, of the numbers to be shot.

In the gulag, malnutrition, overwork, disease, and brutality had few limits. In all, between 1929 and Stalin's death in 1953, perhaps 18 million people passed through the 500 camps of the gulag, and 1 to 3 million died there. More were released when on death's door and died within days or weeks after regaining freedom. In all, Stalin's peacetime policies killed about 10 to 12 million Soviet citizens between 1928 and 1941.

Part of the reason behind Stalin's enthusiasm for educating millions of peasant children was that so many doctors, engineers, and accountants had been killed or imprisoned.

Soviet communism—like Italian fascism and German Nazism—both attracted and repelled people around the world. The overnight industrialization struck many observers as a model path to wealth and power. But rumors of famine, purges, and state terror leaked out, despite the best efforts of Stalin's loyalists to conceal the truth. As of 1939, communism had come to power only in the USSR.

Anti-Colonialism to 1939

Another important political movement that gathered pace after World War I was **anti-colonialism**. Asians and Africans, almost all of them subjects of one or another colonial empire, created new ideologies and social movements that helped them focus their resistance. Their experience of World War I, as participants or observers, generally lowered their estimate of their colonial masters. Fewer than ever now accepted British or French claims to represent a higher civilization. The cynicism and duplicity of the peace settlement invited further contempt for the colonial powers. Thus movements arose calling for self-rule and the end to colonial empires. In most cases it took decades, and another world war, for these movements to bear fruit, but they first came of age during the tumult of World War I and its aftermath.

China and the May Fourth Movement

In China, as we've seen, the Qing dynasty had collapsed during the years 1910–1911. World War I, when it came, at first seemed distant. But in 1915 Japan exploited the European powers' preoccupation with the war to issue an ultimatum, The Twenty-one Demands, calling, in effect, for China to become a de facto colony of Japan.

Many Chinese students and intellectuals responded with defiance. But negotiations between China and Japan resulted in an agreement signed in 1915 by Yuan Shikai—the military man running most of China at this point. The agreement focused popular anger upon the government of China as much as upon Japanese imperialism. Nationalistic intellectuals re-doubled their questioning of China's policies and traditions in the New Culture Movement. Hundreds of new publishing houses and journals sprang up in which debates raged about how best to reform China. An example was the magazine *New Youth*, edited by a dean of Beijing University, Chen Duxiu. In a soul-searching essay, "Our Final Awakening" (1916), Chen wrote:

> We ... must ask ourselves what is the level of our national strength and our civili-
> zation. This is the final awakening. . . . [I]f we open our eyes and take a hard look

at the situation within our country and abroad, what place does our country and our people occupy, and what actions should we take?

At the same time that Chen and others were searching for a new basis for Chinese society, the existing government entered World War I in 1917 against Germany. Its leaders hoped to recover the German territorial concessions established in 1898 in Tianjin, a port near Beijing. Some 600,000 Chinese men served the Allied cause in Europe as laborers, most of them in Russia, and more than 30,000 died—almost all in Russia.

In the spring of 1919, the Chinese learned, to their shock, that the Versailles treaty had transferred German concessions in China to Japan. Britain, France, and Italy had made a secret deal, offering Japan the German holdings, to secure its wartime support for the Allies. The diplomats in Paris had ignored the principle of self-determination and instead supported Japanese imperialism. They had ignored the Chinese contribution to the Allied war effort. As in the Arab Middle East, they had made incompatible promises, justified to themselves by the urgency of winning the war.

That spring, university students in Beijing led protests against Japan, the Versailles treaty, the diplomatic missions of the Allies, and the Chinese government that seemed inclined to accept humiliation. Boycotts and demonstrations swept across the country in the May Fourth Movement, named for the day of the first big protests in Beijing. Police arrested over 1,000 students, but thousands more joined strikes and protests. The government soon concluded it could not endorse the Versailles treaty and would have to risk standing up to Japan.

The insulting terms of the Versailles treaty did much to strengthen the cause of anti-imperialism in China. The treaty's support for Japanese imperialism undermined the appeal of European ways and examples, although one European idea, Marxism, rose in the balance. Many young, educated Chinese in the years 1919–1921 admired the Bolsheviks' swift seizure of power in Russia and their dedication to re-making society. They formed the Chinese Communist Party in 1921.

May Fourth Movement Students join a demonstration outside the seat of Chinese government in Beijing's Forbidden City in 1919. The May Fourth movement, sparked by discontent with the terms of the Versailles treaty, launched a broad examination of Chinese culture and politics.

India

In India, World War I and its aftermath strengthened another nascent anti-colonial movement. After the uprisings of the years 1857–1858, British rule had fastened more tightly upon India. Although many Indians resented British power, they knew that the Indian Army, trained and commanded by British officers, would smash any rebellion. But in the 1880s, elite, educated Indians, mostly Hindus, came together to form the Indian National Congress. At first a group that lobbied for a larger Indian role in government, Congress, as it was called, gradually came to function as a political party, at first with British approval. Meanwhile, educated Muslims created their own political organizations, such as the All-India Muslim League formalized in 1906 and

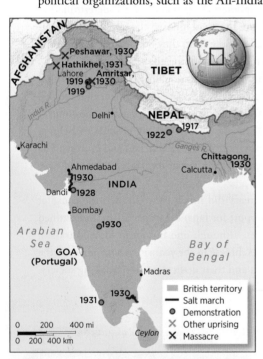

soon led by a brilliant London-trained lawyer, Muhammad Ali Jinnah, also a Congress member. The leaders of Congress were products of schools and colleges established by the British to create a class of men—no women—competent to handle the lower rungs of officialdom. The schools also created a cadre of fluent English speakers well acquainted with British traditions, law, literature—and the merits of representative self-government.

Most of these educated Indians expected that India would one day become ready for self-government—perhaps in 50 or 100 years. World War I reduced their patience. Some 1.2 million Indians served the armies of the British Empire, mainly in campaigns against the Ottomans. About 62,000 died in the war. Indian businessmen and landowners contributed a lot of money to the British war effort. They did so in the expectation that in exchange for its blood and treasure, India would win something akin to the self-governing dominion status within the British Empire already accorded to Canada, New Zealand,

The Indian Independence Movement, 1915–1935 The Indian independence movement, the world's largest decolonization campaign, involved a mixture of peaceful protests and violent insurgency. Gandhi and his followers mounted nonviolent actions designed to undermine colonial British authorities, such as the salt march he led in 1930 from Ahmedabad to the sea. But other Indians clashed with imperial forces, such as those involved in a failed insurrection in Chittagong—also in 1930. By 1935 India was on the road to self-rule.

Australia, and South Africa. Like the Chinese who expected a reward for their contributions to the Allies in World War I, these Indians were soon keenly disappointed.

After the war's end, British authorities showed no eagerness to extend self-rule to India. It was not the Versailles peace settlement that disappointed Indians. Indeed, India was allowed to send its own delegation to the talks. But early in 1919, when the British government of India extended its own wartime powers preventing freedom of speech and assembly, Indian nationalists reacted with outrage. Demonstrations dotted the country. That April, a demonstration in the holy city of Sikhs, Amritsar, ended in bloodshed. A British general ordered his Indian troops to fire into an unarmed crowd, killing some 400 demonstrators and wounding 1,000. Afterward, the general who gave the order was commended by the British House of Lords. To many Indians, the Amritsar massacre showed that Britain would never allow India to enjoy dominion status but would try to rule the country indefinitely.

Gandhi The anti-colonial movement in India was already growing more impatient when **Mohandas K. Gandhi** returned to India in 1915 and joined Congress. He came from a middle-class family, and despite a mediocre school record went to study law in London at age 20. Starting in 1893, he spent 21 years in British South Africa defending the rights of the Indian community there. He suffered various slights at the hands of white South Africans but remained a loyal subject of the British Empire, even winning a medal for his work organizing Indian medics for the Boer War (1899–1902).

In South Africa, he developed the political tactic called *satyagraha* (translated as "truth force" or "soul force"), which amounted to the practice of non-violent civil disobedience in the face of unjust treatment. It drew upon Hindu, Jain, and Christian religious traditions. Gandhi also learned from the writings of the American author Henry David Thoreau and the Russian novelist and philosopher Leo Tolstoy, with whom he corresponded. The South African compound where he trained people in *satyagraha* was called Tolstoy Farm. Gandhi's thought combined many influences, a reflection of the growing interconnectedness of the world in his day.

When he arrived in India in 1915, Gandhi encouraged Indians to join the British armed forces, hoping that by showing loyalty Indians would win political independence after World War I ended. His fellow Congress members found him strange. He had abandoned his lawyer's suit and tie for the *dhoti* worn by poor Indians. He ate sparingly and flaunted his frail physique. The Bombay (Mumbai) police considered him "a psychological case." But in 1919, he more than anyone else converted Indian anti-colonial nationalism from an elite affair into a mass movement.

The spur was the massacre at Amritsar. Gandhi now proclaimed there could be no cooperation with the British "satanic regime." Since armed resistance to British rule was futile, Gandhi, with his non-violent tactics honed in South Africa, became the most effective and prestigious leader of anti-colonialism in India. He pioneered mass

CONSIDERING THE EVIDENCE

Satyagraha: Gandhi's Strategy of Resistance

Before Gandhi returned to India in 1915, he had already spent two decades in South Africa, where he led Indian settlers in protests against laws that limited their rights because of the color of their skin. It was there that he first distinguished *satyagraha* from the campaigns of suffragists and other political movements that he associated with violence. Gandhi taught his followers to disobey unjust laws without resorting to physical force—instead, they dared the British governments in South Africa and India to commit violence against them. Through such suffering, they hoped to shame the British Empire into living up to the principles of justice that Gandhi had studied as a law student in London.

The suffragists had no franchise rights. They were weak in numbers as well as in physical force.... The suffragist movement did not eschew the use of physical force. Some suffragists fired buildings and even assaulted men. I do not think they ever intended to kill any one. But they did intend to thrash people when an opportunity occurred....

But brute force had absolutely no place in the Indian movement in any circumstance,... no matter how badly they suffered, the *satyagrahis* never used physical force. *Satyagraha* is soul force pure and simple, and whenever ... there is room for the use of arms or physical force or brute force, there and to that extent is there so much less possibility for soul force. These are purely antagonistic forces....

[Yet] even a generous friend like Mr. Hosken [an English supporter of Gandhi in South Africa] imagined us to be weak. The power of suggestion is such that a man at last becomes what he believes himself to be. If we continue to believe ... we are weak ... our resistance would never make us strong.... On the other hand, if we ... offer *satyagraha*, believing us to be strong, ... we grow stronger and stronger every day....

Satyagraha and brute force, being each a negation of the other, can never go together.... In *satyagraha* there is not the remotest idea of injuring the opponent. *Satyagraha* postulates the conquest of the adversary by suffering in one's own person.

Questions for Analysis

1. Why did Gandhi reject the idea that *satyagraha* was weak?
2. How did the woman suffrage movement affect Gandhi's approach to anti-colonial resistance?
3. Contrast Gandhi's anti-colonial movement with the fascist and communist movements in Italy, Germany, and Russia.

Source: M. K. Gandhi, *Satyagraha in South Africa*, trans. Valji Govindji Desai. (Madras, 1928).

politics, rousing illiterate peasants to the cause of self-rule. Congress chose him as its president in 1920.

Gandhi's program baffled most other Indian nationalists. He argued for a self-sufficient peasant economy and against factories and industrialization. He claimed that British education, of which he was a product, corrupted India and prevented its liberation. He particularly disliked modern science and technology, preferring Hindu traditions. Yet he was no respecter of caste, campaigning for the rights of the lowest of the low in India's caste system, people called *dalits* ("untouchables"). Gandhi embraced all Indians, Muslim and Hindu alike, and Christians, Jains, and Buddhists too. He spoke out against child marriage, dowry, and the Muslim custom of seclusion of women. He felt India's strength could come from piety and moral righteousness, not factories and armies. He regarded women as natural champions of this cause: "If by strength is meant moral power, then woman is immeasurably man's superior."

His methods included deft use of the weapons of the weak. He lived simply, all the better to be an Indian David against a British Goliath. He went on well-publicized hunger strikes. He and his colleagues in Congress organized marches involving thousands of poor Indians who were trained not to resist violence but to suffer it—in order to seize the moral high ground and undercut British claims to superiority.

To succeed, he had to know his adversary well, and three years of legal education in London helped in that regard. And he required an adversary that was vulnerable to public shaming and moral truth—the weapons of the weak—one that would not be willing to repeat the massacre of Amritsar time and time again.

Gandhi's classic act of civil disobedience was the salt march of 1930. By law, the sale of salt was a government monopoly, and Indians had to pay a salt tax. Gandhi exploited this by organizing a 24-day march from his base near Ahmedabad, in western India, to the coasts of the Arabian Sea in order to scoop up natural sea salt in defiance of the law. Tens of thousands of Indians joined him, and several journalists too. As he expected, Gandhi's act of civil disobedience earned him a jail sentence. Some 80,000 others were arrested. The British authorities undermined their own legitimacy in India, Britain, and around the world by arresting so many poor people over salt—just as Gandhi intended. By 1935, Britain had passed new legislation turning many governmental functions over to Indians. India was on the road to self-rule.

European rule in India had begun in the sixteenth century as a result of a quest for valuable peppers, and it would end in 1947 as a result—in part—of Gandhi's salt march. He was able to make the struggle for self-rule a mass movement after 1919, parallel in this respect, but different in every other, to what Mussolini did with fascism in Italy in 1919. He re-cast a political movement based on novel tactics that fit India's circumstances far better than violent resistance. He made non-violent civil disobedience into a potent political force.

Africa, the Caribbean, and Pan-Africanism

In Africa and the Caribbean, anti-colonial movements also drew strength from the disillusionment that came with World War I and the peace settlement. Recall that in 1914, Africa was almost entirely colonized by European powers, chiefly Britain and France. The Caribbean too was a patchwork of European colonies, with a population mainly descended from Africans brought to the region in the transatlantic slave trade.

In World War I, several hundred thousand Africans and a few thousand West Indians—as people from the Caribbean are known—served in European armies. Some 400,000 black volunteers and conscripts fought for the French Army on the western front and often were assigned the most dangerous tasks. The president of France, Georges Clemenceau, made his views clear in 1918: "We are going to offer civilization to the Blacks. They will have to pay for that. . . . I would prefer that ten Blacks are killed rather than one Frenchman." Some 30,000 to 70,000 Africans died in the French Army in Europe in World War I. The British refused to use African troops in Europe. But, like the French and Germans, they employed large numbers in the campaigns fought in East and West Africa, and a few thousand, as laborers, in the Middle Eastern theater.

Almost all soldiers and laborers came from the lower ranks of African societies. They volunteered, often encouraged by those chiefs and kings who now supported colonial rule, in hopes of improving their status. Chiefs and kings hoped that African contributions to the war effort would win political concessions from France and Britain in the form of more autonomy, political rights, and power for chiefs and kings. These hopes, like Gandhi's during World War I, were to be disappointed. Policy makers in France and Britain believed Africans needed centuries of tutelage to become ready for self-rule.

Soldiers and their sponsors were not the only ones to be disappointed. Africa by 1918 included a small population of men—and far fewer women—equipped with European formal education and a cosmopolitan knowledge of the world. They liked the sound of President Wilson's emphasis on self-determination, until it became clear that neither Wilson nor any of the peacemakers of 1919 intended to apply it to Africa.

Pan-Africanism Many of them found hope in **pan-Africanism**, an idea that had not won much attention before 1914. The war seemed to present new opportunities. African American intellectuals from the Caribbean and the United States, including the Harvard-trained historian and sociologist W.E.B. Du Bois, called for unified political action among Africans and people of African descent. Many saw anti-colonialism in terms of race. In an essay appearing in 1915, Du Bois, after calling for the extension of the "democratic ideal to the yellow, brown, and black peoples," wrote apocalyptically: "The colored peoples still will not always submit to foreign domination. . . . These nations and races, composing as they do the vast majority of humanity, are going to endure their treatment as long as they must and not a moment longer. Then they are going to fight and the war of the Color Line will outdo in savage inhumanity any war this world has yet seen." To avoid this grim prospect, Du Bois concluded, would require an end to racism and colonialism.

Other pan-Africanists looked forward to the imminent liberation of Africa. Marcus Garvey, a Jamaican who lived in London and later New York, organized a political and cultural movement that celebrated black identity. He wanted educated people of African descent to return to their ancestral homeland and "assist in civilizing the backward tribes of Africa." In 1920, he proposed to "organize the 400 million Negroes of the world into a vast organization and plant the banner of freedom on the great continent of Africa."

Several Francophone pan-Africanists shared Garvey's emphasis on culture and identity. In the late 1930s, a black poet from Martinique, Aimé Césaire, and his friend and fellow-poet from Senegal

Pan-Africanism The pan-African movement leader Marcus Garvey pictured here in a New York City parade in 1922.

(West Africa), Léopold Senghor, developed a cultural philosophy they called Négritude (literally: "blackness"). They extolled the qualities of black people, among which they counted generosity, warmth, spontaneity, and honesty. In their own way, which featured literature as much as politics, they too endorsed the notion of solidarity among people of African background both as an end in itself and as a means to end colonial rule. Both men became leading politicians in later decades.

Pan-Africanism had a strong literary and cultural component. Garvey, Senghor, and others shared the view of Chinese intellectuals of the New Culture Movement: a revitalization of culture was required before political independence could be achieved. Theirs was an elite movement, with no equivalent to Gandhi's outreach to the illiterate masses.

To give pan-Africanism political weight, Du Bois and others organized pan-African Congresses in 1919 and 1921, held in Europe. Another took place in New York in 1927. Scores of educated men—no women—from the African diaspora and Africa itself attended. They specifically challenged the continuation of colonial rule in Africa and called for an Africa for Africans.

Anti-Colonialism and the Global Web

Within Africa itself, anti-colonialism consisted of more than pan-Africanism. Every colony had its own groups working toward greater political voice for Africans. In most cases, those groups imagined that one day they would replace the colonial masters themselves and rule independent countries. Indeed, in time this vision—rather than the pan-African ideal of African unification—would come to pass.

All these movements, in China, India, and Africa (and the African diaspora), had local grievances and causes. But they all shared some commonalities too, first and foremost their anti-colonialism. In each case, World War I and the disappointing peace settlement contributed mightily to a sense of disillusionment—and to a sense of new possibilities. The war and the peace showed conspicuously that Europeans were not the morally superior beings they had claimed to be. The rhetoric of self-determination rang hollow when followed by renewed imperialism.

These movements also shared a reliance on European-educated elites. In Africa, as in India, the key to the formation of effective anti-colonial groups was colonial education. In the 1920s and 1930s, a new generation with more formal education arrived on the scene in Africa. A symbol of the ongoing change occurred in Gabon (West Central Africa), where a people called the Fang altered one of their rituals: where once spears were dipped in the water in which baby boys took their first bath, now their parents dipped pencils in the bathwater. Education, they foresaw, was the key to power and status.

In every case, anti-colonial leadership came substantially from young men educated in European schools—often, mission schools. While colonial authorities generally wanted the colonized peoples to confine their educations to job training—such as rudimentary office skills—Africans and Indians wanted to study subjects that, as they saw it, fit people for leadership, such as law, philosophy, and history.

There are two lessons here. One is the irony of colonial rulers creating institutions that contributed to the downfall of colonial rule. The other is the power of the swirl of ideas in the decades after 1914. Growing literacy, and then the advent of radio after 1920, made it easier for Wilson's and Lenin's ideas to reach Chinese students, Tolstoy's ideas to reach Gandhi, or Garvey's ideas to reach black people in Lagos or London. The interconnections of the Global web were now better than ever at spreading ideas and ideologies, offering people everywhere new choices with which to try to fashion their futures. The Global web, which had helped to form and strengthen colonial empires in the nineteenth century, now began to undermine them through the flow of ideas, ideals, and ambitions for self-rule.

Conclusion

World War I wasn't all that worldwide as a war. The combat took place mainly in Europe and the Ottoman lands of Southwest Asia. But as a political event, World War I was truly global. It inspired the mobilization of people and resources on every inhabited continent. More enduringly, the war's horror and destruction posed strong challenges to existing authority in every sphere. If the leaders and institutions of Europe permitted the slaughter of 10 million soldiers, what argument could there be to leave such leaders and institutions in place? Millions thought it must be better to try something new and different, such as fascism or communism. The peace settlement, with its evident hypocrisies, multiplied the challenges to existing authorities by dashing hopes and breaking promises, especially in Asia and Africa. How could such leaders and institutions be permitted to rule over most of the world's population through colonial empires? Millions thought it must be better to end colonial rule as soon as possible. Considering that men—and only men—had directed a brutal war and an unsatisfactory peace, what argument remained for excluding women from politics? Millions found no convincing argument and agreed that women should vote.

Like the influenza virus in 1918 and 1919, the intellectual and political repercussions of the war and the resulting peace spread quickly around the world—but news and ideas traveled even faster than pathogens. The peace settlement in Versailles gave rise to events in China almost instantaneously in 1919.

Of all the meanings and legacies of World War I and its peace settlement, perhaps the greatest was one that took decades to work itself out: the decline of western Europe in world affairs. It is not that European states necessarily grew weaker as a result of the war and its aftermath, although some did. Rather, the United States and soon the USSR grew much stronger, as did, if less obviously, the enemies of empire in Asia and Africa. The growing strength of the United States and the USSR came mainly in the form of material power such as industrial capacity. The enemies of empire in Asia and Africa gained strength through organization, education, and determination. Their material resources were scant—wholly inadequate for a military challenge to colonial rule. But, as Gandhi showed, sometimes the weapons of the weak are enough to change history.

Chapter Review

KEY TERMS

World War I p. 997

alliance networks p. 1000

Russian Revolution of 1917 p. 1007

Vladimir Lenin p. 1009

Treaty of Versailles p. 1012

self-determination p. 1012

Mustafa Kemal p. 1014

suffragism p. 1015

fascism p. 1021

Benito Mussolini p. 1022

Adolf Hitler p. 1024

communism p. 1027

Josef Stalin p. 1028

anti-colonialism p. 1030

Mohandas K. Gandhi p. 1033

pan-Africanism p. 1036

REVIEW QUESTIONS

1. What are the four main strands of global politics in modern times?

2. In order of strength, who were the great powers in 1914, and to which alliance network did each belong?

3. Discuss the two key decisions that contributed to the start of World War I.

4. Why did the German High Command begin unrestricted submarine warfare in the Atlantic, and what effect did it have on the war?

5. Describe the various roles that women filled during World War I, and explain what happened to these positions when the war ended.

6. Compare and contrast the policies of the Provisional Government in spring and summer 1917, the Bolsheviks in 1918, and the Bolsheviks in 1921.

7. What were the chief ambitions behind the post-war peace treaties?

8. What longstanding dynasties did World War I destroy, and what governing structures replaced each one?

9. How did World War I lead to the extension of the vote to women in several large and populous countries?

10. Why did Mussolini's fascism seem an attractive choice to millions of Italians after World War I?

11. What were Hitler's ambitions, and what economic and cultural policies did he introduce after 1933 to achieve them?

12. Identify the significant elements that communist and fascist movements shared, and explain their important differences.

13. What agricultural, economic, and educational policies did Stalin advance?

14. How did World War I contribute to the rise of anti-colonialism as a mass movement?

15. What elements did anti-colonial movements in China, India, Africa, and the Caribbean share?

16. Explore the global aspects of World War I as a political event.

Go to INQUIZITIVE

to see what you've learned—and learn what you've missed—with personalized feedback along the way.

World War II and the Cold War

1937 to 1991

FOCUS QUESTIONS

1. What factors had the biggest impact on the outcomes of World War II?
2. Why was the Cold War a hot one in some parts of the world?

> We rely upon the loyalty and courage of Our subjects in Our confident expectation that the task bequeathed by Our forefathers will be carried forward and that the sources of the evil will be speedily eradicated and an enduring peace immutably established in East Asia, preserving thereby the glory of Our Empire.

With these words the high command of the Japanese armed forces concluded its public declaration of war, issued in the name of Japan's emperor, against the United States and the British Empire on December 8, 1941. Attacks proceeded against American bases at Pearl Harbor (where it was December 7) and the Philippines, and against British positions in Hong Kong, Malaya, and Singapore. In 1941, Japan was a colonial power in East Asia, controlling Korea, Taiwan, Manchuria, and most of eastern China. The leadership appealed to ordinary Japanese citizens to continue the overseas expansion under way since 1895, and to expel European and American colonial powers from East and Southeast Asia, thereby leaving Japan unrivaled in the region. Confidence in the loyalty and courage of the emperor's subjects proved well placed, but Japan lacked the economic resources to defeat its foes. Rather than preserve the glory of Japan's

CHRONOLOGY

1937 Japan attacks China; World War II in Asia begins

Sept. 1939 Germany invades Poland; World War II in Europe begins

June 1941 Operation Barbarossa; war on eastern front begins

Dec. 1941 Japan attacks United States, British Malaya, Philippines; Pacific War begins

June 1942 Battle of Midway

Nov. 1942–Mar. 1943 Battle of Stalingrad

Sept. 1943 Italy surrenders

June 1944 Normandy landings

May 1945 Germany surrenders

Aug. 1945 United States drops atomic bombs on Hiroshima and Nagasaki; Japan surrenders

1945 Start of Cold War

1945–1949 Chinese Civil War

1948 Berlin airlift

1949 Stalin acquires nuclear weapons; NATO is formed; Mao Zedong establishes People's Republic of China

1950–1953 Korean War

1954 Vietnam is divided between north and south

1956 Uprisings in Poland and Hungary

1961 Start of construction of Berlin Wall

Oct. 1962 Cuban missile crisis

1965–1975 Vietnam War

empire, these attacks sealed its doom, which came in August 1945 after 43 months of pitiless combat.

This chapter explores the titanic political battles and unspeakable violence of World War II (1937–1945) and the Cold War (1945–1991). Both were truly global contests, much more so than World War I or any previous struggles. The Global web had grown so strong that politics spilled across boundaries and oceans with ease. In World War II, combat took place on three continents and three oceans. During the Cold War, the United States chose to fight wars in Korea (1950–1953) and Vietnam (1965–1975), whereas it had previously avoided wars in Asia. And the USSR, which had previously had minimal interests in the American hemisphere, chose to support Cuba beginning in 1960.

Three main themes predominate in this chapter. First, these conflicts featured violence on astonishing scales. The technologies of war had grown so efficient that death and suffering outstripped even the carnage of World War I. Ordinary civilians could not keep out of harm's way in World War II, or in the hotspots of the Cold War such as Vietnam or Angola. This marked a return to an older pattern of warfare in which the distinction between military and civilian was often blurry. As a result, the violence of these wars affected women and children at home more often than in World War I. These were hard and dangerous times, none harder than the years between 1937 and 1952—especially if you were Chinese, Japanese, Korean, German, Italian, Greek, or any kind of eastern European, but above all Jewish.

Second, ferocious ideological hatreds sharpened these conflicts. Sometimes these were ethnic or "racial," as in the case of Hitler and his supporters. Such hatreds had long been commonplace, but in World War II they became extreme. During the Cold War, ideological hatreds were based on differing conceptions of how best to organize societies and economies.

Third, this chapter tries to explain why the winners won and the losers lost in both World War II and the Cold War. These struggles, and especially their results, shaped the international political system we live in today, and fundamentally affect all our lives. It is important to grasp why they turned out as they did.

1975 Start of Angolan Civil War

1979–1989 Soviet-Afghan War

1986 Chernobyl disaster

1989 Fall of Berlin Wall

1991 Collapse of USSR

World War II, 1937–1945

By any measure except duration, **World War II** was the biggest war in history. It ranged over more terrain, mobilized more resources, and killed more people than any other war. It also re-configured world politics dramatically, as had World War I. Sometimes scholars like to lump the two world wars together as one extended conflict (1914–1945). In the European context this makes some sense, because in both wars Germany and its allies fought against a coalition including Russia, Britain, France, and the United States. But whereas World War I took place mainly in Europe, World War II involved major theaters of combat in China and the Pacific, and another in North Africa. From the perspective of world history as opposed to European history, it makes sense to treat the world wars separately.

Origins

The origins of World War II are not as complex, accidental, or contested as those of World War I. Most historians agree that its causes lay in the expansionist ambitions of Japan, Germany, and to a lesser extent Italy. Those powers formed a loose alliance in the late 1930s known as the **Axis**. Each was run by an authoritarian clique hostile to pluralist democracy and rule of law. Each felt shortchanged by the international status quo. Each eagerly ran the risks of provoking large-scale warfare in order to acquire more territory and resources. Indeed, many in their governing elites regarded war as something to be sought rather than avoided, because, they thought, it was good for a nation to be tested in blood. The fact that almost no one thinks such things anymore is in large part a consequence of the many horrors of World War II.

As we've seen, both Italy and Germany by the 1930s had fallen under fascist dictatorships, led by Mussolini and Hitler, respectively. Each had consolidated his grip on power by 1935 or before, muzzling the press, squashing legislatures, and filling the court system, the military, and key government ministries with reliable fascists. Outraged by the terms of the Treaty of Versailles, both leaders felt that their country should not shrink from launching wars to achieve a more glorious future for the Italian or German people. Germans and Italians were peppered with messages, in schools and state-run media, encouraging them to embrace nationalism and militarism as solutions to almost all problems.

Both Mussolini and Hitler envisioned futures based on nationalistic fantasies. For Mussolini, that glorious future entailed re-creating the grandeur of ancient Rome. He wanted Italy to dominate the Mediterranean, as the Romans had done, and to acquire colonies in Africa. For Hitler, overseas colonies were not a priority. Instead, he wanted what he called *lebensraum* ("living space") for Germans in Europe. He wanted to unite all Germans, including millions living in Poland, Austria, Czechoslovakia, Ukraine, Russia, and elsewhere, into a greater Germany. His understanding of U.S. history, which relied heavily on adventure stories by the popular German author Karl May, suggested to him that Germans could displace or kill Slavs and Jews in eastern Europe and take it for themselves—as Americans had pushed Amerindians off their lands in the nineteenth century. He was convinced that the German people faced a mortal threat and could survive only by means of expansion at the expense of neighbors—specifically, the Slavs and Jews whom he held responsible for all the misfortunes Germans experienced. Both Mussolini and Hitler concocted mythical pasts to try to justify their future plans.

Italy was poorly positioned for expansionist warfare. In the late 1930s, it had about 43 million people, most of them undernourished peasants. It had almost no coal and only a small military-industrial complex, and it depended on imports for vital goods. Its armed forces were sizeable but neither well trained—one-third of army recruits could not read—nor abundantly supplied, although the quality of their equipment was good.

Germany included about 67 million people. In 1938, Hitler absorbed his native Austria into the German Third Reich (*Reich* means "empire"), raising the population closer to 80 million. The Versailles treaty had officially limited the size of Germany's armed forces; but since coming to power in 1933, Hitler had been building up the military in secret. By the late 1930s, Germany had a formidable and technologically modern military.

The third Axis power was Japan. Since the Meiji Restoration (1868), Japan had industrialized its economy and modernized its state administration and armed forces with astonishing speed, despite a comparative lack of raw materials. It had defeated China (1895) and Russia (1905) in war and had acquired Taiwan and Korea as colonies. In 1919, it took over some former German possessions in the Pacific through the Versailles treaty. The Japanese people increasingly came to see themselves as a special nationality—indeed, a "race," better than their neighbors if not everyone else. Their leaders, like those in Italy and Germany, used schooling and media to hammer home messages of Japanese racial superiority and victimization by foreigners.

Japanese Aggression in Asia Like Italy and Germany, Japan wanted to revise the international system. It aimed to expand its imperial power. But it was thwarted mainly by the United Kingdom and the United States, neither of which wished to see Japan or any other nation become pre-eminent in East Asia. A treaty of 1922 limited the size of Japan's navy to 60 percent of that of either the American or British fleets. Japanese military officers grew impatient with these constraints, and in 1931 they manufactured an incident in Manchuria (in northeast China) to justify seizing it. Rich in natural resources such as coal and iron ore, Manchuria could strengthen Japan's heavy industry, including its weapons industry.

By the mid-1930s, Japan's population stood at about 70 million and was growing rapidly. Its navy was the world's third largest; its army was six times the size of the American army. Japan's rulers felt their nation needed more space and resources. They envisioned Japan leading the peoples of East Asia in throwing off the shackles of European rule. They offered an anti-colonial ideology but in reality intended to make all of East Asia subordinate to Japan. By the late 1930s, the European colonial rulers of Southeast Asia—Britain, France, and the Netherlands—were becoming increasingly anxious about the rising power of Germany in Europe and less inclined to devote military resources to Asia. Japan took advantage of that to attack China in 1937.

China made a tempting target for Japan. Its 511 million people—as of 1937—were politically divided. The central government, run by the Guomindang, a party that had evolved out of Sun Yatsen's 1910 revolution, was famous for corruption and unloved by the masses. It controlled only parts of the country. It had virtually no navy and a poorly equipped army. China was a peasant land, with little industry. Yet it had plenty of raw materials, especially ores and coal, that Japan wanted. Japan's assault on China in 1937 was the beginning of World War II in Asia.

German Aggression in Europe The war in Europe began in 1939 when Germany invaded Poland. France and Britain, the other great powers in Europe, offered no effective response to German expansion. At the Munich Conference in 1938, they signed over the Sudetenland, a mainly German-speaking region of Czechoslovakia, to Hitler in exchange for a promise that he would seek no more territory. A few months later, in March 1939, Hitler seized the rest of Czechoslovakia anyway.

France and Britain proved feeble adversaries in the diplomacy of the late 1930s. Both were haunted by the human losses of World War I and eager to avoid another war at almost any cost. They had a population of 90 million between them, plus reserves of military manpower and resources in their overseas empires. They also had enormous manufacturing capacity but, compared to Germany, poorly equipped armies and air forces. After the seizure of Czechoslovakia early in 1939, their leaders realized that they could not check Hitler's Germany short of going to war.

In August 1939, Hitler's diplomats negotiated a non-aggression pact with the Soviet Union, a stunning reversal of both German and Soviet foreign policy. The agreement reduced Germany's risk of a two-front war against both Soviet Russia and the western allies, a lesson from World War I. Stalin signed it in order to buy time to build up his military, which had suffered greatly from his own purges of top commanders. The agreement included secret protocols for yet another partition of Poland—there had been

Aggressions in Europe, 1936–1939 Germany, under Hitler from 1933, sought to undo the settlement established in the Treaty of Versailles. Among his early violations of the treaty was the stationing of military units in the Rhineland near the French and Belgian border. He followed with territorial annexations of Austria and parts of Czechoslovakia. In 1939, Italy's fascist dictatorship under Mussolini annexed Albania after a brief battle. When World War II in Europe began in 1939, military aggression became much more violent with the German and Soviet invasions of Poland.

three during the eighteenth century. The German Army invaded Poland on September 1, the start of World War II in Europe. France and Britain agreed that they could not allow Germany to gobble up the remainder of Europe, so they declared war against Germany. Two weeks later, the Soviet Red Army invaded Poland too, seizing the share promised to it in the Nazi-Soviet pact.

Four Theaters World War II in effect consisted of four overlapping wars in four different theaters. They began at different times, but all ended in 1945. The first to break out was that between Japan and China in 1937. Most of the fighting took place in China. The second was Germany's and Italy's war against Poland, Britain, France, and most of the rest of Europe, begun in 1939. Fought in Europe, North Africa, and on the waters of the North Atlantic, by the end of 1941 it included the United States aligned against the Axis powers. The third began in June 1941, when Germany attacked the USSR despite the recent Nazi-Soviet pact. It was fought in the lands between Berlin and Moscow. The last was Japan's war against the United States, the United Kingdom, and Australia in the Pacific and Southeast Asia, begun in December 1941. The United States, the Soviet Union, and Britain formed the major Allied forces, or **Allies**, opposing the Axis of Germany, Japan, and Italy.

New technologies such as tanks and long-range aircraft enabled armies and air forces to roam widely, unlike in World War I, and inflict terrible brutalities on civilians especially in China and eastern Europe. Many more civilians than soldiers lost their lives during the course of the war, partly through aerial bombing campaigns and partly because they could not escape rapidly moving invading armies. Millions of women and girls who fell into the hands of marauding soldiers were raped, especially in China, eastern Europe, and Germany.

The Course of the War

Until mid-1942, the Axis—Japan, Germany, and Italy—went from strength to strength. Japan inflicted huge losses on China and took the richest parts of the country. In late 1940, it conquered French Indochina (now Vietnam, Laos, and Cambodia) and reduced Thailand to the status of a dependent ally. Part of Japan's interest in mainland Southeast Asia lay in its rubber and tin supplies, important for military production. Japan's aggression inspired a joint response from the United States, Britain, and the Netherlands, whose colonies in Southeast Asia were now threatened: in August 1941, these countries stopped all oil and steel exports to Japan. They hoped to force Japan to give up expansionist warfare.

Japanese Advances in Southeast Asia and the Pacific The policy backfired. The Japanese leadership, mainly military elites, gambled on a surprise attack on British Malaya, the U.S. colony of the Philippines, and the American naval base at Pearl Harbor in Hawaii. The attacks, in December 1941, were intended to cripple American and British naval power, giving Japan a chance to seize oilfields in the Dutch East Indies (Indonesia today) and time to win its war in China. Once Japan had firmed up its positions in East and Southeast Asia, the thinking went, the United States and the United Kingdom would acquiesce. The Japanese leaders knew the United States had twice the population of Japan and far more industrial might, but they hoped, and many believed, that Americans were too soft and undisciplined to pay the price of war with Japan. President Franklin Roosevelt responded to the December 7 attack on Pearl Harbor by asking Congress to declare war, which it did on December 8, 1941. The Pacific War, as this part of World War II is often called, was under way.

The United States in 1941 was a sleeping giant. It had retreated from international politics after World War I. Its armed forces had shrunk, and its military equipment was obsolete. Its economy was slowly emerging from the Great Depression. But it had the largest industrial capacity of any country in the world. And it had more than 130 million people, who turned out not to be as soft as the Japanese hoped.

Nonetheless, Japanese armed forces thrashed the United States in the first six months after Pearl Harbor. They drove U.S. forces out of the Philippines.

Pearl Harbor The USS *West Virginia* was badly damaged in the Japanese attack on Pearl Harbor, December 7, 1941. The battleship was repaired and later re-entered the war in the Pacific.

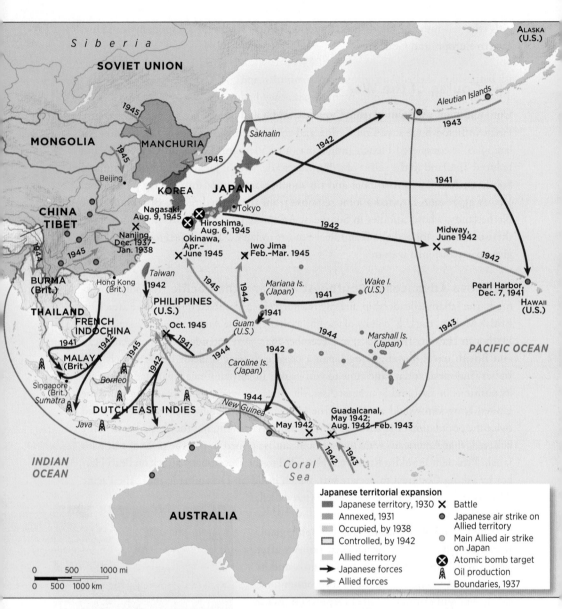

Japanese Expansion and World War II in Asia and the Pacific, 1931–1945 Japan focused its war effort on campaigns in China, beginning with the seizure of Manchuria in 1931. After Japan's attacks of December 7–8, 1941, on Pearl Harbor, the U.S. bases in the Philippines, and British bases in Malaya, the Japanese war widened to include vast spaces of the Pacific, from the Aleutian Islands to Australia. This became a war of movement, fought with ships and aircraft, and therefore a war of oil—which Japan lacked. By late 1942, American forces had begun to turn the tide and were island-hopping toward Japan. By mid-1944, U.S. bombers were pounding Japan relentlessly, ending with the two atomic blasts of August 1945.

They seized Britain's colonies of Malaya and Singapore, as well as the Dutch colony of Indonesia, and
bombed northernmost Australia. Their navy sank British battleships, shelled Australia's Sydney suburbs, and
attacked two Alaskan islands. By mid-1942, they had
won dominion over almost all of Southeast Asia and
the western Pacific.

Axis Advances in Europe Meanwhile in Europe,
the Germans also fared well early on. After conquering
Poland in late 1939, in the spring of 1940 they over-
ran France, Belgium, the Netherlands, Denmark, and
Norway. Only Britain continued to resist. Many in
Britain thought it wise to reach a deal with Hitler. But
the new prime minister, Winston Churchill, in office
since May 1940, refused to consider it. Churchill was
an elderly career politician, nationalistic, imperialist,
and stubborn as a man can be. He had an American
mother, an aristocratic politician father, a fondness for
reading history, and a burning desire to make it. He
also had an eloquence that inspired the British public
when they needed it most.

Winston Churchill British prime
minister Winston Churchill displays a "V for Victory" during the
Battle of Britain in 1940. Churchill's
effectiveness as a political and military leader won him widespread
popular support during the war.

Britain withstood a sustained German air attack—the Battle of Britain—in the summer and fall of 1940. Londoners called this the blitz. They crowded into underground
(subway) stations night after night to avoid the worst of German bombing. Industrial
workers in munitions factories worked long shifts amid the bomb blasts. Fighter pilots of
the Royal Air Force took a sufficient toll upon the German Air Force that Hitler abandoned plans of an invasion of Britain. Churchill famously said of the pilots, "Never in
the field of human conflict was so much owed by so many to so few." Meanwhile, late in
1940 Italy attacked Greece. To nearly everyone's surprise, the Greek Hellenic Army bested
Mussolini's legions. But the German Army made short work of Greece in the spring of
1941, leaving the Axis supreme on the European continent. Romania and Bulgaria both
joined forces with the Axis. Then Hitler made an epic blunder.

Operation Barbarossa and Stalingrad On June 22, 1941, in Operation
Barbarossa—named for a medieval German emperor—Germany attacked the Soviet
Union. Hitler believed its mostly Slavic population was sub-human, inferior to Germans, and therefore ripe for conquest—despite Napoleon Bonaparte's experiences in
Russia in 1812. The population of the USSR in 1941 was about 195 million people,
many of whom were fervently devoted to its ruler, the dictator Josef Stalin. Many more
passively endured Stalinism. Soviet industry was considerable, growing by leaps and

bounds, and by the late 1930s oriented toward military production. The Soviet military had just undergone a political purge in which Stalin ordered many of the best officers killed. But the army was still large and well equipped. The Soviet Union's vast spaces and few roads made movement difficult for attackers. Its stoic population, accustomed to harsh conditions, proved Hitler's low estimation wrong.

Hitler intended to destroy the USSR and settle its western regions with German families. The Nazi-Soviet pact of 1939 had bought him time to conquer western Europe first so he would not have to fight on two fronts. Now, in June 1941, he felt the time had come to complete his life's ambition by shattering the USSR, destroying communism, and—of fundamental importance to him—killing the millions of Jews who lived in eastern Europe and the USSR.

Stalin—surprisingly—was taken by surprise. It is remarkable that anyone as cynical and calculating as Stalin could have been unprepared for Hitler's double-dealing. But he was. He went into hiding for a couple of weeks while the Soviet army was in full retreat. For 16 months the German Army pushed eastward, inflicting tremendous damage along the way. In October 1941, Hitler declared victory, claiming the war was over. But the Soviet state, the Soviet economy, the Soviet people, and the Soviet Red Army did not break. They summoned grim determination, withdrew to the east, and, as their ancestors had done with Bonaparte's legions in 1812, pulled the Germans deeper and deeper into Russia. Late in 1942, they checked the German advance.

The epic **Battle of Stalingrad** was one of the war's turning points. The city, on the banks of the Volga River in Russia's southwest, had both strategic and symbolic importance. With control of Stalingrad, the Germans could prevent oil barges from the Caspian region from chugging upstream on the Volga to supply the Soviet forces around Moscow. Stalingrad carried additional psychological importance because Stalin had named it for himself. Aware that the war's outcome might be decided there, huge German and Soviet armies clashed at Stalingrad between November 1942 and March 1943. In the end, the Soviets encircled and captured the Axis armies, which Hitler had unwisely forbidden to retreat. The Axis lost about 800,000 men. After Stalingrad, Soviet forces began slowly to drive the Germans out of the USSR.

The eastern front, as the Soviet-German war is called, was the scene of unremitting horror before, during, and after Stalingrad. The Soviet army here consisted of 6 to 9 million men and thousands of women. The Axis forces, about 80 percent German, included Finns, Romanians, Hungarians, and Italians, and by 1942 added hundreds of thousands of Soviet citizens—Russians, Ukrainians, Lithuanians—who saw the German invasion as their liberation from communism. At its mid-1943 maximum, the Axis forces on the eastern front counted 4 million. This was the decisive theater of the war in Europe, and the largest in world history. Four-fifths of German war dead fell here, and more than half of the total Axis casualties in all theaters. In total, about 15 million soldiers of all nationalities died on the eastern front, and another 15 million civilians; another 25 million were homeless because of wartime destruction by 1945.

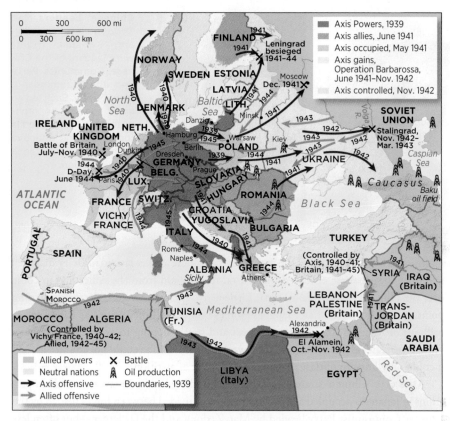

World War II in Europe, Africa, and the Middle East, 1940–1945 Roughly three-quarters of the German war effort was devoted to the eastern front against the Soviet Union. The German drive eastward was stopped at Stalingrad, after which the Soviet Red Army, using great quantities of American equipment, pushed the Germans back to Berlin. In North Africa, the tide turned against the Axis in 1942 at El Alamein in Egypt, which was followed by the Allied invasion of Italy launched from Tunisia in 1943. In the final year of the war in Europe, another major front opened in France with the Allies' D-Day invasion.

In each major theater except China, the Axis suffered defeats that turned the tide against them. In the Pacific, at the Battle of Midway (June 1942), U.S. naval aircraft destroyed a large chunk of Japan's fleet. In North Africa, where the Germans were driving toward British bases in Egypt and the strategic prize of the Suez Canal, the key moment came in October–November 1942 at El Alamein, in the desert of northwestern Egypt, when the British turned back a German-led attack—most of the foot soldiers were Italians. At El Alamein the Axis lost about 50,000 men, or 6 percent of the toll at Stalingrad.

The War in China The war in China (1937–1945) cost about 15 to 20 million lives, 80 percent of them Chinese. Japan by the end of 1938 occupied most of north and eastern

Chinese Leaders Mao Zedong (left) and Chiang Kai-shek (right) were leaders of the Chinese Communist Party and the Guomindang, respectively. Each led an army against the Japanese, with Mao's guerilla forces proving effective in mobilizing resistance to the invasion.

China, and by mid-1942 all of the major ports. Chinese armies lacked military materiel, and once the Japanese occupied the coastal regions, aid from the Allies had to come over the Himalayas to the southwest. Little arrived. Here there was no major turning point, only deadly stalemate. Japanese forces bombed Chinese cities at will. Tens of millions of refugees streamed to the west and south, hoping to escape the Japanese. Hunger, disease, and currency inflation were rampant. China could not counter-attack; it could only hope to outlast the Japanese in a war of attrition.

After 1940, Chinese strategists learned to avoid big battles in favor of smaller operations in Japanese-occupied areas. They remained divided between forces fielded by the Chinese Communist Party headed by Mao Zedong and the far larger—but often less effective—armies loyal to the Guomindang now led by Chiang Kai-shek. After Pearl Harbor, both expected Japan would ultimately lose, which undercut their ability to cooperate as each one intended to rule China after the war. They fought one another frequently after 1938, and as Japanese defeat seemed more certain by late 1944, they prepared for all-out civil war.

The Final Years In 1943, without any key battle, the Allies also prevailed over Germany on the seas of the North Atlantic. The U.S., U.K., and Canadian navies learned how to protect shipping and hunt submarines effectively. That enabled millions of tons of North American food, fuel, weapons, munitions, and other supplies to reach Britain and the USSR safely. After these turning points—Stalingrad, Midway, El Alamein, and the Atlantic—the Axis powers remained on the defensive, their now-slim chances of victory waning with each passing month.

The war dragged on for two and a half more years. Italy quit in 1943, leaving Germany and Japan to fight on. Both fought tenaciously, even after all rational hope was lost. Their forces had committed countless atrocities on foreign soil, and they feared payback if and when the fighting reached their own countries. But desperate tenacity

Hiroshima A trade exhibition hall was the only building left standing near the epicenter of the atomic bomb's explosion over Hiroshima on August 6, 1945. Today the building's ruins are the site of a memorial park.

was not enough. Over the course of 1943 and 1944, the Soviets pushed the Germans out of the USSR. On June 6, 1944—D-Day—the British, Canadians, and Americans landed the largest amphibious invasion force in world history on the beaches of Normandy, in northwestern France, and pushed Hitler's armies back toward Germany. Meanwhile, the Americans island-hopped across the South Pacific, driving the Japanese back toward their home islands.

The end came at last in 1945. In Europe, the Red Army slugged its way into Germany and took Berlin (April 1945), while the Americans and British fought their way into the western half of Germany in early 1945. The Germans were running low on men, fuel, and the will to combat. Relentless bombing campaigns hampered their war production and especially their movement, as rails, roads, bridges, and tunnels were by late 1944 bombed constantly. They surrendered in May 1945 shortly after Hitler committed suicide.

In the Pacific, the Americans pushed the Japanese back, island by island. The fiercest combat took place on Guadalcanal, in the Solomon Islands, and on Iwo Jima and Okinawa, islands close to Japan. In the summer of 1945, the Americans prepared to invade Japan, which they expected would cost a quarter-million American lives—and many more Japanese. But before they embarked on that mission, in early August 1945, the United States dropped an atomic bomb on each of two mid-size cities, **Hiroshima and Nagasaki**. The explosions instantly killed about 105,000 people, 90 percent of them civilians. Radiation poisoning soon killed roughly an equal number. In the same week, the USSR declared war on Japan. The Japanese high command chose to surrender in mid-August 1945.

Why the Allies Won

The Axis won almost every encounter in the years 1937–1941. But time was not on its side. The only realistic chance it had was a quick victory, before the Allies could bring to bear their enormous advantages in manpower and materiel. Until 1941, the Axis held an edge in military manpower and the quantity and quality of weaponry. But after the Axis attacked the USSR and the United States, it was heavily out-numbered and soon out-gunned. Its chances of winning shrank, slowly at first and more quickly after Midway and Stalingrad.

Coalition War The Axis was also out-managed. Germany, Japan, and Italy scarcely cooperated at all and, in the case of Germany and Italy, often worked at cross-purposes. When Hitler occupied Romania in 1940 he did not tell Mussolini, and Mussolini returned the favor when Italy invaded Greece months later. The Italian Fascist Party included Jews until 1938 and did not round up Jews for extermination. The Italian Army protected Jews in areas under its control, which confirmed Hitler's sense of Italian softness. When Italy surrendered to the Allies in 1943, the Germans captured hundreds of thousands of Italian soldiers and took them as slave laborers to Germany. Cooperation between Japan and its Axis partners amounted to little beside information sharing, because their theaters of operations were so distant.

In contrast, the Allies cooperated—not smoothly, but effectively. This was a remarkable achievement, given the ideological chasm between Stalin on one side and Roosevelt and Churchill on the other. Churchill had long been a vocal anti-communist; but after the German invasion of the Soviet Union in 1941, he concluded a pact with Stalin. He justified his position by saying, "If Hitler invaded hell I would make at least a favorable reference to the devil in the House of Commons." The United States provided vast quantities of war materiel to Britain and, despite the U.S. government's disdain for communism, the USSR. The United States and Britain frequently shared secret intelligence with each other, and from time to time shared it with Stalin, who rarely reciprocated.

The biggest tensions in the alliance arose over the American and British caution in opening a second front against Germany. With German armies deep in Soviet territory, Stalin wanted his allies to invade France in 1942. But U.S. and U.K. commanders did not feel ready to mount an amphibious assault on France, and they sent armies to Axis-occupied North Africa instead. Churchill was keen to defend Britain's position in Egypt and the Suez Canal, the lifeline to British India. Stalin suspected his allies were content to see his army bear the brunt of German firepower, and they probably were. But the shaky performance of the U.S. Army against German forces in North Africa in 1942 and 1943 strongly suggested it was not prepared for an invasion of German-occupied Europe. These tensions pitting the USSR against the United States and the United Kingdom, as we will see, helped break the wartime alliance and usher in the Cold War. But holding the alliance together until victory in 1945, across an ideological chasm, was the supreme achievement of Roosevelt, Churchill, and Stalin. It enabled them to make full use of their inherent advantages.

Economic War The biggest advantage the Allies enjoyed was their economic strength. In population, the Allies outnumbered the Axis by 2 to 1, if one counts only the major combatants (the USSR, United States, United Kingdom and its dominions of Canada, Australia, New Zealand, and South Africa on one side; and Germany, Italy, and Japan on the other). If one includes India and China among the Allies, the ratio swells to close to 7:1. The combined economies of the Allies was 2.1 times as large as that of the Axis in 1940—before the United States and the USSR entered the war—and 5 times larger by 1945. In the core years of the war, 1942 through 1944, total Allied military production outstripped that of the Axis by ratios between 3:1 and 10:1. The imbalance came in part from the success of the U.S. and U.K. navies in maintaining access to international trade flows, while the Axis had to rely on its own resources and those of the lands it conquered. Japan in 1940 had adequate supplies of only 2 of the 32 raw materials its high command deemed essential to warfare—graphite and sulfur. By and large, the Axis enjoyed an advantage in the quality of its military goods, but suffered an enormous disadvantage in quantity, partly from shortages of raw materials.

The Allies controlled almost all the world's oil, a crucial advantage. The most effective weapons systems in the 1940s—tanks, ships, and airplanes—all ran on oil. Fighting without oil meant moving men and equipment by rail or draft animal, in effect fighting with one hand tied behind your back. In particular, there was no way to fight an air war without oil. As it happened, most of the world's oil production in 1940 took place in the United States, the USSR, Mexico, Venezuela, and parts of the Middle East mainly under British control. The Axis produced almost none. Japan's initial conquests included oilfields in the Dutch East Indies (now Indonesia), and the Germans took over an oil patch in Romania. They targeted the Soviet oilfields near Baku on the Caspian Sea, but after Stalingrad they had no hope of adding to their oil supplies. Late in the war, the German Air Force could not fly for lack of fuel. Oil was the most important economic resource in warfare, and the Allies had almost all of it. American oilfields pumped 86 percent of the oil used by the Allies.

Economic culture mattered too. For different reasons, both the American and Soviet economies could change almost overnight into effective war economies. The mobilization of the American economy was stunning. Soon after the United States entered the war, one of Hitler's closest comrades, Air Marshall Hermann Goering, scoffed that the Americans were only good at producing razor blades. But in fact the U.S. economy was good at producing mass quantities of anything.

The Detroit area was the center of the world's automobile industry, which had been using electrified assembly lines for decades. This production technique worked superbly for the mass production of tanks, aircraft, jeeps, and trucks. The U.S. auto industry stopped making cars in 1942 to focus entirely on military vehicles and aircraft. The Ford Motor Company alone out-produced Italy during the war. By 1944, Ford workers could assemble a B-24 bomber every 63 minutes. Their counterparts in U.S. shipyards

American Manufacturing
Workers on the assembly line at a Chrysler factory in Michigan manufacture tanks in 1942. Theirs was one of many American auto plants that mobilized to produce war materiel.

could weld together big cargo ships in 8 days. The United States launched 16 warships for each one Japan could build. As President Roosevelt put it, the United States had a "genius . . . for mass-production."

The United States also had the resources to pay for, and found the labor to undertake, a giant war effort. The government sold billions of dollars of bonds to ordinary Americans and raised taxes across the board—the richest Americans paid a 94 percent income tax. As men left for war, American women streamed into war work in factories, offices, and on farms as well. Five million women joined the paid labor force between 1940 and 1945. By 1943, the majority of workers assembling airplanes were women. Thousands of women, including chemists and physicists, worked to create atomic bombs. Some 350,000 women joined the U.S. armed forces, driving trucks, serving as nurses, or handling paperwork. But overall, women made up a smaller proportion—27 to 29 percent—of the American industrial labor force during the war than in the United Kingdom (27 to 32 percent), Germany (27 to 32 percent), or the USSR (about 60 percent). Labor was less of a constraint on the war effort in the United States than it was for other major combatants.

The Soviet economy also performed miracles during the war. Since 1918 it had been a command economy in which the government, not market forces, made most major decisions. Since 1929 it had used five-year plans to run the economy and specialized in heroic mobilization—building a new steel mill in weeks or a factory in days. This helps to explain why the Soviet economy did not collapse in the years 1941–1942 while the Germans hammered ever deeper into the country, occupying lands that formerly had accounted for one-third of Soviet economic output. Soviet factory workers packed up everything they could, took it east, behind the Ural Mountains, and put their factories back together again. Everyone not in uniform or producing food—teenagers, the elderly, political prisoners—was recruited for armaments production. The Soviet economy already made widespread use of female labor before 1941 and, unlike the United States, had no great reserve of labor to mobilize. Nevertheless, the Soviet economy, despite losing many of its most industrialized regions to Hitler's armies and much of its male workforce to active military duty, produced more military materiel than Germany in every year of the war.

Both the Americans and the Soviets relied on mass production of simple designs built with interchangeable parts, which made it easier to maintain and repair machinery. Neither the Americans nor the Soviets made high-quality military goods, at least not until 1944. But they could make much more, much faster than anyone else. The United States was able to ship about 17 percent of its military output to either Britain or the USSR in a program called Lend-Lease, in which the U.S. government "lent" food, fuel, trucks, and aircraft to its allies with little expectation of repayment. When the Red Army marched to Berlin in 1945, it rode in Dodge and Studebaker trucks made in the American Midwest. The top Soviet general, Marshall Georgy Zhukov, said afterward that without the American equipment the USSR could not have continued to fight.

The contrast with the German and Japanese war economies was sharp. Both had strong industrial traditions of skilled craftsmen. They built excellent tanks and airplanes; but lacking electrified assembly lines, they could not make them quickly, and repair was difficult. American jeeps were easy to maintain, but it took prolonged training to maintain German or Japanese high-quality equipment. Skilled labor shortages became a bottleneck in the German and Japanese war economies.

Indeed, labor of any kind became a bottleneck for the Axis economies. They mobilized almost all young men for military service from the outset of war. By 1943 they were conscripting middle-aged men, and by 1945 they were putting 15-year-olds in uniform. For ideological reasons, they—the Japanese especially—did not want women in factories. Women were supposed to stay at home and provide a wholesome environment for children, or perhaps work as teachers and nurses. Half a million German women went to work, mainly as nurses, in occupied territories. The proportion of women in Japan's industrial workforce was about half of Germany's, which in turn was about half that in the USSR. Meanwhile, both Germany and Japan enslaved millions of men from countries they occupied and dragged them into war production. Thus Germany and Japan relied on legions of forced laborers, who if not constantly intimidated would slow production or even sabotage it.

Brainpower War The enormous economic advantages of the Allies told in the long run. But as the war dragged on, the Allies acquired another advantage too. They harnessed the brainpower of their populations more effectively than did the Axis powers.

Part of the Allies' success resulted from the flight of scientists from Germany and Europe as the Nazi threat took shape. Before the rise of the Nazis, Germany had, by far, the world's most advanced centers of physics. Several great physicists, such as Albert Einstein, were Jewish and left Europe to escape from Nazism. A dozen or more worked on the U.S. atomic bomb project. Enrico Fermi oversaw the first self-sustaining

Manhattan Project Members of an all-female engineering team operate equipment at a uranium enrichment facility in Oak Ridge, Tennessee, in 1944. Laboratories and other facilities around the United States were dedicated to the effort to develop a nuclear bomb.

nuclear reaction, which took place in 1942 under the stadium stands at the University of Chicago. He had left Italy in 1938 because his wife was Jewish. Refugees from Nazism contributed significantly to scientific war work in the United States and the United Kingdom.

Moreover, the United States and the United Kingdom converted their industrial laboratories, engineering works, and universities to war work. This strategy paid dividends in the form of weaponry, radar, better bombsights, and much else that helped win the war. The most famous example is the Manhattan Project, the secret project to build an atomic bomb that, starting in 1941, tapped scientists and engineers from several American, British, and Canadian universities and U.S. corporations. Together with hundreds of thousands of laborers, they built the engineering and weapons complex that developed the bombs used to destroy Hiroshima and Nagasaki.

Another important example of war-related technological development was miniaturized radar. The Allies needed to ferry millions of tons of fuel, food, and munitions across the Atlantic, from North America to Britain and the USSR, running a gauntlet of German submarines. To do so successfully, they needed radar devices small enough to fit on airplanes. Two British physicists at the University of Birmingham—one of them, Harry Boot, only 22 years old—developed miniaturized radar technology (used today in microwave ovens), and American factories built the needed devices. Before they had them, the Allies were losing ships to German submarines faster than they could build new ones. After they started using micro-radar in airplanes, they could hunt down and destroy submarines faster than the Germans could build new ones. That enabled North American farms and factories to keep Britain and the USSR supplied by sea.

In addition to engineering improvements in military hardware, the Allies put to use extraordinary advances in medicine. A good example is the use of DDT, a chemical compound that kills insects. (It was later banned in many countries because of its toxic effects on wildlife.) The Americans mass-produced it and sprayed their troops with it to protect them from lice, which can carry typhus, and mosquitoes, which can carry malaria. In the South Pacific and New Guinea campaigns, where malaria was far more deadly than combat, abundant supplies of DDT gave American and Australian troops a major advantage over the Japanese, who had none. The Allies also had an edge in anti-bacterial drugs such as penicillin, which saved countless soldiers from dying from infected wounds.

More generally, the United States and the United Kingdom, and to a lesser extent the USSR, proved better at learning from mistakes than did the Axis powers. Both the United States and the United Kingdom were more open societies, in which information flowed more freely than in Germany or Japan—although this was not true of the USSR. The first requirement of learning from mistakes is admitting them and studying them. Much went wrong for the United States, the United Kingdom, and especially the USSR early in the war, and they could not pretend to themselves they knew how to fight as well as the Germans and Japanese. They had urgent reason to study their failures and improve their performance. After some disastrous experiences, the Americans got very good at amphibious landings on Pacific islands. After costly disasters, the Soviet army learned how to fight tank battles. The Axis proved less able to improve combat performance by learning from failure. The Japanese navy even concealed its loss of one-third of its aircraft carriers at Midway from civilian leaders and the army, which for several months forged its strategy in the false belief that 12 carriers were still available.

Finally, the Allies did much better than the Axis in codebreaking. With the help of Polish mathematicians and intelligence officers, the British learned the secrets to German encoding machines before the war even began. As the Germans changed their codes through the course of the war, British codebreakers, many of them mathematicians, got better at deciphering them. The Germans and Italians broke some of the Allies' codes too, which helped them considerably in the years 1940–1942. The Germans, with Italian help, were reading coded dispatches on Allied plans sent by an American army officer in Cairo. The legendary German general Erwin Rommel, known as the "desert fox," could read these messages within hours. But the Germans and Italians could not keep up with periodic changes in the Allies' codes, and by 1943 were usually operating in the dark.

In the Pacific War, codebreaking was also crucial. The Americans could read the main Japanese diplomatic and naval codes throughout the war. Convinced that their code was too complex to decipher, the Japanese made only small changes that did not baffle codebreakers for long. The Japanese failed to break any important American codes.

The Human Cost

The death toll of World War II reached 60 million, more than any previous war and about 3 percent of humankind. In addition to those killed, many millions more suffered bodily or psychological harm that lasted all their lives. The death and destruction were greatest in eastern Europe and China. The USSR, Poland, Yugoslavia, and Greece lost large proportions of their population. The United States, which made huge contributions in terms of war materiel, paid the lowest human cost of any major combatant— partly because it joined the war later than most, but mainly because after Pearl Harbor no combat took place on American soil. The table on the next page reduces the grisly tragedy to numbers and percentages.

War Crimes War crimes took place on an unprecedented scale. Outside of combat, Germans and their accomplices murdered 10 to 14 million people, including nearly 6

The Human Cost of World War II

	War dead (in millions)	1940 population (in millions)	War dead as a percentage of 1940 population
USSR	25–29	194	13–16%
China	15–20	520	3–4%
Germany	6.9–7.4	70	8–9%
Poland	6	35	17%
Dutch East Indies	3–4	70	4.3–5.7%
Japan	2.5–3.1	72	3.5–4.3%
Yugoslavia	1.0–1.7	16	7–11%
Greece	0.5–0.8	7.2	7–11%
France	0.6	42	1.4%
Italy	0.5	45	1%
United Kingdom	0.5	48	1%
United States	0.4	132	0.3%
Canada	0.04	11.3	0.4%
Australia	0.04	7	0.6%
WORLD	60	2,300	3%

Sources: Gerhard Weinberg, *World at Arms* (1995), 894, and https://en.wikipedia.org/wiki/World_War_II_casualties#Total_deaths_by_country

million Jews (see below). Stalin's henchmen killed at least 1.2 million and perhaps as many as 7 million—the figures are highly controversial. They killed anyone suspected of favoring the Germans, which included many Ukrainians and Poles, among others within the USSR. In addition, they tried to kill all educated people and military officers in the parts of Poland they controlled. Japanese forces murdered or deliberately starved millions more, most notoriously in the Nanjing Massacre of 1937–1938 in which perhaps 200,000 Chinese civilians were slaughtered and 20,000 women and girls raped. In north China in 1941, the Japanese implemented a policy known as the Three Alls: kill all, loot all, burn all. That resulted in nearly 3 million civilian deaths. Of the 30 million prisoners of war, perhaps 6 to 10 million died of starvation and disease, most commonly those held by the USSR, Germany, or Japan.

Bombing of Cities   Aerial bombing of cities, regarded by some as a war crime, killed several hundred thousand civilians in Europe and Japan. War strategists thought, incorrectly, that they could break civilian morale by bombing cities and terrorizing populations. But the bombing only hardened the popular will to resist. Worst hit were

Britain in 1940–1941, Germany in 1943–1945, and Japan in 1944–1945. Squadrons of bombers burned whole cities to the ground. In Tokyo in March 1945, one American air raid killed about 100,000 civilians. In February 1945, British and American bombing of Dresden, in Germany, killed about 25,000.

As we have seen, in August 1945 the United States dropped two atomic bombs, one each on the Japanese cities of Hiroshima and Nagasaki. Counting lingering deaths from radiation exposure, the bombs killed roughly 200,000 people. These were the first and, thus far, the last uses of nuclear weapons in warfare. They succeeded in their immediate purpose: to force a Japanese surrender without the heavy losses expected in an invasion of Japan's home islands. President Truman's decision to use them was welcomed by the Allies at the time, but later became highly controversial because of the uniquely devastating power of atomic weapons.

The Holocaust The horrific human cost of the war included the near destruction of European Jewry. Hitler intended to kill Europe's entire population of 9 to 10 million Jews. Sporadic murders of Jews in Germany, of whom there were more than 400,000, began before the war. In 1939, when the Germans conquered half of Poland, they murdered many more Jews and tried to collect all the rest into ghettoes—in effect, urban prison camps. Larger-scale systematic murder, carried out by specialized death squads called *Einsatzgruppen*, began with the German invasion of the USSR in June 1941.

Hitler intended to win the war quickly and afterward finish off the Jews, but he realized that the war would drag on after two events in December 1941: the first Soviet army counter-attack against German forces, and the Japanese attack on Pearl Harbor, which brought the United States into the war. He decided to kill all of Europe's Jews while the war was still under way, and his underlings convened a conference in early 1942 outside of Berlin at Wannsee to plan what they called "The Final Solution to the Jewish question."

At the Wannsee Conference 15 Nazi officials, nearly half of whom held doctorates in law, worked out the broad outlines of the plan. Even after the tide of battle had turned against them in 1943, the Germans devoted manpower and rail cars to the transport of Jews from all over Europe to dozens of concentration camps—both labor camps and extermination camps. The extermination camp names are synonyms for the deepest abyss in the annals of human morality: Treblinka, Sobibor, Auschwitz. In all, the Germans and their helpers murdered between 5.6 million and 6 million Jews, the vast majority from eastern Europe. Some they worked

Holocaust Emaciated survivors of the Buchenwald concentration camp in eastern Germany were photographed shortly after U.S. troops liberated the camp in April 1945.

to death, some they starved to death, some they shot, and most they gassed in specially built death chambers. A quarter of the victims were children. In Poland, as in Germany, most Christians had a pretty good idea of what was happening to their Jewish neighbors, but judged it was safest for themselves to do and say nothing. In western Europe, where Jews were comparatively few, puppet governments such as the so-called Vichy regime that governed most of France collaborated with the Nazi genocide. German executioners often had eager assistants, especially among those Croats, Ukrainians, Romanians, Hungarians, and Poles who willingly took part in the murders. Croatian fascists even set up their own death camp.

Occasionally Europe's Jews had courageous defenders. Led by a Protestant pastor, one village in the south of France, Chambon-sur-Lignon, hid a thousand or more Jews and helped others escape from France. A Dutch village, Nieuwlande, also inspired by a Protestant clergyman, did much the same. In 1943, when German authorities ordered the mayor of the Greek island of Zakynthos to provide a list of the island's Jews and their property, they received a list with two names: the mayor's and that of the island's bishop. Islanders helped all 275 Jews on Zakynthos to hide, and all survived the Nazi occupation. So, improbably, did the mayor and the bishop. The Swedish diplomat Raoul Wallenberg, posted to Budapest, saved thousands of Hungarian Jews by issuing them documents providing the legal protection of neutral Sweden. (The Soviet army seized Wallenberg when it captured Hungary in 1945, and he perished not long after, probably in a Soviet prison.) The Polish diplomat Jan Karski snuck into the Warsaw ghetto twice, and a Jewish transport camp once, in order to bring authentic

The Holocaust, 1939–1945 This map shows a landscape of death and despair. Beginning in 1933, the Nazi Party set up a system of concentration camps, also called labor camps, which held about 21,000 people when World War II began in Europe in 1939. They held 715,000 at their height in early 1945. A parallel system of seven extermination camps opened in 1942. (Auschwitz, opened in 1940, was both a labor camp and an extermination camp.) Some 800,000 people died in the labor camps of starvation, disease, and brutality. About 3.1 million died in the extermination camps—most of them Jews. Another 2.6 to 2.9 million Jews were murdered outside the camp systems.

information of the fate of Poland's Jews to the attention of the outside world. He went to London and Washington to explain what he knew, but with little result. Churchill and Roosevelt thought the best way to save lives, whether Jewish or not, was to win the war fast.

A few tens of thousands of Jews fought back against Hitler's extermination campaign. Some managed to join Polish or Ukrainian guerillas in the forests and swamps of eastern Europe. Some rose in rebellion in the ghettoes. The largest such rising took place in the Warsaw ghetto, which had once held 400,000 Jews. Less than a quarter remained by January 1943, when renewed deportations to the extermination camps were met with violent resistance by a few hundred poorly armed Jews who had smuggled in weapons over the previous months. They held off German units for 27 days before being overwhelmed.

The mass murder of the Jews was the biggest part of a larger Nazi extermination project. Hitler also regarded Roma (Gypsies) and the mentally ill as unworthy to live in the expanded and racially purified Germany. His supporters murdered roughly 200,000 to 500,000 Roma, most of them in the same camps as the Jews. That amounted to about 20 to 50 percent of Europe's Roma population. Some 300,000 people judged by doctors to have mental or physical disabilities were also killed in Hitler's efforts to safeguard the German "race."

Hitler also regarded all Slavs as sub-human. German soldiers, police, and other units killed millions of Poles, Ukrainians, and Russians. They particularly sought to kill anyone with an education, except those who could be recruited into the German war effort. Of 5.7 million Soviet prisoners of war in German hands, 3.3 million died from starvation, disease, or violence.

Hitler was one of few extreme racists ever to hold sufficient power to put his views into practice. He thought a pure German race existed and deserved to thrive, while Slavs, Roma, and Jews were obstacles to German greatness. He wanted to kill, starve, or enslave them all. German voters, politicians, and military men had put him in a position to realize much of his murderous agenda.

Home Fronts

World War II reached into lives far from the many battle zones. Total war required the involvement of all citizens, whether on the front lines or at home.

Germany In Germany, all was quiet on the home front until 1943. Remembering the privations of World War I, German authorities reserved plenty of food and other necessities for civilians until late in the war when they no longer could. Domestic support for Hitler remained strong, and organized resistance to his regime—extremely dangerous for anyone—was minimal. The most famous anti-Nazi movement was a non-violent and ineffective student group in Munich called the White Rose, almost all

CONSIDERING THE EVIDENCE

Propaganda for the Japanese Home Front

During World War II, the Japanese government produced films, leaflets, plays, radio broadcasts, and posters to unify the home front. But some of the most effective propaganda was *kamishibai*—that is, one-person performances accompanied by 10 to 30 hand-painted illustrations presented in sequence. Before the war, *kamishibai* artists and writers worked under the direction of managers who rented the illustrations, scripts, and bicycles to performers, who made their money by selling candy. The performers visited the same neighborhoods every day, captivating their young audiences with serialized melodramas and adventure stories. After Japan seized Manchuria from China in 1931, government agencies began writing and sponsoring official *kamishibai* performances at factories, farming collectives, and schools to promote the idea that Japan was liberating, rather than conquering, the rest of East Asia. The *kamishibai* also encouraged adults to support wartime policies—for example, by depositing the money saved by rationing into the country's banks. In the following excerpt, members of a group that grows vegetables together speak with their leader, named Sakuta, about the best way to spend the profits from their sales.

Scene 12

Troop member: "Troop Commander, sir! I have run out of face cream; may I purchase some, sir?"

Sakuta: "What? You want to buy face cream? Outrageous! Don't you know that 'Luxury is the Enemy'? Huh?"

Another troop member: "Troop Commander, I would like to buy a pair of socks."... "I would like to eat some bread."... "I am out of tissues."...

Scene 13

Sakuta: "Stop yelling 'Troop Commander' in my ear! 'I need to buy this,

---

of whom were executed in 1943. Three times military officers organized assassination plots against Hitler: all three narrowly failed.

By 1943, the veneer of normalcy in Germany was challenged by growing knowledge of the death camps, the presence of 10 to 12 million slave laborers dragged from occupied territories, and Allied bombing of German cities. Most Germans eventually knew that Jews were disappearing, many knew they were being killed, but almost no one objected publicly. Either they approved of the mass murder, or they feared—with good reason—for their own position and safety. In 1944 and 1945, any appearance of normalcy disappeared. Allied bombing intensified. Shortages of food and supplies became common. A dark joke at the time went like this: "Enjoy the war, because the peace will be horrible." Anxiety about what was to come when the Red Army entered

I want that'—you sound like a bunch of whining babies. I am about to make a speech, so listen up."...

Scene 15

Sakuta continues: "...what Japan needs now is not just money; we also have to use goods as carefully as possible. Buying things just because you have some money...weakens our nation."...

Scene 16

Sakuta continues: "The money that you keep in hand belongs just to the person who has it, but...putting money into savings is an expression of loyalty to the nation....

"What would you do if you had children? Would you eat those adorable little kids?

"Or, instead, would you loyally offer them up to the service of the nation? Hmm? It's just the same with money."...

Scene 17

Sakuta continues: "If you don't understand something as simple as this, even children will laugh at you. In fact, the reason I am making this speech is that I heard it from my son who is in elementary school. These days even children understand the importance of savings."

Questions for Analysis

1. Which parts of the script suggest that this *kamishibai* was intended for adults instead of children?

2. How did the writers of this *kamishibai* use references to children to persuade adults that they should contribute to the war effort?

3. Why was it important to Japan and other countries for their people to ration resources, save money, and invest in war bonds?

Source: Sharalyn Orbaugh, "Record of the Cheerful Troop," in *Propaganda Performed: Kamishibai in Japan's Fifteen Year War* (Boston, 2015).

German lands was commonplace, and well founded: Soviet soldiers raped about 20 percent of the German women they encountered in 1944 and 1945.

Japan and Italy Japan's home front was also quiet into 1943. The military exercised tight control and kept any discouraging information, such as the fate of the Japanese fleet at Midway, from the public. They also suppressed all information about the atrocities at Nanjing. Support for the emperor and the war stayed high. By 1944, the strain hit home. Amidst growing shortages, the government asked women to work in war industries, and half a million "volunteered" before the war's end—they could be fined if they didn't. Hiroko Nakamato, whose Hiroshima high school closed in 1943, went to work in an unheated airplane factory where she toiled long hours, slept on the premises, and got little to eat. Heavy aerial bombing began late in 1944 and intensified thereafter, making the last months of the war a living hell for Japanese. Even then, there was no serious resistance to the imperial government or the war.

In Italy, the war was never popular outside of committed fascist circles. Many Italians thought they were fighting on the wrong side, a conviction deepened by witnessing German atrocities in North Africa and eastern Europe. A steady diet of military defeats sapped morale. In the summer of 1943, when Allied armies invaded Italy's southernmost island of Sicily, Mussolini's hold on the country crumbled, the Fascist Party turned on him, and Italy quit the war. In 1944 and 1945, Italian factions were fighting one another while the Allies occupied the southern part of the country and the Germans the north.

The Soviet Union In the Allied countries, governments were able to demand greater sacrifices sooner from their populations. In the USSR, Stalin had no choice because the war started so badly. Total and immediate mobilization of manpower, womanpower, and all resources followed quickly upon the German invasion and the sudden loss of millions killed or taken prisoner. Women took over most of the farm work and much of the factory work. Nearly a million women served in the armed forces, including in combat roles such as tank commander, infantry sniper, or fighter pilot. Food shortages were widespread and strict rationing imposed. In Leningrad, which the Germans besieged for nearly 900 days, one-third of the population (800,000 people) starved to death.

And yet the Soviet home front did not collapse. Soviet citizens were accustomed to stoic endurance. Many truly idolized Stalin and were prepared to sacrifice for him and their country. His appeals to patriotism helped, which extended to enlisting the Russian Orthodox Church in the war effort, reversing two decades of official atheism and ruthless Soviet persecution of the church. Well-publicized German brutality made it clear to almost everyone that the lesser of the evils available was to work as hard as possible for victory. And for those who doubted it, Stalin's network of informers and secret police stood ready to execute anyone suspected of defeatism, sympathy for the enemy, or just insufficient admiration of Stalin.

Soviet Mobilization In the Soviet army, it was relatively common for women to serve in combat roles. The highly decorated Soviet fighter pilot Lydia Litvyak, posing here with her plane, was shot down in the Battle of Kursk in 1943, at age 22.

The United Kingdom In the United Kingdom, thorough home-front mobilization was also the rule. Strict rationing prevailed and made everyday life drab—except during German bombing raids, when it was terrifying. Morale at times was shaky, despite Churchill's charismatic leadership. Petty crime spiked during air raid blackouts. In 1940 and early 1941, when Britain suffered defeat after defeat, many thought—and some said—that making peace with Germany made sense. Women worked long hours in armaments factories, entrusting their children to relatives and friends. In 1941, they were required to register for national—not military—service, working wherever the government judged they would be most useful. The entry into the war of the USSR and then the United States, and stepped-up deliveries of American and Canadian food, fuel, and other supplies, brightened the outlook by late 1943, as did the improving prospect of victory.

The United States The United States instituted rationing too but experienced no serious deprivations, nor any serious bombing after Pearl Harbor. Most citizens accepted the necessity for sacrifices, and little compulsion was needed. The government worked with business leaders to mobilize the economy for war production. As we've seen, millions of women took on war work in offices, factories, and the armed forces—but not in combat roles. Hundreds of thousands of African Americans and poor whites left the rural South for armaments factories in the Midwest or California. The war against the most uncompromising racists in world history drew heightened attention to racial inequalities at home. Whereas in 1941 only 4,000 African Americans were in uniform, by 1945 about 1.2 million had served, albeit in segregated units and usually in non-combat roles. But the so-called Tuskegee Airmen, fighter pilots who flew out of bases in Italy in 1944 and 1945, were in particular demand by bomber crews who wanted the best fighter escorts they could get for air raids over Nazi-controlled Europe. The United States de-segregated its armed forces in 1948.

The United States and Canada both treated citizens of Japanese ancestry as potential enemies. Most of the Japanese American population on the West Coast, about 110,000 people, was rounded up in 1942 and kept in internment camps for the duration of the war. This was Roosevelt's decision, upheld by the Supreme Court in the *Korematsu* decision of 1944. In contrast, almost none of the larger Japanese Hawaiian population was interned. German Americans were sometimes kept under surveillance, and some 11,000 were interned. Almost all Japanese Canadians, about 22,000 people, most of whom were born in Canada, were put into camps and their property sold to help pay for the war.

Racialist thinking shaped—and often weakened—the war effort of most major combatants. Britain recruited only from Indian and African populations deemed "martial races." South Africa

Japanese Internment The American photographer Dorothea Lange took this photograph of the Mochida family of Hayward, California, preparing for their removal to an internment camp in May 1942.

refused to use black Africans, the vast majority of the population, in military roles, until losses of white troops left it no choice. New Zealand was slow to mobilize Maori. The USSR initially refused to use men from non-Slavic minorities as combat troops, until the death toll obliged the army to pour Tajiks, Uzbeks, Turkmen, and others into battle. It also deported about 2 million people from Muslim minorities in the Crimea and the Caucasus to Siberia or Central Asia on the grounds—often well founded—that they preferred the Germans to Stalin.

Occupations

Lands occupied by Axis troops in Europe or East Asia suffered grievously. In German-occupied western Europe, conditions were grim; in eastern Europe, they were horrific. Food, fuel, and other supplies went first to the Germans; everyone else had to make do with what remained. Germans found willing collaborators, especially early on when it seemed likely they would win. Collaborators throughout Nazi-occupied Europe helped to organize German war production, labor drafts, and the deportation of Jews to death camps.

Occupation also incited resistance, which was strongest in Yugoslavia and the conquered parts of the USSR, but present on some scale everywhere. None of it had much effect until the years 1944–1945, and even then it was far from decisive. Yugoslav partisans operating in mountains and forests at times kept two German Army divisions tied up. Partisans operating in the woods and swamps of eastern Europe, and, late in the war, in the mountains of Italy and France, also gave the Germans trouble. But acts of resistance in German-occupied and Italian-occupied Europe provoked terrible reprisals, typically featuring the murder of dozens or hundreds of civilians taken at random. As a consequence, civilians in occupied Europe often resented resistance fighters as much as those who collaborated with the Germans.

In the parts of China, Southeast Asia, or the Pacific Islands occupied by Japanese forces, the war years were also exceedingly grim. In occupied China, millions collaborated with the Japanese and millions resisted them. Japanese racial ideology encouraged extremely harsh treatment of Chinese, which over time nourished resistance. Both the Guomindang and the Chinese Communist Party (CCP) mounted military resistance in occupied China, generally in small-scale guerilla actions. The Guomindang confined itself to guerilla operations after 1943, but on balance proved less successful at them than the CCP, which did a better job of winning over peasant support and dodging Japanese reprisals.

Throughout China and Southeast Asia, food often ran short, and the Japanese took what they wanted. Epidemics raged. With ship and rail transport serving mainly military purposes, it became next to impossible to transport food or medicine. In Indonesia, 1 million people starved in the years 1944–1945. In the Philippines, where resistance was widespread during the Japanese occupation (1941–1945), some 330,000 starved and another 140,000 were massacred—most famously in the so-called Bataan death march in 1942, when about 9,000 captured Filipino soldiers and 1,000 Americans lost their lives. Millions of men and women were forced into slave labor for the Japanese war effort, most notoriously in 1943 on a railway-building project linking Burma and Thailand, on which 90,000 Southeast Asians—and 12,000 Allied prisoners of war—died.

In another grievous wartime abuse, the Japanese army seized hundreds of thousands of young women in Korea, China, the Philippines, and elsewhere and forced them to work throughout occupied Asia as sex slaves. Only about one-quarter of these **comfort women** survived the abuse meted out to them. A few survivors, such as Maria Rosa Luna Henson, a Filipina who was 15 years old when first raped by Japanese soldiers, wrote harrowing memoirs of their sufferings.

Aftermath

The war's end left much of Europe and East Asia in ruins. Millions of war refugees wandered in search of safety, food, and shelter. Allied troops liberated the remaining Nazi death camps and the shockingly emaciated survivors. Millions of Japanese struggled to get home from China. Millions of Germans who had trudged westward to get away from the Soviet Red Army huddled in camps all over Germany, dependent on Allied charity. Violent clashes continued, as people settled scores with those they had come to resent for personal or political reasons. Many thousands who had collaborated with the Germans or Japanese were casually killed. The Allies formally charged 24 top-ranking Nazis and 28 Japanese political and military leaders with war crimes and conducted trials at Nuremberg (1945–1946) and Tokyo (1946–1948). Almost all were found guilty and sentenced to death or prison.

Human Rights Sorrow and anger at the atrocities and crimes of World War II led to a surge of interest in ways to prevent anyone, governments especially, from doing such things again. One form this took was renewed discussion of individual human rights, usually understood to include at a minimum the right to life, freedom of expression, and equality before the law. The concept had deep roots in western Europe and its offshoots in North America—despite their histories of imperialism, slavery, and disenfranchisement of women. Most cultural traditions in world history, in contrast, understood rights not as held by individuals, but as shared by groups such as clans or tribes. Nonetheless, the principle of human rights held broad appeal—not least in the colonized world, where it lent moral support to independence movements. When the victorious Allies met in San Francisco in 1945 to establish an international body charged with keeping the world at peace, the United Nations, they set up a commission for human rights.

Chaired by Eleanor Roosevelt, widow of the late president, the commission issued a

Universal Declaration of Human Rights in 1948, the preamble of which included these words: "[R]ecognition of the inherent dignity and of the equal and inalienable rights of all members of the human family is the foundation of freedom, justice, and peace in the world." All UN member nations voted to adopt the Declaration as a statement of principles—with the exception of the USSR and those eastern European countries under its control; Saudi Arabia, where slavery was still legal; and South Africa, which had just passed racist laws denying basic rights to its black majority.

The new emphasis on human rights was subsequently expressed in UN agreements on the rights of refugees (1951), women (1979), children (1989), and other conventions. The World War II tradition of tribunals—temporary courts—for war criminals, such as at Nuremberg and Tokyo, led to the establishment in 2002 of the International Criminal Court (ICC), based in The Hague. The ICC has opened 12 prosecutions, 10 of them of African rulers. The ICC and the UN's human rights regime generally are ongoing responses to one of the saddest legacies of World War II and its more recent echoes.

The Post-War Period   Over time, a new normal settled in. Tens of millions of soldiers and sailors went home, shedding uniforms for civilian garb. Millions of women gave up factory or office jobs and returned to domestic roles, some willingly, some only because they were fired in favor of ex-soldiers. In some countries, including France and Italy, the wartime contributions of women translated into political rights in the form of suffrage; the United States during its post-war occupation of Japan imposed a new constitution providing for female suffrage. Food and fuel shortages eased in most countries—but slowly. Starvation stalked the USSR in 1946 and 1947; rationing of some items in the United Kingdom lasted into the 1950s.

In terms of international politics, the new normal was very different from the pre-war world. Two former great powers, Germany and Japan, were defeated, partially destroyed, and now under military occupation. The United Kingdom, although victorious, was financially ruined and dependent on the United States. Its empire—as we shall see—was more unstable than ever. The USSR, also triumphant, was exhausted, hungry, and now without the supplies formerly shipped from North America. Soviet forces remained in most of the lands they had taken from the Germans and soon created communist governments to rule them. China remained at war after the Japanese left, as the Guomindang and the CCP fought to control the ravaged country.

The United States, in contrast, with only 7 percent of the world's population, now accounted for half of its industrial production and a quarter of the global economy. It had the only nuclear weapons in the world, and the biggest air and naval forces by far. It produced most of the world's surplus food and much of its oil. Its science and technology communities, buoyed by the arrival of refugees, were the world's most dynamic and creative. Never before or since has the United States been as dominant in world politics as in late 1945. Never in the history of the world had any single state exercised greater power relative to all others. It could not last.

The Cold War, 1945–1991

The **Cold War** was an ideological and strategic struggle principally between the United States and the USSR. It dominated international politics between 1945 and 1991. Its tensest moments are the closest the human race has yet come to self-destruction. Within societies, it helped support Stalin's continuing dictatorship in the USSR and brought harsh divisions and increased regimentation to life in the United States. It divided Korea and Germany, and it added a dangerous combustibility to conflicts and civil wars in countries such as Greece, China, Korea, Vietnam, Mozambique, Angola, Ethiopia, Somalia, Chile, Guatemala, and Nicaragua. It was a genuinely global struggle. The international system no longer featured multiple great powers but became a "bipolar system," with two superpowers more formidable than all the rest: the United States and the USSR.

Origins: Fractures in the Alliance

In some respects, the Cold War began before World War II ended. The politics of the Allied coalition, although on balance highly successful, showed strains from early on. The biggest strategic differences, noted above, were what Stalin considered the delayed opening of a second front in Europe and, much less important, the late opening, from the American perspective, of a Soviet front against Japan in Manchuria.

Soviet Security and Eastern Europe Other problems also helped to fracture the wartime alliance. When the war ended, the Soviet army occupied the eastern half of Europe and the eastern one-third of Germany. Stalin had no intention of leaving all this territory to its own citizens. In 1945, Stalin's strongest commitment in foreign policy was that the USSR should never again be traumatized by invasion. He wanted all of eastern Europe, including what was to become East Germany, as a buffer under his control.

Stalin's position, although partly a result of his longstanding paranoia, had a rational basis to it. The USSR had lost about 18,000 to 20,000 citizens daily during World War II, albeit many of them from Stalin's own brutalities. In mortality terms, this amounted to the equivalent of a Pearl Harbor every three hours for the duration of the war. Aware of massive invasions by Bonaparte's forces in 1812 and by Germany in 1914 and 1941, most Soviet citizens would have agreed with Stalin: it was wise to control eastern Europe so any future invasions could be challenged before reaching Soviet soil.

In 1945, Stalin annexed to the USSR small slices of Romania and Czechoslovakia to go with the Baltic countries—Latvia, Lithuania, and Estonia—and the eastern half of Poland annexed in 1940–41. In the years 1945–1948, he found willing puppets—or, in his view, loyal and reliable communists—to govern Poland, Czechoslovakia, Hungary, Romania, Bulgaria, and East Germany. He shipped huge amounts of machinery and other goods from eastern Europe, and especially from East Germany, to the USSR.

Collective Security The American leadership, however, preferred a different vision of international security. The United States, in comparison to the USSR, had suffered lightly in World War II. Led now by Harry Truman, who became president when Roosevelt died in April 1945, the U.S. government favored a system of collective security anchored by the United Nations, founded in 1945 as an improved version of the League of Nations. That and the American monopoly on nuclear weapons would theoretically ensure international security.

These incompatible visions defeated any hopes of prolonging Allied wartime cooperation. At a conference in February 1945, held at Yalta in the Soviet Crimea, Stalin, Roosevelt, and Churchill agreed to divide Germany when the war ended and to give the USSR part of the Japanese island of Sakhalin. They formally agreed on free elections in the eastern European countries controlled by the Soviet army, but in fact Stalin had no intention of permitting elections that would not return governments subservient to him. The wartime Allies continued discussions in July 1945 at Potsdam outside Berlin, but they could agree on little aside from details of the treatment of a defeated Germany and the requirement of absolute surrender from Japan. The fate of eastern Europe was the biggest unresolved issue: the United States and the United Kingdom wanted free elections rather than communist rule, but were not prepared to force the Soviet army out of the region in a new war.

Even the United States and the United Kingdom, which had collaborated effectively during the war, discovered that they had postponed some important disagreements. The greatest of those was the future of the British Empire, which Churchill dearly wished to protect but Roosevelt and Truman did not. In need of American money, food, and oil, Britain had to bow to American wishes. Churchill decisively lost a national election in July 1945, and his successors did not share his imperialist bent. The British Empire, as we will see, would soon dwindle to insignificance.

Truman and Stalin also clashed over China's future. After Japan's defeat, China's warring factions—the communists of Mao Zedong and the nationalists, or Guomindang—stepped up their fighting in what is known as the **Chinese Civil War** (1945–1949), the final chapter in their decades-long competition for power. Each side appealed for outside help and received it, one from the USSR and the other from the United States. So the security ambitions of the two greatest powers were fundamentally at odds in eastern Europe and China.

The World Economy In addition, the United States and the USSR held incompatible ambitions for the world economy. Both self-interest and ideology stood behind these ambitions. The United States emerged from the war with the world's most competitive industries and healthiest financial sector. Its leadership supported an international economy with free trade and free flows of capital, lightly regulated by international institutions such as the International Monetary Fund and what would become the

World Bank. These institutions anchored the Bretton Woods system, named for the resort in New Hampshire where a conference in 1944 hammered out agreements to manage monetary policy, currency rates, and debt, with the aim of preventing a return of the Great Depression.

This capitalist vision did not suit Stalin and the USSR. Soviet ideology regarded capitalism as exploitative and as a regrettably necessary stage of history to be replaced as soon as possible by communism. Moreover, the Soviet economy was uncompetitive internationally. Its remarkable growth since 1929 had derived from the enormous, inefficient use of raw materials and the ruthless exploitation of labor. Stalin preferred to shield his economy from the pitiless competition of the market and divide the world into spheres of control, much as the Germans and Japanese had wished to do in the 1930s. Divergent self-interest and ideologies made for incompatible visions of the global economy between the United States and the USSR.

Once the Axis menace disappeared, there was nothing to bind the United States and the United Kingdom to the USSR and much to divide them. So within months after the peace settlements with Germany and Japan, the victorious Allies were allies no longer. They resigned themselves to grim competition and tried to keep it from erupting into outright war.

The Character and Course of the Cold War

Although the United States and the USSR never engaged each other in actual combat during the Cold War, except on a tiny scale, they competed fiercely. Their guiding Cold War strategies were similar: to outlast their opponents rather than to destroy them militarily. The American version of this strategy, called containment, was formulated in 1946 by George Kennan, a diplomat and student of Russian history. The **containment strategy** rested on the faith that Soviet communism would ultimately collapse if the United States prevented communism from expanding elsewhere. It reflected the confidence that people everywhere would prefer greater political freedom and material prosperity than the Soviet system seemed likely to provide. The Soviet version rested on a supposed law of history according to Marxism: that capitalism would inevitably collapse under the weight of its own contradictions—specifically, the rise of a militant, alienated working class that would recognize that its true interest required a revolution to usher in communism. Not everyone believed this doctrine in the USSR, but everyone pursuing a political career had to pretend to believe it. So although ideologically at odds, both the United States and the USSR pursued strategies of patience.

Rather than strike militarily, both tried in several ways to hasten the—theoretically inevitable—collapse of their foe. They built up their armed forces, including nuclear arsenals, in readiness for actual war. They mounted propaganda campaigns aimed at their own citizens and people all over the world. They competed for influence, especially in Europe and East Asia. And they fueled **proxy wars** in which they supported rival factions in local conflicts around the world. The most dangerous of all these undertakings was their nuclear arms race.

Nuclear Weapons   Both the United States and the USSR invested heavily in their armed forces during the Cold War. The most distinctive, expensive, and risky part of this buildup was in their nuclear arsenals. From 1945 to 1949, the United States enjoyed a nuclear weapons monopoly. Then, thanks to good spies and better physicists, Stalin acquired atomic weapons in 1949. Thereafter, the United States and the USSR built thousands of nuclear bombs and missiles, enough to wipe out the human race and perhaps all life on Earth. Before long, Britain (1952), France (1960), and China (1964) were testing nuclear weapons too, although they never built arsenals anywhere near the size of the Soviet or American ones. Of the roughly 2,000 nuclear tests conducted during the Cold War, about 1,000 were American, 700 Soviet, 200 French, 45 British, and 45 Chinese. Until a treaty banned atmospheric testing in 1963, most tests—about 500—involved nuclear explosions that sprinkled toxic radiation downwind of test sites.

Nuclear weapons reinforced the Cold War strategies of patience. Everyone knew that all-out nuclear war would annihilate a large share of the human race. The superpowers did not go to war in part because their leaders understood that neither country could survive nuclear war. Once armed with nuclear weapons, neither side had any incentive to disarm or to use nuclear weapons. Their value lay in what was called deterrence. Paradoxically, both superpowers felt it was vital to their security to have giant arsenals of nuclear weapons and equally vital that the arsenals should never be used.

Nonetheless, at times, the world was a whisker away from self-annihilation. A close call came during the Cuban missile crisis of October 1962. In 1959, a revolution led by Fidel Castro succeeded in ousting a corrupt, pro-American military government in Cuba. After a failed U.S.-backed attempt to overthrow the Castro regime in 1961, the Soviets shipped some nuclear missiles to Cuba, only 90 miles from Florida. When U.S. president John Kennedy insisted on the removal of the missiles, two anxious weeks followed in which the world faced the very real possibility of a nuclear exchange. In the end, the Soviets chose to avoid the worst and removed their missiles, averting nuclear war.

Several even closer calls came as a result of malfunctions in weapons systems. In 1966, a U.S. Air Force plane accidentally dropped four hydrogen bombs—each one many times more powerful than mere atomic bombs—on the coast of southeastern Spain. None exploded. At least five times during the years 1979–1983, leaders of either the United States or the USSR were briefly convinced that enemy missiles had already launched, and they prepared to unleash a devastating counter-attack. Despite these brushes with planetary disaster, nuclear arms races continued amid occasional arms-reduction talks.

The fear of obliteration became part of everyday life during the Cold War. It gave

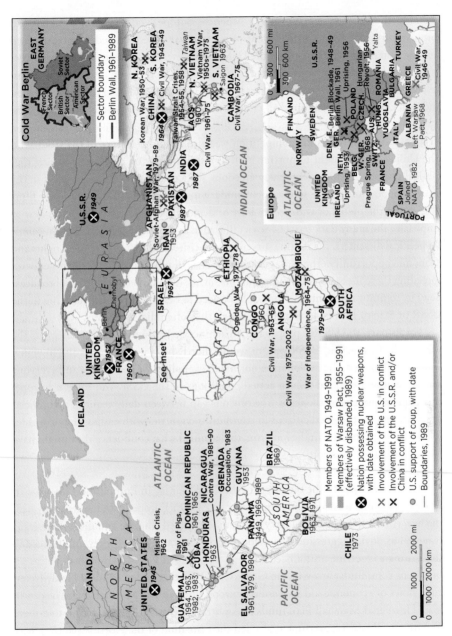

The Cold War World, 1946–1991 The Cold War was a global contest in which the world's superpowers—the United States and the Soviet Union—asserted their power repeatedly in Africa, Asia, and Latin America. The Cold War was particularly tense in Europe, most notably Berlin, and particularly violent in East Asia, most notably Korea and Vietnam. The map shows the most important of the superpowers' military or political interventions, backing one or another faction in civil wars, coups d'état, or other forms of political struggle, with arms, money, intelligence, or training.

rise to civil defense systems in North America, Europe, and the USSR, intended to improve survival chances in the event of nuclear war. These ranged from extra-deep subway systems built after 1950 in the USSR and eastern Europe to "duck-and-cover" drills for schoolchildren in the United States, adopted in the early 1950s. By the 1960s, several societies had built bomb shelters in public buildings and stocked them with food and water. Switzerland required all citizens to maintain bomb shelters in their homes.

Propaganda Propaganda competition was also a regular feature of the Cold War. The United States sought to portray itself as a shining city on a hill, often using that biblical phrase, in which democracy, freedom, justice, and prosperity prevailed in the land of opportunity. The government underwrote hundreds of documentary films illustrating the merits of U.S. technology or democratic governance. It did its best to emphasize the many dark parts of Soviet life, such as the vast network of prison camps for political dissenters, the routine surveillance of citizens, the lack of political rights and economic opportunity. The U.S. government created offices specifically charged with spreading these messages, and radio stations such as Radio Free Europe that broadcast news to communist countries. They did not need to bend the truth to make life in the USSR or eastern Europe look grim, although they often did so anyway.

For its part, the USSR's propaganda machinery tried to paint communism as the wave of the future. The USSR was, or would shortly be, a workers' paradise in which equality triumphed, the exploitation normal in capitalism was banished, and everyone was content and well fed. Given actual conditions in the USSR and eastern Europe, this required routine dishonesty. The obvious gap between daily realities and official pronouncements provided citizens in communist countries with endless opportunities for sarcastic humor and, in the long run, undermined what confidence they might have had in official information.

A Divided Europe The big prizes of the Cold War lay in Europe and East Asia. In Europe, as Stalin was consolidating power in eastern Europe in the years 1945–1948, the new American president, Harry Truman, countered what he and most Americans regarded as Soviet aggression. He made security guarantees to Turkey and Greece in the Truman Doctrine announced in 1946, and helped Greek nationalists defeat an insurgent communist army in the Greek Civil War that ended in 1949. He delivered large flows of economic aid to western Europe through the Marshall Plan, begun in 1947. He offered Marshall Plan funds to countries in eastern Europe; Stalin told them to refuse it. The U.S. government also led the formation of the North Atlantic Treaty Organization (NATO, 1949), a military alliance binding the United States, Canada, and most of western Europe, intended to check Soviet ambitions.

By the end of 1948, the lines were clearly drawn. Eastern and western Europe were divided politically, ideologically, and militarily by what Winston Churchill called the iron curtain, running from the head of the Adriatic to the shores of the Baltic, and right through Germany. The one exception was Berlin, well within the Soviet zone, which by agreement was a divided city with its eastern half under Soviet control and the western half occupied by American, British, and French forces. Cold War Europe was tense, occasionally marked by crises, but generally stable, after 1948.

Crises in Berlin and Eastern Europe The biggest crises in Cold War Europe were sparked by tensions in Berlin or by uprisings of East European populations against Soviet domination. The first Berlin crisis began in 1948 when Stalin, alarmed by the Marshall Plan, ordered a blockade of West Berlin, leaving 2.5 million Germans with no sources of food, fuel, or electricity. The United States and the United Kingdom responded with the Berlin Airlift, flying 270,000 loads of supplies into West Berlin over 11 months until Stalin lifted the blockade.

The second Berlin crisis arose in August 1961, when East Germans at Soviet direction began to erect a wall dividing East and West Berlin, to prevent the escape of East German citizens—one-fifth of whom had already fled to West Germany and 1,500 of whom were leaving every day in Berlin. For the next several weeks, incidents at the boundary between East and West Berlin took place almost daily, and a shooting war seemed likely to break out. But cool heads prevailed, and a new reality took hold in Berlin, dominated by a wall that divided families and symbolized the imprisonment of Eastern Europeans within a political system most of them did not want. The two Berlin crises were moments of high anxiety but not violence.

Violence flared when Eastern Europeans tried to loosen the Soviet grip on their countries. The first major uprising came in East Germany in 1953. In the 24 largest cities, industrial workers led demonstrations against pay cuts and in favor of free elections. Several hundred thousand people took to the streets and in East Berlin almost toppled the government before Soviet military forces intervened, killing dozens before restoring order. In Poland in 1956, a factory workers' uprising met with a similar response and ended with 50 to 80 people dead.

A larger revolt followed later that year in Hungary. Police fired on anti-Soviet demonstrators, leading to wider protests and an effort by the Hungarian communist government to enact reforms and loosen its ties to the USSR. That brought a full-scale invasion by the Soviet army, resisted by units of the Hungarian military and civilian militias. Some 2,500 Hungarians were killed and another 22,000 imprisoned, while 200,000 escaped to other countries. Many Hungarians expected support from the United Nations or the United States, not least because Radio Free Europe broadcasts told them it would come. It did not, because American leaders feared nuclear war.

Berlin Wall Children walk along a street in Kreuzberg, West Berlin, in the 1960s. The street was divided in half by the Berlin Wall, construction on which began in 1961.

Prague Spring Massed demonstrators block Soviet tanks from moving through the streets of Prague in August 1968, during the Prague Spring uprising against Soviet control.

Czechoslovak efforts at reform in 1968 prompted another Soviet invasion. The communist government in Prague, in response to citizen unrest, promised what it called socialism with a human face. In practice, that mainly meant less censorship and more personal and press freedom. That opening, sometimes called the **Prague Spring**, unleashed a torrent of public criticism of the communist system and Soviet domination. The Soviet leadership responded with troops and tanks, killing between 70 and 140 people, despite mostly passive resistance from Czechs and Slovaks.

The brutal suppression of reform efforts in Hungary and Czechoslovakia divided communist parties around the world. The French, Italian, and Finnish communist parties denounced the Soviet invasion of Czechoslovakia. The Chinese foreign minister, Zhou Enlai, called it great-power chauvinism and compared it to Hitler's invasion of Czechoslovakia in 1939. The USSR never recovered the prestige it sacrificed in 1956 and 1968 by invading its allies.

Mao and the Communist Victory in China In East and Southeast Asia the Cold War began hot, with the military victory of the Chinese Communist Party (CCP) over its Guomindang foes in the years 1945–1949. During the war with Japan (1937–1945), as we've seen, both factions fought one another as well as the Japanese. When the Japanese left, the Chinese Civil War grew fiercer.

Mao Zedong (1893–1976), one of the most consequential leaders of the twentieth century, helped organize communist guerilla forces during World War II and rose to the top of the CCP. The son of prosperous peasants from the south-central province of Hunan, he had played a small role in Sun Yatsen's revolution. While working as a grade-school history teacher in Hunan and as an assistant librarian at Peking University, he had become interested in socialism, Marxism, and revolution, and he joined the newly formed CCP in 1921.

During the war against Japan and the Chinese Civil War, the CCP offered a program shaped by Mao and calculated to appeal to China's 400 million peasants. It resembled the Taiping program of a century before: peasants should take farmland from landlords; social equality should replace Confucian hierarchy; women should live free from male oppression; discipline and morality should replace corruption and decadence; and foreigners should go home. Unlike the Taiping, the CCP program had no Christian components, but it used a different foreign idea, Marxism, to lend it prestige and coherence. Mao's main innovation within Marxism was the argument that peasants could lead a communist revolution, whereas Marx and Lenin had believed only industrial workers could do so.

The message worked: peasants increasingly supported the CCP after 1945, and its armies swelled with recruits. By the end of 1949, with some help from Stalin, the communist forces had driven the Guomindang army to the offshore island of Taiwan. China was now in the hands of Mao and his lieutenants, and was aligned with the USSR as the People's Republic of China (or PRC). The Cold War had become more complex, with two major communist powers, the USSR and the PRC, both anti-American and anti-capitalist, but neither fully trusting the other.

War in Korea Once China had joined the communist camp in 1949, the United States deepened its involvement in East Asia. The first challenge came in Korea. With Japan's defeat in 1945, the status of its former colony was thrown into doubt. By agreement between the superpowers, American forces took control south of the 38th parallel and Soviet soldiers occupied the north. Each supported a government that claimed sovereignty over all Korea and denied the legitimacy of the other. That arrangement hardened as the Cold War got chillier. Then, in 1950, with Soviet and Chinese encouragement, the North Koreans launched an invasion across the 38th parallel, starting the **Korean War**.

The UN resolved to defend South Korea and sent a joint force in July 1950. That UN army, 88 percent of which was American, drove the North Koreans back north, which prompted Mao to send in his battle-hardened infantry with Soviet air support. It drove the UN forces back south. For the U.S. Army, this retreat, costing many thousands of lives, was its worst defeat since the American Civil War. The remainder of the Korean War was one of attrition until, with Stalin's death, Soviet leaders decided to end the war, overruling Mao and the North Koreans who still hoped to win, and a cease-fire was agreed on in 1953. No peace treaty was ever signed, so North and South Korea still officially remain at war today.

Korea suffered tremendous damage as armies rampaged up and down the peninsula. The U.S. Air Force bombed North Korea relentlessly. By 1952, no significant buildings remained upright in North Korea. The war killed about 10 percent of Koreans, roughly 3 million people, mostly civilians. Some 35,000 Americans lost their lives, and perhaps 250,000 Chinese.

The Korean War hardened Cold War divisions in East Asia and indeed worldwide. The United States emerged more concerned about China as a regional threat. China, the USSR, and North Korea, now painfully well informed about the American capacity for bomber offensives, emerged more concerned about what they saw as "imperialist" military superiority. The Korean War boosted economic recovery in Japan, which served as a base for American operations, and brought the United States and Japan closer politically. Last, the Korean War showed that there were limits to U.S. power, including its reluctance to use nuclear weapons—which encouraged Mao to consider the United States a "paper tiger." The extraordinarily powerful position in world affairs that the United States had occupied at the end of World War II was already eroding.

War in Vietnam Over the course of the next 25 years it would erode further, for many reasons including American defeat in the **Vietnam War**. Vietnam had been colonized by France late in the nineteenth century and occupied by Japan during World War II. After the war, France tried to reassert its colonial rule, but in 1954 a Vietnamese force—with Chinese army participation—delivered a crushing defeat of the French at Dien Bien Phu. Negotiations followed, and the Geneva Accords of 1954 left Vietnam divided into a communist-nationalist government in the north, aligned with China and the Soviet Union, and an anti-communist state in the south, aligned with the United States. From the mid-1950s onward, the United States crept deeper and deeper into Vietnamese politics and its emerging civil war, trying to support the corrupt government in South Vietnam and prevent communists from taking over the country.

In 1964, after North Vietnamese torpedo boats and a U.S. naval ship clashed off the Vietnam coast, President Lyndon Johnson chose to escalate the struggle. By late 1967, half a million American troops were in Vietnam. The justification was the so-called **domino theory**: Johnson was concerned that if Vietnam went communist, the rest of Southeast Asia would soon follow. As in the Korean War, the United States did most of its damage from the air: it dropped more than three times as much bomb tonnage on Vietnam as it had used in all of World War II. The United States also used chemical defoliants such as Agent Orange on the forests of Vietnam, killing about 10 percent of the country's vegetation. Nevertheless, the United States and its allies, including the ineffective South Vietnamese government, could not prevail on the ground against determined forces employing guerilla tactics. The war became unpopular in the United States, especially among young people subject to the draft. The Americans consequently sought an acceptable way out starting in 1968 but could not find one despite years of peace negotiations. In 1975, as U.S. forces left Saigon, the capital of South Vietnam, communist forces took control of the entire country. The victors put some 250,000 South Vietnamese who had sided with the Americans into labor camps.

Roughly 1.5 million Vietnamese died in the war between 1965 and 1975, as did 59,000 Americans. No further dominoes fell, but the war cost the United States dearly in prestige and popularity around the world: it seemed a contest between David and Goliath, with the North Vietnamese showing enormous courage standing up to a superpower. The war also fueled intense political divisions in the United States.

After 1975, the Cold War in East Asia stabilized. Crises flared up, sometimes between Taiwan and the PRC, sometimes on the Korean Peninsula. But none escalated into serious fighting, and none changed the balance of power significantly.

War in Angola The Cold War reached from Europe and East Asia to every continent. The U.S. and Soviet governments backed rival factions in at least 50 local struggles and civil wars, providing weapons, money, training, and other support. The goal was to show resolve and win an ally or at least prevent the enemy from winning one.

Angola, a Portuguese colony for nearly 500 years, became Africa's biggest cauldron of Cold War competition. During the 1960s, several rival parties and militias eager to oust Portuguese rule emerged. But they found cooperation difficult for two reasons: one of these parties, UNITA, mainly represented the Ovimbundu people of central Angola, and other Angolans feared Ovimbundu domination; the other obstacle was the involvement of foreign powers, whose support enabled groups to fight on even if their popularity within Angola was small. Angola's substantial oil reserve, discovered in 1955, heightened the interest of foreigners.

War in Angola A poster for the MPLA shows a young mother carrying an automatic rifle—signifying the devotion the faction called for ordinary citizens to show to the cause. Supported by the USSR, the MPLA became caught up in a proxy war against the U.S.-backed UNITA.

When a revolution in Portugal in 1974 led to the sudden end of colonial rule in Angola and the departure of 500,000 Portuguese citizens, fighting among anti-colonial factions stepped up. UNITA's main rival was a faction called the MPLA, whose leaders had proclaimed themselves communists. Angola seemed up for grabs. South Africa, Israel, and the United States supported UNITA with weapons, money, and training, while the USSR, several East European governments, and Cuba backed the MPLA. Cuba sent 40,000 soldiers in the mid-1980s to bolster the MPLA. But in 1990 and 1991, as the USSR was coming apart, the MPLA's position weakened, bringing peace talks. The local war continued, at lower intensity, even after Soviet, East European, and Cuban aid ceased. In all, about half a million—of 8 million Angolans—were killed, and another 2 to 4 million became refugees.

War in Afghanistan The USSR, with less capacity to fight proxy wars than the United States, used its own troops sparingly in combat except in Afghanistan. The

Soviet-Afghan War (1979–1989) ranks with Korea and Vietnam as the deadliest of Cold War contests. Afghanistan, on the USSR's southern border, was an extremely poor, mainly Muslim country of 13 million in 1978 when the Afghan Communist Party staged a successful coup. Communist rule provoked widespread rebellion, particularly among committed Muslims called mujahideen ("those who follow jihad," or Islamic struggle). When they appeared likely to topple the government, the Soviet leadership, without consulting its allies, sent in the Red Army in December 1979. The invasion brought wide condemnation.

Soviet forces fought several bands of mujahideen, most of which enjoyed support from Pakistan, Iran, China, Saudi Arabia, the United Kingdom, or the United States. Over a 10-year span, combat and massacres killed about 1.5 million, 90 percent of them Afghan civilians. In addition, about 5 to 6 million Afghans fled the violence, becoming refugees in neighboring Iran or Pakistan. After losing nearly 15,000 soldiers, the Soviets withdrew in 1989, leaving Afghanistan in turmoil.

Other Proxy Wars Smaller proxy wars smoldered in Latin America. For more than a century, the United States had considered Latin America its own backyard and had often intervened, especially in the Caribbean, to support or create friendly governments. After Cuba's alignment with the USSR in 1960 and 1961, the Cold War in Latin America intensified. The U.S. government supported coups and often brutal military dictatorships in Brazil, Argentina, Chile, Guatemala, the Dominican Republic, and elsewhere, as long as their leaders convincingly claimed to be anti-communist. The most sustained combat took place in Central America during the 1980s, where Nicaragua and El Salvador descended into civil wars in which the United States became deeply involved. The loss of life in Cold War conflicts in Latin America, even if one includes political murders in addition to combat, remained far smaller than in Africa or Asia.

When the Americans or Soviets committed large numbers of their soldiers, as in Korea, Vietnam, and Afghanistan, these ventures became costly and unpopular at home. But when they didn't, the costs of backing factions in conflicts in Africa, Asia, or Latin America were low, and therefore the temptation to do so was high. Governments and rebels around the world grew adept at posing as ardent communists or ardent anti-communists in order to receive flows of money and weapons. In this way, while avoiding direct conflict between themselves, the United States and the USSR inflamed conflicts in the poorer parts of the world.

The Decline and Collapse of the USSR

In the end, the Cold War was won and lost at home. The United States survived the Cold War's pressures but suffered deep divisions over domestic campaigns in the 1950s to purge the army, the State Department, the media, and universities of suspected communists and communist sympathizers. Divisions over the U.S. intervention in Vietnam also left lasting effects. The USSR, however, came apart under Cold War pressures. The Soviet regime collapsed during the years 1989–1991, leaving Russia and 14 smaller countries. Among the reasons the USSR crumbled were the cost of nuclear competition, the implausibility of its propaganda, and the toll of war in Afghanistan. But the biggest reasons were the USSR's failure to construct an international economy to rival the American-led one, and the tensions with China that led to an open split.

After World War II the Soviet planned economy, with few incentives for innovation, stagnated technologically except in weapons production. Its growth rate sagged after the 1960s. Soviet agriculture, handicapped by collectivization, could not reliably feed the population by the 1970s. Soviet international economic linkages, such as loans to India or bartering oil for Cuba's sugar, proved a net drain on Soviet resources. At the same time that its economy sputtered, the military commitments of the USSR expanded.

The Sino-Soviet Rift The first big problem to arise was the Sino-Soviet rift. In the late 1950s, cracks began to appear between the two communist powers. Mao resented his treatment by the Soviets as a junior partner and preferred his own version of communist ideology. Mao maintained that peasants, of which China had many, could spearhead a communist transformation, whereas Soviet ideology reserved that role for industrial workers, of which China had few.

Mao also came to see Stalin's successors as disappointingly soft on capitalism. When in the years 1959–1961 Soviet premier Nikita Khrushchev tried to reduce Cold War tensions by meeting with American presidents, Mao sensed treasonous compromise. He began to compete with the USSR for influence and admiration among communists worldwide. Chinese and Soviet leaders started denouncing one another at international communist congresses. Whereas in 1956 Mao had strongly supported the Soviet invasion of Hungary, in 1968 he denounced the invasion of Czechoslovakia. By 1969, their armies were shooting at one another at points along their border.

The Sino-Soviet rift cost the USSR dearly. It had to park roughly 20 percent of its military on the long Chinese border, far from the food and supplies it needed and therefore expensive to sustain. Moreover, in 1972 when the U.S. government wanted Chinese help to make an exit from the Vietnam War, Mao saw an opportunity to bolster his position against the USSR. China suddenly welcomed warmer relations with the United States, adding new strains for the Soviets.

During the 1970s, however, an economic windfall bolstered the USSR. The production of its giant Siberian oil fields spurted in time for spikes in the world price of oil in 1973 and 1979. For a few years, the USSR could afford to import new technology, food, and other goods. But in 1985 and 1986, world oil prices—and Soviet revenues—plummeted. Moscow had grown accustomed to oil money and had no substitute when it dried up. The legitimacy of the Soviet state, long shaky, was crumbling.

Gorbachev's Reforms In 1985, a vigorous new leader, **Mikhail Gorbachev**, age 54, came to power in Moscow. Gorbachev's response to the challenges facing the Soviet Union was to gamble on radical reforms. In some respects, his approach resembled those taken by self-strengtheners in the nineteenth century who recognized that their countries could not compete with the industrial powers, that time was not on their side, and that only radical economic development could stave off political defeat.

Gorbachev's version of self-strengthening featured twinned policies called *perestroika* ("restructuring") and *glasnost* ("openness"). With *glasnost*, he permitted much more free circulation of information, hoping to breathe life into a re-structured Soviet economy through innovation and technological advances. He aligned his foreign policy with these goals and sought to relax tensions with the United States and NATO, and he negotiated arms reductions treaties with President Ronald Reagan. He was trying to buy the USSR some time to reform. But his gamble did not work: the medicine killed the patient.

The Soviet system, without a vibrant economy, could not survive a freer flow of information. In 1986, at Chernobyl (in today's Ukraine), a nuclear reactor blew up, spreading lethal radiation far and wide. At first, ignoring *glasnost*, Soviet authorities tried to cover it up. But the accident was too big to hide. For Ukrainians especially, the Chernobyl meltdown and cover-up underscored the technological backwardness of the USSR and the untrustworthiness of the government.

Gorbachev's *glasnost* also allowed the expression of hopes and ambitions that did not fit with the Soviet system. It let the genie of ethnic nationalism out of the bottle. The USSR contained dozens of ethnicities, some with strong but long-underground nationalist traditions. Now Ukrainians, Lithuanians, Armenians, Georgians, and others found ways to express their national identities and—within limits—denounce Soviet oppression.

By the mid-1980s, keeping the lid on in Eastern Europe was getting harder, especially in Poland. Poles, East Germans, Czechs, and Hungarians had grown more restive, showing their frustration at stagnant living standards, acute environmental pollution, and the ever-present surveillance state. The more they learned about life in Western Europe, the more they resented their own lack of freedoms and comforts.

End of the Cold War Demonstrators take sledgehammers to the Berlin Wall, which fell on November 9, 1989. Soldiers watch from atop the wall, but do not intervene to stop the protesters.

In 1989, Gorbachev decided to take the lid off before the pot boiled over. He signaled, gradually, that Eastern Europe's communist rulers could not count on the USSR's army to suppress demonstrations calling for greater freedoms. East Germans began to flee to West Germany, Czechs into Austria, and Gorbachev did not send in tanks. Soon the Berlin Wall, symbol of the imprisonment—as many saw it—of East European populations, was crumbling. The security forces watched the wall fall on November 9 and did not shoot. By 1991, the USSR itself dissolved. The Russian component declared itself independent of the USSR, and soon the others followed suit. A once-mighty superpower went out with a whimper, not a bang.

The Cold War ended because the strategy of containment worked. The U.S.-led international economy outpaced the Soviet one, and the material comforts and relative freedom of capitalist liberal democracy, for all its flaws, held more appeal to more people than any variant of communism did. The Cold War ended *peacefully* because Gorbachev undertook his desperate gamble to save the USSR from itself, and because he was prepared to let Eastern Europe go. He recognized that in an age of intercontinental missiles, holding Eastern Europe did not actually provide much of a buffer against enemies. Sometimes a single person makes a big difference—especially in autocratic systems.

Conclusion

World War II (1937–1945) and then the Cold War (1945–1991) took about 75 million lives and imperiled many more. Humankind came closer than ever before, or since, to destroying itself.

The half-century between 1937 and 1991 was defined by genuinely global struggles. The world had become a smaller place. Great powers could meddle across oceans with ease. Any small conflict had the potential to blow up. Power struggles in poor places, such as Vietnam or Angola, now attracted superpower support. All the interconnections of the Global web, and the technological and economic power they created, made international politics more unstable, unpredictable, and unsafe than before.

In particular, the uneven prosperity of the globalizing economy, combined with resentments caused largely by the settlement of World War I, encouraged the advent of nationalist regimes. Three of these, in Germany, Italy, and Japan, developed expansionist ambitions that other great powers resisted. World War II was in part a struggle over the future political and economic organization of the globe: spheres of influence dominated by nationalist states, as the Axis hoped; a more open international economy, as the United States wished; or the spread of communism, as Soviet ideologists dreamed.

After the Allies won in 1945, the world fractured along different lines. The Cold War too was a battle over the future organization of the world. Once again, in that contest, the forces favoring internationalism and globalization of the world economy won out. Bonaparte once had said that God is on the side with the bigger battalions, by which he meant bigger armies usually win. In the great political struggles of the twentieth century, the bigger, more productive, more connected economies could field bigger battalions. They could make more of whatever was needed to prevail in international politics, whether oil, tanks, and aircraft, or just plentiful ordinary consumer goods—such as the razor blades that Goering mocked.

|||||||||||||||||||||||||||||||||||||||||||||||||||||||||||||||||||||||||||||||||||||||||||||||||||||||||||||||||||||||||||||||

Chapter Review

KEY TERMS

World War II p. 1043

Axis p. 1043

Allies p. 1046

Battle of Stalingrad p. 1050

Hiroshima and Nagasaki p. 1053

Holocaust p. 1061

comfort women p. 1069

Cold War p. 1071

Chinese Civil War p. 1072

containment strategy p. 1073

proxy wars p. 1074

Prague Spring p. 1078

Mao Zedong p. 1078

Korean War p. 1079

Vietnam War p. 1080

domino theory p. 1080

Mikhail Gorbachev p. 1084

REVIEW QUESTIONS

1. Describe the shared ambitions and beliefs behind Germany, Italy, and Japan's expansionist pursuits.

2. What four overlapping wars and four theaters made up World War II?

3. What key moments caused the tide of the war to turn against the Axis powers?

4. Compare and contrast the cooperation among the Allied powers with the cooperation among the Axis powers.

5. What economic, natural resource, and labor advantages did the Allies have over the Axis powers during World War II?

6. Which groups did Hitler's extermination program target, and why?

7. Compare and contrast the level of home-front mobilization in Germany, Japan, the Soviet Union, the United Kingdom, and the United States.

8. Explain what happened to people of Japanese ancestry living in the United States and Canada during World War II.

9. In terms of international politics, what was different about the post-war world?

10. Discuss the competing U.S. and Soviet visions of international security after World War II.

11. What were the guiding Cold War strategies of the United States and the USSR?

12. In which cities or countries did the biggest crises in Cold War Europe erupt, and why?

13. What was Mao Zedong's program during the Chinese Civil War, and to whom did it appeal?

14. What were the main international consequences of the Korean War?

15. Whom did the Soviets support with their invasion of Afghanistan, and who supported their enemies, the mujahideen?

16. Why did the Cold War end, and why did it end peacefully?

Go to INQUIZITIVE

to see what you've learned—and learn what you've missed—with personalized feedback along the way.

28

Decolonization and the Rise of East Asia

1945 to 1991

FOCUS QUESTIONS

1. What broad factors opened the way to decolonization in the decades after World War II?

2. Why did East Asian nations experience strong economic advances in the late decades of the twentieth century?

3. How did the economic rise of East Asia shift the balance of the Global web?

> It doesn't matter whether the cat is black or white, as long as it catches mice.
>
> —Deng Xiaoping (1962)

Deng Xiaoping, the leader of communist China from 1978 to about 1995, was a practical man. His reference to cats (above) was an assertion that ideological stripes matter less than effectiveness. What he wanted to effect was a transformation of China into a global power, and he did more than anyone else to achieve that. Deng and his allies within the Chinese Communist Party (CCP) revolutionized China by emphasizing practicality. The resulting changes in East Asia were as great as any since the Qing conquests of the seventeenth century. The changes to the global balance of power were as great as any since the Industrial Revolution in the nineteenth century and the rise of Britain, Germany, and the United States.

Usually, shifts in the global distribution of wealth and power are gradual and work themselves out over centuries. But not always. This chapter concerns two sudden shifts in world balances of power under way since World War II—and still afoot today. Just when the United States and the USSR were emerging as Cold War superpowers in the 1940s, colonial empires around the world began to crumble. Asians and Africans found new ways to challenge imperial rule. They succeeded in raising its costs beyond the thresholds that imperial peoples and governments were willing to pay. That brought a spurt of decolonization starting in 1947, a scramble from empire every bit as hasty as the scrambles for empire of the late nineteenth century. Roughly 100 new countries emerged within three decades.

Decolonization opened the door to the second sudden shift, what we might call the rise of the East. Historians for generations have wrestled with what they sometimes call the rise of the West, referring to the accumulation of wealth and power by Atlantic European countries and eventually the United States, Canada, and Australia—a process that began in the sixteenth century and accelerated with industrialization in the nineteenth. Since 1960 or so, a rebalancing of global wealth and power has been under way, led by the rise of East Asia. The centerpiece was the tremendous economic growth in Japan, South Korea, Taiwan, Singapore, and Hong Kong— the "Asian tigers," as journalists and economists called them—and, after 1980, in China.

Just as colonization of much of the world was important in the rise of the West between 1500 and 1914, so decolonization was a crucial pre-condition to the rise of the East. The first step came with the destruction of Japan's empire in World War II. Liberation from Japanese colonial rule was necessary before South Korea and Taiwan could transform themselves into rich countries. Likewise, Singapore shed British rule before becoming a "tiger." Hong Kong, however, became rich while still a British colony—a unique case and the exception that proves the rule.

CHRONOLOGY

1945 Sétif massacre

1945–1952 Allied occupation of Japan

1947 India and Pakistan become independent; formation of United Gold Coast Convention; Japan adopts new constitution

1948 Ceylon and Burma become independent; Dutch invade Indonesia

1948–1956 Land reform in South Korea

1949 Indonesia becomes independent; establishment of MITI in Japan

1954–1962 Algerian war for independence

1957 Ghana becomes independent

1958–1961 Great Leap Forward

1960 UN declares colonialism a violation of human rights

1965 Singapore becomes independent

1966 Kwame Nkrumah is ousted in coup d'état

1966–1976 Great Proletarian Cultural Revolution

1967–1970 Biafra secedes from Nigeria

1971 Bangladesh secedes from Pakistan

1976 Mao Zedong dies

1978 Deng Xiaoping becomes head of China

1980 Gwangju uprising

1989 Tiananmen Square massacre

1992 China's stock exchange re-opens

In the story of the rise of East Asia, China takes center stage. From the 1840s to 1931, foreigners exploited its resources and menaced its independence but never formally colonized the country. Then in Manchuria starting in 1931 and much of the rest of China beginning in 1937, Japan conquered and in effect ruled most of the country. After Japan's empire collapsed in 1945, China could begin its remarkable self-transformation from a weak and divided country to a great power. That process started under Mao Zedong, who led the CCP's re-unification of China in 1949. But the major advances in China's wealth and power came after Mao's death, when Deng Xiaoping took the helm by 1980.

As in the heyday of the Tang and Song dynasties (roughly the seventh through the twelfth centuries), East Asia now became an interconnected space. After 1980 it was the most dynamic part of the global economy, exchanging goods, technologies, and ideas at a feverish pace, thanks to new connections both within East Asia and between the region and the wider world. And its engine, China, engineered the largest shift in global power politics so far in the twenty-first century.

Decolonization as a Global Movement

With the formation of a truly global web in the sixteenth century, overseas empires became easier to create and therefore more numerous. But they were not always easy to keep: there were four pulses of decolonization in recent centuries, all of them linked to major international conflicts.

The Long Arc of Decolonization, 1776–1991

The first pulse of decolonization came between 1776 and 1826 with the liberation of the Americas from European imperial rule during the Atlantic revolutions (see Chapter 21). This burst of decolonization led to the creation of roughly 20 new countries in the Americas. The term *decolonization* can also be applied to the demise of the Habsburg, Ottoman, and Romanov (Russian) empires during the years 1917–1923, brought on by the intense pressures of World War I. As we've seen, this led to the creation of eight new countries in east-central Europe and to an independent Turkey. In Russia's empire, decolonization resulting from the Romanov dynasty's collapse in 1917 was temporary: by 1925, Lenin and his successors put most of the empire back together again as the USSR. The financial and manpower demands of World War I also contributed mightily to the creation of the Irish Free State (Eire) in 1922. After three years of guerilla war and civil disobedience between 1918 and 1921, Irish revolutionaries negotiated independence from an exhausted United Kingdom. In these two pulses of decolonization, during the periods 1776–1826 and 1917–1923, big wars put events into motion. They put pressures on imperial powers, giving anti-imperial forces opportunities they seized.

The third—and biggest—pulse of decolonization came between 1945 and 1975, and it is the focus here. Colonized peoples took advantage of the material pressures that World War II and the Cold War placed on several more empires, notably the Japanese, British, French, Dutch, and Portuguese. This time about 100 new countries emerged, mainly in Africa, Asia, and the Caribbean.

The fall of the USSR was a Cold War story more than a decolonization story. But the USSR too was a vast empire, and when it lost its grip on Eastern Europe in 1989 and then dissolved in 1991, roughly 20 countries acquired independence. Poland, Czechoslovakia, Hungary, Romania, and Bulgaria were officially independent already, but in reality they were controlled by the USSR in all important matters between the late 1940s and the late 1980s. So the destruction of the Soviet empire, during the years 1989–1991, constitutes the fourth great pulse of decolonization.

The Big Pulse, 1947–1975

Empires of one sort or another had been commonplace around the world for millennia; but in the twentieth century, empire suddenly—at least on the time scale of millennia—seemed less inevitable and more illegitimate. The mobilizing rhetoric of the Allies in the World Wars—self-determination of peoples—had something to do with this change in perspective. So did the sorry record of colonial rule on the ground in Africa, Asia, and the Caribbean. In 1960, the United Nations declared colonialism a violation of human rights.

The moral legitimacy of empire was slipping after 1945, but more important were the shifts in power relations between colonized and colonizers. Within many colonies, those people who chafed most under colonial rule organized themselves into political parties or guerilla bands. Anti-colonial movements sometimes made common cause across borders, sharing expertise, weapons, or money. Many future leaders of anti-colonial movements learned about fighting wars during World War II. Others learned about law, politics, and culture as students in British or French universities, and they used their new knowledge to advance the cause of independence. All this gave anti-colonial movements more tools than they had wielded before 1940. Over time, more and more colonized peoples raised the costs of continued empire to colonizers.

For example, anti-colonial leaders seized upon the Allies' rhetoric of liberation from tyranny in World War II, embodied in the Atlantic Charter of 1941 signed by Roosevelt and Churchill. Its third clause endorsed the principle that all peoples should be free to choose their form of government. Although Churchill did not intend that to apply to colonized peoples of the British Empire, the text makes no exceptions, and people in Asian and African colonies logically argued that it should apply to them too.

And while colonized peoples were getting stronger, better organized, and more committed to ending empires, imperial powers were struggling with resources and resolve. World War II had drained the manpower and treasuries of most of the combatants. Defeat in 1945 destroyed Japan's empire. Meanwhile, the effort required for victory in

1945 exhausted Britain and France both. They began to lose the determination necessary to maintain empires, partly because they were strapped for military manpower
and money, but mainly because colonized peoples were raising the costs of continued
empire. Public support for imperialism faded.

Beyond the impacts of World War II, two other aspects of the Global web of the
mid-twentieth century, one economic and the other both technological and cultural,
also propelled the **third pulse of decolonization**. Colonial rule depended financially
on mines and plantations. The sale of gold, diamonds, and mineral ores, and crops such
as cotton or jute, made the money that supported colonial governments. Those ores and
crops normally traveled by rail to seaports for export. Asian and African railway workers

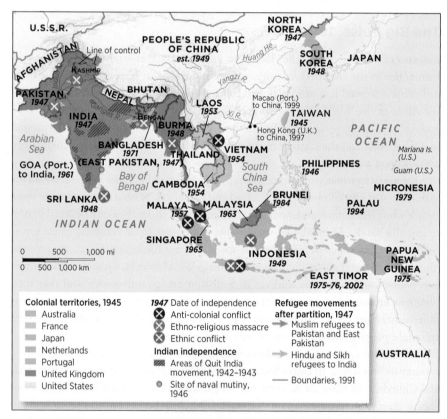

Decolonization in South and Southeast Asia The third pulse of decolonization got under
way in the late 1940s and began in Asia. Anti-colonial movements in Indonesia and Vietnam won independence by militarily facing down the colonial powers—the Netherlands
and France, respectively. Britain's exit from South Asia was negotiated, but the formation
of India as primarily Hindu and of Pakistan as primarily Muslim brought intense violence
and massive refugee movements. Independence for East Timor and Bangladesh required
victory first over European colonial powers and then over rival local powers.

and dock workers thus acquired power over colonial economies: if they refused to work, exports and revenues would both cease. By the late 1940s, strikes among rail and dock workers became increasingly common—undermining the finances of colonial rule.

In addition, the speed with which information now traveled helped spur the process of decolonization. By the 1920s, newspapers used the telegraph networks to report on important events within hours of their occurrence. During the 1930s and 1940s, radio and newsreels—short films of current events—carried news around the world quickly and reached the great majority who could not read. By the 1960s, television added to the flows of information—and of inspiration. When Indians achieved independence in 1947, Indonesians—and many others—were watching. When Algeria won an independence war (1956–1962), everyone was watching. Images of anti-colonial successes coursed through the pathways of the Global web, hurrying the end of empire. Let's look at a few examples.

Asia: India and Indonesia

The movements for decolonization in Asia, Africa, and the Caribbean were all connected. Many activists had studied together in their youth in Lisbon or London. Some had attended the same pan-African congresses or other international gatherings. After 1945 they offered what support they could to one another, as they recognized a common struggle against imperial rule. Everyone keen on ending colonialism paid attention to India, the most populous of all the world's colonies.

India At midnight on August 14, 1947, some 400 million people cast off British colonial rule for independence as the countries of India and Pakistan. Ceylon and Burma, longtime British colonies administratively linked to British India, became independent in 1948. (Ceylon changed its name to Sri Lanka in 1972, and Burma changed to Myanmar in 1989.)

As we've seen, anti-colonial nationalism had a deep tradition in British India. After 1919, Gandhi and the Indian National Congress made it a mass movement. After 1935, British legislation put Indians in more and more government posts and set colonial India on a path toward independence. World War II shortened that path.

India contributed mightily to Britain's efforts in World War II. Several million Indians volunteered for military service, and 87,000 of them died in the war. In summer 1945, Britain's Indian Army counted 2.5 million men, the largest all-volunteer army in world history. Most of them fought against the Japanese in Southeast Asia, some against German and Italian forces in North Africa, and a few in Europe.

At the same time that millions of Indians volunteered to fight for the British Empire, World War II sharpened opposition to British rule in India. Some 40,000 Indians captured by the Japanese chose to switch sides and fight for Japan, or—as they saw it—against the British Empire in Asia. One independence leader, Subhas Chandra Bose, visited Axis leaders in Berlin and Tokyo, and organized Indian forces against Britain. To the British, he was a traitor; to many Indians, a national hero. Most leaders of the Indian National Congress—now operating as a political party—refused to cooperate with the war effort from late 1942 on. Following Gandhi and the British-trained lawyer **Jawaharlal Nehru**, who since the late 1920s had emerged as the second most important figure in Congress, they demanded immediate independence as the price of their cooperation. Britain's viceroy agreed to promise liberation only after the war. Gandhi called that promise "a post-dated cheque on a crumbling bank," not to be trusted.

Instead, Gandhi called for Britain to "quit India" immediately, despite the risk of Japanese invasion. Britain's wartime prime minister, Churchill, who had served in India as a young man, was determined that India should remain British. Relying on loyal police and Indian Army units, the British responded to the Quit India movement by arresting over 100,000 Indians in 1942 and 1943, including Gandhi, Nehru, and all the top leadership of the Congress Party. At the same time, British authorities did little to address a famine in Bengal that killed 2 to 3 million Indians in 1943 and 1944. British rule in India was now more unpopular than ever.

As the war wound down, everyone attentive to politics knew independence was coming, especially when Churchill was voted out of office in July 1945. The Congress Party tried to represent all Indians, not just Hindus, but many Muslims regarded it as deaf to their interests. Muslims, who formed about a quarter of India's population in 1941, had taken the opportunity to fill many administrative positions open by 1943 as a result of the imprisonment of so many Congress Party members. This deepened the divide between the Muslim and Hindu communities. The **Muslim League**, headed by the cosmopolitan and wealthy lawyer Muhammad Ali Jinnah, grew increasingly committed to the idea of a divided post-colonial India with a Muslim state and a Hindu one.

Jinnah and South Asia's Muslims generally feared they would be oppressed by the Hindu majority if independence yielded a united India. Most of them wanted their own state, where they could be in the majority. Many Sikhs (about 3 percent of India's population) wanted their own state too. Many Hindus, however, objected to the idea of a fragmented India and opposed Muslim and Sikh ambitions. Almost everyone wanted independence, but they couldn't agree on how to define the nation.

By this point, most British politicians were almost as eager for Indian independence as Indians were. Indians had succeeded in making India ungovernable for Britain. This became clear in early 1946, when a mutiny among Indian naval units showed that Britain could no longer rely on the loyalty of Indian military manpower. Without it, Britain could not continue as an imperial power in South Asia. Soon the government in London appointed a lawyer who had never been to India to draw a line on the map, based on religious identities, as a border between what were to become two countries.

The lawyer was given a month to draw the line: getting it done fast was more important to all parties than getting it done well. No line, however well drawn, could have tidily divided Hindu from Muslim from Sikh in India. On August 14–15, 1947, India and Pakistan were born. Nehru, whose appetite for politics far exceeded Gandhi's, became prime minister of India, while Jinnah led Pakistan. Gandhi, the pacifist, was murdered in 1948 by an assassin who considered him too sympathetic to Muslims and Sikhs.

Partition Conflict between Hindus and Muslims over the partition of India led to widespread violence and upheaval. Here police in Calcutta use tear gas to suppress rioters attempting to set fire to a Hindu temple in 1948.

The partition of British India into two countries provoked a bloodbath. Roughly 1 million people died in violent clashes. Another 10 to 17 million became refugees, fleeing to one or another side of the new borders to avoid persecution or worse. India and Pakistan quickly became lasting enemies, fighting three wars since 1947 and perpetually skirmishing over Kashmir, a majority Muslim region claimed by India. Pakistan was born in two parts, one in the Indus valley and one in East Bengal, an arrangement that Bengalis often likened to colonial rule. In 1971, Pakistan's Bengalis seceded, fought a brief independence war with India's help, and created their own country, Bangladesh.

Independence in Burma and Sri Lanka brought conflicts too. It plunged Burma into a brief civil war among factions hoping to rule the new country. Sri Lanka suffered from ethnic division between Sinhalese and Tamil groups—the Tamils mainly descended from Indian immigrants. That rivalry escalated into civil war in the 1980s.

Indonesia Indonesia's path to independence was no less rocky than India's. The Dutch had acquired a foothold on this sprawling archipelago of 13,000 islands in the seventeenth century. By 1940, the Dutch East Indies had 70 million people divided by religion, language, and ethnicity—among other things. Muslims were the most numerous religious community, maybe three-quarters of the population; but many Indonesians were Hindu, Buddhist, Christian, or followers of one of several indigenous faiths. Indonesia was then and is now one of the most diverse places in the world, with hundreds of languages spoken and some 600 ethnicities. Nationalism and unity did not come easily there.

Early anti-colonial groups had formed in the 1920s. These included an Islamic group, a communist organization, the Congress of Indonesian Women, and a nationalist political party, the PNI (or Partai Nasional Indonesia). The PNI mainly represented traditional landed elites on the most populous island, Java, but claimed to speak for all Indonesians. Its founder and moving spirit was **Sukarno**, who like most Javanese went by a single name.

Sukarno came from an aristocratic Javanese Muslim family on his father's side, but one that had fallen on hard times. His mother was from a high-caste Hindu family. Sukarno trained as an architect and spoke four Indonesian languages as well as

Indonesian Independence (Left) Sukarno, as president of an independent Indonesia, addresses a crowd of demonstrators in 1950. (Right) Peasants from rural parts of Indonesia—photographed here being trained as guerilla fighters in 1947—were a key component of the opposition to Dutch colonial rule.

Dutch, English, French, Arabic, and Japanese. His greatest talent, though, was political flexibility.

Sukarno's agitation for independence in the late 1920s earned him a prison term. He collaborated eagerly with the Japanese occupation (1941–1945), helping recruit millions of Indonesians as essentially slave laborers for work on railroads, bridges, and airfields throughout Japanese-occupied Southeast Asia. He also helped Japan secure access to Indonesia's natural resources, notably bauxite, from which aluminum is made, and oil. In return, the Japanese helped Sukarno to denounce Dutch colonialism and to spread his version of Indonesian nationalism—together with his own fame and prestige.

The Japanese occupation took a heavy toll on Indonesia. Malaria flared up, and food requisitioning for Japan's army led to starvation. Thousands of Indonesian women, and dozens of Dutch women, were forced into sex slavery as comfort women for Japanese troops. In 1944 and 1945, roughly a million Indonesians died from these and other hardships. The Japanese departed hastily in the summer of 1945, leaving Sukarno and other prominent collaborators in a tight spot.

With the Japanese going and the Dutch not yet returning, some Indonesian nationalists thought the moment of liberation had come. Sukarno was unsure; but after one night held hostage by a fervently nationalist youth group, he agreed to declare independence. He also declared himself president.

In September 1945, the Dutch returned, intending to restore colonial rule. They negotiated with many different groups, following the old strategy of divide-and-rule. They succeeded in rallying people in the outer islands against Javanese domination, Sukarno, and the PNI. Indonesia in the next few years was racked by political violence.

In 1948, the Dutch deployed 150,000 soldiers to try to impose their will. Sukarno and the PNI responded with guerilla warfare. Both the UN and the United States denounced the Dutch action and called for a cease-fire. The U.S. government threatened to stop delivering food and fuel to the Netherlands under the Marshall Plan. The Dutch government was too poor and too indebted to defy that threat.

The Dutch could not turn back the clock in Indonesia without American approval. In 1946, the United States had cautiously supported the Dutch attempt to restore colonial power in Indonesia. But by 1949, with communists about to take over China, American policy makers judged that the best bet for resisting communism—the dominant consideration in Washington—was a resolutely non-communist independent country. The PNI and Sukarno, despite his wartime collaboration with the Japanese, fit the bill. Once the Americans made it clear they preferred Sukarno to continued Dutch colonialism, the Dutch gave up and negotiated a quick exit from Indonesia.

So in 1949 Indonesia acquired the independence the PNI had claimed since 1945, thanks to the disruptions of World War II, the persistence and opportunism of Sukarno and the PNI, the weakness of the Netherlands, and the intervention of the United States. The PNI and Sukarno now undertook an ambitious experiment in democracy in an ethno-linguistic patchwork of a country. Indonesian nationalism proved too weak to overcome the country's diversity. By 1957, the democratic experiment was on hold and the country was an autocracy, with Sukarno and the army in charge.

Africa: Ghana and Algeria

In a broad sense, the story of independence in Africa followed the same lines as in Asia. African anti-colonial nationalists found ways to band together and use what tools they had either to negotiate or to fight their way to freedom. In the late 1940s, France and Britain still intended to keep their African colonies and develop them to strengthen their empires. But by 1956 or 1957, Africans had persuaded them to change their plans.

Let's look at a couple of examples: Ghana and Algeria. Ghana was among the first African countries to achieve independence and among those that took the most peaceful of roads. Algeria was among the last, and it took the most violent road of all.

Ghana The West African peoples of the Gold Coast, as Ghana was called in colonial times, mainly spoke languages of the same group, called Akan. But they did not think of themselves as Akan, or Gold Coasters, or Africans. More local identities, based on clan and village, prevailed. As in Indonesia, national identity did not come easily here.

The British had colonized the Gold Coast beginning in the 1870s and controlled it by 1900. By the 1920s, the Gold Coast economy hinged largely on cocoa production. It became Britain's most prosperous African colony—indeed, Britain's model African colony.

For the Gold Coast, World War II was a lot farther away than for India or Indonesia, but it nonetheless provided a catalyst for independence. Tens of thousands of volunteers from the Gold Coast fought in British armies. To secure fuller cooperation in wartime, British authorities created an advisory body of Gold Coast Africans called the Legislative Council. Its members worked with the British rulers on a new constitution that would delegate some authority to Africans. Almost everyone still thought British rule in the Gold Coast would last far into the future.

But as the war ended, the Gold Coast came to simmer with discontent. The colonial government infuriated peasant farmers when it killed over 2 million cocoa trees to try to stop a crop disease. Many former soldiers, of whom the Gold Coast counted about 63,000, felt dissatisfied with the reward for their military service in World War II on behalf of the British Empire—they wanted bigger pensions. School graduates also stewed with resentments. The Gold Coast in 1950 enrolled 44 percent of school-age children in school, an extraordinarily high percentage for colonial Africa. But schooling raised hopes for jobs and careers that in the late 1940s too often went unfulfilled. Unemployment climbed. Riots broke out in several towns and cities, particularly the capital of Accra.

Broad discontent led in 1947 to the formation of a new political party, the United Gold Coast Convention (UGCC), the first in Africa to adopt independence as its stated goal. Its members were British-educated elites, eager to negotiate better terms within colonial structures, eventually leading to self-rule—not unlike the Indian National Congress in its early decades.

The UGCC's gradualist ambitions did not suit one of its members, **Kwame Nkrumah**, who did not wish to wait for freedom. Nkrumah looms large over Ghana's history. Born in 1909, he came from a poor and illiterate family in a seaside village in the southwest of the Gold Coast. He excelled in Catholic schools and in the late 1920s became a schoolteacher himself. But his intellectual gifts caught the attention of other West Africans who recommended that he go overseas for further education. With money from relatives, Nkrumah enrolled at Lincoln University near Philadelphia. There he grew interested in pan-African ideas in circulation among the African American intelligentsia and came to envision an Africa united and free from foreign rule. In late 1945, having gone to London for PhD work in anthropology, he organized a pan-African congress in England, where he met many prominent African and Caribbean politicians and intellectuals. He gave up his studies for politics, hoping to liberate Africa—beginning with his homeland.

Nkrumah returned to the Gold Coast in 1947 after 12 years abroad. He instantly joined the UGCC and almost as quickly grew impatient with its gradualism. He founded a rival party, the Convention People's Party, to demand independence "now." He sought to appeal not to the intellectuals and well-to-do of the Gold Coast, but to former soldiers, dock workers, students, market women (as the women who dominate West African open-air markets are called), and other groups he thought he could organize politically. He knew how threadbare Britain was in 1947, and he understood the opportunity that presented.

Nkrumah had studied the arts of political organization, particularly the examples from India, and developed his own program of non-violent agitation—demonstrations,

Kwame Nkrumah Here, officials of the newly independent Ghanaian government carry its new prime minister, Nkrumah, on their shoulders in celebration in 1957.

strikes, boycotts—that he called Positive Action. His talents as a political orator and organizer had few rivals within the Gold Coast. Even though the British jailed him, he and his party easily won an election in 1951, the first in African history open to adult male franchise. At this point, the British authorities either had to work with Nkrumah or face massive unrest in their model African colony.

They released Nkrumah from prison and invited him to form a cabinet. In effect, he led a colonial government for the next several years. He and his supporters negotiated an orderly transition to independence, officially achieved in 1957. British policy makers judged it too difficult to hold on to the Gold Coast. A constitutional handover of power suited them—if power could be handed to someone willing to maintain business and military ties with Britain. Nkrumah could seem such a person when he wished.

Ghana—the name was chosen to honor West Africa's ancient kingdom—was the first sub-Saharan African country to slip the bonds of colonial rule. Thanks to the pressure groups organized by Nkrumah and his colleagues, and thanks to British willingness to withdraw, the process happened peacefully with few disturbances of any size after 1951. A wave of hope and optimism splashed over Ghana and indeed all Africa. As Nkrumah put it in a speech to a big crowd at the moment of Ghanaian independence, "We are going to demonstrate to the world, to the other nations, that we are prepared to lay our own foundation. . . . We are going to create our own African personality and identity. It is the only way we can show the world that we are ready for our own battles."

The aftermath proved disappointing. Nkrumah hoped the liberation of Ghana would be only the first step toward the independence of all Africa and the formation of a unified African federation: a united states of Africa. Unity proved elusive, though, even within Ghana. Soon Nkrumah was detaining political opponents and censoring newspapers. Cocoa prices nosedived, and unrest bubbled up. By the early 1960s,

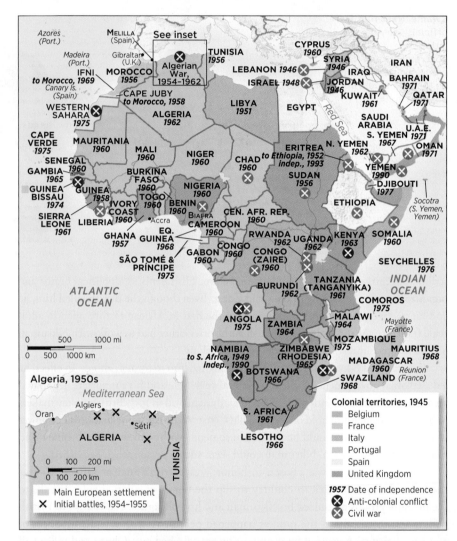

Decolonization in Africa and the Middle East The third pulse of decolonization created almost 50 new countries between 1956 and 1975. Independence involved warfare—particularly in former Portuguese colonies, but also in Algeria and Madagascar and, on a smaller scale, Kenya. Political conflicts with ethnic or religious components were widespread in Africa's newly independent countries, and exploded into warfare most lethally in Nigeria, Angola, and Mozambique.

Nkrumah banned all but his own party and had himself declared "president for life." Unhappy army officers ousted him in a coup d'état in 1966.

The discouraging record of Ghana between 1957 and 1966 was partly a matter of Nkrumah demonstrating the truth of the old saying that "power corrupts." It was also something else: African nationalists—indeed, Asian ones too—promised too much when rallying people against colonial rule. As a motivational tool it made sense to claim that independence would bring peace, justice, and prosperity. But it set up post-colonial rulers for failure, whether in Ghana or Indonesia, when ordinary people found that independence would not necessarily enable them to get jobs or feed their families.

Algeria Algeria's independence struggle took a different, darker form than Ghana's. French armies had claimed Algeria beginning in 1830. Thousands of French, Spanish, and Italians crossed the Mediterranean to settle in Algeria. They often benefited from the colonial government's efforts to push native Algerians off their land. As we've seen, Algeria became a settler colony, and by the 1950s settlers accounted for 10 percent of the population of 10 million. Settlers, known as *pieds-noirs* ("black feet" in French), owned a quarter of the land—including all the best farmland.

Algeria's indigenous population was overwhelmingly Muslim and mainly Arabic-speaking. Large numbers of them learned French, and some tried to advance within the confines of the colonial system. But French Algeria held limited promise for Algerians. Still, few agitated for independence until after World War II.

Once again, the war proved galvanizing. There was no heavy fighting in Algeria, but the rhetoric of the Allies—including the right of all peoples to self-determination—was widely heard. At least 200,000 Algerians served with French armies in the years 1943–1945, fighting in Italy and in the liberation of France from German occupation. Their experiences pushed many of them to think hard about how to liberate Algeria from France.

In May 1945, news of Hitler's defeat prompted a celebration in the eastern Algerian city of Sétif. Somehow—accounts differ—shooting broke out and about 100 *pieds-noirs* were killed. Local police and vigilantes reacted by killing several thousand Muslim Algerians, the great majority of whom had done nothing more than celebrate the Allies' triumph over Nazism.

As the news of Sétif spread, millions of Algerians changed their minds about French rule. Liberation organizations sprouted. In 1954 one of them, known as the FLN (short for "national liberation front" in French), declared a war for independence—a few months after French armies, made up substantially of Algerian soldiers, were crushed at Dien Bien Phu in Vietnam. In Algeria and throughout the French Empire, people followed the news from Vietnam and recognized French weakness.

The **Algerian war for independence** lasted from 1954 to 1962 and cost a million lives. France fought hard to keep Algeria, the most important part of the French Empire. The French fought to protect the *pieds-noirs,* who were in legal fact French citizens, and to preserve its strong business and economic ties to Algeria. The forces of the FLN proved equally committed and just as ruthless.

The French Army—bolstered by tens of thousands of Muslim Algerians, known as *harkis,* who fought against Algerian independence—fared well in combat. But the

CONSIDERING THE EVIDENCE

Sankara Condemns Neo-Colonialism

In 1983, a 33-year-old military officer named Thomas Sankara launched a successful coup against the president of Upper Volta in West Africa, whom he condemned as a French puppet. He promptly re-named the country Burkina Faso, or "Land of Incorruptible People." While the first generation of African nationalists had declared political independence from European colonialism, Sankara and others of his generation sought economic independence from neo-colonialism—the control exercised by the United States, the Soviet Union, and other nations through trade regulations, monetary policy, foreign aid, and loans. Under Sankara's leadership, Burkina Faso supported other countries from Asia, Latin America, and Africa in the Movement of Non-Aligned Countries, which refused to take sides in the Cold War and lobbied for their own interests as members of what was considered an underdeveloped "third world" in the General Assembly of the United Nations. In the following speech to the UN, Sankara expresses support for liberation movements in Palestine, South Africa, Ireland, East Timor, Grenada, Nicaragua, and Afghanistan and decries the exploitation of an international economic order that continues the legacies of colonialism.

I do not intend to enunciate dogmas here. I am neither a messiah nor a prophet. I possess no truths. My only ambition is to...express...the feelings of that mass of people who are disinherited—those who belong to that world maliciously dubbed "the third world"—and to state, even if I cannot make them understood, the reasons that have led us to rise up....

Nobody will be surprised to hear us associate...Burkina Faso with that despised rag-bag, the third world, which the other worlds [i.e., the United States and Europe, and the Soviet Union] invented at the time of our independence in order better to ensure our intellectual, cultural, economic and political alienation. We want to fit in

FLN would not quit. They outlasted the French, who by 1962 had already given up in Vietnam, and conceded independence to all their African colonies, including Algeria's neighbors, Morocco and Tunisia. Fighting on in Algeria was very controversial in France and led to a constitutional crisis and almost to civil war. In the end, a French leader with strong imperialist and nationalist leanings, Charles de Gaulle, decided to quit Algeria in order to save France. The FLN and Algerians had successfully made it clear that the costs to France of continued war would outweigh the benefits of protecting the *pieds-noirs* and preserving French Algeria.

The gruesome war had a gruesome aftermath. Some 800,000 of the million *pieds-noirs*, told to choose between "a suitcase and a coffin" by the FLN, left Algeria for France. France under de Gaulle refused entry to *harkis*, leaving them to the mercy there without at all ... accepting that we are a backward world left behind by the West. Rather, we do so to affirm, ... as one of the non-aligned countries, our deeply felt conviction that a special solidarity unites the three continents of Asia, Latin America and Africa ... [against] political traffickers and economic exploiters.

. . .

There must be no more deceit. The new international economic order ... can be achieved only if we manage to do away with the old order, which completely ignores us, only if we insist on the place which is ours in the political organization of the world, only if we realize our importance in the world and obtain the right to decision-making with respect to the machinery governing trade, economic and monetary affairs at the world level.

The new international economic order is simply one among all the other rights of peoples ... it is a right which can be gained only through the struggle of the peoples. It will never be obtained by any act of generosity by any Power whatsoever.

Questions for Analysis

1. According to Sankara, what "special solidarity" unites the three continents of Asia, Latin America, and Africa?

2. What parts of Sankara's speech would be appealing to "third world" countries but concerning to other countries?

3. How is Sankara's critique of neo-colonialism similar to or different from the grievances that motivated the earlier independence movements in Ghana and Algeria?

Source: Transcript of Thomas Sankara's Address to the United Nations General Assembly, 20th plenary meeting, Thursday, October 4, 1984, New York.

of the FLN, whose supporters murdered about 70,000 and brutalized many more, often by cutting off their noses.

Violence and Legacies of Decolonization

Between 1945 and 1975, the process of decolonization swept away the Japanese and European colonial empires. Japan lost its empire in East and Southeast Asia by losing World War II. For the other imperial powers, the fundamental story was that anti-colonial nationalists found ways to raise the costs of continued colonialism above the threshold that populations and politicians in Europe were prepared to pay.

Decolonization proved a violent process especially in colonies with sizable settler

Casualties of Decolonization, 1945–1975

	PALESTINE, 1945–1948	VIETNAM, 1946–1954	MADAGASCAR, 1947–1960	KENYA, 1953–1963	CYPRUS, 1954–1959	ALGERIA, 1954–1962	MOZAMBIQUE AND ANGOLA, 1961–1975
Number of imperial troops deployed	100,000 British	190,000 French and Africans	30,000 French and Africans	10,000 British and Africans	20,000 British	470,000 French and Africans‡	125,000 Portuguese
Estimated number of people killed (on all sides)	500*	500,000 to 800,000†	30,000 to 50,000	15,000 to 30,000	300	500,000 to up to 1 million	80,000 to 100,000

*and another 15,000 to 20,000 killed in a 1948 war between Arabs and Israelis
†This refers to the Vietnamese war against France. The war with the United States, 1962–1975, is discussed in Chapter 27.
‡not including *harkis*

Sources: Data drawn by author from various sources.

communities, such as Algeria, Kenya, or Mozambique. Madagascar's independence from France also came with a high price in blood, exacted by African troops under French command who suppressed a revolt in 1947 and 1948. The table above shows the size of the military commitments in a few cases of violent decolonization.

In far more cases, decolonization came reasonably peacefully, as in Ghana. This was true in the Philippines and everywhere in the Caribbean. But part of the reason colonial powers did not fight to keep every colony is because they saw—in Vietnam, Kenya, Algeria, and elsewhere—the high price of fighting to hold on.

With few exceptions, former colonies kept their colonial borders when becoming independent countries. In most cases, the borders did not fit snugly around any ethnic or language group, ensuring cultural diversity within almost every former colony. In many countries, diversity produced divisions that led to internal strife. Nigeria, for example, suffered through a secessionist war when the southeastern part of the country proclaimed independence as Biafra in 1967. Biafra collapsed in 1970 amid a famine that killed 2 million, and Nigeria—unlike British India—held together. Only a handful of secession movements have succeeded; Bangladesh is by far the largest. Brief experiments with federations were also tried, uniting Egypt and Syria, for example, in the United Arab Republic, during the years 1958–1961. None lasted, and the borders of the colonial world largely remain in place.

Decolonization remains incomplete. A small number of colonies still exist, relics of earlier empires. They are generally little islands or enclaves, economically subsidized by their colonizers. Examples include Spanish Melilla on the coast of Morocco, British Gibraltar, French Martinique and Guadeloupe (officially a *département* in the Caribbean), and the U.S. territories of Guam and Puerto Rico.

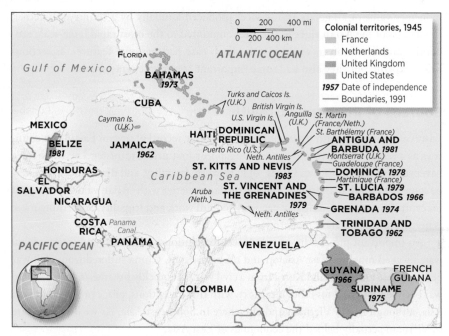

Decolonization in the Greater Caribbean Region The third pulse of decolonization reached the Caribbean in 1962 when Jamaica, and Trinidad and Tobago, won independence. Thirteen new countries emerged, counting the mainland territories of Belize, Guyana, and Suriname. Unlike decolonization in Asia or Africa, in the greater Caribbean no major violence took place. Several territories remain in effect colonies today, such as Puerto Rico, French Guiana, and the Netherlands Antilles (Aruba, Bonaire, and Curaçao).

Decolonization remains incomplete from another point of view as well. Nkrumah and others scorned what they called flag independence, referring to former colonies that were formally independent but still economically and politically dependent on their former imperial masters—a situation sometimes called neo-colonialism. Chad, for example, once part of French Central Africa, still maintains strong ties to France. French companies dominate Chad's economy, and the French military still props up or overthrows Chadian leaders as it pleases. French armed forces have intervened at least 20 times since 1962 in countries that are former French colonies in Africa.

The Rise of East Asia

At least as momentous as decolonization was the rise of East Asia—the economic "miracles" of Japan, South Korea, Singapore, Hong Kong, Taiwan, and mainland China. They all managed sustained economic growth, as measured by GDP, at rates rarely if ever achieved in world history. (GDP—gross domestic product—measures the total monetary value of all goods and services produced annually by a country.) Together, the success of the **Asian tiger economies** amounted to the most rapid large-scale economic transformation in world history. Each case had national features, as sections below explain, but they also had some important common characteristics.

Sources of Economic Growth

East Asians often explain the astonishing economic record of several East Asian countries as a result of culture and values. Singapore's first prime minister, Lee Kuan Yew, never tired of touting "Asian values" of hard work, frugality, and discipline. There may be some truth in that argument, but East Asian societies with "Asian values" were poor for centuries and condemned by necessity to hard work and frugality. Something more is needed to explain their modern rise.

An important pre-condition was peace. Revolutions, civil wars, and international wars ravaged much of East Asia on and off before 1945. China suffered from civil war between 1946 and 1949, and Korea from a civil war that quickly became an international war between 1950 and 1953. But after 1953, with tiny exceptions, peace prevailed in East Asia, although not in Vietnam and elsewhere in Southeast Asia. As we'll see, warfare in Vietnam actually helped the economies of East Asia.

Demographic Change Another factor common to the economic success of East Asia was a gigantic **demographic dividend**. The key to a demographic dividend is a fertility transition that offers a window of time highly favorable for economic growth and development. Under the old biological regime, with high fertility and big families, adults—women especially—devoted great effort to child care. When fertility falls, the age structure changes: the ratio of people of prime working age to children and the elderly rises. That shift makes economic growth and development likelier. In addition, with fewer children to support, families find it easier to pay for education. In short, fertility transitions deliver demographic dividends in the form of economic growth, and nowhere—so far—has this happened faster than in East Asia after 1950.

The demographic dividend in East Asia was in some cases partly a result of government policy encouraging lower birth rates, as we will see. But since it happened everywhere at almost the same speed, and close to the same time, regardless of policy, it is likely that the effect of choices made by hundreds of millions of couples throughout East Asia was more fundamental than policy. As formal education became more important to securing one's future, couples increasingly preferred to invest more heavily in fewer children.

Technology and the Open Economy Another factor contributing to the economic rise of East Asia came from technical changes to shipping, the biggest of which was **containerization**. Before the 1950s, ports were bottlenecks in maritime shipping.

Longshoremen filled and emptied ships, which might take weeks. Beginning in the United States in the late 1950s, entrepreneurs started to use shipping containers—enormous metal boxes—to hold freight. Containers could go on ships, trains, or trucks, and no one had to "break down" the cargo first. Big cranes plucked containers from ships to shore or vice versa. Containerization cut the costs of maritime shipping between the 1950s and 1990s by one-third. Labor costs plunged as longshoremen were let go. Trans-oceanic shipping times fell by nearly 90 percent. The risk of broken or stolen goods declined, and longshoremen's strikes no longer delayed transport. Shipping times became so reliable that companies—led by the Japanese carmaker Toyota—began what is now known as "just-in-time" delivery of product parts. With no inventories sitting around, production costs declined.

The container revolution was global, but East Asia benefited most. Containerization put the big consumer markets of North America and Europe within reach of the East Asian

The Rise of East Asia The "tiger" economies of Japan, South Korea, Taiwan, Hong Kong, and Singapore formed the leading edge of the East Asian economic explosion. China's economic transformation, begun under Deng Xiaoping, was of greater magnitude and global impact, even if uneven across China's interior regions.

economies. Export-oriented growth strategies became much more practical when shipping costs and times were plummeting and more predictable.

Another general factor contributing to the East Asian economic rise is connected to containerization's success: the comparative openness of the world economy, or at least a big slice of it, since 1950. All of the successful East Asian economies prospered on the basis of exports—the imports of other countries. The United States, historically a protectionist country, by 1950 encouraged free trade and low tariffs everywhere around the world. It had the power to persuade many countries in Western Europe and Latin America to lower trade barriers. This opened the door for export-led growth of the sort the East Asian tigers pursued.

Cheap labor was another important factor. Just as Meiji Japan's industrialization at the end of the nineteenth century took advantage of low labor costs, so it was with all of the East Asian tigers in the late twentieth century. Hundreds of millions of very poor people were willing to work for paltry wages. If they asked for higher pay or better working conditions, their bosses—at least in South Korea, Japan, and China—could easily find eager replacement workers in rural villages. Hong Kong and Singapore did not have masses of poor villagers, but they could draw on cheap immigrant labor from China or Malaysia.

Let's now look more closely at the examples of Japan, South Korea, and China. The story of Taiwan is equally remarkable but similar to South Korea's. Hong Kong and Singapore also engineered economic surges, but on the smaller scale of city-states. North Korea missed out entirely. Its leadership did not choose export-led industrial growth as its guiding strategy. It preferred to rely on its own meager resources rather than integrate into the international economy. North Korea suffered mass starvation in the 1990s and remains very poor today. Its record shows, among other things, the economic penalty of isolation from the commercial circuitry of the Global web. Self-reliance, in a global economy, has often proved disastrous.

Japan

Japan's post-1945 economic miracle was its second. It had pulled one off after the Meiji Restoration of 1868. That one featured rapid industrialization, beginning with textiles and shifting to heavy industry. It continued into the 1930s, little troubled by the Great Depression, with a new emphasis on military production and planning.

Bombing during World War II obliterated about one-quarter of Japan's buildings and infrastructure and slashed its GDP in half (1940–1945). In the immediate post-war years, most people were hungry and some starved to death. Malnutrition caused the average heights of children to decline. Japan's currency lost almost all value to inflation in the years 1945–1949. But Japan had expertise, traditions, and institutions that, with a few tweaks, could support another economic surge when conditions improved—as they did markedly in the 1950s.

The U.S. Occupation and Strategic Support From 1945 to 1952, the Allies—mainly the U.S. military—occupied Japan and directed its high-level policy. American army officers wrote a new constitution for Japan, adopted in 1947. Their goals were to eradicate militarism and ensure a stable, democratic, and pro-American Japan. They pushed through land reform that ended the domination of the countryside by big landlords and made Japan into a country of small farmers, a key step on the road to economic transformation.

The new constitution provided for the equality of men and women in articles written by Beate Sirota, a 23-year-old American of Ukrainian parentage. She had grown up in Japan and was working for the occupation authorities as a translator when invited to help draft the constitution. Equality of the sexes was a revolutionary concept in Japan and helped bring about a fertility transition and demographic dividend.

Once communists took over China (1949) and the Korean War broke out (1950), U.S. policy toward Japan shifted. Engineering social change seemed less urgent than re-building Japan as a bulwark against communist expansion in East Asia. After some missteps, the Americans came to understand that on economic policy they needed to work within Japan's cultural traditions, one of which included cooperation between business elites and government bureaucrats to craft national economic and industrial strategies. After 1949, a new ministry for international trade and industry (MITI) took primary responsibility for creating these strategies. It sponsored research and directed investment funds toward chosen industries. Like the leaders of the Meiji era, post-war Japan's government did not trust the free market to make the best economic decisions for Japan.

One important factor sustaining the Japanese economic miracle was its role in supplying the U.S. military during the Korean and Vietnam wars. These war efforts needed vast quantities of supplies, and Japan was close to the war zones, especially to Korea. A Japanese prime minister referred to the Korean War, a bit callously, as "a gift of the gods."

In 1950, Japan's economy, halved by war's ravages, was smaller than that of Colombia, Costa Rica, or Morocco. Its per capita annual growth after 1950 averaged about 8 percent to 1973, a sustained rate never seen anywhere before, and more than twice the global average of those years. During the 1970s, a tough decade for the world economy because of oil price hikes, Japan's economy still grew rapidly, and by 1980 was the third largest in the world. Prosperity—in the form of cars, TVs, washing machines, and the like—reached into the villages and formerly poor neighborhoods of big cities. The expansion slowed in the 1990s and beyond. These trends are evident in the table to the right.

Some of the general factors discussed above help explain Japan's economic takeoff. It benefited from a demographic dividend, containerization, and easy access to the U.S.

Japanese per Capita GDP, 1950–2020 (indexed to 1950)

YEAR	GDP (1950 = 100)
1950	100
1955	144
1960	208
1965	309
1970	506
1975	591
1980	701
1985	803
1990	980
1995	1043
2000	1069
2005	1125
2010	1145
2015	1144
2020	1151 (estimated)

Source: Maddison Project, https://www.rug.nl/ggdc/historical development/maddison/releases/maddison-project-database-2018

Note: Per capita GDP refers to the national GDP divided by the national population.

market. At first, its industrial competitiveness also benefited from cheap labor. But under the Allies' occupation Japanese workers had been encouraged to unionize, which led to rising wages by the mid-1950s. In addition, the supply of poor villagers willing to work for low wages dried up by about 1960, so Japan could not profit for long on the basis of cheap export manufactures such as textiles and toys.

Zaibatsu and *Keiretsu*   Japanese business organizations, especially large, integrated corporate conglomerates, proved especially nimble at exploiting the opportunities of the post-war years. These conglomerates had existed in Japan since the late nineteenth century, when they were called *zaibatsu*. They brought together banks, trading companies, and industries all under the same leaders, often from one family. They had led industrialization in late nineteenth-century Japan, when they emphasized iron, steel, and ship building, and during the years 1937–1945, when they organized war production. The *zaibatsu* tradition was woven into the fabric of Japanese society, culture, and politics.

The Americans had at first tried to break up the *zaibatsu* during the post-war occupation, but the effort withered as U.S. policy shifted to building up Japan to counter communism in East Asia. Called **keiretsu** after 1945, the conglomerates re-grouped and led a new campaign, aimed at capturing foreign markets in select industries. Their success in some areas was stunning: in 1965, nearly two-thirds of the world's new ships were built in Japan.

Like the *zaibatsu* of the Meiji era, the *keiretsu* proved successful at technological innovation, especially adapting foreign technology to Japanese contexts. The rising wages of Japanese workers in the 1950s tempted companies to give up on labor-intensive approaches. With the encouragement of MITI, they shared research costs and pooled resources to buy licenses for foreign technology. They sent people abroad to study the latest production techniques—as Japan had done during the Meiji era. In the 1950s and 1960s, the U.S. government eagerly assisted in transferring industrial technology to Japan. Japanese engineers worked small wonders inventing or improving cameras, computers, printers, electronic keyboards, automated teller machines, and hundreds of other common devices.

The *keiretsu* and other Japanese firms entrenched assembly-line production in Japan and found ways to ensure better quality control than the Americans, the originators of the assembly line. In the 1950s, they succeeded mainly because they made cheaper goods than industry elsewhere could manage; but by the 1970s they did it with high-quality goods: better steel, ships, cars, audio equipment, and TVs than companies elsewhere could make. The *keiretsu* and smaller firms also pioneered miniaturization. Post-war Japan was crowded. Its urban apartments were small and its streets narrow. Japanese industry responded with small TVs, refrigerators, and cars that fit Japanese spaces— and similarly crowded societies elsewhere. In pursuing miniaturization, they developed skills and technologies that proved useful in markets such as personal computers, mobile phones, and robotics.

Economic Miracle Consumer goods and electronics helped to fuel Japan's economic revolution in the mid-twentieth century. During the 1970s, the Nissan factory near Yokohama could turn out three cars per minute for worldwide export. Workers in a 1960s Tokyo factory assemble components of color television sets, which became commonplace even in poorer Japanese households as prosperity increased.

The Japanese economic spurt lasted into the 1970s and made Japan an industrial powerhouse and one of the richest societies in the world. Its growth rates slowed from a sprint to a trot during the 1970s and 1980s, and after 1995 to a crawl. Among the reasons for its economic stagnation was an ageing population, the price Japan pays for its rapid reduction in birth rates between 1950 and 1970. The public and politicians have resisted immigration—which skews young—leaving Japan since 1990 with the world's oldest population. By 2020, 28 percent of Japanese were age 65 or older, and in no other country was the proportion above 23 percent. Japan's total population has been falling since about 2010. In addition, since the 1980s, Japan has also enjoyed less cooperation from the United States, whose automobile and other businesses came to feel threatened by Japan's. And Japan's export sector faced growing competition from South Korea, Taiwan, Singapore, and, by 1990, China.

South Korea

South Korea engineered an economic miracle even more extraordinary than Japan's. Whereas Japan already had decades as an industrial society behind it in the 1950s, South Korea had next to nothing. Its few modern industries had been built to serve the interests of Korea's colonial master, Japan, which siphoned all the wealth and resources that it could from Korea between 1910 and 1945. In the Korean War (1950–1953), Korean, Chinese, and American armies blasted the peninsula into tatters and left it divided in two. South Korea in the late 1950s had virtually no natural resources, and per capita incomes were lower than those of newly independent Ghana—and of communist North Korea. Yet by 1990 South Korea was well on its way to becoming one of the world's best-educated and richest populations. Between 1960 and 2017, its GDP per capita grew roughly 300-fold. How could a former colony ruled so harshly pull off such a self-transformation?

Although harsh, Japanese colonial rule (1910–1945) in Korea left a few useful legacies. The Japanese built the foundations of a modern educational system. They also built a transportation infrastructure, although most of that needed re-building after the Korean War. And they trained some Koreans in industrial skills, both as workers and as managers.

American military occupation of the south beginning in 1945 left another helpful legacy: **land reform**. In 1948, most South Koreans were peasants, renting land from aristocratic landowners called *yangban* who made all important decisions about farming. But by 1956, South Korean peasants owned most of the farmland, grew whatever they liked, and sold as much of their harvest as they wished. Land reform, undertaken under pressure from the U.S. government, was the foundational act of South Korea's economic miracle.

A second step was building a universal education system for both boys and girls. In the 1950s, South Korea's government began an enduring investment in primary and secondary school education that paid off in the decades ahead. In the mid-1950s, school lessons were often held in tents and teachers had to cope with classes of as many as 100 students. By 1960, almost every child over five years of age spent long hours in newly built schools. Soon South Korea's literacy rates were among the highest in the world. By 1980, its workforce was among the world's most educated.

Industrial Policy and U.S. Support Government policy helped in other ways too. In the early 1960s, South Korea's rulers embarked on a series of five-year plans featuring government direction of economic policy but private ownership of most business enterprises. In the latter respect, it was crucially different from communist five-year plans followed in the USSR or China. The government's industrial policy rewarded companies that exported goods. It protected South Korean industry behind tariff barriers. It also increasingly welcomed foreign investment, which came mainly from the United States and Japan.

The United States regarded South Korea, like Japan, as an important Cold War bulwark against communism in Asia. During the 1950s, the U.S. government paid about 80 percent of South Korea's government budget. From 1946 to 1976, the United States gave twice as much aid money to South Korea as it did to all of Africa. The Vietnam War provided South Korean industry, especially construction firms, with an opportunity to win contracts from the U.S. military—as it did for Japanese firms. And most important of all, the United States opened its market to South Korean exports. For decades, it was the main customer for South Korean manufactures.

Economic and Social Change At first, those manufacturing exports were mainly textiles and shoes. Then, in the 1970s, the South Korean government—ignoring advice from U.S. economists—decided to leave textiles behind and invest in heavy industry such as steel, ship building, automobiles, and chemicals, following the Japanese route. By this time, South Korean schools and universities had trained enough scientists and engineers to staff such industries. This gamble on heavy industry worked well, as it had for Japan.

South Korea's leaders were no angels. They had studied the experiences of Meiji Japan and Atatürk's Turkey—both of which fended off foreign domination and used threats, detention, and violence against their own citizens. In 1980, South Korea's military government unleashed the army on peaceful pro-democracy protesters, killing hundreds in the city of Gwangju. Until the late 1980s, South Korea's rulers were authoritarian nationalists, whose aim was to strengthen South Korea economically and to cast off dependence on the United States.

Throughout the decades of its economic surge (1960–1990), South Korea underwent social change that boosted economic growth. The land reform enabled peasants to save enough to educate their children in hopes of upward social mobility. Millions moved from farm to city. And like much of the rest of East Asia in these years, South Korea underwent a lightning-fast fertility transition. In the 1950s, South Korean families averaged more than 5 children. In the decades that followed, partly as a result of government support for birth control, South Korean women changed their ambitions and their lives. Mothers' clubs in thousands of villages spread knowledge of birth control methods, which were eagerly taken up by South Korean women. In 1975, they averaged under 3 children each; and in 2005, only 1.2. This social change delivered a huge demographic dividend to the economy as the proportion of people in the prime of life climbed. In addition, during these decades women took up jobs in offices and factories in unprecedented numbers.

South Korea transformed itself from a poor peasant country to a rich industrial one within a generation. Its economy grew by 8 to 10 percent annually from 1960 to 1985, and in the late 1980s it led the world with annual growth rates of up to 12 percent. The explanation for this spurt lies in shrewd industrial and educational policy; a quick fertility transition and big demographic dividend; and the opportunities presented by U.S. strategic support such as massive aid, access to U.S. markets and technology, and U.S. guarantees of security that made South Korea an attractive destination for investment.

China

China's economic rise is the most miraculous of all. It has lifted several hundred million people out of grinding poverty. It has taken place under the rule of an authoritarian and often brutal Communist Party that has embraced capitalism and the unabashed pursuit of private gain. And it has achieved all this without the support from the United States that helped Japan and South Korea.

In longer historical perspective, China's economic transformation is not so miraculous. Chinese society and culture had deep-seated traditions of entrepreneurship and technological innovation. China—as we've seen—was the first market society, dating back to the Song dynasty (960–1279 CE). Chinese culture was suited to competition in a global economy. But first China's economy had to survive a century of imperialist exploitation, revolution, war, and Maoist rule.

Concerted efforts to modernize and industrialize China began in the late nineteenth century under the wobbling Qing dynasty. These efforts continued after the revolution of 1910 under Guomindang rule, but the results were modest: in 1936, factories accounted for only 3 percent of China's economic output—compared to 25 percent in Japan. Textiles in the area around Shanghai made up most of that industrial output. The only other industrial cluster in the 1930s was in Manchuria, which was under Japanese control after 1931.

As we've seen, World War II (1937–1945) and the Chinese Civil War (1946–1949) took a terrible toll on China. Violence, disease, and starvation killed about 7 to 8 percent of the population in those 12 years. The standard of living fell to levels of the early nineteenth century. In 1945 and 1946, hyperinflation reduced the currency to near worthlessness. China was among the poorest countries in the world when Mao Zedong and the Chinese Communist Party came to power in 1949. It remained overwhelmingly rural with only small pockets of industry.

The Economy under Maoism Mao Zedong ruled China from 1949 until his death in 1976. His economic policies were ambitious and erratic. He thrived on chaos and used sudden reversals in policy as a political tool to destroy rivals. Given the economic history of China's neighbors since 1950, and that of China itself since Mao's death, it is tempting to conclude that the main impact of Mao and Maoism was to slow the economic rise of China by 30 years.

In the early years of the People's Republic of China (PRC), Mao and his fellow communists aimed to make China stronger, richer, and fairer. Their reforms drew on Chinese precedents and, despite their frictions, the record of Stalin's USSR, which had stood the test of World War II. So they tried to build a hierarchical communist party, a one-party state, a robust military, and a highly regulated society. They shared the standard communist faith in five-year plans and heavy industry, which they hoped would make China economically and militarily strong and give it a proletariat with which to build communist society. They began with collectivization of agriculture, as Stalin had done.

Collectivization began with the murder of a few million landlords in the early 1950s and the intimidation of the rest. Once the power and authority of the landed gentry was eliminated, the CCP re-organized peasants into communal "work units" that shared land, tools, and animals. Party-appointed leaders of work units decided almost everything for peasant families, including who could marry and who could have children. Peasant families were allowed to keep about 10 percent of the farmland for themselves. Collectivization in China proved unpopular with peasants, as it had in the USSR. In the far south, many slipped over borders to the British colony of Hong Kong or to Burma. The hundreds of millions who remained usually worked much harder on their own tiny plots than on the communal fields—if they could get away with it.

In Japan and South Korea, breaking the hold of landholding elites and turning land over to peasants was a crucial step in launching their economic upsurges. In China, crushing the landlords and turning land over to communal work units was a disaster. At Mao's death in 1976, agricultural efficiency, measured in yields per hectare or per acre, were lower than in 1956. The tiny private plots were the only exceptions: their yields were 5 to 10 times higher than those on collectively farmed land. China became a food importer from 1961 to 1996, despite Mao's ambitions for self-reliance.

In embracing heavy industry as a path to growth, Mao was also following in Stalin's footsteps. In what could be the most massive technology transfer in world history, China imported industrial machinery from the USSR and Eastern (Sovietized) Europe in the 1950s. By 1955, two-thirds of China's foreign trade was with the USSR, and Moscow paid for one-third of the projects undertaken in China's first five-year plan (1953–1957). Thousands of Soviet experts flocked to China, giving advice on factory construction, mining, dam building, and much else. Millions of Chinese peasants now became factory workers. In sheer quantitative terms, Mao's program of industrialization was a success. Starting from a very low base, it achieved roughly 11 percent annual growth in industrial output between 1952 and 1978. But the growth in output came only from using more labor, coal, ores, and other raw materials. Chinese industry remained inefficient, wasting energy and raw materials. The quality of goods remained shoddy.

The most spectacularly inefficient—and tragic—of Mao's policies was the **Great Leap Forward** of 1958 through 1961. To strengthen his hand in domestic politics, Mao decided to make a massive economic push involving both industry and agriculture. Instead of building modern steel mills, for which China did not have the capital or expertise, he required the work units to produce steel in a million "backyard furnaces." For Mao, steel had a symbolic value. He wanted to outstrip British and American production levels and show that he could build a steel industry from scratch even faster than Stalin. Even students and faculty at China's elite Peking University had to meet steel quotas. Through heroic effort, China doubled its steel output, melting down doorknobs, bedsprings, bicycle frames, and cooking pots. But steel made this way was usually brittle and useless, a waste of vast quantities of coal, charcoal, and labor, not to mention bikes, beds, and pots.

Great Leap Forward
Workers manufacture steel in the "backyard furnaces" mandated by Mao's Great Leap For-ward economic policy of the period 1958–1961.

The Great Leap Forward also featured fiascoes in agriculture. Skeptical of scientific expertise, Mao maintained that seeds of the same species even if planted close together would not compete for nutrients and water. When food ran short, he demanded that the village work units hand over more grain for the cities, the army—and even for export. Fearing the consequences if they did not deliver, party workers took so much grain that peasants starved. Estimates vary greatly, but between 1958 and 1961 some 20 to 50 million Chinese starved to death—3 to 8 percent of the population of 650 to 700 million. It was by far the worst self-inflicted famine in world history. The Great Leap Forward coincided with a rupture in Sino-Soviet relations, resulting in the expulsion of Soviet advisers and the isolation of China.

The Cultural Revolution   Mao's reliance on political mobilization campaigns con-tinued to hamper China's economy. The biggest of these was the Great Proletarian Cultural Revolution (1966–1976), an effort to re-kindle revolutionary spirit and oust some of Mao's critics within the CCP. He shut down schools and universities, urging young people to organize themselves as Red Guards and to assault everything old. The Red Guards destroyed temples and texts, and attacked elders from teachers to party cadres to their own parents. They beat up foreigners, including Soviet and East German diplomats. They targeted ethnic minorities, killing thousands, especially Mongolians and Tibetans. They inflicted public humiliations on their targets, exhibiting them to jeering crowds. One Red Guard recalled: "We were told that we needed to use vio-lence to destroy a class, spiritually and physically. That was justification enough for torturing someone. They weren't considered human anymore. If they were the enemy, they deserved to be strangled to death, and they deserved to be tortured. This was the education we received."

In 1967 and 1968, Mao called out the army, in some cases to tame the Red Guards and in others to support them. The Cultural Revolution was now virtually a civil war with 1 to 2 million killed by either the Red Guards or the army. It was also an economic disaster, costing the country about 7 to 8 percent of its GDP in each of 1967 and 1968—a more severe decline than any two-year period of the Great Depression in any major country. By keeping young people out of school for several years, and by encouraging them to memorize the quotations of Chairman Mao rather than learn to read and write, it cost China in the longer run too. As the economic growth surge swept the rest of East Asia in the 1960s, Mao's policies, whatever their motives, kept China poor and, after the Sino-Soviet split, isolated.

At the same time, however, Mao laid a foundation for future economic growth. He and the CCP re-unified China in the 1940s and then, despite domestic turmoil, kept it together as one country. He succeeded where Gandhi, Nehru, and Jinnah in India failed. In effect, he established a new dynasty—not of a family or lineage as in China's past, but of the CCP. National unity would help vault China's economy upward after his death.

Cultural Revolution Red Guards humiliate victims—forcing them to wear dunce caps proclaiming their crimes—as crowds look on. Humiliation tactics were characteristic of the ideological warfare of the Cultural Revolution.

Also, in obliterating the landlord class, Mao achieved through murder and brutality what American-imposed land reform achieved in South Korea and Japan. When collectivized agriculture ended after Mao's death, land did not revert to landlords but went to the peasants in long-term leases. His reliance on Soviet machinery and expertise in the 1950s trained a few million Chinese in how to handle machine tools, truck engines, and other useful skills. And as we've seen, Mao thawed relations with the United States in the early 1970s, setting the stage for the full participation of China in the international economy. But it took Mao's death in 1976, and a few other favorable developments, for China to embark on its epic rise.

Deng Xiaoping In the years following Mao's death, **Deng Xiaoping** emerged as China's supreme leader—head of the party, the government, and the army. His re-orientation of Chinese economic policy led to a genuine great leap forward and a real cultural revolution.

Deng was born in the southwestern province of Sichuan in 1904 to a family of middling gentry status. His father had attended university and played a local role in Sun Yatsen's nationalist revolution. As a schoolboy Deng became an ardent nationalist, eager to rescue China from weakness, poverty, and humiliation. As a teenager he joined a work-study program in France, where over a six-year stay (1920–1926) he worked in factories and joined the European branch of the Chinese Communist Party. Like several young Chinese, he saw communism as a way to make China strong. In 1926, Deng went to Moscow to study at a university set up by the Soviets to train Chinese revolutionaries. A year later, he returned to China and began political work.

For the next several decades, Deng rose through the ranks of the CCP. He worked as an ideological enforcer in the CCP's army units during the long struggles against Japan and Chiang Kai-shek's Guomindang party. After the CCP took power in 1949, he served as mayor of a major city, Chongqing, and in many central government posts in the 1950s and 1960s. By and large he supported Mao's policies, but he occasionally ran afoul of Mao anyway and was stripped of his posts more than once. During the Cultural Revolution he and his family were attacked by Red Guards, and his son thrown out of a fourth-story window (he survived as a paraplegic).

Patience and shrewdness were among Deng's hallmarks. He weathered all the storms of Mao's rule and the power struggles after Mao's death. When he took power beginning in 1978, Deng was well over 70 years old and about to embark on a world-changing program of reform to make China strong again.

In 1978, Deng visited Japan and Singapore. At the time, China was poor and technologically backward—its per capita income was less than half of sub-Saharan Africa's. Singapore dazzled Deng with a shiny vision of wealth combined with one-party rule and an orderly society—and all overseen by a local population of ethnic Chinese. Thousands of CCP officials visited Singapore after 1978, and Singapore's autocratic leader, Lee Kuan Yew, traveled to China many times. Lee's Singapore had the prosperity of Western countries and all the advantages of an open, technologically modern economy, but no political opposition, no litter or graffiti, and almost no drugs or decadence. Why couldn't China be more like Singapore?

In fact, it could. Deng cautiously allowed the profit motive to operate within limits prescribed by the Communist Party and called it "socialism with Chinese characteristics." In fact, he was dismantling Maoist socialism and gradually replacing it with capitalism—with Chinese characteristics. Deng's economic reforms unleashed the rise of contemporary China while keeping the CCP's monopoly on political power intact.

Deng's Economic Reforms Deng's first task was replacing the Maoist economy. He allowed peasant families to lease farmland long-term, ending the commune work-unit system. Agricultural production skyrocketed. Between 1978 and 1990, the average Chinese calorie intake doubled, and by 1991 China no longer needed to import food. Between 1979 and 1988, Deng, working with provincial party bosses, created several "special economic zones," at first next door to Hong Kong and across from Taiwan, and invited foreign investment and trade in these zones. Small businesses, such as textile workshops, sprouted alongside the older state-owned factories built under Mao. China's stock exchange, closed since 1949, re-opened in 1992.

Whereas Mao had tried to raise production by means of political exhortation and threat, Deng let economic incentives do that work. He allowed local governments to make most of their own decisions about how to invest, produce, and trade.

Following the path blazed by the East Asian tigers, he encouraged export-oriented industry and welcomed foreign technology and factory management techniques. Deng unchained the profit motive, claiming that in China markets and socialism were compatible. He translated his earlier remark—that the color of a cat doesn't matter, only that it catches mice—into action: economic growth mattered more than ideological purity. His pragmatic policies sparked an industrial revolution in China, focused on textiles and consumer electronics—just as in South Korea and Taiwan. Deng retired in the early 1990s and died in 1997, but his successors steered China along the same path.

Deng was no democrat. He ordered mass executions to encourage obedience and reduce corruption. He maintained oppressive policies toward ethnic minorities such as Uighurs and Tibetans. Whereas Gorbachev in 1989 declined to use the Soviet army to crush East Europeans' efforts to win greater freedom, Deng in 1989 called out the army against peaceful democracy protesters at Tiananmen Square in the heart of Beijing, leading to a massacre much larger than the one South Korea's army perpetrated in Gwangju in 1980. His commitment to one-party rule was as firm as Mao's.

His ruthless authoritarian streak did not interfere with his liberalization of the economy, the results of which were of world historical importance. By 2004, China was receiving more foreign investment than any other country in the world. Between 1980 and 2020, the economy grew 50-fold, posting annual growth rates of 8 to 11 percent. No big country had ever done this before, or even come close. The United States achieved such rates only during World War II.

Comparison between the world's two most populous countries helps show how extraordinary China's economic trajectory was. China and India between 1950 and 1990 were twins in poverty. In both countries, most people barely had enough to eat. After 1990 both got richer; but China did so far faster, so that in 2020 its per capita GDP was roughly five times that of India.

Tiananmen Square An Associated Press photojournalist took this iconic photo of a single Chinese man attempting to block tanks on their way to Tiananmen Square in order to crush peaceful pro-democracy protests on June 5, 1989. As many as several thousand protesters may have been killed by the Chinese military during the protests.

Economic Effects and Global Reach   The Chinese government and some Chinese citizens were getting rich. By 2000, government revenues were about 30 times the level of Mao's last years and rising fast. The wealth of the central and provincial governments allowed tremendous investment in infrastructure: China built 54 new airports between 2000 and 2010 and a network of bullet trains covering much of the country. Millionaire and billionaire entrepreneurs sprouted up. According to World Bank figures, about 800 million Chinese climbed out of poverty between 1990 and 2020. This represents the largest and fastest escape from mass poverty in world history.

By 2015, China was the workshop of the world—as Britain was called in the mid-nineteenth century. It was the world's largest carmaker, having overtaken the United States in 2009. It built 90 percent of the world's personal computers and mobile phones, 80 percent of the air conditioners, 70 percent of the solar panels, and 65 percent of the shoes. Its biggest cities—Beijing, Shanghai, Guangzhou—became nodes of the Global web.

Economic prosperity also brought China international prestige and power. By the mid-1990s, China was doubling its military budget every few years and converting uninhabited islands in the South China Sea into military bases. It became a major arms dealer, especially to Pakistan. It offered loans to many governments in Asia and Africa, in exchange for control of commercial ports and military bases around the Indian Ocean. It purchased long-term leases on farmland in Africa. Some 10,000 Chinese companies were active in Africa as of 2020, creating new factories, mines, and plantations, and building roads, bridges, dams, and hotels. Outside of Lagos, Nigeria, for example, a Guangdong-based firm opened a new industrial zone, which its Chinese manager said was "like managing a country. We have our own customs, our own police, our own operations." There is irony in the resemblance of these quasi-imperial arrangements to the autonomous commercial compounds run in the nineteenth century by Europeans in Guangzhou, the capital of today's Guangdong. By the early twenty-first century, the Chinese state had become a major force not only in East Asia but in global politics as well.

Sources of China's Economic Surge   Deng's economic reforms took advantage of several favorable circumstances with roots in the Mao period. The diplomatic opening to the United States that Mao had engineered in the early 1970s enabled China's return to the global economy. It joined the World Trade Organization (WTO) in 2001, symbolizing its economic re-integration. The Chinese economy also benefited from the millions of overseas Chinese living in Singapore, Hong Kong, Taiwan, and scattered throughout Southeast Asia. These communities included bankers and entrepreneurs who spoke Chinese, understood Chinese cultural contexts, and were willing to trade with and invest in Deng's China. For the first two decades after Deng's reforms, the majority of investment in China came from overseas Chinese and from South Korea.

Education was another source of China's economic surge. When the CCP took power in 1949, only about 20 percent of Chinese could read. By 1964, thanks to intensive efforts in primary education, about 65 percent could. The Cultural Revolution (1966–1976) slowed progress, so that the figure remained about the same in 1980—and women were still much less likely to be literate than men. But by 2018, fully 97 percent of Chinese could read, and the gender gap had almost vanished. By 2020, 8 million Chinese graduated from universities each year, and another 400,000 were studying in U.S. universities.

Additionally, Deng and his successors inherited a growing demographic dividend. During the 1950s and 1960s, Mao urged Chinese to have big families on the theory that a country's strength lies in its people and there could never be too many Chinese. In 1967, Chinese women averaged six births over their lifetime. By 1978, the average had dropped to only three. As the graph below shows, it took the United Kingdom 95 years (1815–1910) to reduce fertility from six to three births per woman over her lifetime. The United States took 82 years (1844–1926). China did it in 11—and did not stop there.

Fertility Declines from More Than 6 to Fewer Than 3 Children per Woman

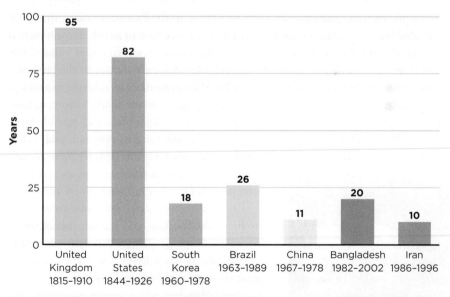

This bar graph shows the timing and pace of fertility transitions in seven countries. The earlier transitions—in the United Kingdom and the United States—were slower. Those occurring from 1960 on were far faster. Fast transitions created an age structure—lots of people in the prime of life and fewer who were very old and very young—that sped up economic growth for a few decades. China and Iran were among the countries with the fastest fertility transitions in world history.

Source: OurWorldinData.org (data from Gapminder fertility dataset, version 6, and World Bank World Development Indicators).

In the years 1978–1980, with the birth rate already falling rapidly, the CCP abandoned Mao's position on population and imposed a "one-child rule" that penalized families with two or more children. Birth rates continued to slide; by 1990 the average fell to two children per woman. It is likely that urbanization and the education of females had more to do with this fall in fertility than did the government restriction. But whatever the causes, it delivered an enormous demographic dividend. Some economists credit this factor alone with one-quarter of China's economic growth since 1980. Today, China's birth rate is a little over one child per woman—the lowest fertility rate in the world. Faced with a rapidly aging population, China abandoned the one-child policy in 2016.

So Deng, his allies, and his successors took advantage of some favorable circumstances that, combined with shrewd policies, ignited an era of economic growth in China that fit the earlier regional pattern. While Japan launched the economic rise of East Asia, and South Korea, Taiwan, Singapore, and Hong Kong confirmed it, China—because of its size—completed it.

Environmental and Social Problems

Economic growth spurts usually come at a price. In the East Asian cases, that price included heavy pollution loads affecting air, water, and human health. Environmental protection carried a low priority in East Asia while countries were trying to industrialize and escape poverty. Japan suffered many episodes of acute pollution in the 1950s and 1960s. The most famous of these was so-called **Minamata disease**, referring to a seaside bay teeming with mercury from a nearby chemical plant. Many people who ate seafood from Minamata developed nerve damage, and their babies often had horrible birth defects. By the 1970s and 1980s, Japan got around to addressing its environmental health. South Korea and Taiwan followed a similar trajectory. China today is trying to address monumental pollution problems, but air and water pollution still kill a few million Chinese annually.

East Asia's concentrated economic growth also produced the frictions and resentments of social inequality. Some people got very rich while others did not. Japan suffered less strife from this cause than South Korea or China. Today, China is—depending how you measure it—among the most spectacularly unequal societies in the world. In 1978, its top 1 percent of earners took in 6 percent of national income, but by 2015 they received 15 percent. One-quarter of its population remains dirt-poor, and in the interior, away from the more prosperous coasts, the proportion is much higher.

Minamata Disease A mother in the village of Minamata in southern Japan holds her 12-year-old daughter, who was born with severe nerve damage due to exposure to the mercury that polluted Minamata Bay.

A demographic inequality affected China as well, one that empowers young women and deprives tens of millions of Chinese men of a chance to marry and raise families. Chinese families for centuries have had a strong preference for boys, and in difficult times had often sold or killed girl babies. When ultrasound technology became available around 1990, and the government permitted most families only one child, many couples turned to selective abortion in their effort to ensure that they got a boy. As a result, China's population in recent decades developed a shortage of females. The ratio of boys to girls among newborns peaked at 1.22 to 1.0 in 2008, by far the highest in the world. Today, Chinese women of marriageable age are in short supply and consequently enjoy unprecedented choice in selecting partners. Their good fortune came at the expense of tens of millions aborted because they were female, and tens of millions of men unhappily unmarried.

Economic development also brought corruption. Where governments take a strong role in the economy, as in every East Asian economic surge, officials have countless opportunities to accept bribes and kickbacks. Hong Kong and Singapore minimized this problem, partly because they are small and easy to monitor, but also because those in charge chose to suppress corruption rather than revel in it. Japan tackled the problem and today ranks with Singapore and Hong Kong among the least corrupt societies when it comes to business practices. China, however, has suffered from widespread corruption that, despite occasional crackdowns, often involves top government officials and their families.

Despite these and other dark clouds, almost no one in East Asia regrets the economic transformation of the past two generations. Their full meaning, of course, is impossible to assess because the process is still under way.

Rebalancing in the Global Web

By the second half of the twentieth century, the Global web was no longer expanding much. It had drawn in just about every population on Earth. But, as always, the web of connections was changing shape, with some pathways carrying more traffic and others slowing down. And just what those circuits carried—political ideas, trade goods, investment funds, cultural fashions, human migrants, and microbes—also evolved.

Decolonization and the rise of East Asia both re-shaped the Global web. At warp speed they reversed the longstanding process whereby Atlantic Europe had accumulated wealth and power and had established imperial rule over much of the world. Colonization and the rise of the West had taken several centuries; decolonization and the rise of East Asia took several decades. The difference in the pace of change is rooted in the densely connected world of the mid- and late twentieth century: the end of empire in India could instantly inspire people in Indonesia or the Gold Coast, and the prosperity of Singapore could inspire reformers in Beijing.

East Asia became one of the Global web's most interactive zones. During the 1930s and 1940s, Japan had tried to unify most of East Asia within an imperial system that it called the Greater East Asian Co-Prosperity Sphere. It collapsed with Japan's defeat in 1945. But a more successful version soon followed, held together by modern communications and container shipping. Sometimes called Asia-Pacific, this tightly integrated space centered on the humming economies of China and the neighboring Asian tigers. Overseas Chinese, often bilingual in English, played crucial roles bringing this integration to East Asia; but students, entrepreneurs, diplomats, and others from Chinese-speaking lands, and from Japan and South Korea as well, took part.

East Asia also became firmly linked—economically, culturally, and politically—to the United States and to some extent almost everywhere else. Japanese businesses built links to companies based on the Pacific coasts of Canada, the United States, and South America by the 1960s. China and Brazil had had almost nothing to do with each other before 1980, but by 2009 China was Brazil's biggest trade partner, importing soybeans and ores and building new ports and railroads in South America. Flows of investment, joint research ventures, diplomatic visits by heads of state, and much else bound them together. South Korea developed strong business connections to the Persian Gulf, pioneering another new strand of the Global web.

Conclusion

Decolonization resulted from the weakening of the imperial powers and the rising strength of colonized populations. The big colonial empires teetered under the impacts of World War II. Whether defeated in war or merely enfeebled by it, Japan, France, Britain, and the Netherlands could not easily continue as colonial powers after 1945. Colonial populations made it too hard to continue by building better political organizations and in some cases acquiring new military skills. During the third big pulse of decolonization in modern history, between 1945 and 1975, some 100 new countries were born.

Decolonization prepared the way for the rise of East Asia. The defeat of Japan's empire enabled it to integrate into the global economy, and gave South Korea and Taiwan their chance to engineer their own economic miracles. Singapore remained a poor and ragged place when it acquired independence in 1965, but it achieved a similar economic surge soon thereafter. China's economic transformation owed much to the examples of Singapore, Taiwan, and South Korea, and at least as much to the end of empire and the subsequent liberalization of global trade and investment flows. Without decolonization, the rise of East Asia would have come much more slowly, if at all.

A new architecture of the international system, shaped by the outcomes of World War II and the ongoing Cold War, also favored the rise of East Asia. First, peace prevailed in the region after 1953. Second, the United States provided a security umbrella for Japan, South Korea, and Taiwan, and most of the time they happily accepted it. The U.S. government underwrote a liberal economic order in which the East Asian tigers could export to American markets even if their own markets were protected. Third, after Mao and Nixon defrosted China-U.S. relations in the early 1970s, even communist China could, and shortly did, enter the liberal economic order. These developments proved highly favorable for trade and investment flows in and out of East Asia.

Decolonization and the rise of East Asia are much more significant for the early twenty-first century than the rise or fall of any single state or empire since 1960—even the fall of the USSR. They represent fundamental shifts in the international order and the distribution of wealth and power around the world.

|||||||||||||||||||||||||||||||||||||||||||||||||||||||||||||||||||||||||||||||||||||||||||||||||||||||||||||||||||||||||||||||||||||||||||||||||||

Chapter Review

KEY TERMS

third pulse of decolonization p. 1092

Jawaharlal Nehru p. 1094

Muslim League p. 1094

Sukarno p. 1095

Kwame Nkrumah p. 1098

Algerian war for independence p. 1101

Asian tiger economies p. 1106

demographic dividend p. 1106

containerization p. 1106

keiretsu p. 1110

land reform p. 1112

Great Leap Forward p. 1115

Deng Xiaoping p. 1117

Minamata disease p. 1122

REVIEW QUESTIONS

1. What two sudden shifts in world balances of power emerged after World War II?

2. How and why did power relations between the colonized and colonizers change after World War II?

3. What were the short- and long-term outcomes of the partition of British India?

4. How and why did the United States support Sukarno and Indonesian independence?

5. Explain why Ghana's transition to independence was peaceful.

6. Why did Charles de Gaulle decide to quit the Algerian war for independence?

7. What was the consequence of former colonies keeping colonial borders?

8. Identify the common demographic, technological, and global economic factors that led to the economic success of East Asia.

9. How did the *keiretsu* contribute to the Japanese economic miracle?

10. What social changes facilitated South Korea's economic surge?

11. Discuss the economic consequences of the Great Proletarian Cultural Revolution.

12. What chief agricultural and economic policies did Deng Xiaoping introduce?

13. Identify and explain the main environmental and social problems associated with rapid industrialization.

14. What international developments favored the rise of East Asia?

Go to **INQUIZITIVE**

....

to see what you've learned—and learn what you've missed—with personalized feedback along the way.

A Shrinking World

GLOBALIZATION SINCE 1980

FOCUS QUESTIONS

1. What major environmental changes have become evident in recent decades?

2. How have population trends and public health interacted since 1980?

3. What major developments have occurred in global politics since 1980?

4. What major changes has the global economy undergone since 1980?

5. How have music and sports reflected the intense globalization of the period?

6. What limits to global integration have become evident in recent decades?

Wangari Maathai was persistent. Born in 1940 in a farming village in the central highlands of Kenya, a British colony at the time, she started school at age eight. A good student, she mastered English, won a scholarship to attend high school, and was selected in 1960 as one of 300 young Kenyans to study in the United States. After studying biology at a small Catholic women's college in Kansas, she won another scholarship for graduate work at the University of Pittsburgh, where she grew interested in grassroots movements to combat the Steel City's notorious air pollution. After further study in Germany and at the University of Nairobi, in 1971 she became the first woman in the history of East Africa to earn a PhD.

Maathai embarked on an academic career in Nairobi while raising a family, but she was drawn to grassroots environmental activism. In her analysis, environmental problems such as soil erosion and water contamination underlay Kenya's economic and social ills. She established the Green Belt Movement in 1976, which encouraged women to stand up for their rights and for the environment. She objected when Kenya's

CHRONOLOGY

1961 Amnesty International is founded

1964 Beginning of worldwide TV broadcasts of Olympics

1970s Eradication of smallpox

1971 Médecins Sans Frontières (Doctors without Borders) is founded

1973 End of Bretton Woods system of currency and debt management

1977 Likud Party rises to power in Israel

1979 Iranian Revolution

1980s HIV/AIDS pandemic begins

1986 Overthrow of Ferdinand Marcos

1988 Intergovernmental Panel on Climate Change is founded; Osama bin Laden founds al-Qaeda

1991 Launch of Women's World Cup of soccer

1992 Hindu extremists destroy Babri mosque

1994 South Africa ends apartheid

1996 Rise of the Taliban

1997 Kyoto Protocol

1998 Indonesia ends military rule

2001 Vladimir Putin ends democracy in Russia

Sept. 11, 2001 Terrorist attacks in New York, Virginia, and Pennsylvania

2002 Islamist party in Turkey wins election

2003 U.S. invasion of Iraq

autocratic president proposed to build a skyscraper with a giant statue of himself in a public park. Police beat and arrested her more than once. The president said she should behave like a proper African woman, respect men, and be quiet. But she persisted.

The Green Belt Movement eventually planted 30 million trees in Kenya. A figure of national and international prominence, **Wangari Maathai** was elected to Kenya's parliament in 2002, and two years later she was awarded the Nobel Peace Prize. Before her death in 2011, she had garnered 15 honorary degrees and nearly 50 public service awards in 11 countries. She raised funds all over the world for the Green Belt Movement and for women's rights in Africa. Wangari Maathai operated—skillfully and persistently—within a Global web of educational, environmental, and fundraising communities.

The main themes in this chapter are the scale and pace of contemporary environmental change, the ongoing—but imperiled—golden age of human health and longevity, and the meanings of globalization for politics, economics, and culture. In many respects, the strands of the Global

Wangari Maathai The successful leader of the Green Belt Movement was also a strong proponent of women's rights in Africa.

web since 1980 have grown thicker and stronger, carrying more goods, ideas, data, and microbes than ever before—and at faster speeds. That is a shared human experience, but everyone lived it—and lives it—differently.

2006 Shakira and Wyclef Jean record best-selling song (to date) of twenty-first century

2007–2009 Great Recession

2011 Arab Spring

2016 Paris Agreement

2019 COVID-19 pandemic begins

Some 400 years ago, the English adventurer, politician, and historian Sir Walter Raleigh observed that "Whosoever is writing a modern History, shall follow truth too neare the heeles, it may haply strike out his teeth." This chapter enters the treacherous terrain of contemporary history. It is easy to know what happened in recent decades but hard to know what it means. The Bantu migration, the rise of the Mughal Empire, and the Meiji Restoration happened long enough ago that their consequences have worked themselves out. With a little effort, we can hope to know what they meant and mean for today. But we can't yet know the full significance of recent events or how ongoing trends will unfold. What seems important now may seem superficial in years to come, and what now seems trivial might loom large. Treacherous terrain indeed, but no reason to shy away from trying to understand the human experience.

Environmental Change: Into the Anthropocene?

According to geologists, the Earth for the last 11,700 years has been in an epoch called the Holocene (from the ancient Greek for "wholly recent"). But since 2000, increasing numbers of scientists have argued that the Holocene is over and a new interval of geological time has begun. They call it the **Anthropocene**, to highlight the role of humankind (*anthropos* in Greek) in changing big natural systems, including global climate. Most earth scientists who embrace the concept of the Anthropocene think it began in the middle of the twentieth century.

It is important to bear two points in mind here. First, the Earth's natural systems have always been changing. So, for example, the Earth's climate over the past 3 billion years has undergone ice ages that come and go as a result of regular changes in the Earth's orbit. So the mere fact of change to the Earth's natural systems is nothing new. What is new, as we shall see, is the scale and pace of change in the recent past, and what lies behind it.

Second, humans have been causing major environmental changes mainly by accident. The concept of the Anthropocene does not mean that humans now control the global environment. Far from it. We influence the global environment, now more than ever, but mainly in ways no one intends and no one fully understands. The Anthropocene is an age of unintended consequences.

Climate Change and Climate Politics

Earth's climate is affected by many variables, including changes in the Earth's orbit, how much energy the sun emits, and how well the atmosphere traps heat. Climate has never been changeless. But in the past 30 to 40 years it has been changing faster than at any other time in human history.

The main reason for the current pulse of **climate change** is that the atmosphere now traps heat from the sun more efficiently than it has for the last 3 million years. That is a consequence of rising concentrations of the gases that do the trapping, called greenhouse gases, the most important of which is **carbon dioxide** (CO_2). Air bubbles trapped in polar icecaps show that for the entire human career—some 300,000 years—carbon dioxide levels in the atmosphere have ranged between 180 and 280 parts per million (ppm). For the past 12,000 years, carbon dioxide concentrations fluctuated a little bit on either side of 280 ppm. That made for unusually stable climate by the standards of the last few million years.

After 1840 or so, CO_2 concentrations slowly climbed above 280 ppm. The causes lay in the Industrial Revolution and the burning of fossil fuels and, to a lesser extent, the extension of agriculture and the burning of forests. For a century, the impact on climate was tiny.

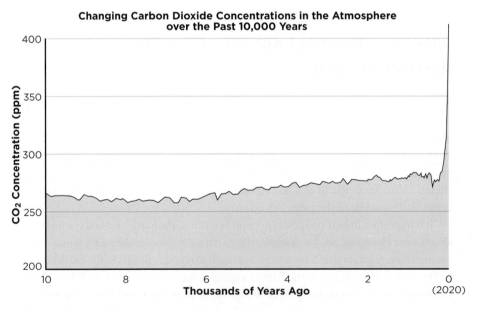

Through most of human history, the amount of atmospheric CO_2—the main greenhouse gas that helps to regulate climate—was fairly stable. The Industrial Revolution in the nineteenth century and the widespread adoption of fossil fuels in the twentieth ended that age of stability. Since 1950 or so, the atmosphere has been changing faster than at any time in many millions of years.

Source: Scripps Institution of Oceanography and NOAA.

Then, after 1950 or so, fossil fuel combustion around the world took off. By 1960, the CO_2 level had climbed to 315 ppm and by 2020 it topped 417 ppm (see the graph on the previous page), a level not previously touched in 3 million years and not consistently topped in 16 million years. At 2 ppm per year, the current rate of increase in atmospheric CO_2 levels is roughly 10 times faster than ever before—as far as we know. But there have been times in the deep past (about 500 million years ago, long before any mammals existed) when CO_2 levels stood much higher than today's, and the Earth was a lot hotter. We know about CO_2 concentrations in the past from measurements taken since 1958 on Mauna Loa, a Hawaiian mountain, and before that from air bubbles trapped in ice cores taken from Greenland and Antarctica.

Burning billions of tons of carbon every year amounts to a gigantic unintentional experiment on the planet. It has helped power machinery that allowed billions of people to enjoy more comfortable lives. But together with other greenhouse gases, the added carbon in the atmosphere has also raised average temperatures on Earth by about 2 degrees Fahrenheit (1.1 degree Celsius) since widespread temperature measurement began in the 1880s. As is evident in the graph below, most of that warming took place after 1980. It has also raised sea level by about 11 inches (28 cm) since 1880, because warmer air temperatures melt glacial ice and warmer sea temperatures expand the

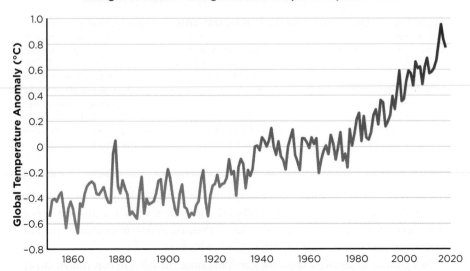

Changes in Global Average Surface Temperature, 1850–2018

This chart of global average surface temperature shows a strong warming trend from the 1850s to the present, especially pronounced since 1980. This warming trend is occurring far faster than any known in the deeper past. The main cause of the warming measured here is the atmospheric carbon dioxide trend shown in the figure on page 1130.

Source: Land data prepared by Berkeley Earth and combined with ocean data adapted from the UK Hadley Centre.

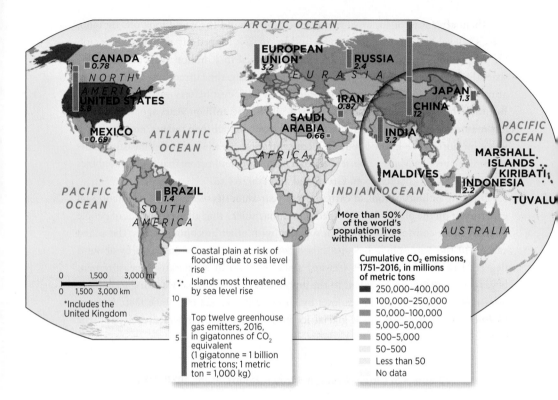

Climate Change: Emissions and Sea Level Rise, 1751–2016 The international politics of climate change is complicated by the fact that the countries most responsible over centuries for the buildup of greenhouse gases—carbon dioxide being the most important—are not necessarily the same as those now emitting the most greenhouse gases. The United States now releases far less greenhouse gas than China, but over time has emitted far more. In addition, the countries most likely to suffer from ongoing climate change are often those with low emissions such as Egypt, Bangladesh, Mozambique, Vietnam, or the Maldives—all of which have densely populated areas just above sea level. The key to the future of climate change lies in South, Southeast, and East Asia, where half of humankind lives, tens of millions are at risk of sea level rise, and greenhouse gas emissions are rising rapidly.

oceans' volume. The extra carbon also seeps into seawater, making it more acidic— about 30 percent more since 1800. Over the last 500 million years, oceans have grown notably more acidic about 30 times. On four of these occasions, more than 75 percent of marine animal species went extinct.

This gigantic experiment upon the Earth has since the 1980s drawn climate issues into politics. One issue was the validity of the science that points overwhelmingly to human-caused climate change. In some societies, notably Russia, the United States, and Australia, constituencies developed that encouraged some politicians either to deny the existence of climate change or, if they accepted it, to deny that humans had a role in it. In most of the world, however, these arguments got nowhere in the face of strong evidence and near-unanimous consensus among scientists. Only in countries where the fossil fuel industry was politically powerful did the existence of rapid climate change become controversial.

The second focus of climate politics was on what to do internationally about rising temperatures and greenhouse gas levels. Most nations contended that others should burn less carbon. Chinese diplomats, for example, noted correctly that the United States and Europe had burned more fossil fuels over the past 200 years than anyone else, and, the Chinese argued, should therefore reduce their carbon emissions first. American diplomats noted, also correctly, that Chinese CO_2 emissions (as of about 2013) were the highest in the world, and they argued that China should curtail its emissions. Poorer countries argued that they needed to burn more fossil fuel energy in order to escape poverty and should be exempt from any reductions in carbon emissions. Such differences proved hard to reconcile, resulting in the trends shown in the graphs on pages 1130 and 1131. The major international agreements that sought to slow climate change—the Kyoto Protocol of 1997 and the Paris Agreement of 2016—had no visible effect on carbon dioxide levels. The U.S. government chose not to ratify Kyoto and withdrew from the Paris Agreement, refusing to accept restrictions on its greenhouse gas emissions—a position that undermined both agreements.

Environmental Turbulence

Climate change was only one of several global environmental concerns that emerged in the late twentieth century. Biologists documented rapidly accelerating rates of animal and plant extinctions. Over the long history of life on Earth, on average about one in every million species has gone extinct each year. By the early twenty-first century, that annual rate had climbed to several hundred, perhaps several thousand, suggesting that life on Earth was entering a sixth spasm of mass extinction. The previous one, about 66 million years ago, led to the disappearance of dinosaurs. The sixth one, if it is indeed that, is in its early stages and its consequences thus far remain modest. The driving force behind the acceleration of extinction is destruction of habitat, notably tropical forests, which are rich in species diversity. Vigorous efforts at species conservation dating from the 1960s have rescued some creatures, such as whooping cranes, California condors, and grizzly bears—at least for now.

Other acute environmental issues affected people more directly than the loss of species. For example, after the 1980s over-fishing brought several of the world's economically important fisheries, such as the North Atlantic cod or Atlantic bluefin tuna, to the point of collapse, depriving fisherfolk of their livelihoods. Air pollution in hundreds of cities reached levels sufficient to kill millions of people every year, especially in India, China, and elsewhere that people breathed too much coal soot into their lungs.

Most of these environmental issues were more difficult to address politically than technologically. Reducing air pollution, for example, proved feasible in cities in Western Europe, Japan, and North America once citizen activism, between 1965 and 1980, produced enough political will to nudge public policy toward tighter regulations. But in many cases, political will remained weak. Some environmental problems, such as climate change or the accumulation of plastics in the oceans' food webs, were slow-brewing, so that ignoring them for another year or two seemed unlikely to make matters much worse. Moreover, the economic activities behind environmental problems produced winners as well as losers, and winners fought to preserve their gains. Thus coal miners and coal companies checked regulation of carbon emissions. Fishermen fought regulations on fishing—even if it meant their catch would shrink with each passing year.

Although it is hard to say what all this global environmental flux may mean in the long run, we can be sure of a few things. First, while human-caused environmental change is not new, the pace, scale, and scope of it in the last couple of human generations are unique. Second, global averages, whether of temperature, biodiversity loss, or the reduction in fish stocks, don't reveal much about specific places. Arctic regions, for example, have warmed far more than the tropics in the past 30 years. The collapse of the Atlantic cod fishery in the early 1990s brought bitter consequences for people living in Newfoundland, while the global marine fish catch has held steady since 1980 at about 75 million tons annually. Hundreds of millions of people within reach of tropical storms in places such as the Philippines, Bangladesh, or the Caribbean had to face more frequent and larger typhoons, cyclones, and hurricanes. Meanwhile, the hundreds of thousands of people who live in northern Siberia, Scandinavia, Greenland, Canada, and Alaska experienced longer growing seasons and much milder winters.

Just why the world became so environmentally turbulent over the last 70 years is easy to explain. Many factors contributed, among them culture. Most people around the world clung to, or adopted, a culture of consumption, preferring more clothes, more furniture, more travel—more of just about everything. Cultural traditions such as Buddhism or Christianity, which historically had associated virtue and godliness with poverty and asceticism, proved extremely flexible in this regard. So did the Chinese Communist Party, which in the 1950s had trumpeted poor peasants as the most admirable of classes, but after 1980, as we've seen, converted to the gospel of wealth. In India, Gandhi's emphasis on simplicity lost out to a political culture that idolized industry, wealth, and power. Bhutan, a tiny kingdom high in the Himalaya, formed an exception: there the government since 2008 tried to measure, and to maximize, gross national happiness rather than gross national product.

Politics reinforced the impact of culture. Neither elected officials nor dictators thought asking anyone to consume less was good politics. Moreover, leaders concerned with national security normally thought a wealthier society would help fund a bigger military, which would make everyone safer. Rulers for 5,000 years had thought the same way. But now the consequences were different.

Energy Use since 1975 (in millions of tons of oil equivalent)						
	WORLD	United States	China	Japan	India	Egypt
1975	5,762	1,698	337	329	82	10
1995	8,545	2,117	917	489	236	38
2015	13,105	2,276	3,006	446	685	87

Source: BP Statistical Review of World Energy, various years.

At the same time as these notions of consumption and security prevailed, an enormous expansion in energy use made mass consumption much easier. We last looked at energy in the chapter on the Industrial Revolution, which emphasized the transition to fossil fuels. As late as 1960, however, that transition was mainly confined to North America, Europe, and Japan. Since then, the continuing rise of energy-intensive activities, such as motor vehicle use or the production of nitrogen-based fertilizer, has changed the picture. The world's vehicle fleet (cars, buses, trucks), for example, grew from 250 million in 1970 to 1.2 billion by 2015. Nitrogen fertilizer use rose sevenfold between 1961 and 2020. As the table above shows, the total quantity of energy used globally more than doubled between 1975 and 2015. China, India, and Egypt by 2015 used eight or nine times their 1975 totals.

About 80 percent of this surge in energy use came in the form of fossil fuels. So this global trend led to considerable increases in urban air pollution, especially in India and China. It also led to more oil spills—notably in the oilfields of Siberia and Nigeria, and in the world's shipping lanes, where tankers occasionally ran aground or broke up in storms. And, as noted above, the increased use of fossil fuels elevated CO_2 concentrations in the atmosphere, warming the Earth.

Population Trends since 1950

Population growth was another powerful driving force behind environmental change and much else in recent decades. We last looked at the subject in Chapter 23 in the context of the Vital Revolution, which carried the story up to 1950.

Population and Public Health

The population history of planet Earth since 1950 is unique, although almost everyone alive has known nothing else and so considers it normal. In the span of one human lifetime (1950–2020), global population more than tripled, from 2.5 billion to 7.8 billion, growing at well over 1 percent per year. For the previous 10,000 years, the annual

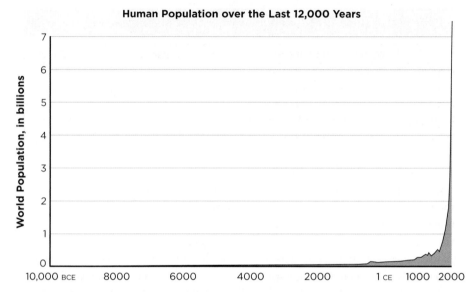

Human Population over the Last 12,000 Years

This chart shows the size of the human population over the past 12,000 years. It reached 1 billion around 1820 and 2 billion by 1930. Since 1960, it has grown by 1 billion every 12 or 15 years. Although the rate of growth is now slowing, the record of the recent past through to the present is an extreme departure from the pattern of the longer past.

Source: World Population Data from the United Nations, the U.S. Census Bureau, and others, found at https://en.wikipedia.org/wiki/Estimates_of_historical_world_population#/media/File:Population_curve.svg

rate was closer to 0.05 percent. Put another way, two-thirds of the population growth in all 300,000 years of human history took place after 1950. We now outnumber any other large mammal on Earth, and we account for about 5 percent of the globe's animal biomass (although ants easily outweigh us—because there are so many of them). The graph above shows how peculiar the last few decades are in light of longer patterns.

The key to this unique development has been better public health programs since 1945. One way to think of it is that humankind invented and adopted effective "death control" measures before we adopted much birth control. It began in the nineteenth century but took a giant stride forward in World War II when medical personnel figured out how to administer vaccines and antibiotics to large military populations. After 1945, similar techniques applied more broadly reduced mortality, especially for infants and children, especially in Asia, Africa, and Latin America. A glorious landmark came in the late 1970s, when international health teams wiped out smallpox, ridding the human race of one of its greatest killers. Even when we count deaths caused by the COVID-19 pandemic, the global death rate in 2020 stood at less than half the 1950 rate, mainly through reductions in infectious diseases such as measles, smallpox, and typhoid. Average life expectancy around the world exceeded 71 years. In almost every country except India, women outlived men.

The surge in life expectancy—one of the signal social changes of recent history—was a global phenomenon achieved mainly by the quick spread of new vaccines, anti-bacterial drugs, and public health measures. But improved nutrition and a rollback of famines also helped. More fertilizers and irrigation, better crop breeding and weather forecasting, and a host of other changes to agriculture enabled the global food supply to grow even faster than global population. In addition, better transport enabled people to move food faster to places where it was in short supply. All these changes reduced the frequency and size of killing famines. While hundreds of millions of people remained persistently malnourished, after the 1980s mass starvation occurred only in war zones and the hermit country of North Korea.

Estimated Life Expectancy in 2020

	YEARS		YEARS
Japan	85	Mexico	75
Switzerland	83	Egypt	72
Australia	83	Russia	72
New Zealand	82	Indonesia	72
Greece	82	India	69
United Kingdom	81	Pakistan	67
		Haiti	64
United States	79	South Africa	64
China	77	Uganda	63
Vietnam	76	Nigeria	54
Brazil	76	Central African	
Jamaica	75	Republic	53

Source: United Nations Development Program data, found at https://en.wikipedia.org/wiki/List_of_countries_by_life_expectancy

The consequences of improved public health and food supply played out differently around the world. Richer, more stable countries could provide the means of death control more thoroughly than could poorer or unstable countries, as the table above suggests. Lives are briefest in Africa, which accounts for 32 of the 33 countries with the shortest life expectancy. Even the poorest and most unstable countries, however, now have life expectancies almost twice as long as the richest places in the world two centuries ago.

Counter-Currents in Public Health: Emerging Diseases

Recognition of this golden age of human health and longevity should not overshadow some grim exceptions. In the former Soviet Union, especially Russia and Ukraine, life expectancy fell in the 1990s mainly because of illnesses associated with alcohol and smoking. It has rebounded since. In the United States, where overall life expectancy crept upward after 2000, it fell for the middle-aged white male population through suicides, alcoholism, and drug overdoses—so-called deaths of despair. It has not yet rebounded.

New infectious diseases also imperiled the golden age of human health. The viruses that caused AIDS in the 1980s, SARS in 2003, MERS in 2012, and COVID-19 beginning in 2019 all mutated and leapt successfully from animal to human populations. As more people brushed up against wild and domestic animals more frequently, they gave viruses more opportunity to evolve so as to survive in human bodies. **HIV/AIDS**, genomic evidence tells us, was an infection of chimpanzees until the 1940s, when it first became a human infection. It did not spread much until the 1980s, when growing connectivity within Africa enabled it to travel farther and faster, igniting a global pandemic that took some 30 million lives as of 2020. HIV/AIDS was much worse in Africa than elsewhere. In South Africa, for example, it shortened average life expectancy by about 10 years from 1990 to 2005. (It has rebounded, thanks to medical interventions.) SARS and MERS had killed fewer than 1,000 each as of 2020.

The so-called novel coronavirus (SARS CoV-2), which causes the disease COVID-19, apparently lived only in bat colonies until late in 2019. It mutated into a human pathogen in or near Wuhan in central China and spread quickly around the world, causing another global pandemic and killing hundreds of thousands. To prevent far greater death tolls, people worldwide adopted social distancing to slow the virus's spread, which seriously damaged the inter-connected world economy.

The devastating health impact of **COVID-19** was the result of four conditions. First, the pathogen itself is easily transmitted from human to human. For days before showing symptoms, infected people shed virus with every breath, cough, or sneeze. Normal gatherings, such as weddings, concerts, or religious services, could create clusters of infection anywhere. Second, nobody carried any resistance or immunity to the disease, because it was new to humans. Third, air travel moved so many people so far and so fast that they carried the virus out of central China to every other country

within two months. About 13 million people flew in airplanes every day in 2019—about 16 times the daily air traffic in 1970. And fourth, the world's public health systems were—like individual immune systems—unprepared for what hit them. The main exceptions were effectively governed countries such as Costa Rica, South Korea, Vietnam, New Zealand, Jamaica, and Iceland. Partly because of their experience of either SARS or MERS, South Korea, Singapore, and Hong Kong took COVID-19 seriously weeks or months sooner than other countries, and they escaped the first wave with minimal mortality. National leaders in China, Western Europe, Brazil, and the United States, in contrast, reacted only after the virus had already spread widely within their countries, and their populations—indeed, the entire human population—paid a price for that.

Viral Epidemics COVID-19 patients fill a temporary hospital erected in a sports center in Wuhan, China, in February 2020. Wuhan was at the center of the first outbreak of COVID-19, when the virus that causes the illness made the jump from bats to humans.

Whether or not these newly emerging infectious diseases mark the end of the golden age of human health, or a temporary setback, it is too soon to say. None of them equaled the 1918 influenza, which killed perhaps 50 million people worldwide. But more new diseases are sure to come, because humans so frequently are in contact with animals such as bats and rodents that harbor an immense variety of viruses. And when new diseases are highly infectious, even in people showing no symptoms, as with COVID-19, they will spread around the world in days or weeks, because air travelers course throughout the Global web every day.

Fertility Declines

Regardless of the impact of emerging diseases, the anomalous moment of supercharged population growth after 1950 is now slowing because birth control is catching up to death control. The rate of population growth reached its maximum in the 1960s, briefly exceeding 2 percent per year. It now stands at 1.1 percent per year, because birth rates have fallen almost everywhere. By 2019, roughly three out of every four women of reproductive age around the world used some form of birth control. About 140 million babies were born that year (and about 55 million people died).

The main reasons behind the downward fertility trend were urbanization and the spread of formal education for females. On average, women with more education prefer not to have large families, and couples living in cities want smaller families than do their country cousins. The places where fertility did not fall much—Afghanistan and parts of Africa, mainly—are places where urbanization and formal education for females made little headway in the past 70 years.

The **declines in fertility** around the world amount to an enormous change in the lives of families and women in particular. Adult women came to spend far less of their lives pregnant, and a good deal less time attending to the needs of small children than their mothers and grandmothers had done. Instead, they spent much more time in school and working in factories and offices. Each trend—lower fertility and time spent outside the home—reinforced the other.

Humans grew bigger as well as more numerous after 1950. The greatest changes came in East Asia, southern Europe, and the Baltic countries. South Koreans topped the list, growing 7 to 9 inches (18–23 cm) taller on average between 1950 and 2015, an indication of better diets especially among the poor. A few populations, mainly in Africa, have not grown taller since 1950. Egyptians and Ugandans, because of malnutrition, have been shrinking since 1990.

On average, people grew heavier as well as taller. More sedentary lifestyles and more food have caused the average person to gain weight in just about every country since 1980. In the United States, the average adult in 2015 weighed 15 lbs. (7 kg) more than in 1990. Taking both height and weight together, the average human has expanded in size far faster in the past 50 years than ever before.

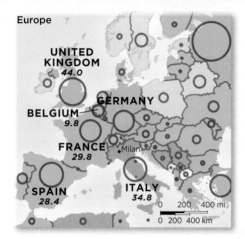

Europe

UNITED KINGDOM
44.0

GERMANY

BELGIUM
9.8

FRANCE
29.8
•Milan

SPAIN
28.4

ITALY
34.8

0   200   400 mi
0 200 400 km

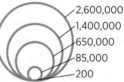

Reported cases and deaths, by July 1, 2020

Number of reported cases, by country

2,600,000
1,400,000
650,000
85,000
200

34.8 12 countries with the highest number reported of deaths, in thousands

29.5 10 states of the United States with the highest number of reported deaths, in thousands

See inset

To New York City

Milan

RUSSIA
9.5

EURASIA

TURKEY

IRAN
11.0
PAKISTAN

EGYPT
SAUDI
ARABIA

INDIA
17.4
Bangkok

Beijing
CHINA   Seoul

Wuhan

JAPAN

TAIWAN

AFRICA

INDIAN OCEAN

PACIFIC OCEAN

ATLANTIC
OCEAN

SOUTH
AFRICA

AUSTRALIA

NEW ZEALAND

Questions for Analysis

Based on this feature and your chapter reading, consider the following questions:

1. How did the COVID-19 pandemic reveal connections between your life and the Global web?

2. Did the public health emergency of COVID-19 show the need for stronger national and global coordination of response measures or more local autonomy? Explain your response.

The COVID-19 Pandemic

KEY

 Initial spread of infection from Wuhan, China, January 1– 31, 2020. Arrow thickness indicates approximate number of travellers.

● City with recorded outbreak, by January 31, 2020

Stay-at-home requirements in place, by March 24, 2020

▨ Required, with virtually no exceptions

▨ Required, except for daily exercise, food shopping, and essential trips

☐ Recommended

☐ None

☐ No data

CANADA

NORTH AMERICA

IL 7.1
MI 6.2
MA 8.1
From Italy

Seattle

UNITED STATES
125.2

New York

CT 4.3
NY 29.5
NJ 15.0
PA 6.6
LA 3.2
FL 3.7

CA 6.0

MEXICO
27.8

ATLANTIC OCEAN

BRAZIL
59.6

PERU
9.7

SOUTH AMERICA

0   1000   2000 mi
0 1000 2000 km

CHILE

LATE IN 2019, A CORONAVIRUS new to humans burst upon the world, causing a disease called COVID-19 in those infected. The outbreak began in Wuhan, a provincial capital in central China, and spread rapidly within the country aided by travel at the Chinese New Year. The virus then spread around the world and grew to pandemic proportions. By July 1, 2020, global agencies had recorded about 10 million confirmed cases and half a million deaths from COVID-19, with the numbers continuing to rise. The stay-at-home and shut-down orders adopted in many countries and large cities shook the global economy.

The pandemic was entangled in the Global web in three main ways. First, the virus itself moved along every pathway of the Global web. It spread by jet from China to the hubs of the world's airline systems in cities such as Milan, London, and New York. From the hubs it eventually traveled out to every city and town of any size everywhere in the world.

Second, information about the virus and how to combat it spread at electronic speed throughout the Global web. The virus was formally identified in China on January 7, 2020, and its genome was published on the Internet on January 10. Scientists around the world collaborated in the effort to find effective drugs and a vaccine. Strategies for slowing the virus, such as social distancing, stay-at-home requirements, and the use of face coverings, also spread almost instantly, although authorities often delayed implementation at the cost of many thousands of lives.

Finally, the necessary measures to slow the virus resulted in economic hardship wherever web connections were strong. Tens of millions of people lost jobs and billions lost income. The COVID-19 pandemic led to more economic pain than the far deadlier 1918 flu pandemic because economic globalization was stronger in 2020 than in 1918. The world economy in 2020 was built on dense and active international supply chains, trade, and travel. These strong global connections made the world economy more vulnerable to interruption than at any earlier time in world history.

Urbanization in Overdrive

While humans have been growing more numerous, and on average bigger, we have also become primarily urban animals. For most of the last 10,000 years, the typical human habitat was the farming village. A century ago, only about 10 to 15 percent of the world's people lived in cities. By 1950 that figure reached 29 percent, and by 2020 some 55 percent of people were city-dwellers, about 4.2 billion in all.

Big cities got bigger. In 1800, only one, Beijing, had more than 1 million inhabitants. By 1950, there were about 70, led by New York, London, Tokyo, and Moscow. By 2015, some 540 cities reached the 1 million threshold, and 39 of those had more than 10 million people. The biggest were in Asia: Tokyo, Jakarta, Seoul, Karachi, Shanghai, and Manila all counted more than 24 million in their metro areas.

Two trends drove this spurt of accelerating urbanization. First, city life stopped killing people quite so fast. Until about 1880, cities everywhere were so unhealthy that their residents died at faster rates than new ones were born. Cities survived only because villagers moved in looking for better lives. Between 1880 and about 1950, cities around the world became healthy enough that their birth rates came to exceed their death rates. That happy trend grew stronger after 1950. Meanwhile, streams of migration from the countryside swelled to torrents: population growth and land shortages in the villages drove young people to seek their futures in cities. The largest and fastest urbanization in world history took place in China after 1980.

Migrants from village to city rarely had it easy. Carolina María de Jesus moved from a Brazilian village to the metropolis of São Paulo and lived in its shantytowns (called *favelas* in Brazil) for several decades. She had only a second-grade education and struggled to make a living as a single mother, protect her three children from violence, and avoid falling into the despair that claimed so many of her neighbors. She kept a diary,

Favelas Houses built from scrap wood line a hillside in 1950s Rio de Janeiro. *Favelas*, or shantytowns, became sites of poverty and overcrowding in rapidly urbanizing Brazil.

translated as *Child of the Dark*, which gives an unsparing picture of *favela* life in the late 1950s with its daily fare of domestic violence, alcoholism, jealous gossip, and the constant struggle to put food on the table—which she did by selling paper she scavenged from garbage heaps. Hundreds of millions of women around the world lived similar lives after leaving their native villages for the slums of Bangkok, Nairobi, or Lima.

Another who went to the big city to better himself is the uncle of one of my students. Alim (not his real name) was born in 1960 in a village in what was then East Pakistan, now Bangladesh. He spent his early years in a corrugated tin hut. His life changed when he was sent to live with a relative whose village had a school. He loved school, did well in it, and began to win scholarships—as Wangari Maathai did. He kept winning them and studied electrical engineering at a polytechnic institute. That allowed Alim to get a job helping the government build an electrical grid in rural Bangladesh. In the 1980s he tried his hand at business, distributing fertilizer, but ended up in debt. In the 1990s he moved to the capital, Dhaka, seeking better opportunities because he now had a family to feed. They stayed in the countryside while Alim, feeling lonely and economically insecure, worked in Dhaka. Hundreds of millions of men around the world found themselves in similar predicaments, able to make a better living in the big city than in their native village but unable to support their families comfortably.

In Australia, Argentina, Japan, and a few smaller countries, more than 90 percent of people live in cities. In the United States, 82 percent do. But in South Asia and sub-Saharan Africa, only a third of the people live in cities, although cities there are growing fast. Across the globe, urban population is growing at about twice the rate of total population, a little above 2 percent annually.

It is still too soon to tell the full meaning of this overnight urbanization of the human species. It has contributed to lowering fertility—a social revolution in and of itself. It has also helped raise levels of education, because providing such services is easier where people are close together. On average, it has made people slightly richer. But it surely has also made them more acutely aware of inequality, as rich and poor live close together. And it has created opportunities for infectious diseases, such as COVID-19, to flourish in tightly packed neighborhoods.

International Migration

The movement of hundreds of millions from village to city was not the only important migratory flow in recent decades. In 1980, some 100 million people lived in a country other than where they were born. In 2019, roughly 270 million people, or 3.5 percent of humankind, did so. About 10 percent were officially refugees who fled war or persecution. The table on the next page shows the five biggest population groups living abroad in 2019.

Largest Populations Living Abroad, 2019	
Indians	18 million
Mexicans	12 million
Chinese	11 million
Russians	10 million
Syrians	8 million

Source: United Nations Department of Social and Economic Affairs, www.un.org/development/desa/en/news/population/international-migrant-stock-2019.html

In 2019, some 51 million **international migrants** lived in the United States, with the next largest totals in Germany and Saudi Arabia, with 13 million each. In 2012, a Gallup poll concluded that 640 million people *wanted* to migrate to another country but couldn't. International migration remains highly restricted. Much of it goes uncounted. Each year since 2010, about 8 to 16 million people have migrated internationally, of whom about one-quarter were going back home.

This surge of migration is best understood in longer context. Between 1840 and 1940, inexpensive, steam-powered transport enabled over 170 million people, mostly young men, to move to another country. They left home for factories in Detroit and Dortmund, for mines in Manchuria and Minnesota, for plantations in Thailand and Trinidad. The number of international migrants peaked in 1913 and again in the late 1920s at a little more than 3 million per year.

Broadly speaking, there were three main currents of migration in the century before 1940. One involved 55 to 60 million people moving to the Americas from Europe and the Middle East. The British Isles, Germany, Italy, Poland, and Russia provided the most emigrants, two-thirds of whom went to the United States and most of the others to Canada, Argentina, or Brazil. A second current featured 45 to 55 million Indians and southern Chinese going to Southeast Asia and other rimlands of the Indian Ocean such as Burma and Ceylon (now Sri Lanka). A third current took 45 to 55 million northern Chinese, Koreans, and Russians to Manchuria or Central Asia. But there were smaller flows too, such as the 2 to 3 million Canadians who migrated to industrial cities in the United States, and a few million from all over southern Africa who went to the mines of South Africa.

After a downturn during the Great Depression and World War II, international migration revived in 1945. The first pulse came in the form of perhaps 10 million war refugees in Europe and East Asia. Then came the flows provoked by decolonization, such as the 10 to 17 million Muslims and Hindus who were uprooted because of the 1947 partition of India.

A more sustained pulse began in the 1960s. Northern European countries, especially West Germany, began to recruit large numbers of supposedly temporary workers from southern Europe and Turkey. Called guest workers, many of them wound up staying for life. Meanwhile the United States, Canada, and Australia changed their immigration rules, which had been overtly racist, opening doors for more migrants from Asia, the Caribbean, and Latin America. And in the 1970s, an oil boom attracted millions of migrants to the Arabian Peninsula, mainly the tiny countries of the Gulf. Most came from South Asia and the Philippines. So, since the 1970s, the main destinations for migrants have been Western Europe, North America, and the Gulf. The numbers of migrants increased a bit after 1990. The dissolution of the USSR led to migrations of ethnic Russians out of several formerly Soviet territories. The booming U.S. economy of the 1990s attracted many job seekers from Mexico and the rest of Latin America.

The share of migrants in the world population in the quarter-century 1990–2015 was about the same as that in 1890–1915. But there were two big differences in the makeup of the migrant populations. In 1890–1915, the great majority of migrants were men, the normal pattern until recently. Since 1990, however, nearly half of all international migrants have been women, mainly because families are likelier to migrate together. In many European countries, a small majority of immigrants are women.

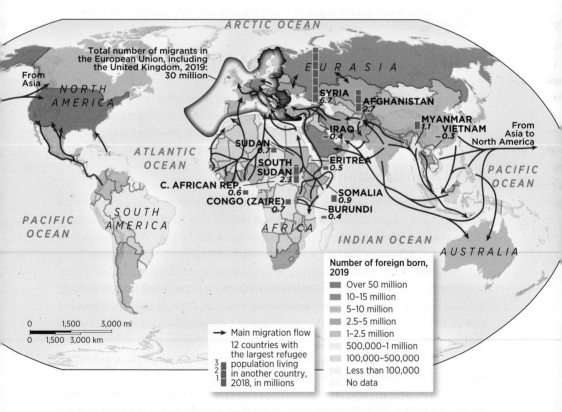

International Migration and Refugee Flows, ca. 2015-2020 The broadest pattern in recent migration history is movement from poor countries to richer ones. Several million people migrated every year in the 2010s, mainly to North America, Europe, the Persian Gulf region, and Australia. Latin Americans went chiefly to the United States; Africans to Europe; East and Southeast Asians to both North America and Australia. Refugees left war-torn lands, especially Syria, Afghanistan, and several countries of central and eastern Africa. Those leaving Myanmar fled religious persecution rather than war.

The other big difference is education. Before 1940, the overwhelming majority of migrants were uneducated. Their skill set was usually confined to what they learned growing up in farming villages. Since 1990, in contrast, roughly 20 percent of migrants brought with them university educations and professional training. This change reflects immigration policy, especially in the United States, Australia, and Canada, which gave preference to people with skills expected to be economically useful. It also results from the more globalized world of multinational corporations, in which business managers from Italy or India might work a few years in Hong Kong, then a few in London or Rio de Janeiro. There is, then, in addition to a majority of migrants who are poor (as before), a sizeable share who are among the world's richest 1 percent.

Migration contributed powerfully to the recent spurt of globalization. Although uneven in impact from place to place, the net effect was to tie the Global web a little tighter, bringing more people into more frequent contact with strangers from afar.

Politics and the Global Web

In the decades since the end of the Cold War (1989), the most important political trends were the rise of China (discussed in Chapter 28), the growing role of international institutions, a revival of religious politics, and a cresting wave of democratization.

International Institutions

Many of the powerful **international institutions** still with us were created in the 1940s as leaders sought to avoid future crises of the sort that had brought on the Great Depression and World War II. The most important were the United Nations and the pair tasked with looking after the world economy—the International Monetary Fund and the World Bank. Some others are a little older, such as Interpol, founded in 1923, which facilitates cooperation among law enforcement agencies around the world. Some are more recent, such as the Intergovernmental Panel on Climate Change, formed in 1988 under the authority of the UN, which reports periodically on all aspects of global climate.

With the rise of problems and challenges that are global in scale, such as international drug trades, human trafficking, and climate change, states around the world came together more often to create such institutions and to rely on them to an unprecedented extent. The United Nations grew particularly active after the end of the Cold War, for example, mounting far more peacekeeping operations than previously, helping to end 21 civil wars between 1991 and 2017.

The UN's peacekeeping record, however, was mixed. UN forces grew from about 20,000 in 1990 to about 100,000, in 2010, mainly provided by the armed forces of South Asian and African countries. While its interventions in Cambodia (1991–1993) and El Salvador (1989–1995) contributed to lasting peace, it failed to prevent genocide in Rwanda, in East Africa, in 1994, or massacres in Bosnia (part of the former Yugoslavia) in 1995. As of 2020, it maintained 14 peacekeeping operations, half of them in Africa. Since the UN, like other international institutions, had no armies, its authority ultimately came from the support of countries—only some of which consistently proved supportive. This problem limited the impact of the UN and at times made people and politicians skeptical of its value.

Also over the last half-century, an increasing number of international nongovernmental organizations emerged to play larger and larger roles. Médecins Sans Frontières (Doctors without Borders) took shape in 1971 as a volunteer group of medical professionals who donated their services, particularly in war-torn areas. Amnesty International, formed in 1961, sought to protect people against governmental abuses. Such outfits, and many like them, gradually became part of the fabric of international affairs. So too (less happily) did criminal cartels, which also responded to global opportunities by internationalizing their businesses—for example, moving cocaine from Peru and Bolivia to high-priced markets in the United States and Europe. In some cases, such as the Russian mafia since the 1990s, international criminal cartels were informally allied with governments. All these organizations and groups arose in response to a more globalized world and by their actions helped to globalize it further.

Revivals of Religious Politics

A second powerful trend around the world was a revival of religious politics. Most societies throughout world history blended political and religious authority together. Religious politics are as old as religion itself. But during the nineteenth and twentieth centuries many states had distanced themselves from formal religion, following a tradition born in the French and American revolutions, both of which put barriers between church and state. Most communist states, including the USSR, China, and Cuba, were officially atheist. But in the 1970s, religious politics made a comeback.

Political Islam The most conspicuous case is the rise of political Islam. Religion had always mattered in the politics of Muslim societies—both Shi'a, who predominated in Iran and Iraq, and Sunni, the majority almost everywhere else. But between the 1920s and 1960s, it mattered less and national and class identities mattered more. Nationalist regimes, often run by military men, held sway in several countries such as Turkey from the 1920s, Egypt from the 1950s, and Algeria after independence in 1962.

By the 1970s, the governments of most Muslim societies struck their citizens as corrupt and ineffective. Despite decades in office, they had failed to live up to promises of social justice or national wealth and power. Religious leaders called for more virtuous, godly, and efficient rule. In Iran, mullahs—meaning Muslims learned in Islamic law and tradition—seized power in a revolution in 1979. They overthrew a monarch whom they regarded, with justification, as corrupt and subservient to foreign powers. They installed an Islamic republic, enforcing a Muslim law code and imposing rules about personal conduct and dress—mainly for women—that they deemed consistent with their religious heritage.

The dominant form of Islamic political revival was party politics. Muslims, like everyone else, had been adapting to electoral systems for decades when the revolution in Iran added to the inspiration of a new generation of politically active Muslims. In Turkey, an Islamic party grew prominent in the 1990s and started winning elections in 2002. It gradually re-asserted the authority of religion in Turkish society, undoing some of the Atatürk revolution of the 1920s that, as we've seen, had built a secular state in Turkey. Islamic parties did well in elections in Algeria, Tunisia, Bangladesh, Indonesia, and elsewhere. They typically promised a more just and godly society, and in particular an end to corruption. They proved adept at providing social services such as food kitchens and support for widows and orphans. They funded school systems intended to instill the teachings of Islam in the young.

In some cases, Islamic politics took extremist, intolerant forms. Religious parties often struggle with notions of compromise and negotiation, because some believers consider any compromise with divine will to be immoral. Several factions claiming to represent the will of Allah in the politics of Islamic societies resorted to terrorist violence. The Taliban in Afghanistan, active since 1996, are a leading example, but many others arose across the Islamic world from Mali to the Philippines. In places where repressive monarchs or military rule quashed all forms of opposition, terrorist tactics seemed— to those who adopted them—the only weapon at their disposal. Most Muslim societies by 2010 had some experience with terrorist factions operating in the name of Islam. The proportion of civil wars around the world that involved an Islamist faction was below 10 percent in the decades before 1990, but thereafter climbed to about 40 percent, where it remains in 2020.

Al-Qaeda Rescue workers remove casualties from the wreckage of the U.S. Embassy in Nairobi, Kenya, following a 1998 al-Qaeda attack that killed more than 200 people. The Nairobi bombing was one of several international terrorist attacks that Osama bin Laden orchestrated in the 1990s and 2000s.

A small proportion of these factions flourished internationally. The most successful was **al-Qaeda** (its name means "the base" in Arabic), begun in 1988 by a charismatic and wealthy Saudi Arabian and Sunni zealot, Osama bin Laden. He acquired his prestige helping to defeat the Soviet army in its war in Afghanistan from 1979 to 1989. He based his ideology of militant jihad—as warfare in the name of Islam is often called—on his selective interpretation of the Qur'an. He promoted the notion of a restored Islamic caliphate and sanctioned violence against Shi'a Muslims and other minorities within Islam, as well as against non-Muslims.

In the 1990s, after the Soviets left Afghanistan, bin Laden turned his sights on new enemies, especially the United States. At that time, the United States had troops stationed in bin Laden's home country. He regarded foreign armies in Saudi Arabia as an intolerable affront and organized anti-American terrorist assaults. He was the paymaster behind the terrorist attacks of September 11, 2001, that killed nearly 3,000 people in New York, in Arlington, Virginia, and in Shanksville, Pennsylvania. Al-Qaeda also flourished in Iraq after an American invasion of that country in 2003, undertaken in the mistaken belief that Iraq had weapons of mass destruction, left it in chaos. Offshoots of al-Qaeda engaged in terrorism, usually targeting other Muslims, in several countries such as Somalia, Syria, and Yemen. American forces killed bin Laden in Pakistan in 2011, but al-Qaeda lived on. Its franchises and affiliates continued to operate in at least 20 countries, sharing funding, training, and propaganda using international banks, air travel, the Internet, and other sinews of the Global web.

Other Religions Like Islam, other major religious traditions after the 1970s served as fuel for political ideologies. In India, for example, organizations promoting various versions of Hindu values grew more active. A political party (the Bharatiya Janata Party, or BJP) devoted to making India more authentically Hindu took shape in the 1980s. Since the 1990s, the BJP has been in and out of power, and always one of the two biggest parties in Indian politics. Its leaders wanted to see India become more forceful in international affairs, especially in its stance toward its Muslim neighbor Pakistan. Many of its members wished to stop Muslim immigrants from entering India. In 1992, Hindu extremists destroyed the old Babri mosque in Ayodhya, in northern India, with the aim of building a temple to the Hindu god Rama on the site. Deadly riots followed. Various Hindu terrorist cells stood behind bombings of mosques, attacks on Christian missionaries, and assaults on representatives of India's secular state. But, as with other cases of religious politics, the primary expression of Hindu political revival was in Indian party politics.

Christianity, especially its Protestant evangelical forms, has also been increasingly enlisted in political struggles since the 1970s. Evangelical Christians in the United States, often motivated by social issues such as the legality of abortion, overcame their traditional distaste for politics. Evangelical Protestantism became a political force in several Latin American countries, such as Brazil and Guatemala, from the 1980s onward. In 1960, the Protestant population of Latin America was tiny, but by 2015 some 15 to 20 percent of Latin Americans considered themselves Protestants, usually Pentecostalists. They typically pressed their governments to restrict abortion and gay marriage. In Africa too, evangelical Protestant faiths acquired many recruits after 1980, and by 2015 they accounted for perhaps 20 to 25 percent of all African Christians. Both Kenya and Zambia elected presidents who identified as evangelical Protestants, and Zambia's, Frederick Chiluba, officially declared his country a Christian nation in the 1990s.

Buddhism too acquired a new political edge. Since 2000, in majority-Buddhist countries such as Thailand, Burma, and Sri Lanka, small groups, sometimes called Buddhist fundamentalists, have organized militant wings that target Muslims and Christians. Many Buddhists in these countries felt that their religion and culture were under threat from foreign values, including those of Islam, Christianity, and the marketplace. They appealed to their governments for laws that would ban uncomplimentary remarks about the Buddha or make it illegal for Buddhist women in Burma to marry anyone of another faith.

Israel, the only country with a Jewish majority, also developed a more religious politics after the 1970s. Officially a Jewish state since its foundation in 1948, its central political issue was that it claimed land—the land of the ancient Hebrews—that Palestinian Arabs regarded as their own. So Israelis had to choose whether to try to co-exist with Palestinians or dominate them, a dilemma complicated by Israel's vulnerability to the often hostile Arab states surrounding it. In its early decades, Israel was led by secular Jews of European background. But in 1977, several religious factions, calling for a more observant society and less compromise with Palestinians, helped put the nationalistic Likud Party in power. Thereafter, religious groups provided crucial support for nationalist parties that consistently did well in elections. What unified them was the wish for a more aggressive policy toward Palestinians and the so-called West Bank, land that the Israeli army conquered in 1967 but that Palestinians—and most of the world—considered theirs. Governments in Israel encouraged Jews to settle in the West Bank, guaranteeing frictions with Palestinians, and used those frictions to justify stricter controls on Palestinians.

Everywhere, globalization created problems that people hoped religion would solve. Some of those problems were economic, and some cultural. The sudden ups and downs of a globalized economy cost many people their economic security. When in distress, they felt grateful for the charity and social support that religious groups typically provided. The rapid urbanization in Latin America and parts of Africa and South Asia uprooted people from their communities, leaving emotional and psychological voids in their lives. Religious groups offered comfort and companionship for those in need. Religion also offered an affirmation of identity and community for those who felt their culture was under siege by strangers with alien values.

Democracy Rising

One of the signal trends of world politics in the late twentieth century was the **spread of democracy**. In 1974, the world had twice as many authoritarian states as liberal democracies. Then, in the mid-1970s, dictatorships in Portugal, Spain, and Greece fell in near-bloodless revolutions that led to durable parliamentary democracies. Between 1978 and 1990, military dictatorships in 11 Latin American countries collapsed and were replaced by democracies. The Iranian Revolution, mentioned above, also replaced an authoritarian monarchy with a parliamentary system. In the Philippines, a popular revolution overthrew a dictator in the late 1980s. In 1989 and 1990, Eastern Europe's communist regimes tumbled down with the Berlin Wall, giving way to much more democratic states. Communist Yugoslavia fragmented in the late 1980s, giving rise to six new republics, two of which, Slovenia and Croatia, built more or less democratic political systems by the late 1990s. In Mexico, what was essentially a one-party system became a more pluralistic multi-party one in the 1990s. South Korea and Taiwan replaced authoritarian regimes with more democratic ones in the 1980s and 1990s. Indonesia ended military rule in 1998. In Africa, where authoritarian rule had become the norm after independence, 13 one-party dictatorships fell in the early 1990s. South Africa in 1994 ended decades of *apartheid* ("separateness"), a political system of democracy for whites only that excluded nearly 90 percent of South Africans. The result—thanks in large part to the commitment of Nelson Mandela, a longtime foe of racial politics who had spent 26 years as a political prisoner—was a more inclusive and pluralist system.

By 2010, the world had twice as many democracies as authoritarian regimes—a remarkable turnaround since 1974. Durable dictatorships, such as those of Fidel Castro in Cuba, Hosni Mubarak in Egypt, Robert Mugabe in Zimbabwe—or the Communist Party in China—now were the exception.

Contributing Conditions Three forces, all connected to late twentieth-century globalization, help explain this worldwide upsurge of democracy. First, in Latin America and Eastern Europe especially, governments with large amounts of debt ran into trouble in the early 1980s when interest rates spiked. New loans became expensive, and governments had to impose austerity on their populations. This cost them what little legitimacy they had and strengthened dissent.

Second, the end of the Cold War proved bad news for dictators. Not only did the end of the USSR mean the end of Soviet support for communist dictatorships, but it normally meant the end of American support for anti-communist dictatorships. During the Cold War, the U.S. government had propped up dozens of brutal military rulers because they were anti-communist, but after 1991 the United States lost interest. Most of these dictators could not survive in power without the weapons and money that had formerly flowed from Washington.

Third, the power of example helped propel the spread of democracy. The case of Argentina, which in the years 1982–1983 overthrew a brutal military regime, was inspirational throughout Latin America. The "people power" on display in the Philippines

Mothers of the Plaza de Mayo A 1987 demonstration in Buenos Aires by mothers whose children had been "disappeared" by the Argentine dictatorship.

CONSIDERING THE EVIDENCE

Social Media in the Arab Spring

On January 25, 2011, over 50,000 Egyptians marched into Tahrir Square in downtown Cairo to demand the resignation of their president, Hosni Mubarak. They accused him of corruption and negligence, but they were also angry at his plans to pass the presidency to his own son in the next election. The protesters overwhelmed police who assaulted them with tear gas, rubber bullets, and water cannons. To keep the protest going, organizers throughout Egypt used social media to announce and organize events, communicate with one another, and share news independently of the state media. When the government responded by shutting down the Internet and cell phone networks, the protests gained even more support. By February 11, when the president resigned, the crowds in Tahrir Square alone had swelled to over 250,000 people. As Adel Abdel Ghafar writes in his recollection of the protest, organizing on Facebook could never compensate for getting people out onto the streets.

Revolutions are not hatched in smoke-filled rooms or by activists armed with Twitter and Facebook accounts; rather, revolutions are made by everyday people who are no longer afraid. That is the profound change that happened in Egypt on January 25. Egyptians, who had bowed down to their pharaohs for seven thousand years, simply said, no more.

As the riot police approached us with their armor and batons raised high, they noticed that we were not moving, something they had never seen before. The line of soldiers started to slow down until they abruptly stopped a few meters in front of us. For a moment, both crowds stared at each other, polar opposites on an urban battlefield. That

in 1986, when Ferdinand Marcos was overthrown, resonated in Southeast Asia. The well-televised scenes of ordinary Germans hacking apart the Berlin Wall in 1989 struck chords everywhere, as did the courage, in a losing battle, of Chinese protesters at Tiananmen Square. Modern communications, especially television news, spread sound and image of these events far and wide, helping to motivate and mobilize people who had for years grudgingly accepted their life under authoritarian rule. They accepted it no longer.

Authoritarian Responses Some autocrats withstood the global wave of democratization. In China, as we have seen, the communist leadership crushed a democratization movement in 1989 and retained its monopoly on politics. In Central Asian countries such as Uzbekistan or Turkmenistan, the end of Soviet rule led merely to new dictatorships run by men who had formerly served Moscow's will. Some dictators such as Mugabe or Castro managed to out-maneuver and outlast their enemies until feeble with age.

moment will be etched in my memory forever; time almost seemed to stand still.

Then the most incredible thing happened. The riot police turned back and started running for their lives. We chased them, captured a few, hit them, and took away their weapons and helmets. They ran back to their lines, psychologically broken. Although they would still fight us in the coming days, we all knew that something profound had just taken place. There was a raised collective consciousness among us. A realization. An epiphany. Simply that we will no longer be afraid. We drew strength, courage, and resolve from one another, from our numbers, and from our conviction. Our small group right there reached that conclusion, just as other Egyptians had reached it across the country that day. And in that moment, the Mubarak regime had lost its most significant weapon: fear. Eighteen days later, the tyrant stepped down.

Questions for Analysis

1. According to Adel Abdel Ghafar, why were the protesters successful this time?

2. How did the Internet help protesters organize support on the streets during the Arab Spring?

3. How were the actions taken by the protesters in Egypt similar to or different from the methods promoted by Gandhi as *satyagraha*?

Source: Adel Abdel Ghafar, "The Moment the Barrier of Fear Broke Down," in *Voices of the Arab Spring: Personal Stories from the Arab Revolutions*, ed. Asaad al-Saleh (New York, 2015).

In several countries, experiments with democracy left many citizens unsatisfied. Ambitious authoritarian politicians learned how to rig elections, intimidate the opposition, use social media for propaganda purposes, and cut deals with billionaires who owned media empires. These tactics enabled them to undermine democracy even while preserving its outward forms. In Russia, Vladimir Putin proved a master of this general strategy. In 2001, he ended a chaotic flirtation with democracy and thereafter ruled Russia with the help of billionaire oligarchs whose businesses he protected.

In the so-called Arab Spring in 2011, democracy protesters challenged several long-standing dictatorships, and in Tunisia and Egypt overthrew them. But only in Tunisia did democracy endure. In Egypt and Bahrain authoritarian rulers recovered, and in Syria, Libya, and Yemen civil wars resulted from popular efforts to topple dictators. Meanwhile, Turkey, the Philippines, Venezuela, Uganda, Hungary, Poland, Brazil, South Africa, and several other countries drifted toward more authoritarian rule in the early twenty-first century.

Two main factors lay behind this revitalization of authoritarianism. One was the rise of China, the best example of an undemocratic state that achieved wealth and power rapidly. China also provided economic support for rulers without imposing conditions about human rights or democracy. Another factor was the frequent failure of democracies to protect their citizens from the economic dislocations of globalization. Millions who lost their jobs after a major economic downturn in 2007 and 2008 also lost their faith in their system of government. And in 2020 the COVID-19 pandemic enabled many governments to claim emergency powers, which in India, Sri Lanka, Cambodia, Bolivia, Hungary, and elsewhere they used to detain political opponents illegally.

The Role of Social Media Twenty-first-century politics was also shaped by the rise of the Internet, and by social media in particular. Social media are online platforms designed for communication and for sharing, via computers and mobile devices, information including images, videos, news, stories, and opinions. They include social networking sites such as Facebook, launched in 2004; microblogging platforms such as Twitter (2006) and Tumblr (2007); and platforms used mainly for image and video sharing such as YouTube (2005), Instagram (2010), and Snapchat (2011). The most frequented social media networks in 2020 were offered by either American or Chinese companies. Facebook had more than 2.5 billion users, YouTube and WhatsApp (owned by Facebook) both around 2 billion. Approximately 3.8 billion people—half the human race—used social media in 2020, and some 4.5 billion used the Internet.

The Internet has been used for political purposes practically since its inception, and by the late 2000s pro-democracy movements around the globe were using social media to advance their agendas. As one Egyptian activist of the Arab Spring tweeted in 2011, "We use Facebook to schedule the protests, Twitter to coordinate, and YouTube to tell the world." Popular protests in Turkey, Iran, Russia, the United States, Hong Kong, and many other places did so as well.

At first governments were outflanked, less by the technology itself than by the online tactics of young, technologically savvy activists. But within a few short years, authoritarian governments began to restrict unwelcome online content and block social media platforms or users. They also arrested people who organized dissent through social media, and they used the platforms themselves to create and spread lies designed to discredit their critics. Their security services used data collected from online communications companies and social media platforms to monitor citizens, improving the efficiency of surveillance operations. In 2017 in Myanmar, the military used Facebook to incite violence against a Muslim minority population, the Rohingya.

States found that they could use social media at minimal expense to influence political opinions in other countries as well as their own, and undertook to sway elections or even incite riots abroad. Meanwhile, terrorist organizations such as ISIS (the Islamic State of Iraq and Syria, or Daesh) also found that social media served their ambitions, especially for recruiting volunteers, spreading propaganda, and coordinating attacks. Every new communications technology in world history—writing, printing, telegraph, radio, TV—carried political consequences, sometimes empowering states, sometimes weakening them. Often the new technologies at first weakened states by enabling subjects and citizens to share information more rapidly and cheaply, but states eventually learned how to exploit the new tools for their own purposes.

The Global Economy since 1980

As usual, political changes were tightly bound up with economic ones. Other than the rise of East Asia, which we have seen, the major developments in economic history since the 1980s are a surge in global connectedness and the increase of inequality within most countries. To see the significance of the recent tightening of economic integration, it helps to look backward first.

The international economy before 1914 had been knitting itself together rapidly. But with world wars and the Great Depression, the decades between 1914 and 1945 were a time of economic de-globalization. International trade and investment flows fell to levels below those of 1880. So did labor migration. After 1945, the global economy resumed its integration, limited by the Cold War. Indeed, it might be better to say that two rival processes of economic integration began—a communist one under Soviet leadership, and a capitalist one anchored by the United States. In the years 1989–1991, the end of the Cold War gave globalization another boost by opening the former Soviet bloc to stronger connections with the capitalist world. The two most important features of this entire process—integration, disintegration, re-integration—were trade and finance.

The Growth of International Trade

In 1913, about 20 to 25 percent of the world's goods were traded internationally. During the 1930s and 1940s, that fell to about 10 percent. The proportion recovered to 20 to 25 percent by 1980, and then it skyrocketed. In the decade between 2008 and 2017, it reached a plateau at about 55 to 60 percent. Machinery, consumer electronics, and oil have lately topped the list of goods traded across borders.

Why this sudden change since 1980? Part of the explanation is illusion: there are more countries than before. Shoes exported from Russia to Ukraine in 1980 were not international trade; but after 1991 and the breakup of the USSR, they were. However, the fuller explanation involves basic changes in the organization of the global economy, the result of several shifts in ideas, policy, business organization, and technology.

Free Trade Policy In the realm of ideas and policy, the 1980s marked a major shift in favor of **free trade**. It was led by the United States and the United Kingdom, in particular by President Ronald Reagan and Prime Minister Margaret Thatcher, who spearheaded efforts to get other countries to liberalize trade. Most big American businesses by now had abandoned their support for high import tariffs because much of their own production took place overseas. Since the United States remained by far the biggest national economy and the most powerful country in the world, especially after the collapse of the USSR, its ideas, policies, and preferences carried considerable weight internationally in the 1990s.

A second key policy shift was the effort to reduce barriers to trade within Europe, which dated back to the 1950s. The main idea then was to make Western Europe stronger and richer through cooperation and integration, so it would not be eclipsed by the Cold War superpowers. But the biggest steps toward free trade in Europe took place in the early 1990s, with the formation of the European Union (EU), symbolized by the adoption of a common currency, the euro, which replaced more than a dozen national currencies. Between 2004 and 2013, the EU expanded to include almost all the countries of the former Soviet bloc, creating a highly integrated trade zone accounting for about 22 percent of the world economy.

As the policies of free trade spread around the world, multinational corporations got bigger and better at scattering parts of their operations in several countries. For labor-intensive jobs, they chose low-wage countries. Reagan and Thatcher regarded labor unions as obstacles to the economic changes they wished to see, and both succeeded in reducing the power of unions—making it easier for firms to move manufacturing jobs from the United States or the United Kingdom to Mexico, India, or China. Meanwhile, firms put technology-intensive work in countries with a highly educated labor force. They located their pollution-intensive operations in countries with minimal environmental regulation. This trend accelerated after 1980, in part owing to the trade liberalization pushed by Reagan and Thatcher. So by 2015, a Ford truck might be designed in Michigan, have a transmission built in China, an engine from Brazil, and be assembled in Kentucky. Most big companies in the auto, petrochemical, pharmaceutical, electronics, and computer industries found ways to cut costs by globalizing their supply chains. When big companies did this, they "traded" internationally with themselves to prepare finished products for market. By 2015, roughly 80 percent of international trade took place within such global firms.

Information Technology Much of the success of globalized firms came from new technology, some of which we've seen with containerization. **Information technology** (IT)—the use of computers to store, transmit, and process data—did at least as much to enable firms to conduct global operations. Together, these innovations reduced the cost of transporting goods from factory to customer by about 95 percent between 1980 and 2015, making global supply chains much cheaper than any alternative.

The keys to the impact of IT were cheaper computing power and the Internet. In 1946 there were 10 computers in the world, and in 1960 about 5,000. By 2020 there were 2 billion laptops and desktops, each one more than 100 billion times more efficient than the computers of 1946. And there were 3.5 billion smartphones, each one with more computing power than NASA could wield in 1969 when it put men on the moon. In the 1990s, the Internet connected computers into one vast network, enabling each one to access an almost infinite quantity of digitized information.

With the advent of this digital revolution, a firm could learn the preferences of its customers from their web-browsing habits and almost instantly revise production schedules for everything from shoes to cars. With quick and reliable shipping, it could move components anywhere at minimal cost, reduce inventories in warehouses, and rely on so-called just-in-time delivery both at assembly plants and at retail shops. This system, sometimes

Early Computing A Bell Labs mainframe computer, developed for the U.S. Army, 1946.

called lean production, rested on IT, free trade, and container shipping. Firms also increasingly enticed consumers to buy goods online with vast selection, secure ordering, and quick delivery. In 2019, consumers spent some $3.5 trillion online globally, roughly 16 percent of total retail sales for the year. Many brick-and-mortar stores that did not adjust to the new model were forced to close.

Lean production and globalized supply chains relied fundamentally on peace and health. During the twentieth century, world wars interrupted international flows of goods in a much less globalized economy, bringing shortages, rationing, and hunger. In 2020, the vulnerabilities of a much more globalized economy, especially firms reliant on just-in-time delivery, were laid bare by the COVID-19 pandemic, which threw sand in the gears of supply chains everywhere. So the enormous expansion of international trade after 1980 carried risks as well as rewards.

By 2020, businesses also found that social media could boost their global profiles and profits. Some platforms allowed advertising—which could potentially reach billions of people. Other platforms did not, but clever marketers could achieve the same effect by creating messages that went viral—or by encouraging satisfied customers to do so for them. Businesses also purchased data about potential customers harvested from social media platforms to learn how best to target their marketing efforts. New firms with limited brand awareness were especially likely to turn to social media to expand their global customer base.

Global Finance

While world trade was booming, international financial flows were gushing. Finance is basically the business of pooling savings and investing them in other businesses expected over time to become profitable. Before 1980, it was done mainly by banks. Once again, it helps to take a brief backward glance.

International financial flows flourished during the 1870–1913 surge in economic integration. Like trade, financial flows then dropped with the world wars and Great Depression. As World War II ended, the victors (except the USSR) re-built the world's banking systems with tight restrictions on capital flows and fixed exchange rates for currencies.

In 1973, the so-called Bretton Woods system came apart when the currency inflation of the Vietnam War era caused the U.S. government to withdraw its support. In the following decade, the international financial system underwent major reforms, most of which reduced regulations and eased international capital flows.

Financiers responded with investment innovations that opened the floodgates of finance. New communications and information technology sped the movement of money. In the mid-1970s, employees of the investment bank Goldman Sachs in New York would send faxes of the *Wall Street Journal*'s page on stocks to British colleagues so they could begin their day in London knowing where New York markets closed the day before. By 1990, new digital technology instantly alerted investors in London, New York, and Tokyo to every shift in interest rates and stock prices.

Finance now became far more lucrative than trade or manufacturing. Tiny differences in the value of a currency from one market to the next would cause an overnight stampede of billions of dollars. By the late 1990s, foreign exchange markets every week handled more money than the annual GNP of the United States, and by 2016 they did so every three days.

De-regulation and Economic Instability The **financialization** of the world economy (as it came to be called) meant money could flow easily and instantly to wherever it might earn the best return on investment. De-regulation meant that insurance companies, hedge funds, and pension funds could all get into the finance business. The brave new world of de-regulated finance attracted reckless speculators. In 1995, a 28-year-old financier working in Singapore, because his ethical lapses had barred him from employment in England, lost every penny entrusted by customers to Baring Brothers, a 233-year-old bank.

The boom in finance brought much more economic instability. During the period 1870–1913, most international capital supported building durable enterprises such as railroads or mines that investors hoped would pay off for them over decades. After 1990, the sums that traders could move around the world with a few keystrokes exceeded the value of the entire economy of a mid-sized country. So governments in Argentina or Thailand had to obey the preferences of international investors with respect to their budgets, currencies, and banking regulations, or risk a massive withdrawal of money. Governments occasionally chose not to obey financial pressures because they did not wish to face the political consequences of firing thousands of government workers or cutting the military budget.

The Great Recession The ease with which big investors could withdraw vast sums made major financial crises more common in the 1990s. The biggest came in Mexico in 1994, Southeast Asia in 1997, and Russia in 1998. These crises all became more or less global, although none reached the proportions of the 2007 financial crisis that originated in the housing market and financial system of the United States. That one rippled throughout the world, causing massive bankruptcies, layoffs, and dis-investment in the Great Recession of

Global Financial Crisis A trader on the Philippine Stock Exchange shows his disgust as red deficit figures fill up a screen behind him. The collapse of the U.S. investment bank Lehman Brothers in September 2008 led to economic shocks worldwide.

2007–2009. The U.S. Treasury bailed out the biggest banks, insurance companies, and investment firms, including European ones, to keep the crash from getting worse. Countries with big debt problems, such as Greece and Ireland, needed foreign bankers to bail them out too, and with those bailouts came brutal austerity in the form of higher taxes and slashed public services. Tens of millions of people around the world lost their jobs or homes. Street protests in the United States and Europe lasted for months, and citizens voted out existing governments in favor of more radical parties. Countries with no debt loads, and those least linked to the world's financial system— China, India, Indonesia, Australia, and several African nations—managed to weather the crisis comparatively well.

The financialization of the world economy thus led to a spike in economic volatility. It amounted to a rising tide that lifted some boats but swamped others. It added to the hunger felt around the world for economic stability and security, especially among older citizens who remembered less volatile times and who had more in the way of savings or property to lose. Politicians capitalized on this hunger, winning support with promises of a return to stable jobs and economic security, which none of them could deliver.

Heightened Inequality

Like every earlier surge in economic globalization, the rapid one after 1980 created winners and losers. Globally there were more winners than losers. In poor countries, roughly 500 to 700 million people with few options found new opportunities in the years between 1980 and 2015. They left their villages to accept low wages and sometimes dangerous working conditions in new factories. They may not have won much, but they were the bulk of the winners from economic globalization. Most of the winnings—a different thing—went to the few people who had the education, skill, connections, and luck to profit from either the growth in finance or the migration of manufacturing from high-wage to low-wage countries. This profit flowed to a few million people around the world, most of whom became super-rich.

One of those was the Mexican business magnate Carlos Slim, born in 1940. He was a first-generation Mexican whose ancestors hailed from Lebanon. He parlayed a modest inheritance into diverse business holdings in Mexico, the rest of Latin America, the United States, and Europe. He became one of the world's 10 richest people in the 1990s, thanks in part to the growth of several manufacturing businesses he owned in Mexico, most of which exported goods to the newly open U.S. market. He owned Latin America's biggest mobile phone company when mobile phones took off. As of 2015, he owned about 200 companies. Slim took full advantage of de-regulation of telecoms, insurance, and financial industries, as well as the reduction in barriers to transactions among Mexico, the United States, and other countries. He is among the biggest beneficiaries of economic globalization (and says his favorite subject in high school was history).

The losers from globalization included the tens of millions of people in high-wage countries who saw the market for their skills disappear. In the 1970s, it was possible for a Seattle steelworker to support a family by himself, to own a home and a car, and take foreign vacations. But as steel production migrated to South Korea, Mexico, and elsewhere, high-paying jobs of this sort gradually disappeared in the United States, much of Europe, and Japan. Secure industrial jobs also disappeared in Russia and Eastern Europe after 1989 as communist-era factories could not compete internationally. Automation of factory work also replaced high-wage laborers everywhere. In the United States, the proportion of the economy that went to wages and salaries peaked at around 50 to 52 percent between 1945 and 1970, and it fell thereafter as a result of global competition and automation in American factories. By 2020, it had slid to 42 percent. Wage earners struggled to keep what they regarded as decent jobs in the globalized economy.

All this re-shuffling of income as a result of economic globalization changed patterns of inequality in the world. On most measures, **income inequality** of the global population declined after 1990. Rising wages in China and to a lesser degree India accounted for most of that change. Apart from these cases, there was very little reduction in global inequality. By and large, Africa did not close any gaps.

Income inequality within—as opposed to among—countries was a simpler story. Throughout the twentieth century up to about 1980, a strong trend toward greater equality had prevailed just about everywhere. Then, in the 1970s through the 1980s, that trend leveled off in Europe. In the United States, the United Kingdom, Canada, and Australia it reversed direction sharply. Those societies developed mega-rich classes, known colloquially after 2008 as "the one percent." In the United States in 2017, the top 1 percent got 18 percent of all national income—up from 8 percent in 1970. Most of the countries with the greatest income inequality were poor countries with super-rich elites such as South Africa, Botswana, and Panama. Those with the least income inequality were mainly in Europe.

Measured by wealth—what people owned, rather than their incomes—inequality widened even more sharply after 1990. By 2015, the richest eight individuals on Earth owned as much as the poorest 3.7 billion people.

All of these post-1980 economic trends—the growth in international trade, the power of finance, and heightened inequality—were jolted by the consequences of the COVID-19 pandemic beginning in 2020. The need for social distancing to reduce the loss of life proved disastrous for business sectors that required either international transport or crowds. International trade fell abruptly. Tourism and professional sports halted almost overnight. Auto manufacturers could not get parts for assembly, and customers put off purchases. Many sectors, including education and finance, shifted on the fly to tele-working. Countries that struggled to mount a coherent pandemic response or relied heavily on global trade suffered the greatest economic dislocation. In the United States, for example, unemployment skyrocketed to levels experienced only during the depths of the Great Depression. Canada suffered a smaller spike in unemployment. Outside of North America, job losses remained minimal, but global economic output in 2020 slumped by about 4 percent.

Cultural Globalization

Recent decades witnessed globalization in the realm of culture as well as economics. Thanks to technical advances in communication and to the upswing in international migration, people more frequently came in contact with unfamiliar languages, customs, food, and music. This proved unsettling for many people but also sparked a surge of creativity around the world.

Everything from food fusion (such as sushi burritos) to Facebook friendships (15 percent of which were international in 2015) has globalized lately. Here we'll look more carefully at two aspects of the broader cultural trend: music and sport.

Music

Music is one of the cultural forms that travels well through the Global web. People can enjoy it without words, or without understanding the words. Until the 1880s, music was always experienced live. It traveled most easily when musicians traveled, bringing, for example, Celtic ballads (from Ireland and Scotland) to North America in the eighteenth and nineteenth centuries. Religious music traveled wherever religions did. Sufi ceremonial music and dance went everywhere that Sufism went, from Morocco to Mindanao (in the Philippines) and every Islamic land in between.

The globalization of music accelerated with the invention of recording technology beginning in the 1880s and radio in the 1920s. Those technologies took hold first in the richer countries, so in the first half of the twentieth century European and North American music proved the most mobile. Classical music—the symphonies, sonatas, and concertos that Europeans had raised to a high art during the eighteenth and nine-teenth centuries—found audiences around the world. Today more people are trained in classical music in East Asia than anywhere else. European musical styles often traveled in the footsteps of European empire.

In the 1950s, a dramatic change in the history of music took place with recordings marketed exclusively to youth—a growing share of the world's population after 1945, owing to the widespread "baby boom." The change began in the United States and proved lucrative. Young people came to define themselves partly by the music they liked, and to mark themselves off from their elders with their musical preferences. This development, combined with cheaper recordings, led to an even faster surge of musical globalization.

The engine room of this musical movement was the American South, the home of jazz and blues. In the late 1950s, when John Lennon and Paul McCartney were Liverpool teen-agers, they eagerly awaited the arrival of American ships because sailors brought records made by black American artists with roots in the South. Lennon and McCartney imitated the music of Chuck Berry and Little Richard, got good at playing it in bars in Germany, and soon became the core of one of the most popular musical acts of all time, the Beatles.

The music they learned, at the time called rhythm and blues in the United States, was itself derived partly from West African traditions, including polyrhythmic drumming used in jazz. Black Americans in the 1950s and 1960s combined those traditions with vocal styles from gospel church choirs. In their lyrics they replaced gospel music's intense longing for salvation with longing for love and sex. This proved a magic formula, generating a youth music—including soul and rock 'n' roll, among others—that exploded on the scene in the 1960s.

In an ironic twist, the wealth and power of the United States by the 1960s helped to spread the cultural influence of its most underprivileged population, black Ameri-cans from the South or from the inner cities of Detroit or Chicago. During the Cold War years, the economic and political clout of the United States was at its height. The U.S. State Department sponsored global goodwill tours by American jazz musicians. U.S. soldiers and sailors stationed around the world served as unofficial ambassadors for American popular music. In earlier centuries, the power and wealth of the Roman Empire had helped to spread the tastes and fashions of its aristocrats throughout Europe and North Africa. The prestige of China's Song dynasty had a similar impact in Korea and Southeast Asia. Now the United States wielded even broader influence, but, in music at least, the influence came not from the higher echelons but from the lower rungs of the social hierarchy.

Musicians all over the world developed their own styles blending local and international—often American—influences. Brazilians made bossa nova—a style combining their own tradition of samba and American jazz—internationally popular in the 1960s. The South African singer Miriam Makeba melded a style from Johannesburg's dance halls with American pop to create an international hit in the Xhosa language. Other African musicians—perhaps most notably the Nigerians King Sunny Ade, who sang in Yoruba, and Fela Kuti, who sang in Nigerian English—enjoyed international popularity in the 1980s with styles that incorporated instruments from American popular music such as the pedal steel guitar and synthesizers, but relied on West African drumming traditions. Both were in the forefront of what since 1987 has been called world music, a loose category of popular music made by people outside of North America or Europe but influenced by the popular music traditions of the United States.

Fela Kuti The Nigerian musician Fela Kuti with his band in 1980. Fela's music, called Afrobeat, was a blend of American rhythm and blues, jazz, and Yoruba traditions.

American country music also went global, finding audiences especially in Europe and Australia. Bal Kishore Das Loiwal, born to a prosperous family in northern India, learned to play and sing country music from records sent home by an aunt who had moved to Nashville, the mecca of country music. He changed his name to Bobby Cash and after 2005 broke into the Australian market as well as creating a following at home, calling himself the Indian cowboy and dressing the part.

One of the world's most popular musical forms by the 1970s was the Jamaican invention called reggae, a blend of older Caribbean styles with American jazz and rhythm and blues. It was associated with the Rastafarian religion, a Jamaican innovation of the 1930s, which revered the Ethiopian king Haile Selassie as a prophet. Reggae's most successful artist was Bob Marley, a global star from the early 1970s until his death in 1981. By the 1980s, Jamaican reggae was popular everywhere: even Iceland and Japan had their own reggae bands.

Few musicians blended as many global influences as Shakira, whose name means "grateful" in Arabic. Born in Colombia, her ancestors came from Spain, Italy, and Lebanon. By her teenage years she was performing throughout Colombia, singing in Spanish and occasionally in Arabic. She learned from an eclectic mix of music, from Lebanon, Latin America, the United States, and the United Kingdom. Her Lebanese dance style translated well to music video, a genre that became popular in the 1980s. In the early 2000s she began to record in English, expanding her audience. Together with a Haitian American rapper, Wyclef Jean, she recorded the best-selling song of the twenty-first century (so far) in 2006. Asked in 2001 to describe herself, Shakira said: "I'm a fusion between black and white, between pop and rock, between cultures—between my Lebanese father and my mother's Spanish blood, the Colombian folklore and Arab dance I love and American music."

Drake and Rihanna were almost as international in their inspirations as Shakira and even more successful as global stars. Drake, whose Canadian mother had Eastern European Jewish roots and whose father was an African American musician from Tennessee, grew up in Toronto. He helped develop a rap style that proved enormously popular around the world by 2010. Rihanna began singing in outdoor markets in her hometown of Bridgetown, Barbados. She moved to the United States in her late teens and launched a recording career that mixed Caribbean reggae and dancehall styles with American pop, rap, and dance music. By 2020 she stood among the 10 best-selling recording artists ever, and the only one among them born after 1960. Like Drake and Shakira, she became a movie star and entrepreneur with a global following.

Nowadays, thanks to YouTube, Spotify, and their successors, music swirls around the world as never before. Traditions rubbed up against one another, leading to new forms every year. Rap stars from Korea (Psy) could become global celebrities overnight. Opera, whose fans usually expect rigid adherence to tradition, also globalized: one of the most admired sopranos of the last 40 years, Kiri Te Kanawa, who sang in Italian and German, as opera singers normally do, was raised in a Maori family in New Zealand.

Sport

Modern sport took shape at the end of the nineteenth century with the reincarnation of the ancient Greek Olympic games and the formation of leagues for team sports such as soccer in Britain and baseball in the United States. These became spectacles for crowds as well as competitions for athletes, like chariot racing in the ancient world. All the major global sports developed first in Europe and America, and often spread along the trails of empire. Polo, originating in Iran, is the closest thing to an exception. Cricket became popular in South Asia, Australia, and the Anglophone Caribbean—all regions within the former British Empire. Baseball took root in Mexico and those parts of the Spanish Caribbean with the strongest historical links to the United States such as Puerto Rico, Cuba, the Dominican Republic, and Panama. It acquired a following in those parts of East Asia where the U.S. presence, especially military presence, was strong, such as Japan, Taiwan, and South Korea. Basketball by the 1990s spread far and wide, aided by its minimal need of equipment, unlike ice hockey, a Canadian invention played only in cold and prosperous countries, or American football, which won only minor followings outside North America.

The most global of sports was soccer, which first took shape in Britain during the nineteenth century. Britain's global reach in the nineteenth century brought soccer to every continent. It found especially fertile soil in South America and continental Europe, which to this day produce most of the best male players, lately joined by West Africa. The secret to soccer's global appeal lay in how little one needs to play it: some open space and a ball.

The women's game also originated in Britain, where a public match was played as early as 1895 and one in 1920 drew 53,000 spectators. France and Italy had amateur leagues by the 1930s. But it took until late in the twentieth century before professional women's soccer leagues sprang up in Europe and the United States, aided by the development of girls' sports programs in schools, the launching of the Women's World Cup in 1991, and the inclusion of women's soccer as an Olympic sport in 1996.

The men's soccer World Cup began in 1930 with only 13 national teams taking part. The first TV broadcasts came in 1954, and soon the World Cup was a global cultural event held every four years. Decolonization led to increased participation, so that by 2006 nearly 200 national teams competed for slots in the 32-team tournament. The World Cup attracted more TV viewers than the Olympics or any other sporting competition. Since 2006, the final match of each tournament has been seen live by 10 to 12 percent of the global population. The Women's World Cup, at first a 12-team tournament, expanded to a 24-team event and between 1999 and 2019 attracted many millions of spectators on TV and major corporate sponsorships.

Global Sport A member of the U.S. women's national soccer team plays in a match against Sweden during the 2019 Women's World Cup tournament. The world's most popular sport, soccer is today played on every inhabited continent.

Sports changed less when traveling than did music. The rules of baseball were very much the same in Korea and Panama as in Kansas and Pennsylvania. Styles of play differed a bit more than rules, but any innovations that brought competitive advantage spread almost instantly, because of modern communications and the intense competition in sport. Stable rules through the decades were important to the public appeal of sports, so fans could enjoy arguing whether Walter Payton was a better football player than Christian McCaffrey (he was), whether Serena Williams was better at tennis than Margaret Court (she was), or whether Pelé was better at soccer than Lionel Messi (he wasn't).

Television helped convert international competitions such as the World Cup and the Olympics into global cultural phenomena and arenas of peaceful national competition. The modern Olympics began in Europe in 1896 as a gentlemanly competition, mainly in track and field. Women—at first only golfers and tennis players—began to take part in 1900. With the beginning of worldwide TV broadcasts at the Tokyo games in 1964, the Olympics began to attract global audiences. Decolonization increased the number of teams and competitors, and it made the Olympics more interesting to Africans and Asians. The increasing participation of female athletes also increased the popularity of the Olympics. Women runners competed in the 1500-meters beginning in 1972, and the women's marathon debuted in 1984. In the most recent Olympiads, about 42 to 44 percent of athletes were women.

During the Cold War, the Olympics became one of the stages on which the USSR and the United States tried to demonstrate the superiority of their sociopolitical systems. Both supported officially "amateur" athletes for the purpose of winning medals. Sports fans—and politicians too—developed an obsession with medal counts. In East Germany and China, which entered Olympic competition in 1980, all sports organizations were directly under government control, and party leaders went to great lengths to use sport to show the vigor of their brand of communism. East German politicians, desperate to outdo West Germany, encouraged the nation's sports federation to administer performance-enhancing drugs to the best athletes, often without the athletes' consent. Some as young as 10 years of age were fed testosterone, steroids, and amphetamines. They did bring home a bumper crop of Olympic medals—at the price of health problems later in life. The Olympics, which officially admitted professional athletes by 1992, remains one of the most politically meaningful sporting events today even if the intensity of the Cold War years is gone.

The advent of TV in the 1950s and 1960s made many sports into big businesses and enabled some athletes—a few hundred in all—to become exceedingly rich. In most years, all of the top 30 earners among athletes were male. The top women were always tennis players, with Serena Williams recently leading the way. Prize money for men and women in tennis was equalized at major tournaments between 1973 and 2007, though at lesser tournaments around the world women players as of 2020 earned 80 percent as much as men.

Imagined Global Community and Its Limits

Strong as they are in light of the past, all these currents of globalization are much weaker than people think they are. A survey of people in 138 countries undertaken in 2015 revealed that on average, people imagine that international migrants make up 30 percent of the world's population, whereas 3.5 percent is about right. Respondents thought that 22 percent of university students came from abroad; the real figure was 2 percent. They thought foreign trade was twice as large as it was. Across dozens of variables, the survey showed that people around the world imagined globalization was about five times more prevalent than it actually was in 2015.

The fast pace of cultural and economic globalization after 1980 has had its limits. First of all, many people feared globalization as a threat to their livelihood, their identity, or both. Elections in the United States and several European countries after 2012 reflected this sentiment. More fundamentally, there are big and basic obstacles checking globalization. People in Nigeria and Norway have good reason not to dress alike, because it's always warm in Nigeria and often cold in Norway. And it seems most unlikely that anyone other than Icelanders will ever regard fermented shark meat as a delicacy.

The long trend, nevertheless, remains toward greater integration of the Global web. Since its formation in the sixteenth century, it has expanded and tightened despite several setbacks along the way. The COVID-19 pandemic is another setback, but hardly a reversal. The web-building process has been woven into world history since the earliest times, and it has rebounded from shocks, including world wars and pandemics a hundred times more deadly than COVID-19. No one planned it and many people resent its effects, but almost everyone by pursuing their own economic, intellectual, cultural, and religious interests contributes to the ongoing life of the Global web.

Conclusion

The post-1980 world at the moment looks like one of tumultuous change. Climate change sped up dramatically. Population growth slowed down with reduced fertility, as women increasingly devoted more time to schooling and paid work and less to child rearing and household chores. Emerging viruses threatened human health on every continent, perhaps heralding a counter-trend to the remarkable centuries-long reduction in the burden of disease. Nevertheless, population growth as of 2020 remained more rapid than at any time in human history before about 1940. Humankind became predominantly urban for the first time ever. Politics evolved so as to become more democratic, more religious, and more influenced by global international institutions—and all three trends sparked smaller counter-trends in the form of authoritarian revivals that fed on anti-globalization sentiment. Cheap travel and cheap communications brought a kaleidoscopic swirl of cultural interaction, vividly expressed in music. The same trends made sport into an international spectacle of immense popularity.

But to people in 50 or 100 years, the world of 1980 to 2020 will look very different from what it seems to any of us now. We are following truth too near the heels to know for sure just where we are.

Chapter Review

KEY TERMS

Wangari Maathai p. 1128
Anthropocene p. 1129
climate change p. 1130

carbon dioxide p. 1130
HIV/AIDS p. 1138
COVID-19 p. 1138

declines in fertility p. 1139
international migrants p. 1144
international institutions p. 1146
al-Qaeda p. 1148
spread of democracy p. 1150

free trade p. 1155
information technology p. 1156
financialization p. 1158
income inequality p. 1160

REVIEW QUESTIONS

1. What is new about climate change since 1840?
2. Culturally and politically, why did the world become so environmentally turbulent over the last 70 years?
3. What key innovations in medicine and agriculture led to population growth after 1950?
4. What four conditions contributed to the devastating health impact of COVID-19?
5. Explain the main reasons behind the worldwide downward fertility trend since 1960.
6. What two trends drove the spurt of urban growth since 1950?
7. Compare and contrast the characteristics of international migrants in the periods 1890–1915 and 1990–2015.
8. Why have so many international organizations arisen since World War II?
9. What factors caused political Islam to grow in popularity in Muslim societies after 1970?
10. Identify and describe three forces related to late-twentieth-century globalization that help explain the worldwide upsurge of democracy.
11. Why did multinational corporations get bigger and globalize their supply chains?
12. Describe the consequences of the financialization of the world economy.
13. Who were the winners and losers of economic globalization after 1980?
14. Compare how music and sport changed when traveling worldwide.
15. Discuss the long trend of global integration.

Go to INQUIZITIVE

to see what you've learned—and learn what you've missed—with personalized feedback along the way.

FURTHER READING

Chapter 16 Convergence: The Discovery of the Oceans and Biological Globalization, 1400 to 1800

John Logan Allen, ed., *A New World Disclosed* (1997). A detailed account of European voyaging to, and into, North America from the Vikings to about 1680.

Judith Carney, *Black Rice* (2002). A detailed study of how African rice got to the Americas.

Alfred Crosby, *The Columbian Exchange: Biological and Cultural Consequences of 1492* (1972). A classic analysis that essentially invented the idea of the Columbian exchange of plants and animals.

Edward Dreyer, *Zheng He: China and the Oceans in the Early Ming Dynasty, 1405–1433* (2007). The best general treatment of the Ming voyages.

Felipe Fernández-Armesto, *Pathfinders* (2006). A general (and well-written) history of exploration, with several chapters on European maritime efforts from 1400 through 1800.

Linda Newsom, *Conquest and Pestilence in the Early Spanish Philippines* (2009). A careful analysis of how some of this chapter's themes worked out in one archipelago.

Chapter 17 Disruption: Africa, the Americas, Siberia, and Oceania, 1492 to 1850

James Belich, *Making Peoples* (1996). The first several chapters recount Polynesian and contact-era history of New Zealand with insight, wit, and verve.

J. H. Elliott, *Empires of the Atlantic World* (2006). A work by a master historian on the Spanish and British Empires in the three centuries after Columbus.

David Eltis and David Richardson (2010). *Atlas of the Transatlantic Slave Trade*. The authoritative source on the size, sources, and destinations of the slave trade. See also the website based on the same research: http://www.slave-voyages.org/

Janet Hartley, *Siberia: A History of the People* (2014). A readable overview of that vast land, with good chapters on the Russian absorption of Siberia.

Andrés Reséndez, *The Other Slavery: The Uncovered Story of Indian Enslavement in America* (2016). The author shines a spotlight on a neglected aspect of the history of the Caribbean, Mexico, and the U.S. Southwest.

John Richards, *The Unending Frontier* (2003). A massive study of environmental change around the period 1450–1800.

Randy Sparks, *The Two Princes of Calabar* (2004). A true story that explores how the Atlantic slave trade worked in the late eighteenth century.

John K. Thornton, *A Cultural History of the Atlantic World, 1250–1820* (2012). An excellent transatlantic history, with a broad sense of what counts as "cultural."

Chapter 18 Cultural Upheavals: Religious and Intellectual Movements, 1500 to 1750

Rula Jurdi Abisaab, *Converting Persia: Religion and Power in the Safavid Empire* (2015). A work that focuses on the Shi'a clerics imported into Iran by the Safavids.

Daniel Bays, *A New History of Christianity in China* (2011). Chapter 2 discusses the Jesuits in the sixteenth century.

H. Floris Cohen, *The Rise of Modern Science Explained: A Comparative History* (2015). An excellent and readable study.

Carlos Eire, *Reformations: The Early Modern World, 1450–1650* (2016). A massive, insightful work with a focus on Europe.

Philip Ivanhoe, *Ethics in the Confucian Tradition: The Thought of Mengzi and Wang Yangming* (2002). A dense but thorough exploration of Wang's ideas.

Gurinder Singh Mann, *The Sikhs* (2004). A basic primer on Sikh history and belief.

Colin Mitchell, *The Practice of Politics in Safavid Iran: Power, Religion and Rhetoric* (2011). A work of serious scholarship rather than an introductory text, but the author contextualizes religion well through the time of Shah Abbas I.

Lawrence Principe, *The Scientific Revolution: A Very Short Introduction* (2011). A perceptive look into the mindset of the time.

Lyndal Roper, *Martin Luther: Renegade and Prophet* (2017). The 500th anniversary of Luther's 95 theses inspired several new biographies, of which this serious but readable account might be the best.

Chapter 19 University of War: Empires and Power, 1450 to 1800

Jos Gommans, *Mughal Warfare* (2002). This remains the most careful assessment of the military revolution in India.

Xing Hang, *Conflict and Commerce in Maritime East Asia* (2015). The standard work on the Zheng family enterprise.

Peter Lorge, *The Asian Military Revolution* (2008). A handy summary of cases in South, Southeast, and East Asia. Especially good on China.

Alfred Rieber, *The Struggle for the Eurasian Borderlands: From the Rise of Early Modern Empires to the End of the First World War* (2014). One of a few comparative studies of multiple empires—the Qing, Mughal, Safavid, Ottoman, Russian, and Habsburg.

Brian Sandberg, *War and Conflict in the Early Modern World, 1500–1700* (2016). A work that is attentive to questions of organization and culture as well as technology.

Douglas Streusand, *Islamic Gunpowder Empires: Ottomans, Safavids, and Mughals* (2011). An accessible summary of its subject.

Joanna Waley-Cohen, *The Culture of War in China: Empire and the Military under the Qing Dynasty* (2006). A very readable and compact study, emphasizing cultural sides of the Qing military buildup.

Chapter 20 The First Global Economy, 1500 to 1800

Robert C. Allen, Tommy Bengtsson, and Martin Dribe, eds., *Living Standards in the Past: New Perspectives on Well-Being in Asia and Europe* (2005). A good source of information about consumption, wages, nutrition, and height for Eurasian populations.

Femme Gaastra, *The Dutch East India Company: Expansion and Decline* (2003). Perhaps the best of several histories of the VOC.

Arturo Giraldez, *The Manila Galleons and the Dawn of the Global Economy* (2015). An accessible account of world trade, and especially good on silver.

Geoffrey Gunn, *History without Borders: The Making of an Asian World Region, 1000–1800* (2011). A seriously scholarly economic history of the connections among Japan, China, and Southeast Asia.

Wim Klooster, *The Dutch Moment: War, Trade, and Settlement in the Seventeenth-Century Dutch Atlantic* (2016). A general study of the Dutch activities in North America, Brazil, and Africa with plenty on the economy.

Lodewijk Petram, *The World's First Stock Exchange* (2014). Explains how Amsterdam developed modern financial institutions in the seventeenth century.

Marjorie Shaffer, *Pepper: A History of the World's Most Influential Spice* (2013). An enjoyable popular history of the early modern spice trade.

Zheng Yangwen, *China on the Sea: How the Maritime World Shaped Modern China* (2012). The early chapters deal with the Ming and Qing regulation of overseas trade.

Chapter 21 The Best and Worst of Times: Atlantic Revolutions, 1640 to 1830

Jeremy Adelman, *Sovereignty and Revolution in the Iberian Atlantic* (2006). An insightful and thorough study of the Spanish American revolutions.

Robert Allison, *The American Revolution: A Very Short Introduction* (2015). Just what the title suggests, and very readable.

John Chasteen, *Americanos* (2008). A readable narrative of Spanish American revolutions.

Laurent Dubois, *Avengers of the New World: The Story of the Haitian Revolution* (2005). A crisp narrative by one of the top historians of the subject.

Brian Hamnett, *The End of Iberian Rule on the American Continent, 1770–1830* (2017). A handy synthesis of independence in Brazil and Spanish America.

Anne Hilton, *The Kingdom of the Kongo* (1985). This remains one of the key books on Kongo.

Wim Klooster, *Revolutions in the Atlantic World: A Comparative Perspective* (2009). Provides brief narratives together with an analysis that emphasizes Atlantic dimensions.

Peter McPhee, *Liberty or Death* (2016). A general summary of the French Revolution, unusually sympathetic to Robespierre.

Janet Polasky, *Revolutions without Borders* (2015). Explores the circulation of ideas among revolutionary societies.

Chapter 22 Fossil Fuels and Mass Production: Industrial Revolutions around the World, 1780 to 1914

Robert C. Allen, *The British Industrial Revolution in Global Perspective* (2009). A summary statement by one of the foremost economic historians.

Gareth Austin and Kaoru Sugihara, eds., *Labour-Intensive Industrialization in Global History* (2013). The best way to get access to Sugihara's important take on industrialization in East Asia.

Emma Griffin, *A Short History of the British Industrial Revolution* (2010). A very handy summary of the story and the controversies among earlier historians.

Toni Pierenkemper and Richard Tilly, *The German Economy during the Nineteenth Century* (2004). A basic survey with a focus on industrialization.

Eiichi Shibusawa, *The Autobiography of Shibusawa Eiichi: From Peasant to Entrepreneur*, translated by Teruko Craig (1994). The life story of the "father of Japanese capitalism."

Robert C. H. Sweeny, *Why Did We Choose to Industrialize? Montreal 1819–1849* (2015). A detailed study of one city contexualized in the world history of industrialization.

Barrie Trinder, *Britain's Industrial Revolution: The Making of a Manufacturing People* (2013). A thorough examination of the subject with endless interesting detail.

Peer Vries, *Averting a Great Divergence: State and Economy in Japan, 1868–1937* (2019). An analysis of the state's role in Japanese industrialization.

Richard White, *The Republic for Which It Stands: The United States during Reconstruction and the Gilded Age, 1865–1896* (2019). A general history with a lot on industrialization and its consequences.

E. A. Wrigley, *Energy and the English Industrial Revolution* (2010). The most accessible version of the ideas of this master historian.

Chapter 23 Two Liberations: The Vital Revolution and the Abolitions of Slavery and Serfdom, 1750 to 1950

Matt Childs, *The 1812 Aponte Rebellion in Cuba and the Struggle against Atlantic Slavery* (2006). On the risings in eastern Cuba and their connections to antislavery activities elsewhere.

David Brion Davis, *Inhuman Bondage: The Rise and Fall of Slavery in the New World* (2006). An overview by one of the most prominent historians of slavery; includes historiographical context providing a sense of what others have had to say.

Dale Graden, *Disease, Resistance, and Lies: The Demise of the Transatlantic Slave Trade to Brazil and Cuba* (2014). Emphasizes the role of slave revolts and pressure from the British navy in changing elite opinion against the slave trade.

Adam Hochschild, *Bury the Chains: The British Struggle to Abolish Slavery* (2005). A lively popular history, with excellent sketches of the principal actors.

Peter Kolchin, *Unfree Labor: American Slavery and Russian Serfdom* (1987). Still the only extended study that puts both these systems of forced labor in direct comparison.

David Northrup, *Indentured Labor in the Age of Imperialism, 1834–1922* (1995). The best overview of the subject.

James Riley, *Rising Life Expectancy: A Global History* (2001). A handy synthesis of the Vital Revolution.

Manisha Sinha, *The Slave's Cause: A History of Abolition* (2016). A comprehensive history of abolition in the United States, with some attention to Britain, and due recognition of slaves' roles.

Emilia Viotta da Costa, *Crowns of Glory, Tears of Blood: The Demerara Slave Rebellion of 1823* (1994). A classic in-depth study of one of the key revolts.

Chapter 24 Nationalism and Imperialism: Tightening the Global Web, 1800 to 1930

David Abernethy, *The Dynamics of Global Dominance* (2000). A political scientist's systematic and comprehensive history of European imperialism.

Alexander Bulatovich, *Ethiopia through Russian Eyes* (2000). The 1897–1898 diary of a Russian soldier serving under Menelik II in Ethiopia. A fascinating document.

Pekka Hamalainen, *Comanche Empire* (2008). A masterpiece of research and analysis.

E. J. Hobsbawm, *Nations and Nationalism since 1780* (2012). A readable and excellent work on languages and their links to nationalisms.

Adam Hochschild, *King Leopold's Ghost* (1999). A detailed narrative of the Belgian king's pillaging of the Congo.

Heather Streets-Salter and Trevor Getz, *Empires and Colonies in the Modern World* (2016). A broad overview, thematic in structure.

Chapter 25 Making the Modern World: Confronting Industrialization, Nationalism, and Imperialism, 1850 to 1920

Michael Adas, *Prophets of Rebellion: Millenarian Protest Movements against the European Colonial Order* (1979). A work on millenarian movements in East Africa, South and Southeast Asia, and New Zealand.

C. A. Bayly, *The Birth of the Modern World, 1789–1914* (2004). A very imaginative and thoughtful take on connections around the world.

Man-houng Lin, *China Upside Down: Currencies, Society, and Ideologies, 1808–1856* (2006). An in-depth account of China's struggles before the Taiping Rebellion.

Jürgen Osterhammel, *The Transformation of the World: A Global History of the Nineteenth Century* (2014). A gigantic book with lots of insight about globalization, imperialism, nationalism. His main emphases are on China and Europe.

Gungwu Wang, *Anglo-Chinese Encounters since 1800* (2003). A readable and slender book emphasizing intellectual and technological transfers from Britain to China, mainly through overseas Chinese.

Louis Warren, *God's Red Son: The Ghost Dance Religion and the Making of Modern America* (2017). An authoritative and accessible study.

O. Arne Westad, *Restless Empire: China and the World since 1750* (2012). A highly readable book, and strong on the international dimensions of the decline of the Qing.

Chapter 26 International Politics: War, Peace, and Ideologies, 1870 to 1940

Volker Berghahn, *Europe in the Era of Two World Wars* (2006). A brief overview of European affairs, with useful sketches of fascism and communism.

Laura Engelstein, *Russia in Flames: War, Revolution, and Civil War* (2018). A massive narrative of momentous events, with many insights along the way.

Adrian Gregory, *A War of Peoples, 1914–1919* (2014). A short overview of World War I, with a chapter on how historians have presented it for the last hundred years.

Erez Manela, *The Wilsonian Moment* (2009). A study of the reception of the 1919 peace agreement in Egypt, India, China, and Korea.

David Reynolds, *The Long Shadow: The Legacies of the Great War in the Twentieth Century* (2015). A readable and insightful study of the meanings of World War I.

Vladimir Tismaneanu, *The Devil in History: Communism, Fascism and Some Lessons of the Twentieth Century* (2012). A thoughtful reflection on the origins and character of communism and fascism, mainly in the USSR, post-1945 Eastern Europe, and Germany.

Chapter 27 World War II and the Cold War, 1937 to 1991

Svetlana Alexievich, *The Unwomanly Face of War* (2017). Narratives of the lives of women who served in the Soviet armed forces during World War II.

Anonymous, *A Woman in Berlin* (2016). First published in the early 1950s, this diary details the grim experiences of a young woman in the weeks after the Soviet army marched into Berlin.

Pierre Asselin, *Vietnam's American War* (2017). A well-researched account of how North Vietnam prevailed over the United States in the Vietnam War.

Paul Kennedy, *Engineers of Victory* (2013). A very clear analysis of how the Allies learned to do things better during the course of World War II.

Xiaobing Li, *The Cold War in East Asia* (2017). A synthesis strong on the Chinese role.

Richard Overy, *Why the Allies Won* (1995). A readable and insightful analysis of World War II.

S.C.M. Paine, *The Japanese Empire: Grand Strategy from the Meiji Restoration to the Pacific War* (2017). A brief narrative and analysis of Japan's rise and overreach.

Peipei Qiu, *Chinese Comfort Women: Testimonies from Imperial Japan's Sex Slaves* (2013). A study based on recent and disturbing interviews of women who survived terrible ordeals.

O. Arne Westad, *The Cold War: A World History* (2017). A massive and detailed work by a dean of Cold War historians.

Vladislav Zubok, *A Failed Empire* (2007). A good study of the USSR during the Cold War.

Chapter 28 Decolonization and the Rise of East Asia, 1945 to 1991

Kent Deng, *China's Political Economy in Modern Times* (2012). A work presenting lots of data not easily available elsewhere.

Barry Eichengreen, Dwight Perkins, and Kwanho Shin, *From Miracle to Maturity: The Growth of the Korean Economy* (2012). An authoritative and readable book on South Korea's economic transformation.

Dane Kennedy, *Decolonization: A Very Short Introduction* (2016). A thematic study and the quickest way to get a good general picture.

Yasmin Khan, *The Great Partition* (2007). A mix of analysis and personal stories from the saga of Indian independence and partition.

Robert McMahon, *Colonialism and Cold War: The United States and the Struggle for Indonesian Independence, 1945–49* (2011). A detailed study of the evolution of U.S. policy.

Tessa Morris-Suzuki, *The Technological Transformation of Japan* (1994). A compelling analysis, strong on how Japanese traditions proved favorable for its post-war surge.

Kwame Nkrumah, *I Speak of Freedom: A Statement of African Ideology* (1961). The leader of Ghana's independence movement in his own words.

Martin Thomas, *Fight or Flight: Britain, France, and Their Roads from Empire* (2014). An authoritative comparative study, strong on international context and the stories of Algeria, Madagascar, India, Kenya, and Malaysia.

Ezra Vogel, *Deng Xiaoping and the Transformation of China* (2011). A detailed assessment arguing that Deng stands among the titans of twentieth-century history.

Chapter 29 A Shrinking World: Globalization since 1980

Richard Baldwin, *The Great Convergence: Information Technology and the New Globalization* (2016). An economist's take on recent trends, written informally.

Angus Deaton, *The Great Escape: Health, Wealth, and the Origins of Inequality* (2013). A work that's strong on health trends and the economics of globalization.

Edward R. Dickinson, *The World in the Long Twentieth Century: An Interpretation* (2018). A very useful look at political, economic, and environmental trends.

Wangari Maathai, *Unbowed: A Memoir* (2006). An account of her path from a Kenyan village girl to international environmental activist.

J. R. McNeill and Peter Engelke, *The Great Acceleration* (2016). A brief account of global environmental changes since 1945.

Branko Milanovich, *Global Inequality: A New Approach for the Age of Globalization* (2016). A book that's packed with data but highly readable (as economists' prose goes).

GLOSSARY OF KEY TERMS AND PRONUNCIATION GUIDE

AH *a* sound, as in *far*
IH short *i* sound, as in *hit*
OO long *o* sound, as in *snooze*
UH short *u* sound, as in *cup*
A short *a* sound, as in *tap*
EE long *e* sound, as in *sneeze*
OH long *o* sound, as in *bone*
EH short *e* sound, as in *very*
AY long *a* sound, as in *say*
EYE long *i* sound, as in *white*
OW diphthong *o* sound, as in *how*
AW diphthong *a* sound, as in *saw*

Emphasis: Syllables in capital letters receive the emphasis. If there is no syllable in capitals, then all syllables get equal emphasis.

1918 flu pandemic: A flu mutation that spread worldwide after World War I, killing 50 to 100 million people mostly between the ages of 15 and 40. Due to tighter global connections, it spread quickly and widely.

Abbasid caliphate [ah-BAH-sihd KA-lih-fayt]: The Islamic successor state (750–1258) to the Umayyads. Based in Baghdad, the Abbasids consolidated power over most of the Islamic world, profited from widespread trade, supported scholars and artists, and had learned works from Chinese, Sanskrit, Hebrew, Greek, and Latin translated into Arabic and Persian.

Abdelkadir [ab-dehl-KAH-dihr] (1808–1883): A Sufi scholar and the leader of the biggest revolt against French rule in Algeria, which reached its height in the 1830s. The French captured and exiled Abdelkadir in 1847.

aboriginal Australians: Also known as Aborigines, aboriginal Australians were mobile hunter-foragers. They spoke 200 to 250 related languages and shared consistent animist religious beliefs across the continent.

Achaemenids [ak-KEE-muh-nids] (559–330 BCE): A dynasty that came from what is now southwestern Iran. They conquered all major powers from Egypt to northwest India, making their empire unprecedented in size.

Adi Granth [ah-dee GRAHNTH]: The scripture of the Sikhs. Written in Punjabi, it is a collection of Nanak's hymns, or teachings, as well as some additional hymns.

Adolf Hitler (1889–1945): The fascist head of the Nazi Party who became chancellor of Germany in 1933. Wanting to return Germany to great power status, he introduced social and economic reforms, including national purification, which targeted Jews, Slavs, and Roma for elimination.

Ahura Mazda [uh-HOOR-uh MAHZ-duh]: A benevolent, all-knowing god and the preferred deity of the Achaemenid dynasty from Darius onward. A priesthood called the Magi led Ahura Mazda worship, which involved outdoor fire ceremonies and sacrifices.

Akbar [AHK-bah] (r. 1556–1605): A Mughal emperor who spearheaded the unification of most of South Asia. He used a combination of horses, guns, and siegecraft along with tolerant religious policy to assert and maintain power.

Aksum: An African state south of Kush that reached its peak between 300 and 500 CE. It traded African products to Egypt, the Mediterranean world, and Mesopotamia, which enabled it to amass wealth and power.

al-Andalus [al-ANN-duh-luhs] (711–1492): The Muslim-controlled part of Spain that the last Umayyad dynast founded in 711 and the Córdoba caliphate ruled from 929 to 1031. Afterward, it remained fragmented until Christian armies defeated it in 1492.

al-Qaeda: An extremist Islamist political faction begun in 1988 by Osama bin Laden that funded the September 11, 2001, terrorist attacks on the United States. It became powerful in Iraq after 2003, and its offshoots have engaged in terrorism targeting other Muslims in several countries.

Alexander II (1818–1881): The tsar of Russia who emancipated the serfs due in part to his commitment to military reform. He wanted a standing army and hoped the abolition of serfdom would lead to a cheaper and better-educated army without the risk of rebellion.

Alexander Hamilton: An American politician who prescribed tariffs to protect U.S. industry when he was secretary of the Treasury in 1791. His recommendations guided U.S. trade policy for a century and inspired the German economist Friedrich List.

Alexander the Great (356–323 BCE): Born in Macedonia to the king of Macedon, Alexander was one of the most skilled military commanders in history. He continued and completed his father's conquest of the Greek world and claimed the Achaemenid throne, uniting both regions in a vast empire.

Alexandria (founded 331 BCE): A wealthy Mediterranean seaport city during the Hellenistic age that fostered trade linkages among Egypt, Africa, the Mediterranean, and Southwest Asia. It was a center for manufacturing, medicine, mathematics, commerce, and culture.

Algerian war for independence (1954–1962): The conflict between the FLN, Algerian independence fighters, and the French Army, along with its collaborators, over France's colonial presence. It led to Algerian independence; the massacre of Muslim Algerians, known as harkis; and the mass expulsion of French settler-colonists, the pieds-noirs.

alliance networks: Two groups into which the great European powers were divided in order to uphold peace in Europe after the Napoleonic Wars. In 1914, Germany, Austria-Hungary, and Italy belonged to the Triple Alliance; and France, Russia, and Great Britain belonged to the Triple Entente.

Allies: A coalition of countries that fought against the Axis powers in World War II, most prominently the United Kingdom, United States, USSR, and China. The alliance also included many other countries, colonies, and members of the British Commonwealth.

American Revolution (1775–1781): An anti-colonial, revolutionary war between thirteen British colonies in America and the British government. The colonists won and created the United States, an independent country.

Ancestral Pueblo Inhabitants of the high-plateau Four Corners area in today's U.S. Southwest who developed a dispersed agricultural society around the ninth century. Their distinctive architectural style of cliff dwellings and ceremonial spaces called *kivas* is evident at their central settlement of Chaco Canyon. Their settlements declined in the twelfth and thirteenth centuries as a probable result of long-lasting drought cycles. They are also known as the Anasazi, which means "ancestors of our enemies" in the Navajo language.

Anthropocene: The proposed new geological age defined by the influence of humans on big natural systems, such as climate. Around 2000, many scientists started to argue that the Holocene ended in the mid-twentieth century and that we are now living in the Anthropocene.

anti-colonialism: A mass political and social movement that developed after World War I. Supporters, disillusioned with European rulers and post-war peace settlements, advocated for self-rule and the end of colonial empires.

Antônio Conselheiro [kohn-say-YAY-roo] (1830–1897): A traveling preacher in Brazil who eventually settled in Canudos. He attracted many followers with his sermons on salvation, denunciations of the state, and promise of the imminent return of Jesus Christ.

Arabs: At the time of Muhammad's birth, Arabs were a group of polytheistic, loosely connected, mostly nomadic tribes who lived in the Arabian Peninsula and made a living herding, trading, and raiding. In the seventh century, united under Muhammad, they became a formidable military force, conquering lands from India to Spain.

Asian tiger economies: Collective name for the economies of certain East Asian countries—Japan, South Korea, Taiwan, Singapore, Hong Kong, and China—that experienced massive economic growth after World War II.

Assyrian [uh-SEER-ee-uhn] **Empire** (ca. 911–609 BCE): A large and multicultural empire based in northern Mesopotamia; its power rested partly on raising horses and forging iron tools and weapons.

Augustine (354–430): A North African bishop whose prolific moralistic writings influenced the creation of a more uniform Christianity called Catholicism.

Axis: A loose coalition among Germany, Italy, and Japan. The Axis powers instigated World War II through their expansionist aims and fought against the Allies during the conflict.

Bantu [BAN-too]: A language group that originated in the area of the modern-day Cameroon-Nigerian border. It is made up of 600 related languages now spoken in East, central, and southern Africa.

Battle of Stalingrad (1942–1943): A brutal, months-long conflict between Soviet and German armies on the eastern front. The German loss of the battle was a major turning point in World War II and part of a broader Axis decline.

Beatriz Kimpa Vita (ca. 1684–1706): A young woman in Kongo who was drawn to Catholicism, became a preacher, and sought the re-unification of Kongo. She gained thousands of followers by telling them God spoke through her, but her movement threatened other aspirants to power and she was burned at the stake as a witch and heretic.

bell beaker ware: Clay containers shaped like an upside-down bell that became popular across Europe and North Africa between around 2900 and 1800 BCE. Used mainly for beer, their widespread presence points to commercial and cultural connections among elites in Europe.

Benito Mussolini (1883–1945): The fascist and authoritarian ruler of Italy who took power in 1922. He manipulated the media, promoted Italian nationalism, and capitalized on Italians' anxieties, particularly about communism, to build support.

Bhakti [BAHK-tee] **movement**: A popular form of Hinduism that emerged in the seventh century in India and appealed to a broad segment of the population. The religion stressed intense, personal devotion to one god (usually Shiva, Vishnu, or Devi) and used local languages (not Sanskrit) spoken by the common people.

Big Bang: The origin of our universe and the start of time, space, and energy. It occurred about 13.8 billion years ago, and the universe has been cooling and expanding since that time.

biological globalization: A worldwide exchange of plants, animals, and microbes that followed the discovery of the oceans and of which the Columbian Exchange was a part. It led to connections among ecosystems and a change of flora, fauna, and diseases across the world.

biological old regime: Conditions of human health that preceded the Vital Revolution. Deadly crowd diseases, gastrointestinal infections, high infant mortality, malnutrition, and starvation defined it.

bipedalism: The ability to stand upright that evolved 6 million to 4.5 million years ago; a trait that distinguishes hominins from apes and ape-like ancestors.

Bourbon Reforms: Changes reflecting Enlightenment thought that the Spanish Crown introduced in Spanish America to revitalize its empire. They included new taxes, strengthened fortifications, administrative reorganization, and freer trade.

British Raj [rahj] (1858–1947): British colonial rule in India, which relied on the cooperation of local Indian elites and the exploitation of existing societal divisions. It reordered the Indian economy with the introduction of free trade and new infrastructure.

bronze: An alloy, or combination, of the two metals copper and tin; used in many cultures for armor and weapons as well as for ornamentation.

Byzantine [BIHZ-ann-teen] **Empire**: The eastern part of the Roman Empire and all that remained of the empire after 476. At its height in the sixth and seventh centuries, it included Egypt, the Levant, Anatolia, and the Balkans; it lasted until 1453.

cabotage: Port-to-port, local trade links. In the Indian Ocean world, shorter-distance cabotage trade in everyday goods supported long-distance trade in luxuries.

Cahokia [kuh-HOH-kee-uh] (ca. 1000–1350): A large Amerindian city that was located in the floodplain of the Mississippi River in present-day Illinois and home to mostly farming people. Cahokians engaged in coordinated efforts to build ceremonial plazas and over 100 mounds used mostly for sacrifices and burials.

Calicut: An important commercial port city on the southwest coast of India. Its merchants traded various spices that were highly sought by Arab, Persian, and European merchants.

caravanserais: In Eastern countries, inns along major trade routes that accommodated large numbers of traders, their animals, and their wares.

carbon dioxide (CO_2): Released by burning fossil fuels, it is one of the most important greenhouse gases. The rise of fossil fuel use since around 1840—especially since 1950 or so—has contributed to increased concentrations of CO_2 in the atmosphere and, in turn, the current pulse of climate change.

Carolingians (ca. 750–843): A dynasty that ruled a comparatively modest and poor state in western Europe and introduced feudalism. The state became an empire during the reign of Charlemagne (r. 768–814) but fell apart after his death.

Carthage: A Phoenician colony on the Mediterranean Sea's North Africa coast that became a formidable seaborne empire based on commerce. Carthage flourished between approximately 800 and 146 BCE.

cassava [kuh-SAH-vuh]: Native to Brazil, as part of the Columbian Exchange cassava (also called manioc) became a staple food in many parts of Africa. It is drought resistant, does well in poor soils, and remains edible even if left in the ground for long periods of time.

caste system: A hierarchical and hereditary division of society that developed in the Ganges basin. The early caste system split people into four main tiers: Brahmins, Kshatriya, Vaishya, and Sudra.

Catholic Reformation: Also called the Counter-Reformation, a period of major reforms in the Catholic Church undertaken in response to the Protestant Reformation. The Catholic Church became more centralized and standardized; popes, bishops, and abbots cut back on high living; efforts were made to root out heresy and ban certain books.

Celts: A loose grouping of various peoples in Atlantic Europe who spoke similar languages and shared cultural features. They emerged between 1300 and 700 BCE. They migrated south from the Alps and Danube in droves during the fifth to third centuries BCE.

Chaco Canyon: A settlement in northern New Mexico that was likely the center of the broader Ancestral Pueblo (Anasazi) region spread throughout the Four Corners area. All roads built by Ancestral Pueblo led to Chaco Canyon, and it was the home of religious and political elites until its collapse due to drought in the twelfth century.

champa rice: A variety of rice that matures quickly, is drought resistant, and ripens at higher and cooler elevations than other strains. After the Chinese imported it from Vietnam in the eleventh century, it became a reliable food supply that spurred massive population growth.

chariot: A two-wheeled carriage pulled by horses and often used as a weapon of war. Chariots appeared first in western Asia around 2100 BCE and were widespread in Eurasia by 1500 BCE.

chartered joint-stock companies: Companies to which governments grant monopoly rights by charter and in which hundreds or thousands of investors own shares. These innovative measures, developed during the sixteenth century, helped share the risks and increase the scale of long-distance trade.

Chinese Civil War (1945–1949): Conflict between the Chinese Communist Party, led by Mao Zedong, and the nationalist Guomindang. The CCP won and created the People's Republic of China.

Chinese Revolution (1880s–1910s): A long revolution that ultimately overthrew the Qing dynasty. Yuan Shikai, an army general, along with Sun Yatsen and other revolutionaries, took advantage of an army mutiny to force the last Qing emperor to abdicate.

choke point: A narrow route providing strategic, affordable passage from one large body of water to another—such as the Straits of Malacca between Sumatra and the Malay Peninsula, or the strait between India's southern tip and Sri Lanka. Those who controlled choke points often were able to profit economically and politically.

Chola [CHOH-lah] **kingdom** (ca. 970–1300): A state that arose in southeastern India and ultimately controlled Indian Ocean trade passing along south Indian coasts and Sri Lanka. Partly an alliance of merchant trading guilds, the Chola flourished through commercial and naval activity, and even attacked Srivijayan cities while under the expansionary rule of Rajendra I (r. 1012–1044).

Christopher Columbus: Born in Genoa, Italy, Christopher Columbus secured funding from the king and queen of Castile (a powerful state in Spain) to sail west from Europe and find a route to China in 1492. He instead found islands in the Caribbean and inaugurated a new age of global interconnection.

Cimmerians: Horse nomads from the Russian and Ukrainian steppe who began arriving on the Hungarian plain around 900 BCE, bringing with them steppe traditions. Many waves of nomads and semi-nomads followed, migrating from the steppes to eastern Europe in subsequent centuries.

city: A large settlement with elaborate divisions of labor, social hierarchies, tightly packed living spaces, open public areas, and large buildings. Trade, exchange, and markets feature prominently in cities.

civil service examinations: The use of written examinations on Confucian ideology to select public administrators in China (and in Korea while under Tang influence). This system fostered cultural unity and an educated elite.

classic Hinduism (begun ca. 400 BCE): An evolution of Vedic traditions of caste, ritual, and sacrifice. Hindus added several new beliefs to Vedic foundations, including the endless migration of souls based on moral conduct, or *karma*.

climate change: Recent, rapid change in Earth's climate patterns that is unprecedented in human history and largely human-caused. It is due mainly to a significant increase in fossil fuel use in the past 30 to 40 years, which created high concentrations of greenhouse gases in the atmosphere and caused Earth's temperature to rise.

Clovis points (ca. 12,000–11,000 BCE): Stone spearheads used throughout North America; their broad dissemination indicates widespread cultural and technological diffusion across the continent.

coal: A fossil fuel made up of ancient plant remains that can be converted into motor power. Cheap, low-lying coal gave rise to the Industrial Revolution in Britain and fueled industrialization around the world.

coaling stations: Pacific ports where imperial powers' naval ships refueled during the late nineteenth century. European powers seized Pacific islands largely for their strategic use as coaling stations and the low cost of controlling them.

Cold War (1945–1991): An ideological and political struggle, primarily between the United States and the USSR, that led to a proliferation of nuclear weapons and pervasive propaganda campaigns. It also intensified conflicts around the world through the two countries' participation in proxy wars.

Columbian Exchange: The transfer of plants, animals, and microbes among Eurasia, Africa, and the Americas that followed Columbus's initiation of contact.

Comanche [kuh-MAN-shee] **Empire** (1730–1870): The Comanche rule of the southern plains of the present-day United States, resulting from their near monopoly of the regional gun trade and mastery of horses.

comfort women: Hundreds of thousands of women that the Japanese army captured from various places, including Korea, China, and the Philippines, and forced to work as sex slaves in occupied areas.

commercial revolution: The increased commercialization and specialization, coupled with frontier expansion and territorial conquest, that occurred especially in China and Atlantic Europe during the period 1500–1800. In combination, these factors caused the regions' economies to grow and their societies to become richer.

communism: A broadly appealing international movement and political theory based on the ideas of Karl Marx and Vladimir Lenin. Communists opposed capitalism and private property and believed that inevitable revolution would bring about a prosperous, equitable world.

Communist Manifesto (1848): A political pamphlet co-authored by Karl Marx and Friedrich Engels arguing that class struggle propels history. It describes the inevitability of a communist revolution and calls for the working classes around the world to join together in the struggle against the ruling elite.

complex society: A social unit characterized by a large hierarchical society, regulatory institutions, and a complex division of labor. Complex societies often developed states and cities.

Confucius [kuhn-FYOO-shuhs] **(Kong Qiu)** (ca. 551–479 BCE): A *shi* whose followers wrote down his ideas in the book *Analects*, which emphasized ethical conduct, ritual, social hierarchy, and the importance of scholars.

Constantine (r. 306–337 CE): A Roman emperor who established a second Roman capital in Byzantium (modern-day Istanbul), renamed it Constantinople, and split the Roman Empire into two halves. He converted to Christianity, ultimately making it an imperial, state-supported religion.

containerization: The transition to the use of shipping containers for the transport of goods that led to decreased shipping and labor costs as well as shorter shipping times. Containers facilitated the connection between East Asian export economies and large North American markets.

containment strategy: An approach guiding U.S. Cold War policy toward the USSR based on defeating it with patience and endurance rather than military strength. The strategy was based on the belief that Soviet communism would collapse if the United States prevented its spread.

cotton: Lightweight and durable cloth woven from the cotton plant. During the early modern period Atlantic Europeans expanded the trade of cotton to new markets in Africa, Europe, and the Americas, and it became an essential global trade commodity.

cotton gin: A machine, invented in the United States and patented in 1794, that separated cotton seeds from cotton fiber, thereby easing cotton production. It contributed to the rise of cotton manufacturing and the spread of cotton production and slavery in the U.S. South.

COVID-19: An easily transmittable infectious disease caused by the novel coronavirus (SARS CoV-2), which apparently originated in bat colonies before mutating into a human pathogen in or near Wuhan, China, in late 2019. In 2020, COVID-19 quickly spread around the world, causing a global pandemic that killed hundreds of thousands.

creole cultures: Societies in the Americas, particularly in the plantation zone, that blended various features from Africa and Europe to create hybrid cultures, religions, and languages.

crowd diseases: Infections such as smallpox, mumps, or measles that require large populations in order to stay in circulation. In large populations, these pathogens mostly affect children.

Crusades (1096–1231): Waves of small-scale wars and attacks on the Levant that were motivated by both religious and military aims. Over 200 years, Crusaders of mostly French, German, and English origin established small kingdoms that all fell by the thirteenth century.

culture of imperialism: Celebratory literature, theater, music, and public ceremony that supported the belief in the right and duty of one group to rule over others. It was most prominent in Britain but also existed in the United States, France, Germany, Italy, and Japan.

cuneiform: The earliest known form of writing, cuneiform developed in Uruk around 3400 to 3300 BCE and consisted of scratches made on wedges of clay.

Darius (r. 522–486 BCE): A lance-bearer who staged a coup d'état and became an Achaemenid king. He introduced many innovations that helped him effectively manage the vast Achaemenid territory.

dark earth: Human-made patches of nutrient-rich soil in Amazonia. People used these areas to raise crops that supported thousands of settlements.

declines in fertility: The global drop in birth rates since about 1960 due to growing urbanization, the spread of female education, and the increased use of birth control.

de-industrialization: During the Industrial Revolution, the decline of industries that could not compete with the price and quality of factory-made products.

Delhi sultanate (ca. 1206–1400): A military aristocracy established in northern India by Turkic horsemen from Central Asia who fostered an Indo-Islamic culture fusing Indian, Turkic, Persian, and Arabic elements. Its legacy includes palace and mosque architecture, and Urdu poetry—a blend of Hindi and Persian.

demographic dividend: A shift in fertility patterns that aids economic growth and development. Demographic dividends in East Asia after 1950 contributed to the Asian tigers' economic success.

demokratia [day-moh-kra-TEE-uh]: After 508 BCE, a form of government that the Athenian *polis* introduced wherein all citizens directly participated in governance. It was based on an elected ruling council of 500 that was responsible to a larger assembly of all free Athenian men over age 18 who had completed military training.

Deng Xiaoping [DUHNG show-pihng] (1904–1997): The head of China beginning in 1978 and leader of its economic transformation. His economic reforms, which essentially replaced socialism with capitalism, included the end of the commune work-unit system, re-introduction of profit motives, and encouragement of export-oriented industry.

dhows [dows]: Ships used by Arab seafarers in the Indian Ocean. Dhows featured slanting, triangular sails to efficiently capture the wind and hulls sewn with coconut fiber for maximum flexibility.

disease disasters: As a result of entry into the expanding Global web, the introduction of deadly diseases to previously isolated areas of the world that had no experience with them. In combination with violence and declining fertility, these diseases led to devastating demographic collapses in the Americas, Siberia, many Pacific Islands, and parts of southern Africa.

dolmens: Stacks of stones, erected mainly between 1500 and 500 BCE, that mark burial sites and imply growing social stratification. Although they were built in many places in Eurasia, Korea contains almost half the world's dolmens.

domestication: The genetic modification of plants or animals through human selection or breeding. Domestication enables humans to produce food instead of searching for it.

domino theory: Conjecture among U.S. policymakers that if one country fell to communism, then the countries surrounding it would follow. This theory drove U.S. involvement in the Vietnam War because officials feared that if Vietnam became entirely communist, the rest of Southeast Asia would too.

dreamtime: One of the religious beliefs of aboriginal Australians according to which a distant past linked to the birth of the world when supernatural entities crossed Australia, forming the continent and tracing paths that became "songlines."

Dutch East India Company (VOC): A very successful chartered joint-stock company created to control the Dutch spice trade. During the seventeenth and eighteenth centuries, the VOC's heavily armed ships dominated the Indonesian archipelago as the company used force and violence to gain advantageous trade terms.

economies of scale: Economies of scale occur when a producer's costs per unit of output decline as the scale of the enterprise grows. This condition, which exists in only some industries such as sugar production, benefits large-scale enterprises.

Eiichi Shibusawa [ay-EE-chee shih-boo-SOW-ah] (1840–1931): A Japanese government official and businessman who was passionate about bringing industrialization to his country. He set up Japan's first modern cotton mill in Osaka with the help of Takeo Yamanobe.

emancipation for serfs (1861): A labor liberation granted by a statute that, in theory, liberated serfs by granting them freedoms they previously lacked. In practice, it introduced many new legal constraints to which former serfs remained subject.

encomienda [ehn-koh-mee-EHN-dah]: Granted by Spanish rulers to colonizers in Spanish America, the legal right to conscript Amerindians as unpaid laborers.

Epic of Gilgamesh: A long poem written down around 2100 BCE in cuneiform and the oldest surviving epic poem in world history. It is about a legendary Uruk king, Gilgamesh, who lived around 2600 BCE.

Eurasian steppe: A broad grassland that stretches from eastern Europe to East Asia.

fascism: A political movement and ideology that formed the basis of Benito Mussolini and Adolf Hitler's governments. It emphasized militant nationalism, purification of the nation, a cult of the leader, and showy displays of national strength.

Ferdinand Magellan: A Portuguese explorer whom the Spanish Crown funded to find a route to the Moluccas by sailing west from Europe and along the southern coast of South America in 1519. He died in the Philippines after crossing the Pacific, but his crew became the first people to sail around the world and attained knowledge of the vastness of the Pacific Ocean.

field artillery and fortifications: Large and heavy mobile guns and cannon deployed in the field, and the highly engineered structures used to defend against them. These elements increased the cost and intricacy of war during the early modern period.

financialization: The rise in the prominence, prevalence, and profitability of finance worldwide due to de-regulation and digital technology. It has eased the global flow of money and contributed to increased economic volatility.

firestick farming: Intentional burning of landscapes and methodical use of fire that promotes the growth of edible plants and attracts animals for hunting. Aboriginal Australians employed firestick farming to increase their food supply.

flint maize: A form of maize, developed in the American Midwest around the ninth or tenth century, that matured faster than other varieties and with bigger kernels. It boosted food supplies and enabled North American farmers to subsist mainly on agricultural crops and less on hunting and foraging.

Florentine Codex: A comprehensive catalogue of Aztec history and culture, complied between 1545 and 1590 by a Spanish priest and his Aztec students. The *Codex* incorporates about 2,000 illustrations of Aztec daily life along with text in Nahuatl expressed in the Roman alphabet.

fractional reserve banking: The practice of banks lending out more money than they have in their reserves in order to create money in the form of credit. The Bank of Amsterdam pioneered this practice, which promoted commerce by reducing its costs.

free trade: De-regulation of trade beginning in the 1980s that Ronald Reagan and Margaret Thatcher spearheaded. Free trade policy spread around the world, leading to bigger multinational corporations and globalized supply chains.

French Revolution (1789–1799): A political revolution within France aimed at reforming the hierarchical social order. It led to sweeping changes, descended into terror and dictatorship, and was largely reversed when the monarchy was re-established in 1814.

Friedrich List (1789–1846): An economist born in Germany who wrote newspaper articles and books that guided state-sponsored industrialization. He advocated for protectionist policies and the construction of railroads.

Ganges [GAN-jeez] **basin**: Rich alluvial lands surrounding the Ganges River that supported the development of a new Indian culture and complex society starting around 1500 BCE. It is also known as the Gangetic plain.

Genghis Khan (ca. 1165–1227): Born as Temujin, Genghis Khan was the founder and leader of the Mongol Empire. Under his command, the Mongols conquered territory from China to Ukraine.

germ theory of disease: The scientific theory developed after 1850 that pointed to bacteria's role in infection. It led to sanitation reforms that reduced death and illness from water-borne diseases and paved the way for understanding infections.

Germanic tribes: Groups originating from east of the Danube River and north of the Rhine River in Europe, including Goths, Vandals, and Franks. Beginning in the 370s, the Germanic tribes migrated to Roman territory as they fled from the Huns, or when the Romans hired them to fight against other tribes or to fight for one set of Romans against another in civil wars.

Ghost Dance: A spiritual movement that arose in response to disruptions in Amerindian life during the nineteenth century. Inspired by Wovoka's prophecy, participants performed a community circle dance in hopes that this ceremony would bring the return of peace, joy, and plenty.

Glorious Revolution (1688–1689): The nearly bloodless replacement of James II with William of Orange on the throne of England, organized by Protestant British elites. It cemented the increased power of Parliament in relation to the monarchy.

Göbekli Tepe [goh-behk-LEE teh-peh]: A site in southeastern Turkey; likely a religious temple that a sedentary or semi-sedentary group built around 9000 BCE and abandoned by 7000 BCE.

gracialization: The thinning and shrinking of skeletons through evolution. Humans underwent this process as social groups grew and relied less on their physical strength for survival.

Grand Canal: A massive public works project, started under the Sui dynasty (581–618), that linked north and south China, promoting unity and enabling emperors to move troops and food quickly and easily.

Great Leap Forward (1958–1961): Mao Zedong's massive and disastrous campaign to improve China's industry and agriculture. He called for citizens to produce steel in their own backyards, the output of which proved to be useless, and introduced new agricultural policies that caused a devastating famine.

Great Zimbabwe (ca. 1250–1450): A city and center of power in southern Africa based on cattle wealth and a thriving gold trade. The rulers at Great Zimbabwe had enough authority and wealth to erect great stone buildings beginning in 1275.

gross world product (GWP): The size of the world economy, which is calculated by using the combined value of all goods and services produced worldwide. Between 1500 and 1800, the GWP almost doubled.

Guanches [GWAHNCH-ihz]: Descendants of North African Berbers, the Guanches were inhabitants of the Canary Islands who fought against Spanish conquest and settlement from 1402 to 1496. Spanish weapons technology and the diseases they carried with them eventually led to the defeat of the Guanches.

Gulf Stream: The counterclockwise movement of North Atlantic Ocean currents that warms the climates of western Europe's coastal areas from Portugal to Norway.

Gupta [GOOP-tah] **dynasty** (ca. 330–550): A dynasty that ruled the north of India and supported religious institutions, math, science, and arts. Samudragupta (r. 335–375) and

Chandragupta II (r. 375-415) were two successful Gupta kings.

Habsburgs (1282–1918): Originating as Swiss and German nobles, the Habsburgs extended their territory with military force and advantageous political marriages. They built a global empire and became a major European power but were unable to unify Europe.

Haitian Revolution (1791–1804): An anti-colonial, political, and anti-slavery revolution rooted in racial tensions and led primarily by Toussaint L'Ouverture, a former slave. It began with the largest slave rebellion in history and ended in victory, but it left Haiti fractured in its aftermath.

Hammurabi [hahm-uh-RAH-bee] (r. 1792–1750 BCE): A king of Babylon who formed a short-lived empire; he erected a stone monument inscribed with 282 laws that survives today.

Han dynasty (206 BCE–220 CE): Emperor Gaozu founded the Han dynasty following Qin rule. Han rulers expanded Chinese territory and promoted Confucian ideology; under their leadership the economy and population grew, and land and maritime trade flourished.

Hannibal Barca (247–ca. 182 BCE): A member of the Carthaginian Barca clan who transformed Carthage's presence in Spain into an empire there. Hannibal led the fight against Rome in the Second Punic War and gained renown for his skills as a military commander.

Harrapans [hah-RAP-puhnz] (ca. 2600–1700 BCE): The name of the Indus valley populations and culture; its two largest cities were Harappa and Mohenjo Daro.

Hawaiian kings: Between 1450 and 1700, several Hawaiian chiefs responded to shortages of resources and increased competition by making themselves kings, thereby initiating a ruling class, an administrative bureaucracy, and struggles for succession to the throne. Kings and kingdoms were unique in the Pacific world; no other Polynesians outside of Hawaii had them.

heavy cavalry: One of Darius's military innovations. Instead of arming mounted warriors with only light equipment, heavy cavalry rode on large, strong horses with full armor and weaponry.

Heian [HAY-ahn] **Japan** (734–1185): A period of rule in Japan, based at Heian (modern Kyoto), during which Chinese influence waned, indigenous religious traditions (especially Shinto) became dominant, aristocratic social order prevailed, and refined courtly life produced the first substantial body of literature written by women anywhere in world history.

heliocentric system: The idea, which Nicholas Copernicus wrote down in 1514, that planets rotate around the sun as opposed to the idea that the sun moves around the Earth. Johannes Kepler, Galileo Galilei, and Isaac Newton built on this work, and the heliocentric system won acceptance in 1687.

Hellenistic age (323–31 BCE): The age of Greek and Macedonian rule in Greece, Egypt, and Southwest Asia. It began after Alexander died and his generals Ptolemy, Antigonus, and Seleucus divided his empire among themselves.

herders: People who mainly lived off of domesticated grazing animals that they raised in arid and semi-arid grassland and scrubland regions.

hieroglyphs [HEYE-ruh-gliphs]: The primary Egyptian writing system, which eventually contained nearly 1,000 symbols; it developed around 3000 BCE, possibly influenced by Sumerian cuneiforms.

Hiroshima and Nagasaki: Two Japanese cities and centers of military production onto which the United States dropped nuclear weapons in August 1945. The bombs killed 105,000 people immediately and were the first, and so far only, nuclear weapons used in warfare.

HIV/AIDS: The infectious and deadly disease that spread from chimpanzees to humans in the 1940s and caused a global pandemic beginning in the 1980s. Africa was the hardest hit. As of 2020, the disease has killed 30 million people.

Holocaust: The outcome of a Nazi-led effort to racially purify Germany through the mass murder of groups Hitler deemed inferior, particularly Jews. During the Holocaust, Nazis murdered millions of Jews, as well as Roma (Gypsies), the mentally ill, and the physically disabled.

Holocene: The name given to the roughly 11,700-year period beginning with the end of the Younger Dryas and continuing until today.

hominins [HAWM-ih-nihms]: The term used to describe all humans, extinct human branches, and ape-like human ancestors who have lived in the last 7 million years. Fossil hunters have discovered 18 species of hominin so far.

Homo erectus [HOH-MOH ee-REHK-tuhs]: A hominin species that emerged 1.5 million years ago and went extinct 190,000 years ago. *Homo sapiens*, Neanderthals, Denisovans, and Flores Island "Hobbits" are all probably descended from *Homo erectus*.

Homo sapiens [HOH-MOH SAY-pee-uhns]: A type of hominin and the name for our species, human beings. *Homo sapiens* emerged 300,000 to 200,000 years ago in Africa.

Hyksos [HICK-sohs]: A group of people, probably from the area of modern-day Lebanon, who migrated to and invaded Egypt. They ruled Egypt from around 1700 to 1500 BCE.

imperial consolidation: The general trend during the early modern period of empires growing bigger and more powerful at the expense of smaller powers.

income inequality: The growing divergence in incomes beginning in the 1980s. Globalization caused a vast share of the world's wealth to be concentrated in the hands of the few, creating the mega-rich class.

indentured labor: Commitment to a fixed period of bonded labor, usually between two and eight years. Although signing indenture contracts was technically voluntary, labor recruiters often used predatory practices to secure laborers.

Indian Ocean monsoon: Regular and predictable alternating winds that made the Indian Ocean relatively easy to sail.

Indian Rebellion (1857–1858): A rebellion that began with an army mutiny and spread to include many regional revolts. The rebels' aims were to get rid of British rule and restore old regimes; but many Indians remained loyal to Britain, and the rebellion collapsed.

Indus River: A river 2,000 miles (3,000 km) long that runs from the Himalayan glaciers to the Arabian Sea. The Indus was central to agriculture and trade for the complex Indus valley cities.

Industrial Revolution: A monumental switch to factory-scale production using machinery driven by water power and fossil fuels instead of human muscle and hand tools. It began in Britain in the late eighteenth century and spread to other countries and continents, with global consequences.

information technology (IT): Innovations in information storing, processing, and sharing, particularly via the Internet and computers. IT reduces the costs of transportation and production, thus aiding in the growth of globalized supply chains.

Inka (ca. 1300–1532): An empire located in the Andean region with its capital in Cuzco. Using a combination of military force and cultural influence, it quickly became one of the two largest polities in the Americas prior to 1492.

international institutions: Governmental, non-governmental, and illicit organizations that operate internationally due to the rise of challenges, problems, and opportunities that are global in scale. Prominent examples include the United Nations, Amnesty International, and drug cartels.

international migrants: People who live in a country other than that in which they were born. Since the 1970s, the majority of migrants have moved to Western Europe, North America, and the Arabian Gulf; by 2019, international migrants made up about 3.5 percent of the global population.

iron: Made from a relatively common ore, iron was cheaper and better than bronze in many ways. However, it required a lot of fuel to smelt and highly skilled ironsmiths to shape it into useful objects.

iron working: The complex process of transforming a raw material, iron ore, into a metal useful for tools and weapons. It appeared in Europe around 1000 BCE and in Africa at roughly the same time.

irrigation: The process of diverting water from lakes, streams, and rivers and supplying it to fields and gardens to ensure crop growth. Irrigation enabled farmers to cultivate land that was otherwise too dry for growing crops.

Islam: A monotheistic religion established in the seventh century whose followers are called Muslims. Its scripture is the Qur'an, which contains God's revelations to Muhammad.

Islamization: The widespread conversion to, and adoption of, Islam. India underwent Islamization beginning in 1000; coastal East African Islamization mostly occurred between the seventh and thirteenth centuries.

Istanbul [ihs-tan-BOOL]: Formerly named Constantinople, it was the capital of the Ottoman Empire from 1453, after Mehmet the Conqueror seized it from the Byzantine Greeks. Istanbul gave the Ottomans control of profitable trade routes and was a launching point for several successful attacks in the Balkans and along the Black Sea coasts.

Jack Gladstone: A slave in British Guiana who led the Demerara revolt of 1823 with his father, Quamina. Gladstone believed that legal abolition had passed in London and called Guiana's slaves to freedom, causing 10,000 slaves to revolt.

Jacobins: A political faction made up of mostly middle-class lawyers who increasingly dominated the government of revolutionary France. They ended elections in 1793, introduced wide-reaching reforms, and ushered in the Terror—a period of widespread suspicion and public executions.

James Watt (1736–1819): A Scottish-born engineer who designed and built more efficient steam engines. He was among a group of engineers who made steam engines more appealing to and useful for manufacturers.

janissaries [JAN-ih-sehr-eez]: Slave soldiers who formed an elite infantry under the Ottoman sultan and developed volley fire with muskets. They were taken as young boys from Christian homes in the Balkans and trained in warfare and administration.

Jawaharlal Nehru [jah-WAH-hah-lahrl NAY-roo] (1889–1964): Instrumental leader of the Indian independence movement and first prime minister of India. Next to Gandhi, he was the second most important figure in the Indian National Congress.

Jenne: An archeological site in West Africa where either a cluster of villages or a city stood by 450 CE. It offers evidence of long-distance trade along the Niger River.

Jesuits: Founded in 1540 in Spain, an order of priests in the Catholic Church dedicated to evangelizing non-Catholics and to rigorous education. During the sixteenth and seventeenth centuries, Jesuit missionaries worked to counter Protestantism in places as varied as Poland, Germany, Japan, China, India, and the Americas.

Jomon culture: A group that became sedentary around 7000 BCE, mostly along the east-central Pacific coast of Japan. They lived off of shellfish,

fish, acorns, and chestnuts and were among the first inventors of pottery.

José Aponte [HOH-say uh-POHN-tay]: A Yoruba-speaking free black who led a slave revolt in Cuba in 1812. This revolt was part of a rise in resistance in Cuba and Brazil due to the growing number of Yoruba-speaking slaves being shipped to these slave markets.

Josef Stalin (1878–1953): The leader of the USSR who consolidated power in the years 1927–1928. He introduced policies of industrialization and collectivization and headed state-led mass terror and brutal coercion.

Julius Caesar (100–44 BCE): A skilled military commander who gained prominence and the loyalty of legions of soldiers, which he refused to disband when the Roman Senate instructed him to. This decision led to civil war, from which Caesar emerged successful and then ruled as dictator from 49 BCE until his assassination five years later.

Justinian (r. 527–565): A Byzantine emperor who built the famous church Hagia Sophia in Constantinople and sought to reconstitute the old Roman Empire by re-conquering territories the Romans had once controlled. He was militarily successful, but he drained the empire of money and his successors lost many of his gains.

keiretsu [kee-REHT-soo]: Large, often family-based Japanese corporate conglomerates made up of banks, trading companies, and industries. They led Japan's post–World War II economic miracle by spearheading technological innovation, assembly-line production, and miniaturization.

Khazaria [kuh-ZAHR-ee-uh] (ca. 640–ca. 970): A Turkic-speaking, multireligious kingdom located in the grasslands of the North Caucasus. The leaders converted to Judaism in the ninth century.

Khoi [KOH-ay]: African hunters and cattle raisers who lived in the southern tip of Africa and clashed with Dutch colonists. Many Khoi eventually died, and their culture largely disappeared due to dispossession and disease epidemics.

King Afonso (r. 1506–1543): A king in Kongo, West Central Africa, whose father, also a king, had converted to Catholicism. Afonso learned to speak, read, and write Portuguese, and as king he made Catholicism the state religion in Kongo. His power grew with the help of Portuguese advisers and military technology.

King Kamehameha [kah-MAY-hah-MAY-hah] (r. 1782–1819): A ruler who unified Hawaii as a single kingdom by using imported military and sailing technology that he strictly controlled. His monarchy lasted a century.

Kongo monarchy: Elected rulers of the kingdom of Kongo whose legitimacy and backing largely rested on protecting their subjects from enslavement.

Korean War (1950–1953): A conflict that began when Soviet-backed, communist North Korea invaded U.S.-backed South Korea. Chinese and United Nations forces joined the fight, which became a war of attrition until a cease-fire was agreed to in 1953.

Koryo [KOHR-yoh] (918–1392): A kingdom in Korea that was based on an alliance of aristocratic families known as *yangban*. It was started due to the threat of steppe nomads.

Kwame Nkrumah [KWAH-may n-KROO-mah] (1909–1972): An influential anti-colonial agitator and chief negotiator in the Gold Coast's transition from British colony to the independent country of Ghana. He was Ghana's first leader and ruled in an increasingly authoritarian way until his ouster in 1966.

La Marseillaise [MAHR-say-yehz]: The song chosen as the French national anthem in 1795. It inspired many countries to designate national anthems, which became a part of growing nationalist cultures around the world.

Lakshmibai [lahk-SHMEE-beye]: A local Indian ruler, also known as the Queen of Jhansi, in north-central India who continued to rule in defiance of British East India Company armies until she died in combat. She remains a national hero in India.

land empires: Empires that used industrial technologies and/or nationalist ideas to extend control over large areas of land rather than overseas. These empires included Russia, the United States, Canada, Brazil, and Argentina. The Comanche Empire in North America and the Ethiopian Empire in northeastern Africa were secondary land empires.

land reform: In South Korea, the transition from the majority of peasants renting land from wealthy landowners to the majority owning their own land. Pursued under pressure from the U.S. military during the post–World War II occupation, land reform laid the foundation for South Korea's economic growth.

Lapita: An Oceanic group that sailed out into the Pacific Ocean from the Bismarck Archipelago around 1300 BCE. They settled most of Remote Oceania, including Fiji, Tonga, and Samoa.

latte stones: Large stone pillars erected on several islands of the Marianas that probably formed the bases of buildings. The Chamorro of Guam began to build latte stones around 1000.

League of Peace and Power: An Iroquois confederacy forged sometime before 1450 among the five Iroquois nations; the League united them and stopped them from warring among one another.

Legalism: A political philosophy that emphasized law, punishment, regimentation, and the power of the state. Lord Shang (390–338 BCE), one of Legalism's chief advocates, promoted intimidation as an ideal governing method.

Levant: The eastern Mediterranean coast and its hinterland. It forms the western edge of the Fertile Crescent and is the location of the first strong evidence of farming.

Lucy: Discovered in 1974 in Ethiopia, a fossilized skeleton of a hominin called *Australopithecus afarensis* who lived 4 million to 3 million years ago.

Magdalenian culture: A semi-settled group that lived between Portugal and Poland and intercepted seasonal migrations of reindeer for sustenance. Magdalenians painted the famous cave art at Lascaux and Altamira.

maize [mayz]: A staple food crop indigenous to the Americas; also known as corn. Part of the Columbian Exchange, maize flourished in southern Europe, China, and western and southern Africa.

malaria: A disease originating in Africa that is transmitted by mosquitos and was particularly deadly in warm, humid, and populous locations. Malaria spread widely around the world, including to the Americas, as part of the Columbian Exchange.

Mandate of Heaven: A cultural formula positing the divine authority that allowed kings to rule. It was a provisional legitimacy that rulers had to convince their subjects they maintained.

Manichaeism [man-ih-KEE-iz'm]: A dualistic religion derived from the preachings of Mani around the third century CE. A blend of Christianity, Zoroastrianism, and Buddhism, it emphasized a struggle between good and evil and a code of conduct including non-violence, fasting, and restraint.

Mao Zedong [MOW tsay-TOHN] (1893–1976): Head of the Chinese Communist Party beginning in World War II and founder of the People's Republic of China. He developed a novel perspective on Marxist theory, arguing that peasants, not just industrial workers, could lead a communist revolution.

Maori [mow-ree]: Polynesians who live in New Zealand. They arrived from central or eastern Polynesia around 1280 and experienced two centuries of peace and prosperity until population growth led to scarcity and warfare at the end of the fifteenth century.

Mauryan [MAWR-yuhn] **Empire** (ca. 321–230 BCE): Indian prince Chandragupta Maurya united the Indus and Ganges valleys for the first time and established the Mauryan Empire; it ended after his grandson Ashoka's reign.

Maya [MEYE-uh] (ca. 600 BCE–900 CE): A complex hierarchical Mesoamerican society that was culturally and linguistically united but politically fragmented. Its rulers amassed wealth through the export of products such as salt, jade, and obsidian, and the Mayan glyphs were the most complete Mesoamerican writing system.

Meiji [MAY-jee] **Restoration** (1867–1868): A political revolution in Japan that ended in the reinstatement of rule by emperor and the introduction of a new elite. Meiji reformers were committed to strengthening Japan and promoting its industrialization.

Menelik II [MEHN-eh-lihk] (1844–1913): Architect and ruler of the Ethiopian Empire who used foreign military technology and skills to conquer surrounding lands and defeat Italian forces at the Battle of Adowa. He also introduced foreign technologies and institutions, such as railroads and public schools.

menhirs: Large oblong stones, standing upright, that began appearing in Europe in about 5500 BCE, marking a shift in spiritual practices that spread across the region. One example is Stonehenge, built around 2500 BCE in southern England.

merchant trading guilds: Formal organizations of groups of traders who worked together to facilitate trade and ease the risks associated with it. An alliance of merchant trading guilds formed the foundation of the Chola kingdom's power (ca. 970–1300).

Meroë [MEHR-oh-wee]: A kingdom in Kush located on the Nile between Egypt and sub-Saharan Africa that reached its peak around the first century BCE. It was the center of iron working in Africa and controlled the export of African goods to Egypt.

Mesopotamia: A largely agricultural region in the Tigris and Euphrates river valleys where Sumer, Akkad, Assyria, and Babylon were located.

metallurgy: The process of separating metals from ore—the rock in which they are found—and then fashioning metals into objects.

Mexican Revolution (1910–1920): A social and national revolution that remade Mexico. It began when a succession struggle led to the jailing of presidential candidate Francisco Madero, which sparked insurgencies across the country and led to a decade of fighting.

Middle Passage: The months-long journey of slave ships between Africa and the Americas. Slaves were tightly packed below deck, usually naked and in chains, and many died due to unsanitary conditions and violence.

Mikhail Gorbachev [mihk-HEYEL gohr-bah-CHUHV]: The reform-minded final leader of the USSR who came to power in 1985. He introduced policies of perestroika ("restructuring") and glasnost ("openness"), defused international tensions, and pursued nuclear arms reduction treaties but ultimately could not prevent the collapse of the Soviet Union.

military revolution: An increase in the complexity and expense of war between 1450 and 1800. It comprised several innovations in weaponry, defense, technique, and administration.

millenarian movements: Religious movements whose adherents believe that spiritual or divine intervention will transform the world for the better.

millet system: The Ottoman Empire's tolerant religious policy: the Ottomans taxed non-Muslims at a higher rate than Muslims but also welcomed Christians and Jews and left them alone to oversee their own communities.

Minamata disease: The effects of mercury poisoning that those who ate seafood from the Minamata bay in Japan developed due to pollution from a nearby chemical plant. It was one among many acute pollution disasters in the 1950s and 1960s that arose from East Asia's rapid industrialization.

Ming voyages (1405–1433): Seven large maritime voyages arranged by Zheng He under the Yongle Emperor of China during the Ming dynasty. The extent of the voyages and the size of their wooden ships were unprecedented, and they served to project power as far as East Africa.

mita [MEE-tah]: The forced labor draft imposed on Andean peoples by the Inka. Under Spanish rule in South America, the *mita* provided unfree labor to work in the brutal conditions of the silver mines.

Mohandas K. Gandhi (1869–1948): The Indian anti-colonial activist who developed the practice of non-violent civil disobedience called *satyagraha*. His activism led to a widespread nationalist movement in India and contributed to the end of British rule in 1947.

Moluccas [moh-LUH-kuhz]: Part of the islands of Indonesia, also known as the East Indies, where nutmeg and cloves grew. Because Europeans placed great value on these spices, trade connections to these islands were very attractive to merchants.

monasticism: A way of life long prominent in Christianity and Buddhism that involves voluntary withdrawal from society, including a rejection of marriage and family, in favor of dedication to rigorous spiritual work.

Mongol western campaigns (1219–1260): A series of campaigns beginning under Genghis Khan and carried on by his grandsons Batu and Hulegu. By 1260, Mongol rule stretched from Russia and the Black Sea to Mongolia.

monotheism [MAW-noh-thee-iz'm]: A religious system that espouses a belief in one god, or the oneness of God. Judaism, Christianity, and Islam are all monotheistic religions.

Muhammad [muh-HAH-mehd] (570–632): The founder of Islam who was born in the city of Mecca in Arabia and had visions at age 40 telling him he was God's prophet. He subsequently gathered a group of followers, called Muslims, and embarked on a successful military campaign in 622, establishing Islam as both a political and a religious movement.

Mulla Sadra [MOO-lah SA-drah] (1571–1640): An influential Shi'a theologian living in Safavid Iran. His writings attempted to reconcile Sufi mysticism with Islamic philosophical traditions and helped create an intellectual foundation for the Safavid theocracy.

multiethnic empire: A polity comprising different linguistic and religious groups and containing many ethnic minorities and multilingual people. The Habsburg, Russian, and Ottoman empires were all multiethnic.

Muslim League: The organization of Muslims in British India that advocated for the division of post-colonial India into a Muslim state and a Hindu state. Muhammad Ali Jinnah, who became the first head of Pakistan, was its leader.

Mustafa Kemal [MUHS-tah-fah kuh-MAHL] (1881–1938): Leader of Turkey's nationalist revolution and its first president. Also known as Atatürk, he introduced a set of educational and legal policies, the Atatürk Reforms, aimed at strengthening and secularizing Turkey.

Nalanda: A Buddhist monastery in northeast India that was a center of learning and science in the Indian Ocean world, reaching its height in the sixth to the ninth centuries. Nalanda was part of the thriving intellectual scene in India between 500 and 1000.

Napoleon Bonaparte (1769–1821): A military man who ascended to power in France in 1799 by way of a coup d'état and became a dictator. He won numerous military victories against foreign armies but abdicated in 1814 after a string of disastrous campaigns.

Narmer: The first ruler of Upper and Lower Egypt who completed unification around 2950 BCE; also known as Menes.

National Policy: A Canadian program that was launched in 1879 to stimulate industrialization. It involved the introduction of tariffs on foreign goods and investment in railroads.

nationalism: A set of beliefs, ideas, and attitudes that provides a sense of solidarity for a group. The group usually occupies a defined territory and claims to share language, culture, ethnicity, ancestry, political values, civic values, or some combination of these.

Natufians (ca. 12,500–9,500 BCE): Sedentary residents of the Levant who showed the earliest known signs of plant cultivation and farming.

natural selection: The process whereby organisms that are better adapted to their environments pass down advantageous genetic traits through generations.

Neanderthals [nee-ANN-duhr-tawls]: An extinct "cousin" of human beings that lived from 400,000 to 40,000 years ago in Europe, Siberia, and southwestern Asia.

neo-Confucianism: An ideology originating in the Song dynasty (960–1279) that emphasized rigorous study and academic learning as the path to morality and righteousness. In the sixteenth century, Wang Yangming—also considered a neo-Confucianist—claimed that book learning was not necessary for obtaining wisdom and acting ethically.

new imperialism: A pervasive and widespread form of empire that arose after 1870 due to the power and wealth gaps that industrialization caused and the popular support that nationalism stirred.

Nile River: A river 4,000 miles (nearly 7,000 km) long that flowed through Nubia and Egypt, bringing precious water and fertile silt.

Norte Chico (ca. 3100–1600 BCE): The collective name for a group of roughly 25 settlements in the Andes. Norte Chico was the earliest complex society in the Andean world, and its elites' power was based on the control of dried fish, a staple in the food supply.

Nubia [NOO-bee-uh]: A region south of Egypt and upriver from it on the Nile. Egypt mostly traded with or ruled over Nubia, but on occasion Nubia asserted control over parts of Egypt.

Oceania: The Southeast Asian region that includes the islands in the Pacific Ocean, including Melanesia, Micronesia, and Polynesia. Near Oceania consists of New Guinea, the Bismarck Archipelago, and the Solomon Islands; Remote Oceania reaches as far as Hawaii and Easter Island.

Octavian (Augustus): Caesar's grandnephew, adopted son, and heir, who became emperor of Rome and changed his name to Augustus. He was a ruthless emperor who ruled for 40 years, consolidated the Roman state, and built a strong administrative foundation for subsequent emperors.

Oda Nobunaga [oh-DAH noh-boo-NAH-gah] (1534–1582): A Japanese warlord who unified southern Japan and may have invented volley fire. He met his political aims by militarizing peasants and arming them with widely produced Japanese guns.

Olmecs: Concentrated in the urban centers of San Lorenzo (ca. 1600–900 BCE) and La Venta (ca. 900–300 BCE) in southern Mexico, the Olmecs were the first Mesoamerican group to develop complex hierarchical societies. They were builders of giant basalt heads and pioneers of pyramid construction in the Americas.

oracle bone inscriptions: The first evidence of Chinese writing, oracle bone inscriptions are questions posed to the gods written on turtle shells and cattle bones. Diviners heated the bones until they cracked and then interpreted the gods' answers using the fragments.

Paleolithic: The period lasting from 2.6 million years ago to 13,000 years ago; the latter part, the late Paleolithic, saw a profusion of cultural change.

pan-Africanism: The call for Africans and people of African descent to liberate Africa and end racism through unified political action. The movement also supported literary and cultural revitalization. W.E.B. Du Bois and Marcus Garvey were prominent pan-Africanists.

Parliament: A British legislative body comprising elected officials and hereditary nobles. Following the British Civil Wars and Revolution, Parliament became the chief governing authority in Britain.

Parthians (247 BCE–224 CE): Successors of Seleucid rule that emerged from a group of mobile pastoralists. They are particularly notable for successfully cultivating long-distance trade.

partition of Africa: The dividing up of African lands among Britain, France, Germany, Belgium, Spain, and Portugal between 1874 and 1890. It began as an informal process, until the Berlin Conference convened to officially partition the African continent in 1884–1885.

***patío* process:** A technology involving the use of mercury to separate silver from its surrounding rock. This process made the task of silver extraction easier in the sixteenth and seventeenth centuries, thus increasing the value of lower-grade silver ores.

Pax Mongolica (ca. 1260–1350): Meaning "Mongolian Peace," a relatively calm period during which the Mongolian Empire boosted trade along the Silk Road by creating an environment of largely peaceful exchange.

pharaohs [FARE-ohs]: Egyptian kings; there were about 170 pharaohs between around 2950 and 30 BCE.

Phoenicia [fih-NEE-shuh]: The Greek name for the cities on the eastern coast of the Mediterranean, including Tyre. The word *Punic* is derived from *Phoenicia* and is used to describe things Carthaginian.

pirates: Seafaring bandits who took advantage of periods when long-distance trade was widespread and navies were weak. The beginning of global trade was a very lucrative period for pirates such as the Zhengs and those organized by the North African beys.

plague pandemic (1346–1351): A disastrous outbreak of plague that is historically unmatched in its death toll. At the time incurable, plague killed 30 to 50 percent of the Eurasian population and continued to return regularly for centuries.

plantation zone: An area stretching from the Chesapeake to Brazil where the majority of African slaves were used. Plantations grew tobacco, rice, and sugar on a large scale as part of the transatlantic economy.

plebeians [plih-BEE-uhns]: Roman citizens who did not come from elite families. Plebeians were commoners who often performed the same work as slaves, although plebeians were reimbursed for their labor whereas slaves were not.

plow agriculture: The use of large domesticated animals to pull plows—a piece of farm equipment that tills soil. Farmers could cultivate five times more land using plows.

polis [POH-lihs]: A political institution, a type of city-state, developed by the Greeks around 700 BCE, that included governance by magistrates, citizenship for adult males, and required military duties for citizen-soldiers.

political decentralization: The weakening of centralized kingdoms and the diminishing of links among transatlantic empires, all as a result of the Atlantic revolutions.

Pontiac's War (1763–1765): An Amerindian uprising against the British. Named after one of the uprising's leaders, the Ottawa chief Pontiac, it was a military standoff but resulted in the designation of all North American lands between Appalachia and the Mississippi River as an "Indian reserve."

population surge: A nearly twofold growth of the global population in the three centuries between 1500 and 1800.

Porfiriato [POHR-fihr-ee-AH-toh] (1876–1910): The decades of Porfirio Díaz's authoritarian rule in Mexico. During this period the Mexican economy grew rapidly, as did increasing inequality, due to Díaz's encouragement of foreign investment and support of dispossessing poor peasants.

Potosí [poh-toh-SEE]: Site of large-scale, dangerously deadly silver mining in the Andes under Spanish authorities during the sixteenth and seventeenth centuries; laborers were mostly conscripted Amerindians and, later, African slaves who suffered harsh conditions, frequent accidents, and mercury poisoning. Silver was the most valuable transatlantic commodity.

praetorian guard: A select group of 4,500 men that Augustus created in order to protect the emperor. On five occasions, the praetorian guard assassinated emperors deemed ineffectual or corrupt, including Caligula and Elagabalus.

Prague Spring (1968): A Czechoslovak reform effort that called for less censorship and more freedom during post–World War II communist rule. The Soviets repressed it with a violent military invasion, causing widespread criticism of communism and the USSR.

printing press: A device invented by Johannes Gutenberg in the mid-fifteenth century that involved the use of movable metal type. It allowed for easier, faster, and cheaper production and dissemination of written information.

Protestantism: A branch of Christianity, initiated by the monk Martin Luther (1483–1546), that took issue with the Catholic Church. Luther's writing and preaching emphasized scripture over tradition and salvation by inner faith. Many variations of Protestantism arose, but all denominations generally emphasized the importance of individual relationships with God.

proxy wars: Local conflicts around the world in which the United States and the USSR supported rival factions, with each superpower indirectly engaging the other as part of broader Cold War competition. There were at least 50 proxy wars, including the Korean War, the Vietnam War, the Angolan Civil War, and the Soviet-Afghan War.

Punic Wars (264–241 BCE, 218–201 BCE, 149–146 BCE): A series of three wars between the Romans and the Carthaginians. Rome won all three wars and razed Carthage after the Third Punic War.

pyramids: Monumental tombs, containing provisions for an eternal afterlife, that Old Kingdom pharaohs used conscripted peasants to build. The largest was Khufu's Great Pyramid at Giza.

Qin [chihn] **dynasty** (221–207 BCE): A state, under the ruthless leadership of Shi Huangdi, that conquered the Warring States, expanded to the south, and made unifying reforms that left a legacy of a large and united China.

Qing [chihng] **dynasty** (1644–1911): An imperial dynasty descended from a group of Manchu elite. Using innovative military techniques such as banners (units that cut across kin lines) and improved centralized command, the Qing vastly expanded Chinese territory and power.

Quakers: A Protestant sect originating in England that began the organized antislavery movement. Quaker beliefs stress the fundamental equality of all human beings, and their moral objections were instrumental to antislavery efforts in Britain and the United States.

Queen Boudica: A British queen who led an uprising against the Roman Empire in the years 60 to 61 CE. The Roman army ultimately defeated Queen Boudica and her followers.

railways: Transportation infrastructure that was central to industrialization and an outgrowth of the coal and iron industries. Railways and locomotives lowered transportation costs, connected markets, and linked countries together.

raised-field agriculture: A labor-intensive and very productive, early farming technique used in the Americas from today's Bolivia to Mexico. It is a form of amphibious agriculture that involves creating islands in wetlands and raising crops on them.

Reconquista [ray-kohn-KEE-stah]: A centuries-long Christian campaign to retake Iberia from Muslim rulers. Europeans, especially Iberians, viewed sailing expeditions as a way to continue the Reconquista in new lands by spreading Christianity and depriving Muslim states of wealth from trade.

Renaissance: A fascination among European elites with the intellectual and artistic traditions of the ancient Greeks and Romans. Humanism, the focus on human bodies and experiences, was a defining feature of the Renaissance.

rising merchant classes: Those of modest backgrounds who traded goods in the Atlantic world and became wealthy. With their newly accumulated fortune, they sought liberties and political voice to ease their commerce and preserve their position.

Russian Revolution of 1917: The overturning of imperial rule in Russia that started with a coup d'état led by the Bolsheviks, a minority Marxist faction. They eventually seized control of the government and set out to reform Russia based on the ideology of communism.

Saadians [SAHD-ee-ihnz]: Dynasts who successfully used guns and cannon to unify Morocco and defeat the Songhai in West Africa. They ultimately were unsuccessful in further attempts to gain wealth and power.

Safavids [SAH-fah-vihds]: A dynasty that originated as a Sunni-Sufi brotherhood but adopted Shi'a Islam and then conquered Iran and most of Iraq. They made Shi'a Islam the state religion, reformulated its theology, and pursued mass conversions.

Sahel: An area of semi-arid grassland that stretches east to west and is located on the southern edge of the Sahara Desert. The Senegal and Niger rivers are in the western Sahel, and ancient Ghana and Mali were located in their floodplains.

Sargon of Akkad: A king who pioneered the political format of empire and united the city-states of southern and central Mesopotamia around 2340 BCE; he built the first professional army, promoted trade, and reigned for about 56 years.

Sassanid [suh-SAH-nid] **dynasty** (224–651 CE): Successors of the Parthians and leaders of the Sassanian Empire who popularized the term *Iran* to refer to Persia. They built up irrigation works, introduced new agricultural crops, promoted long-distance trade, and made Iran into a great regional power.

schisms [SIH-zuhms]: Formal divisions generally based on opposing beliefs, especially within young religions. Early Christian schisms included Arianism, Nestorianism, and Monophysitism. Islam split into Shi'a and Sunni branches soon after its inception.

Scientific Revolution: The adoption of mathematics, observation, and systematic experimentation to understand the world instead of relying solely on scripture and ancient texts, as had been done previously.

sedentary: A term that describes people who stay in one place and form settlements instead of moving around.

self-determination: U.S. president Woodrow Wilson's idea that every

European nationality had the right to its own, self-ruled nation. This concept was an important feature of the post–World War I peace treaties and an inspiration for anti-colonialists.

Seljuk [sahl-JYOOK] **Turks** (ca. 980–1090): A pastoral, Sunni Muslim group that rode into Iran, took Baghdad, and conquered Byzantine territory in Anatolia. They spearheaded the lasting Turkification and Islamization of the eastern Mediterranean.

serfs: Peasants who worked as forced labor on large, grain-producing estates for the gentry in Prussia, Poland-Lithuania, and Russia. Land-lords of these estates controlled the movement, economic activity, and personal lives of serfs.

Sergei Witte [SAYR-gay VIHT-tee] (1849–1915): A Russian statesman who was deeply involved in the coun-try's industrialization. He directed the government to build railroads, create technical schools, and introduce pro-tectionist tariffs.

settlement houses: During the Indus-trial Revolution, institutions that elite and middle-class women set up to research and help improve the condi-tions in which poor and working-class people lived and labored.

settler colony: A form of imperialism in which migrants from a conquering nation establish colonies in con-quered lands. Settlers often seek land and dominance, and settler colonies are more violent than colonies with-out settlers.

shabti [SHAH-tee]: Miniature figurines buried with pharaohs to aid them in the afterlife. Pharaohs sacrificed humans to be their otherworldly attendants until 2600 BCE, after which the use of *shabti* supplanted this practice.

shamanism [SHAH-mah-niz'm]: A broad set of religious beliefs and practices, including direct communication with the supernatural realm and a belief in the existence of a spirit world where the dead live.

Shang dynasty (ca. 1600–1046 BCE): A highly militarized and hierarchical society based in the lower Huang He basin that worshipped the deity Di. During Shang rule, Chinese writing was invented.

shari'a: Meaning "the path" in Arabic, shari'a is the body of Islamic holy law and ethics that governs every aspect of Muslim life. Originally developed on the basis of the Qur'an and accounts of Muhammad's life, it has evolved to form the basis of several schools of Islamic legal practice today.

shi: A cultural elite that emerged under the Zhou and consolidated much of Chinese culture. During the Warring States period, they transformed from being just scholars, to being both scholars and men of war.

Shi Huangdi [shee HWAHNG-dee] (259–210 BCE): Also known as King Zheng and Qin Shi Huang, Shi Huangdi was a successful military commander who conquered vast amounts of land, put an end to the Warring States period, and began the Qin dynasty. He pro-moted Chinese unity and created a base of unification for subsequent dynasties.

Shi'a [SHEE-ah] **Islam**: An orthodox branch of Islam that was adopted as the state religion in Iran under the Safavid dynasty in the sixteenth and seventeenth centuries. Followers of Shi'a Islam believe that only members of Muhammad's lineage can hold reli-gious and political authority.

shifting agriculture: A type of farming in which farmers cleared land, farmed it for a few years, and then moved to a new patch of land once soil was depleted; often used in forest zones with poor soils.

Shinto [SHIHN-toh]: Meaning "the way of the gods," Shinto is an indigenous Japanese religion that is animistic and polytheistic. It emphasizes ritual and is based on tradition, folklore, shrines, and monuments.

Siddhartha Gautama [sih-DAHR-tuh GOW-taw-mah]: A Kshatri caste prince, born in the sixth or fifth century BCE, who rejected his privileged background and became the Buddha (the Enlightened One); his followers established the religion known as Buddhism.

Sikhism [SIHK-ihzm]: A religion that developed in India in the sixteenth century based on the teachings of Nanak (1469–1538), who asserted that Hinduism and Islam were one and the same. Nanak rejected elaborate ceremony and the caste system, promoted pacifism, and stressed the importance of humankind over other living creatures and the equality of all people before God.

Silk Road: Relay trade routes that crossed the steppes and deserts of Asia from China to the shores of the Mediterranean; named after one of the most valuable commodities transported on these routes—Chinese silk.

silkworms: Domesticated caterpillars that provided the raw materials for the silk industry in China. Women and girls produced silk, a lucrative trade item, from the threads that silkworms excreted.

silver trade: The worldwide buying and selling of silver that sustained the global economy and grew increasingly important as more people used silver as money. In particular, governments and merchants sought silver to engage more easily in state spending or long-distance trading.

Simón Bolívar [see-MOHN boh-LEE-vahr] (1783–1830): A Venezuelan creole revolutionary leader who fought the Spanish Crown and hoped to found a united states of South America.

Simon Kimbangu [KIHM-ban-goo] (1887–1951): The Congolese founder and leader of the independent African Kimbanguist Church, whom the Belgians imprisoned for 30 years until his death. He preached faith healing, non-violence, monogamy, and sobriety.

slave soldiers: Slaves used in the military; most had been sold by their families in Central Asia to the armies of caliphs and sultans. A few slave soldiers managed to overthrow their masters and install themselves on thrones. The Ghaznavids and Turkic horsemen who established the Delhi sultanate were slave soldiers, and they spread the practice of slave soldiery into India.

slave-and-sugar plantations: Profitable, extensive commercial sugar farms in Brazil and the Caribbean that were larger and more efficient than their predecessors. They relied on the brutal exploitation of slaves who worked in notoriously unhealthy conditions and faced a life expectancy shorter than that of slaves anywhere else in the Americas.

Slavery Abolition Act (1834): Passed in Britain, the first large abolition of slavery. When the Whig Party took power in British Parliament, it introduced the act with widespread support from petitioners. It inspired abolitionists around the world.

smallpox inoculation: The intentional infection of humans with cowpox to produce an immunity against smallpox. It replaced riskier methods of inoculation, quickly spread around the world, and reduced worldwide deaths from smallpox.

social Darwinism: The pseudo-scientific application of Charles Darwin's ideas to subsets of the human species. Arguing that some humans were more fit than others, social Darwinism appealed to science to support racism and racial hierarchies.

socialists: People who sought to alter social and political institutions with an emphasis on the rights of the working class. They often supported ideas such as strong unions, worker cooperatives, and communal ownership of industry.

Sons of Africa: A London-based abolitionist organization. It was made up of former slaves, including Ottobah Cugoano and Olaudah Equiano, who wrote detailed descriptions of their experiences as slaves to strengthen the anti–slave trade movement.

spice trade: The exchange of spices that became increasingly widespread in the early modern period and acted as a driving force of global trade. Portuguese, English, and Dutch merchants dominated the spice trade after 1511.

spices: The most frequently traded raw materials in the Indian Ocean world. Spices—including nutmeg, cloves, cinnamon, and a variety of peppers—largely came from Southeast Asia and southern India; the greatest importers were China, Egypt, Arabia, and Iran.

spread of democracy: The shift from the world having twice as many authoritarian states as liberal democracies in 1974 to the reverse by 2010 due to a rise in interest rates, the end of the Cold War, and the power of example.

Srivijaya [sree-VIH-juh-yuh] (ca. 670–1300): A Southeast Asian, Buddhist kingdom based in Sumatra that Indian culture influenced. It controlled the Straits of Malacca, gaining income from taxes on Indian and Chinese shipping.

state: A territorial unit and political community with a formal government. States always have bureaucrats, judges, and soldiers, and usually have ideologies.

steam engine: A machine that converts the chemical energy in fossil fuels into mechanical energy, called steam power. Steam engines powered the defining technologies of the Industrial Revolution and vastly expanded production levels.

steppe nomads: Mobile peoples, including Khitans, Jurchens, and Mongols, who came from the steppe grasslands north of China. Often clashing militarily with the Chinese, they conquered north China three times and all of China once.

suffragism: A mass political and ideological movement that sought to give women the right to vote. It originated in the nineteenth century, and World War I greatly facilitated its progress and success.

Sufi [SOO-fee] **movement**: A form of mystical Islam that sprang up in the ninth century in response to official attempts to enforce orthodoxy. Instead of following scholarly traditions, Sufism promoted a more personal relationship with God and incorporated song, poetry, and dance into its rituals.

Sukarno [soo-KAHR-noh] (1901–1970): Javanese aristocrat, Indonesian independence activist, and founder of the nationalist Partai Nasional Indonesia. He became the first president of Indonesia after collaborating with the Japanese during World War II and then fighting off the return of Dutch colonialism.

Sumer [SOO-mehr]: The region and culture of southern Mesopotamia, located in today's southern Iraq; the early cities Ur and Uruk were in Sumer.

Sun Tzu [suhn-zoo]: Attributed author of *The Art of War*, possibly written in the sixth or fifth century BCE. The classic work gives insight on military strategy, diplomacy, statecraft, and espionage.

Sun Yatsen [suhn YAHT-suhn] (1866–1925): A physician and revolutionary who opposed the Qing and wanted to reform China in the image of powerful Western countries. He led the Chinese Revolution and became president of China's new constitutional republic until his ouster and exile to Japan in 1913.

Swahili [swah-HEE-lee] **coast**: The coast of East Africa where Arab and Persian traders interacted with local Africans. A distinct Swahili culture and language rooted in Indian Ocean trade developed along this coast.

Tacky's War (1760): An uprising in Jamaica of nearly 1,500 slaves, led by Akan-speaking slaves from what is now Ghana, that lasted for several months before it was brutally suppressed.

Taíno [TAY-noh]: The indigenous population of the Spanish-controlled Caribbean island of Hispaniola. Disease, violence, and enslavement led to a demographic catastrophe among the Taíno.

Taiping [TEYE-pihng] **Rebellion** (1850–1864): A large rebellion led by Hong Xiuquan and his army, the Taiping. Motivated by political, nationalist, and Christian goals, the Taiping managed to control much of the Yangzi Valley for 10 years until their defeat and Hong's death.

Tenochtitlán [thuh-NOCH-tee-tlahn]: The large, populous capital of the Aztec Empire located on an island in Lake Texcoco in the Basin of Mexico.

textiles and metallurgy: The two main industries at the forefront of industrial revolutions around the world. Both cloth making and iron making were well suited to steam-powered mass production.

third pulse of decolonization: The comparatively rapid emergence of around 100 new countries that occurred between 1945 and 1975, mainly in Africa, Asia, and the Caribbean.

Thirteenth Amendment (1865): Introduced at the end of the Civil War, an amendment to the U.S. Constitution that abolished slavery. It led to the liberation of 4 million people, making it the largest emancipation in world history.

Thomas Clarkson (1760–1846): A member of the Anglican elite and a staunch anti–slave trade and abolitionist activist. He allied with the Quakers to publicize the atrocities of the slave trade and was influential in the British abolition of the slave trade and slavery.

Tibetan Empire (ca. 618–842): Also known as Yarlung, the Tibetan Empire was located north of the Himalaya, and its influence spread from India to Mongolia. It was a formidable competitor to the Tang.

Tigris and Euphrates Rivers: Twin rivers that flow into the Persian Gulf; they supported agriculture and trade in Mesopotamia.

Tiwanaku [tee-wahn-AH-koo] (ca. 100–1100 CE): An Andean city and empire that amassed wealth and power through its control of the supply of llamas. The city was a religious center located near Lake Titicaca in what is now Bolivia; its empire and influence reached as far as northern Chile, lowland Bolivia, and the Peruvian Andes.

Tlacélel [tlah-KAY-luhl] (ca. 1398–1480): A successful and influential Aztec king who fortified the cultural legacy and importance of the Aztecs. He invented a glorious Aztec history and strengthened the Aztecs' religious importance by putting them in charge of sustaining the sun god.

Tokugawa shogunate [TOH-koo-GAH-wah SHOH-guh-nayt] (1600–1868): A ruling dynasty in Japan made up of the descendants of Tokugawa Ieyasu, who completed the task of unifying Japan in 1600.

Toussaint L'Ouverture [TOO-sahn LOO-vehr-toor] (ca. 1743–1803): The main leader of the Haitian Revolution. He was born a slave on St. Domingue but was freed around age 30, after which he led the Haitian slave insurrection and became a successful commander in the Haitian army.

Toyotomi Hideyoshi [tohih-yoh-TOH-mee hee-day-OH-shee] (1537–1598): Oda Nobunaga's successor; a Japanese warlord whose soldiers liberally employed guns and nearly united all of Japan. He invaded Korea, enslaving thousands, but retreated from a failed invasion in China.

transatlantic slave trade (1519–ca. 1860): The transportation by European traders of 12 to 14 million slaves from Africa to the Americas, mainly to work on plantations. This trade constituted the largest forced migration in world history.

transition to agriculture: The switch between human populations finding or cultivating food and settled human populations producing food through domestication. This process occurred in various places independently of one another.

Trans-Siberian Railway: A railway from Moscow to the Pacific Ocean that was completed in 1903. A remarkable feat of engineering and construction, the almost 6,000-mile-long railway built by 9,000 laborers was a defining symbol of the Russian Industrial Revolution.

Treaty of Tordesillas (1494): Spain and Portugal used this agreement to demarcate a line halfway between Columbus's discoveries in the Americas and the Cape Verde islands off the coast of West Africa. It gave all lands west of the line to Spain and all lands east to Portugal.

Treaty of Versailles [vehr-SEYE] (1919): A peace treaty written by the victorious Allies that imposed strict and punitive policies on Germany in the aftermath of World War I. The treaty provoked outrage in Germany due to its reparations and war guilt clauses, as well as among Chinese because it gave German concessions in China to Japan.

Treaty of Waitangi [weye-TANG-ee] (1840): A treaty in which the Maori of New Zealand agreed to become British subjects in exchange for land guarantees. British settlers soon broke this treaty, fought the Maori for land, and ended Maori independence.

tsar [ZAHR]: The title Russian rulers adopted after 1547. The tsars, particularly Ivan the Terrible (r. 1547–1584) and Peter the Great (r. 1682–1725), built an expansive and centralized Russian empire by modernizing the military and asserting control over the Russian elite.

Túpac Amaru II [too-pak ah-MAHR-oo] (1738–1781): A Jesuit-educated mestizo revolutionary descended from the Inka ruling family. He led a tax revolt in the Andes beginning in 1780 and emphasized justice and the end of ethnic oppression.

Tyre: A merchant town that linked the trade of Egypt, northern Mesopotamia, Syria, and Anatolia and specialized in a highly desirable maroon-purple dye. In order to expand their metals trade, Tyre's

merchants established Carthage as well as several other colonies along the Mediterranean coast.

Umayyad caliphate [oo-MEYE-ahd KA-lih-fayt]: The first genuine Islamic state (661–750), based in Damascus and led by caliphs ("deputies of God") who claimed to be successors of the prophet Muhammad. They expanded their empire through conquests and exerted "soft power" through monumental architecture such as the Dome of the Rock mosque.

universities: The first opened in Cairo in the tenth century, followed by several in Europe in the twelfth century. European universities, as comparatively free spaces of inquiry and debate, prompted the development of science and art.

university of war: The state of constant military competition and chaos in Europe during the early modern period. These conditions increased the power of successful states and made them skilled in warfare, efficient at tax collection, and able to adapt quickly to innovations.

Vasco da Gama: A low-ranking Portuguese noble who led an expedition in 1497 around the southern tip of Africa and into the Indian Ocean in search of Christian allies and valuable spices for the Portuguese Crown. He helped set up a lasting Portuguese presence in India and East Africa.

Vedas [VAY-duhs]: Four texts, which probably originated as oral traditions, that are the earliest existing examples of literature in Sanskrit and the oldest sacred texts of Hinduism. The culture of the Ganges basin is called Vedic after them.

vertical archipelago: The system by which Andean clans, called *ayllus*, placed people from a given lineage in communities at each elevation level of the mountains in order to exploit the resources of the different environments. The Inkas did not invent this system, but greatly expanded it.

Vietnam War (1965-1975): A proxy conflict between communist North Vietnam, aligned with China and the USSR, and anti-communist South Vietnam, aligned with the United States. The United States committed hundreds of thousands of troops to the domestically unpopular war, which the North Vietnamese ultimately won.

Vikings: A group of seaborne marauders from Scandinavia that looted, slaved, and conquered nearby territories beginning around 800 CE. They settled land from Russia to Greenland and established several enduring trade links.

Vital Revolution: The steady improvement of human health and life expectancy after 1750. Better nutrition, microbial unification, control of smallpox, and sanitation reform contributed to this shift.

Vladimir Lenin (1870-1924): A Russian-born revolutionary and influential member of the Bolsheviks. He consolidated power by 1921 and was the first leader of the USSR.

Wang Yangming [wang YAHN-mihng] (1472-1529): A Chinese philosopher who challenged prevailing neo-Confucian thought and gained followers by arguing that ordinary people could attain moral perfection through inherent knowledge rather than through book learning.

Wangari Maathai [wahn-GAH-ree MAH-theye] (1940-2011): A prominent political, environmental, and women's rights activist. The first woman in the history of East Africa to earn a PhD, founder of the Green Belt Movement, member of the Kenyan parliament, and Nobel Peace Prize laureate.

witch hunts: The spike in accusations of witchcraft between 1500 and 1700, which resulted in the widespread use of torture and execution of accused witches. Unmarried women over age 40 were the main targets.

working class: A section of society, formed during the Industrial Revolution, that comprised factory and mine workers who performed shift work for wages. Workers' lives at this time were precarious and dangerous, and they were politically divided between seeking reform and inciting revolution.

World War I (1914-1918): A conflict between the Central Powers (Germany, Austria-Hungary, the Ottoman Empire) and the Entente or Allied Powers (France, Russia, Britain, Italy) fought mainly in Europe. Many smaller European nations joined in, as well as ultimately the United States. The war required mass mobilization of populations and resources and led to unprecedented violence and destruction.

World War II (1937-1945): The most expansive and deadliest war in history, fought between the Axis powers and the Allies. It involved four overlapping wars, fought primarily in Europe, China, the Pacific, and North Africa.

Wu Zetian [woo ZAY-shihn] (624-705): The only woman who both ruled China in her own name and was the most powerful person on Earth when in power. Wu was a controversial ruler who was ruthless toward her enemies, adept at foreign affairs, a great patron of Buddhism, and a supporter of commerce.

Yamato race theory: A fictional idea developed in the 1930s. It held that all Japanese people shared a common ancestry to an ancient race that was superior to other nearby peoples, including Koreans and Chinese.

Yamato region: A state in the southeast of Japan that began to expand its influence in the 600s. It ruled several rice-producing regions, emphasized military skill, adopted Buddhism, and imported cultural ideas from the Tang.

Yangzi [YAHNG-zuh] **River**: A river in China whose valley was home to the second transition to agriculture, which occurred about 7000 BCE and was rice-based.

Yermak [yehr-MAHK]: A Cossack who pioneered the expansion of the Russian fur trade into Siberia during the 1580s. His success also spearheaded the introduction of disease and practices of brutality that ultimately killed many native Siberians.

Yoshinogari [yoh-shih-noh-GAH-ree]: A site on Japan's southern island of Kyushu where evidence of weaving, bronze casting, and other crafts has been found, as well as mainland trade goods such as Korean-made bronze daggers and Chinese bronze mirrors.

Young Turk Revolution (1908): A coup d'état in the Ottoman Empire that nationalist army officers, called the Young Turks, led. They were frustrated with foreign encroachment on Ottoman territory and successfully imposed a constitution.

Younger Dryas (10,700–9,700 BCE): A severe cold and dry period that temporarily reversed the process of slow global warming that occurred after the coldest part of the last ice age.

Yuan [yoo-AHN] **dynasty** (1279–1368): The dynasty established by the Mongols after the defeat of the Song by Khubilai Khan. Despite their rough-edged steppe-nomad nature, the Yuan allowed religious diversity, promoted scientific creativity and cultural exchange, and encouraged trade throughout the many lands they controlled.

Zanj revolt (868–883): A massive uprising of slaves from East Africa who worked on plantations in Iraq. One of the most successful slave rebellions in world history, it dealt an immense blow to southern Iraq and ended the practice of plantation slavery in Iraq for around a millennium.

Zheng He [SHENG-hah]: An admiral and an important ally of the Yongle Emperor. He arranged and led the Ming voyages during the fifteenth century.

Zhou [JOH] **dynasty** (1045–256 BCE): The dynasty that began the process of Chinese unification, developed irrigation, promoted iron farm tools, and began using chariots in war. In 771 BCE, Zhou rulers lost much of their territory; only part of their kingdom, the Eastern Zhou, survived until 256 BCE.

ziggurats [ZIG-uh-rahts]: A pioneering form of monumental architecture, ziggurats are temple-palaces dedicated to local gods.

Zoroastrianism [zohr-oh-ASS-tree-ahn-iz'm]: A monotheistic religion that arose in Persia around the prophecies of Zoroaster sometime between the tenth and sixth centuries BCE. With priests called magi, it emphasized the creator-god Ahura Mazda, human choice between good and evil, and divine judgment.

TEXT CREDITS

CHAPTER 16

Malyn Newitt, ed. "Duarte Pacheco Pereira Tries to Come to Terms with 'Difference,'" in *The Portuguese in West Africa, 1415–1670: A Documentary History*. Cambridge, U.K. Published by Cambridge University Press. © Malyn Newitt 2010. Reproduced with permission of The Licensor through PLSclear.

CHAPTER 17

Malyn Newitt, ed. "Duarte Pacheco Pereira Tries to Come to Terms with 'Difference,'" in *The Portuguese in West Africa, 1415–1670: A Documentary History*. Cambridge, U.K. Published by Cambridge University Press. © Malyn Newitt 2010. Reproduced with permission of The Licensor through PLSclear.

"Letter of the King of Kongo to King of Portugal Dom João III, 1526,'" in *Converging on Cannibals: Terrors of Slaving in Atlantic Africa 1519–1670 (Africa in World History Series)* Jared Staller ed. and trans. Athens, Ohio. (Ohio University Press, © 2019). This material is used by permission of Ohio University Press, www.ohioswallow.com.

CHAPTER 18

"A Hymn from the Kabir," from Dass, Nirmal, *Songs of Kabir from the Adi Granth/translation and introduction by Nirmal Dass*, pp. 251–252. Albany: State University of New York Press, [1991].

CHAPTER 21

ADAMS FAMILY CORRESPONDENCE, VOLUME 1 AND 2: DECEMBER 1761–MARCH 1778, edited by L. H. Butterfield, Cambridge, Mass.: The Belknap Press of Harvard University Press, Copyright © 1963 by the Massachusetts Historical Society.

"A revolutionary's letter from Jamaica," from *Selected Writings of Bolivar, Vol 1: 1810–1822*, edited by Harold A. Bierck, Jr. Compiled by Vicente Lecuna. Translated by Lewis Bertrand. New York, N.Y.: The Colonial Press Inc. 1951. © 1951 Banco de Venezuela.

CHAPTER 22

"Approximate Share of Global Industrial Production, 1800–1900," from J. R. McNeill and Kenneth Pomeranz, ed., *The Cambridge World History: Volume 7, Production, Destruction, and Connection, 1750–Present*, p 122. Cambridge, U.K. (Cambridge University Press, © 2015). Reproduced with permission of The Licensor through PLSclear.

"Riots," Leeds Mercury, 25 Apr. 1812, in *British Library Newspapers*.

CHAPTER 23

Excerpts from the testimony of Abina Mansah in "SCT 5/4/19 *Regina V. Quamina Eddoo, 10 Nov 1876*" from Getz, Trevor R. and Liz Clarke, *Abina and the Important Men: A Graphic History*, pp 87–89, 92, 94, 97. Oxford, U.K. (Oxford University Press, © 2016). Reproduced with permission of The Licensor through PLSclear.

CHAPTER 24

Excerpts from *Ethiopia Through Russian Eyes, Country in Transition 1896–1898* by Alexander Bulatovich; Richard Seltzer, trans. Reprinted by permission of Richard Seltzer and Red Sea Press.

CHAPTER 27

Excerpts from "Record of the Cheerful Troop," presented by Nippon Kyoiku Kamishibai Kyokai. From *Propaganda Performed: Kamishibai in Japan's Fifteen Year War, 2015,* Sharalyn Orbaugh, ed., pp. 24–25, 27–29. (Copyright © by Koninklijke Brill NV, Leiden), reprinted by permission of Brill.

CHAPTER 29

From "The Moment the Barrier of Fear Broke Down" by Adel Abdel Ghafar in *Voices of the Arab Spring: Personal Stories From the Arab Revolutions,* Asaad Alsaleh, ed. Copyright © 2015 Columbia University Press. Reprinted with permission of Columbia University Press.

PHOTO CREDITS

Images; p. 796: Archivart/Alamy Stock Photo; p. 797: The Picture Art Collection/Alamy Stock Photo; p. 803: Chronicle/Alamy Stock Photo; p. 806: © Isadora/Bridgeman Images; p. 808: Erich Lessing/Art Resource, NY; p. 812: Bridgeman Images; p. 816: Photo 12/Alamy Stock Photo; p. 818: (left): Album/Alamy Stock Photo; (right): Bridgeman Images; p. 822: Album/Alamy Stock Photo; p. 826: Pictures Now/Alamy Stock Photo.

Chapter 22: Page 835: ©Archives Charmet/ Bridgeman Images; p. 838: akg-images/Liszt Collection; p. 841 (left): Heritage-Images/The Print Collector/akg-images; (right): 19th era 2/Alamy Stock Photo; p. 843: akg-images; p. 847: Isadora/Bridgeman Images; p. 852: ullstein bild via Getty Images; p. 855: Boorne & May/Library and Archives Canada/C-006686B; p. 859: Snark/Art Resource, NY; p. 864: Album/Alamy Stock Photo; p. 869: Chicago Daily News/Chicago History Museum/ Getty Images.

Chapter 23: Page 878: Bridgeman Images; p. 881: INTERFOTO/Alamy Stock Photo; p. 884: Chronicle/Alamy Stock Photo; p. 885: Arterra Picture Library/Alamy Stock Photo; p. 887: Niday Picture Library/Alamy Stock Photo; p. 889: akg-images/Pictures From History; p. 892: Everett/Shutterstock; p. 893: Private Collection/AF Fotografie/Alamy Stock Photo; p. 894: Heritage Image Partnership Ltd/Alamy Stock Photo; p. 898: Photo © Christie's Images/Bridgeman Images; p. 902: Look and Learn/Illustrated Papers Collection/Bridgeman Images; p. 908: Heritage Images/Fine Art Images/akg-images; p. 910 (left): HIP/Art Resource, NY; (right): North Wind Picture Archives/Alamy Stock Photo.

Chapter 24: Page 919: © Archives Charmet/ Bridgeman Images; p. 921: Chronicle of World History/Alamy Stock Photo; p. 924: Fine Art Images/Heritage Images; p. 927: World History Archive/Alamy Stock Photo; p. 929: The Print Collector/Alamy Stock Photo; p. 933: North Wind Picture Archives/Alamy Stock Photo; p. 936: Felice Beato/Hulton Archive/ Getty Images; p. 941: Chronicle/Alamy Stock Photo; p. 944: akg-images; p. 947: Granger.

Chapter 25: Page 966: Drawn by Frederic Remington from sketches taken on the spot. Illus. in: Harper's weekly, 1890 Dec. 6, p. 960-961/Library of Congress; p. 972 (left): CPA Media Pte Ltd/Alamy Stock Photo; (right): Pictures from History/Bridgeman Images; p. 975: akg-images/British Library; p. 977: Pictorial

Press Ltd/Alamy Stock Photo; p. 981: World History Archive/Alamy Stock Photo; p. 984: Pictures from History/Bridgeman Images; p. 987: Granger; p. 990: Everett Collection Historical/Alamy Stock Photo.

Chapter 26: Page 999: Historical Images Archive/Alamy Stock Photo; p. 1003: Sueddeutsche Zeitung Photo/Alamy Stock Photo; p. 1006: Pictures from History/Bridgeman Images; p. 1010: Pictorial Press Ltd/Alamy Stock Photo; p. 1014: Keystone-France/ Gamma-Keystone via Getty Images; p. 1017: Bancroft Library, University of Berkeley; p. 1020: Everett Historical/Shutterstock; p. 1023 : Hi-Story/Alamy Stock Photo; p. 1025: Pictorial Press Ltd/Alamy Stock Photo; p. 1029: Universal History Archive/UIG/Bridgeman Images; p. 1031: Pictures from History/Bridgeman Images; p. 1037: Everett Collection Historical/Alamy Stock Photo.

Chapter 27: Page 1047: Library of Congress; p. 1049: Chronicle/Alamy Stock Photo; p. 1052 (left): akg-images; (right): Bridgeman Images; p. 1053: Pictorial Press Ltd/Alamy Stock Photo; p. 1056: William Vandivert/ Life Magazine/The LIFE Picture Collection via Getty Images; p. 1058: DOE Photo/Alamy Stock Photo; p. 1061: Pictorial Press Ltd/ Alamy Stock Photo; p. 1066: akg-images/ UIG/Sovfoto; p. 1067: FDR Library, National Archives; p. 1077: akg-images/ullstein bild; p. 1078: Sovfoto/UIG/Bridgeman Images; p. 1081: Look and Learn/Elgar Collection/ Bridgeman Images; p. 1084: AF archive/ Alamy Stock Photo.

Chapter 28: Page 1095: Matteo Omied/Alamy Stock Photo; p. 1096 (left): Everett Collection Inc/Alamy Stock Photo; (right): Bridgeman Images; p. 1099: Bettman/Getty Images; p. 1111 (left): ZUMA Press, Inc./Alamy Stock Photo; (right): Alan Band/Fox Photos/Getty Images; p. 1116: CPA Media Pte Ltd/Alamy Stock Photo; p. 1117: Everett Collection Inc/ Alamy Stock Photo; p. 1119: AP Photo/Jeff Widener; p. 1122: AP Photo.

Chapter 29: Page 1128: William Campbell/ Sygma via Getty Images; p. 1138: Xinhua/Xiao Yijiu/eyevine/Redux; p. 1142: Mario De Biasi per Mondadori Portfolio via Getty Images; p. 1148: AP Photo/Khalil Senosi, File; p. 1151: Andrew Hasson/Alamy Stock Photo; p. 1157: The Book Worm/Alamy Stock Photo; p. 1159: AP Photo/Bullit Marquez; p. 1163: David Corio/Redferns/Getty Images; p. 1165: MB Media Solutions/Alamy Stock Photo.

INDEX

Aquinas, Thomas, 774
Arabia and Arabs
  coffee plantations of, 620
  slavery and, 888, 890, 911
  See also Islam; Muslims
Arabian Peninsula, biological exchange in,
  616
Arab Spring, 1129*c*, 1152–53*b*, 1153, 1154
Arakan (or Magh) pirates, 744
archeology and archeologists, 662
architecture
  Manueline, 610
  Renaissance, 677–78
  See also specific structures
Argentina, 919, 1143, 1151, *1151*
aristocrats in British society, 845
Aristotle, 774, 887
Armenian genocide, 1006, *1006*
arms industry, 853
artistic techniques and art, Renaissance, *677*,
  678
Asante kingdom, 594*m*, 620, 645
Asian tiger economies, 1089, 1105–23, **1106**,
  1107*m*, 1119, 1124
  See also East Asia
Askia Muhammad, 634, 637
Asma'u, Nana, 635
astrolabes, 602
astrology, 686
astronomy
  heliocentric system and, 686–87, *687*
  Ptolemaic, 686
  Scientific Revolution and, 686–87
  telescopes and, 673–74, 687
Atatürk (Mustafa Kemal), 1014–15, 1021, 1148
Atlantic Africa, 593*c*, 605–6
Atlantic Charter, 1091
Atlantic Europe, 631–32, 676, 745, 750,
  757–58, 779–80, 994
Atlantic Ocean
  currents and prevailing winds of, 598, *599*,
    605, 607
  European navigation of, 602–5, 604*m*, 611*m*
Atlantic revolutions (1640–1830), 788–828
  Atlantic connections and, 823–25, *826*
  in global perspective, 790–91, 822–27
  outcomes of, 825–27
  overview of, 789–80*c*
  political decentralization and, 823
  quest for new liberties, 790
  See also rebellions; *and specific countries*
atomic bomb. *See* nuclear weapons
Augustine, Saint, 681
Aurangzeb, 707*c*, 712, 722, 724–25
Auschwitz concentration camp, 1061
Australia
  Aborigines in, 614, 624, 664–65
  biological exchange in, 617
  Christianity and missionaries in, 664

disease and depopulation in, 663, 665
European exploration and settlement of,
  614, 664–65, 665*m*
Federation, 917*c*, 940
Global web and, 662–68
Great Depression and, 1020
"one percent" in, 1160
population in 1750, 662–63
as settler colony, 939–40
suffrage movement in, 1017
trade goods and plants and animals
  introduced to, 664
World War II and, 1049, 1060*t*
Austria
  independence after World War I, 1013
  suffrage movement in, 1019
Austria-Hungary
  ethnic diversity of, 999–1000, 1000*t*
  as great power (1870–1914), 999–1000,
    1001*m*
  World War I and, 1000, 1001–2, 1003, 1006,
    1007, 1009
  See also Habsburg Empire
authoritarianism, revitalization of, 1152–54,
  1167
Avicenna (Ibn Sina), 688, 887–88
Axis, **1043**, 1085
  advances in Europe, 1049, 1051*m*
  countries of, 1043, 1047
  in course of the war, 1047–53, 1048*m*,
    1051*m*
  early successes of, 1047–49
  losses and defeat of, 1050–51, 1052–53
  occupations by, 1068–69
  reasons for losing war, 1053–59
  See also World War II
Azores, 604, 605
Aztecs
  Florentine Codex on, *618*
  overthrow by Cortés, 647, *648*, 650, 652,
    669
  Tenochtitlán and, 618
  See also Mexica

Bahadur Shah II, 974
Bahamas, Columbus in, 592, 593*c*, 608
Bahrain, 1153
Bakongo, 791, 795
Bangladesh, 844, 1089*c*, 1095, 1104, 1143, 1148
banks and banking
  bank notes and credit, 776–77
  Bank of Amsterdam, 749*c*, 775–76
  Bank of England, 776
  Bank of Sweden, 776
  Baring Brothers, 1158
  as economies of scale, 773, 777
  in first global economy (1500–1800),
    749–50, 773–77
  fractional reserve banking, 776

coal and Industrial Revolution in, 831, 832, 835-37, 839-40
Cold War origins in, 1072
Combination Acts of, 868
Commonwealth and Protectorate in, 789c, 795
cotton industry in, 840-41
culture of imperialism, 932
environment and health impacts of industrialization in, 846-47, *847*
family life and Industrial Revolution in, 846
fascism and, 1023
fertility declines in, 1121, *1121*
free trade policy and, 1155-56
German aggression (1936-1939) and, 1045
as great power (1870-1914), 998, *999*, 1001*m*, 1008
India ruled by, 866, 935-37, *936*, 940
industrialists in, 845
in Industrial Revolution, 873
iron industry in, 841-42
labor activism during Industrial Revolution in, 869
labor costs and technological change in, 839
Labour Party of, 832c, 870
middle classes in, 844-45
Munich Conference in 1938 and, 1045
nuclear weapons and, 1074
"one percent" in, 1160
population of, 998-99
protectionist tariffs and, 838-39, 841
railways in, 831c, 842
settlement in North America, 652-53
society during Industrial Revolution, 843-46
steamships in, 842
suffrage movement in, 1016, 1017-18
working classes in, 844
World War I and, 1001, 1002-3, 1005, 1005*t*, 1006
World War II and, 1046, 1049, 1052, 1054, 1055, 1060*t*, 1061, 1066-67, 1070
See also England; Scotland; Wales
British Civil Wars, 789*c*
British Guiana, 897-98
British North America Act, 921
British Raj, 916*c*, **936**, 937, 975-76
Brittain, Vera, 1007
Brunias, Agostino, *657*
bubonic plague, 726
See also plague and plague pandemic
Buddha. *See* Siddhartha Gautama (Buddha)
Buddhism and Buddhists
in Japan, 672
Mahayana, 683
militant Buddhist fundamentalists, 1150
Theraveda, 683
Bulatovich, Alexander, 954*b*

Bulgaria, 916*c*, 927, 1007, 1049, 1091
Burkina Faso, 1102*b*
Burma (Myanmar)
as British colony, 935, 1093, 1115
Buddhism and, 1150
independence of, 1089*c*, 1093, 1095
militant Buddhist fundamentalists in, 1150
pirates in, 744, 745
social media use by military in, 1154
state formation of, 739
World War II and, 1069
Bussa, 897
Byzantine Church, 678

Cabot, John, 593*c*, 608-9, 611*m*
Cabral, Pedro de, 593*m*, 610-20, 611*m*
Calicut, 593, **609**, 610
caliphs, 727, 1014
Calvinism, 681
Calvin, John, 681, 682, 683, 701
Cambodia, 946, 1047, 1146-47, 1154
Canada
British North America Act and, 921
Chinese labor on railroad building in, *855*
Confederation, 855, 916*c*, 921, 923, 940
First Nations and assimilation, 922
French settlement and population (1750-1790) in, 799
Great Depression and, 1020
Industrial Revolution in, 855-56
nationalism and, 921-23, 924-25
National Policy of, 831*c*, 855
North-West Rebellion and, 922
"one percent" in, 1160
as settler colony, 939-40
suffrage movement in, 1018, 1019
World War I and, 1003, 1005, 1007
World War II and, 1052, 1060*t*
Canary Islands, 593*c*, 604-5, 606, 608
Cantino Planisphere, *607*
Canudos rebellion, 960*c*, 961, 967-68
Cape Colony, 960
Cape of Good Hope, 630*c*, 639-40, 646, 657
Cape Verde Islands, 612
carbon dioxide (CO_2), **1130**, *1130*, 1130-31, 1132*m*, 1135
Caribbean region
anti-colonialism and, 1036
biological globalization and, 620
British territories claims in, 654
Columbus and, 608, *608*, 611*m*
decolonization of, 1104, 1105*m*
disease and depopulation in, 646-47
piracy and, 744
sugar plantations in, 654, 749*c*, 769-70
winds, 598 (*See also* Cuba; West Indies)
See also Cuba; West Indies
Caribs, 649
Caroline Islands, 596

Heyn, Piet, 744

Hideyoshi, Toyotomi, 707*c*, **715**, 715–16, 717, 728, 740, 765

Hinduism
  Bharatiya Janata Party (BJP) and, 1149
  in India, 936
  militancy and, 1149
  terrorism and, 1149

Hiroshima and Nagasaki, 1042*c*, **1053**, *1053*, 1058, 1061

Hispaniola, 608, 647, 769

Hitler, Adolf, 997*c*, 998*c*, **1024**, 1054, 1063, 1101
  aggression in Europe (1936–1939), 1045, 1046*m*
  assassination plots against, 1064
  lebensraum and, 1027, 1044
  Munich Conference and, 1045
  Operation Barbarossa and Stalingrad and, 1049–50
  plans to invade Britain, 1049
  plans to kill Jews and *untermenschen*, 1025, 1044, 1050, 1061
  racial purification efforts of, 1025, 1026, 1044, 1050, 1061–63
  rise to power, 1013, 1024–27, 1043
  See also Nazi Germany; World War II

HIV/AIDS, 1128*c*, 1137–38, **1138**

hockey, ice, 1164

Holocaust, *1061*, 1061–63, 1062*m*

Holocene era, 1129

Holy Roman Empire, 680

Hongi Hika, 916*c*, 953–54

Hong Kong
  as Asian tiger economy, 1089, 1105, 1108
  ceded as British colony, 969
  corruption minimized in, 1123
  Japanese attack on, 1041

Hong Taiji, 718, 720–21

Hong Xiuquan, 970–71, *972*, 973, 991

Horace, 997

horse nomads, 742–43
  See also nomads; steppe nomads

horses
  Americas and, 619
  Columbian Exchange and, 619
  See also nomads; steppe nomads

House of Hohenzollern, 1013

Hudson Bay, 614

Hudson's Bay Company, 771

Huerta, Victoriano, 987, 988

Hugo, Victor, 812

Hull House, 832*c*, 869, *869*, 870

humanism, 678

human web
  Columbian Exchange and, 622–23
  COVID-19 pandemic and, 1140–41
  metallic web and, 860–61
  See also webs

Hungary, 1153
  COVID-19 and, 1154
  fascism and, 1023
  independence after World War I, 1013
  independence from USSR, 1091
  nationalism and, 925–26
  Ottoman control of, 727
  revolt against Soviet control, 1042*c*, 1077, 1078, 1083
  See also Austria-Hungary

Hus, Jan, 679, 682

Iberia, 604, 604*m*
  See also Portugal; Spain

Ibn al-Nafis, 688

Ibn Battuta, 635

Ibn Sina (Avicenna), 688, 887–88

ice hockey, 1164

Iceland, 879

Igbo, 644–45

I. G. Farben, 1026

Iliad (Homer), 610

Il-Khanids, 690

imperial consolidation, **729**
  Mughal Empire, 723–25
  Ottoman Empire, 728
  Qing consolidation in China, 717–21
  in Russia, 729–33
  Tokugawa consolidation in Japan, 714–17

imperialism
  Berlin Conference and, 940–41, *941*
  civilizing mission (*mission civilisatrice*) of, 930, *933*
  in colonial Africa to 1930, 942–45
  concepts of manliness and muscular Christianity in, 934
  cultures of, 932–35
  economic exploitation in Africa, 942–43
  European, in Southeast Asia, 945–46
  geopolitical rivalry and, 930, 932, 940
  Global web and, 955, 956
  growth of empires (1830–1914), 928, 931*m*
  intellectual responses to, 934–35
  land empires and, 948–55, 949*m*, 951*m*, 953*m*, 954*b*
  nationalism in support of, 930, 932
  new, **928**, 935
  overview of, 786, 916–17*c*, 928–29
  partition of Africa (1874–1890) and, 940, *941*, 952
  responses to (1850–1920), 959–91, 960–61*c*
  settler colonies and, 667, 939–40, 948, 956
  social Darwinism and pseudo-scientific racism of, 933–34
  steamships and, 929
  technologies and, *929*, 929–30
  See also colonies and colonization

Inazo, Nitobe, 933–34

income inequality, **1160**, 1160–61

Minamata disease, **1112**, *1122*
Ming dynasty, 593*c*, 599–602, 698, 707*c*,
  717–18, 719*m*, 720, 738, 749*c*, 752, 778–79
Ming voyages, 599–602, *600*, **601**, 601*m*,
  711–12
mining
  in colonial Africa, 942–43
  in Japan, 764
  in Mexico, 764
  in South America, 649, 654–55
  Spanish, 649
  in Spanish America, 765
Miranda, Francisco, 820, 824
missionaries
  in Africa, 934, 943–44, *944*
  during Catholic Reformation, 683
  in Hawaii, 667
  in Japan, 698, 700, *700*, 703
  in Kongo, 637–38, 639
  Maori and, 667
  in New Zealand, 667
  in Oceania and Australia, 664
  in Spanish America, 649–50, 656, *656*
mita, **649**, 654
Moche (Mochicas), 652
Moluccas, **612**, 614
Mongolia, 918
Mongols
  Atlantic European mariners compared to,
    632
  Genghis Khan and, 918
  Golden Horde (Kipchak Khanate) and, 659
  Ming dynasty and, 600, 601
  Pax Mongolica and, 594
  Zunghars, 718, 720, 721, 742, *742*, 743
Monroe Doctrine, 948
monsoons, 595, 598
More, Thomas, 888
Mormons, 964–65, 964*b*, 1016
Morocco
  independence of, 1102
  military battles of, 739, *739*
  mobile pastoralists in, 742
  pirates and, 744
  Portuguese in, 593*c*, 604, 605
  sugar plantations and, 641, 767
Morris, Esther Hobart, 1016
Morse, Samuel, 854
Mothers of the Plaza de Mayo, *1151*
*Motion of the Heart and Blood in Living
  Beings, The* (Harvey), *688*
Mott, Lucretia, 1016
moveable type, 674–75, *675*
Movement of Non-Aligned Countries, 1104*b*
Mozambique, 614, 638–39, 1104
MPLA, 1081, *1081*
Mubarak, Hosni, 1151, 1152–53*b*
mudlarks, 844
Mugabe, Robert, 1151, 1152

Mughal Empire, 707*c*
  Akbar and, 696, 721–24, *722*, 729
  Aurangzeb and, 712, 722, 724–25
  British termination of, 866, 935
  conquests of, *722*, 724, 724*m*
  consolidation and, 723–25
  decline of, 725–26
  destruction during Indian Rebellion, 961,
    973, 975
  military innovations and, 712, 723–24
  pirates and, 745
  religious policy of, 723–24
  silver and, 763
Muhammad, 774
  See also Islam
mujahideen, 1082
mulattos, 817
mullahs, 1147–48
Mulla Sadra, **692**, 692–93, 698
multiethnic empires, **925**
multinational states, defined, 919
mumps, 879
Mumtaz Mahal, 724
Munich Conference in 1938, 1045
Muscovy, 659–60, 660*m*
  See also Russia
muscular Christianity, 934
music and global culture, 1161–64, *1163*
Musket Wars, 630*c*, 666
Muslim League, 1032, **1094**
Muslims
  da Gama's treatment of, 610
  Sunni, 595, 683, 690
  See also Islam; Shi'a Islam
Mussolini, Benito, 997*c*, **1022**, 1022–23, *1023*,
    1035, 1043, 1044, 1049, 1054, 1066
Myanmar. *See* Burma

Nader Shah, 725
Nagasaki, 1042*c*, 1053, 1058, 1061
Nairobi bombing, *1148*
Nakamato, Hiroko, 1065–66
Namban screen, *615*
Namibia, 942
Nanak, 672*c*, 694–96
Nanjing Massacre of 1937, 1060, 1065
National Assembly (France), 808, 809
nationalism, **917**
  Canadian, 921–23, 924–25
  civic, 917–18, 920, 923
  ethnic, 917, 918
  French, 918–20, *919*
  German, 923–25, *924*
  Global web and, 955–56
  Hungarian, 925–26
  Japanese, 918, 920–21, *921*, 924, 956
  Mexican, 918, 986, 989
  militarism and, 920, 921, 924
  minority, 927–28

in Germany, 851–52
in Russia, 857
Trans-Siberian Railway, 832c, 857, 949, 999
U.S. transcontinental railroad, 977
Raleigh, Walter, 1129
Rastafarianism, 1163
Read, Mary, 744
Reagan, Ronald, 1084, 1155, 1156
rebellions
  Boxer Rebellion, 960c, 981–82, 984
  Canudos rebellion (Brazil), 960c, 961, 967–68
  Cold War uprisings in Eastern Europe, 1077–78
  Indian Rebellion, 935, 936, 960c, 961, 972–76, 974m, 975
  in Ireland (1641), 797
  Ming China and, 600
  North-West Rebellion (Canada), 922
  Taiping Rebellion, 768–972, 960c, 961, 970m, 972, 976
  White Lotus Rebellion, 969
  See also Atlantic revolutions; and specific rebellions and revolts
Reconquista, **603-4**
recording technology, 1162
Red Guards, 1116, 1117
reggae music, 1163
Regulators, 802
religion
  Buddhism (See Buddhism and Buddhists)
  Christianity (See Christianity and Christians)
  of creole cultures, 656–57
  in Europe, 682m
  Hinduism (See Hinduism)
  Islam (See Islam)
  Judaism (See Jews and Judaism)
  oceanic navigation and, 604
  Old World web and, 595
  religious movements, 1500–1750, 672c
  religious politics since 1970, 1147–50
  Shinto, 672
  Sikhism, 694–97, 697, 700
  slaves and, 656–57
Remington, Frederic, 966
Remote Oceania, 662
Renaissance, **677**, 677, 677–78
Renan, Ernst, 918
Republican Party (United States), 900
rheas, 743
Rhodes, Cecil, 933
rhythm and blues music, 1162
Ricardo, David, 840
rice, 620
rice plantations, 654
Riefenstahl, Leni, 1026
Riel, Louis, 922

Riffaiyya, 690
Rihanna (Robyn Rihanna Fenty), 1164
rinderpest, 916c, 941–42, 947, 952
rivers, 596
  See also specific rivers
roads and road systems of Britain, 837–38
Roberts, Bartholomew, 708c, 744
Roberts, Issachar, 970
Robespierre, Maximilien, 810–11
Robin John, Ancona Robin, 644–45
Robin John, Little Ephraim, 644–45
Robinson Crusoe (Defoe), 763
Rohingya, 1154
Roma (Gypsies), 1025, 1063
Romania
  independence from USSR, 1091
  nation-state establishment of, 927
  World War I and, 1007
  World War II and, 1049, 1054
Romanovs, 732, 1009, 1013, 1090
Rome, early expansion of, 709
Roosevelt, Eleanor, 1069–70
Roosevelt, Franklin, 1047, 1054, 1056, 1063, 1067, 1072, 1091
Roosevelt, Theodore, 934
root crops
  cassava, 620, 621, 621, 792
  manioc, 621, 645
  potatoes, 620
Rousseau, Jean-Jacques, 867
Rowbotham, Titus, 843
Russia
  abolition of slavery, 905
  Bolshevik Revolution in, 997c, 1010, 1010, 1023, 1025, 1027
  Bolsheviks in, 1010, 1010–11, 1022, 1023, 1027, 1031
  Bonaparte's invasion of, 812, 812, 906
  conquest of Siberia, 661, 729
  Cossacks and, 659–62, 907
  Crimean War and, 856, 858, 906–7, 950
  Duma in, 1008–9, 1010
  emancipation of serfs in, 877c, 904–8, 905m, 908, 1008
  expansion in 1400–1800 of, 660m, 661, 729–30
  financial crisis in 1998, 1159
  as great power (1870–1914), 998, 999, 1001m
  imperial consolidation in, 729–33
  imperialism and, 948–50
  Industrial Revolution and, 856–57, 862–63
  land empire of, 948–50, 949m, 949–50
  land reform in, 1008–9, 1010
  migration and, 1144, 1144t, 1145
  Napoleon and, 812, 949, 1049
  nationalism in, 926–28, 949
  population of, 999, 1008
  protectionist tariffs and, 857

WORLD POLITICAL MAP

GREENLAND
(Denmark)

ICELAND

Faro
(Denma

ALASKA
(U.S.)

CANADA

Hudson
Bay

KI

IRELA

Bering Sea

Gulf of
Alaska

Aleutian Is.

UNITED STATES

Bermuda (U.K.)

Azores
(Portugal)

PORTUG.

Madeira Is.
(Portugal)

MORO

Canary Is.
(Spain)

WESTERN
SAHARA

HAWAII
(U.S.)

Gulf of
Mexico

MEXICO

THE BAHAMAS

CUBA

DOMINICAN REPUBLIC
PUERTO RICO (U.S.)

SAINT KITTS AND NEVIS
ANTIGUA AND BARBUDA
DOMINICA
SAINT LUCIA
BARBADOS
GRENADA
TRINIDAD AND TOBAGO

MAURITAN

JAMAICA

HAITI

BELIZE

Caribbean Sea

CAPE VERDE

SENEGAL

GUATEMALA
EL SALVADOR
HONDURAS
NICARAGUA
COSTA RICA

ST. VINCENT
AND THE GRENADINES

GAMBIA

GUINEA BISSAU

GUINE.

PACIFIC OCEAN

SIERRA LEONE

LIBERIA

PANAMA

VENEZUELA

GUYANA

FRENCH GUIANA
(France)

ATLANTIC
OCEAN

COLOMBIA

SURINAME

KIRIBATI

Galapagos Is.
(Ecuador)

ECUADOR

SAMOA

FRENCH POLYNESIA
(France)

PERU

BRAZIL

TONGA

BOLIVIA

Easter I.
(Chile)

CHILE

PARAGUAY

URUGUAY

Chatham Is.
(N.Z.)

ARGENTINA

Falkland Is.
(U.K.)

S. Georgia
(U.K.)

S. Sandwich Is.
(U.K.)

Abbreviations			
ARM.	Armenia	**K.**	Kosovo
AUS.	Austria	**LUX.**	Luxembourg
AZ.	Azerbaijan	**MO.**	Montenegro
BEL.	Belgium	**NETH.**	Netherlands
B.H.	Bosnia and Herzegovina	**N.MAC.**	North Macedonia
CR.	Croatia	**SE.**	Serbia
CZ.	Czech Republic	**SLK.**	Slovakia
GEO.	Georgia	**SLN.**	Slovenia
HUNG.	Hungary	**SWITZ.**	Switzerland

ARCTIC OCEAN

RUSSIA

Bering Sea

Sakhalin

NORWAY
SWEDEN
FINLAND
MARK
ESTONIA
LATVIA
LITHUANIA
POLAND BELARUS
RMANY
CZ. SLK.
AUS. HUNG.
SLN. CR. ROMANIA
ITALY MO.
BULGARIA
N. MAC.
ALBANIA GREECE
MALTA CYPRUS
NISIA Mediterranean

KAZAKHSTAN

MONGOLIA

Black Sea
GEO.
ARM.
AZ.
Caspian Sea
UZBEKISTAN
TURKMENISTAN
TAJIKISTAN
KYRGYZSTAN

N. KOREA
Sea of
Japan
S. KOREA
JAPAN

TURKEY
LEBANON
ISRAEL
SYRIA
IRAQ
JORDAN
IRAN
AFGHANISTAN
CHINA

East
China
Sea

KUWAIT
BAHRAIN
QATAR
U.A.E.
PAKISTAN
BHUTAN
NEPAL
TAIWAN

LIBYA
EGYPT
SAUDI
ARABIA
OMAN
INDIA
BANGLADESH

GER
CHAD
SUDAN
ERITREA
YEMEN
DJIBOUTI
Arabian
Sea
Bay of
Bengal
MYANMAR
THAILAND
LAOS
VIETNAM
South
China
Sea
PHILIPPINES
PACIFIC OCEAN

ERIA
CENTRAL
AFRICAN REP.
CAMEROON
SOUTH
SUDAN
ETHIOPIA
SRI
LANKA
CAMBODIA
BRUNEI
FEDERATED STATES
OF MICRONESIA
MARSHALL
ISLANDS

GABON
CONGO
UGANDA
KENYA
SOMALIA
MALDIVES
MALAYSIA
PALAU
KIRIBATI

MÉ
PE
DEM. REP.
OF THE
CONGO
RWANDA
BURUNDI
TANZANIA
SINGAPORE
Sumatra
Borneo
INDONESIA
NAURU

SEYCHELLES
Java
New Guinea
PAPUA NEW
GUINEA
SOLOMON
ISLANDS

ANGOLA
ZAMBIA
MALAWI
COMOROS
INDIAN
OCEAN
TIMOR-
LESTE
TUVALU

NAMIBIA
BOTSWANA
ZIMBABWE
MOZAMBIQUE
MADAGASCAR
MAURITIUS
Réunion
(France)
VANUATU
New Caledonia
(France)
FIJI

SOUTH
AFRICA
ESWATINI
LESOTHO
AUSTRALIA

Kerguelen Is.
(France)
Tasmania
NEW
ZEALAND

UTHERN OCEAN

ANTARCTICA

0   1,000   2,000 mi
0 1,000 2,000 km